Corrections
in the 21st Century

Corrections
in the 21st Century

2024 Release

Frank Schmalleger, PhD
Distinguished Professor Emeritus
University of North Carolina at Pembroke

John Ortiz Smykla, PhD
Professor and Director (Retired)
Florida Atlantic University
Distinguished University Professor (Retired)
University of West Florida
Professor (Retired)
University of Alabama

Foreword by Dr. Ryan Thornell
Director
Arizona Department of Corrections, Rehabilitation and Reentry

1 2 3 4 5 6 7 8 9 LKV 29 28 27 26 25 24

ISBN 978-1-266-30274-9 (bound edition)
MHID 1-266-30274-3 (bound edition)

ISBN 978-1-266-90859-0 (loose-leaf edition)
MHID 1-266-90859-5 (loose-leaf edition)

Associate Portfolio Manager: *Katie Reuter*
Marketing Manager: *Kim Schroeder-Freund*
Lead/Senior Content Project Managers: *Melissa M. Leick/Laura Payne*
Manufacturing Project Manager: *Nancy Flaggman*
Content Licensing Specialist: *Melissa Homer*
Cover Image: *Shutterstock.AI*
Compositor: *MPS Limited*

Library of Congress Cataloging-in-Publication Data

Names: Schmalleger, Frank, author. | Smykla, John Ortiz, author.
Title: Corrections in the 21st century / Frank Schmalleger, Distinguished
    Professor Emeritus,University of North Carolina at Pembroke, John Ortiz
    Smykla, Professor and Director (Retired), Florida Atlantic University,
    Distinguished University Professor (Retired), University of West Florida.
Other titles: Corrections in the twenty first century
Description: 2024 release. | New York : McGraw Hill LLC, 2024. | Includes
    bibliographical references and index.
Identifiers: LCCN 2023043401 (print) | LCCN 2023043402 (ebook) |
    ISBN 9781266302749 (hardcover) | ISBN 9781266908590 (spiral bound) |
    ISBN 9781266889950 (ebook)
Subjects: LCSH: Corrections—United States. | Corrections—Vocational
    guidance—United States.
Classification: LCC HV9471 .S36 2024 (print) | LCC HV9471 (ebook) |
    DDC 365/.973—dc23/eng/20231113
LC record available at https://lccn.loc.gov/2023043401
LC ebook record available at https://lccn.loc.gov/2023043402

mheducation.com/highered

dedication }

For my granddaughters, Ava and Malia
—*Frank Schmalleger*

For my granddaughter, Harper Grace, and my grandson, Holden Fate
—*John Smykla*

About the Authors

Frank Schmalleger

Frank Schmalleger, PhD, is Distinguished Professor Emeritus at the University of North Carolina at Pembroke.

Dr. Schmalleger holds a bachelor's degree from the University of Notre Dame and both a master's and a doctorate in sociology from The Ohio State University with a special emphasis in criminology. From 1976 to 1994, he taught criminal justice courses at the University of North Carolina at Pembroke, serving for many years as a tenured full professor. For the last 16 of those years, he chaired the Department of Sociology, Social Work, and Criminal Justice. As an adjunct professor with Webster University in St. Louis, Missouri, Dr. Schmalleger helped develop a graduate program in security management and loss prevention that is currently offered on U.S. military bases around the world. He taught courses in that curriculum for more than a decade, focusing primarily on computer and information security. Dr. Schmalleger also has taught in the New School for Social Research online graduate program, helping build the world's first electronic classrooms for criminal justice distance learning.

Dr. Schmalleger is the author of numerous articles and many books, including *Criminal Justice Today* (Pearson, 2024), *Criminal Justice: An Introduction* (Pearson, 2024), *Criminology Today* (Pearson, 2021), and *Criminal Law Today* (Pearson, 2016). He is founding editor of the journal *Criminal Justice Studies* (formerly *The Justice Professional*) and has served as imprint advisor for Greenwood Publishing Group's criminal justice reference series.

Dr. Schmalleger is also the creator of a number of award-winning websites (including the former cybrary.info and crimenews.info). He is a member of the Academy of Criminal Justice Sciences, the American Society of Criminology, and the Society of Police Futurists International (where he is a founding member). Schmalleger's author page on Amazon.com can be viewed at amazon.com/author/frankschmalleger. Follow him on Twitter @schmalleger.

John Ortiz Smykla

John Ortiz Smykla, PhD, is Retired director and professor of the School of Criminology and Criminal Justice at Florida Atlantic University. He also held appointments at the University of Alabama, where he served as professor and chair of the Department of Criminal Justice; the University of South Alabama, where he served as professor and chair of the Department of Political Science and Criminal Justice; and the University of West Florida, where he served as professor and chair of the Department of Criminal Justice and Legal Studies and was named Distinguished University Professor. He earned the interdisciplinary social science PhD in criminal justice, sociology, and anthropology from Michigan State University. He holds bachelor's and master's degrees in sociology from California State University at Northridge.

Dr. Smykla has authored or edited five corrections books, including *Probation, Parole, and Community Based Corrections* (2013) and *Offender Reentry: Rethinking Criminology and Criminal Justice* (2014). His coauthored data set *Executions in the United States, 1608–2003: The Espy File,* funded by a grant from the National Science Foundation, is one of the most frequently requested criminal justice data files from the University of Michigan's Inter-University Consortium for Political and Social Research. Dr. Smykla testified to its authenticity in hearings on death qualification and executions occurring after repeals.

Dr. Smykla has published more than 75 research articles on corrections and policing issues. He recently studied why null findings are rarely reported in leading criminology and criminal justice journals, published the results of a multiyear analysis of federal reentry court, and reported on the perceptions of the public, police officers and their supervisors, and police executive leadership on the impact of police-worn body cameras.

In 1986, Dr. Smykla was a Senior Fulbright Scholar in Argentina and Uruguay. He is a member of the Academy of Criminal Justice Sciences and the Southern Criminal Justice Association. In 1996, the Southern Criminal Justice Association named him Educator of the Year. In 1997, he served as program chair for the annual meeting of the Academy of Criminal Justice Sciences in Louisville, Kentucky. In 2000, he served as president of the Southern Criminal Justice Association. In 2017, Dr. Smykla and his colleagues received Springer's Outstanding *American Journal of Criminal Justice* Article Award for their research on police body cameras, and in the same year, another of their articles on police body cameras was named Most Read in *Criminal Justice and Behavior.* He was inducted into the Michigan State University School of Criminal Justice Wall of Fame in 2019.

Brief Contents

Expanded Contents

PART 3 INSTITUTIONAL CORRECTIONS 123

Julie Jacobson/AP Image

Daniel Russell/Hobbs News-Sun/AP Image

David R. Frazier/Science Source

PART 4 THE PRISON WORLD 235

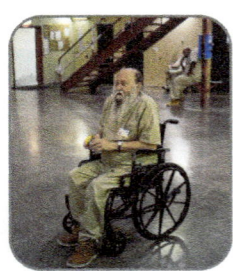

Andrew Burton/
Staff/Getty Images

CHAPTER 12

SPECIAL POPULATIONS

People in Prison with Substance Use Disorders, HIV/AIDS, Mental Illness, and the Elderly   335

Boxed Features

CAREER PROFILES

FOREWORD

This 2024 release of Dr. Frank Schmalleger's and Dr. John Smykla's *Corrections in the 21st Century* highlights the forward momentum of a field that's historically opposed to reconciling the need for punishment with the social responsibility of rehabilitation.

America's corrections system is at a crossroads, and the pendulum of correctional ideology is teetering. On the one end, more of the same: criticism, shame, punishment, power, and control, all in the name of public safety and justice. On the other end: meaningful programming designed specifically for engaged and dynamic rehabilitation, the prioritization of personal wellness, and the investment of resources that have proven, sustainable long-term outcomes.

This release, by two distinguished scholars in the criminal justice field, is sure to spark new thought and prompt new action among students like yourself, new correctional officers, career correctional administrators, and policymakers.

But why should you care which way correctional ideology swings? What difference does it make to you?

There are many reasons.

Perhaps, like me, you believe the system of power and punishment embedded for centuries within corrections is archaic. Or perhaps you recognize that corrections is a $100 billion industry, with very little return on investment when measured against recidivism and public safety. Or, maybe, as someone just entering the field of corrections, you have an interest to elevate the profession, to debunk myths and negative connotations, and to move your chosen profession beyond the punishing "guard" persona often seen as caricatures in the TV and movies.

The result of caring about correctional ideology is a more professional, cost-efficient, healthier, and safer correctional environment for staff and the incarcerated.

For nearly 20 years, I have witnessed first hand what happens inside U.S. prisons and on community supervision. It hasn't always been pretty. Stress, violence, force, and conflict have all been visible around the various corners of the system. In 2004, as a newly trained correctional officer in South Dakota, I was taught from the traditional school of thought that safety and security relied primarily on force, compliance, and discipline and required little meaningful communication or engagement. This school of thought has prevailed for decades, even centuries. But I've learned from this. I've learned that respectful communication, meaningful engagement, and

therapeutic intervention produce better outcomes—better for individuals and better for communities. As a senior correctional administrator in Maine and Arizona, I've demonstrated that a system built on modern, humanizing principles can produce increased safety and security while also promoting rehabilitation and wellness. My early days as an officer looked a lot different than my more recent days as a senior leader. Societal views on the nature of punishment inside correctional facilities have started to change, fortunately, and with it a reimagining of the foundational principles of public safety and rehabilitation has been borne. The moment in time to seize the opportunity and redefine punishment, to reinvent actual rehabilitation, and to strengthen public safety in a more sustained manner has arrived.

Updated chapters in this textbook capture the pivotal decisions and changes happening in current-day corrections. Changes that ask those in the profession to:

- Emphasize, through action, the importance of meaningful human engagement and respectful connectivity. Humanity belongs inside correctional complexes, practiced by staff and the population.
- Allow for growth and change and encourage and continue dialogue around the social need for punishment with the social responsibility of rehabilitation. Power and control dynamics are outdated and ineffective.
- Realign and reinvest fiscal resources both inside the prison walls and in communities to positively impact families and groups that historically have been trapped by the justice system.
- Balance the needs of victims, public safety, and reduction of recidivism, with programming and stigma reduction.
- Expect a higher level of performance, accountability, and outcome from the fiscal and human capital investment.

These aims are accomplished by reimagining the foundational principles on which the system functions, by providing meaningful access to programming, education, and treatment, along with other rehabilitative objectives to the wide masses of incarcerated and supervised individuals. Further, it requires an investment in the actual profession of corrections. Better outcomes require attention to recruiting, training, and retaining professionals who embody the values, integrity, and moral responsibility required to teach, lead, and prepare individuals to return to our local communities.

When done right, this new model of corrections will help address the acute impacts of major social challenges like the opioid epidemic or the housing crisis.

The result, as has been demonstrated by a few early-adopter states, is an improved correctional environment contributing to increased safety and stronger communities. I've witnessed healthier, more fulfilled staff, motivated and engaged populations, and strong continuity of care reintegrated into communities. In this reimagined correctional environment, staff and population exist without the historic concerns associated with high rates of violence or lockdowns. Instead, there is participation in career and technical education classes and substance use disorder treatment, among others. We all should want corrections, whether in the community or a facility, to have less tension, improved health, and meaningful engagements. Think about this opportunity as you read the pages in this text and explore the career pages throughout.

What keeps me engaged as a corrections leader, and what I hope this textbook helps you contemplate, is that we can learn from our past, especially to get smarter about our future, while continuing to strive for healthier, systemic outcomes.

We can cut through all the partisan politics and resistive influences pushing against this change. As a nation, we will finally see reimagined corrections. There should be no other option. It makes sense. And it works.

Ryan Thornell, Ph.D.
Director
Arizona Department of Corrections, Rehabilitation
    and Reentry

PREFACE

Corrections, when seen as the control and punishment of convicted offenders, has been an important part of organized society from the earliest days of civilization. It has not always had a proud past, however. In pre-modern times, atrocious physical punishment, exile, and unspeakable torture were the tools used all too often by those called upon to enforce society's correctional philosophies—especially the strongly felt need for vengeance.

Important changes in correctional practice began around the time of the American Revolution when the purposes of criminal punishments were closely examined by influential reformers. More recently, corrections has become an important field of study in which scientific techniques are valued and reasoned debate is encouraged.

The best, however, is yet to come. Only within the past 30 years have conscientious corrections practitioners begun to embrace the notion of professionalism—wherein ethics, a sense of high purpose, a personal long-term career commitment, a respect for the fundamental humanity of those supervised, and widely agreed-upon principles and standards guide the daily work of correctional personnel. Corrections professionalism, although not yet as well-known as police professionalism, has garnered support from policymakers and is winning respect among the public. It serves as this textbook's organizing principle.

Corrections in the 21st Century:

- provides an in-depth look at the past, present, and future of corrections;
- identifies the many *subcomponents* of modern-day corrections;
- highlights the *process* of modern-day corrections;
- focuses on the *issues* facing the correctional enterprise today;
- provides an appreciation for contemporary real-world correctional *practice;*
- examines the opportunities represented by new and developing corrections *technologies;* and
- points students in the direction of the still emerging ideal of corrections *professionalism.*
- features the Foreword by Dr. Ryan Thornell, Director, Arizona Department of Corrections, Rehabilitation and Reentry.

It is our belief that a new age of corrections is upon us. It is an age in which the lofty goals of corrections professionalism will take their place alongside the more traditional components of a still developing field. It is our hope that this textbook will play at least some small part in helping bring about a new and better correctional enterprise—one that is reasonable and equitable to all involved in the justice process.

2024 RELEASE

The following changes have been made in this 2024 Release of *Corrections in the 21st Century* to better focus reader attention on the key learning materials in each chapter:

- Web-based instructional videos featuring the authors, and emphasizing key learning points are now available.
- Enhancement of the photo program to better grab student interest and draw readers into the text.
- Integration of additional evidence-based information throughout the book and frequent citation of the literature relating to such practices.
- A number of new stories, many focusing on what's happening in corrections, now open the chapters.
- Incorporation of reviews of the most recent data and literature throughout.
- Updates to statistics and data throughout the book.

Significant chapter-specific content changes include the following:

Chapter 1

- The chapter now opens with a new story about Norwegian and German prison, asking whether some European models of imprisonment might be applied to American corrections.
- The "carceral state" is discussed in the context of the growing use of imprisonment.
- New key terms include "social justice," "correctional supervision," and "carceral state."
- Statistics describing the growth in the use of imprisonment in this country are discussed, and questions raised about where prison population numbers are headed.

- A new photo of former police officer Derek Chauvin has been added to the chapter, along with a discussion of what social justice means for corrections.

Chapter 2

- The chapter-opening story has been completely rewritten, and a number of photos have been replaced.
- A new Crime Solutions box has been added about the Milwaukee, Wisconsin, County Diversion Program.
- "Social diversity" has become a key term and is now defined.
- The career profile of Rhianna Johnson has been updated.

Chapter 3

- A new story now opens the chapter.
- The Crime Solutions box has been replaced with a new one.
- "Victim services" has been added as a key term and is now defined.
- The discussion of capital punishment has been updated along with exhibits (line art) that relate to it.
- The American Correctional Association Public Correctional Policy has been updated in keeping with changes made by the Association.

Chapter 4

- The title was changed to emphasize that probation is the most used form of punishment.
- The account of Jussie Smollett's sentence to probation opens the chapter.
- Characteristics of persons on probation have been updated.
- The Crime Solutions box—Reduced Probation Caseload (Oklahoma City)—highlights the importance of evidence-based practices.
- There is a new exhibit on the risk-needs-responsivity framework.
- There is a new discussion on the application of procedural justice to probation.
- There is a new exhibit comparing the cost of probation to other sentencing options.
- The career profile of Clarissa Grissette has been updated.

Chapter 5

- The chapter title was revised to better reflect chapter content.

- The chapter-opening story discusses the "stacked" sentences given to former NFL player Clinton Paris.
- We provide a new material on problem-solving courts.
- There is a new career profile of Tim Czaja, Director of Berkeley County Community Corrections.
- We include an updated map of the United States showing the number of drug courts by state.
- The Crime Solutions box features an evidence-based program featuring gender specific drug treatment.
- We feature a new exhibits outlining the pros and cons of day fines and electronic monitoring.
- The photo library was updated.

Chapter 6

- The chapter title was revised to better reflect chapter content.
- The story and sentence of Richard Tobin who conspired with other members of a white supremacist hate group to vandalize minority-owned properties opens the chapter.
- There is new coverage on the link between election politics and jail administration.
- We provide updated BJS data on the jail population and facility characteristics.
- We include a new Crime Solutions box on a jail-based evidence-based reentry program.
- There is an updated exhibit on the American Jail Association's mission statement.
- There are new exhibits on jail incarceration rates and jail-based reentry initiatives.
- We include a new career profile of Reese Walker, Deputy Administrator of Operations/Program Services Shelby County Division of Corrections.
- We expand our discussion on bail reform, preventive detention, and reentry from jail to the community.

Chapter 7

- The case of Jacob Chansley, the so-called QAnon Shaman, who disrupted the joint session of the U.S. Congress on January 6, 2021 opens the chapter.
- There is updated data on characteristics of persons in prison.

- There is a new Crime Solutions box on an evidence-based rehabilitation program for adults.
- We expanded the discussion of mass incarceration.
- We include a new career profile of Courtney McCoy, Corrections Sergeant, Lancaster County Department of Corrections.
- We report on the first-of-its kind reporting on gender identity in prison.
- We include new exhibits on prison rates by race/ethnicity, minimum wage for persons in prisons, and on justice reinvestment in six states.
- There is new coverage of the return of Pell grants for incarcerated persons.
- We revised the discussion of vocational training, prison industries, and work assignments in prison.
- We offer new data on the cost of incarceration and the efforts to limit the use of supermax-like confinement.
- We reorganized and expanded the discussion on technocorrections.

Chapter 8

- We reorganized major chapter headings to better understand who is in prison before learning about the parole-releasing authority.
- Data on the characteristics of persons in prison has been updated.
- There is new material on the collateral consequences of reentry that make it difficult to reintegrate into society and increase the chances for recidivism.
- There are new exhibits on the top ten employment fields with the most licensing restrictions and new material on federal reentry legislation and fair chance licensing.
- We include new material on how the practice of returning persons to prison for violating the technical conditions of their parole supervision contributes to mass incarceration.
- There is a new Crime Solutions box on the reentry court in Harlem, New York.
- We present a new career profile of Palm Beach County Deputy Sheriff Nakisha Bishop Zambrana.
- There is new material on felony disenfranchisement and voting, and a new exhibit on state voting restrictions for persons convicted of a felony.
- We include the latest information on the effectiveness of reentry court.

Chapter 9

- Statistics on the pay of correctional officers have been updated.
- The discussion of the terrorist threat inside of America's prisons has been expanded.
- The career profile of Dr. Tracy Andrus, Executive Director of the Tracy Andrus Foundation has been added.

Chapter 10

- A new story opens the chapter, highlighting New York Governor Kathy Houchl's announced changed in official vocabulary used when referring to people in prison.
- "Inmate subculture" has become "prison subculture," and "inmates" and "prisoners" are now generally referred to as "people in prison." "Inmate roles" have become "prison roles," and "inmate code" has become "prison code."
- Some photos have been replaced to update the chapter.
- A new career profile box featuring Craig A. Waleed, author, educator, and counselor, has been added to the chapter.
- The section on "Sexuality in Men's Prisons" has been completely rewritten.
- The section on overcrowding has been revised, and updated PREA data have been added.
- The discussion of gender-related issues has been revised and enhanced.

Chapter 11

- A new story about the Arizona Department of Corrections, Rehabilitation, and Reentry opens the chapter.
- The 2021 U.S. Supreme Court case of *Ramirez* v. *Collier* has been added.
- A new careers box about Evan M. Touchette, Unit Manager for the Intensive Mental Health Unit at the Maine State Prison, has been added.

Chapter 12

- The settlement between the Vermont Department of Corrections and the U.S. Department of Justice Civil Rights Division to remedy conditions in state prisons opens the chapter.
- There is new data on the number of persons in prison with vision, hearing, and ambulatory disabilities and a new exhibit comparing the percent of people with disabilities in prisons to the U.S. adult population.

- There is new data on the number of persons in prison with a substance use disorder and a new Crime Solutions box on using motivational interviewing for persons with a substance use disorder.
- There is new information on persons in prison with HIV and AIDS and HIV testing in prison.
- We expanded the discussion of people in state and federal prison with mental health problems.
- We expand coverage on the aging of the prison population, prison hospice, and geriatric units in prison.
- We present new and updated information on compassionate release and the cost of incarcerating the elderly.
- The career profile of Jose Ortiz-Cruz has been updated.

ORGANIZATION

This 2024 Release of *Corrections in the 21st Century* has been shortened to better reflect aspects of the correctional process. Chapters are grouped into four parts, each of which is described in detail in the following paragraphs.

Part One, "Introduction to Corrections," provides an understanding of corrections by explaining the problem of mass incarceration and the goals underlying the correctional enterprise and by describing the how and why of criminal punishments. Part One identifies professionalism as the key to managing correctional personnel, facilities, and populations successfully. Standard-setting organizations such as the American Correctional Association, the American Jail Association, the American Probation and Parole Association, and the National Commission on Correctional Health Care are identified, and the importance of professional ethics for correctional occupations and correctional administrators is emphasized.

Part Two, "Community Corrections," explains what happens to most convicted offenders, probation, and intermediate sanctions.

Part Three, "Institutional Corrections," provides a detailed description of jails, prisons, and parole. The reentry challenges facing persons released from jail and prison are explained. Education, vocational preparation, and drug treatment programs that are intended to prevent reoffending also are explored.

Part Four, "The Prison World," provides an overview of life inside prison from the points of view of both persons in prison and staff. Part Four also describes the responsibilities and challenges surrounding the staff role. Chapter 12 focuses attention on special correctional populations, including individuals who are elderly, have HIV/AIDS, are substance abusers, and are mentally and physically challenged. We have chosen to integrate our coverage of women in corrections—including information about the important NIC report titled "Gender Responsive Strategies: Research, Practice, and Guiding Principles for Women Offenders"—throughout the body of the text rather than isolating it.

PEDAGOGICAL AIDS

Working together, the authors and editor have developed a learning system designed to help students excel in the corrections course. In addition to the many changes already mentioned, we have included a wealth of new photographs to make the book even more inviting and relevant.

To this same end, our real-world chapter-opening vignettes give the material a fresh flavor intended to motivate students to read on; our photo captions, which raise thought-provoking questions, actively engage students in the learning process. Carefully updated tables and figures highlight and amplify the text coverage. And chapter outlines, objectives, and reviews, plus marginal definitions and an end-of-book glossary, all help students master the material.

The Schmalleger/Smykla learning system goes well beyond these essential tools, however. As mentioned, *Corrections in the 21st Century* offers a unique emphasis on corrections professionalism, an emphasis that has prompted us to create a number of innovative learning tools that focus on the real world of corrections:

- A concentration on *Evidence-Based Corrections*—What actually works in correctional settings? that is, what correctional programs are effective in reducing recidivism and in preventing future crimes? Evidence-based corrections is an exciting new development in the corrections field, and a number of agencies, institutions, and organizations now emphasize the use of scientific evidence. Evidence-based policy, which builds on evidence-based corrections, is an approach that helps people make well-informed decisions about policies and programs by putting the best available evidence from research at the heart of policy development and implementation.
- *Career Profiles*—enlightening minibiographies of corrections professionals, such as a college professor who once served time in prison, a deputy sheriff who received a Medal of Honor, and a unit manager of an intensive mental health unit.
- *CrimeSolutions.Gov*—boxes that use the National Institute of Justice's research to rate the effectiveness of programs and practices in achieving criminal justice-related outcomes in order to inform practitioners and policymakers

about what works, what doesn't, and what's promising in criminal justice.

In addition to the features we have developed to further our goal of creating a uniquely practical, professionally oriented text, we also have included end-of-chapter review material to help students master the concepts and principles developed in the chapter:

- *Chapter Summary*—a valuable learning tool organized into sections that mirror the chapter-opening objectives exactly; the summary restates all of the chapter's most critical points.
- *Key Terms*—a comprehensive list of the terms defined in the margins of the chapter, complete with page references to make it easy for students to go back and review further.
- *Questions for Review*—objective study questions (exactly mirroring the chapter-opening objectives and summary) that allow students to test their knowledge and prepare for exams.
- *Thinking Critically About Corrections*—broad-based questions that challenge students to think critically about chapter concepts and issues.
- *On-the-Job Decision Making*—unique experiential exercises that enable students to apply what they have learned in the chapter to the daily work of correctional personnel.

Finally, we should add that people under correctional supervision are referred to in this text under a number of different legal statuses. They are often referred to as detainees, inmates, probationers, parolees, and offenders. Based on person-first language, we refer to persons under correctional supervision as "individuals" or "people" whenever possible.

Proctorio Remote Proctoring & Browser-Locking Capabilities

Remote proctoring and browser-locking capabilities, hosted by Proctorio within Connect, provide control of the assessment environment by enabling security options and verifying the identity of the student.

Seamlessly integrated within Connect, these services allow instructors to control the assessment experience by verifying identification, restricting browser activity, and monitoring student actions.

Instant and detailed reporting gives instructors an at-a-glance view of potential academic integrity concerns, thereby avoiding personal bias and supporting evidence-based claims.

ReadAnywhere® App

Read or study when it's convenient with McGraw Hill's free ReadAnywhere® app. Available for iOS and Android smartphones or tablets, give users access to McGraw Hill tools including the eBook and SmartBook® or Adaptive Learning Assignments in McGraw Hill Connect®. Students can take notes, highlight, and complete assignments offline—all their work will sync when connected to Wi-Fi. Students log in with their Connect username and password to start learning—anytime, anywhere!

OLC-Aligned Courses

Implementing High-Quality Instruction and Assessment through Preconfigured Courseware

In consultation with the Online Learning Consortium (OLC) and our certified Faculty Consultants, McGraw Hill has created preconfigured courseware using OLC's quality scorecard to align with best practices in online course delivery. This turnkey courseware contains a combination of formative assessments, summative assessments, homework, and application activities, and can easily be customized to meet an individual instructor's needs and desired course outcomes. For more information, visit https://www.mheducation.com/highered/olc.

Test Builder in Connect

Available within McGraw Hill Connect®, Test Builder is a cloud-based tool that enables instructors to format tests that can be printed, administered within a Learning Management System, or exported as a Word document. Test Builder offers a modern, streamlined interface for easy content configuration that matches course needs, without requiring a download.

Test Builder allows you to:

- access all test bank content from a particular title.
- easily pinpoint the most relevant content through robust filtering options.
- manipulate the order of questions or scramble questions and/or answers.
- pin questions to a specific location within a test.
- determine your preferred treatment of algorithmic questions.
- choose the layout and spacing.
- add instructions and configure default settings.

Test Builder provides a secure interface for better protection of content and allows for just-in-time updates to flow directly into assessments.

Writing Assignment

Available within McGraw Hill Connect®, the Writing Assignment tool delivers a learning experience to help students improve written communication skills and conceptual understanding. Assign, monitor, grade, and provide feedback on writing more efficiently and effectively.

Polling

Every learner has unique needs. Uncover where and when you're needed with the new Polling tool in McGraw Hill Connect®! Polling allows you to discover where students are in real time. Engage students and help them create connections with your course content while gaining valuable insight during lectures. Leverage polling data to deliver personalized instruction when and where it is needed most.

Evergreen

Content and technology are ever-changing, and it is important that you can keep your course up to date with the latest information and assessments. That's why we want to deliver the most current and relevant content for your course, hassle-free.

Corrections in the 21st Century by Frank Schmalleger and John Ortiz Smykla is moving to an Evergreen delivery model, which means it has content, tools, and technology that is updated and relevant, with updates delivered directly to your existing McGraw Hill Connect® course. Engage students and freshen up assignments with up-to-date coverage of select topics and assessments, all without having to switch editions or build a new course.

Create

Your Book, Your Way

McGraw Hill's Content Collections Powered by Create® is a self-service website that enables instructors to create custom course materials—print and eBooks—by drawing upon McGraw Hill's comprehensive, cross-disciplinary content. Choose what you want from our high-quality textbooks, digital products, articles, cases, and more. Combine it with your own content quickly and easily, and tap into other rights-secured, third-party content such as cases, articles, readings, cartoons, and labs. Content can be arranged in a way that makes the most sense for your course, and you can select your own cover and include the course name and school information as well. Choose the best format for your course: color print, black-and-white print, or eBook. The eBook can be included in your Connect course and is available on the free ReadAnywhere® app for smartphone or tablet access as well. When you are finished customizing, you will receive a free digital copy to review in just minutes! Visit McGraw Hill Create®—www.mcgrawhillcreate.com—today and begin building!

Reflecting the Diverse World Around Us

McGraw Hill believes in unlocking the potential of every learner at every stage of life. To accomplish that, we are dedicated to creating products that reflect, and are accessible to, all the diverse, global customers we serve. Within McGraw Hill, we foster a culture of belonging, and we work with partners who share our commitment to equity, inclusion, and diversity in all forms. In McGraw Hill Higher Education, this includes, but is not limited to, the following:

- Refreshing and implementing inclusive content guidelines around topics including generalizations and stereotypes, gender, abilities/disabilities, race/ethnicity, sexual orientation, diversity of names, and age.
- Enhancing best practices in assessment creation to eliminate cultural, cognitive, and affective bias.
- Maintaining and continually updating a robust photo library of diverse images that reflect our student populations.
- Including more diverse voices in the development and review of our content.
- Strengthening art guidelines to improve accessibility by ensuring meaningful text and images are distinguishable and perceivable by users with limited color vision and moderately low vision.

IN APPRECIATION

Writing a textbook requires a great deal of help and support. We gratefully acknowledge the contributions of the following individuals who helped in the development of this textbook.

Steve Abrams, Ret.
California Department of Corrections and Rehabilitation
Santa Rosa, California

Stanley E. Adelman
University of Arkansas School of Law
Little Rock, Arkansas
University of Tulsa College of Law
Tulsa, Oklahoma

Colleen Andrews
Ozarks Technical Community College
Springfield, Missouri

Cassandra Atkin-Plunk
Florida Atlantic University
Boca Raton, Florida

John Augustine
Triton College
River Grove, Illinois

Tom Austin, Ret.
Shippensburg University
Shippensburg, Pennsylvania

Ken Barnes
Arizona Western College
Yuma, Arizona

Jeri Barnett
Virginia Western Community College
Roanoke, Virginia

Valerie R. Bell
Loras College
Dubuque, Iowa

Rose Johnson Bigler
Curry College
Milton, Massachusetts

Kathy J. Black-Dennis
University of Louisville
Louisville, Kentucky

Robert Bohm, Ret.
University of Central Florida
Orlando, Florida

Paul Bowdre
SUNY Canton
Canton, New York

David A. Bowers Jr.
University of South Alabama
Mobile, Alabama

Ed Bowman
Lock Haven University
Lock Haven, Pennsylvania

Greg Brown
Westwood College of Technology
Denver, Colorado

David C. Cannon
Henry Ford College
Dearborn, Michigan

Samantha Carlo
Miami Dade College
Miami, Florida

David E. Carter
Southern Oregon University
Ashland, Oregon

Kelley Christopher
University of University of West Georgia
Carrollton, Georgia

Jason Clark-Miller
Tarrant County College
Fort Worth, Texas

Matthew Crow
University of West Florida
Pensacola, Florida

Karen Curls
Metropolitan Community College–Penn Valley
Kansas City, Missouri

Lonnie DePriest
Albany Technical College
Albany, Georgia

Kenneth L. Done
Coahoma Community College
Clarksdale, Mississippi

Vicky Dorworth
Montgomery College
Rockville, Maryland

Don Drennon
Gala Federal Bureau of Prisons
Atlanta, Georgia

Carrie L. Dunson
Central Missouri State University
Warrensburg, Missouri

Michael Earll
Western Technical College
La Crosse, Wisconsin

Hilary Estes
Southern Illinois University
Carbondale, Illinois

Cory Feldman
LaGuardia Community College
New York, New York

Robert Figlestahler
Eastern Kentucky University
Richmond, Kentucky

Lynn Fortney, Ret.
EBSCO Subscription Services
Birmingham, Alabama

Harold A. Frossard
Moraine Valley Community College
Palos Hills, Illinois

Michelle Furlow
Moraine Valley Community College
Palos Hills, Illinois

Craig Goforth
Mars Hill University
Mars Hill, North Carolina

Paul D. Gregory
University of Wisconsin–Whitewater
Whitewater, Wisconsin

Donna Hale Ret.
Shippensburg University
Shippensburg, Pennsylvania

Homer C. Hawkins
Michigan State University
East Lansing, Michigan

Nancy L. Hogan
Ferris State University
Big Rapids, Michigan

Michael Hollingsworth
University of South Alabama
Mobile, Alabama

Amanda Humphrey
Mount Mercy University
Cedar Rapids, Iowa

Ronald G. Iacovetta
Wichita State University
Wichita, Kansas

Connie Ireland
California State University
Long Beach, California

James L. Jengeleski. Ret.
Shippensburg University
Shippensburg, Pennsylvania

Brad Johnson
Las Vegas, Nevada

Kathrine Johnson
University of West Florida
Ft. Walton Beach, Florida

Frank E. Jones
New England College
Henniker, New Hampshire

John Calvin Jones
North Carolina A&T State University
Greensboro, North Carolina

Kay King
Johnson County Community College
Overland Park, Kansas

Mike Klemp-North
Ferris State University
Big Rapids, Michigan

Julius Koefoed Kirkwood
Community College
Cedar Rapids, Iowa

Michael Kwan
Salt Lake Community College
Taylorsville, Utah

James Lasley
California State University
Fullerton, California

Michael Leary
Hawkeye Community College
Waterloo, Iowa

Walter B. Lewis
St. Louis Community College at Meramec
Kirkwood, Missouri

Shelley Listwan
Kent State University
Kent, Ohio

Jess Maghan
Forum for Comparative Correction
Chester, Connecticut

Iryna Malendevych
University of Central Florida
Orlando, Florida

Preston S. Marks
Keiser University

Laurie A. Michelman
Cayuga Community College
Auburn, New York

Rosie Miller
Coahoma Community College
Clarksdale, Mississippi

Alvin Mitchell
Delgado Community College
New Orleans, Louisiana

Etta Morgan
Pennsylvania State University
Capital College, Pennsylvania

Kathleen Nicolaides
University of North Carolina
Charlotte, North Carolina

Jessica Noble
Lewis and Clark Community College
Godfrey, Illinois

Sarah Nordin
Solano Community College
Suisun City, California

Michael F. Perna
Broome Community College
Binghamton, New York

Kristin Pickett
Waldorf University
Forest City, Iowa

Terry L. Pippin
College of Southern Nevada
Henderson, Nevada

Lisa Pitts
Washburn University
Topeka, Kansas

Scott Plutchak
University of Alabama at Birmingham
Birmingham, Alabama

Bobby B. Polk
Metropolitan Community College
Omaha, Nebraska

Wayne D. Posner
East Los Angeles College
Monterey Park, California

Melissa L. Ricketts
Shippensburg University
Shippensburg, Pennsylvania

Brittany Rodriguez
Tarleton State University
Mansfield, Texas

Barbara R. Russo
Wayne Community College
Goldsboro, North Carolina

John Sloan
University of Alabama at Birmingham
Birmingham, Alabama

Walter Smith
Hazard Community and Technical College
Hazard, Kentucky

Larry E. Spencer
Alabama State University
Montgomery, Alabama

Quanda Stevenson
Athens State University
Athens, Alabama

James M. Stewart
Calhoun Community College
Decatur and Huntsville, Alabama

Anthony C. Trevelino
Camden County College
Blackwood, New Jersey

Sheryl Van Horne
Radford University
Radford, Virginia

Shela R. Van Ness
University of Tennessee at Chattanooga
Chattanooga, Tennessee

Gennaro F. Vito
University of Louisville
Louisville, Kentucky

Brenda Vos
University of North Florida
Jacksonville, Florida

Kiesha Warren-Gordon
Ball State University
Muncie, Indiana

Anthony White
Illinois Central College
East Peoria, Illinois

Earl White
Illinois Central College
Peoria, Illinois

Ed Whittle
Florida Metropolitan University at Tampa College
Tampa, Florida

Beth Wiersma
University of Nebraska at Kearney
Kearney, Nebraska

Robert R. Wiggins
Cedarville College
Cedarville, Ohio

Jeffrey Zack
Fayetteville Technical Community College
Fayetteville, North Carolina

Kristen M. Zgoba
Rutgers University
Piscataway, New Jersey

Dawn Zobel
Federal Bureau of Prisons
Alderson, West Virginia

We would like to thank the following reviewers for taking time and effort necessary to review the previous manuscript.

Dywane Thompson, University of South Carolina, Aiken, South Carolina

AnneMarie Garmon, Central Piedmont Community College, Charlotte, North Carolina

Curtis R. Blakely, University of Wyoming, Laramie, Wyoming

Wayne Posner, East Los Angeles College, Monterey Park, California

Joanna Daou, University of South Carolina, Aiken, South Carolina

LaNina Cooke, Farmingdale State College, Farmingdale, New York

Finally, we want to acknowledge the special debt that we owe to the McGraw Hill team, including managing director Tim Vertovec, product developer Katie Reuter, editorial coordinator Soo-Jin Lea, marketing manager Kim Schroeder-Freund, program manager Jolynn Kilburg, content project managers Melissa M. Leick and Laura Payne, buyer Nancy Flaggman designer Urvi Rustagi, and content licensing specialist Melissa Homer. The professional vision, guidance, and support of these dedicated professionals helped bring this project to fruition. A hearty "thank you" to all.

Frank Schmalleger

John Smykla

A complete course platform

Connect enables you to build deeper connections with your students through cohesive digital content and tools, creating engaging learning experiences. We are committed to providing you with the right resources and tools to support all your students along their personal learning journeys.

65%
Less Time Grading

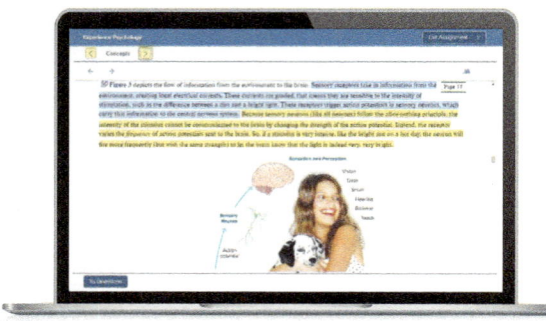

Laptop: Getty Images; Woman/dog: George Doyle/Getty Images

Every learner is unique

In Connect, instructors can assign an adaptive reading experience with SmartBook® 2.0. Rooted in advanced learning science principles, SmartBook 2.0 delivers each student a personalized experience, focusing students on their learning gaps, ensuring that the time they spend studying is time well spent. **mheducation.com/highered/connect/smartbook**

Study anytime, anywhere

Encourage your students to download the free ReadAnywhere® app so they can access their online eBook, SmartBook® 2.0, or Adaptive Learning Assignments when it's convenient, even when they're offline. And since the app automatically syncs with their Connect account, all of their work is available every time they open it. Find out more at **mheducation.com/readanywhere**

I really liked this app—it made it easy to study when you don't have your textbook in front of you.

Jordan Cunningham, a student at *Eastern Washington University*

Effective tools for efficient studying

Connect is designed to help students be more productive with simple, flexible, intuitive tools that maximize study time and meet students' individual learning needs. Get learning that works for everyone with Connect.

Education for all

McGraw Hill works directly with Accessibility Services departments and faculty to meet the learning needs of all students. Please contact your Accessibility Services Office, and ask them to email **accessibility@mheducation.com**, or visit **mheducation.com/about/accessibility** for more information.

Affordable solutions, added value

Make technology work for you with LMS integration for single sign-on access, mobile access to the digital textbook, and reports to quickly show you how each of your students is doing. And with our Inclusive Access program, you can provide all these tools at the lowest available market price to your students. Ask your McGraw Hill representative for more information.

Solutions for your challenges

A product isn't a solution. Real solutions are affordable, reliable, and come with training and ongoing support when you need it and how you want it. Visit **supportateverystep.com** for videos and resources both you and your students can use throughout the term.

Updated and relevant content

Our new Evergreen delivery model provides the most current and relevant content for your course, hassle-free. Content, tools, and technology updates are delivered directly to your existing McGraw Hill Connect® course. Engage students and freshen up assignments with up-to-date coverage of select topics and assessments, all without having to switch editions or build a new course.

Introduction to Corrections

Part One develops an understanding of corrections by examining the purposes of corrections and by describing the forces molding contemporary corrections.

Today, crime rates are falling but the number of people under correctional supervision (on probation or parole or in jail or prison) has only just started to decline from historical highs. Get-tough-on-crime attitudes, the War on Drugs, and the reduction in the use of discretionary parole explain what some have seen as the overuse of imprisonment in the past few decades. The current period of mass incarceration has led to concerns about the development of a carceral state in this country, and social justice proponents decry the huge numbers of persons who remain confined.

Professionalism is the key to effectively managing correctional populations—and

that is especially true today as the mass incarceration era begins to wind down. Standard-setting organizations such as the American Correctional Association, the American Jail Association, the American Probation and Parole Association, and the National Commission on Correctional Health Care offer detailed sets of written principles for correctional occupations and correctional administrators.

Nevertheless, professional credentialing in corrections is relatively new.

The professional nature of corrections is also seen in the way sanctions are developed. From a time when theory and practice advocated indeterminate sentences to the legislatively mandated determinate sentences of today, correctional decision makers have had to use their knowledge of human behavior,

philosophy, and law to construct sanctions that are fair and just. The correctional goals of retribution, just deserts, deterrence, incapacitation, rehabilitation, and restoration have produced the sanctions of probation, intermediate sanctions, jail, prison, parole, and capital punishment.

Part One also discusses evidence-based corrections (EBC) or the use of social scientific techniques to determine the most workable and cost-effective programs and initiatives. Choosing the best programs means understanding the political, social, economic, human, and moral consequences of crime control. For that reason, corrections is a field in which complex decision making requires the skills of trained professional staff and administrators.

Jim West/Alamy Stock Photo

[1]

CORRECTIONS
An Overview

CHAPTER OBJECTIVES

After completing this chapter you should be able to do the following:

1. Describe the corrections explosion that began in the United States in the 1980s, and tell how American prison populations have finally started to decline.

2. Describe how crime is measured in the United States, and list the kinds of crimes that cause people to enter correctional programs and institutions.

3. List and describe the various components of the criminal justice system, including the major components of the corrections subsystem.

Mass imprisonment [has been] shown to be irrational, unscientific, inhumane, and bereft of a future.

—Francis T. Cullen, 2022[1]

Recently, the California-based Vera Institute of Justice announced that three new states have been selected to join a model national initiative designed to test whether imprisonment strategies used in Germany and Norway can be successfully applied to American correctional institutions that house youthful offenders.[2] The new states, North Dakota, Colorado, and Idaho, will join three others that are already in the "Restoring Promise" program run by the institute. Organizers say that the Restoring Promise program "disrupts and transforms" the "living and working conditions inside American prisons and jails." It uses input from people who are incarcerated to "repurpose" existing housing units and replaces traditional rigid discipline with more compassionate practices. Early studies of the program already show a "staggering improvement in the life of all people who live and work" in participating correctional facilities. Vera adds that "at its core, Restoring Promise is about deepening our understanding of how the American legacy of slavery and genocide has shaped our current prison system."

Introduction to Corrections
What is corrections, and why should you learn about it?

Jugendanstalt prison in Lower Saxony, Germany. American corrections officials have begun to examine European prisons for clues on how to improve those in the United States. What might they learn?
Erich Häfele/agefotostock/Alamy Stock Photo

THE CARCERAL STATE: WHERE DO WE GO NOW?

One amazing fact stands out from all the contemporary information about American corrections: While serious **crime** in the United States consistently declined throughout much of the 1990s, and while such declines continued into the first two decades of the 21st century, the number of people under **correctional supervision** in this country—not just the number of people who have been convicted and sent to **prison**—started to skyrocket during the 1980s, and only began to drop after 2010. Crime rates are approximately 20 percent lower today than they were in 1980. In fact, they are near their lowest level in 35 years. But the number of people under correctional supervision increased almost 300% between 1980 and 2010—when it finally started to decline. During that period, the federal prison population went from 11 incarcerated persons for every 100,000 U.S. residents to 68. Annual spending on the federal prison system rose 600 percent, from $970 million to more than $6.7 billion in inflation-adjusted dollars. States, like the federal government, recorded sharp increases in incarceration and corrections costs over the three decades from 1980 to 2010. Numbers like these show that the era of **mass incarceration,** created a widescale reliance on the use of imprisonment to address the nation's problems. By the turn of the 21st century, the provision of correctional services of all kinds had become a major strain on government budgets at all levels.

Today, progress is being made in bringing imprisonment rates down.[3] By 2020, the imprisonment rate at the federal level had fallen to 43 persons out of every 100,000 U.S. residents—and it continues to decline. In just one

The Corrections Explosion
What is the "corrections explosion"? What brought it about? How can we control it?

CO1-1

crime
A violation of the criminal law.

correctional supervision
A term that refers to all persons under the supervision of adult correctional systems and includes those who are supervised in the community under the authority of probation or parole agencies and those held in state and federal prisons or local jails.

prison
A state or federal confinement facility that has custodial authority over adults sentenced to confinement.

mass incarceration

The overuse of correctional facilities, particularly prisons, in the United States as determined by historical and cross-cultural standards. We live in an era of mass incarceration.

carceral state

The social conditions that exist when government power is used to incapacitate, incarcerate, detain, or otherwise limit the physical freedom of vast numbers of people, extending beyond that necessary to ensure a safe and just society.

social justice

An ideal that embraces all aspects of civilized life and is linked to fundamental notions of fairness and to cultural beliefs about right and wrong.

year (between 2019 and 2020), federal prisons showed a 40% decrease in new admissions. State prisons showed similar declines, with the largest percentage declines in admissions in California, which had 66% fewer admissions in 2020 than in 2019, and in New York where admissions to prison decreased by 60%. Although some of the decline in prison admissions was the result of new government policies, the bulk of it was due to the fact that courts across the country altered their operations during the COVID epidemic, leading to delays in trials and the sentencing of persons.

Alongside fewer admissions, there have also been increases in the number of persons released from prison, but when viewed historically American prison populations continue to be extraordinarily high (Exhibit 1-1). Critics of today's continued high rates of imprisonment sometimes refer to our country as a **carceral state**. The term *carceral state* implies that government power is being used to incapacitate, incarcerate, detain, or otherwise limit the physical freedom of vast numbers of people, extending far beyond that necessary to ensure a safe and just society. Of course, the words "safe" and "just" are critical and reveal that **social justice** concerns need to be balanced with public safety in determining appropriate levels of incapacitation not only in the United States but in any society.

Those who support the widespread use of incarceration argue that public safety can be assured only through incapacitation of those who are dangerous. But "dangerousness" can be a slippery concept when applied to social activity that may not physically harm others directly—as when those who use (or even traffic in) illicit drugs are arrested and prosecuted. Nora Krinitsky, Director of the Carceral State Project at the University of Michigan, says, "The term *carceral state* often calls to mind institutions of confinement like jails, detention centers, prisons, but … it also comprises a wide range of policies, practices, and institutions that scrutinize individuals and communities both before and after their contact with the criminal justice system."[4] We might also add that, in a true carceral state, the justice system employs millions of men and women who directly depend upon high rates of imprisonment and detention to earn a living.

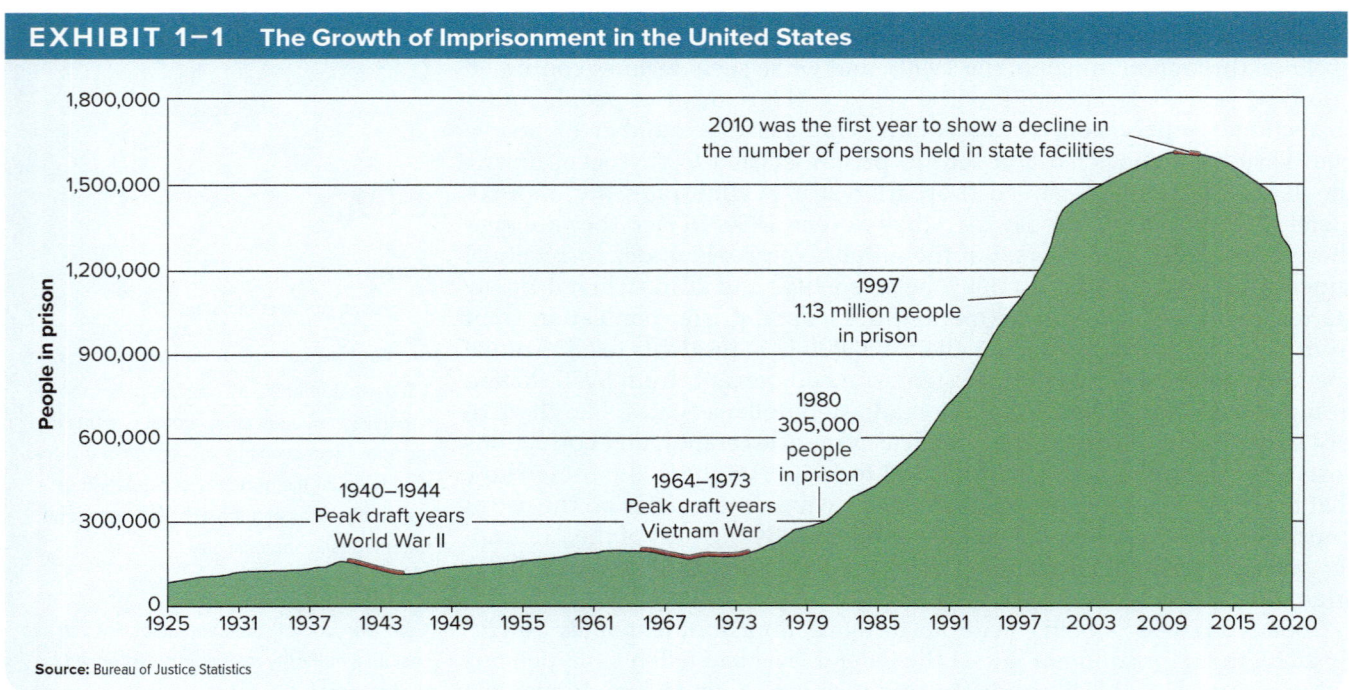

EXHIBIT 1–1   The Growth of Imprisonment in the United States

Y-axis: People in prison — 0 to 1,800,000

Annotations on chart:
- 2010 was the first year to show a decline in the number of persons held in state facilities
- 1997 — 1.13 million people in prison
- 1980 — 305,000 people in prison
- 1940–1944 Peak draft years World War II
- 1964–1973 Peak draft years Vietnam War

X-axis: 1925, 1931, 1937, 1943, 1949, 1955, 1961, 1967, 1973, 1979, 1985, 1991, 1997, 2003, 2009, 2015, 2020

Source: Bureau of Justice Statistics

The question that needs to be answered is, "Why?" Why did the American correctional population increase so dramatically in recent decades even in the face of declining crime rates? And why is the United States still in the midst of an era of mass incarceration? The answer to these questions, like the answers to most societal enigmas, is far from simple, and it has a number of dimensions. We identify four such dimensions in the material that follows.

First, it is important to recognize that get-tough-on-crime laws, such as the three-strikes (and two-strikes) laws that were enacted in many states during the mid-1990s, fueled rapid increases in prison populations. The conservative attitudes that gave birth to those laws are still largely with us, and much of the increase in state prison populations has come from imprisoning more people for violent crimes for longer periods of time.[5] At the federal level, the Violent Crime Control and Law Enforcement Act of 1994 encouraged longer prison sentences for more crimes and led to the adoption of harsher sentencing regimes throughout the nation.

A second reason that correctional populations increased rapidly during the 1990s and the decade that followed can be found in the Twentieth Century's War on Drugs. The War on Drugs led to the arrest and conviction of many people, resulting in larger correctional populations in nearly every jurisdiction (especially within the federal correctional system). The congressional Colson Task Force on Federal Corrections, which issued its report ten years ago, found that "The biggest driver of growth" in the federal prison population was "federally sentenced drug offenders, almost all of whom were convicted of drug trafficking" (see Exhibit 1–2 for drug arrests, and compare it with Exhibit 1–1 to see the impact of drug arrests on prison populations). Many drug arrestees—especially traffickers—are sentenced to lengthy prison terms, further increasing the number of people in prison, and many such people have multiple convictions, including use (or possession) of a firearm during a drug transaction.[6] So although today's drive to legalize marijuana and other previously illicit substances may lead to fewer imprisoned persons in the future, the last century's War on Drugs goes a long way toward explaining the

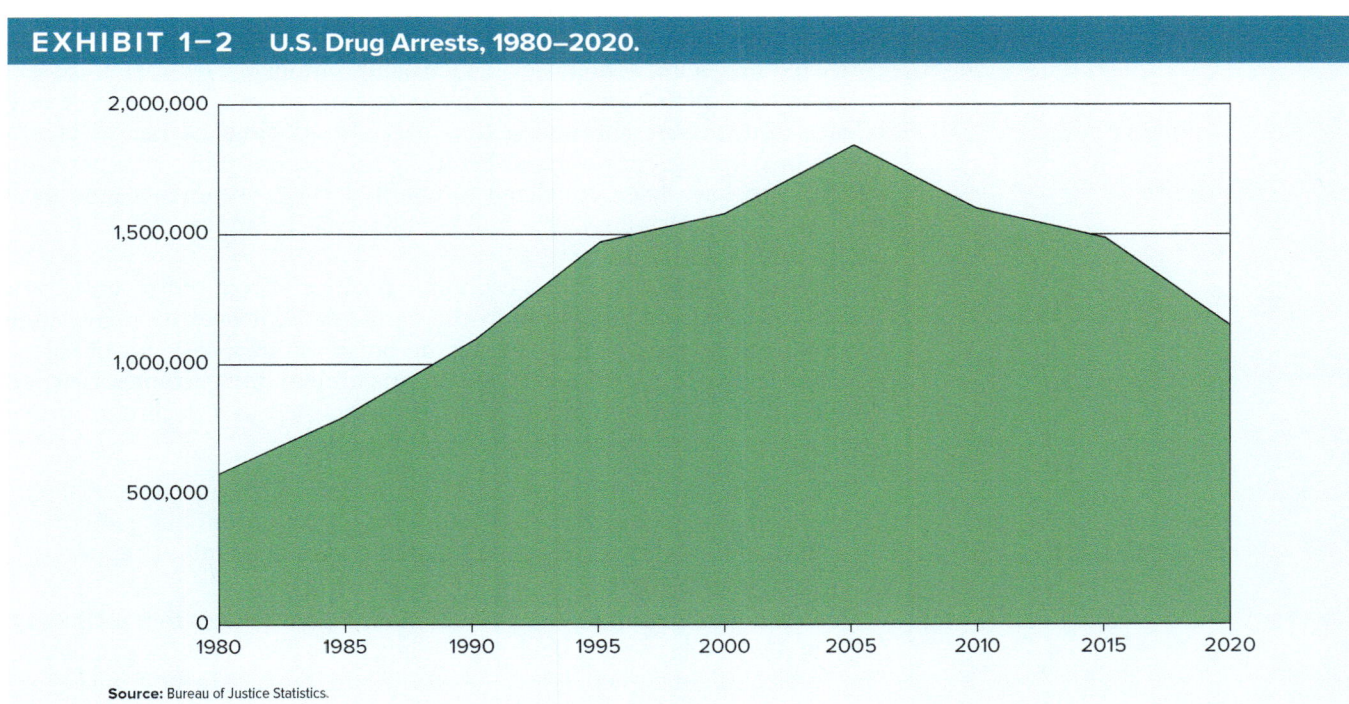

EXHIBIT 1–2   **U.S. Drug Arrests, 1980–2020.**

Source: Bureau of Justice Statistics.

U.S. correctional populations have grown dramatically over the past 40 years, as this image of incarcerated persons living in a modified gymnasium at the Mule Creek State Prison in Ione, California, illustrates. What factors led to a substantial increase in the use of imprisonment in this country beginning in the 1980s?

Justin Sullivan/Getty Images

historical growth in correctional populations even while the rate of "serious crime" in the United States was declining.

Third, parole authorities became increasingly reluctant to release people on parole for fear of the civil liability that they could face should those people commit new crimes. This contributed to a further expansion of prison populations.

Fourth, as some observers have noted, the corrections boom created its own growth dynamic. As ever increasing numbers of people were placed on probation, the likelihood of probation violations increased. Prison sentences for more and more violators resulted in larger prison populations. When people who have been in prison are released, they swell the numbers of those on parole, leading to a larger number of parole violations, which in turn can still fuel further prison growth. Statistics show that the number of persons convicted of violating the criminal law and then sent to prison for at least the second time has increased steadily, accounting for approximately 35 percent of the total number of admissions.[7]

One analysis of the dramatic increase in imprisonment, found that it "was not driven by a centralized national-level strategy for dealing with crime and was not based on a coherent body of empirical knowledge demonstrating that prisons improved public safety."[8] Instead, said the report, "it was the product of layers of legislative decisions, primarily enacted at the state level, to charge and imprison more offenders, increase sentences, limit prison releases, and expand" prison capacity. These decisions led to a new era in which prisons became primary weapons in what was then seen as the nation's war on drugs and on crime.

Turning the Corner in U.S. Prison Populations

While get-tough-on-crime attitudes continue to persist among significant segments of American society today, they have largely been trumped by economic realities. State budgets have been hard pressed to continue funding prison expansion, and the number of people behind bars began to show a slow decline beginning around 2010. Alternatives to imprisonment, most of which will be discussed in coming chapters, are many and include probation, fines, and community service—to which people who have been convicted are being sentenced in increasing numbers. In order to reduce correctional expenditures even further, some states are using forms of early release from prison, shortening time served, reducing the period of probation or parole supervision, and shifting the responsibility of supervising people who have been convicted to county-level governments (and away from state responsibility). We will examine these innovations at various places throughout this text.

As states grappled with the economic realities of reduced revenues and constrained budgets beginning in the early 2000s, it became increasingly important to get the most "bang for the buck," so to speak, out of correctional programs. The realization that imprisonment had become too expensive, combined with a number of other factors, led to a decline in prison populations. Other reasons for the decline include:

1. Criminal justice reform policies—Many states have enacted policies aimed at reducing the use of imprisonment and promoting alternatives to incarceration, such as drug courts and community supervision programs.
2. A decrease in crime rates—In recent years, crime rates in the United States have generally been declining (contrary to what the popular media might depict), which has contributed to a reduction in the number of people being sentenced to prison.

3. Reforms to sentencing laws—Some states have passed laws to reduce mandatory minimum sentences and provide greater discretion to judges in imposing sentences, which has, in turn, led to fewer people being sentenced to long prison terms.

4. Decarceration initiatives—In response to overcrowding, budget constraints, and public pressure, some states have implemented initiatives to safely reduce their prison populations, such as early release programs and parole reforms.

5. Changes in drug enforcement policies—Some states have adopted reforms to their drug enforcement policies, such as reducing sentences for drug offenses and expanding access to treatment, all of which have reduced the number of people incarcerated for drug-related crimes.

In her incoming presidential address to the Academy of Criminal Justice Sciences, Melissa Hickman Barlow outlined a plan for the implementation of **sustainable justice.** Barlow defined sustainable justice as "criminal laws and criminal justice institutions, policies, and practices that achieve justice in the present without compromising the ability of future generations to have the benefits of a just society."[9] Barlow's call for affordable justice, based on principles and operating practices that can be carried into the future without bankrupting generations yet to come, represents an important turning point in our nation's approach to corrections and other justice institutions.

These and other factors have contributed to a reduction in the number of people being incarcerated in the United States and a growing recognition of the need to adopt evidence-based policies. As we will see in the next chapter, the evidence-based movement in corrections seeks to evaluate programs and services to see which are the most effective relative to their costs. Evidence-based practices play an important role in correctional administration today—and should contribute much to the call for sustainable justice and continue to contribute to a decline in the use of imprisonment.

sustainable justice

Criminal laws and criminal justice institutions, policies, and practices that achieve justice in the present without compromising the ability of future generations to have the benefits of a just society.

Correctional Employment

As correctional populations peaked, increasing budgets led to a dramatically expanding correctional workforce and enhanced employment opportunities within the field. Much of that momentum continues into the present day. In 2023, for example, the North Carolina Department of Public Safety offered a $7,000 hiring bonus for new correctional officers (COs), and the Tennessee Department of Corrections provided a $5,000 bonus to newly hired officers. At the same time, the Nebraska Department of Correctional Services provided a bonus of $15,000 for experienced COs (i.e., for those at the rank of corporal or higher) who were willing to work at the Nebraska State Penitentiary and other select facilities.[10]

According to historical reports, persons employed in the corrections field totaled approximately 27,000 in 1950.[11] By 1975, the number had risen to about 75,000. Estimates published by the Bureau of Labor Statistics (BLS) in 2021 show that over 400,000 government employees throughout the United States worked in corrections, with a total monthly payroll of around $3 billion.[12] BLS also found that the average hourly and annual wage for COs and jailers was $25.69 and $53,420, respectively. Of course, supervisors and those at higher rank earned more than the average. Similarly, those who begin work with college degrees are paid more. Exhibit 1–3 shows some of the employment possibilities in corrections.

EXHIBIT 1–3   Careers in Corrections

Academic teacher	Field administrator	Psychologist
Activity therapy administrator	Fugitive apprehension officer	Recreation coordinator
Business manager	Human services counselor	Social worker
Case manager	Job placement officer	Statistician
Chaplain	Mental health clinician	Substance abuse counselor
Chemical dependency manager	Parole caseworker	Unit leader
Children's services counselor	Parole officer	Victim advocate
Classification officer	Presentence investigator	Vocational instructor
Clinical social worker	Probation officer	Warden/superintendent
Correctional officer	Program officer	Youth services coordinator
Dietary officer	Program specialist	Youth supervisor
Drug court coordinator	Programmer/analyst	

Prisons mean jobs and can contribute greatly to the health of local economies. Some economically disadvantaged towns—from Tupper Lake, in the Adirondack Mountains of upstate New York, to Edgefield, South Carolina—recently cashed in on the corrections industry, having successfully competed to become sites for new prisons. Although prison populations have recently fallen, a number of states are building new prisons to replace failing prison infrastructure with safer, more secure facilities that accommodate the rehabilitation of incarcerated people.[13] In 2021, for example, the state of Alabama announced the planned construction of two new correctional facilities to be built on state-owned land. The two new facilities, each designed to hold 4,000 persons in confinement will cost approximately $700 million to build and will contribute about $30 million a year to the local economy.[14]

CRIME AND CORRECTIONS

The crimes that bring people into the American correctional system include felonies, misdemeanors, and minor law violations that are sometimes called *infractions.*

Felonies are serious crimes. Murder, rape, aggravated assault, robbery, burglary, and arson are felonies in all jurisdictions within the United States, although the names for these crimes may differ from state to state. A general way to think about felonies is to remember that a **felony** is a serious crime whose commission can result in confinement in a state or federal correctional institution for more than a year.

In some states, a felony conviction can result in the loss of certain civil privileges. A few states make conviction of a felony and the resulting incarceration grounds for uncontested divorce. Others prohibit people who have been convicted of felonies from running for public office, voting, or owning a firearm, and some exclude them from professions such as medicine, law, and police work.

Huge differences in the treatment of specific crimes exist among states. Some crimes classified as felonies in one part of the country may be misdemeanors in another. In still other states, they may not even be crimes at all! Such is the case with some drug law violations and with social order offenses such as sex work and gambling.

felony

A serious criminal offense; specifically, one punishable by death or by incarceration in a prison facility for more than a year.

Misdemeanors, which comprise the second major crime category, are relatively minor violations of the criminal law. They include crimes such as petty theft (the theft of items of little worth), simple assault (in which the victim suffers no serious injury and in which none was intended), breaking and entering, the possession of burglary tools, disorderly conduct, disturbing the peace, filing a false crime report, and writing bad checks (although the amount for which the check is written may determine the classification of this offense). In general, misdemeanors can be thought of as any crime punishable by a year or less in confinement.

Within felony and misdemeanor categories, most states distinguish among degrees, or levels, of seriousness. Texas law, for example, establishes five felony classes and three classes of misdemeanor—intended to guide judges in assessing the seriousness of particular criminal acts. The Texas penal code then specifies categories into which given offenses fall.

A third category of crime is the **infraction.** The term, which is not used in all jurisdictions, refers to minor violations of the law that are less serious than misdemeanors. Infractions may include such violations of the law as jaywalking, spitting on the sidewalk, littering, and certain traffic violations, including the failure to wear a seat belt. People committing infractions are typically ticketed—that is, given citations—and released, usually upon a promise to appear later in court. Court appearances may be waived upon payment of a fine, which is often mailed in.

misdemeanor

A relatively minor violation of the criminal law, such as petty theft or simple assault, punishable by confinement for one year or less.

infraction

A minor violation of state statute or local ordinance punishable by a fine or other penalty, or by a specified, usually very short term of incarceration.

MEASURING CRIME

CO1-2

Two important sources of information on crime for correctional professionals are the FBI's Uniform Crime Reporting Program (UCR) and the Bureau of Justice Statistics' National Crime Victimization Survey (NCVS). Corrections professionals closely analyze these data to forecast the numbers and types of **correctional clients** that they can expect to see in the future. The forecasts can be used to project the need for different types of detention and rehabilitation services and facilities. It is important to note that the UCR program is transitioning to a new set of reporting criteria under the National Incident-Based Reporting System (NIBRS). NIBRS, which should have been fully implemented by 2021, provides more detailed data about criminal incidents than had previously been available under the older UCR. Unfortunately, however, many police agencies did not successfully meet the FBI's deadline for data submission in NIBRS format because of COVID-induced delays and other factors. As a result, the most reliable data on crimes committed in the United States now comes primarily from the NCVS.

correctional clients

Prison inmates, probationers, parolees, individuals assigned to alternative sentencing programs, and those held in jails.

The Crime Funnel

Not all crimes are reported, and not everyone who commits a reported crime is arrested, so relatively few people who violate the criminal law actually enter the criminal justice system. Of those who do, some are not prosecuted (perhaps because the evidence against them is insufficient), others plead guilty to lesser crimes, and others are found not guilty. Some who are convicted are diverted from further processing by the system or may be fined or ordered to counseling. Hence, the proportion of people who eventually enter the correctional system is small, as Exhibit 1–4 shows.

EXHIBIT 1–4   The Crime Funnel

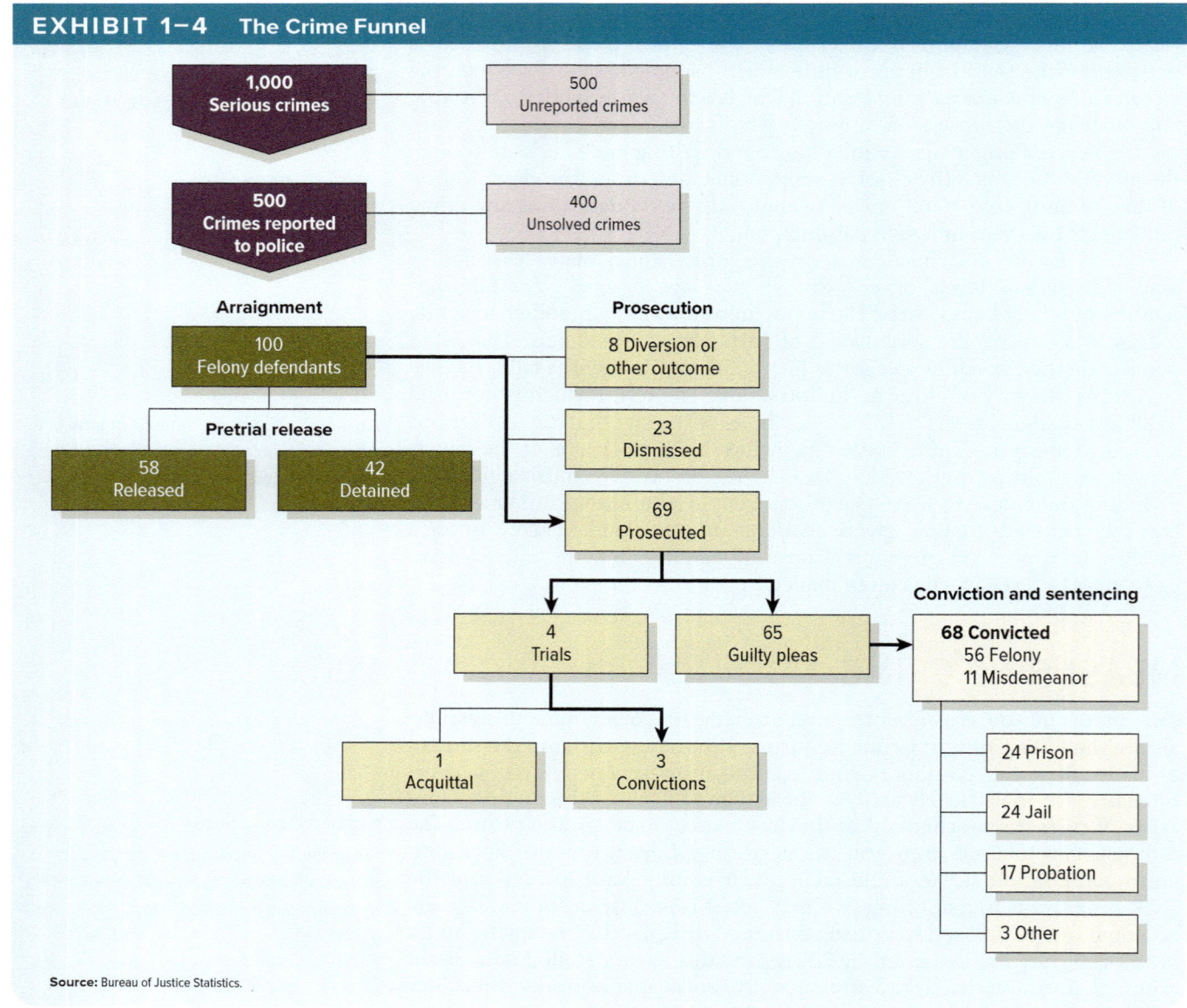

Source: Bureau of Justice Statistics.

CO1-3   CORRECTIONS AND THE CRIMINAL JUSTICE SYSTEM

criminal justice

The process of achieving justice through the application of the criminal law and through the workings of the criminal justice system. Also, the study of the field of criminal justice.

criminal justice system

The collection of all the agencies that perform criminal justice functions, whether these are operations or administration or technical support. The basic divisions of the criminal justice system are police, courts, and corrections.

Corrections is generally considered the final stage in the criminal justice process. Some aspects of corrections, however, come into play early in the process. Keep in mind that although the term **criminal justice** can be used to refer to the justice *process,* it can also be used to describe our *system* of justice. Criminal justice agencies, taken as a whole, are said to compose the **criminal justice system.**

The components of the criminal justice system are (1) police, (2) courts, and (3) corrections. Each component, because it contains a variety of organizations and agencies, can be termed a *subsystem.* The subsystem of corrections, for example, includes prisons, agencies of probation and parole, jails, and a variety of alternative programs.

The *process* of criminal justice involves the activities of the agencies that make up the criminal justice system. The process of criminal justice begins when a crime is discovered or reported, and it often ends when persons who have been convicted of crimes are released from correctional supervision.

Court decisions based on the due process guarantees of the U.S. Constitution require that specific steps be taken in the justice process. Although the exact nature of those steps varies among jurisdictions, the description that follows portrays the most common sequence of events in response to serious criminal behavior. Exhibit 1–5, which diagrams the American criminal justice system, indicates the relationships among the stages in the criminal justice processing of adults who have been criminally convicted.

Entering the Correctional System

The criminal justice system does not respond to all crime because most crimes are not discovered or reported to the police.[15] Law enforcement agencies learn about crimes from the reports of citizens, through discovery by a police officer in the field, or through investigative and intelligence work. Once a law enforcement agency knows of a crime, the agency must identify and arrest a suspect before the case can proceed. Sometimes a suspect is found at the scene; other times, however, identifying a suspect requires an extensive investigation. Often no one is identified or apprehended—the crime goes unsolved. If a person is arrested, booked, and jailed to await an initial court appearance, the intake, custody, confinement, and supervision aspects of corrections first come into play at this stage of the criminal justice process.

Prosecution and Pretrial Procedure

After an arrest, law enforcement agencies present information about the case and about the accused to the prosecutor, who decides whether to file formal charges with the court. If no charges are filed, the accused must be released. The prosecutor can also drop charges after filing them. Such a choice is called *nolle prosequi;* and when it happens, a case is said to be "nolled" or "nollied."

A suspect charged with a crime must be taken before a judge or magistrate without unnecessary delay. At the initial appearance, the judge or magistrate informs the accused of the charges and decides whether there is probable cause to detain them. Often, defense counsel is also assigned then. If the offense charged is not very serious, the determination of guilt and the assessment of a penalty may also occur at this stage.

In some jurisdictions, a pretrial release decision is made at the initial appearance, but this decision may occur at other hearings or at another time during the process. Pretrial release on bail was traditionally intended to ensure appearance at trial. However, many jurisdictions today permit pretrial detention of defendants accused of serious offenses and deemed dangerous in order to prevent them from committing crimes in the pretrial period. The court may decide to release the accused on their own recognizance, into the custody of a third party, on the promise of satisfying certain conditions, or after posting a financial bond. Conditions of release may be reviewed at any later time while charges are still pending.

In many jurisdictions, the initial appearance may be followed by a preliminary hearing. The main function of this hearing is to determine whether there is probable cause to believe that the accused committed a crime within the jurisdiction of the court. If the judge or magistrate does not find probable cause, the case is dismissed. However, if the judge finds probable cause for such a belief, or if the accused waives the right to a preliminary hearing, the case may be bound over to a grand jury.

EXHIBIT 1–5   The Adult Criminal Justice System

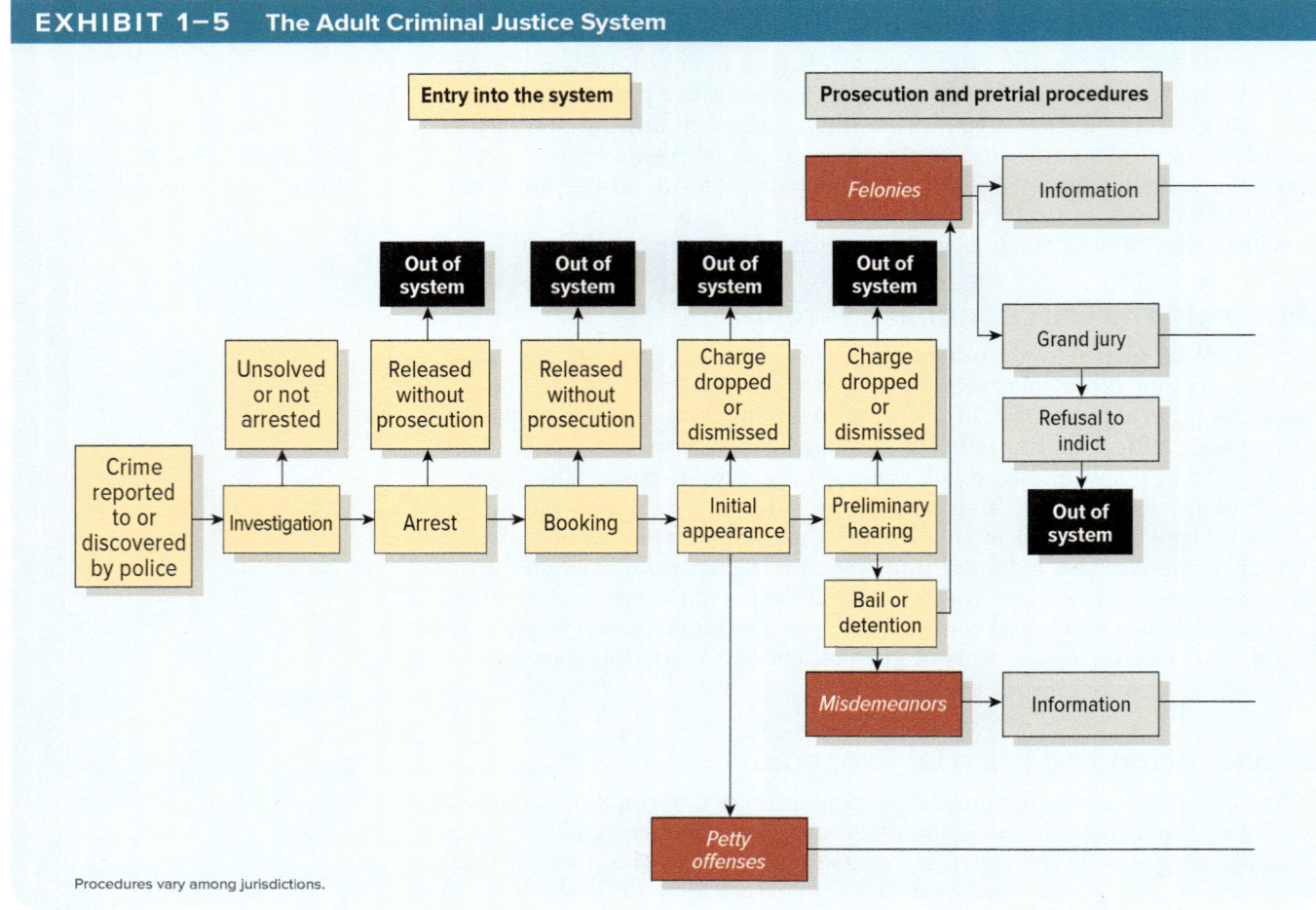

Procedures vary among jurisdictions.

A grand jury hears evidence against the accused, presented by the prosecutor, and decides whether there is sufficient evidence to cause the accused to be brought to trial. If the grand jury finds sufficient evidence, it submits an indictment to the court.

Not all jurisdictions use grand juries. Some require, instead, that the prosecutor submit an information (a formal written accusation) to the court. In most jurisdictions, misdemeanor cases and some felony cases proceed by the issuance of an information. Some jurisdictions require indictments in felony cases. However, the accused may choose to waive a grand jury indictment and, instead, accept service of an information for the crime.

Judicial Procedures

Adjudication is the process by which a court arrives at a decision in a case. The adjudication process involves a number of steps. The first is **arraignment.** Once an indictment or information is filed with the trial court, the accused is scheduled for arraignment. If the accused has been detained without bail, corrections personnel take them to their arraignment. At the arraignment, the accused is informed of the charges, advised of the rights of criminal defendants, and asked to enter a plea to the charges.

If the accused pleads guilty or pleads *nolo contendere* (accepts a penalty without admitting guilt), the judge may accept or reject the plea. If the plea is accepted, no trial is held and the person is sentenced at this proceeding or at a later date. The plea may be rejected if, for example, the judge believes that the accused has been coerced. If this occurs, the case

adjudication

The process by which a court arrives at a final decision in a case; or the second stage of the juvenile justice process in which the court decides whether the individual is formally responsible for (guilty of) the alleged offense.

arraignment

An appearance in court prior to trial in a criminal proceeding.

nolo contendere

A plea of "no contest." A no-contest plea may be used by a defendant who does not wish to contest conviction. Because the plea does not admit guilt, however, it cannot provide the basis for later civil suits.

EXHIBIT 1–5 **The Adult Criminal Justice System** *(Continued)*

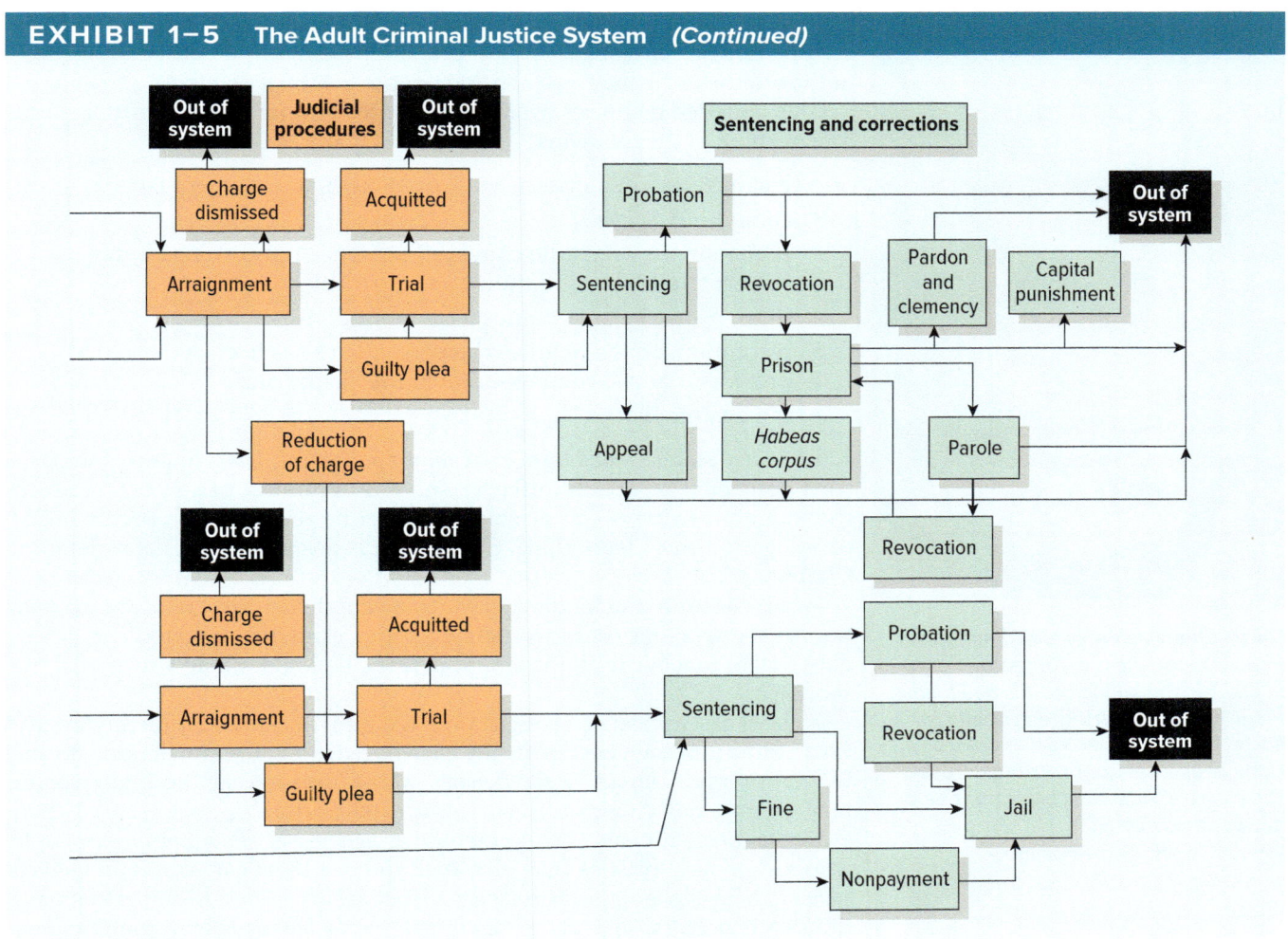

may proceed to trial. Sometimes, as the result of negotiations between the prosecutor and the defendant, the defendant enters a guilty plea in expectation of reduced charges or a light sentence. *Nolo contendere* pleas are often entered by those who fear a later civil action and who therefore do not want to admit guilt.

If the accused pleads not guilty or not guilty by reason of insanity, a date is set for trial. A person accused of a serious crime is guaranteed a trial by jury. However, the accused may ask for a bench trial, in which the judge, rather than a jury, serves as the finder of fact. In both instances, the prosecution and defense present evidence by questioning witnesses, and the judge decides issues of law. The trial results in acquittal or conviction of the original charges or of lesser included offenses. A defendant may be convicted at trial only if the government's evidence proves beyond a reasonable doubt that the defendant is guilty, or if the defendant knowingly and voluntarily pleads guilty to the charges.

Sentencing and Sanctions

After a guilty verdict or guilty plea, sentence is imposed. In most cases, the judge decides on the sentence, but in some states, the sentence is decided by the jury, particularly for capital offenses, such as murder.

To arrive at an appropriate sentence, a court may hold a sentencing hearing to consider evidence of aggravating or mitigating circumstances.

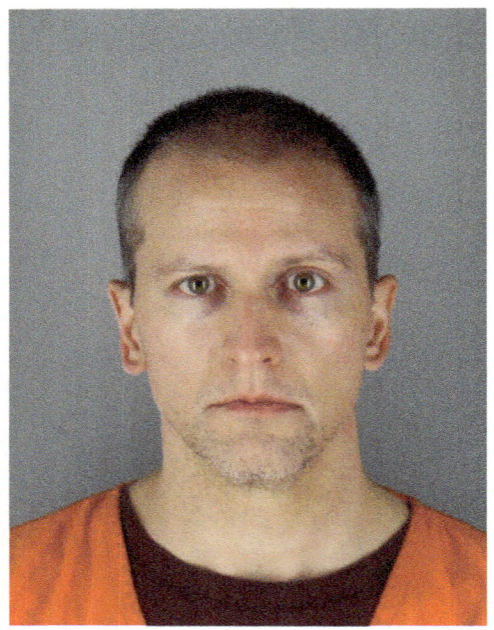

Derek Chauvin, one of the Minneapolis Police Department officers convicted in 2021 in the killing of George Floyd. Floyd's death contributed to calls for social justice and led to demonstrations against police brutality across the country. How can corrections help answer those calls?

Hennepin County Sheriff/AP Images

In assessing the circumstances surrounding a criminal act, courts often rely on presentence investigations by probation agencies or other designated authorities. Courts may also consider victim impact statements.

The sentencing choices available to judges and juries frequently include one or more of the following:

- incarceration in a prison, a jail, or another confinement facility;
- community service;
- probation, in which the convicted person is not confined but is subject to certain conditions and restrictions;
- fines, primarily as penalties for minor offenses;
- restitution, which requires the person who has been convicted to provide financial compensation to the victim; and
- the death penalty.

In many states, *mandatory minimum* sentencing laws require that persons convicted of certain offenses serve a minimum prison term, which the judge must impose and which may not be reduced by a parole board or by "good-time" deductions. Sentencing is discussed in greater detail in Chapter 3.

After the trial, a defendant may request appellate review of the conviction to see whether there was some serious error that affected the defendant's right to a fair trial. In some states, the defendant may also appeal the sentence.

At least one appeal of a conviction is a matter of right. Any further appeal (to a state supreme court or in the case of federal court convictions, to the U.S. Supreme Court) is *discretionary,* which means that the higher court may or may not choose to hear the further appeal. After losing all their available *direct* appeals (also known as *exhaustion of state remedies*), people who are in state prisons may also seek to have their convictions reviewed *collaterally* in the federal courts via a writ of *habeas corpus.* In states that have the death penalty, appeals of death sentences are usually automatic, and extensive federal *habeas corpus* review often takes place before the sentence of death is actually carried out.

The Correctional Subsystem

After conviction and sentencing, most defendants enter the correctional subsystem. Before we proceed with our discussion, it is best to define the term *corrections.* As with most words, a variety of definitions can be found.

In 1967, for example, the President's Commission on Law Enforcement and Administration of Justice wrote that *corrections* means "America's prisons, jails, juvenile training schools, and probation and parole machinery." It is "that part of the criminal justice system," said the commission, "that the public sees least of and knows least about."[16]

Years later, in 1975, the National Advisory Commission on Criminal Justice Standards and Goals said in its lengthy volume on corrections, "*Corrections* is defined here as the community's official reactions to the convicted offender, whether adult or juvenile."[17] The commission noted that "this is a broad definition and it suffers ... from several shortcomings." Today, the Bureau of Justice Statistics (BJS) says that "**corrections** refers to the supervision of persons arrested for, convicted of, or sentenced for criminal offenses."[18] It is this definition that we will use in this text.

We can distinguish between institutional corrections and noninstitutional corrections. A report by the BJS says that **institutional corrections** refers to "persons housed in secure correctional facilities."[19] BJS goes on to say

corrections

The supervision of persons arrested for, convicted of, or sentenced for criminal offenses.

institutional corrections

A term that refers to persons housed in secure correctional facilities.

that correctional institutions are prisons, reformatories, jails, houses of correction, penitentiaries, correctional farms, workhouses, reception centers, diagnostic centers, industrial schools, training schools, detention centers, and a variety of other types of institutions for the confinement and correction of adults who have been convicted, or of juveniles who are adjudicated delinquent or in need of supervision. [The term] also includes facilities for the detention of adults and juveniles accused of a crime and awaiting trial or hearing.

According to BJS, **noninstitutional corrections,** which is sometimes called **community corrections,** includes "pardon, probation, and parole activities, correctional administration not directly connectable to institutions, and miscellaneous [activities] not directly related to institutional care."

As all these definitions show, in its broadest sense, the term *corrections* encompasses each of the following components, as well as the process of interaction among them:

- the *purpose* and *goals* of the correctional enterprise;
- jails, prisons, correctional institutions, and other *facilities*;
- probation, parole, and alternative and diversionary *programs*;
- federal, state, local, and international correctional offices and *agencies*;
- counseling, educational, health care, nutrition, and many other *services*;
- risk *assessment* and risk *management*;
- correctional *clients*;
- corrections *volunteers*;
- corrections *professionals*;
- fiscal appropriations and *funding*;
- various aspects of criminal and civil *law*;
- formal and informal *procedures*;
- effective and responsible *management*;
- community *expectations* regarding correctional practices; and
- the machinery of *capital punishment*.

When we use the word *corrections,* we include all of these elements. Central to this approach is the recognition that corrections—although it involves a variety of programs, services, facilities, and personnel—is essentially a management activity—especially one that focuses on risk assessment and risk management (particularly as it relates to the likelihood of reoffending). Rather than stress the role of institutions or agencies, our take on corrections emphasizes the human dimension of correctional activity—especially the efforts of the corrections professionals who undertake the day-to-day tasks. Like any other managed activity, corrections has goals and purposes. Exhibit 1–6 details the role of corrections as identified by the American Correctional Association (ACA).

noninstitutional corrections

That aspect of the correctional enterprise that includes "pardon, probation, and parole activities, correctional administration not directly connectable to institutions, and miscellaneous [activities] not directly related to institutional care." *Also known as* community corrections.

community corrections

A philosophy of correctional treatment that embraces (1) decentralization of authority, (2) citizen participation, (3) redefinition of the population of individuals for whom incarceration is most appropriate, and (4) emphasis on rehabilitation through community programs.

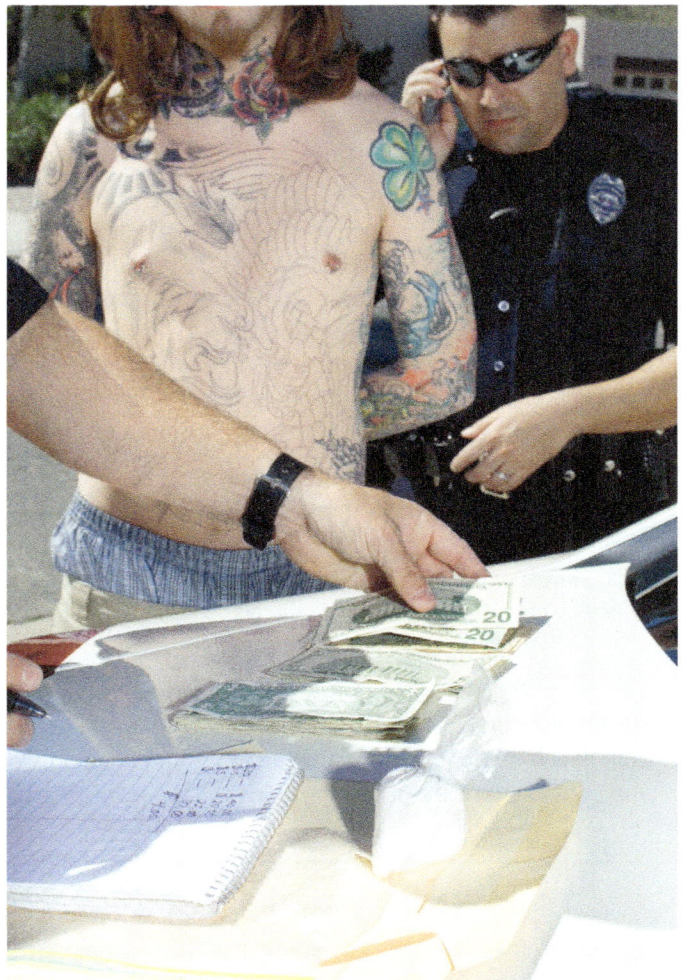

Police arrest a person who was charged with dealing in illegal drugs. While marijuana and some other previously illicit drugs are freely available in many states today—especially to those who are sick—not all drugs have been decriminalized. What role does corrections play in the maintenance of social order, and why is social order important?

moodboard/Getty Images

EXHIBIT 1–6 **American Correctional Association**

Public Correctional Policy on the Role of Corrections

The overall role of corrections is to enhance public safety and social order. Adult and juvenile correctional systems should:

- implement court-ordered sanctions and provide supervision of those accused of unlawful behavior prior to and after adjudication in a safe and humane manner;
- offer the widest range of correctional programs that are based on exemplary practices, supported by research and promote pro-social behavior;
- provide gender- and culturally-responsive programs and services for preadjudicated and adjudicated offenders that will enhance successful reentry to the community and that are administered within the least restrictive environment consistent with public, staff and offender safety;
- address the needs of victims of crime;
- routinely review correctional programs and reentry services to ensure that they are addressing the needs of offenders, victims, and the community; and
- collaborate with other professions to improve and strengthen correctional services and to support the reduction of crime and recidivism.

Source: Reprinted with permission of the American Correctional Association, Alexandria, VA.

REVIEW AND APPLICATIONS

SUMMARY

1 Although crime rates are at their lowest level in more than 30 years, correctional populations have increased for decades because of get-tough-on-crime attitudes, the nation's War on Drugs, and the reluctance of parole authorities, fearing civil liability and public outcry, to release people from prison. Consequently, we have witnessed the growth of what some call the carceral state. At the same time, growth in correctional populations and in spending on prisons and jails led to a dramatically expanding correctional workforce and to enhanced employment opportunities within the field. Today, however, political realities, heightened concerns about social equality, and budgetary limitations have led to a reduction of the numbers of people held in our nation's prisons—a reduction that is likely to continue into the future.

2 Two important sources of crime statistics are the FBI's Uniform Crime Reporting Program (UCR) and the National Crime Victimization Survey (NCVS), published by the Bureau of Justice Statistics. The crimes that bring people into the American correctional system include felonies, which are relatively serious criminal offenses; misdemeanors, which are less serious crimes; and infractions, which are minor law violations. It is important to note that the traditional UCR has now been officially replaced by the FBI's new National Incident-Based Reporting System (NIBRS).

3 The main components of the criminal justice system are police, courts, and corrections. Each can be considered a subsystem of the criminal justice system. The major components of the corrections subsystem are jails, probation, parole, and prisons. Jails and prisons are examples of institutional corrections, while probation and parole are forms of noninstitutional corrections. This chapter stresses that the management of correctional resources and clients is a central part of the correctional enterprise—including the assessment and management of risk for reoffending.

KEY TERMS

crime, p. 3
correctional supervision, p. 3
prison, p. 3
mass incarceration, p. 4
carceral state, p. 4
social justice, p. 4
sustainable justice, p. 7

felony, p. 8
misdemeanor, p. 9
infraction, p. 9
correctional clients, p. 9
criminal justice, p. 10
criminal justice system, p. 10
adjudication, p. 12

arraignment, p. 12
nolo contendere, p. 12
corrections, p. 14
institutional corrections, p. 14
noninstitutional corrections, p. 15
community corrections, p. 15

QUESTIONS FOR REVIEW

1 Why did correctional populations in the United States increase dramatically in the 30 years between 1980 and 2010? Why have they since declined?

2 What are the kinds of crimes that cause people to enter correctional institutions? To enter other kinds of correctional programs?

3 What are the major components of the criminal justice system? What aspects of the corrections subsystem can you identify?

THINKING CRITICALLY ABOUT CORRECTIONS

Vision

In 2022, then newly appointed Director of the Bureau of Justice Statistics, Alexis R. Piquero, said, "Now, more than ever, the need is great for timely, accurate, relevant, and easy to understand data on crime and justice issues."[19] What did he mean, and how does what he said apply to corrections in particular?

ON-THE-JOB DECISION MAKING

Training

Today is the first day of your job as a correctional officer. A severe statewide shortage of officers required you to begin work immediately before training, which you are scheduled to attend in three months. When you arrive at the facility, you are ushered into a meeting with the warden. She welcomes you and gives you a brief pep talk. She asks if you have any concerns. You tell her, "Well, I feel a little uneasy. I haven't gone through the academy yet." "Don't worry," she says, "all our new recruits get on-the-job experience before a slot in the academy opens up. You'll do fine!" She shakes your hand and leads you to the door. After you leave the warden's office, you are given a set of keys and a can of mace. The shift supervisor, a sergeant, gives you a brief tour of the prison. Then he tells you that as you learn your job, you will spend most of your time with another officer, though pairing up will not always be possible.

The officer you are assigned to accompany is Latasha Gates. At first, you follow Officer Gates across the compound, getting more familiar with the layout of the facility. Then you spend an uneventful afternoon working with Officer Gates in the yard. At 4:30, Officer Gates instructs you to make sure that all correctional clients have left the classroom building in preparation for a "count." As you enter the building, you encounter a group of six clients heading toward the door. Before you can move to the side, one of them walks within an inch of you and stares at you. The others crowd in behind him. You can't move. You are pinned to the door by the men. The man directly in front of you is huge—over 6 feet tall and about 280 pounds. His legs look like tree trunks, and his arms are held away from his body by their sheer bulk. You're staring at a chest that could easily pass as a brick wall. With a snarl he growls, "What do you want?"

1. How do you respond? Would you feel more confident responding to a situation like this if you had had some training?

2. If you tell correctional clients in your facility that it's time for a count and to move along, what will you do next? Will you ask anyone for guidance in similar future situations or just chalk up the encounter to a learning experience? To whom might you talk about it?

3. Suppose you are a manager or supervisor at this facility. How would you handle the training of new recruits?

Leadership

You are a correctional officer at the McClellan Correctional Facility. You and your coworkers have been following, with high interest, the events at Brownley, another correctional facility located approximately 35 miles away. Rioting at Brownley during the past four days has left 4 correctional officers and 19 incarcerated people seriously hurt. It now appears, though, that while tensions remain high, the riot has been contained and the people held at Brownley are settling back down. The uneasy truce, however, mandates resolution of the issues that led to the riot in the first place.

The main issue leading to the riot was a claim of mistreatment at the hands of certain members of the Brownley correctional staff. State correctional administrators have determined that an essential first step in preventing future riots is replacement of certain members of the correctional staff at Brownley. You are called to your supervisor's office, where she informs you that you are being reassigned temporarily to Brownley, with a possibility that the reassignment may become permanent.

This news does not make you happy. The logistical impact alone is irritating because it will mean a significant commute each day. More important, though, is that you will be leaving a cohesive team of skilled and dedicated correctional officers with whom you have developed a close bond. You trust one another, and you trust your leaders. There's no telling what you will encounter at Brownley.

Your worst fears are realized when you report for your first shift and your new sergeant takes you aside. "We can't let them win on this," he says. "You know the drill. Stay on 'em hard, and don't cut 'em any slack. We need to let them know from the get-go that things haven't changed—we're still in charge, whether they like it or not, and we ain't gonna take any guff from the likes of them!"

It is immediately apparent to you that your sergeant has a strong "us-against-them" perspective. Your experience tells you that such an attitude at the leadership level likely induces similar, often stronger attitudes at the correctional officer level, and your common sense tells you that this is probably the root of the problem at Brownley.

1. How do you respond to your new sergeant?
2. If you elect to keep your thoughts to yourself, how will you establish yourself with the Brownley clients as a CO who does not subscribe to the other CO's practices without appearing weak or exploitable?
3. If you elect to bring your thoughts to the attention of someone higher up in the supervisory chain, how will you deal with potential adverse reactions from your new coworkers?

ENDNOTES

1. Francis T. Cullen, "The End of American Exceptionalism: An Enlightened Corrections," *Criminology and Public Policy,* November 15, 2022, https://doi.org/10.1111/1745-9133.12605 (accessed March 18, 2023).

2. "'Disrupting Prison' Reform Initiative Expands to Six States," *The Crime Report,* November 19, 2019, https://thecrimereport.org/2019/11/19/model-prison-reform-initiative-expands-to-six-states (accessed January 5, 2023)

3. "U.S. Prison and Jail Populations Flat or Rising Again After 2020 Decline Spurred by Pandemic," *Prison Legal News,* June 1, 2022, https://www.prisonlegalnews.org/news/2022/jun/1/us-prison-and-jail-populations-flat-or-rising-again-after-2020-decline-spurred-pandemic (accessed February 5, 2023).

4. Nora Krinitsky, "What Is the Carceral State?" https://storymaps.arcgis.com/stories/7ab5f5c3fbca46c38f0b2496bcaa5ab0 (accessed May 20, 2023).

5. John F. Pfaff, "The Causes of Growth in Prison Admission and Populations," http://web.law.columbia.edu/sites/default/files/microsites/criminal-law-roundtable-2012/files/Pfaff_New_Admissions_to_Prison.pdf (accessed January 5, 2020).

6. *Charles Colson Task Force on Federal Corrections* (Washington, DC: Urban Institute, 2015).

7. See, for example, Jory Farr, "A Growth Enterprise," www.press-enterprise.com/focus/prison/html/agrowthindustry.html (accessed March 28, 2020).

8. Michael C. Campbell, Matt Vogel, and Joshua Williams, "Historical Contingencies and the Evolving Importance of Race, Violent Crime, and Region in Explaining Mass Incarceration in the United States," *Criminology,* 2015. doi: 0.1111/1745-9125.12065

9. Melissa Hickman Barlow, "Sustainable Justice: 2012 Presidential Address to the Academy of Criminal Justice Sciences," *Justice Quarterly,* 2012, pp. 1–17, 1 First Article.

10. Nebraska Department of Correctional Services, "Apply Now," https://corrections.nebraska.gov/hiring-bonuses (accessed January 5, 2023); North Carolina Department of Public Safety, "Correctional Officers Careers," https://www.ncdps.gov/careers-matter/correctional-officer-careers (accessed January 5, 2023); and Tennessee Department of Corrections, "Correctional Officer," https://www.tn.gov/correction/eo/choose-a-career/correctional-officer.html (accessed January 5, 2023).

11. Cahalan, *Historical Corrections Statistics.*

12. Bureau of Labor Statistics, "Correctional Officers and Jailers," *Occupational Employment and Wage Statistics,* https://www.bls.gov/oes/current/oes333012.htm (accessed January 5, 2023).

13. Isaac Barzso, "As States Turn to New Construction to Combat Nationwide Prison Overcrowding, Construction Delays Add Issues," *Levelset,* July 30, 2021, https://www.levelset.com/news/prison-overcrowding-construction-delays (accessed January 5, 2023).

14. Erin Davis, "Plans for Alabama's New Mega-Prisons Outlined," WSFA 12 News, October 6, 2021, https://www.wsfa.com/2021/10/06/plans-alabamas-new-mega-prisons-outlined (accessed March 3, 2023).

15. Some of the historical material is adapted from Bureau of Justice Statistics, *Report to the Nation on Crime and Justice,* 2nd ed. (Washington, DC: Bureau of Justice Statistics, 1988), pp. 56–58.

16. President's Commission on Law Enforcement and Administration of Justice, *The Challenge of Crime in a Free Society* (Washington, DC: U.S. Government Printing Office, 1967), p. 159.

17. National Advisory Commission on Criminal Justice Standards and Goals, *Corrections* (Washington, DC: U.S. Government Printing Office, 1975), p. 2.

18. Bureau of Justice Statistics, *Glossary,* https://bjs.ojp.gov/glossary?title=&page=4#glossary-terms-block-1-whw1p81svq11v0je (accessed January 20, 2023).

19. Bureau of Justice Statistics, "A Message from the Director," August 18, 2022, https://bjs.ojp.gov/message-bjs-director (accessed January 20, 2023).

CORRECTIONS TODAY

Evidence-Based Corrections and Professionalism

Omar Antonio Negrin/Shutterstock

An evidence-based approach involves an ongoing, critical review of research literature to determine what information is credible, and what policies and practices would be most effective given the best available evidence.

National Institute of Corrections, Evidence-based Practices (EBP)

In 2023 California officials announced the planned closing of Chuckwalla Valley State Prison in Riverside County and cutbacks at six other prisons—including a facility for women in Sacramento County. The closing comes on the heels of two other California prison closings—including the Deuel Vocational Institution in Tracy and the California Correctional Center in Lassen County. All three closings were facilitated by two California laws passed within the past 12 years.[1]

A smash-and-grab robbery in a California jewelry store. Some say that certain California laws intended to reduce prison populations have led to increases in this type of crime. Where is the evidence?
Noah Berger/AP Images

One of those laws was California's 2011 Public Safety Realignment (PSR) Act, which shifted selected persons convicted and sentenced for nonviolent low-level felonies out of state-run prisons and into county lockups. It essentially transferred jurisdiction and funding for managing lower-level offenders from the state to the counties. In doing so, it shifted the post-release supervision of most persons who were released and reentered society *away* from state parole agents and *to* county probation officers (or to other county-specified offices).

Another law, California's Proposition 47, a measure approved by voters in November 2014, permitted persons who were serving felony prison sentences for certain nonviolent crimes to apply to have their sentences reduced to misdemeanors—meaning that they would likely be released and placed on probation. The law also upped the limit for classifying thefts as felonies to $950, meaning that anyone who steals goods worth less than that amount faces only misdemeanor charges. Although some claimed that Proposition 47 led to an increase in shoplifting and "smash-and-grab" burglaries, efforts to rescind the law failed in 2022.

Importantly, Proposition 47 redirected the savings that were achieved from reductions in incarceration to treatment interventions, with the goal of reducing recidivism.

Realignment, however, is not without its issues. According to the California Board of State and Community Corrections, the state's jail population has risen significantly as more and more people who have been convicted of criminal offenses are sent to jail in lieu of state prison.[2]

Consequently, when comparing state incarceration rates and when examining national statistics on imprisonment, it may make more sense to talk about the number of persons sentenced to confinement rather than merely counting those held in state prisons—especially when talking about California.

Although thorough assessments of California's experiment with realignment and sentence reductions have yet to be made, one report by a Los Angeles County advisory board found that responsibility for a large number of high-risk offenders, many with mental illness, has been shifted to counties (and to county jails) that may be ill-prepared to deal adequately with those offenders.

Even so, California's efforts to lower prison populations are clearly working. As of January 2023, prisons in California held 94,000 people, but those numbers are down significantly from the 120,000 that the state's prison held in 2019 and the 160,000 held in 2011.

EVIDENCE-BASED CORRECTIONS (EBC)

The scientific study of corrections and of correctional policies and programs is referred to as **evidence-based corrections (EBC).** The evidence-based model uses empirical data to determine what works in correctional settings—that is, which correctional programs are effective at meeting correctional goals, such as reducing recidivism and preventing future crimes. EBC is a hallmark of contemporary corrections and is regarded as the gold standard by which correctional programs and services are evaluated today. EBC uses ongoing, critical reviews of research literature to identify credible scientific evidence and involves rigorous quality assurance to ensure that evidence-based practices are replicated with fidelity and that new practices are evaluated to determine their effectiveness.

The National Institute of Corrections says that **evidence-based practice (EBP)** (1) implies that there is a definable outcome(s), (2) works to identify the best available strategy or program, (3) uses measurable program features and measurable outcomes, and (4) is defined according to practical realities (i.e., public safety, recidivism, victim satisfaction, etc.) rather than immeasurable moral- or value-oriented standards or beliefs.[3]

EBP refers to the implementation of programs that have been studied and found to be effective. Although EBC and EBP are different sides of the same coin, EBC is primarily concerned with study and evaluation, while EBP focuses on the practical use of programs that have been found to be effective.

One important component of EBC is **cost-benefit analysis,** which seeks to assess the effectiveness of correctional approaches relative to their costs. While EBC is a theme of this text, another theme is economic realities in corrections. As you will see, the two themes go hand in hand.

Evidence-Based Corrections

What is evidence-based corrections? Why is it regarded as the gold standard in assessing the effectiveness of correctional programs?

evidence-based corrections (EBC)

The application of social scientific techniques to the study of everyday corrections procedures for the purpose of increasing effectiveness and enhancing the efficient use of available resources. Also known as evidence-based penology.

evidence-based practice (EBP)

The implementation of programs that have been studied and found to be effective.

cost-benefit analysis

A systematic process used to calculate the costs of a program relative to its benefits. Programs showing the largest benefit per unit of expenditure are seen as the most effective.

The History of EBC

The evidence-based model began to be used in this country in 1992 when it was first applied to the medical sciences. Soon, the value of EBP was recognized in many fields, including education, psychology, psychiatry, sociology, and criminal justice.

In the mid-1990s, two separate efforts were made to identify crime and justice-related programs that were effective and to assess the methodological quality of each of the studies.[4] The first effort was undertaken by the Center for the Study and Prevention of Violence (CSPV) at the Institute of Behavioral Science, University of Colorado–Boulder, when it developed its Blueprints for Violence Prevention program. The program, which remains well-known today, identified 10 model programs for delinquency prevention and intervention that met strict scientific standards of program effectiveness. About that same time, Congress mandated a "comprehensive evaluation of the effectiveness of Department of Justice grants to assist state and local law enforcement communities in preventing crime." The result was a highly visible effort to identify EBPs in criminal justice. The evaluations were undertaken by faculty members at the University of Maryland, who reviewed research studies carried out in various settings nationwide.

Susan Turner, director of the Center for Evidence-Based Corrections at the University of California, Irvine. Turner is shown at the Orange County (California) jail. What is evidence-based corrections?

Courtesy of the University of California, Irvine

The Maryland study was one of the first large-scale efforts to "score" the criminal justice studies that it reviewed based on the strength of the scientific methods that they employed.

Shortly afterward, in what many say was the official beginning of the evidence-based movement in corrections, came the publication of a lengthy report to the U.S. Congress, entitled *Preventing Crime: What Works, What Doesn't, What's Promising.*[5] The report, known as a meta-analysis because it assessed more than 500 previously completed studies of various crime prevention programs, looked at the effectiveness of correctional programs in seven different settings: families, police, community, place security, labor markets, schools, and the criminal justice system. Researchers discovered that a number of the evaluated programs could be declared successful. Successful efforts became known as *what works* programs—defined as those that are reasonably certain to reduce recidivism. Other programs were found likely to fail to reduce recidivism and were listed in the category of what does not work. Finally, some programs, which fell into a middle ground, were termed *promising.*

It was not long before other universities focused on EBPs, and soon the University of California–Irvine announced the creation of its Center for Evidence-Based Corrections. The center, which continues to thrive today, seeks "to put science before politics when managing state correctional populations" and to help "corrections officials make policy decisions based on scientific evidence."[6] Similarly, the Center for Advancing Correctional Excellence at George Mason University, another well-known institution of higher learning, espouses an evidence-based model.

EBC has become worldwide in scope. Australia's famed Griffith University, for example, runs the Global Centre of Evidence-Based Corrections and Sentencing, and other major universities around the world have similar programs or are developing them.

Today, the federal government, through the National Institute of Justice, identifies and showcases successful EBPs via its Crime Solutions website (crimesolutions.gov). The site lists hundreds of programs that have been evaluated by expert reviewers who rate them as "effective," "promising," or having "no effect."

What Is Evidence?

In any discussion of EBC (also known as *evidence-based penology*), it is important to remember that the word *evidence* refers to scientific evidence, not to criminal evidence. Corrections professionals who adhere to an evidence-based philosophy acknowledge the problem-solving potential of social science research methods, read correctional publications and journals, and keep abreast of the latest findings in their field. They also work to implement the most successful evidence-based programs of relevance to their programs or jurisdictions.

How EBP Is Utilized in Corrections

Law enforcement and correctional agencies are always seeking the best methods to deter individuals from committing crimes or to prevent them from reoffending. When crimes are committed, law enforcement professionals apprehend the perpetrators, and correctional professionals process, monitor, and rehabilitate those individuals throughout their confinement.

In order to reduce recidivism, an ever increasing number of correctional programs and agencies at both the federal and state level are instituting EBP as the standard for all policies and procedures. Instead of using procedures

Crime SOLUTIONS.gov

RELIABLE RESEARCH. REAL RESULTS.

Enter your keyword(s) 🔍 | Search Site | Advanced Search

Home | Help | Contact Us | Site Map | Glossary

EVIDENCE-BASED CORRECTIONS

Milwaukee (Wisconsin) County Diversion Program

This is a prosecutor-led pretrial diversion program to rehabilitate individuals with misdemeanor or felony offenses who are at low risk of reoffending. The program is rated effective. There were statistically significant reductions in the rearrest rate, days to rearrest, and cases dismissed for treatment group individuals, compared with comparison group individuals, at the two-year follow-up.

The Milwaukee County Diversion Program is a prefiling program in which the prosecutor receives the case from law enforcement but opts not to file charges with the court, provided the defendant completes diversionary programming. The program was established in Milwaukee County, Wisconsin, in 2007. The program targets individuals with a wide range of misdemeanors and felonies who are classified as low risk on the Level of Services Inventory Short Version (LSI-R:SV). The goal is to rehabilitate individuals who are at low risk for reoffending.

Participants receive a relatively low service dosage, responsive to their low risk, consisting mainly of community service, educational programs, required restitution, and, if needed, drug treatment and attendance at a restorative justice conference. The individualized treatment is for six months. If a participant successfully completes the program's individualized treatment and social services and remains crime free for the program period, the participant's case will never be filed with the court. Program failure results in the participant's case being filed in court.

Source: Adapted from the Bureau of Justice Statistics.

that may work in one situation but not in another, EBP provides guidelines that determine the most effective strategy for a given locale based on the results of research.

Recently, for example, the state of West Virginia formed the Justice Center for Evidence-Based Practice (JCEBP) whose job it is to use the best available evidence for informed decision making in justice agencies throughout the state. Similarly, the Pennsylvania Commission on Crime and Delinquency (PCCD) created the Resource Center for Evidence-Based Prevention and Intervention Programs and Practices to help increase the use of EBPs throughout Pennsylvania's justice-related agencies. Finally, Colorado's Department of Public Safety has created a statewide Evidence-Based Practices Implementation for Capacity (EPIC) program intended to enhance the capabilities of the state's justice system within existing budgetary limits.

The National Criminal Justice Association (NCJA) notes that the state-level programs described here "all represent a shift from reliance solely on outside experts to having internal subject matter experts and a state driven commitment to utilizing evidence-based practices and programs."[7] NCJA believes that "as policymakers around the country continue to see and understand

Graduates from a corrections academy attend a ceremony at the completion of their studies. What are the components of corrections professionalism?
SOPA Images Limited/Alamy Stock Photo

the potential for using EBP's to decrease crime, victimization, and criminal justice expenditures, other states may soon adopt similar programs." With the sobering budget realities of the coming years, the work of state-level centers for EBPs provide a blueprint for not only continuing the success of state programs but also for protecting the investments of time and energy that have already gone into changing the way that the criminal justice system uses resources, sees research and evaluation, and reacts to new and innovative ways of protecting the public.

The Reach of Evidence-Based Studies in Corrections

Some evidence-based studies focus on particular programs and practices, while others are more far-reaching. An example of the former is a study conducted by the Minnesota Department of Corrections, which found that prison visitation has a significant impact on recidivism, with "frequent and recent visits" being closely associated with a decreased risk of recidivism. A surprising finding from the study was that "any visit reduced the risk of recidivism by 13 percent for felony reconvictions."[8]

One large-scale evidence-based assessment of the effectiveness of imprisonment, in general, concluded that "there is little evidence that prisons reduce recidivism and at least some evidence to suggest that they have a criminogenic effect." The study authors noted that "the policy implications of this finding are significant, for it means that beyond crime saved through incapacitation, the use of custodial sanctions may have the unanticipated consequence of making society less safe."[9]

If the findings of studies like this are validated by further investigation, then it would seem that the wider use of community corrections, reentry programs, and sentences that divert people from prison will serve the rehabilitative goals of society better than imprisonment and will likely lead to a reduction in corrections-related budgets.

Corrections Professionalism
What is corrections professionalism?
Why is it important?

profession

An occupation granted high social status by virtue of the personal integrity of its members.

CO2-2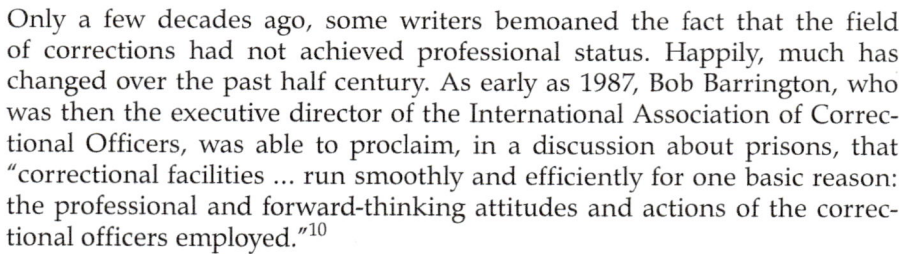

PROFESSIONALISM IN CORRECTIONS

Only a few decades ago, some writers bemoaned the fact that the field of corrections had not achieved professional status. Happily, much has changed over the past half century. As early as 1987, Bob Barrington, who was then the executive director of the International Association of Correctional Officers, was able to proclaim, in a discussion about prisons, that "correctional facilities ... run smoothly and efficiently for one basic reason: the professional and forward-thinking attitudes and actions of the correctional officers employed."[10]

Writers on American criminal justice have said that the hallmark of a true profession is "a shared set of principles and customs that transcend self-interest and speak to the essential nature of the particular calling or trade."[11] This description recognizes the selfless and ethical nature of professional work. Hence, professionals tend to have a sense of commitment to their professions that is usually not present among those in other occupational groups. Work within a profession is viewed more as a "calling" than as a mere way of earning a living. "Professionals have a love for their work that is above that of employment merely to receive a paycheck."[12]

Although it is important to keep formal definitions in mind, for our purposes, we will define a **profession** as an occupation granted high social status by virtue of the personal integrity of its members. We can summarize the *attitude* of a true professional by noting that it is characterized by the following:

- a spirit of public service and interest in the public good;
- the fair application of reason and the use of intellect to solve problems;
- self-regulation through a set of internal guidelines by which professionals hold *themselves* accountable for their actions;
- continual self-appraisal and self-examination;
- an inner sense of professionalism (i.e., honor, self-discipline, commitment, personal integrity, and self-direction);
- adherence to the recognized ethical principles of one's profession (see the Ethics and Professionalism box in this chapter); and
- a commitment to lifelong learning and lifelong betterment within the profession.

Ethics and Professionalism

American Correctional Association Code of Ethics

1. Members shall respect and protect the civil and legal rights of all individuals.
2. Members shall treat every professional situation with concern for the welfare of the individuals involved and with no intent to gain personally.
3. Members shall maintain relationships with colleagues to promote mutual respect within the profession and improve the quality of service.
4. Members shall make public criticism of their colleagues or their agencies only when warranted, verifiable, and constructive.
5. Members shall respect the importance of all disciplines within the criminal justice system and work to improve cooperation with each segment.
6. Members shall honor the public's right to information and share information with the public to the extent permitted by law subject to individuals' right to privacy.
7. Members shall respect and protect the right of the public to be safeguarded from criminal activity.
8. Members shall refrain from using their positions to secure personal privileges or advantages.
9. Members shall refrain from allowing personal interest to impair objectivity in the performance of duty while acting in an official capacity.
10. Members shall refrain from entering into any formal or informal activity or agreement which presents a conflict of interest or is inconsistent with the conscientious performance of duties.
11. Members shall refrain from accepting any gifts, services, or favors that is or appears to be improper or implies an obligation inconsistent with the free and objective exercise of professional duties.
12. Members shall clearly differentiate between personal views/statements and views/statements/positions made on behalf of the agency or Association.
13. Members shall report to appropriate authorities any corrupt or unethical behaviors for which there is sufficient evidence to justify review.
14. Members shall refrain from discriminating against any individual because of race, gender, creed, national origin, religious affiliation, age, disability, or any other type of prohibited discrimination.
15. Members shall preserve the integrity of private information; they shall refrain from seeking information on individuals beyond that which is necessary to implement responsibilities and perform their duties; members shall refrain from revealing nonpublic information unless expressly authorized to do so.
16. Members shall make all appointments, promotions, and dismissals in accordance with established civil service rules, applicable contract agreements, and individual merit, rather than furtherance of personal interests.
17. Members shall respect, promote, and contribute to a workplace that is safe, healthy, and free of harassment in any form.

Adopted by the Board of Governors and Delegate Assembly in August 1994.

Source: Reprinted with permission of the American Correctional Association, Alexandria, VA.

Offices of the American Correctional Association (ACA) in Alexandria, Virginia. The ACA is a leading proponent of professionalism in corrections. What does corrections professionalism entail?

Reprinted with permission of the American Correctional Association, Alexandria, VA.

Most high-status occupations have developed practices that foster professionalism among their members.

Standards and Training

Historically, professional corrections organizations and their leaders have recognized the importance of training. It was not until the late 1970s, however, that the American Correctional Association's (ACA) Commission on Accreditation established the first training standards. The commission did the following:

- set specified standards for given positions within corrections;
- identified essential training topics;
- set specific numbers of hours for preservice (120) and annual in-service training (40); and
- specified basic administrative policy support requirements for training programs.[13]

Following ACA's lead, virtually every state now requires at least 120 hours of preservice training for correctional officers working in institutional settings; many states require more. Probation and parole officers are required to undergo similar training in most jurisdictions, and correctional officers working in jails are similarly trained.

Through training, new members of a profession learn the core values and ideals, the basic knowledge, and the accepted practices central to the profession. Setting training standards ensures that the education is uniform. Standards also mandate the teaching of specialized knowledge. Standards supplement training by doing the following:

- setting minimum requirements for entry into the profession;
- detailing expectations for those involved in the everyday life of correctional work; and
- establishing basic requirements for facilities, programs, and practices.

From the point of view of corrections professionals, training is a matter of personal responsibility. A lifelong commitment to a career ensures that those who think of themselves as professionals will seek the training needed to enhance their job performance.

Basic Skills and Knowledge

By the start of the 21st century, the Professional Education Council of the American Correctional Association had developed a model entry-level test for correctional officers. The test was intended to increase professionalism in the field and to provide a standard criminal justice curriculum.

The council suggested that the test could act "as a quality control measure for criminal justice education, much as does the bar exam for attorneys." The standard entry test was designed to "reveal the applicant's understanding of the structure, purpose, and method of the police, prosecution, courts, institutions, probation, parole, community service, and extramural programs." It was also designed to "test for knowledge of various kinds of corrections programs, the role of punitive sanctions and incapacitation, and perspective on past experience and current trends."

Mark S. Fleisher of Illinois State University has identified four core traits essential to effective work in corrections.[14] The traits are as follows:

- **Accountability.** "Correctional work demands precision, timeliness, accountability and strong ethics." Students may drift into patterns of irresponsibility during their college years. Once they become correctional officers, however, they need to take their work seriously.

- **Strong writing skill.** Because correctional officers must complete a huge amount of paperwork, they need to be able to write well. They should also be familiar with the "vocabulary of corrections."

- **Effective presentational skills.** "A correctional career requires strong verbal skills and an ability to organize presentations." Effective verbal skills help officers interact with their peers, correctional clients, and superiors.

- **A logical mind and the ability to solve problems.** Such skills are essential to success in corrections because problems arise daily. Being able to solve them is a sign of an effective officer.

In sum, we can say that a **corrections professional** is a dedicated person of high moral character and personal integrity who is employed in the field of corrections and takes professionalism to heart. He or she understands the importance of standards, training, and education and the need to be proficient in the skills required for success in the correctional enterprise. The corrections professional recognizes that professionalism leads to the betterment of society, to enhanced social order, and to a higher quality of life for all.

corrections professional

A dedicated person of high moral character and personal integrity who is employed in the field of corrections and takes professionalism to heart.

Standard-Setting Organizations

A number of standard-setting **professional associations** in the field of corrections have developed models of professionalism. Among them are the ACA, the American Probation and Parole Association (APPA), and the American Jail Association (AJA).

professional associations

Organized groups of like-minded individuals who work to enhance the professional status of members of their occupational group.

certification

A credentialing process, usually involving testing and career development assessment, through which the skills, knowledge, and abilities of correctional personnel can be formally recognized.

Standard-setting organizations like these offer detailed sets of written principles for correctional occupations and corrections administration. The ACA, the APPA, and the AJA, for example, all have developed standards to guide training and to clarify what is expected of those working in corrections. Moreover, many professional associations have developed codes of ethics, outlining what is moral and proper conduct. Some of these codes will appear in later chapters.

Correctional associations also offer training, hold meetings and seminars, create and maintain job banks, and produce literature relevant to corrections. They sometimes lobby legislative bodies in an attempt to influence the development of new laws that affect corrections.

Future chapters will present ACA policies. The ACA policies are important because they guide the development of training and because they influence the work environment of many agencies and institutions.

The ACA, through its national Commission on Correctional Certification, has established a program for certifying correctional staff, from line officers to executive leaders. **Certification** is part of a process called *credentialing* that focuses specifically on the individual. Its counterpart is accreditation, a formal process that highlights the quality of a facility in an effort to ensure that it meets health, safety, and other correctional standards. ACA certification began officially in January 2000 when the first Certified Corrections Executive (CCE) application was accepted by the ACA. Today, the ACA says that "the Corrections Certification Program is designed to advance the overall knowledge level of practitioners in the corrections field, promote the capabilities of corrections professionals to the public, and enhance society's image of corrections personnel, thereby aiding in the recruitment of new, talented staff members."[15]

Students, who are in a course developed by San Joaquin Valley (California) College for the regional corrections academy, jog in unison along a bike path. What role do training and education play in the professionalization of corrections?

ZUMA Press Inc/Alamy Stock Photo

There are four categories of ACA Certified Corrections Professional (CCP), extending from those who work at the highest organization levels to personnel employed at the line level, working directly with correctional clients. Those categories are (1) Certified Corrections Executive (CCE), (2) Certified Corrections Manager (CCM), (3) Certified Corrections Supervisor (CCS), and (4) Certified Corrections Officer (CCO). Applicants for certification must pass a written examination, document their corrections experience, show compliance with the ACA's Code of Ethics, and meet minimum requirements for formal education. Educational requirements increase with each certification level. While a high school diploma or equivalent is required of those seeking CCO certification, CCS and CCM certification seekers are required to hold a two-year college degree (or its equivalent), while those applying for certification at the CCE level must hold a four-year college degree (or equivalent). According to the ACA, the organization's certification program creates the *opportunity* for a lifetime of progressive professional achievement. Anyone successfully completing the certification process is designated as a CCP.[16] Recertification happens at three-year intervals and requires a specified number of continuing education contact hours.

The purpose of the ACA Professional Certification Program is "to uphold standards for competent practice." Moreover, certification provides an opportunity "for staff to be recognized as qualified correctional practitioners."

Like the ACA, the AJA, through its five-member Jail Manager Certification Commission (JMCC), offers a program for the certification of jail administrators, managers, and supervisory personnel. In 2019, the AJA introduced the Certified Jail Supervisor certification, designed for mid-level managers. As of early 2023, 25 people had been recognized as Certified Jail Managers across the country.[17]

Education

Education is another component, in addition to basic job skills and job-specific training, of true professionalism. Training, by itself, can never make one a true professional because complex decision-making skills are essential for success in any occupation involving intense interpersonal interaction—and they can be acquired only through general education. Education builds critical-thinking skills, it allows the application of theory and ethical principles to a multitude of situations that are constantly in flux, and it provides insights into on-the-job difficulties.

Correctional education that goes beyond skills training is available primarily from two- and four-year colleges that offer corrections curricula and programs of study (see Exhibit 2–1). Courses in corrections are also typically found in undergraduate and graduate programs in criminal justice. The day will come when at least a two-year degree will be required for entry into the corrections profession.

EXHIBIT 2–1   American Correctional Association

Public Correctional Policy on Higher Education

The field of corrections, in cooperation with higher education, should contribute to the improvement of the professional practice of corrections. Academic programs concerned with criminal justice, including juvenile justice and corrections should:

- provide competency-based education to prepare qualified candidates for correctional service, and assist in the delineation of dimensions of work responsibilities that may emerge as a result of changing social, economic, political and technological trends;
- promote understanding, both for correctional practitioners and for the public at large, of the complex social, ethical, political and economic factors that influence all areas of corrections;
- challenge assumptions about crime and corrections, and stimulate change when change is needed;
- partner with criminal justice, juvenile justice and corrections organizations to promote and support ethical standards in research, planning and evaluation in all areas;
- engage in public service related to corrections, including informational programs, volunteer programs and opportunities for training, such as internships and practicums to enhance the relationship between the academic community and corrections;
- encourage colleges and universities to provide opportunities for research and the publication of research findings;
- support, through program and faculty development, the evolution of corrections as a distinct professional discipline;
- implement programs in corrections at the associate degree level and higher that can serve as a minimum requirement for full professional status as a correctional employee; and
- partner with correctional agencies to promote and facilitate learning initiatives for employees, to include but not limited to the offering of professional development opportunities, and articulating college credit for experience and training obtained while working in the corrections field.

Reprinted with permission of the American Correctional Association, Alexandria, VA.

Rhianna Johnson

Rhianna Johnson
Education Director, Larch Corrections Center, Yacolt, Washington

Rhianna Johnson is the education director at Larch Corrections Center, a minimum security male prison camp in Washington State. The facility houses approximately 480 clients who are less than four years from their release dates. The Education Department at Larch Corrections Center operates through a partnership between Clark College and Washington Department of Corrections. It provides classes in vocational programs, GED, and other skills. All Washington State prison facilities provide educational programming for correctional clients.

Mrs. Johnson worked in higher education as an instructor, advisor, and manager for several years before moving into corrections education. With a master's degree in sociology, she was interested in issues related to criminology, social equity, and reentry. She decided to take her experience supporting students on a college campus into the prison setting in order to prepare correctional clients for career and personal goals. Working in a prison, she says, was somewhat of an adjustment. "At times, it is challenging because of the political disagreements associated with educating inmates," she adds. Johnson thoroughly enjoys working with people who are imprisoned and challenging stereotypes. She supervises faculty who agree that teaching in a prison setting is highly rewarding.

> *The challenges of educating clients lead to huge personal rewards.*

CO2-3   SOCIAL DIVERSITY IN CORRECTIONS

The corrections profession faces a number of social issues that are of special concern to Americans today. Contemporary issues include questions about the purposes and appropriateness of punishment in general and the acceptability of capital punishment in particular; the usefulness of alternative or nontraditional sanctions; the privatization of correctional facilities; and the rights and overall treatment of people who are imprisoned. At the forefront of today's issues are those involving concerns about gender, race, ethnicity, and other forms of social diversity and social justice (which was defined and briefly discussed in Chapter 1).

While a number of these issues are discussed in later chapters, this brief section provides definitions of some of the terms that will be discussed and suggests some structure for what is to follow.

Some terms, such as *race,* are not easy to define. Historical definitions of race have highlighted some supposed biological traits, such as skin color, hair type, or shape of the skull and face. Eighteenth-century European physical anthropologists distinguished among white, Black, and Asian (or "yellow") races. The notion of race, however, is now generally recognized as a social construct and is not seen as an objective biological fact. Moreover, racial distinctions have blurred throughout American society, which has long been characterized as a melting pot. Nonetheless, when asked, the majority of Americans today still identify themselves as members of a particular racial group.

To say that race is a social construct means that racial distinctions are culturally defined. It does *not* mean, however, that such distinctions are without consequences. On the contrary, great social significance is often attached to biological or other indicators of race, and race plays a crucial role in social relations. *Racism,* which is also socially constructed, can be the result. **Racism** can be defined as the systemic oppression of a racial group to the social, economic, and political advantage of another.[18] In the field of corrections, as in other social endeavors, racism (rather than race itself) is the real issue because it can lead to forms of racial discrimination, including inequities in hiring and

racism

The systemic oppression of a racial group to the social, economic, and political advantage of another.

promotion for those working in corrections, and to unfairness in the handling of correctional clients because of their perceived race.

Considerable overlap exists between the concept of race and that of *ethnicity*. In contemporary usage, both terms imply the notion of lineage, or biological and regional as well as cultural background and inheritance. Of the two, however, ethnicity is most closely associated with cultural heritage. Members of an ethnic group generally share a common racial, national, religious, linguistic, and cultural origin. Hence, from an ethnic perspective, a person might identify himself or herself as Hungarian, even though he or she has never lived in Hungary, does not speak Hungarian, and knows little of the history of the Hungarian nation. Ethnic differences can lead to serious consequences as prison gangs built around ethnicity demonstrate.

At first blush, the term *gender* seems more straightforward than race or ethnicity because it has traditionally been associated with differences between the sexes. Today, however, gender has become a more fluid concept, and gender preference and gender identity are often personal choices that do not always correlate with the sex of a person at birth. Even so, one critical issue that concerns correctional administrators today reflects a rapid increase in the number of women entering correctional service and in the increased number of correctional clients who self-identify as women.

For many years, corrections was a male-dominated profession. Although the correctional process has always involved some staff members who are women, historically most women in the profession have attended to the needs of the relatively small number of females held in confinement. It wasn't until the 1970s that women began to enter the corrections professions in significant numbers. Many went to work in facilities that housed males, where they soon found themselves confronting *gender bias* from an entrenched macho culture.

Today, women working in correctional facilities have been not only accepted but welcomed—as evidenced by the fact their proportion is more than double the proportion of female law enforcement officers: Thirty-five percent of correctional officers in the United States are women, while only 12 percent of police officers are female. As Exhibit 2–2 shows, however, women working in

Colette Peters, Director of the Federal Bureau of Prisons. In recent years, the number of women working in corrections has increased significantly. Do you think that gender bias exists within the correctional career field today?

Reprinted with permission of State Corrections Director Colette S. Peters

EXHIBIT 2–2   Corrections Personnel by Gender and Rank

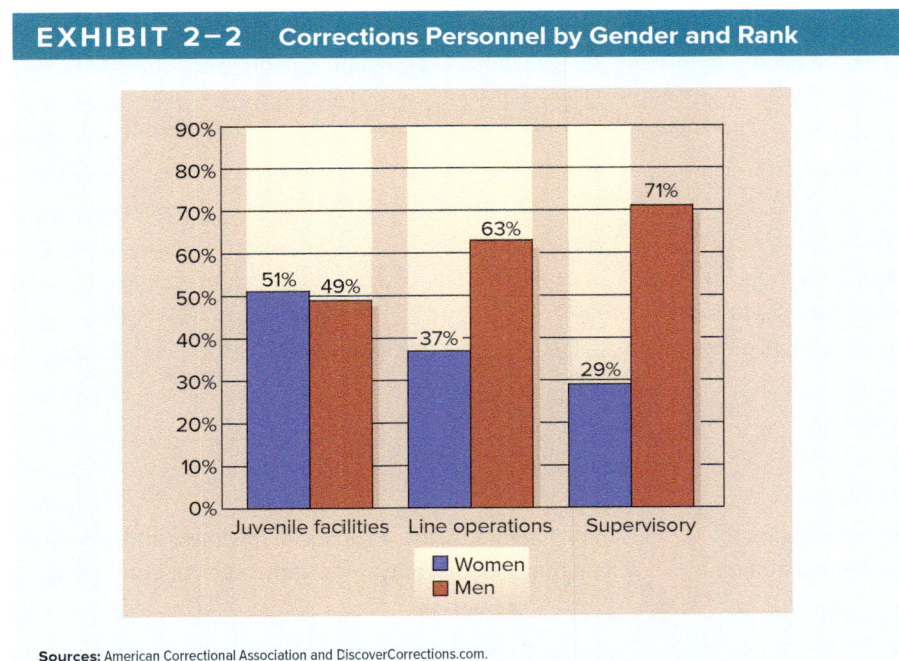

Sources: American Correctional Association and DiscoverCorrections.com.

corrections tend to be concentrated in the lower ranks and are underrepresented in supervisory positions. Today, women of color hold 12.9 percent of corrections positions, 9.7 percent of top command positions, and 9.1 percent of supervisory positions.[19] A new nationwide advocacy movement, known as the 30 × 30 initiative, is working to reach the goal of having 30% of new police recruits be women by the year 2030. Some administrators and policy makers today have adopted a similar goal in the field of corrections.[20]

social diversity

Differences between individuals and groups in the same society, including differences based on culture, race, religion, ethnicity, age, gender identity, and disabilities.

Race, ethnicity, and gender are all aspects of **social diversity**—although diversity in society extends to many other areas as well, such as economics, religion, education, intellectual ability, and politics. Keep in mind, as you read through this textbook, that in the field of corrections diversity issues can be described from four perspectives: (1) as they impact individual correctional clients; (2) as they determine correctional populations and trends; (3) as they affect the lives and interests of those working in the field of corrections; and (4) as they change the structure and functioning of correctional institutions, facilities, and programs.

REVIEW AND APPLICATIONS

SUMMARY

1 Professionalism in corrections is important because it can win the respect and admiration of others outside the field. Moreover, professionals are regarded as trusted participants in any field of endeavor. This chapter also discussed seven aspects of a professional attitude.

2 Evidence-based corrections is the application of social scientific techniques to the study of everyday corrections procedures for the purpose of increasing effectiveness and enhancing the efficient use of available resources. When discussing evidence-based corrections, it is important to remember that the word *evidence* refers to scientific, not criminal evidence.

3 Social diversity encompasses differences of race, gender, and ethnicity and is important in corrections today because it impacts individual correctional clients, influences correctional populations and trends, affects the lives and interests of those working in the field of corrections, and may help determine the structure and functioning of correctional institutions, facilities, and programs.

KEY TERMS

evidence-based corrections (EBC), p. 21
evidence-based practice (EBP), p. 21
cost-benefit analysis, p. 21

profession, p. 24
corrections professional, p. 27
professional associations, p. 27

certification, p. 28
racism, p. 30
social diversity, p. 32

QUESTIONS FOR REVIEW

1 Explain the importance of professionalism in corrections, and list the seven characteristics of a professional attitude.

2 What is evidence-based corrections? What role does it play in corrections professionalism today?

3 What is meant by the term *social diversity*, and why is the issue of social diversity important in corrections today?

THINKING CRITICALLY ABOUT CORRECTIONS

Professionalism

The Website of the U.S. Department of Justice says this: "The true measure of professionals is their attitude and behavior toward the people they serve. Correctional personnel need to be problem solvers rather than task oriented, put the concerns of others before their own, prevent inmates from setting the ground rules for the relationship, recognize their limitations, respect inmates, and take pride in their work and their profession."[21] Do you agree? Why or why not?

ON-THE-JOB DECISION MAKING

Evidence-Based Decisions

You are a captain in charge of programs at a large state correctional facility. The programs that you oversee offer a variety of opportunity to correctional clients, including jobs training, general education, and psychological counseling. The programs under your area of responsibility have the following names: "Alcoholics and Narcotics Anonymous," "Anger Management," "Arts on the Inside," "Batterers Intervention," "Bible Study," "Developing Adults with Necessary Skills (DAWNS)," "Employability Skills Class," "First Step," "General Equivalency Classes," "Prison Fatherhood," "Learn to Read," "Meditation on the Inside," "A New Leash on Life," "Residential Substance Abuse Treatment (RSAT)," "Self-Esteem Class," "SISTA/NIA-HIV Awareness," "Vocational Training," "Yoga 4 Change," "Thinking 4 a Change," and "WorkNet Solutions."

Unfortunately, the state legislature has decided to cut prison budgets, and prison programs are targeted for substantial cost reductions. This means that you will have to decide which programs to keep and which to reduce in size or eliminate entirely.

Your boss, the prison warden, has asked you to draft a written plan that identifies the programs whose funding will be reduced. You have begun to think about what you will write into the plan, keeping in mind the needs of the residents in your facility. You think about their personal and psychological well-being and recognize that counseling programs are important, but you also know that job skills training programs provide a valuable opportunity for success upon release.

As you continue your internal dialogue, you remember what you learned in a class that you took at the local college. The class entitled "Introduction to Corrections" taught you that the best decisions are usually evidence-based—that is, made on the basis of scientific findings that demonstrate what is most effective at achieving the goals that you've set. As you continue thinking, a number of questions arise. They are:

1. What are the most important programs in the institution over which I have control?
2. Which are likely to meet their goals?
3. Where can I find evidence-based studies that will help me make the best decisions?

How will you answer those questions?

ENDNOTES

1. California Board of State and Community Corrections, BSCC Data Dashboards, https://www.bscc.ca.gov/s_datadashboard (accessed January 20, 2023).
2. California Assembly Bill 109/117, Public Safety Realignment (2011).
3. National Institute of Corrections, "Evidence-Based Decision Making," https://info.nicic.gov/ebdm (accessed June 20, 2023).
4. Justice Statistics Research Association, "An Introduction to Evidence-Based Practices," April 2014, http://www.jrsa.org/projects/ebp_briefing_paper1_summary.pdf (accessed February 16, 2023).
5. Lawrence W. Sherman et al., *Preventing Crime: What Works, What Doesn't, What's Promising* (Washington, DC: National Institute of Justice, 1997). Web available at https://www.ojp.gov/ncjrs/virtual-library/abstracts/preventing-crime-what-works-what-doesnt-whats-promising-report (accessed March 10, 2023).
6. Center for Evidence-Based Corrections, University of California, Irvine, http://ucicorrections.seweb.uci.edu (accessed January 30, 2023).
7. National Criminal Justice Association, *How Three States Are Using Evidence to Build State Criminal Justice Policies*, https://cdpsdocs.state.co.us/ccjj/Meetings/2011/2011-02-11_JusticeBulletin-Jan2011.pdf (accessed August 23, 2023).
8. Minnesota Department of Corrections. *The Effects of Prison Visitation on Offender Recidivism* (Rochester: Minnesota DOC, 2011).
9. Cullen, Francis T., Cheryl Lero Jonson, and Daniel S. Nagin. "Prisons Do Not Reduce Recidivism: The High Cost of Ignoring Science," *The Prison Journal*, vol. 91, no. 3 (2011), pp. 48S–65S.
10. Bob Barrington, "Corrections: Defining the Profession and the Roles of Staff," *Corrections Today*, August 1987, pp. 116–120.

11. Arlin Adams, "The Legal Profession: A Critical Evaluation," *Dickinson Law Review*, vol. 93 (1989), p. 643. Web available at https://ideas.dickinsonlaw.psu.edu/cgi/view content.cgi?article=3183&context=dlra (accessed January 23, 2023).

12. Adams, "The Legal Profession."

13. Harold E. Williamson, *The Corrections Profession* (Newbury Park, CA: Sage, 1990), p. 20.

14. Mark S. Fleisher, "Teaching Correctional Management to Criminal Justice Majors," *Journal of Criminal Justice Education*, vol. 8, no. 1 (Spring 1997), pp. 59–73. Published online, August 15, 2006, https://doi.org/10.1080/10511259700083951 (accessed March 10, 2023).

15. See American Correctional Association, "Benefits of Certification," https://www.aca.org/ACA_Member/ACA/ACA_Member/Certification/Certification_Overview.aspx (accessed February 10, 2023).

16. For more information, see the ACA's Professional Certification Program Web, https://www.aca.org/ACA_Member/ACA/ACA_Member/Certification/Certification_Types_and_Levels.aspx (accessed February 10, 2023).

17. See American Jail Association, *Certified Jail Supervisor*, https://www.americanjail.org/cjs (accessed February 10, 2023).

18. Merriam-Webster Dictionary, "Racism," https://www.merriam-webster.com/dictionary/racism (accessed February 20, 2023).

19. All Criminal Justice Schools, "Women in Law Enforcement—History, What to Expect and Why You Should Join," September 21, 2022, https://www.allcriminaljusticeschools.com/blog/women-in-law-enforcement (accessed March 1, 2023).

20. The 30 × 30 Initiative, "The Under-Representation of Women in Policing Undermines Public Safety," https://30x30initiative.org (accessed February 10, 2023).

21. U.S. Department of Justice, "Professionalism in Corrections," https://www.ojp.gov/ncjrs/virtual-library/abstracts/professionalism-corrections (accessed February 20, 2023).

SENTENCING
To Punish or to Reform?

[3]

White House Photo/Alamy Stock Photo

CHAPTER OBJECTIVES

After completing this chapter you should be able to do the following:

1. Describe the central purpose of criminal punishment.

2. Name the seven goals of criminal sentencing.

3. List and explain the sentencing options in general use today.

4. Explain capital punishment, and discuss its pros and cons.

5. Discuss federal and state sentencing trends and reforms.

6. Describe four issues related to fairness in sentencing.

When and if the will to roll back mass incarceration and to create just, fair, and effective sentencing systems becomes manifest, the way forward is clear.

—Michael Tonry, Professor of Law and Public Policy, University of Minnesota Law School

In 2021, 83-year-old Muhammad Abdul Aziz (aka Norman 3X Butler) was one of two men exonerated for the 1966 assassination of Malcolm X.[1] Aziz had been convicted of the murder in 1966 and served 20 years in prison before his release in 1985. The other exonerated man, Khalil Islam (aka Thomas 15X Johnson), left prison in 1987 after the completion of his sentence, but died in 2009. The exoneration of Aziz and Islam followed a nearly two-year investigation by the Manhattan district attorney's office. That investigation concluded that the FBI, in conjunction with the NYPD and the city's prosecutors, had withheld crucial evidence at the original 1966 murder trial and that evidence would have likely demonstrated that the two men were innocent. A lawsuit that was later filed by Aziz said that "As a result of his wrongful conviction and imprisonment, [he had] spent 20 years in prison for a crime he did not commit and more than 55 years living with the hardship and indignity attendant to being unjustly branded as a convicted murderer of one of the most important civil rights leaders in history."

Muhammad Abdul Aziz, exonerated in 2021 for the 1966 assassination of Malcolm X. What social justice issues can corrections help solve?
Spencer Platt/Staff/Getty Images

During the exoneration ceremony, then-Manhattan district attorney Cyrus Vance Jr. apologized to the families of the two men, saying, "I apologize ... for this decades-long injustice, which has eroded public faith in institutions that are designed to guarantee the equal protection of the law." Vance was acknowledging long-standing problems with American criminal justice that have led to recent calls for de-policing and the shuttering of prisons, along with a system-wide overhaul.

While it is true that the justice system—of which corrections is a crucial part—has made many mistakes in the past, it is working hard to fix its problems, champion social justice, and embrace positive change. As we approach the middle of the 21st century, a new and progressive system has finally begun to emerge.

CO3-1 SENTENCING: PHILOSOPHY AND GOALS

Philosophy of Criminal Sentencing

Sentencing Goals
What are the goals of criminal sentencing? How can those goals be achieved?

sentencing
The imposition of a criminal sanction by a sentencing authority, such as a judge.

sentence
The penalty a court imposes on a person convicted of a crime.

social order
The smooth functioning of social institutions, the existence of positive and productive relations among individual members of society, and the orderly functioning of society as a whole.

This chapter discusses criminal sentencing and criminal sentences. **Sentencing** is a court's imposition of a penalty on a convicted offender. A **sentence** is the penalty imposed.

This chapter also introduces you to the goals of sentencing, sentencing options and types of sentencing, sentencing trends and reforms, and issues in fair sentencing.

Philosophers have long debated *why* a wrongful act should be punished. Many social scientists suggest that criminal punishment maintains and defends the **social order.** By threatening potential law violators and by making the lives of violators uncomfortable, they say, punishments reduce the likelihood of future or continued criminal behavior.

Still, one might ask, instead of punishing people who have been convicted of crimes, why not offer them psychological treatment, educate them, or address the social conditions that lead people into criminality— so that they are less prone to future law violation? The answer to this question is complex and involves many different perspectives and values. Although criminal sentencing today has a variety of goals, and educational and treatment programs are more common now in corrections than they used to be, punishment still takes center stage in justice system philosophy.

THE GOALS OF SENTENCING

Sentencing has a variety of purposes. As shown in Exhibit 3–1, the goals of sentencing are (1) revenge, (2) retribution, (3) just deserts (or the fact of deserving punishment), (4) deterrence, (5) incapacitation, (6) rehabilitation or reformation, and (7) restoration.

Revenge

One of the earliest goals of criminal sentencing was revenge. **Revenge** can be described as both an emotion and as an act in response to victimization. Victims sometimes feel as though an injury or insult requires punishment in return. When they act on that feeling, they have taken revenge.

While we think of vengeance as a primitive need, it continues to play a role in contemporary societies. For example, following the November 2015 terrorist attack in Paris, which claimed 129 lives, French President François Hollande announced his intention of finding his inner-Robespierre and employing the guillotine to execute ISIS-linked terrorists. Some philosophers of the law argue that today's criminal laws legitimize society's collective desire for revenge. They suggest, however, that other sentencing rationales are more appropriate for use in a civilized nation.

Retribution

Retribution involves the payment of a debt to both the victim and society and, thus, atonement for a person's offense. Historically, retribution was couched in terms of "getting even," and it has sometimes been explained as "an eye for an eye, and a tooth for a tooth." *Retribution* literally means "paying back" the person who has offended for what he or she has done. Retribution is predicated on the notion that victims are *entitled* to reprisal.

Because social order suffers when a crime occurs, society is also a victim. Hence, retribution, in a very fundamental way, expresses society's disapproval of criminal behavior and demands the payment of a debt to society. It is not always easy to determine just how much punishment is enough to ensure the debt is paid.

Just Deserts

Retribution is supported by many sentencing schemes today—although the concept is now often couched in terms of **just deserts** even though there is a difference between retribution and just deserts. The concept of just deserts de-emphasizes the emotional component of revenge by claiming that criminal acts are *deserving* of punishment, that people who break the criminal law are *morally blameworthy,* and that they must be punished. In this way, just deserts restores the moral balance to a society wronged by crime.

In a now-classic work, Andrew von Hirsch identified the rationales underlying criminal punishment, saying that when someone "infringes the rights of others ... he deserves blame [and that is why] the sanctioning authority is entitled to choose a response that expresses moral disapproval: namely, punishment."[2] Hence, from a just deserts point of view, justice *requires* that punishments be imposed on criminal law violators.

revenge

Punishment as vengeance; an emotional response to real or imagined injury or insult.

retribution

A sentencing goal that involves retaliation against a criminal perpetrator.

just deserts

Punishment deserved. A just deserts perspective on criminal sentencing holds that people who violate the criminal law are morally blameworthy and are therefore deserving of punishment.

A crowded city street. Many social scientists say that criminal punishments help maintain social order. Do you agree? What would a society without order be like?

Glowimages/Getty Images

EXHIBIT 3-1 Goals of Criminal Sentencing

Goal	Rationale
Revenge	Punishment is equated with vengeance and involves an emotional response to criminal victimization.
Retribution	Punishment involves a "settling of scores" for both society and the victim.
	Victims are entitled to "get even."
Just deserts	People who offend are morally blameworthy and deserving of punishment.
	Punishment restores the moral balance disrupted by crime.
Deterrence	Punishment will prevent future wrongdoing by the person who has been convicted of a crime and by others.
	Punishment must outweigh the benefits gained by wrongdoing.
Incapacitation	Some wrongdoers cannot be changed and need to be segregated from society.
	Society has the responsibility to protect law-abiding citizens from those whose behavior cannot be controlled.
Rehabilitation or Reformation	Society needs to help those who violate the law to learn how to behave appropriately.
	Without learning acceptable behavior patterns, those who violate the law will not be able to behave appropriately.
Restoration	Crime is primarily an offense against human relationships and secondarily a violation of a law.
	All those who suffered because of a crime should be restored to their previous sense of well-being.

Of all the purposes of punishment discussed here, only retribution and just deserts are past oriented. That is, they examine what has already occurred (the crime) in an effort to determine the appropriate sentencing response.

Deterrence

A third goal of criminal sentencing is deterrence. **Deterrence** is the discouragement or prevention of crimes similar to the one for which a person is being sentenced. Unlike retribution and just deserts, deterrence is future oriented in that it seeks to prevent crimes from occurring. Two forms of deterrence can be identified: specific and general.

Specific deterrence is the deterrence of the individual being punished from committing additional crimes. Long ago, specific deterrence was achieved through corporal punishments that maimed law violators in ways that precluded their ability to commit similar crimes in the future. Spies had their eyes gouged out and their tongues removed, rapists were castrated, thieves had their fingers or hands cut off, and so on. Even today, in some countries that follow a strict Islamic code, the hands of habitual thieves are cut off as a form of corporal punishment.

General deterrence occurs when the punishment of an individual serves as an example to others who might be thinking of committing a crime—thereby dissuading them from their planned course of action. The **pleasure-pain principle,** which is central to modern discussions of general deterrence, holds that actions are motivated primarily by the desire to experience pleasure and avoid pain. According to this principle, the threat of loss to anyone convicted of a crime should outweigh the potential pleasure to be gained by committing the crime.

deterrence

The discouragement or prevention of crimes through the fear of punishment.

specific deterrence

The deterrence of the individual being punished from committing additional crimes.

general deterrence

The use of the example of individual punishment to dissuade others from committing crimes.

pleasure-pain principle

The idea that actions are motivated primarily by a desire to experience pleasure and avoid pain.

For punishment to be effective as a deterrent, it must be relatively certain, swiftly applied, and sufficiently severe. *Certainty, swiftness,* and *severity* of punishment are not always easy to achieve. Although it may not be easy for all people who violate the law to get away with crime, the likelihood that any individual person will be arrested, successfully prosecuted, and then punished is far smaller than deterrence advocates would like it to be. When an arrest does occur, a person who offends is typically released on bail, and, because of an overcrowded court system, the trial, if any, may not happen until a year or so later.

Incapacitation

Proponents of **incapacitation** say that people who offend should be prevented from committing further crimes either by their (temporary or permanent) removal from society or by some other method that restricts their physical ability to reoffend. Prison is synonymous with incapacitation because as long as a person who has been convicted of a criminal offense is incarcerated, he or she cannot commit crimes against the rest of us. The belief is the pain or suffering imposed on a person through incapacitation is justified because it reduces or prevents the further harm that would have been caused to the rest of society by the future crimes of convicted person. From the point of view of incapacitation, concern is with the victim or potential victim. The rights of the convicted person merit little consideration.

Incapacitation in the form of imprisonment is considered to be a strategy that "works" because, for the duration of their prison sentence, people who have offended are restricted from committing crimes within the community. However incarcerated persons commit crimes in prison against staff and other inmates, and there is evidence that some people who are in prison can continue to commit crimes even beyond the walls of the prison. For example, Sheikh Omar Abdel-Rahman, the blind sheikh who was serving a life sentence in New York for conspiring to bomb a number of New York landmarks, was accused of sending messages from prison through visiting attorneys to members of Gama'a al-Islamiyya, Egypt's largest militant group (Abdel-Rahman died in prison in 2017). Other persons who are imprisoned use smuggled-in cell phones to threaten victims and witnesses and to commit credit card fraud.

Incarceration prevents those who have violated the criminal law from being able to engage in other crimes in free society. Incarceration incapacitates the convicted person by physically removing her or him from society. **Truth-in-sentencing** and **three-strikes** laws have incapacitation as their goal.

The most severe and permanent form of incapacitation is capital punishment. What is indisputable is that, once put to death, an individual is incapable of committing further offenses. Capital punishment is, therefore, undeniably "effective" in terms of eliminating recidivism.

Rehabilitation or Reformation

The goal of **rehabilitation** or **reformation** is to change criminal lifestyles into law-abiding ones. Rehabilitation has been accomplished when previous criminal patterns of thought and behavior have been replaced by allegiance to society's values. Rehabilitation focuses on medical and psychological treatments and on social skills training, all designed to "correct" the problems that led the individual to crime. In 2022, for example, a Neo-Nazi in Portland, Oregon, was sentenced to probation for a hate crime committed against a community refugee center. As conditions of his probation, Jarl J. Rockhill, 35, was ordered to write a report on anti-Semitism along with a letter of apology to the organization where he had pasted racial purity stickers.[3]

incapacitation

The use of imprisonment or other means to reduce a convicted person's capability to commit future offenses.

truth in sentencing (TIS)

The sentencing principle that requires a person who has been convicted to serve a substantial portion of the sentence and reduces the discrepancy between the sentence imposed and actual time spent in prison.

three-strikes laws

Three-strikes laws impose mandatory prison sentences, generally a life sentence, on those convicted of an offense if they have been previously convicted of two prior serious criminal offenses.

rehabilitation (also *reformation*)

The changing of criminal lifestyles into law-abiding ones by "correcting" the behavior of people who have been convicted of criminal offenses through treatment, education, and training. *Also known* as reformation.

As a goal of sentencing, incapacitation restrains offenders from committing more crimes by isolating them from society. Does this threat of social isolation encourage law-abiding behavior?
Courtesy of the Justice Research Association

reintegration

The process of making the individual a productive member of the community.

A subgoal of rehabilitation is **reintegration** with the community. Reintegrating those with criminal convictions back into the community means making them productive members of society—who then contribute to the general well-being of the whole.

Rehabilitation, which became the focus of American corrections beginning in the late 1800s, led to implementation of indeterminate sentencing practices (soon to be discussed), probation, parole, and a separate system of juvenile justice. During the 1970s, however, rehabilitation came under harsh criticism. As American society experienced disruptions brought about by economic change, the decline of traditional institutions, and fallout from the war in Vietnam, conservatives blamed the rehabilitative ideal for being too liberal, and liberals condemned it for providing an unfair basis for coercive action against disenfranchised social groups.[3] About the same time, an influential and widely read study by Robert Martinson, which evaluated rehabilitation programs nationwide, reported that few, if any, produced real changes in the attitudes of those who participated in them.[4] Dubbed the "nothing works doctrine," Martinson's critique of rehabilitation as a correctional goal led some states to abandon rehabilitation altogether or to de-emphasize it in favor of the goals of retribution and incapacitation. In other states, attempts at rehabilitation continued but were often muted.

Today, many state governments and private organizations are re-embracing rehabilitation, emphasizing the cost savings that can result from lowering prison populations and successfully reintegrating past offenders into society. According to Francis T. Cullen and Paul Gendreau, it is time to give the rehabilitative ideal a second chance. They call for *reaffirming rehabilitation*. "Many [rehabilitative] programs fail to work," say Cullen and Gendreau, "because they either are ill-conceived (not based on sound criminological theory) and/or have no therapeutic integrity (are not implemented as designed)." "We would not be surprised," they write, "if young children turned out to be illiterate if their teachers were untrained, had no standardized curriculum, and met the children once a week for half an hour."[5] Until recently, contend Cullen and Gendreau, many correctional treatment programs were in such a state.

Other writers hold that continued efforts at rehabilitation are mandatory for any civilized society as a moral obligation, not merely as an effort to save money. "In order to neutralize the desocializing potential of prisons," says Edgardo Rotman, "a civilized society is forced into rehabilitative

Enter your keyword(s) 🔍 | Search Site | Advanced Search

Home | Help | Contact Us | Site Map | Glossary

EVIDENCE-BASED CORRECTIONS

Ignition Interlock Program (Maryland)

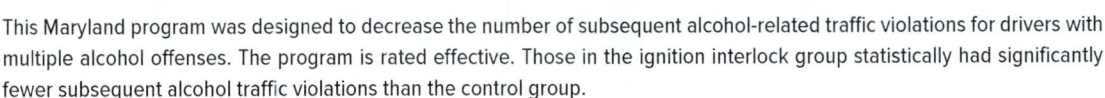

This Maryland program was designed to decrease the number of subsequent alcohol-related traffic violations for drivers with multiple alcohol offenses. The program is rated effective. Those in the ignition interlock group statistically had significantly fewer subsequent alcohol traffic violations than the control group.

Maryland introduced the Ignition Interlock Program for drivers with multiple alcohol offenses to decrease the number of subsequent alcohol-related traffic violations. Breath-analyzed ignition interlock devices have become popular across the nation as one way to combat alcohol-related vehicular accidents.

The program targets drivers applying for license reinstatements who have two or more alcohol-related traffic violations in their lifetimes and who have been approved by the Maryland Medical Advisory Board to apply for the reinstatement. As currently structured, the program may also be required for drivers who violate a previously imposed alcohol-related driving restriction.

Source: Adapted from the Bureau of Justice Statistics.

undertakings. These become an essential ingredient of its correctional system taken as a whole. A correctional system" with no "interest in treatment," says Rotman, "means ... de-humanization and regression."[6]

Restoration

Over the past few decades, a goal of criminal sentencing known as **restoration** has developed. **Restorative justice** is based on the belief that criminal sentencing should involve restoration and justice for all involved in or affected by crime.

Advocates of restorative justice (or, as some agencies refer to it, *community justice* or *reparative justice*) believe that crime is committed not just against the state but also against victims and the community. Restorative justice is especially concerned with repairing the harm to the victim and the community. Harm is repaired through negotiation, mediation, and empowerment rather than through retribution, deterrence, and punishment. A restorative justice perspective allows judges and juries to consider **victim-impact statements** in their sentencing decisions. These are descriptions of the harm and suffering that a crime has caused victims and their survivors. Also among efforts on behalf of victims and their survivors are victim assistance and victim compensation programs.

Advocates of restorative justice believe not only that the victim should be restored by the justice process but also that the person convicted of a crime and society should participate in the restoration process. To this end, efforts at restoration emphasize the successful reintegration of offenders into the community as well as victims' rights and needs. Another aspect of involving people who have been convicted in restoration is having them actively address the harm they have caused. The system strives to accomplish this by holding them directly accountable and by helping them become productive, law-abiding members of their community.[7] Restorative justice programs try to personalize crime by showing people who commit criminal offenses the consequences of their behavior. As such, restorative justice efforts often involve the efforts of **victim services** representatives, who work to ensure that people who are convicted of law violations help to address victims' concerns.

restoration

The process of returning to their previous condition all those involved in or affected by crime—including victims, offenders, and society.

restorative justice

A systematic response to wrongdoing that emphasizes healing the wounds of victims, offenders, and communities caused or revealed by crime.

victim-impact statement

A description of the harm and suffering that a crime has caused victims and survivors.

victim services

Any organized efforts to assist victims; to promote their safety, security, or recovery; to help them participate in the criminal justice system; or to meet other victims' needs.

Restorative justice is based on the premise that because crime occurs in the context of the community, the community should be involved in addressing it. Particular restorative justice or community justice programs might use any of the following: (1) victim–offender mediation, (2) victim–offender reconciliation, (3) victim-impact panels, (4) restorative justice panels, (5) community reparative boards, (6) community-based courts, (7) family group conferences, (8) circle sentencing, (9) court diversion programs, and (10) peer mediation.

Restorative justice seeks to restore the health of the community, repair the harm done by the crime, meet victims' needs, and require the people convicted of the crime to contribute to those repairs. Thus, the criminal act is condemned, people who violate the law are held accountable, offenders and victims are involved as participants, and repentant offenders are encouraged to earn their way back into the good graces of society.

CO3-3 SENTENCING OPTIONS AND TYPES OF SENTENCES

Legislatures establish the types of sentences that can be imposed. The U.S. Congress and the 50 state legislatures decide what is against the law and define crimes and their punishments in the jurisdictions in which they have control. Chapter 1 taught you the stages of criminal justice processing of adults who have been convicted of crimes. Chapters 4 through 8 detail the types of state sentencing options that are frequently used. For example, Chapter 4 discusses probation goals, history, characteristics of probationers, how it is organized and administered, private probation, what probation officers do, issues of caseload size and technology, and probation revocation hearings. Similar detail is covered in subsequent chapters for intermediate sanctions (Chapter 5), jails (Chapter 6), prisons (Chapter 7), and parole (Chapter 8).

One sentence that is becoming less frequently used across the United States is capital punishment. The trends in capital punishment today are these: Death sentences are down, executions are down, and public support for capital punishment is questionable. For these reasons, we have chosen not to devote a complete chapter to a sentencing option that is waning. Instead, we will highlight the major themes of capital punishment in this chapter after reviewing the kinds of sentences that are more frequently imposed by criminal courts. Unlike capital punishment, probation, intermediate sanctions, jail, prison, and parole are being transformed through evidence-based practices.

Exhibit 3–2 is a guide to the sentencing options and sanctions in use across the United States. Our intent here is to review briefly the sequence of sentencing options that judges have following conviction, recognizing that they are discussed in more depth in chapters that follow.

Probation

The sentencing options that may be available to judges and juries begin with probation and end with capital punishment. If a defendant is sentenced to probation, she or he is on conditional release into the community and under the supervision of a probation officer. It is conditional because it can be revoked if certain conditions are not met. On January 1, 2021, about 1 in 84 adults was on probation. And even though more adults are on probation than in jail and prison, the majority of the $60 billion corrections budget is given to jails and prisons, causing problems with high probation caseloads, case investigations, and supervision.

EXHIBIT 3–2 Types of Sentences

capital punishment Lawful imposition of the death penalty.

community service A sentence to serve a specified number of hours working in unpaid positions with nonprofit or tax supported agencies.

consecutive sentences Sentences served one after the other.

concurrent sentences Sentences served together.

day fine A financial penalty scaled both to the defendant's ability to pay and the seriousness of the crime.

deferred sentence A sentence that is postponed for a specific period to allow the court to evaluate the conduct of the convicted person during the deferred period (usually community supervision). If the defendant successfully completes the court order, the charges are normally dismissed and do not remain on the defendants' record.

determinate sentence (also *fixed sentence*) A sentence of a fixed term of incarceration, which can be reduced by good time (days or months prison authorities deduct from a sentence for good behavior and other reasons).

fine A financial penalty used as a criminal sanction.

flat sentences Those that specify a given amount of time to be served in custody and allow little or no variation from the time specified.

habitual offender statute A law that (1) allows a person's criminal history to be considered at sentencing or (2) makes it possible for a person convicted of a given offense and previously convicted of another specified offense to receive a more severe penalty than that for the current offense alone.

indeterminate sentence A sentence in which a judge specifies a maximum length and a minimum length and an administrative agency, generally a parole board, determines the actual time of release.

intensive supervision probation (ISP) Control of offenders in the community under strict conditions, by means of frequent reporting to a probation officer whose caseload is generally limited to 30 offenders.

intermediate sanctions New punishment options developed to fill the gap between traditional probation and traditional jail or prison sentences and to better match the severity of punishment to the seriousness of the crime.

jail Locally operated correctional facilities that that confine people before or after conviction.

life sentence (also *life imprisonment* and *life without parole [LWOP]*) A sentence condemning a person who has been convicted of a serious crime to spend the rest of her or his life in prison.

mandatory minimum sentencing Sentences required by statute for those convicted of a particular crime or a particular crime with special circumstances, such as robbery with a firearm or selling drugs to a minor within 1,000 feet of a school, or for those with a particular type of criminal history.

mandatory sentences Those that are required by law under certain circumstances—such as conviction of a specified crime or of a series of offenses of a specified type.

maximum sentence The maximum amount of time a convicted person can be held in custody.

minimum sentence The minimum amount of time a convicted person can be held in custody.

parole The conditional release of a person from prison, prior to completion of the imposed sentence, under the supervision of a parole officer.

presumptive sentence The expected sentence; sentences that are presumed to be appropriate and that judges are expected to follow unless they document reasons for departing from the guidelines.

prison A state or federal confinement facility that has custodial authority over adults sentenced to confinement.

probation The conditional release of a convicted offender into the community, under the supervision of a probation officer. It is conditional because it can be revoked if certain conditions are not met.

restitution Payments made by a criminal offender to his or her victim (or to the court, which then turns them over to the victim) as compensation for the harm caused by the offense.

sentencing commission A group assigned to create a schedule of sentences that reflect the gravity of the offenses committed and the prior record of the criminal offender.

sentencing enhancements Legislatively approved provisions that mandate longer prison terms for specific criminal offenses committed under certain circumstances (such as a murder committed because of the victim's race or a drug sale near a school) or because of the criminal record of a person who has been convicted of a crime.

suspended sentence A legal term for a judge's delaying of a defendant's serving of a sentence after they have been convicted or found guilty in order to allow the defendant to perform a period of community supervision. If the defendant does not break the law during the probationary period, the sentence is normally eliminated. However, unlike a deferred sentence, a suspended sentence remains on a defendant's criminal record permanently.

straight (also flat) sentence A fixed sentence with no maximum or minimum associated with it.

three-strikes laws Statutes that impose mandatory prison sentences, generally a life sentence, on those convicted of an offense if they have been previously convicted of two prior serious criminal offenses.

truth in sentencing (TIS) The sentencing principle that requires a person who has been convicted of a crime to serve a substantial portion of the sentence (usually 85 percent) and reduces the discrepancy between the sentence imposed and actual time spent in prison.

Many jurisdictions have people on probation for a variety of offenses (e.g., property offenses, domestic abuse, misdemeanor and felony offenses, and sex offenses). It all boils down to the capacity of the individual jurisdiction, what the community will tolerate, state statutes, resource availability, etc. How well individuals do on probation depends on how well their needs are assessed, how well they are supervised, and what resources the agency

has available to assist in their supervision and rehabilitation. The motivation of the people being supervised is also a factor that has to be considered. Assessing a probationer's risk and needs and providing the right treatment at the right level is an evidence-based practice that contributes to successful probation outcomes and is discussed in more depth later.

Intermediate Sanctions

Probation can either stand alone as a criminal sanction or be combined with any of the intermediate sanctions discussed in Chapter 5. As you will learn, intermediate sanctions have been developed to fill the gap between traditional probation and traditional jail or prison sentences and to better match the severity of punishment to the seriousness of the crime. Among the more frequently used intermediate sanctions are *intensive supervision probation* (ISP), *community service,* and *fines.* ISP is control of people who have offended in the community under strict conditions by means of frequent reporting to a probation officer whose caseload is generally limited to 30 clients. Community service is a sentence to serve a specified number of hours working in unpaid positions with nonprofit or tax-supported agencies. And a fine is a financial penalty used as a criminal sanction. Community service and fines are seldom, if ever, used as stand-alone criminal sanctions in the United States as they are in Western Europe. In the United States, they are added as conditions of probation.

Jail and Prison

You often hear the terms *jail* and *prison* used interchangeably. However, there are big differences between the two. Whether a person is confined in jail or prison says something important about the crime committed and the stages of criminal justice processing. The major difference between jail and prison is the length of the individual's sentence. Jails are used to hold people who have been recently arrested or people who are charged with a crime and unable to post bail. It can also house people who are given short sentences, generally one year or less.

By contrast, a prison is designed for long-term confinement. The majority of people who receive criminal convictions serve their sentences in a prison. Under closer scrutiny, however, the distinction between jail and prison in terms of the length of an offender's sentence blurs. Because of crowding in state and federal prisons, more than 100,000 persons serving sentences longer than one year were held in local jails as of January 1, 2021, a decline of almost 10 percent from the year before.[8] Montana houses more than 50 percent of people who have been convicted in local jails—more than any other state.

Jails are locally run. Except for six states that run combined jail/prison systems (Alaska, Connecticut, Delaware, Hawaii, Rhode Island, and Vermont), jails are local correctional facilities, paid for mostly by local tax dollars (although most receive some state funding) and, in most counties, administered by locally elected sheriffs. Prisons, on the other hand, are state facilities, supported by state taxpayers (most prisons also receive some type of federal funding) and are administered by wardens who are appointed by the governor.

In spite of their differences, however, most jails and prisons face the same challenges: crowding, high recidivism rates, large numbers of residents who are mentally ill, and overrepresentation of minorities. On January 1, 2021, approximately 400 people out of every 100,000 persons were in prison: 734,470 persons were confined in our nation's jails, and 1,215,800 were held in state and federal prisons.

Parole

Persons leaving jail or prison are often released under some type of community supervision (sometimes known as *parole*). However, over the past 30 years, almost one-third of the states and the federal government eliminated parole for reasons you will learn about in Chapter 8. Many argue that sentencing policies and practices—mandatory minimum sentences, truth in sentencing statutes, three-strikes laws, life without parole, punitive sentencing guidelines, and the movement to abolish parole—fueled the mass incarceration in the United States that we still see today.

Parole, like probation, faces challenges. The biggest is client reentry. Almost 2,000 persons leave prison every day. Their job prospects are generally dim, their chances of finding a place to live are bleak, and their health is likely to be poor. Is it any wonder that two-thirds are rearrested within three years and one-half are reincarcerated?

To change this cycle of failure, the U.S. Congress and state and local governments are creating opportunities to provide employment assistance, substance abuse treatment, housing, family programming, mentoring, victim support, and other services that can make a person's transition from prison or jail safer and more successful. Three major initiatives include the Second Chance Act, the "ban the box" movement, and reentry court—opportunities unknown just 20 years ago—and which are discussed in more detail in Chapter 8.

- The national Second Chance Act supports state, local, and tribal governments and nonprofit organizations in their work with grants to reduce recidivism and improve outcomes for people returning from state and federal prisons and local jails.
- The "ban the box" movement encourages local, state, and federal governments to remove barriers to qualified workers with criminal records by prohibiting employers from requiring disclosure of past convictions on *initial* job applications. Employers can ask about criminal backgrounds and run background checks after determining that an applicant meets minimum job qualifications.
- Reentry courts are specialized courts (much like drug courts) that manage the return to the community of people who have been released from jail or prison and into the community using the authority of the court to apply graduated sanctions and positive reinforcement and to marshal resources to support the individual's reintegration.

Exhibit 3–3 displays the types of sentences imposed on people who have been convicted of felonies in state courts.

EXHIBIT 3–3   The Sentencing of People Convicted of Felonies in State Courts, by Type of Sentence

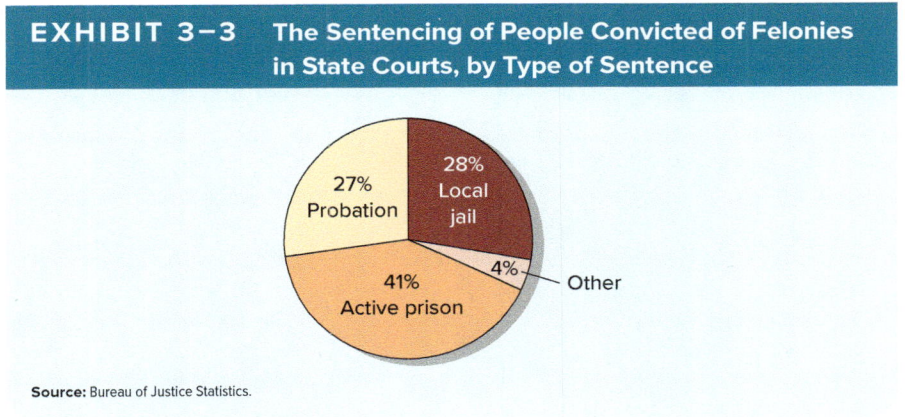

Source: Bureau of Justice Statistics.

CO3-4
CAPITAL PUNISHMENT

capital punishment

Lawful imposition of the death penalty.

Capital Punishment
Is capital punishment an effective sentencing strategy? That is, does it prevent future serious, violent crime? If so, by whom?

Capital punishment was once common throughout the world and imposed for many crimes, including murder, rape, stealing, witchcraft, piracy, desertion, sodomy, adultery, concealing the birth or death of an infant, aiding runaway slaves, counterfeiting, and forgery. Those who had broken the criminal law were sometimes boiled, burned, roasted on spits, drawn and quartered, broken on wheels, disemboweled, torn apart by animals, gibbeted (hung from a post with a projecting arm and left to die), bludgeoned (beaten to death with sticks, clubs, or rocks), or pressed (crushed under a board and stones).

Capital punishment began changing in the 18th century during the Enlightenment. This philosophical movement led to many new theories on crime and punishment. One of these theories proposed that punishment should fit the crime. Penalties involving torture began to disappear, and the use of the death penalty diminished.

By 1950, as prosperity followed World War II, public sentiment for capital punishment faded. The number of executions dropped. Support for capital punishment was at its lowest in 1966 (42 percent), and constitutional challenges were starting to surface. The watershed case in capital punishment took place in 1972 when the Court decided *Furman* v. *Georgia.*[9] The Court held that Georgia's death penalty statute, which gave the sentencing authority (judge or trial jury) complete sentencing discretion without any guidance as to how to exercise that discretion, could result in arbitrary sentencing and was therefore in violation of the Eighth Amendment's ban against cruel and unusual punishment.

Four years later, in *Gregg* v. *Georgia,* the Supreme Court upheld guided discretionary capital statutes, opining that "such standards do provide guidance to the sentencing authority and thereby reduce the likelihood that it will impose a sentence that fairly can be called capricious and arbitrary." The first person executed after *Gregg* v. *Georgia* was Gary Gilmore, who gave up his right to appeal and was executed by firing squad on January 17, 1977, by the State of Utah. Since then, over 1,500 capital offenders have been executed throughout the United States. Almost 45 years later, the trends in capital punishment are these: Death sentences are at a historic low, executions reached a 25-year low, and since 1973, 166 persons have been **exonerated** and freed from death row.

exonerate

To clear of blame.

The now unused gas chamber in the historic Colorado Territorial Correctional Facility in Cañon City, Colorado. Colorado was the last state to use the gas chamber prior to the decisive 1972 U.S. Supreme Court case of Furman v. Georgia. *That case required the rewriting of capital punishment laws nationwide. What do evidence-based studies tell us about the effectiveness of capital punishment?*
Courtesy of the Justice Research Association

Capital Punishment Around the World

In 2020 Amnesty International documented 483 executions in 18 countries, but the total did not include figures from China, which executes more people than the rest of the world combined. Most executions took place in China, Iran, Saudi Arabia, Viet Nam and Iraq—in that order.[10]

By January 1, 2021, the majority of countries had abolished the death penalty in law or in practice.[11] Eighteen countries, however, actively employed it. See Exhibit 3–4 for the number of state-ordered criminal executions that occurred around the world in a recent year.

States With and Without Capital Punishment

By 2021, 22 states and the District of Columbia had abolished the death penalty. Twenty-eight states, the U.S. military, and the federal government still retain it (see Exhibit 3–5).

Today in the United States, what constitutes a **capital crime**—a crime that is punishable by death—is defined by law. This definition varies among jurisdictions. In Delaware, for example, first-degree murder with at least one statutory aggravating circumstance is a capital crime. In Nevada, first-degree murder with at least 1 of 15 specified aggravating circumstances is a capital crime. In Texas, criminal homicide with one of nine aggravating circumstances is a capital offense.[12]

capital crime

A crime for which the death penalty may be imposed but need not necessarily be.

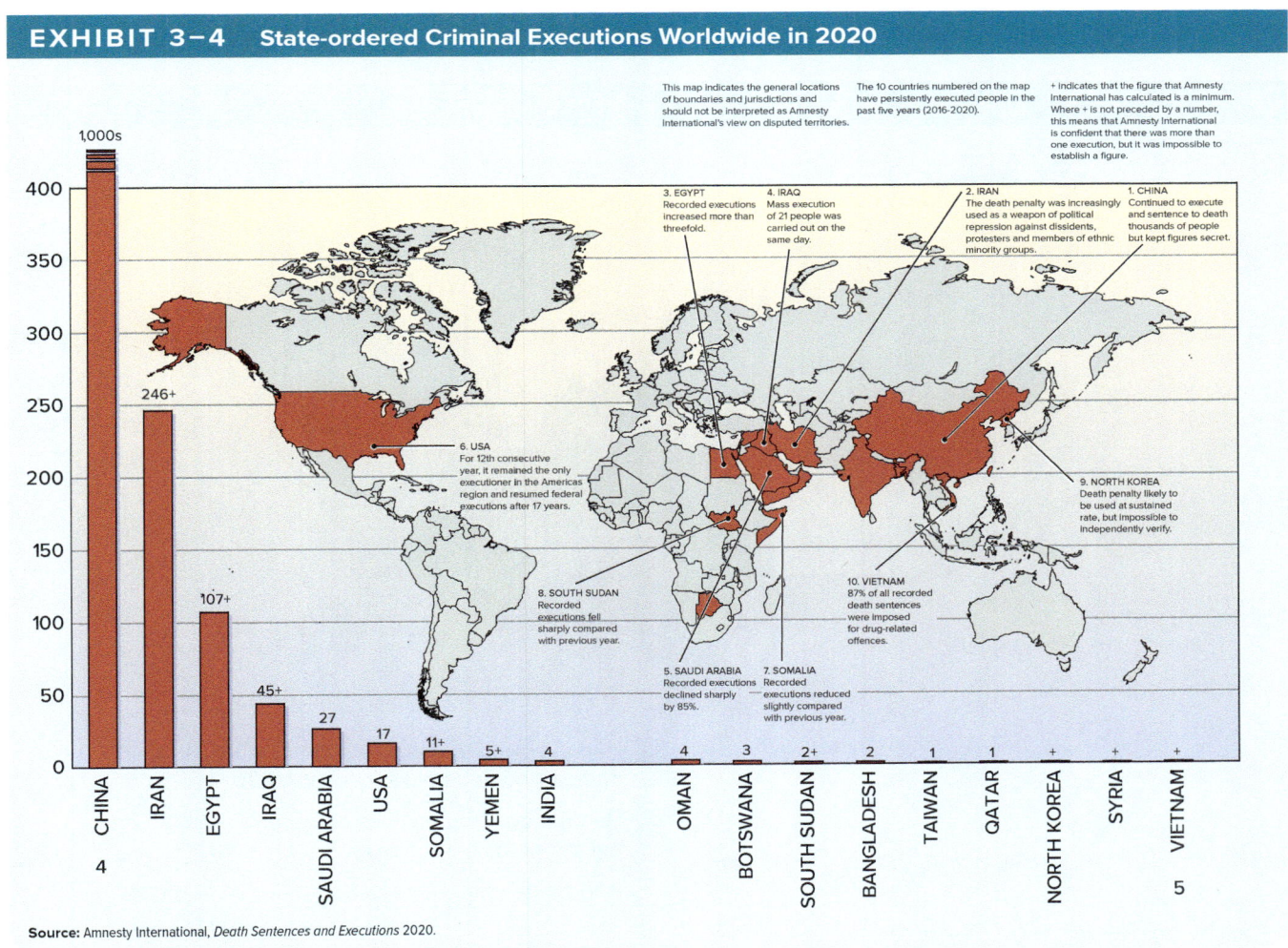

EXHIBIT 3–4 State-ordered Criminal Executions Worldwide in 2020

This map indicates the general locations of boundaries and jurisdictions and should not be interpreted as Amnesty International's view on disputed territories.

The 10 countries numbered on the map have persistently executed people in the past five years (2016-2020).

+ indicates that the figure that Amnesty International has calculated is a minimum. Where + is not preceded by a number, this means that Amnesty International is confident that there was more than one execution, but it was impossible to establish a figure.

Source: Amnesty International, *Death Sentences and Executions* 2020.

Maryland governor Martin O'Malley signing legislation that abolished capital punishment and replaced it with the sentence of life in prison without the possibility of parole. Do you think that other states will abolish the death penalty in coming years? Why or why not?

Patrick Semansky/AP Photo

Characteristics of Persons on Death Row

At the start of 2021, around 2,470 persons were awaiting execution, a decrease of over 600 from a decade earlier. At the time of Gary Gilmore's execution on January 17, 1977, there were 423 people on death row. Ten years later, the number was 1,984. After more than 20 years of continued

---

EXHIBIT 3–5   Jurisdictions With and Without Capital Punishment

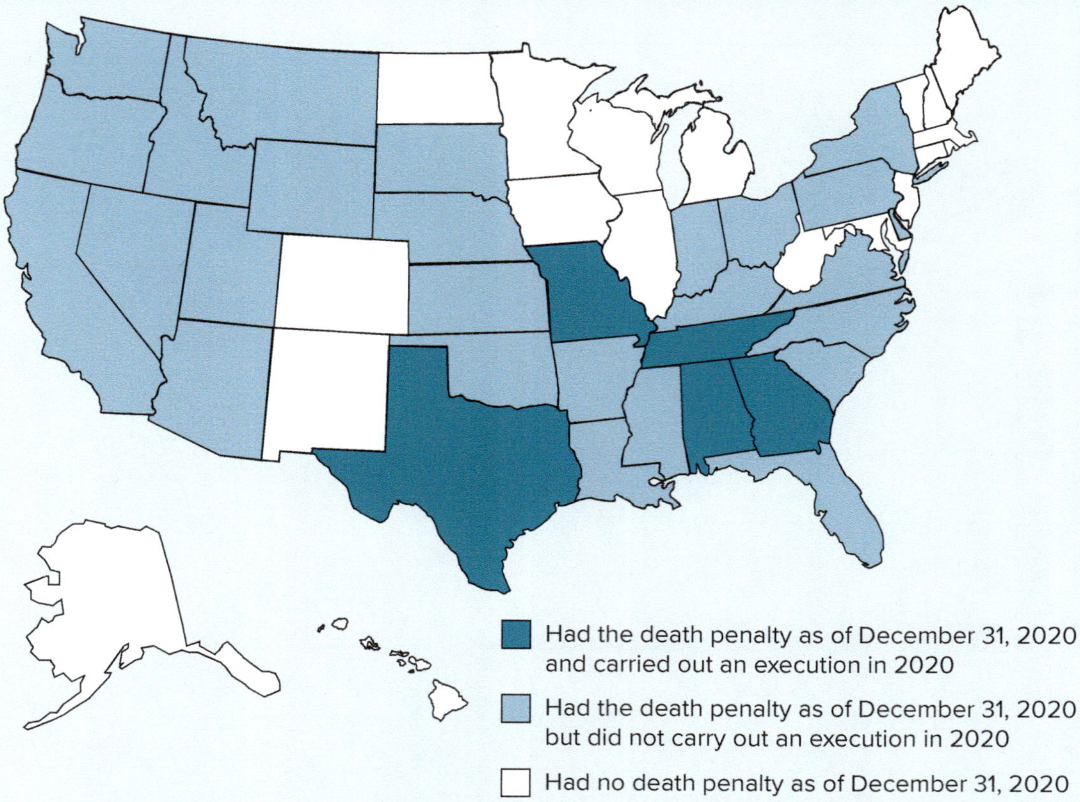

■ Had the death penalty as of December 31, 2020 and carried out an execution in 2020

■ Had the death penalty as of December 31, 2020 but did not carry out an execution in 2020

□ Had no death penalty as of December 31, 2020

Source: Bureau of Justice Statistics, National Prisoner Statistics program.

Few issues generate more public controversy than that of the death penalty. In some states there are movements to end the death penalty, but in others, the move is to speed up death row appeals and complete the sentence of execution. Do you believe that demonstrations such as these influence the public policy implemented by state legislatures?

Left: Alexandros Michailidis/Shutterstock; Right: Alex Wong/Getty Images

increase in the number of people sentenced to die in the United States, the number on death row peaked in 2000 to 3,593 and has been decreasing ever since.

Today, U.S. juries are imposing fewer death sentences than they did on average during the 1990s. In the 1990s, an average of almost 300 people were sentenced to death each year. In the first decade of the 21st century, the average was almost 135 per year. Since 2011, the average has dropped to 74 per year. Almost 50 percent of today's death row population is in three states: California (703), Florida (337), and Texas (206). Exhibit 3–6 shows additional characteristics of inmates under sentence of death.

EXHIBIT 3–6 Characteristics of People Under Sentence of Death, January 1, 2021

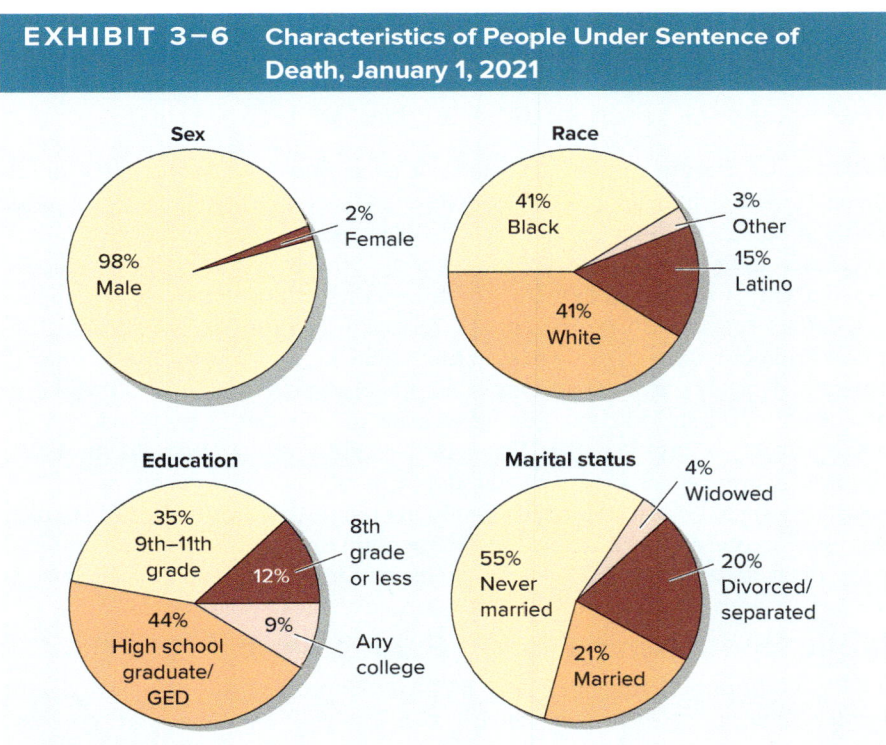

Source: Bureau of Justice Statistics.

Victim Race and Capital Punishment

Defendant–victim racial combinations have been the subject of considerable discussion.[13] Recognizing that whites and minorities are murder victims in approximately equal numbers, why is it that more than 75 percent of the victims in cases resulting in executions since 1977 have been white? Does it imply that white victims are considered more important by the criminal justice system? Some have argued that Blacks and Hispanics are more likely than whites to be sentenced to death and executed because they are more likely to be arrested on facts that can support a capital charge and because whites are more likely to negotiate plea bargains that spare their lives. Others disagree, citing consistent patterns of racial bias.[14] Since the General Accounting Office first studied the issue of interracial murders and sentencing in 1990 and reported that the race of the victim is correlated with the likelihood of being charged with capital murder or receiving the death penalty, many scholars have found the same pattern. For example:

- Jurors in Washington state were three times more likely to recommend a death sentence for a Black defendant than for a white defendant in a similar case (consequently, the Washington supreme court, in 2018, ruled capital punishment unconstitutional).
- In Louisiana, the odds of a death sentence were 97 percent higher for those whose victim was white than for those whose victim was Black.
- A study in California found that those who killed whites were more than three times more likely to be sentenced to death than those who killed Blacks and more than four times more likely than those who killed Latinos.
- In 96 percent of states where there have been reviews of race and the death penalty, there was a pattern of either race-of-victim or race-of-defendant disproportionality, or both.

The public also believes that decision making in homicide cases is not influenced by the same factors in all cases. According to the American Values Survey by the Public Religion Research Institute, 53 percent of all Americans agreed with the statement, "A black person is more likely than a white person to receive the death penalty for the same crime," while 45 percent disagreed.

Methods of Execution Five methods of execution are used in the United States: (1) lethal injection, (2) electrocution, (3) lethal gas, (4) hanging, and (5) firing squad. All states and the federal government prefer to use lethal injection as their primary method of execution. States use a variety of protocols involving one, two, or three drugs. The three-drug protocol uses an anesthetic or sedative, typically follpancuronium, followed by bromide to paralyze the inmate and potassium chloride to stop the inmate's heart. The one- or two-drug protocols typically use a lethal dose of an anesthetic or sedative and avoid the controversy of the short-acting sedative wearing off and leading to consciousness of the inmate. A problem that has arisen recently is that manufacturers of anesthetics are refusing to provide departments of corrections drugs for executions. In 2018, as a result of difficulty in obtaining lethal drugs, the state of Tennessee executed two inmates by electrocution, and in 2022 South Carolina had to delay its first-planned firing squad execution because of legal action.

Public Opinion and Capital Punishment

A 2021 Gallup poll revealed that 54% of Americans support the death penalty.[15] Support, however, varies considerably by race and gender. About six in ten men support it, while less than 50 percent of women are in favor of it. About 59 percent of white people favor its use, but only 47 percent of Hispanics and 36 percent of Blacks do. In a wider gap, persons in death penalty states are divided about evenly in their preference for capital punishment versus life without the possibility of parole (LWOP). However, in states without capital punishment, LWOP is preferred by a 20-point margin.[16] The poll results are consistent with other signs of declining support for the death penalty: Eight states have abolished the death penalty over the past decade, and death sentences are at their lowest level since capital punishment was reinstated. Even with historic lows in death sentencing, the poll reports the highest ever percentage of Americans now saying that the death penalty is imposed too often (27 percent). Many arguments favor capital punishment, and many arguments oppose it. Some of the arguments—pro and con—are summarized in Exhibit 3–7.

The Courts and Capital Punishment

When the Supreme Court ruled in *Furman* v. *Georgia* in 1972, it also voided the death penalty statutes of 40 states, commuted the death sentences of all

EXHIBIT 3–7	Arguments Favoring and Opposing the Death Penalty

PRO

- It deters people from crime through fear of punishment; it exerts a positive moral influence by stigmatizing crimes of murder and manslaughter.
- It is a just punishment for murder; it fulfills the "just deserts" principle of a fitting punishment; life in prison is not a tough enough punishment for a capital crime.
- It is constitutionally appropriate; the Eighth Amendment prohibits cruel and unusual punishment, yet the Fifth Amendment implies that, with due process of law, one may be deprived of life, liberty, or property.
- It reduces time spent on death row to reduce costs of capital punishment and the attendant costs of postconviction appeals, investigations, and searches for new evidence and witnesses.
- It protects society from the most serious and feared offenders; it prevents the reoccurrence of violence.
- It is more humane than life imprisonment because it is quick; making the person suffer by remaining in prison for the rest of his or her life is more torturous and inhumane than execution.
- It is almost impossible for an innocent person to be executed; the slow execution rate results from the process of appeals, between sentencing and execution.

CON

- It does not deter crime, and no evidence exists that the death penalty is more effective than other punishments.
- It violates human rights; it is a barbaric remnant of an uncivilized society; it is immoral in principle; and it ensures the execution of some innocent people.
- It falls disproportionately on racial minorities; those who murdered whites are more likely to be sentenced to death than are those who murdered Blacks.
- It costs too much; $2 million to $5 million are poured into each execution while other criminal justice components such as police, courts, and community corrections lack sufficient funding.
- It boosts the murder rate; this is known as the *brutalizing effect;* the state is a role model, and when the state carries out an execution, it shows that killing is a way to solve problems.
- Not everyone wants vengeance; many people favor alternative sentences such as life without parole.
- It is arbitrary and unfair; people who commit similar crimes under similar circumstances receive widely differing sentences; race, social and economic status, location of crime, and pure chance influence sentencing.

mandatory death penalty

A death sentence that the legislature has required to be imposed upon people convicted of certain offenses.

guided discretion

Decision making bounded by general guidelines, rules, or laws.

bifurcated trial

Two separate hearings for different issues in a trial, one for guilt and the other for punishment.

mitigating circumstances

Factors that, although not justifying or excusing an action, may reduce the culpability of the individual.

aggravating circumstances

Factors that may increase the culpability of the individual.

629 death row inmates around the United States, and suspended the death penalty because existing statutes were no longer valid. It is important to note that the Court majority did *not* rule that the death penalty itself was unconstitutional but that only the way in which it was administered at that time.

States responded to the *Furman* decision by rewriting their capital punishment statutes to limit discretion and avoid arbitrary and inconsistent results. The new death penalty laws took two forms. Some states imposed a **mandatory death penalty** for certain crimes, and others permitted **guided discretion,** which sets standards for judges and juries to use when deciding whether to impose the death penalty.

In 1976, the U.S. Supreme Court rejected mandatory capital punishment statutes but approved guided discretion statutes in *Gregg* v. *Georgia.* In its ruling, the Court approved automatic appellate review, a proportionality review whereby state appellate courts compare a sentence with those of similar cases, and a **bifurcated trial,** or special two-part trial. The first part of a bifurcated trial, the *guilt phase,* decides the issue of guilt. If the defendant is found guilty, the second part of the trial, the *penalty phase,* takes place. The penalty phase includes presentation of facts that mitigate or aggravate the circumstances of the crime. **Mitigating circumstances** are factors that may reduce the culpability of the offender (make the defendant less deserving of the death penalty). **Aggravating circumstances** are factors that may increase the offender's culpability (make the defendant more deserving of death).

In 2002, the U.S. Supreme Court handed down another decision that shaped capital sentencing. In *Ring* v. *Arizona,* the Court held that only juries, not judges, can determine the presence of "aggravating factors" to be weighed in the capital sentencing process. Although judges may still reduce sentences, the Court held that a defendant may not receive a penalty that exceeds the maximum penalty that he or she would have received if punished according to the facts in the jury verdict.

The U.S. Supreme Court has continued to refine its death penalty decisions over the years. In 2005, the Court, in *Deck* v. *Missouri,* found that the Constitution forbids the use of visible shackles during a capital trial, unless that use is "justified by an essential state interest"—such as courtroom security—specific to the defendant. In 2008, in *Kennedy* v. *Louisiana,* the Court held that the U.S. Constitution bars states from imposing the death penalty for the rape of a child, but only where the crime did not result and was not intended to result in the child's death. In 2016, the state of Florida's death penalty sentencing procedure was found to be unconstitutional in *Hurst* v. *Florida* because it allowed a judge to find and weigh aggravating circumstances independently of the jury.

In 2018, the supreme court of the state of Washington found that the death penalty violated the state's constitution because it was applied unequally. The race of the defendant and the budget available to county prosecutors, said the court, often determined who was condemned to death.

Support for capital punishment, at least among politicians, seems to be waning. In 2019, the Oregon legislature restricted the types of murders eligible for the death penalty. Under Oregon's law, sentences of capital punishment are limited to defendants who kill two or more people as an act of organized terrorism; kill a child younger than 14 intentionally and with premeditation; kill another person while locked in jail or prison for a previous murder; or kill a police, correctional, or probation officer. In 2020, outgoing Oregon governor Kate Brown commuted the sentences of those on death row and ordered the dismantling of the state's execution chamber.

Colorado abolished the death penalty in 2020, although it is still possible in that state for anyone who committed a capital crime before July 1, 2020, to receive a capital sentence.

In 2021, U.S. Attorney General Merrick B. Garland imposed a moratorium on federal executions saying that "the Department of Justice must ensure that everyone in the federal criminal justice system is not only afforded the rights guaranteed by the Constitution and laws of the United States, but is also treated fairly and humanely, That obligation has special force in capital cases."

Similarly, in 2022, the governor of Oregon commuted the entire death row population, although capital punishment remains "on the books" in that state. Also, in 2022, Alabama governor Kay Ivey halted executions indefinitely after a series of botched executions in that state.

In 2023, California governor Gavin Newsom effectively invalidated that state's death penalty with an announcement that persons sentenced to death and under the care of the state's Department of Corrections and Rehabilitation (CDCR) would be moved off of death row and into the general population of prisons across the state. Newsom called the death penalty in America unjust and racially and class biased, and said that it had little connection to justice. "The prospect of your ending up on death row has more to do with your wealth and race than it does with your guilt or innocence," he said.[17]

Appealing the Death Penalty

Capital punishment cases may pass through as many as 10 courts in three stages: trial and direct review, state postconviction appeals, and federal *habeas corpus* appeals (see Exhibit 3–8).

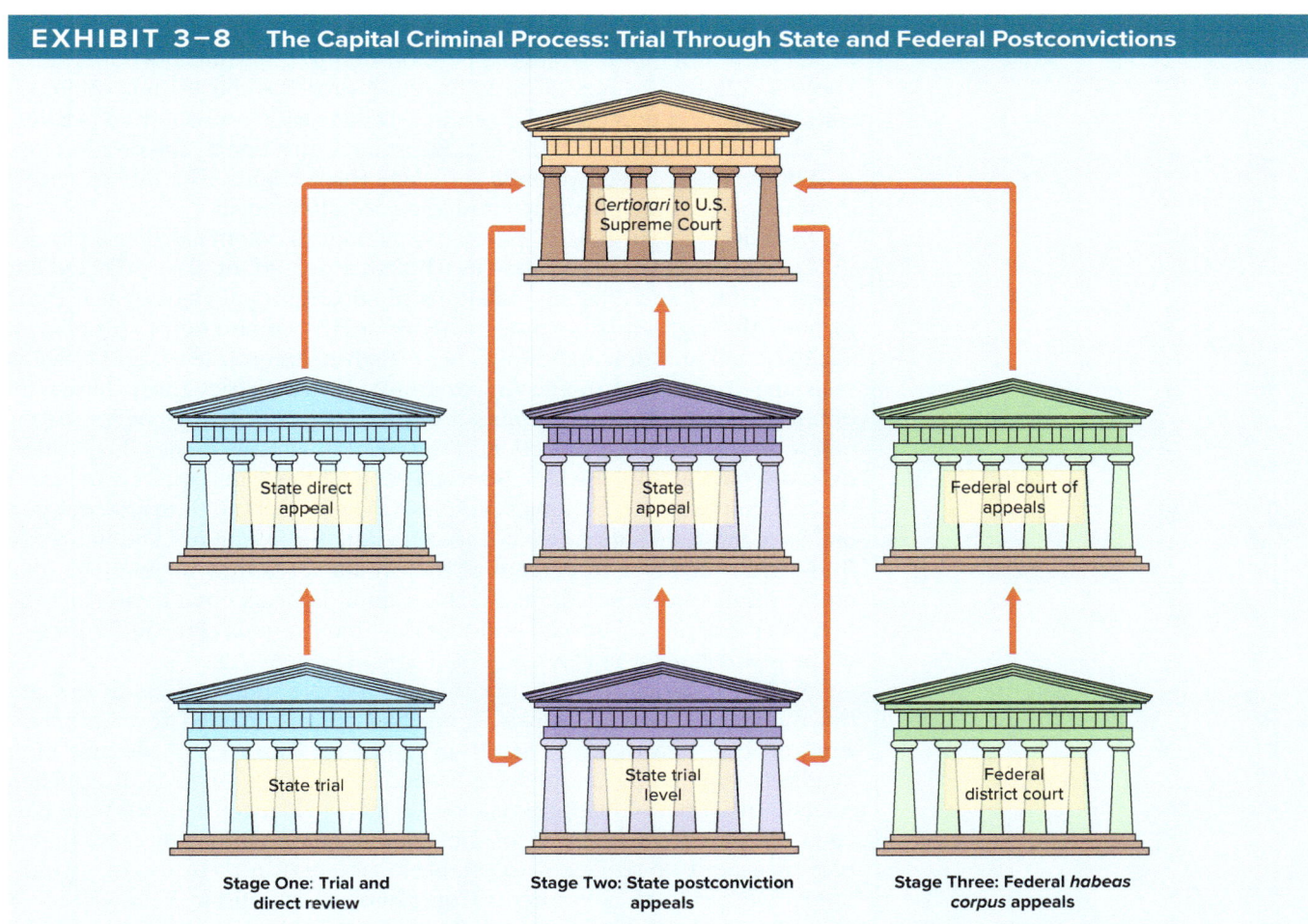

EXHIBIT 3–8   The Capital Criminal Process: Trial Through State and Federal Postconvictions

Certiorari to U.S. Supreme Court

State direct appeal

State appeal

Federal court of appeals

State trial

State trial level

Federal district court

Stage One: Trial and direct review

Stage Two: State postconviction appeals

Stage Three: Federal *habeas corpus* appeals

Source: James S. Liebman, Jeffrey Fagan, and Valerie West, *A Broken System: Error Rates in Capital Punishment Cases, 1973–1995* (New York: Columbia University School of Law, 2000), p. 23.

serious error

Error that substantially undermines the reliability of the guilt finding or death sentence imposed at trial.

In stage one, trial and direct review, a death sentence is imposed. The laws of all states require that legal issues about the trial and sentence automatically be appealed to the state appellate courts. Alabama and Ohio have two rounds of appeals in the direct review process; this means that the legal issues may be heard first in the state court of criminal appeals before reaching the state supreme court. These courts evaluate the original trial for legal or constitutional errors and determine whether the death sentence is consistent with sentences imposed in similar cases. State appellate courts seldom overturn a conviction or change a death sentence. The defendant then frequently petitions the U.S. Supreme Court to grant a petition for a writ of *certiorari*—a written order to the lower court whose decision is being appealed to send the records of the case forward for review. Stage one, direct review, consumes about five years—half of the time required for the entire appeals process. Nationally, the rate of **serious error** (error that substantially undermines the reliability of the guilt finding or death sentence imposed at trial) discovered on direct review is 41 percent.

If the defendant's direct appeals are unsuccessful and the Supreme Court denies review, stage two—state postconviction appeals—begins. At this point, many death row inmates allege ineffective or incompetent trial counsel, and new counsel is appointed. The new counsel petitions the original trial court with newly discovered evidence; questions about the fairness of the trial; and allegations of jury bias, tainted evidence, incompetence of defense counsel, and prosecutorial or police misconduct. If the trial court denies the appeals, they may be filed with the state's appellate courts (either directly to the state supreme court or, if there exists a dual level of appellate review as in Alabama and Ohio, through a petition first to the state court of criminal appeals, followed by a petition to the state supreme court. Most often, the state appellate courts deny the petition. Defendant's counsel then petitions the U.S. Supreme Court. If the U.S. Supreme Court denies the petition for a writ of *certiorari,* stage two ends and stage three begins. The rate of serious error found on state postconviction appeals is 10 percent.

In stage three, the federal *habeas corpus* stage, a defendant files a petition in U.S. district court in the state in which the defendant was convicted and is incarcerated and alleging violations of constitutional rights. Such rights include the right to due process (Fourteenth Amendment), prohibition against cruel and unusual punishment (Eighth Amendment), and effective assistance of counsel (Sixth Amendment). If the district court denies the petition, defense counsel submits it to the U.S. court of appeals for the circuit representing the jurisdiction. If the court of appeals denies the petition, defense counsel asks the U.S. Supreme Court to grant a writ of *certiorari.* If the U.S. Supreme Court denies *certiorari,* the office of the state attorney general asks the state supreme court to set a date for execution. Federal courts find serious error in 40 percent of the capital cases they review. The Eleventh Circuit—the nation's most active capital appeals circuit with jurisdiction over Alabama, Georgia, and Florida—finds serious error in 50 percent of the death cases it reviews.

In 1996, in an effort to reduce the time people spend on death row and the number of federal appeals, the U.S. Congress passed the Antiterrorism and Effective Death Penalty Act (AEDPA). The AEDPA defines filing deadlines and limits reasons for second, or successive, federal appellate reviews to (1) new constitutional law, (2) new evidence that could not have been discovered at the time of the original trial, or (3) new facts that, if proven, would be sufficient to establish the applicant's innocence. Under the AEDPA, if the U.S. Supreme Court denies the petition for a writ of *certiorari* in the final federal *habeas corpus* appeal, defense counsel may once again petition the federal courts; however, before a second, or successive, application for a writ of *habeas corpus* may be filed in a U.S. district court, defense counsel must petition the appropriate U.S. court of appeals for an order authorizing the district court to consider the application. The petition to the U.S. court of appeals is decided by a three-judge panel; the panel must grant or deny the authorization to file the second, or successive, application within 30 days after the petition is filed. If the panel approves the petition, the district court must render a decision regarding the application within 180 days. If the motion is appealed to the court of appeals representing the jurisdiction, the court must render its decision within 120 days. If the petition is filed with the U.S. Supreme Court, the Court may grant the petition for *certiorari* or let the lower court's decision stand.

Wrongful Convictions and Capital Punishment

Four times as many people have had their death sentences overturned or received clemency than were executed since 1977. At the turn of the 21st century, Columbia law professor James Liebman and colleagues calculated the frequency of error in capital cases.[18] Liebman studied what happened when 4,578 capital cases were appealed. His conclusion was powerful: The overall rate of prejudicial error in the U.S. capital punishment system was found to be 68 percent. More than two of every three capital judgments reviewed by the courts were found to be seriously flawed. Ten states (Alabama, Arizona, California, Georgia, Indiana, Maryland, Mississippi, Montana, Oklahoma, and Wyoming) had overall error rates of 75 percent or higher. Almost 1,000 of the cases sent back for retrial ended in sentences less than death, and 87 ended in *not guilty* verdicts.

Liebman and his colleagues found two types of serious error. The first is incompetent defense lawyering (accounting for one-third of all state post-conviction appeals). A review of death penalty cases in Pennsylvania spanning three decades found that lawyers who handle such cases—typically at taxpayers' expense because the defendants are indigent—are often overworked and underpaid and present only the barest defense.[19] These lawyers neglect basic steps, including interviewing defendants, seeking witnesses, and investigating a defendant's background (See Exhibit 3–9).

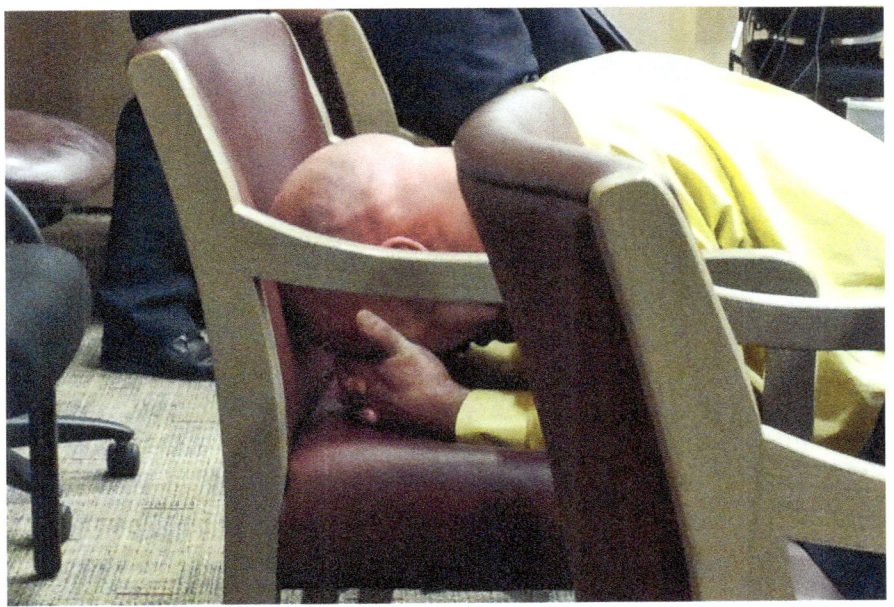

Former Florida death row inmate Seth Penalver cries into his chair after an appellate court overturned his death sentence. Penalver was aquitted of all charges and freed from Florida's death row 13 years after being sentenced to death. At the time of his exoneration, Penalver was the 24th person released from death row in Florida, the most of any state. Since 1973, 190 persons have been released from death row, and news of their innocence has set off a new debate over capital punishment in the United States. How are exonerations seen by death penalty advocates? By those opposed to the death penalty?

Sun-Sentinel/ZUMAPRESS.com/Alamy Stock Photo

EXHIBIT 3–9   Factors that Can Lead to a Wrongful Conviction

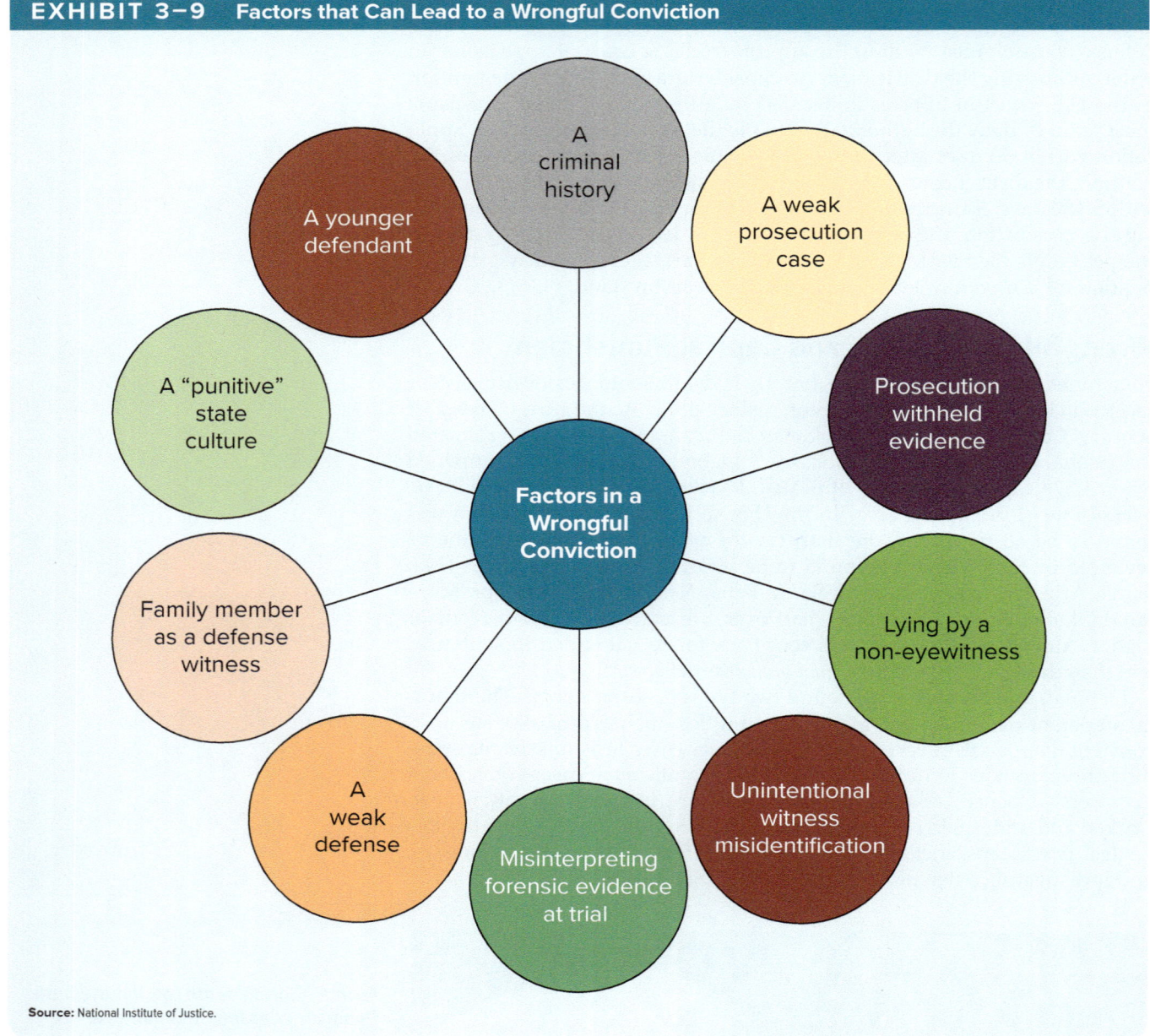

Source: National Institute of Justice.

If death sentences are not reliable and persons are wrongfully convicted and sentenced, the error has serious consequences for the wrongly convicted, for the family of the victim whose search for justice is incomplete, for the family of the person wrongly convicted in terms of the prolonged and distorted grief they suffer, for subsequent victims of the real offender still at large, and for the public in terms of lost confidence in the criminal justice system. The actual perpetrators remain in society to commit additional crimes, and many death row exonerees remain under a cloud of police suspicion because law enforcement failed to find the true offender.

Today, 30 states, the District of Columbia, and the federal government have passed laws that compensate people wrongfully convicted. Although laws vary from one jurisdiction to another, recommendations are for a minimum payment of $50,000 for each year spent imprisoned as a result of a wrongful conviction.[20]

At the national level, the Innocence Project leads the fight against wrongful convictions and has played a role in many exonerations. The Innocence Project had its start in 1992 when two public defenders, Barry Scheck and Peter Neufeld of the Bronx Legal Aid Society, met at the Benjamin N. Cardozo School of Law in New York City to discuss using DNA technology to free the wrongfully convicted. Seth Miller, executive director of the Innocence Project of Florida, says that "the innocence project has been a leader in the expansion of the Innocence network from a handful of tiny like-minded organizations to an international movement."[21] As of 2021, at least 190 people who had been wrongly convicted and sentenced to death in the United States have been exonerated.[22]

Banning the Execution of Juveniles and Persons With Mental Impairment

On June 19, 2002, the U.S. Supreme Court held in *Atkins* v. *Virginia* that execution of offenders who are mentally impaired is cruel and unusual punishment prohibited by the Eighth Amendment. The Court argued that a national consensus has developed against executing this group of people. At that time, 12 states banned executions altogether. However, beginning in 1988, Arizona, Arkansas, Colorado, Connecticut, Florida, Georgia, Indiana, Kansas, Kentucky, Maryland, Missouri, Nebraska, New Mexico, New York, North Carolina, South Dakota, Tennessee, Washington, and the federal government passed statutes banning the execution of offenders suffering from substantial mental impairment. The Court reasoned that it was not so much the number of states that had passed similar statutes but the consistency of the direction of change. In the words of the Court, "Given the well-known fact that anti-crime legislation is far more popular than legislation providing protections for persons guilty of violent crime, the large number of states prohibiting the execution of people with mental retardation (and the complete absence of states passing legislation reinstating the power to conduct such executions) provides powerful evidence that today our society views these offenders as categorically less culpable than the average criminal. The evidence carries even greater force when it is noted that the legislatures that have addressed the issue have voted overwhelmingly in favor of the prohibition."[23] However, the Court left the definition of what it referred to as "mental impairment" up to individual states, and some states, like Florida, set a rigid IQ threshold of 70 to determine whether or not a person suffers from serious mental impairment and would not allow other evidence showing substantial limitations in intellectual functions of reasoning or problem-solving, limitations in adaptive behavior or "street smarts," or evidence of the condition before age 18.

But on May 27, 2014, the U.S. Supreme Court ruled in *Hall* v. *Florida* that Florida's strict IQ cutoff for determining a person's eligibility for the death penalty was unconstitutional. The majority of justices said that Florida must take into account that intellectual disability is a *condition,* not a number, and that Florida cannot ignore the standard error of measurement in all IQ tests. The Court pointed to the American Medical Association's finding that IQ scores have a standard error of approximately five points. The IQ score of Freddie Lee Hall, the Florida death row inmate whose case was before the Court, was 71, one point above the Florida cutoff of 70. Viewing Hall's IQ using the standard error of measurement, the justices reasoned that Hall's

IQ is realistically between 66 and 76, and they reversed the judgment of the Florida Supreme Court.

Some years earlier, the U.S. Supreme Court, by a narrow 5–4 vote in *Roper* v. *Simmons,* said it was unconstitutional and in violation of the Eighth Amendment's ban on cruel and unusual punishment to execute people for crimes they committed before turning age 18. The Court's ruling vacated the death sentences of 72 people on death rows across the United States. The offenders wound up with life sentences, many without parole.

In deciding *Roper* v. *Simmons,* the justices reasoned several things. First, they said that the trend toward banning capital punishment for juveniles reflected "evolving standards of decency that mark the progress of a maturing society."

Second, and perhaps most importantly, the justices cited scientific literature from the American Academy of Child and Adolescent Psychiatry, the American Medical Association, and the American Psychological Association showing that adolescents lack mature judgment, are less aware of the consequences of their decisions and actions, are more vulnerable than adults to peer pressure, and have a greater tendency toward impulsiveness and lesser reasoning skills, regardless of how big they are or how tough they talk.

CO3-5 SENTENCING TRENDS AND REFORMS

There is growing momentum for sentencing reform in the United States. Those reforms have been evolving in a direction that emphasises being smart on crime and evidence-based approaches to public safety. Bipartisan support at the federal, state, and local levels has shaped new sentencing and reentry policies and addressed the runaway expenditures incurred over the past four decades due to the overuse of imprisonment. The American Correctional Association's policy on sentencing is shown in Exhibit 3–10.

At the federal level, the Fair Sentencing Act of 2010 reduced the disparity in sentencing between crack and powder cocaine offenses; the Second Chance Act of 2008 funded some $70 million in reentry services annually across the United States; and in 2005, the U.S. Supreme Court's decision in *Booker* made federal sentencing guidelines advisory, thereby giving federal judges a greater degree of sentencing discretion.

President Trump signs the First Step Act into law in 2018. What is the purpose of the legislation?
SHAWN THEW/EPA-EFE/Shutterstock

EXHIBIT 3–10 American Correctional Association

Public Correctional Policy on Sentencing

The American Correctional Association actively promotes the development of sentencing policies that should:

- promote the principle of proportionality, whereby the sentence imposed should be commensurate with the seriousness of the crime and the harm done;
- ensure impartiality with regard to race, ethnicity, and economic status as to the discretion exercised in sentencing;
- include a broad range of options for custody, supervision, and rehabilitation of offenders;
- ensure that purpose-driven policies are based on clearly articulated purposes. They should be grounded in knowledge of the relative effectiveness of the various sanctions imposed in attempts to achieve these purposes;
- encourage the evaluation of sentencing policy on an ongoing basis. The various sanctions should be monitored to determine their relative effectiveness based on the purpose(s) they are intended to have. Likewise, monitoring should take place to ensure that the sanctions are not applied based on race, ethnicity, or economic status;
- recognize that the criminal sentence must be based on multiple criteria, including the harm done to the victim, past criminal history, the need to protect the public, and the opportunity to provide programs for offenders as a means of reducing the risk for future crime;
- provide the framework to guide and control discretion according to established criteria and within appropriate limits and allow for recognition of individual needs;
- recognize that a major purpose of restorative justice is righting the harm done to the victim and the community that includes the victim or his or her representative in the "justice" process;
- promote the use of community-based programs whenever consistent with public safety; and
- consider the resources needed to implement the policy. The consequential cost of various sanctions should be assessed. Sentencing policy should not be enacted without the benefit of a fiscal-impact analysis. Resource allocations should be linked to sentencing policy so as to ensure adequate funding of all sanctions, including total confinement and the broad range of intermediate sanction and community-based programs needed to implement those policies.

Source: Reprinted with Permission of the American Correctional Association, Alexandria, VA.

In 2016, the Charles Colson Task Force on Federal Corrections released its report. The report found that

the federal prison population should be reduced by 60,000 people over the coming years and thereby achieve a savings of over $5 billion, allowing for reinvestment in programs proven to reduce crime.[24]

The task force found that punitive mandatory minimum sentences for drug crimes represent "the primary driver" of prison overcrowding. It's report recommended that mandatory minimum sentences be reserved for the most violent offenders and found that almost 80 percent of federal inmates convicted of drug crimes had no prior criminal history. The panel urged Congress to create a path for people in prison who have served more than 15 years to apply for shorter sentences by giving judges a "second look" at their cases. The report also urged more oversight and resources for the Federal Bureau of Prisons (BOP)—and for programs that return inmates to their communities and foster bonds with their families. In line with one of the themes of this book, reforms suggested by the task force can be achieved through evidence-based policies that protect public safety.

In 2018, President Trump signed the First Step Act into law. The act reduced the sentences of about 3,000 people who were incarcerated in federal prisons for offenses involving crack cocaine, and mandated changes to the federal

Former Oklahoma Representative J.C. Watts, Chairman of the Charles Colson Task Force on Federal Corrections, speaks at a conference in New Orleans. What did the task force find?

Bill Haber, File/AP Photo

prison system that would help inmates earn sentence reductions. Central to the First Step Act are risk and needs assessments that are to be applied to every federal inmate and that use evidence-based recidivism reduction strategies. Inmates released under the provisions of the act spend time in prerelease custody—either under a home confinement program or in a residential reentry center (RRC) in the community. RRCs are essentially halfway houses intended to provide help to those who are nearing release. However, in 2021, in the case of *Terry* v. *U.S.*, the U.S. Supreme Court held that a crack offender is eligible for a sentence reduction under the First Step Act only if convicted of a crack offense that triggered a mandatory minimum sentence.

Reducing Prison Populations and Costs

In recent years, legislators in many states have become aware of the questionable benefits as well as the fiscal and social costs of many of the hallmarks of the tough-on-crime era. For example, state legislatures in Colorado, Georgia, Hawaii, Illinois, Indiana, Kansas, and Oregon have repealed, limited, or suspended mandatory minimum penalties if certain conditions are present in the case. Colorado, Connecticut, Indiana, Maryland, Oregon, South Dakota, Vermont, and Washington reclassified low-level crimes from felonies to misdemeanors. Colorado, Maryland, Oregon, and South Dakota made probation the presumptive sentence for some offenses that previously allowed for prison. Maryland repealed capital punishment, substituting LWOP. Changes in drug laws have also lowered prison populations. A number of states, including Alaska, Arizona, Colorado, California, Connecticut, Illinois, Nevada, Maine, Maryland, Massachusetts, Michigan, New York, Oregon, Virginia, and Washington, legalized the use of recreational marijuana, while many others now allow marijuana use for medical purposes.

In addition to these sentencing reforms, several states implemented mechanisms for the safe and early release of persons already in custody. Louisiana, for example, expanded the availability of good-time credits from 250 to 360 days for people in prison who complete education, job skills training, and therapeutic programs. Other states (New Hampshire, North

Dakota, and West Virginia) advanced parole eligibility dates for certain nonviolent offenders.

In general, six types of reforms have been implemented by states and the federal government in an effort to reduce prison populations over the past decade or two:

1. **Sentencing modifications**. Sentencing modifications generally make use of risk and needs assessments prior to sentencing (but following conviction) in order to divert nonviolent people who experience a criminal conviction from prison. They also increase the use of community resources to help prevent reoffending.

2. **Probation and parole revocation reforms**. These reforms replace confinement (or reimprisonment) with intense community-level supervision and require relatively serious violations of the conditions of probation and parole before a person who has been convicted of a crime can be incarcerated.

3. **Changes in the criminal law**. A number of states have reclassified lower-level felonies, generally making them misdemeanors; reformed their drug laws to require treatment and counseling in lieu of a prison sentence; and reduced the amount of punishment that can be imposed on people who have been convicted of specified crimes.

4. **Using jails instead of prisons**. A prime example of this approach is California's realignment strategy, under which people who have been convicted of nonviolent crimes can be ordered to serve time in local jails rather than in state prisons.

5. **Early release**. Early release is now utilized in an increasing number of jurisdictions to permit the earned release of people who are in prison prior to the expiration of their sentence if they meet specified conditions while behind bars.

6. **Juvenile sentencing reforms**. A number of states have instituted reforms in juvenile sentencing, giving judges greater leeway in the handling of justice-involved youth—meaning that fewer young people who have been adjudicated "delinquent" will spend time in confinement.

Make Better Informed Criminal Justice Policy Using Evidence-Based Practices

Most states have created independent bodies to increase their reliance on data-driven policy development.

Legislatures now typically require cost and benefit analysis of specific criminal justice interventions. The public and legislators are asking what else might be done to achieve public safety goals if incarceration is failing to have a positive impact on persons who are released from jail or prison. Oregon, Vermont, and a handful of other states now require fiscal impact statements for all bills brought before the legislature that either modify or create new sentencing or corrections policies.

Taken together, these sentencing trends and reforms show the direction that the American public and their legislators are crafting for the second half of the 21st century. States are reexamining the ways they respond to people who are accused of crimes at every stage of criminal justice processing. The pendulum has swung from tough-on-crime policies to employing what is *effective* in terms of cost and outcomes. Evidence-based, data-driven practices, and reliance on the support of external groups of experts and stakeholders are being used to reduce prison populations, strengthen community-based punishments, balance budgets, and improve public safety.

ISSUES IN SENTENCING

CO3-6

Many sentencing reforms have been an attempt to reduce disparity in sentencing and make the process fairer. The term **fair sentencing,** or **fairness in sentencing**, has become popular in recent years. Although fair sentencing today often refers to fairness for *victims,* many suggest that any truly fair sentencing scheme must incorporate fairness for both victims and offenders. The issues related to fairness in sentencing are:

- proportionality;
- equity;
- individualization; and
- parsimony.

Proportionality

Proportionality is a sentencing principle which says that the severity of punishment should match the seriousness of the crime for which the sentence is imposed. This does not mean that sentences for comparable crimes should be identical but rather that there must be good reasons for substantial variations in sentences and that the seriousness of the crime must have an upper limit on the severity of the sentence that may be imposed for it.

Equity

Equity is a sentencing principle which holds that similar crimes and offenders who are similarly situated should be treated alike. Sentencing should be guided by established, regularly applied standards or guidelines, thereby making the process more transparent, the procedures fairer, and judges more accountable. Equity requires judges to sentence regularly with applicable standards or to explain why they do not give people who have been sentenced a basis on which to appeal decisions they believe to be unjust.

Individualization

Fairness in sentencing was also addressed by the blue ribbon Colson Task Force on Corrections mentioned earlier. The panel concluded that sentencing decisions and correctional interventions should be **individualized**. The unique circumstances and attributes of each case and each person entering the criminal justice system should inform sentences as well as the rehabilitation programs, treatment, and services provided.

Parsimony

Sentences should be the least necessary in a given situation to attain its end. That is to say that sentences should be no more severe, disruptive, or harmful to an offender's ability to live a law-abiding life than is minimally necessary. Two-and-one-half centuries ago, Cesare Beccaria, founder of the

fair sentencing

Sentencing practices that incorporate fairness for both victims and offenders. Fairness is said to be achieved by implementing principles of proportionality, equity, social debt, and truth in sentencing.

proportionality

A sentencing principle which holds that the severity of punishment should match the seriousness of the crime for which the sentence is imposed.

equity

A sentencing principle which holds that similar crimes and defendants who are similar should be treated alike, and that sentences should be guided by established, regularly applied standards or guidelines.

individualization

A sentencing principle which holds that unique circumstances and attributes of each case and each person entering the criminal justice system should inform sentences as well as the rehabilitation programs, treatment, and services provided.

Classical School of Criminology, said that imposition of a sentence more severe than is necessary is "superfluous and for that reason tyrannical."[25] Such sentences are wasteful expenditures of capital and serve no good purpose. **Parsimony** means that sentences should be the least necessary in a given situation to attain its end.

parsimony

Sentences should be the least necessary in a given situation to attain its end. Imposition of a sentence more severe than is necessary is harmful.

REVIEW AND APPLICATIONS

SUMMARY

1 The central purpose of criminal punishment is to maintain social order.

2 The goals of criminal sentencing today are (1) revenge, (2) retribution, (3) just deserts, (4) deterrence, (5) incapacitation, (6) rehabilitation or reformation, and (7) restoration.

3 Sentencing options in use today include probation, intermediate sanctions, jail and prison, parole, and capital punishment.

4 Today, around 2,470 people are on death row, a decrease of over 600 from a decade earlier. Almost 50 percent of the nation's death row population is in three states: California, Florida, and Texas. Ninety-eight percent of all people on death row are male, 56 percent are minority, 53 percent have a high school diploma (or GED) or higher, and 55 percent have never married.

5 At the federal level, the U.S. Supreme Court's decision in *Booker* made federal sentencing guidelines advisory; the Second Chance Act of 2008 provided millions of dollars for reentry services annually across the United States; and in 2010, the Fair Sentencing Act reduced the disparity in sentencing between crack and powder cocaine offenses. Elsewhere in the federal system, the Charles Colson Task Force on Federal Corrections recommended that (1) the federal prison population should be reduced by 60,000 people in order to achieve a savings of more than $5 billion for reinvestment in evidence-based programs proven to reduce crime; (2) mandatory minimum sentences should be reserved for the most violent offenders; and (3) Congress should create a path for people in prison who have served more than 15 years to apply for shorter sentences by giving judges a "second look" at their cases. Finally, the federal First Step Act, which became law in 2018, reformed the federal prison system by ensuring a smooth transition for people reentering society. The Act makes use of evidence-based risk assessment strategies and provides for prerelease custody either under home confinement or to a residential reentry center (RRC).

6 The four principles of fairness in sentencing are (1) proportionality, (2) equity, (3) individualization, and (4) parsimony. Any truly fair sentence must consider justice for both victims and offenders.

KEY TERMS

sentencing, p. 36

sentence, p. 36

social order, p. 36

revenge, p. 37

retribution, p. 37

just deserts, p. 37

deterrence, p. 38

specific deterrence, p. 38

general deterrence, p. 38

pleasure-pain principle, p. 38

incapacitation, p. 39

truth in sentencing (TIS), p. 39

three-strikes laws, p. 39

rehabilitation, p. 39

reintegration, p. 40

restoration, p. 41

restorative justice, p. 41

victim-impact statement, p. 41

victim services, p. 41

capital punishment, p. 46

exonerate, p. 46

capital crime, p. 47

mandatory death penalty, p. 52

guided discretion, p. 52

bifurcated trial, p. 52

mitigating circumstances, p. 52

aggravating circumstances, p. 52

serious error, p. 54

fair sentencing, p. 62

proportionality, p. 62

equity, p. 62

individualization, p. 62

parsimony, p. 63

QUESTIONS FOR REVIEW

1 What is the central purpose of criminal punishment?

2 What are the goals of criminal sentencing?

3 What are the major sentencing options in wide use in the United States today?

4 What are the characteristics of persons on death row today?

5 Defend the need for federal and state sentencing trends and options.

6 Justify the four principles of fairness in sentencing.

THINKING CRITICALLY ABOUT CORRECTIONS

Rehabilitation

Edgardo Rotman says, in *Beyond Punishment*, "Rehabilitation ... can be defined tentatively and broadly as a right to an opportunity to return to (or remain in) society with an improved chance of being a useful citizen and staying out of prison."[26] Do you agree that people who have been convicted of a crime and sentenced to prison have a right to rehabilitation? Why or why not?

Murder Rates and the Death Penalty

According to the Death Penalty Information Center, death penalty states record higher murder rates than non-death-penalty states. A recent study shows that the average murder rate among death penalty states is 4.7 per 100,000 population; for non-death-penalty states, the rate is 3.9. The South executes the largest percentage of offenders who are convicted of a capital crime (81 percent) and records the highest murder rate; the Northeast executes the fewest and records the lowest murder rate. What kinds of factors might explain these data? How might we prevent geographical unfairness?

Federal Corrections

The Colson Task Force issued a report calling for the federal Bureau of Prisons to reduce its inmate population by 60,000 people and to reserve mandatory minimums only for people convicted of violent crimes, and it urged Congress to create a path for imprisoned people who have served more than 15 years to apply for shorter sentences by asking their judges to give their cases a second look. How would you defend these reforms to persons who advocate for tough-on-crime approaches?

ON-THE-JOB DECISION MAKING

Recidivism

You have spent the past six years as a counselor at a minimum-security state correctional facility. Your effectiveness has earned you a strong reputation throughout the Department of Corrections as a specialist in prerelease counseling, a program designed to prepare people who are about to be released on parole or upon completion of their sentences.

Lately, a series of highly publicized violent crimes have been committed by people who had been formerly incarcerated at the state's super–maximum-security facility. All were released recently upon completion of their sentences, and all had moved almost directly from their cells back to the criminal lifestyles that originally landed them in prison.

Hard-line correctional officers insist that because those incarcerated in "supermax" are the most likely to reoffend, they cannot be trusted to behave following prerelease counseling. The safety risks such potentially dangerous people represent, they say, make leaving them in their cells until the law requires they be set free the only sensible course of action. What happens after that, in the hard-liners' opinions, is both the decision and responsibility of the formerly incarcerated.

Reformers insist that immediate recidivism is the likely outcome of releasing people directly from a harsh, totally controlled lockdown environment. They call for significant transitional counseling as essential for helping people who are in prison to adjust to free society and for defusing any anger that they may carry with them upon release.

Both the governor and the commissioner of corrections face daily media demands to explain what the administration is going to do about this problem. In particular, the governor is hard pressed because her opponent in the upcoming and hotly contested gubernatorial race has seized on this as an issue that demonstrates "this governor's inability, or unwillingness, to take the tough steps necessary to protect the good citizens of our state."

You have been asked to speak at a meeting to develop potential courses of action to address this problem. The meeting will be chaired by the corrections commissioner, and various wardens, assistant wardens, and senior correctional specialists from throughout the state will attend. It is likely but not yet confirmed that the governor will also attend. Think about the federal and state trends in sentencing and corrections discussed in this chapter.

1. What issues will you address?

2. How might you resolve the conflict between the need to protect counselors and staff from the often violent behavior of people who are held in supermax, and the need to provide critical prerelease counseling to these troubled people?

3. How would you respond to hard-line corrections officers who contend that what happens after release is not their problem?

ENDNOTES

1. Daniele Selby, "Two Innocent Men Spent 20 Years in Prison for Malcolm X's Murder," *The Innocence Project*, https://innocenceproject.org/malcolm-x-murder-innocent-aziz-butler (accessed January 2, 2023).

2. Andrew von Hirsch, *Doing Justice: The Choice of Punishments* (New York: Hill & Wang, 1976), pp. 48–49.

3. Zane Sparliing, "Man Convicted of Hate Crime Against Portland Refugee Center Ordered to Write Report on Genocide, Ta-Nehisi Coates Book," *The Oregonian*, https://www.oregonlive.com/crime/2022/12/man-convicted-of-hate-crime-against-portland-refugee-center-ordered-to-write-reports-on-genocide-ta-nehsi-coates-book.html (accessed March 10, 2023).

4. Robert Martinson, "What Works? Questions and Answers About Prison Reform," *Public Interest*, vol. 35 (Spring 1974), pp. 22–54.

5. Francis T. Cullen and Paul Gendreau, "Assessing Correctional Rehabilitation: Policy, Practice, and Prospects," in Julie Horney (ed.), *Criminal Justice 2000*, Vol. 3 (Washington, DC: National Institute of Justice, 2000). It is worthwhile noting that Francis T. Cullen was the recipient of the highly regarded Stockholm Prize in Criminology in 2022 (along with Peggy C. Giorano) for his research into the effectiveness of offender rehabilitation strategies (see https://www.su.se/english/news/winners-of-the-stockholm-prize-in-criminology-2021-and-2022-1.581009).

6. Edgardo Rotman, *Beyond Punishment: A New View on the Rehabilitation of Criminal Offenders* (Westport, CT: Greenwood, 1990), p. 11.

7. Marty Price, "Crime and Punishment: Can Mediation Produce Restorative Justice for Victims and Offenders?," https://restorativejustice.org/rj-archive/crime-and-punishment-can-mediation-produce-restorative-justice-for-victims-and-offenders/ (accessed March 10, 2023).

8. E. Ann Carson, *Prisoners in 2020* (Washington, DC: U.S. Department of Justice, Bureau of Justice Statistics, December 2021), p. 25.

9. *Furman* v. *Georgia*, 408 U.S. 238 (1972).

10. Amnesty International, "Death Penalty 2021," https://www.amnestyusa.org/reports/death-penalty-2021-state-sanctioned-killings-rise-as-executions-spike-in-iran-and-saudi-arabia (accessed March 10, 2023).

11. Amnesty International, "Death Penalty 2021," https://www.amnestyusa.org/reports/death-penalty-2021-state-sanctioned-killings-rise-as-executions-spike-in-iran-and-saudi-arabia (accessed March 10, 2023).

12. Tracy L. Snell, *Capital Punishment, 2020—Statistical Tables* (Washington, DC: U.S. Department of Justice, Bureau of Justice Statistics, December 2021).

13. See, for example, Death Penalty Information Center, "Executions by Race and Race of Victim," https://deathpenaltyinfo.org/executions/executions-overview/executions-by-race-and-race-of-victim (accessed March 10, 2023).

14. John Boger, "Landmark North Carolina Death Penalty Study Finds Dramatic Racial Bias," https://deathpenaltyinfo.org/resources/publications-and-testimony/studies/race-and-the-death-penalty-in-north-carolina (accessed January 20, 2023).

15. "2021 Gallup Poll: Public Support for Capital Punishment Remains at Half-Century Low," *Gallup News Service*, November 19, 2021, https://deathpenaltyinfo.org /news/2021-gallup-poll-public-support-for-capital -punishment-remains-at-half-century-low (accessed January 2, 2023).

16. Damla Ergun, "New Low in Preference for the Death Penalty," *ABC News*, June 5, 2014, http://abcnews. go.com/blogs/politics/2014/06/new-low-in-preference-for -the-death-penalty/ (accessed January 30, 2023).

17. Eric Westervelt, "California Says It Will Dismantle Death Row. The Move Brings Cheers and Anger," *National Public Radio*, January 13, 2023.

18. James Liebman, Jeffrey Fagan, and Valerie West, A Broken System: *Error Rates in Capital Cases, 1973–1995* (New York: Columbia University School of Law, 2000).

19. Nancy Phillips, "In Life and Death Cases, Costly Mistakes," *The Philadelphia Inquirer*, October 23, 2011, https://www.inquirer.com/philly/news/homep-age/20111023_Mistakes_in_life_and_death_cases-gallery. html (accessed January 30, 2023).

20. See Stephanie Slifer, "How the Wrongfully Convicted Are Compensated for Years Lost," CBS News, https://www .cbsnews.com/news/how-the-wrongfully-convicted-are -compensated (accessed January 30, 2023).

21. The Innocence Project, "About," https://innocenceproject .org/about (accessed January 30, 2023).

22. Death Penalty Information Center, "Innocence," https:// deathpenaltyinfo.org/policy-issues/innocence (accessed March 10, 2023).

23. *Atkins* v. *Virginia*, 536 U.S. (2002).

24. *Transforming Prison, Restoring Lives: Final Recommendations of the Charles Colson Task Force on Federal Corrections*, https://www.urban.org/research/publication/transform-ing-prisons-restoring-lives (accessed March 10, 2023).

25. Cesare Beccaria, *On Crimes and Punishment. Trans.* Henry Paolucci (Englewood Cliffs, NJ: Prentice Hall, 1963 [1764]).

Community Corrections

Part Two examines probation, intermediate sanctions and community corrections.

Probation is the conditional release of persons convicted of crime under community supervision. The degree of supervision depends on the person's level of risk. Some individuals pose no risk to the community. For them, checking in monthly at an automated probation kiosk may be all that is necessary. On the other hand, persons who are high risk receive intensive face-to-face supervision and

sometimes random drug testing, community service, and home confinement with remote-location monitoring.

Sanctions more punitive than probation but not as restrictive as incarceration are called *intermediate sanctions.* Drug court, economic sanctions, community service, day reporting centers, remote-location monitoring, residential centers, and boot camps are some intermediate sanctions.

Community corrections is a set of programs that provide for the supervision of individuals convicted of crimes in their local community versus placing them in a secure correctional facility. Probation, intermediate sanctions and parole are classified as community corrections.

Today, the current probation and parole workforce of 50,000

investigates and supervises almost 4 million adults under probation, parole, and intermediate sanctions. These officers are faced with enormous case investigation and supervision challenges that include increasing caseloads without new resources, deciding on what information to include in a presentence report, figuring out how to structure the report so it is read, and incorporating novel forms of technology into their day-to-day jobs.

Whether supervision is low level or intense, many probationers will violate its technical conditions. Others will commit new crimes. Tightening supervision without resorting to incarceration is a challenge that probation officers face. The decision to revoke probation and incarcerate a person is influenced by legal, social, political, and economic issues.

John Flournoy/McGraw Hill

Mark Dierker/McGraw Hill

PROBATION

The Most Used Form of Punishment

CHAPTER OBJECTIVES

After completing this chapter you should be able to do the following:

1 Define *probation* and know its goals.

2 Explain the reasons for using probation.

3 Describe some of the characteristics of adults on probation.

4 Explain the different ways that probation is administered.

5 Describe the measures used to evaluate probation.

6 Describe the investigation and supervision functions of probation officers.

7 Explain revocation hearings.

We won't get true public safety and protection for crime victims until we invest in community corrections—because most persons who commit crime are not behind bars, but living as our neighbors.

—Anne Seymour, national crime victim advocate

In January 2022, *Empire* actor Jussie Smollett was sentenced to 150 days in jail followed by 30 months of probation and ordered to pay $120,106 in restitution to the city of Chicago, as well as a fine of $25,000 for staging and falsely reporting to police that he was the victim of a hate crime in Chicago.[1] Two years earlier, the *Empire* actor told Chicago police that around 2 a.m. in the city's Streeterville neighborhood two men wearing ski masks beat him, wrapped a rope around his neck, poured an unknown chemical substance on him, hurled racial and homophobic slurs at him, and ran off. In the aftermath of the incident, Smollett received swift support from the *Empire* crew and others. Police questioned Smollett's alleged attackers—brothers Abimbola and Olabinjo Osundairo, both of whom worked with Smollett on *Empire*. Abimbola Osundairo was also Smollett's personal trainer. According to the police, those interviews "shifted the trajectory of the investigation."

Smollett's attorneys argued that Abimbola, Smollett's personal trainer, tried to exploit the "sexual tension" between them to advance his own acting career. Abimbola denied having a sexual relationship with Smollett but said that, as the actor's trainer and occasional drug dealer, he agreed to "fake beat him up" because he "felt indebted to Jussie."

Prosecutors zeroed in on money Smollett paid the Osundairos, including a $100 bill—said to be for the supplies needed to stage the incident—as well as a check for $3,500. Abimbola Osundairo testified that he believed the check was intended as payment to cover for both the attack and a training plan he had devised for Smollett. However, Smollett said it was just for the training plan.

The jury deliberated for more than nine hours before finding Smollett guilty. Cook County Judge James Linn told Smollett that he staged the attack "to make himself more famous." He accused Smollett of "throwing a national pity party" for himself and said the actor betrayed his more charitable instincts by acting upon the side of him that is "profoundly arrogant and selfish and narcissistic." Do you believe the sentence that Judge Linn imposed is fair? (Refer back to Chapter 3 and the issues surrounding fairness in sentencing.) Are there evidence-based probation strategies that would reduce someone's propensity to stage and falsely report a hate crime?

In this chapter you will learn about the history of probation and its goals and purposes. We discuss who is on probation, how the overuse of probation contributes to mass incarceration, what outcomes should be looked at to measure probation's success, what probation officers do, what revocation is, and how revocation for technical violation can also drive mass incarceration.

In January 2022, three years after Jussie Smollet told Chicago police that two men wearing ski masks beat him, wrapped a rope around his neck, poured an unknown chemical substance on him, hurled racial and homophobic slurs at him, and ran off, Smollett was convicted of staging and falsely reporting to police that he was the victim of a hate crime in Chicago. Smollett was sentenced to 150 days in jail followed by 30 months of probation, and ordered to pay $120,106 in restitution and a fine of $25,000. Do you believe Smollett's sentence was fair?
E. Jason Wambsgans/Pool/Getty Images

PROBATION

CO4-1

Probation is the most frequently used form of criminal punishment. Of the 5.5 million persons under the supervision of adult correctional systems across the United States (probation, prison, parole, and local jails), over one-half (55 percent) were on probation, 22 percent in prison, 15 percent on parole, and 10 percent in local jails. Probation is a way to keep people at home

Probation

The conditional release of a person convicted of crime into the community, under the supervision of a probation officer. It is conditional because it can be revoked if certain conditions are not met.

Probation

What is probation, and why is it used?

in the community, avoid incarceration, and carry out sanctions imposed by the court or the probation agency. **Probation** is the conditional release of a person convicted of crime into the community under the supervision of a probation officer (PO). It is conditional because if the individual violates the conditions of probation, the judge may either set more restrictive conditions of probation or revoke probation and sentence the person to prison. Later in this chapter, we discuss the impact that revoking even a small percentage of the probation population can have on the jail population.

 Reasons for and Goals of Probation

Probation is used for at least four reasons. First, probation permits the person convicted of crime to remain in the community for reintegration purposes. Reintegration is more likely to occur if social and family ties are not broken by incarceration.

Second, probation avoids prison institutionalization and the stigma of incarceration. Prison institutionalization is the process of learning and adopting the norms and culture of institutional living. Living in the artificial environment of an institution does not teach people how to live in the free world. Persons on probation do not experience prison institutionalization, nor do they have to worry about the negative effects of being treated like they were incarcerated, which decrease even further their ability to function as law-abiding citizens when released.

The third reason for probation is that it is less expensive than incarceration, more humanitarian, and at least as effective as incarceration in reducing future criminal activity.

The final reason for probation is that it is fair and appropriate sentencing for persons whose crimes do not merit incarceration. Furthermore, probation is the base from which more severe punishments can be built. Not all crimes deserve incarceration, nor do all crimes deserve probation. Probation is preferred when there is no threat to community safety, when community correctional resources are available, and when probation does not unduly deprecate the seriousness of the offense.

Most probation programs share five goals:

1. Protect the community by preparing the presentence report (PSR) to assist judges in sentencing and supervision. (We return to the PSR later in this chapter.)
2. Carry out sanctions imposed by the court.
3. Conduct a risk–needs assessment to identify the appropriate level of supervision and the services that are needed. (Risk-needs assessment is discussed in more detail later in this chapter and again in Chapter 6).
4. Support crime victims by collecting information that describes the losses, suffering, and trauma experienced by a crime victim or by the victim's survivors.
5. Coordinate and promote the use of community resources. Such programs include drug and alcohol treatment, job training, vocational education, anger management, and life skills training.

Not all probation agencies achieve these objectives in the same way. A probation department's orientation is a function of many things, including department philosophy, leadership, the community served, and the persons supervised. Some departments lean more toward treatment; others lean more toward control. It is likely that the majority of probation departments do both, depending on the need and the situation. The American Probation and Parole Association (APPA) policy on probation is found in Exhibit 4–1. What are the beliefs upon which probation is premised?

EXHIBIT 4−1 **American Probation and Parole Association Position Statement on Probation**

Probation

Probation is premised upon the following beliefs:

The purpose of probation is to assist in reducing the incidence and impact of crime by probationers in the community. The core services of probation are to provide investigation and reports to the court, to help develop appropriate court dispositions for adult offenders and juvenile delinquents, and to supervise those persons placed on probation. Probation departments in fulfilling their purpose may also provide a broad range of services including, but not limited to, crime and delinquency prevention, victim restitution programs and intern/volunteer programs.

Position

The mission of probation is to protect the public interest and safety by reducing the incidence and impact of crime by probationers. This role is accomplished by:

- assisting the courts in decision making through the probation report and in the enforcement of court orders;
- providing services and programs that afford opportunities for offenders to become more law-abiding;
- providing and cooperating in programs and activities for the prevention of crime and delinquency; and
- furthering the administration of fair and individualized justice.

Probation is premised upon the following beliefs:

Society has a right to be protected from persons who cause its members harm, regardless of the reasons for such harm. It is the right of every citizen to be free from fear of harm to person and property. Belief in the necessity of law to an orderly society demands commitment to support it. Probation accepts this responsibility and views itself as an instrument for both control and treatment appropriate to some, but not all offenders. The wise use of authority derived from law adds strength and stability to its efforts.

Offenders have rights deserving of protection. Freedom and democracy require fair and individualized due process of law in adjudicating and sentencing the offender.

Victims of crime have rights deserving of protection. In its humanitarian tradition, probation recognizes that prosecution of the offender is but a part of the responsibility of the criminal justice system. The victim of criminal activity may suffer loss of property, emotional problems, or physical disability. Probation thus commits itself to advocacy for the needs and interests of crime victims.

Human beings are capable of change. Belief in the individual's capability for behavioral change leads probation practitioners to a commitment to the reintegration of the offender into the community. The possibility for constructive change of behavior is based on the recognition and acceptance of the principal of individual responsibility. Much of probation practice focuses on identifying and making available those services and programs that will best afford offenders an opportunity to become responsible, law-abiding citizens.

Not all offenders have the same capacity or willingness to benefit from measures designed to produce law-abiding citizens. Probation practitioners recognize the variations among individuals. The present offense, the degree of risk to the community and the potential for change can be assessed only in the context of the offender's individual history and experience.

Intervention in an offender's life should be the minimal amount needed to protect society and promote law-abiding behavior. Probation subscribes to the principle of intervening in an offender's life only to the extent necessary. Where further intervention appears unwarranted, criminal justice system involvement should be terminated. Where needed intervention can best be provided by an agency outside the system, the offender should be diverted from the system to that agency.

Punishment. Probation philosophy does not accept the concept of retributive punishment. Punishment as a corrective measure is supported and used in those instances in which it is felt that aversive measures may positively alter the offender's behavior when other measures may not. Even corrective punishment, however, should be used cautiously and judiciously in view of its highly unpredictable impact. It can be recognized that a conditional sentence in the community is, in and of itself, a punishment. It is less harsh and drastic than a prison term but more controlling and punitive than release without supervision.

Incarceration may be destructive and should be imposed only when necessary. Probation practitioners acknowledge society's right to protect itself and support the incarceration of offenders whose behavior constitutes a danger to the public through rejection of social or court mandates. Incarceration can also be an appropriate element of a probation program to emphasize the consequences of criminal behavior and thus effect constructive behavioral change. However, institutions should be humane and required to adhere to the highest standards.

Where public safety is not compromised, society and most offenders are best served through community correctional programs. Most offenders should be provided services within the community in which they are expected to demonstrate acceptable behavior. Community correctional programs generally are cost-effective and they allow offenders to remain with their families while paying taxes and, where applicable, restitution to victims.

Source: Reprinted with permission of American Probation and Parole Association.

John Augustus (1785–1859) was a Boston shoemaker who invented probation in 1841 and became the first "unofficial" PO. He is called the founder of probation. Which aspects of Augustus's probation system are still in use today?
Courtesy of American Probation and Parole Association

History of Probation

Probation in America developed in the mid-19th century from a rehabilitative paradigm of addressing the causes of criminal behavior. What started as a charitable and volunteer movement took almost 125 years to become available to adults in every state across the country.

Probation Begins in America In 1841, when 57-year-old John Augustus, a wealthy Boston shoemaker, became interested in the operation of the courts, the practice of probation began to emerge. Augustus was particularly sensitive to the problems of persons charged with violating Boston's vice or temperance laws. He was a member of the Washington Total Abstinence Society, an organization devoted to the promotion of temperance. By posting bail in selected cases, persons were released to his care and supervision, and so began the work of the nation's first PO, an unpaid volunteer.

By the time of his death in 1859, Augustus had won probation for almost 2,000 adults and several thousand children. Several aspects of his probation system are still in use. Augustus investigated the age, character, and work habits of each person. He identified individuals he thought redeemable and "whose hearts were not fully depraved, but gave promise of better things." He made probation recommendations to the court. He developed conditions of probation and helped with employment, education, and housing. Supervision lasted, on the average, about 30 days.

After Augustus's death in 1859, unpaid volunteers continued his work. In 1878, the Massachusetts legislature passed the first statute authorizing probation and provided for the first paid PO.[2] The second state to pass a probation statute was Vermont, in 1898. As more and more states passed laws authorizing probation, it became a national institution. On March 4, 1925, President Calvin Coolidge signed the National Probation Act. The act authorized each federal district court to appoint one salaried PO with an annual income of $2,600.[3] By 1925, probation was available for juveniles in every state; by 1956, it was available for adults in every state.

CO4-3 # Characteristics of Adults on Probation

At year end 2020, an estimated 3.1 million adults were on probation, a decrease of almost 300,000 from one year earlier due mainly to emergency responses to COVID-19 to delay trials and sentencing. The adult probation population is at its lowest since 2000.[4] An estimated 1 in 66 adults in the U.S. are under probation.[5]

Probation can be either standard or intensive. Almost 85 percent of adults are on standard probation. Their level of risk to the community is considered low. They contact their POs once or twice a month, either remotely or face-to-face. The cost of supervision for persons on standard probation ranges from $3,000.00 to $5,000.00 a year. Almost all adults on standard probation also pay a monthly supervision fee, a topic we turn to shortly.

Fifteen percent of adults on probation are under intensive community supervision. Their level of risk to the community is higher, and they are required to contact their POs frequently. The cost of their supervision is more than the cost of standard probation. Adults on probation may also be required to pay an additional programming fee for mandatory mental health counseling, electronic monitoring, and drug testing.

Exhibit 4–2 presents selected characteristics of the 3.1 million adults on probation. Of those whose characteristics are known, 75 percent are male and 25 percent are female, 54 percent are white, 30 percent are Black, 13 percent are Hispanic, and each one of the following races is 1%: American

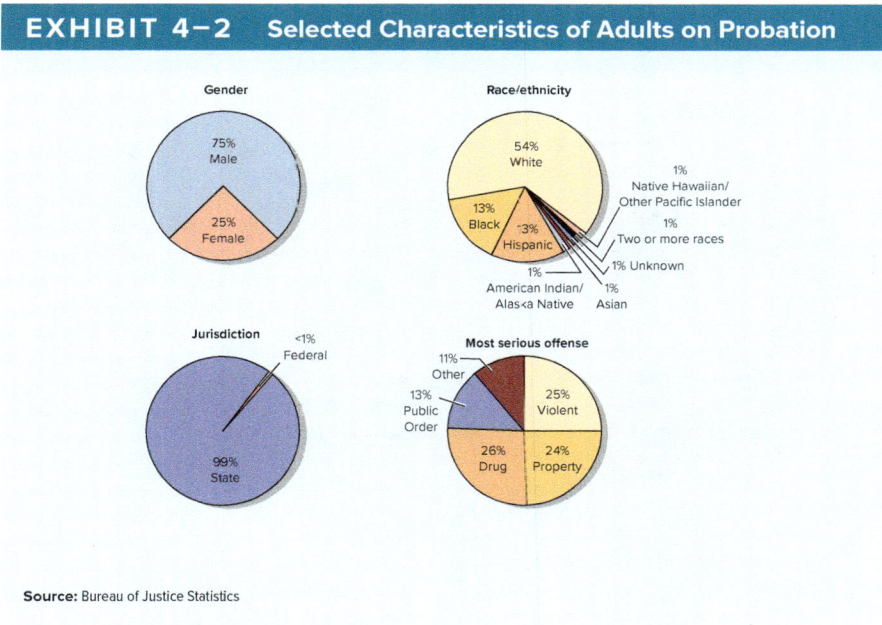

EXHIBIT 4–2 **Selected Characteristics of Adults on Probation**

Gender

75% Male
25% Female

Race/ethnicity

54% White
13% Black
3% Hispanic
1% American Indian/Alaska Native
1% Asian
1% Unknown
1% Two or more races
1% Native Hawaiian/Other Pacific Islander

Jurisdiction

<1% Federal
99% State

Most serious offense

11% Other
13% Public Order
26% Drug
24% Property
25% Violent

Source: Bureau of Justice Statistics

Indian/Alaska Native; Asian; Native Hawaiian/Other Pacific Islander; two or more races; and unknown. Almost three-fourths are currently under supervision. The remaining may have fled, are under warrant, or have financial conditions outstanding. Most adults on probation share other characteristics such as low educational attainment, limited employment history or job skills, mental illness, or gang involvement. Studies have also shown that at the time of their arrest, three-fourths of adults on probation used illegal drugs, and half were under the influence of drugs or alcohol.

Researchers at the Department of Justice (DOJ) learned from hour-long interviews that 9 percent of men on probation and 28 percent of women on probation had been physically or sexually abused before their sentence and before age 18.[6] (Prevalence estimates of child abuse in the general population are 5 to 8 percent for males and 12 to 17 percent for females.) They told DOJ researchers that the abuser was either a family member or someone they knew intimately. Researchers are just beginning to study the link between child abuse and offending.

Today 1,186 adults are on probation for every 100,000 persons age 18 and older in the United States, down from 1,818 per 100,000 in 2000. The largest adult probation populations are in Georgia (341,434) and Texas (334,353). The smallest adult probation populations are in Alaska (2,438) and New Hampshire (2,723). Slightly more than 12,000 persons are on federal probation.

The two states that use probation the most are Georgia (4,136 per 100,000 adult population) and Ohio (2,206). The two states that use probation least are Nevada (374 per 100,000 adult population) and New Hampshire (244). Exhibit 4–3 shows a state-by-state breakdown of how adult probation is administered.

Who Administers Probation?

CO4-4

As probation spread throughout the United States in the late 19th and early 20th centuries, its organization and administration depended on local and state customs and politics. Currently, probation in the 50 states

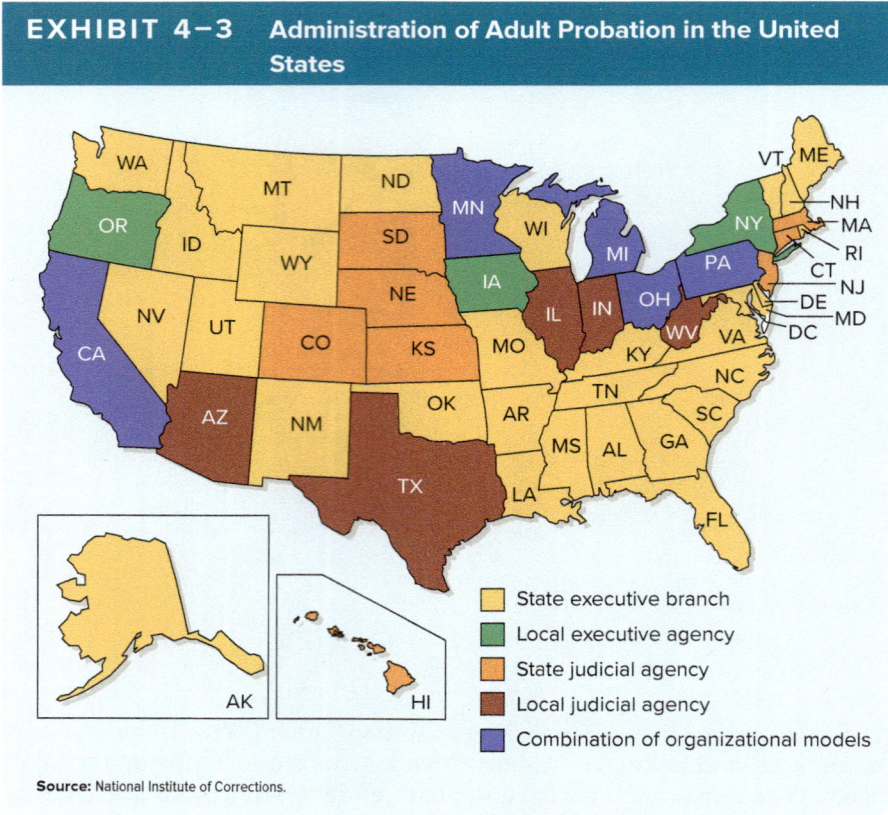

EXHIBIT 4–3 Administration of Adult Probation in the United States

- State executive branch
- Local executive agency
- State judicial agency
- Local judicial agency
- Combination of organizational models

Source: National Institute of Corrections.

is administered by more than 2,000 separate agencies, reflecting the decentralized and fragmented character of contemporary corrections. The agencies have a great deal of common ground, but because they developed in different contexts, they also have a lot of differences in goals, policies, staffing, salaries, budgets, operation, and funding. Exhibit 4–3 shows the five ways adult probation is administered.

Probation Fees

Probation agencies, as with the rest of the criminal justice system, have steadily shifted the costs of probation to those accused and convicted of breaking the law—anywhere from $50 to over $300 per month.[7] The most often cited rationale for charging probation fees is to offset burgeoning correctional budgets. The second most cited justification is based on the theory that forcing persons to pay for their community supervision "teaches them a lesson" that is grounded in rehabilitation/deterrence.

However, the debate over charging probation fees has its critics. Opponents argue that since society has chosen to punish individuals, it should be prepared to pay the cost of punishment. They argue that to ask persons on probation to pay the cost of their probation is unjust because it is like punishing them again by charging them for a multitude of services. Opponents also point to the burden on most families when probation fees take away groceries, mortgage and rent, child care, and utilities.[8]

Following the Department of Justice's March 2015 report on practices in Ferguson, Missouri, that highlighted the overreliance on court fines as a primary source of revenue for the city,[9] three states eliminated monthly supervision fees (California, Massachusetts, and Oregon). However, persons on

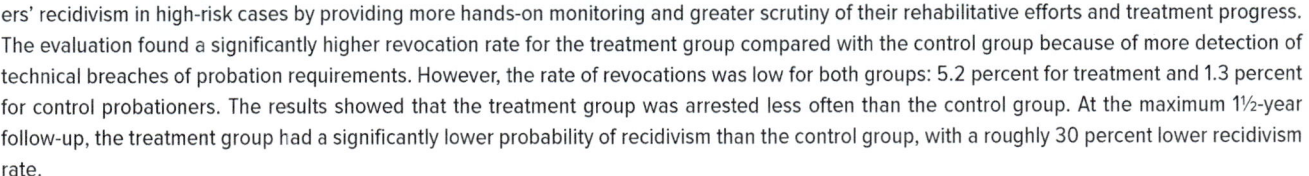

EVIDENCE-BASED CORRECTIONS

Reduced Probation Caseload in Evidence-Based Setting (Oklahoma City)

The program aims to reduce recidivism of high-risk probationers by assigning them to intensive supervision by an officer with a reduced caseload and through the use of evidence-based practices. The reduction in caseloads aims to reduce probationers' recidivism in high-risk cases by providing more hands-on monitoring and greater scrutiny of their rehabilitative efforts and treatment progress. The evaluation found a significantly higher revocation rate for the treatment group compared with the control group because of more detection of technical breaches of probation requirements. However, the rate of revocations was low for both groups: 5.2 percent for treatment and 1.3 percent for control probationers. The results showed that the treatment group was arrested less often than the control group. At the maximum 1½-year follow-up, the treatment group had a significantly lower probability of recidivism than the control group, with a roughly 30 percent lower recidivism rate.

The Reduced Probation Caseload in Evidence-Based Setting (Oklahoma City) is rated *Effective*.

Source: Adapted from Bureau of Justice Statistics

probation in these three states may still be required to pay programming fees such as an electronic monitor, which can cost as much as an additional $300 a month. Forty-seven states charge a monthly supervision fee. The amount depends on the state and offense.

Privatizing Probation

There is also a movement toward privatization in community corrections, including the use of assessment tools, drug testing and treatment, electronic monitoring, halfway house management, and probation field services. There is no census on the number of persons who are under private community supervision. However, at least 1,000 courts in several states allow private companies to oversee probation for minor offenses, collecting outstanding debts and court costs, and oftentimes adding their own fees for services such as ankle monitors and late payment.

In most states, the impetus for privatizing community supervision was similar: Staffing and resources were not keeping pace with increasing caseloads. Community supervision officials believed they had exhausted the use of interns and volunteers, and obtaining funding for new staff was not possible. States partnered with the private sector to monitor persons charged with nonviolent offenses, a group who generally has few needs, whose past records reflect little or no violence, and who successfully completes probation about 90 percent of the time.

Consider the situation in Georgia. The Georgia legislature passed SB 474 that transferred supervision of 25,000 convicted misdemeanants from the state

Probation officers often refer their clients to community agencies to help them overcome the problem that led to their offending behavior. What obstacles might POs face in making referrals to a community agency?

Mark Harvey/Alamy Stock Photo

Department of Corrections to individual counties and permitted each county to contract with a for-profit probation agency to supervise persons convicted of misdemeanors. This number has grown to over 150,000 individuals supervised by more than 40 private probation agencies. Those agencies employ over 850 POs and serve over 600 courts statewide. In Georgia, every person who cannot pay their misdemeanor fine on the day of court is placed on probation under the supervision of a private, for-profit company until the fine is paid. For example, assume you are ordered to pay $200 for a traffic fine. If you have enough money to pay it on the day you go to court, you can avoid probation. If you cannot, you must pay your fine and a monthly supervision fee in the range of $35–$44 to a private company in weekly or biweekly installments over a period of three months to a year. By the time your probation is over, you may have paid more than two or three times the amount that the judge had ordered. In Americus, Georgia, one high school student convicted of violating the terms of his learner's permit served seven months on probation and paid $505 in court fines and probation fees. Had he been able to pay the fine the day he was sentenced, he would have paid only $155.

CO4-5 Does Probation Work?

The most common question asked about probation is, "Does it work?" In other words, do persons granted probation refrain from further crime? **Recidivism**—generally defined as **rearrest**—continues to be the primary outcome measure for probation, as it is for all corrections programs. And if recidivism is the only measure of probation's effectiveness, the reality is that probation works. Nationally, two out of three adults on probation successfully complete their community supervision. The rest have been incarcerated, given a sentence other than incarceration, died, or unknown.[10]

recidivism

The repetition of criminal behavior; generally defined as rearrest. It is the primary outcome measure for probation as it is for all corrections programs.

Today, the push for evidence-based corrections highlights the importance of using scientific research to study correctional policy and increase probation's success. Although the body of scientific evidence to make informed decisions about whether probation strategies reduce criminal activity is not large, we know from sophisticated evaluations in Florida, Maryland, and Washington that control-focused strategies (for example, intensive supervision and remote location monitoring) alone do not reduce criminal activity. However, when control-focused strategies are combined with treatment strategies, there is scientific evidence that probation achieves, on average, a statistically significant 8 to 22 percent reduction in the recidivism rates of program participants compared with a treatment-as-usual group.[11]

To further the success of persons on probation, the vast majority of correctional systems are adopting **risk and needs assessments (RNA)** to identify how likely a person is to commit another crime or violate the rules of prison, jail, or community supervision once they have been convicted and/or sentenced. The risk and needs assessment uses data collected on people who have committed crimes similar to the individual in question. RNAs create categories and show the statistical likelihood that certain kinds of behavior may happen.

Prior to 1970, risk assessments were based on professional judgment which opened the door to bias and racial and ethnic disparities. Actuarial-based tools that became available in the 1920s to predict everything from insurance quotes, financial lending, and health care were later adopted in criminal justice to predict recidivism. However, even actuarial tools are not free from bias. Researchers with the Pretrial Justice Institute argue that RNAs are biased against minorities and people of color because they are based partly on criminal records where biases in the deployment of police, arrest, policies, charging decisions, pretrial decisions, and sentencing practices have been uncovered. On the other hand, supporters argue that a large

risk and needs assessments (RNA)

Tools to identify how likely a person is to commit another crime or violate the rules of prison, jail, or community supervision once they have been convicted and/or sentenced.

body of social science evidence shows that objective, reliable, and valid RNAs are more accurate in assessing risk than human judgments alone. The RNA is one tool that can aid judges in better decision-making.

To lessen bias and disparity in RNAs and achieve better recidivism outcomes, the National Institute of Justice lists four principles to govern the development and implementation of RNAs.

The first principle is fairness. To reduce bias and disparity in outcomes, RNA instruments must be properly designed and implemented. The second principle is efficiency. RNA tools are more efficient when they are automated. The third principle is effectiveness. RNA tools should be customized to fit the needs of the correctional client. The final principle is communication. RNA tools must help persons under correctional supervision understand how their risks and needs can be addressed with programming.

The most influential risk and needs assessment is the **risk-needs-responsivity (RNR) model**, which states that the risk and needs of the person under correctional supervision should determine the strategies appropriate for addressing the individual's criminogenic factors—changeable risk factors that are proven through research to affect recidivism such as antisocial values, antisocial friends, isolation from prosocial others, substance abuse, impulsiveness, low levels of education, and family dysfunction.

As suggested by its name, the model is based on three principles: (1) the risk principle asserts that criminal behavior can be reliably predicted and that treatment should focus on persons classified as higher-risk offenders; (2) the need principle highlights the importance of assessing the major risk factors associated with criminal conduct in the design and delivery of treatment; and (3) the responsivity principle describes how the treatment should be provided. RNR is derived from decades of research demonstrating that the best outcomes are achieved when the intensity of supervision is matched to risk, interventions focus on conditions responsible for participants' crimes, and participants receive the services they need that match their personality and learning styles. Risk-needs-assessment tools play a major role in bail reform and efforts to reduce mass incarceration. For that

risk-needs-responsivity (RNR) model

A risk and needs assessment which states that the risks and needs of the person under correctional supervision should determine the strategies appropriate for addressing the person's criminogenic factors.

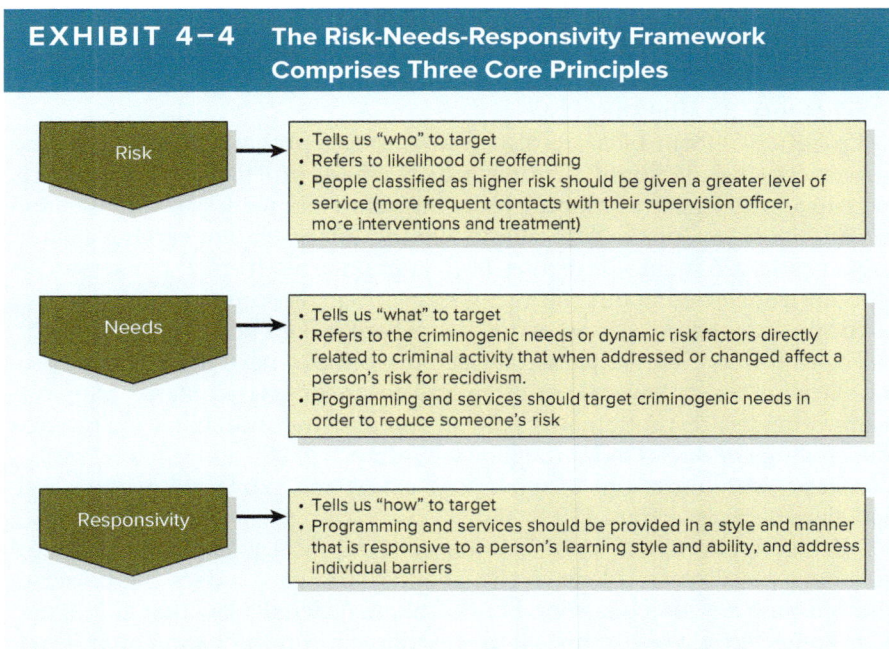

EXHIBIT 4−4   The Risk-Needs-Responsivity Framework Comprises Three Core Principles

Risk
- Tells us "who" to target
- Refers to likelihood of reoffending
- People classified as higher risk should be given a greater level of service (more frequent contacts with their supervision officer, more interventions and treatment)

Needs
- Tells us "what" to target
- Refers to the criminogenic needs or dynamic risk factors directly related to criminal activity that when addressed or changed affect a person's risk for recidivism.
- Programming and services should target criminogenic needs in order to reduce someone's risk

Responsivity
- Tells us "how" to target
- Programming and services should be provided in a style and manner that is responsive to a person's learning style and ability, and address individual barriers

reason we return to a discussion of RNAs in Chapter 6. Exhibit 4–4 details the risk-needs-responsivity model.[12]

We also know that recidivism rates vary from place to place, depending on the seriousness of offenses, population characteristics, average length of probation, and the amount and quality of intervention, surveillance, and enforcement. James Gondles, former executive director of the American Correctional Association, argues that, by the time persons reach probation, other institutions of social control have failed. If the offending behavior could have been controlled, families, neighborhoods, schools, and other social institutions would have controlled it. Offending behavior is not easy to correct and for that reason, Gondles believes that probation systems across the United States need help.

> [Probation officers] are often held accountable for the failures of other elements of the criminal justice community. Therefore, all of us in corrections must help them by doing our own jobs better, to escape the perception that they are ineffective. We must work together to ensure that all elements of the criminal justice system receive adequate funding and that all elements of the criminal justice system work closer together to provide persons with the services they require.[13]

The APPA, representing U.S. POs nationwide, argues that recidivism rates measure just one probation task while ignoring others. The APPA has urged its member agencies to collect data on other outcomes, such as the following:

- amount of restitution collected;
- number of persons employed;
- amounts of fines and fees collected;
- hours of community service performed;
- number of treatment sessions attended;
- percentage of financial obligations collected;
- rate of enrollment in school;
- number of days of employment;
- educational attainment; and
- number of days drug free.

Advocates of measures other than recidivism tell us that probation should be measured by what persons do while they are in probation programs, not by what they do after they leave.

Probation reform bills are also changing the probation landscape and how success is measured. The push to overhaul probation follows efforts to reduce mass incarceration by reducing sentences for lesser offenses and moving more persons to community supervision instead of serving jail and prison time. Changing probation laws is popular with fiscal conservatives who are concerned about the rising costs of corrections and social justice advocates concerned that too many people are locked up.

For example, Georgia passed legislation to move persons on felony probation who are at low risk of offending to unsupervised status after two years provided restitution was paid in full and the individual maintained law abiding conduct. Under the new law, almost 18,000 active felony probation cases were moved to unsupervised status and probation officer caseload sizes decreased from 170 to 130.

Michigan shortened punishments for technical violations (technical violations are discussed later in this chapter) and gave judges the power to shorten time for good behavior. South Dakota enacted a law that allows persons convicted of lesser crimes to be discharged from probation after a year

Clarissa Grissette

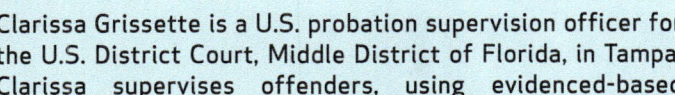

Clarissa Grissette

U.S Probation Officer, U.S. District Court, Middle District of Florida, Tampa, Florida

Clarissa Grissette is a U.S. probation supervision officer for the U.S. District Court, Middle District of Florida, in Tampa. Clarissa supervises offenders, using evidenced-based practices, who have committed federal crimes. She helps offenders reintegrate back into society by providing them with resources based on their needs. She uses evidence-based tools such as the "post-conviction risk assessment" that evaluates offenders' personal needs and the "substance abuse subtle screening inventory" to evaluate whether they need substance abuse treatment.

Clarissa earned her bachelor's degree in criminology and criminal justice from Florida Atlantic University (FAU) in 2009. She interned with the Broward County Sheriff's Office and worked closely with the homicide unit. During her internship, she participated in police ride-alongs, observed autopsies, completed summary reports, and organized case files.

Prior to federal appointment, she worked as a state probation officer for the Florida Department of Corrections for five years, and in January 2015, she was promoted to a drug offender probation officer and intensively monitored offenders with substance abuse and mental health problems. During her time as an officer with the Florida Department of Corrections, she received her master's degree in criminology and criminal justice from FAU in 2014, which helped her obtain her current position as a federal officer.

Grissette has a genuine desire to help offenders reintegrate back into the community while motivating them to exercise prosocial behaviors and engage in prosocial activities. Her passion for offender success placed her in a perfect occupation that she dedicates her life into perfecting. She believes everyone deserves a second chance, sometimes even a third. Her position requires exceptional communication skills, organization, patience, love for people, and commitment. She is under the direction of Chief Joe Collins, who instilled in her that "People can do amazing things when challenged and supported." The point is to have students realize the need to be positive and respectful around everyone they encounter.

As a PO, Clarissa conducts prerelease home visits and interviews family members to determine whether the environment is suitable for an inmate once he or she is released from federal custody. Once probationers are released, she evaluates the totality of their circumstances and prior criminal history and creates a case plan tailored to their needs to ensure they are given the tools/resources to successfully complete supervision.

> *People can do amazing things when challenged and supported.*

of good behavior. Missouri uses **earned discharge** that gives persons time off for complying with the conditions of their sentences such as completing a drug treatment program. In the first three years, Missouri reduced the length of probation by 14 months and probation officer case-loads dropped by 18 percent. Persons serving time in federal prisons are also eligible to shorten their sentences with "time credits"—10 to 15 days of credit for every 30 days they participate in recidivism reduction programs such as anger management, drug treatment, education, and work and social skills classes. Other states are considering bills that would limit the length of probation, limit a judge's ability to jail persons for technical violations that do not threaten public safety, and incentivize good behavior by allowing judges to reduce probation time.

earned discharge

A probation reform measure that allows individuals to earn time off for complying with the conditions of their sentences.

CO4-6
WHAT PROBATION OFFICERS DO

There are almost 54,000 probation officers in the United States, and the majority (54.6 percent) are women. The most common ethnicity of probation officers is white (63 percent), Black (17.6 percent), Hispanic (13.4 percent), and Asian (2.7 percent).[14] POs have two important roles: case investigation and client supervision.

Case Investigation

case investigation

The first major role of probation officers, consisting of interviewing the defendant and preparing the presentence report (PSR).

Case investigation includes the preparation of a PSR, which the judge uses in sentencing. The PSR is prepared by the probation department of a court; it provides a social and personal history as well as an evaluation of a defendant as an aid to the court in determining a sentence. The PSR also sets forth recommended sentencing options and programming needs. In some states, for example, Missouri, the report is called a *sentence assessment report.*[15]

Purposes of the Presentence Report The PSR has two main purposes. First, and most important, the PSR assists the court in reaching a fair sentencing decision. The specific content areas of the PSR vary from jurisdiction to jurisdiction, but common areas include (1) information regarding the current offense, (2) past adult and juvenile criminal record, (3) family history and background, and (4) personal data about education, health, employment, and substance abuse history. In addition, some state statutes dictate content areas such as victim-impact statements. It is not uncommon for jurisdictions to include a sentencing recommendation in the PSR. However, sentencing reforms are limiting judicial sentencing discretion, so the PSR recommendation is much less important than it once was.

Keeping in mind the RNR discussed earlier, the second purpose of the PSR is to outline a treatment plan. During the investigation, in addition to determining the degree of risk the individual poses to the community, the PO identifies programming needs (counseling, treatment, education, community service, restitution, employment, and some form of supervision).

A PO interviews a person referred by the court in preparation of the presentence report (PSR). Case investigation is the first major role of a PO. What is the role of the RNR in the PSR? What questions should a PO ask the defendant?

Pat Sutphin/The Times-News/AP Image

Creating a Presentence Report The PSR starts with an interview between the PO and the defendant. The interview follows a structured format for obtaining information on the offense and the individual.

In the PSR, the PO uses an evidence-based assessment tool to classify persons into levels of risk (e.g., low, medium, and high) and to identify and target interventions to address individual needs (e.g., antisocial attitudes, antisocial peer groups) that are related to recidivism. An evidence-based assessment tool does not indicate whether a particular individual will actually recidivate; rather it identifies the *risk* or *probability* that the person will recidivate. The probability is based on the extent to which an individual has characteristics like those of other persons who have recidivated.

The PO summarizes the information gathered and, in most jurisdictions, makes a sentence recommendation. If the sentence recommended is incarceration, in most jurisdictions the length must be within guidelines set by statute (see Chapter 3). However, if the sentence recommended is probation or some other intermediate sanction (see Chapter 5), few jurisdictions have guidelines for sentence length. Only recently have some states (e.g., Delaware, Minnesota, North Carolina, and Pennsylvania) begun to design sentencing guidelines for nonprison sentences such as probation. Copies of the PSR are filed with the court and made available to the judge, the prosecutor, and the defense attorney. Exhibit 4–5 is an example of a short-form federal PSR. Space does not allow us to include everything. Not shown here is the officer's summary of the defendant's pretrial adjustment, substance abuse history, education and vocational skills, employment record, financial condition, and necessary monthly living expenses.

Supervision

The second major role of probation officers is client supervision. Probation **supervision** has three main elements: resource mediation, surveillance, and enforcement. *Resource mediation* means providing persons on community supervision access to a wide variety of services if needed, such as job development, substance abuse treatment, counseling, and education. *Surveillance* means monitoring the activities of person on probation through office meetings, home and work visits, drug and alcohol testing, and contact with family, friends, and employers. *Enforcement* means making individuals accountable for their behavior and making sure they understand the consequences of violating the conditions of probation. Supervision officers who follow a structured approach to their interactions with their clients, by adhering to the risk, needs, and responsivity principles, are key for reducing recidivism in probation.

Today researchers are also asking if procedural justice strategies could improve the relationship between POs and persons on community supervision and lead to fewer rearrests and convictions. **Procedural justice** describes the idea that how individuals regard the justice system is tied more to the perceived fairness of the *process* and how they were treated rather than to the perceived fairness of the *outcome*. It is a framework for POs to treat people with fairness and respect. If persons on probation feel the PO has treated them in a procedurally fair and just way and decisions and outcomes were arrived at fairly, they will rate the system favorably even if the outcome is not what they hoped for.

Procedural justice is based on five central principles: voice, respect, trust, understanding, and neutrality.

1. **Voice.** The perception that the person had the opportunity to tell their side of the story

supervision
The second major role of probation officers, consisting of resource mediation, surveillance, and enforcement.

procedural justice
The idea that how individuals regard the justice system is tied more to the perceived fairness of the process and how they were treated rather than to the perceived fairness of the outcome.

EXHIBIT 4–5 Sample Presentence Report

**IN THE UNITED STATES DISTRICT COURT
FOR THE NORTHERN DISTRICT OF ALABAMA**

UNITED STATES OF AMERICA	)	PRESENTENCE
	)	REPORT
v.	)	
EDDIE PALMER	)	Docket No. CR 16-H-248-S

Prepared For:	Honorable Casandra Phillips U.S. District Judge
Prepared By:	Noelle Koval U.S. Probation Officer Birmingham, AL (205)555-0923
Offense:	Count One: Possession With Intent to Distribute a Schedule II Controlled Substance (Cocaine Base), not less than 10 Years and not more than Life and/or $4,000,000 Fine. With Enhancement, Mandatory Life and/or $8,000,000 Fine.
Release Status:	Released on $25,000 unsecured bond Remanded to custody

Identifying Data

Date of Birth:	1/9/90
Age:	35
Race:	B
Sex:	M

Charge(s) and Conviction(s)

Eddie Palmer was indicted on two counts by the Grand Jury for the Northern District of Alabama. Count One charged the defendant unlawfully possessed with intent to distribute approximately 500 grams of a mixture or substance containing a detectable amount of cocaine, Schedule II controlled substances, in violation of 21 USC § 841(a)(1). Count Two charged that the defendant carried a firearm during the commission of a drug trafficking crime in violation of 18 USC § 924(c)(1). The Grand Jury returned a superseding indictment in which the defendant was charged in two counts. Count One charges that the defendant intentionally possessed with intent to distribute approximately 100 grams of a mixture or substance containing a detectable amount of cocaine base and approximately 240 grams of a mixture or substance containing a detectable amount of cocaine, Schedule II controlled substances, in violation of 21 USC § 841(a)(1). Count Two charges that the defendant carried a firearm during the commission of a drug trafficking crime in violation of 18 USC § 924(c)(1). Palmer pled guilty to Count One, and Count Two was dismissed on motion of the government. Sentencing was continued to a later date.

---

2. **Respect.** The perception that the PO treated the person with respect and dignity
3. **Trust.** The perception that the PO is sincere, authentic, and listens and cares about the person's personal situation
4. **Understanding.** The perception that the person understands the decisions being made and the conditions by which they are bound
5. **Neutrality.** The perception that communication is consistent, transparent, and trustworthy and the basis for exceptions when they occur

Procedural justice is now an evidence-based practice. Research has consistently shown that when authorities act in a procedurally just manner, people view the law and its enforcers as more legitimate and are more likely to comply and cooperate voluntarily. In the criminal justice context, most procedural justice research has focused on citizen–police interactions. Only

EXHIBIT 4–5 **Sample Presentence Report (*continued*)**

SENTENCING RECOMMENDATION
UNITED STATES DISTRICT COURT
FOR THE NORTHERN DISTRICT OF ALABAMA

UNITED STATES V. EDDIE PALMER   **DOCKET NO. CR 16-H-248-S**

TOTAL OFFENSE LEVEL: 29

CRIMINAL HISTORY CATEGORY: III

	Statutory Provision	Guideline Provisions	Recommended Sentence
CUSTODY:	Mandatory Life	Mandatory Life	Life
PROBATION:	N/A	N/A	N/A
SUPERVISED RELEASE:	Not Less Than 10 Years	10 Years	10 Years
FINE:	$8,000,000	$15,000 to $8,000,000	$15,000
RESTITUTION:	N/A	N/A	N/A

Justification

The sentence of life is mandatory. Supervised release must be 10 years. A $15,000 fine is recommended because it is incumbent upon the defendant to demonstrate that he does not have the financial ability to pay a fine. He and his attorney have not cooperated in providing information, and it appears that he does have the ability to pay the minimum fine based on his purported monthly income from trafficking in illegal drugs.

Voluntary Surrender

The defendant is in custody.

Respectfully Submitted,

Noelle Koval

Noelle Koval
U.S. Probation Officer

recently have researchers begun to investigate procedural justice interventions in community supervision. The Urban Institute analyzed how applying procedural justice techniques in community supervision affects persons on probation in a pilot program in Georgia. Analyses of officer–supervisee interactions, survey responses regarding perceptions of supervision, and analyses of administrative data provide support that the procedural justice training had its intended effects. Respondents reported high levels of procedurally just practices from supervision officers, as well as their consistently high satisfaction with their supervision officers and with the Georgia Department of Community Supervision staff.[16]

Caseload Because **caseload size** (the number of people on a probation or parole officer's caseload) varies from place to place depending on the seriousness of the offense, population characteristics, average length of probation, and agency resources, among other factors, there is no universally accepted standard for caseload size. However, caseload size is important because it allows officers to more meaningfully engage with the people under their supervision and help them change their behavior. The American

Olmsted County (Rochester, Minnesota) PO Bernie Sizer (right), tests Kevin Rood for alcohol during a visit to Rood's apartment. Case supervision is the second major role of a PO. What are the three main elements of case supervision?

Ann Heisenfelt/AP Photo

caseload size

The number of people on a probation officer's caseload.

Probation and Parole Association advocates building caseload size on the type of case and level of supervision required. An example is shown in Exhibit 4–6.

Some states like Texas keep caseloads low enough to enable supervision officers to work intensively with people at a high risk of reoffending, from a low of 14 people per officer for the most intensive supervision, to a high of 75 people at a low risk of reoffending per officer. Minnesota prescribes that caseloads for its intensive supervision program be no more than 30 people per two officers. The limited caseload allows officers to closely supervise people at a high risk of reoffending. In Alabama, after reinvesting $38.5 million to hire 100 new community supervision officers, caseloads dropped from 200 per officer to an average of 110. Alabama also limited the number of high-risk people on an officer's caseload to 20.[17]

A number of jurisdictions are also experimenting with Probation Automated Management (PAM). The PAM kiosk is similar to an ATM and allows persons who are low-risk to report in 24 hours a day, seven days a week, with their fingerprints as biometric identifiers. The fingerprints are compared to the ones collected when the person first began probation. Some kiosks also take a digital face photo.

Once a match is established, the individual can interact with the kiosk by pressing buttons on the touch screen. Data are entered to verify address and employment status and to respond to questions asked by the PO. Advocates of probation kiosks argue that the kiosks save scarce jail beds for those persons who pose a serious risk to the community.

Researchers in Oklahoma City studied whether using evidence-based practices with reduced medium- to high-risk caseloads improves probation outcomes. They found that reducing probation officer medium- to high-risk caseloads from 107 to 54 can reduce criminal recidivism by roughly one-third when delivered in a setting where probation officers apply evidence-based practices.[18] Reduced caseloads, in combination with evidence-based practices, can lead to improved recidivism outcomes.

Regardless of their level of supervision, all persons on probation are subject to "general" conditions of supervision. These include reporting to a PO as directed, paying court-ordered

At the entrance to the Olmsted County jail in Rochester, Minnesota, persons convicted of drunk driving are required to appear before the automated kiosk once a month and check in by handprint to answer questions about their progress. Probation kiosks are used to supervise low-risk individuals who do not require face-to-face contact with a PO. What advantages and disadvantages do you see in this approach?

Ann Heisenfelt/AP Images

EXHIBIT 4–6   Adult and Juvenile Caseload Standards

ADULT STANDARDS

Case Type	Cases-to-Staff Ratio
Intensive	20:1
Moderate to high risk	50:1
Low risk	200:1

JUVENILE STANDARDS

Case Type	Cases-to-Staff Ratio
Intensive	15:1
Moderate to high risk	30:1
Low risk	100:1

Source: American Probation and Parole Association.

monies, working, obeying all laws, and being "of general good behavior." Exhibit 4–7 presents, as an example, the general conditions of probation in Georgia. The court may also order "special conditions" that relate directly to the individual's particular crime or history. For example, a person convicted of cybercrime may be subject to the special conditions shown in Exhibit 4–8.

Technology and Supervision There is also a wide variety of technological tools to help POs in client supervision that only a few years ago did not exist. Computer programs can track fine and probation payments, alert POs when their clients are behind on payments, and help them track whether they have satisfied the conditions of their sentences. Kiosk reporting, secure remote alcohol detection, voice verification, facial recognition, and microchips that fit under the skin are electronic tools that have the potential to enhance community supervision.

Another technological innovation, one of the more interesting strategies for managing the three elements of probation supervision, is mapping technology or geographic information systems (GIS). Mapping has helped law enforcement locate hot spots of crime. Probation departments use mapping as a tool to supervise persons on community supervision. Mapping also helps ensure that probation and parole officers are dispersed in areas with high concentrations of persons under community supervision.

EXHIBIT 4–7   State of Georgia General Conditions of Probation

The court shall determine the terms and conditions of probation and may provide that the probationer shall:

1. avoid injurious and vicious habits;

2. avoid persons or places of disreputable or harmful character;

3. report to the probation supervisor as directed;

4. permit the supervisor to visit him at his home or elsewhere;

5. work faithfully at suitable employment insofar as may be possible;

6. remain within a specified location;

7. make reparation or restitution to any aggrieved person for the damage or loss caused by his offense, in an amount to be determined by the court. Unless otherwise provided by law, no reparation or restitution to any aggrieved person for the damage or loss caused by his offense shall be made if the amount is in dispute unless the same has been adjudicated;

8. make reparation or restitution as reimbursement to a municipality or county for the payment for medical care furnished the person while incarcerated pursuant to the provisions of Article 3 of Chapter 4 of this title. No reparation or restitution to a local governmental unit for the provision of medical care shall be made if the amount is in dispute unless the same has been adjudicated;

9. repay the costs incurred by any municipality or county for wrongful actions by an inmate covered under the provisions of paragraph (1) of subsection (a) of Code Section 42-4–71;

10. support his legal dependents to the best of his ability;

11. violate no local, state, or federal laws and be of general good behavior; and

12. if permitted to move or travel to another state, agree to waive extradition from any jurisdiction where he may be found and not contest any effort by any jurisdiction to return him to this state.

Source: Georgia Department of Corrections.

EXHIBIT 4−8	Specific Probation Conditions for Computer Crime		

(A = Internet Access Permitted; B = Limited or 0 Access to Internet)	A	B
You shall consent to your probation officer and/or probation service representative conducting periodic unannounced examinations of your computer(s) equipment which may include retrieval and copying of all memory from hardware/software to ensure compliance with this condition and/or removal of such equipment for the purpose of conducting a more thorough inspection; and consent at the direction of your probation officer to having installed on your computer(s), at your expense, any hardware or software systems to monitor your computer use or prevent access to particular materials. You hereby consent to the periodic inspection of any such installed hardware or software to insure it is functioning properly.	X	X
You shall not possess encryption or steganography software.	X	X
You shall provide your probation officer accurate information about your entire computer system and software; all passwords used by you; and your Internet Service Provider(s).	X	X
You shall possess only computer hardware or software approved by your probation officer. You shall obtain written permission from your probation officer prior to obtaining any additional computer hardware or software or Internet Service Provider(s).	X	X
You shall refrain from using a computer in any manner that relates to the activity in which you were engaged in committing the instant offense or violation behavior.	X	X
You shall provide truthful information concerning your identity in all Internet or e-mail communications and not visit any "chat rooms" or similar Internet locations/sites where minors are known to frequent.	X	
You shall maintain a daily log of all addresses you access via any personal computer (or other computer used by you), other than for authorized employment, and make this log available to your probation officer.	X	
You shall not create or assist directly or indirectly in the creation of any electronic bulletin board, Internet Service Provider, or any other public or private network without the prior written consent of your probation officer. Any approval shall be subject to any conditions set by the U.S. Probation Office of the Court with respect to that approval.	X	X
You shall not possess or use a computer with access to any "on-line" computer service at any location (including employment or education) without prior written approval of the U.S. Probation Office of the Court. This includes any Internet Service Provider, bulletin board system, or any other public or private computer network. Any approval shall be subject to any conditions set by the U.S. Probation Office or the Court with respect to that approval.		X
You shall not purchase, possess, or receive a personal computer which utilizes a modem, and/or an external mode.		X
You will have an occupational condition that you can not be employed directly or indirectly where you are an installer, programmer, or "trouble shooter" for computer equipment.	X	X

Source: Arthur L. Bowker and Gregory B. Thompson, "Computer Crime in the 21st Century and Its Effects on the Probation Officer," *Federal Probation*, vol. 65, no. 2 (September 2001), p. 21.

revocation hearing

A due process hearing that must be conducted to determine whether the conditions of probation have been violated before probation can be revoked and the individual removed from the community.

For example, the Wisconsin Department of Corrections found through mapping that "if you have an area with a drug usage problem, we would bring drug programming to that area. Really, our experience was we got better attendance and better completion rates with that."[19] The Center for Alternative Sentencing and Employment in New York uses mapping to monitor employment rates in areas where persons on probation live and, with the assistance of community agencies, to help them find a job link upon leaving prison.

 ## Revocation of Probation

If the person on probation willfully violates the conditions of their probation, a **revocation hearing** is usually the next step. A revocation hearing is a due process hearing that must be conducted by the court or probation authority to determine whether the conditions of probation (or parole as we will see in Chapter 8) have been violated before probation can be revoked and the individual removed from the community. **Revocation** is the formal termination of conditional freedom.

Revocation is a serious matter for four reasons. First, the person might lose their freedom to remain in the community. Second, the handling of probation violators by supervision agencies and courts consumes a significant portion of the court's time, energy, and resources. One jurisdiction estimated that the probation violation process consumes the equivalent of a full-time judge, prosecutor, and courtroom staff. In 41 states covered in a study by the Council of State Governments Justice Center, people returning to prison from community supervision cost those states more than $8 billion in 2021.[20] Third, the cost of probation supervision is much lower than the cost of incarceration (see Exhibit 4–9). And fourth, incarcerating persons who otherwise would have been placed on probation force families to go on welfare and make greater demands on community resources.

But the question remains, which sanction to use if someone violates the conditions of their community supervision? Is incarceration more effective than continued community supervision in controlling probation violations? The public and criminal justice practitioners often view community-based punishments such as probation and those discussed in Chapter 5 as less onerous and less effective than incarceration. However, persons on probation, especially those with prior prison experience, do not hold the same views. Wood and May and others have shown that persons under correctional supervision would rather serve a year of incarceration rather than any amount of time under community supervision as evidence that the conditions of probation can sometimes restrict freedom more than incarceration.[21] Wodahl, Boman, and Garland looked at more than 800 probation violations in Wyoming and found no evidence to suggest that jail sanctions were any more effective than community supervision. They write:

> The imposition of a jail sanction for offender noncompliance as opposed to a community-based sanction did not affect the number of days until the next violation, the number of subsequent violations, or the overall likelihood of completing supervision. Furthermore, the number of times an offender went to jail, the number of days spent in jail, or the timing of the jail sanction did not influence offender outcomes.[22]

Findings like these, along with the financial, social, and potentially criminogenic effects of incarceration, call into question the use of jail as a means of punishing persons for violating probation.

revocation

The formal termination of an individual's conditional freedom.

EXHIBIT 4–9   Cost of Probation versus Incarceration

To supervise a person in the community: $3,000–$5,000

To place a person in a residential reentry center: $29,000–$35,000

To incarcerate a person in jail: $30,000–$63,000

To imprison a person: $27,000–$76,000

Source: Bureau of Justice Statistics.

A supervision officer interviews a crime victim. Case investigation is one of a supervision officer's most important tasks. What questions would you ask a crime victim as part of the investigation?
sturti/Getty Images

Violations That Trigger Revocation Revocation is triggered in one of two ways. Either someone willfully violate the *technical* conditions of their probation or they commit *new offenses.*

A **technical violation** is failure to comply with the conditions of probation. It is not a criminal act. Most revocations are the result of technical violations, actions that would not otherwise be considered a crime but become punishable due to the conditions of supervision. The most commonly committed technical violations are positive urinalysis, failure to participate in treatment, **absconding** (fleeing the jurisdiction without permission), and failure to report to the PO.

We know that two out of three people in jail have a substance use disorder; therefore it is not unusual for them to violate supervision by submitting positive drug tests.[23] Most of them will violate the conditions of their probation in the beginning when they are adjusting to the rules. Thus, violations for failure to report, failure to maintain employment, failure to complete community service restitution, or failure to pay court-ordered fees are not uncommon. The question is, what should the PO do?

Most POs do not ask the court to revoke probation for an occasional technical violation. They understand that technical violations are supervision issues and best handled by program or treatment referrals. To ensure compliance, POs can tighten supervision with a reprimand, increase reporting requirements, limit travel or other privileges, increase drug/alcohol testing, make treatment/education referrals, restructure payments for persons who demonstrate an inability to pay in accordance with the court-established payment plan, or extend the terms of probation.

One analyst with the National Institute of Corrections wrote, "If our jails and prisons are filled with offenders who are merely noncompliant, there will be no room for the dangerous offender."[24] Overreliance on incarceration as punishment for conditional supervision violations when alternatives exist like those discussed in Chapter 5 contributes to unnecessary incarceration and the problem of mass incarceration first presented in Chapter 1.

A **new offense violation** is the arrest and prosecution for the commission of a new crime. Depending upon the seriousness of the new offense, the court may, in response to a violation of probation (or parole, see Chapter 8),

technical violation

Actions that would not otherwise be considered a crime but become punishable due to the conditions of supervision.

absconding

Fleeing the jurisdiction in which the individual is required to stay without the permission of the PO.

new offense violation

Arrest and prosecution for the commission of a new crime.

impose a sentence of incarceration *plus* any new sentence of incarceration that may be imposed for the new offense. The two sentences may be imposed to run concurrently or consecutively (see Chapter 3). In the case of parole, a new offense violation may trigger return to prison to serve out the unexpired sentence *plus* the sentence for the new offense.

Data show that persons who violate the conditions of their probation or parole represent 18 percent of the jail population (or about 108,000 persons) and about 30 percent (also about 108,000) of the prison population.[25] Unfortunately, U.S. Department of Justice data on persons in jail and prison do not specify what percent are incarcerated for either a new offense or a technical violation. Imagine the reduction in mass incarceration if persons who violate the technical conditions of their supervision are sentenced instead to an intermediate sanction. You will learn in Chapter 8 that California's "nonrevocable" parole is a step in that direction.

Revocation Hearings   Revocation hearings usually begin with a violation report prepared by the PO. The hearings are governed by the 1973 U.S. Supreme Court decision known as *Gagnon* v. *Scarpelli.* In this case, the Court said that there was no difference between probation and parole revocation because both of them resulted in loss of liberty. The Court extended the same rights to persons on probation that it had granted to persons on parole a year earlier in *Morrissey* v. *Brewer.* The Court ruled that probation cannot be revoked without observing the following elements of due process:

1. written notice of the charge;
2. disclosure of the evidence;
3. the opportunity to be heard in person and to present evidence as well as witnesses;
4. the right to confront and cross-examine witnesses;
5. the right to judgment by a detached and neutral hearing body;
6. a written statement of the reasons for revoking probation; and
7. the right to counsel under "special circumstances" depending on the competency of the individual, case complexity, and mitigating circumstances.

REVIEW AND APPLICATIONS

SUMMARY

1 *Probation* is the conditional release of a person convicted of crime into the community under the supervision of a PO. Most probation programs are designed to (1) protect the community by assisting judges in making sentencing and supervision decisions, (2) carry out sanctions imposed by the court, (3) facilitate behavioral change, (4) support crime victims, and (5) coordinate and promote the use of community resources.

2 Probation is used for four reasons: (1) It permits persons to remain in the community for reintegration purposes, (2) it avoids institutionalization and the stigma of incarceration, (3) it is less expensive than incarceration and more humanitarian, and (4) it is appropriate for individuals whose crimes do not necessarily merit incarceration.

3 Today federal, state, and local probation agencies supervise almost 3.1 million adult U.S. residents, with nonviolent convictions accounting for 85 percent. Twenty-five percent of the adult probation population were women, and 38 percent were white.

4 In 29 states, a state or local agency delivers adult probation services. In three states, adult probation services are delivered exclusively through county or multicounty agencies in the executive branch. In eight states, the judicial branch of government is responsible for adult probation services. In five states, local agencies in the judicial branch deliver adult probation services. And in five states, adult probation services are delivered through some combination of state executive branch, local executive agencies, or local agencies in either the judicial or the executive branch.

5 Corrections professionals urge evaluators to collect data on outcomes other than recidivism, such as amount of restitution collected, number of persons employed, amounts of fines and fees collected, hours of community service, number of treatment sessions completed, percentage of financial obligations collected, rate of enrollment in school, number of days employed, educational attainment, and number of days drug free.

6 Case investigation and client supervision are the two major roles of POs. Investigation includes the preparation of a presentence report (PSR), which the judge uses in sentencing. Supervision includes the functions of resource mediation, surveillance, and enforcement.

7 A *revocation hearing* is a due process hearing that must be conducted to determine whether the conditions of probation have been violated before probation can be revoked and the individual is removed from the community. Probation can be revoked when persons fail to comply with the technical conditions of probation or commit new crimes.

KEY TERMS

Probation, p. 70

recidivism, p. 76

risk and needs assessments, p. 76

risk-needs-responsivity
model, p. 77

earned discharge, p. 79

case investigation, p. 80

supervision, p. 81

procedural justice, p. 81

caseload size, p. 84

revocation hearing, p. 86

revocation, p. 87

technical violation, p. 88

absconding, p. 88

new offense violation, p. 88

QUESTIONS FOR REVIEW

1 Explain probation and its goals.

2 Defend the reasons for using probation.

3 Construct a profile of the characteristics of adults on probation.

4 Summarize the different ways that probation is administered.

5 Evaluate the measures of probation.

6 Distinguish between the investigation and supervision functions of probation, and provide an example of each.

7 Summarize what occurs at a revocation hearing.

THINKING CRITICALLY ABOUT CORRECTIONS

Privatizing Probation

With at least 1,000 courts in several states allowing private companies to oversee probation for minor offenses, collecting outstanding debts and court costs, and oftentimes adding their own fees for services such as ankle monitors and late payment, how can government continue to privatize probation and avoid a charge similar to the one brought by the U.S. Department of Justice's Civil Rights Division against the municipal court in Ferguson, Missouri, that it handles most charges not with the primary goal of administering justice or protecting the rights of the accused but of maximizing revenue?

Probation Effectiveness

Recidivism is one current measure of probation effectiveness. Others include the amount of restitution collected, the number of persons on community supervision who are employed, the amounts of fines and fees collected, the number of hours of community service performed, the number of treatment sessions completed, the percentage of financial obligations collected, the rate of school enrollment, the level of educational attainment, the number of days employed, and the number of days drug free.

1. How important to you, as a taxpayer, is recidivism as a measure of program success?
2. Do you believe probation officers can really keep people from committing new crimes or violating the conditions of their probation?
3. If you were a probation officer today, by which outcome measures would you want to be judged? Why?
4. If recidivism is used as a measure of probation's effectiveness, how should it be defined?

ON-THE-JOB DECISION MAKING

Responding to Program Violations

The new diversion program in your county was developed to help persons charged with misdemeanor drug offenses avoid incarceration and seek help in controlling their dependency. Your job as the new diversion officer is to set the conditions of the diversion program and then monitor and enforce compliance. One of your first clients fails the required weekly drug test. Think about Wodahl, Boman, and Garland's research on the effectiveness of jail and community-based sanctions and argue in favor of jail or a community-based sanction.

Probation and Recidivism

At a recent staff meeting, the chief PO reported that the department's recidivism rate exceeded the national average by 5 percent. The chief asks what can be done about it. You say, "Look at other measures besides recidivism." The chief asks you to explain. What do you say?

ENDNOTES

1. Sonia Rao, "Actor Jussie Smollett Sentenced to 150 Days in Jail, Thousands in Fines for Falsely Reporting a Hate Crime," *The Washington Post*, March 10, 2022, https://www.washingtonpost.com/arts-entertainment/2022/03/10/jussie-smollett-hate-crime-sentence/ (accessed May 30, 2022).
2. Robert Panzarella, "Theory and Practice of Probation on Bail in the Report of John Augustus," *Federal Probation*, vol. 66, no. 3 (December 2002), pp. 38–43.
3. Sanford Bates, "The Establishment and Early Years of the Federal Probation System," *Federal Probation*, vol. 14 (1950), pp. 16–21; Joel R. Moore, "Early Reminiscences," *Federal Probation*, vol. 14 (1950), pp. 21–29; Richard A. Chappell, "The Federal Probation System Today," *Federal Probation*, vol. 14 (1950), pp. 30–40.
4. Department of Justice, *Probation and Parole in the United States, 2000* (Washington, DC: U.S. Department of Justice, Bureau of Justice Statistics, August 2001); United States Courts, "Supervision Costs Significantly Less Than Incarceration in Federal System," July 18, 2013, https://www.uscourts.gov/ (accessed October 20, 2022).
5. Danielle Kaeble, *Probation and Parole in the United States, 2020* (Washington, DC: U.S. Department of Justice, Bureau of Justice Statistics, December 2021).
6. Caroline Wolf Harlow, *Prior Abuse Reported by Inmates and Probationers* (Washington, DC: Department of Justice, Bureau of Justice Statistics, April 1999).
7. Interstate Commission for Adult Offender Supervision, Fees (ICAOS: Lexington, KY, 2020).
8. Fines and Fees Justice Center, *50 State Survey: Probation and Parole Fees*, May 10, 2022, https://finesandfeesjusticecenter.org (accessed October 20, 2022).
9. Matt Apuzzo and John Eligon, "Ferguson Police Tainted by Bias, Justice Department Says," *The New York Times*, March 4, 2015, www.nytimes.com/2015/03/05/us/us-calls-on-ferguson-to-overhaul-criminal-justice-system.html?_r=50 (accessed September 15, 2019); Joseph Shapiro, "As Court Fees Rise, the Poor Are Paying the

Price," *National Public Radio*, May 23, 2014, www.npr .org/2014/05/19/312158516/increasing-court-fees-punish -the-poor (accessed September 15, 2022).

10. Danielle Kaeble, *Probation and Parole in the United States, 2020* (Washington, DC: U.S. Department of Justice, Bureau of Justice Statistics, December 2021).

11. Steve Aos, Marna Miller, and Elizabeth Drake, *Evidence-Based Adult Corrections Programs: What Works and What Does Not* (Olympia, WA: Washington State Institute for Public Policy, 2006); and Jennifer L. Sheem and Sarah Monchak, "Back to the Future: From Klocklar's Model of Effective Supervision to Evidence-Based Practice in Probation," *Journal of Offender Rehabilitation*, vol. 47, no. 3 (2008), pp. 220–247.

12. Mario Paparozzi and Matthew DeMichele, "Probation and Parole: Overworked, Misunderstood, and Under-Appreciated: But Why?" *The Howard Journal*, vol. 47, no. 3 (July 2008), pp. 275–296.

13. James A. Gondles Jr., "The Probation and Parole System Needs Our Help to Succeed," *Corrections Today*, vol. 65, no. 1 (February 2003), p. 8.

14. Zippia, *Probation Officer Demographics and Statistics in the US, 2022*, https://www.zippia.com/probation-officer-jobs /demographics/ (accessed November 12, 2022).

15. "Missouri Considers New Sentencing System," *Corrections Compendium*, vol. 29, no. 6 (November/December 2004), p. 39.

16. The Urban Institute, *Applying Procedural Justice in Community Supervision* (Washington, DC: The Urban Institute, March 2021). See also Carmen L. Diaz, Staci Rising, Eric Grommon, Miriam Northcutt Bohmert, and Evan Marie Lowder, "A Rapid Review of Literature on Factors Associated with Adult Probation Revocations," *Corrections: Policy, Practice and Research*, doi: 10.1080/23774657.2022.2136116.

17. Council of State Governments, *50-State Report on Public Safety* (New York: Council of State Governments, 2018).

18. Sarah Kuck Jalbert and William Rhodes, "Reduced Caseloads Improve Probation Outcomes," *Journal of Crime and Justice*, vol. 35, no. 2 (July 2012), pp. 221–238.

19. Michelle Gaseau, *Mapping to Improve Supervision and Community Corrections*, October 23, 2000, www.corrections.com (accessed December 18, 2015); Jaishankar Karuppannan, "Mapping and Corrections: Management of Offenders with Geographic Information Systems," *Corrections Compendium*, vol. 30, no. 1 (January/February 2005), pp. 7–9, 31–33.

20. Peggy Burke, "Probation and Parole Violations: An Overview of Critical Issues," in Madeline M. Carter (ed.), *Responding to Probation and Parole Violators* (Washington, DC: National Institute of Corrections, April 2001), p. 6. See also Council of State Governments Justice Center, *The Cost of Recidivism: The High Price States Pay to Incarcerate People for Supervision Violations* (NY: Council of State Governments, April 2023).

21. Peter B. Wood and David C. May, "Prison, Reentry, and Offenders' Perceptions of Correctional Punishments," in Matthew S. Crow and John Ortiz Smykla (eds.), *Offender Reentry: Rethinking Criminology and Criminal Justice* (Boston: Jones & Bartlett, 2013), pp. 385–398.

22. Eric J. Wodahl, John H. Boman, and Brett E. Garland, "Responding to Probation and Parole Violations: Are Jail Sanctions More Effective Than Community-Based Graduated Sanctions?" *Journal of Criminal Justice*, vol. 43, no. 3 (May–June 2015), pp. 242–250.

23. Jennifer Bronson, Jessica Stroop, Stephanie Zimmer, and Marcus Berzofsky, *Drug Use, Dependence, and Abuse Among State Prisoners and Jail Inmates, 2007–2009* (Washington, DC: U.S. Department of Justice, Bureau of Justice Statistics, June 2017).

24. Burke, "Probation and Parole Violations," p. 5.

25. Todd D. Minton and Zhen Zeng, *Jail Inmates in 2020—Statistical Tables* (Washington, DC: U.S. Department of Justice, Bureau of Justice Statistics, December 2021) and E. Ann Carson, *Prisoners in 2020—Statistical Tables* (Washington, DC: U.S. Department of Justice, Bureau of Justice Statistics, December 2021).

INTERMEDIATE SANCTIONS AND COMMUNITY CORRECTIONS

Between Probation and Incarceration

Larry French/AP Photo for NADCP

CHAPTER OBJECTIVES

After completing this chapter you should be able to do the following:

1. Define *intermediate sanctions* and describe their purpose.

2. Describe how intensive supervision probation works.

3. Explain what drug courts are.

4. Explain how day fines differ from traditional fines.

5. Describe what a sentence to community service entails.

6. Explain what day reporting centers are.

7. Describe how remote-location monitoring works.

8. Explain what residential reentry centers are.

9. Identify the major features of correctional boot camps.

10. Define *community corrections.*

11. Explain what community corrections acts are.

For many people, being arrested and sent to drug court is what saved their lives, allowed them to get treatment, and gave them a second chance.

—The President's Commission on Combating Drug Addiction and the Opioid Crisis

Ron Hurst/Southcreek Global/ Zuma Press, Inc/
Alamy Stock Photo

In 2004, Clinton Portis was the highest-paid running back in National Football League history with career earnings of more than $43 million. But a combination of bad investments and extravagant spending led to Portis declaring bankruptcy in 2015. That's when Portis and 14 other former NFL players started a scheme to defraud NFL's health care benefit program. The program was designed in 2006 to help retired players pay for medical expenses that were not covered by insurance. Portis received $99,624 in reimbursement for himself for expensive medical equipment for which he did not have a medical need while also falsifying prescriptions, medical letters, and invoices.[1]

In January 2022, U.S. District Court Judge Karen Caldwell "stacked" Portis's sentences: six months in federal prison followed by six months home confinement, and restitution to repay the $99,624 in false claims he received. Portis served his time at the Federal Correctional Institution, Edgefield, South Carolina before beginning his period of home confinement.

Is Portis's sentence fair? (Refer back to Chapter 3 and the issues surrounding fairness in sentencing.) Is it evidence-based?

You learn in this chapter that home detention and financial penalties are forms of intermediate punishments. As you learn about intermediate punishments and community corrections, ask yourself if they are evidence-based correctional practices. If they are not, should they be used in sentencing?

CO5-1

INTERMEDIATE SANCTIONS

intermediate sanctions

New punishment options developed to fill the gap between traditional probation and traditional jail or prison sentences and to better match the severity of punishment to the seriousness of the crime.

Intermediate Sanctions

What are intermediate sanctions, and why are they used?

Sanctions less restrictive than prison but more restrictive than probation are not new. Variations of **intermediate sanctions** like many of those discussed later in this chapter (restitution, fines, and community service) were used as sentences in ancient Israel, Greece, and Rome. Other intermediate sanctions—such as drug court, remote-location monitoring, day reporting centers, and day fines—started in the 1980s as a way to respond to the increase in the number of persons under correctional supervision and widescale prison overcrowding. Prior to this, sentencing options were limited to incarceration or probation. However, there was growing sentiment that some crimes were too severe to be punished by probation alone, but those same crimes were not severe enough to warrant incarceration. Therefore, states started to develop a series of intermediate sanctions that fell somewhere between probation and incarceration. What is new today is the effort to bring all these sanctions together into an evidence-based comprehensive graduated sentencing system like the one shown in Exhibit 5–1. It offers judges an expanded menu of sanctions. Punishment increases from left to right as the seriousness of an offense increases. For example, simple assault may be punished with regular probation where the individual checks in monthly either in person or electronically. If the conditions of probation are violated, the judge can "stack" punishments, meaning instead of checking in monthly, the judge may order weekly face-to-face meetings with the probation officer. However, a conviction of a more serious offense, for example auto theft, may require some type of incarceration.

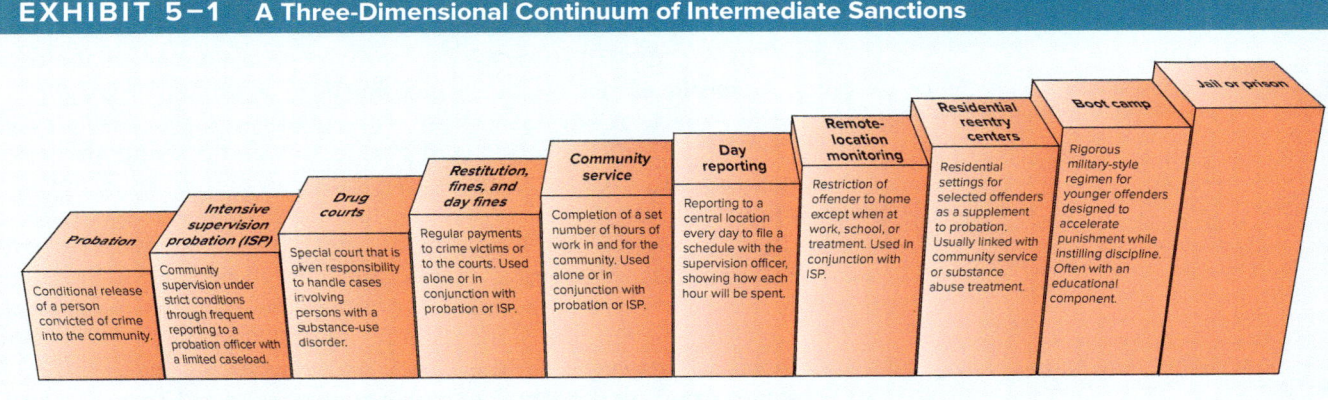

EXHIBIT 5–1 A Three-Dimensional Continuum of Intermediate Sanctions

Intermediate sanctions are sometimes referred to as *alternatives to incarceration.* As you will learn in this chapter, they may be used at initial sentencing, after someone has made progress in compliance and treatment, or as a way to reduce the correctional population. The intermediate sanctions discussed in this chapter form the subfield of community corrections discussed in Chapter 1.

Value of Intermediate Sanctions

For the past two decades, over two million persons each year have been incarcerated in jail and state and federal prisons, placing a heavy economic burden on taxpayers. That burden includes not only the estimated $80 billion a year states pay to build, maintain, and operate prisons and jails, but also the hidden physical, emotional, economic, and social costs on the families and communities left behind. Today, policymakers and politicians are thinking "outside the cell" and turning to evidence-based intermediate sanctions that are less expensive than incarceration and have the same or better outcomes with respect to public safety.

Professional associations too are calling for greater use of intermediate sanctions. The American Jail Association, for example, believes that intermediate sanctions—not prison—should be the backbone of the corrections systems (see Exhibit 5–2). This kind of thinking enables criminal justice officials to sanction persons convicted of crime with intermediate

EXHIBIT 5–2 American Jail Association Resolution

Intermediate Punishments

WHEREAS, the American Jail Association (AJA) recognizes the detrimental impact that crowding places on local jails; and

WHEREAS, many of those who are incarcerated in jails do not pose a known danger to themselves or to society;

THEREFORE BE IT RESOLVED THAT AJA supports the expansion of intermediate punishments in states and localities throughout America for offenders who do not pose a known danger to public safety. AJA believes that intermediate punishments address real concerns of constituents.

Source: Copyright © American Jail Association. Reprinted with permission.

sanctions, thereby teaching them accountability for their actions and heightening their chances for success in the community while reserving expensive prison and jail space for persons who pose a danger to the community. Advocacy of intermediate sanctions by professional organizations such as the American Jail Association, the American Correctional Association, the American Probation and Parole Association, and the International Community Corrections Association can significantly advance career opportunities.

The public's support for intermediate sanctions with treatment over incarceration has also given policymakers and legislators breathing room on moves to reduce the prison population.[2] "When the public is made aware of the possible range of punishments and is given information about how and with whom they are used, they support alternatives to incarceration."[3] Surveys sponsored by the Pew Center on the states found that a majority of registered voters believe that too many people are incarcerated; one-fifth could be released without posing a threat to the community; less expensive alternatives than incarceration yield the same results with respect to public safety; and expanding those alternatives is the best way to reduce the crime rate.

Researchers have also found that the public supports a balanced intermediate approach for persons with mental health issues who commit violent offenses.[4] The belief in a person's redeemability is fairly widespread today, perhaps due to increased interpersonal contact members of the public have with people they know who have committed crimes. Eligibility for the range of treatment and supervision sanctions shown in Exhibit 5–1 has application across many types of offenses and persons awaiting sentencing.

Before proceeding, a word of caution. Research and experience indicate that intermediate sanctions are often given to persons who would have received a less severe sanction prior to the availability of the intermediate sanction. Criminologists refer to this as **net widening,** the risk of new reforms expanding social control over individuals more than the program had originally intended. It's used because it is there—persons are subject to more intrusive sanctions than needed. For example, if someone who would have been fined or sentenced to regular probation is now sentenced to ISP and drug court as a result of the jurisdiction implementing new intermediate sanctions, the net of social control has widened when it was not necessary.

net widening

The risk of new reforms expanding social control over individuals more than the program had originally intended.

Some believe that net widening is an appropriate increase in the severity of punishment. Others argue that net widening increases cost rather than decreasing it by placing persons who would otherwise have received a less expensive sanction (generally, the closer the supervision, the higher the costs) on a more expensive form of supervision.

Perhaps the major concern over net widening is the issue of social control. By using new sanctions to impose more severe penalties on individuals rather than diverting those who do not require a more restrictive sentence, the concern is that the criminal justice system is further expanding its intrusiveness into and control over the lives of members of the community.

Varieties of Intermediate Sanctions

The specific varieties of intermediate sanctions discussed in the following subsections include intensive supervision probation, drug and other accountability courts, fines, community service, day reporting centers, home confinement and remote-location monitoring, residential reentry centers, and correctional boot camps.

Intensive Supervision Probation Probation with frequent contact between the probation officer and the person on probation, strict enforcement of conditions, random drug and alcohol testing, and other requirements is known as **intensive supervision probation (ISP).**

ISP was initially the most popular intermediate sanction. It emerged in the 1960s as an effort to improve rehabilitation by reducing probation and parole caseloads from 100 or more to 30. However, researchers soon discovered that small caseloads led to enhanced supervision and control (and more violations) but not necessarily to enhanced treatment.[5] It wasn't until ISP combined supervision and control with evidence-based treatment components and skill development programs and reinforced clearly identified behaviors that it became effective.[6]

Today, ISP has gained wide popularity. It allows persons to live at home but under more restrictive conditions than those of conventional probation. The primary purpose of ISP is to protect the community, deter the individual from breaking the law or violating the conditions of release, and providing services that match the person's needs and risk.

Requirements of ISP usually include performing community service, attending school or treatment programs, working or looking for employment, meeting with a probation officer (or team of officers) as often as five times a week, and submitting to curfews, employment checks, and tests for drug and alcohol use. Because of the frequency of contact, unannounced drug tests, and rigorous enforcement of restitution, community service, and other conditions, ISP is thought more appropriate for individuals who are high risk.

Today's smartphone is used as a supervision tool across all the varieties of intermediate sanctions discussed in this chapter. With 8 out of 10 U.S. adults having a smartphone, leveraging this new technology for community supervision can be accomplished without great expense.

Text messaging is ideal for giving immediate positive feedback when a client meets curfew or shows up for a counseling session on time. A program in Arkansas sends text messages to clients under community supervision to help reduce missed appointments. Those who received one or two texts the day before the appointment were significantly less likely to cancel or not attend appointments. Sending texts two or more days before the appointment, however, had no effect. The National Institute of Justice's CrimeSolutions.gov rated the program as "Promising."

Instead of traveling to a field office, clients can respond to questions about employment, housing, and other issues at any point between scheduled meetings and give the supervision officer timely information and an opportunity to intervene if necessary. Supervision officers can add appointments and periodic reminders such as a court date or reminder about a scheduled drug test to a person's smartphone. Because smartphones are equipped with GPS or other location-based services, possession of the smartphone can be verified through biometric systems such as voice verification software, and thumbprint and iris scans. Skype and Facebook can also be used to confirm possession of the smartphone. And although not yet widely available, apps to detect alcohol testing and drug monitoring are available from some vendors.

Evidence-based research on ISP has produced two main findings. First, increasing surveillance and control alone does *not* reduce criminal activity.[7] Individuals sentenced to surveillance-oriented ISP programs commit new

CO5-2

intensive supervision probation (ISP)

Supervision in the community under strict conditions, by means of frequent reporting to a probation officer whose caseload is generally limited to 30 persons.

A supervision officer explains court-ordered sanctions to a woman on ISP. Frequent face-to-face contact is a condition of ISP. How can a smartphone help a supervision officer to more efficiently manage their caseload?
Aaron Roeth Photography

crimes at about the same rate as comparable individuals receiving different sentences. Also, technical violation and revocation rates are typically higher for ISP surveillance-oriented programs because more frequent contact makes misconduct more likely to be discovered. Early proponents of surveillance-oriented ISP programs argued that ISP would reduce recidivism rates, offer more rehabilitation, and save money and prison resources. However, most evaluations suggest that the combination of high revocation rates and the cost of processing revocations makes savings unlikely.[8]

On the other hand, scientific analysis of 10 treatment-oriented ISP programs indicates, on average, a significant 22 percent reduction in the recidivism rates of program participants compared with a treatment-as-usual group[9]—what some call "extremely successful."[10] One ISP program that the U.S. Department of Justice says has strong evidence indicating that it achieved its intended outcome is the Reduced Probation Caseload program in Oklahoma City. The results showed that persons on ISP were arrested less often than persons not on ISP. At the maximum 1½-year follow-up, the ISP group had a significantly lower probability of recidivism than those not on ISP with a roughly 30 percent lower recidivism rate.[11] The lesson to be learned is that intensive supervision can be more successful when it is coupled with treatment and paired and customized for an individual's risk and needs using the principles of RNR presented in Chapter 4.

CO5-3

problem-solving courts

Relatively new intermediate sanctions that target serious problems underlying criminal conduct. Also known as *specialty courts, treatment courts and accountability courts*).

drug court

A specialized court to help people who have alcohol and other drug dependency problems. *Also known as* accountability court or problem-solving court.

Problem-Solving Courts **Problem-solving courts (PSC)** (also known as specialty courts, treatment courts, and accountability courts) are relatively new intermediate sanctions that target serious problems underlying criminal conduct. PSC emerged during the rehabilitation and community corrections era of the 1960s when researchers, policy makers, legislatures, and advocacy groups recognized that the traditional criminal court model of adversarial prosecution focused on punishment was not working for persons with addiction, their victims, or communities.

The Miami-Dade Felony **Drug Court** is considered to be the nation's first PSC. Troubled by the devastating impact of drugs and drug-related crime in Dade County, Florida, in 1988, Miami Judge Herbert M. Klein developed the nation's first drug court, a specialized court docket program to help people who have alcohol and other drug dependency problems.

What began as a narcotics docket evolved into a national drug court movement supported by extensive research on "what works." The Bureau of Justice Assistance estimates that almost 4,000 drug courts (also known as recovery courts) are in existence today, about half of which are adult treatment courts serving over 150,000 adults per year.[12] Adult drug court is the largest group of PSCs, representing almost 40 percent of all PSCs.[13]

Drug courts vary across jurisdictions, and no drug court is exactly the same as the next, but there are two general types: deferred prosecution programs and postplea. Deferred prosecution means the prosecutor agrees to withhold charges for a period of time in exchange for the defendant agreeing to fulfill certain conditions. If the conditions are fulfilled, the court may waive, reduce, or dismiss the charge or a combination of these. However, if a participant fails to complete the drug court program, their case is generally processed through the traditional justice system.

Postplea programs require participants to plead guilty to the charges against them and have their sentences deferred or suspended while they are in the program. The sentence will be waived or reduced, and the offense may be expunged from their record if they complete the program. However, the case will be returned to court, and the individuals will face sentencing on their previously entered guilty plea if they fail to satisfy the drug court requirements. The majority (almost 60 percent) of adult drug courts follow a postplea model.

The drug court model inspired the development of other types of problem-solving courts. They share in common a multidisciplinary team approach that combines supervision with treatment and rehabilitation services to reduce relapse and recidivism. The courts are not mutually exclusive. For example, a veterans treatment court may also involve the use of mentors and focus on mental health issues of veterans.[14]

1. DWI Court is dedicated to changing the behavior of persons with alcohol-use disorder arrested for DWI.
2. Family Drug Court targets parental substance abuse in juvenile abuse, neglect, and dependency cases.
3. Felony Domestic Violence Court promotes victim and community safety by increasing the court's monitoring of those who are assessed to be of high risk of lethal domestic violence and placed on felony probation.
4. Gambling Court provides supervision and treatment for those whose offenses were caused by an addiction to gambling.
5. Juvenile Drug Court handles selected delinquency cases and in some instances, children who are identified as having problems with alcohol and/or other drugs.
6. Mental Health Court provides supervision and treatment for individuals with a severe persistent mental illness or intellectual disability where there is some correlation between the offense and their diagnosis.
7. Mentoring Court matches persons on probation (called "mentees") with mentors, provides case management, and requires participants to attend monthly status hearings with a judge.
8. Reentry Court provides treatment and sanction alternatives to address behavior, rehabilitation, and community reentry for persons leaving prison and reentering the community.
9. Tribal Healing to Wellness Court is a component of the tribal justice system that incorporates and adapts a wellness concept to meet the specific substance abuse needs of each tribal community.
10. Veterans Treatment Courts support persons with military service who are in the criminal justice system and have been diagnosed with substance use disorders or mental health issues and other rehabilitation needs. The courts use veterans as mentors to help other veterans engage in treatment and counseling to address their unique needs.

Mariann Avery spent 15 months in a Los Angeles diversion drug court program and graduated with 17 other women and men. The program enables successful participants to earn reduced sentences for their crimes. Superior Court Judge Michael Tynan administers the drug court. Almost 75 percent of those who complete the 18-month program test clean and remain free from arrest 2 years later. "It takes a lot of patience and tough love. I will put people back in jail for tune-ups if they mess up," Tynan says. Drug courts treat, sanction, and reward persons with a substance-use disorder with punishment more restrictive than regular probation but less severe than incarceration. What are the key components of drug court?

Rick Loomis/Contributor/Getty Images

As mentioned earlier, the majority of research on PSCs has focused on drug courts. The key components of drug court first introduced in 1988 by Judge Klein are guideposts that are still in use today.

The 10 key components of drug courts shown in Exhibit 5–3 include such elements as immediate sanctions and incentives, a non-adversarial approach, an ongoing schedule of judicial status hearings, frequent drug testing, immediate access to a continuum of substance abuse treatment services, and a partnership between drug courts, public agencies, and

---

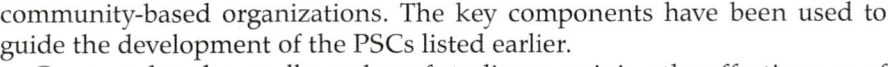

EXHIBIT 5–3   Ten Key Components of Drug Courts

1. Drug courts integrate alcohol and other drug treatment services with justice system case processing.

2. Using a nonadversarial approach, prosecution and defense counsel promote public safety while protecting participants' due process rights.

3. Eligible participants are identified early and promptly placed in the drug court program.

4. Drug courts provide access to a continuum of alcohol, drug, and other related treatment and rehabilitation services.

5. Abstinence is monitored by frequent alcohol and other drug testing.

6. A coordinated strategy governs drug court responses to participants' compliance.

7. Ongoing judicial interaction with each drug court participant is essential.

8. Monitoring and evaluation measure the achievement of program goals and gauge effectiveness.

9. Continuing interdisciplinary education promotes effective drug court planning, implementation, and operations.

10. Forging partnerships among drug courts, public agencies, and community-based organizations generates local support and enhances drug court program effectiveness.

Source: National Association of Drug Court Professionals.

community-based organizations. The key components have been used to guide the development of the PSCs listed earlier.

Compared to the small number of studies examining the effectiveness of other intermediate sanctions on reducing criminal activity, a large body of research has examined the effectiveness of drug courts and concluded that drug courts lead to significant reductions in "serious" drug use and recidivism. Two major studies shed light on PSC outcomes.

The National Institute of Justice conducted an unprecedented five-year longitudinal evaluation of 2,000 adults in 23 drug courts and 6 comparison courts in eight states (FL, GA, IL, NY, PA, NC, SC, and WA).[15] The Institute found (1) drug courts produce significant reductions in drug use than non-drug courts (56 vs. 76 percent); (2) drug court participants are less likely to test positive for drug use (29 vs. 47 percent); (3) drug courts produce significant reductions in criminal activity (40 vs. 53 percent); and (4) drug court participants are arrested less often (52 vs. 62 percent).

At the federal level, researchers examined the records of almost 14,000 federal defendants who participated in a specialty court within one of seven federal districts.[16] Individuals who successfully completed their programs were (1) less likely to be arrested for a new offense; (2) employed a greater percentage of the days; (3) tested positive less often; (4) had their cases dismissed; and (5) were less likely to receive a prison sentence or if they did, the sentences were significantly shorter than the matched comparison group.

Drug courts are also cost-effective. Evaluations of drug courts nationwide find that they save taxpayers' money compared to probation and/or incarceration. The NIJ five-year evaluation of drug court referenced earlier estimated a savings of $2.21 for every dollar spent on drug court. Drug courts save money through improved outcomes, primarily savings to victims from significantly fewer crimes, rearrests, and days incarcerated.[17]

Despite the successes of drug courts, they remain available to less than 10 percent of persons with substance-use disorders. Although every state has at least one drug court, only a handful of states—like New Jersey and

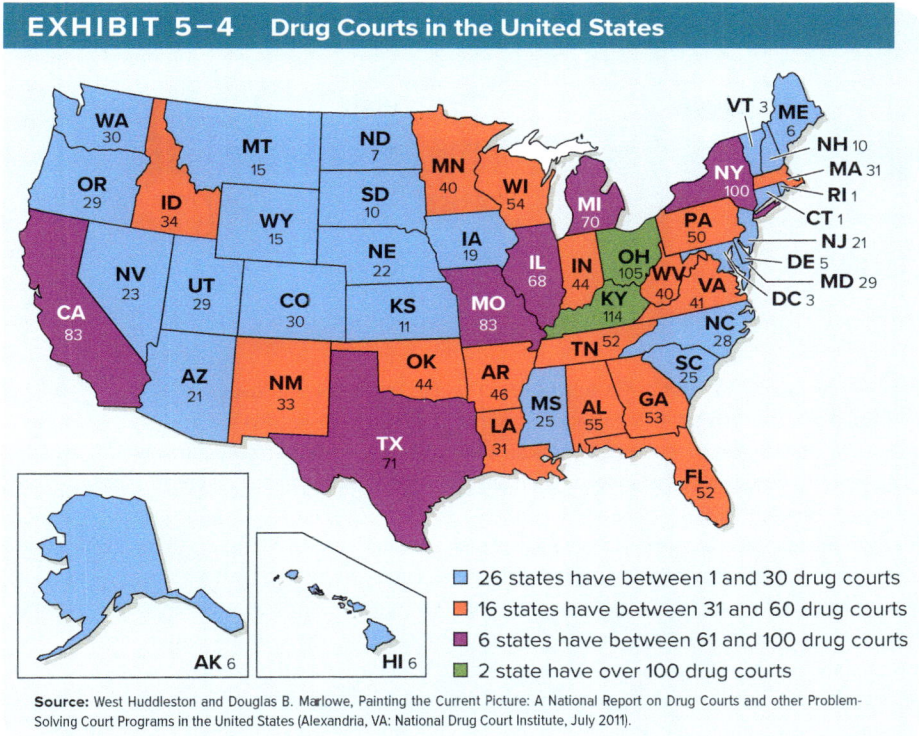

EXHIBIT 5-4   **Drug Courts in the United States**

- ☐ 26 states have between 1 and 30 drug courts
- ☐ 16 states have between 31 and 60 drug courts
- ☐ 6 states have between 61 and 100 drug courts
- ☐ 2 state have over 100 drug courts

Source: West Huddleston and Douglas B. Marlowe, *Painting the Current Picture: A National Report on Drug Courts and other Problem-Solving Court Programs in the United States* (Alexandria, VA: National Drug Court Institute, July 2011).

New York—have one in every county.[18] Approximate numbers of drug courts in each state is shown in Exhibit 5–4.

fine

A financial penalty used as a criminal sanction.

CO5-4

Fines   A **fine** is a financial sanction requiring someone who has been convicted to pay a specified sum of money. The fine is one of the oldest forms of punishment. It is, in practice, the criminal justice tool for punishing minor misdemeanors, traffic offenses, ordinance violations, and corporations. In the United States, fines are rarely regarded as a tough criminal sanction. They are not taken seriously for at least four reasons. First, judicial, legislative, and prosecutorial attitudes restrict the use of fines to traffic offenses, minor misdemeanors, and ordinance violations. Second, a judge seldom has enough reliable information on a person's personal wealth to impose a just fine. Third, mechanisms for collecting fines are often ineffective. Far too often, the responsibility for collecting fines has been left to probation officers, who are already overburdened and have no interest in fine collection. As a result, fines are seldom paid. Over 300,000 people owe the federal government almost $136 billion in criminal debt, nearly 90 percent of which the federal government categorizes as uncollectible due to the individuals'

Most courts accept credit and debit cards for payment of fixed and structured fines. How can technology improve the rate at which persons under community supervision pay their fines?

Kilito Chan/Moment/Getty Image

RELIABLE RESEARCH. REAL RESULTS.

Enter your keyword(s)   🔍   Search Site   Advanced Search

Home | Help | Contact Us | Site Map | Glossary

EVIDENCE-BASED CORRECTIONS

Gender-Specific Drug Treatment Court

The goal of the gender-specific drug treatment court program is to meet the unique needs of women in the criminal justice system and reduce their risk of recidivism The gender-specific drug treatment court program began in 2007 to address the growing number of women becoming involved in the criminal justice system and provide treatment services to women on probation to reduce their risk of reoffending. The program gives preference to women who have higher need and risk profiles, are mothers, and have substance use problems.

Women are referred to the gender-specific drug treatment court program as a condition of their sentence or as an alternative to revocation while on probation. The drug treatment court operates in phases similar to a traditional mixed-gender drug court. The women typically move through four phases. Phase 1 consists of court case managers and the female participant together developing a case plan based on assessment information and the needs of the participant. Phase 2 involves the participant undergoing treatment services and programming, based on her specific needs. Phase 3 involves a decrease in the frequency of services, if the participant is progressing in treatment. The fourth and final phase focuses on continuing care under court supervision. The participant may continue to participate in programming and receive support from alumnae meetings. The average completion time for all four phases of the drug treatment court program is about 15 months.

Researchers found that women in the treatment group were statistically significantly less likely to have a new conviction, compared with similar women on probation who did not participate in the program, at the 2-year follow-up.

Gender-Specific Drug Treatment Court is rated *Promising*.

Source: Adapted from Bureau of Justice Statistics

---

day fine

A financial penalty scaled both to the person's income and to the seriousness of the crime.

Day Fines

What are day fines, and how do they adjust for economic inequality?

limited financial resources.[19] But when persons are informed on a regular basis showing what they owe and paid to date, they pay more, and they pay more often than those not so notified. Earlier we mentioned the program in Arkansas that sends text messages to clients under community supervision to help reduce missed appointments. The National Institute of Justice's CrimeSolutions.gov rated the program "Promising" because it reduced no-shows by 43 percent. Text messages are an efficient way to remind persons under community supervision of their financial obligations. The fourth reason the use of fines is not widely used in the U.S. as a criminal sanction is because many have argued that fines inflict a hardship on the poor while affluent people feel no sting.

Outside the United States, however, day fines are popular. A **day fine** is a financial penalty based on the seriousness of the offense and the defendant's income. Day fines, also called *structured fines,* were introduced in Sweden in the 1920s and were quickly incorporated into the penal codes of other European countries and used as the primary sanction for low-level and misdemeanant offenses, including speeding.[20]

Under the day fine system, the world's most expensive speeding ticket was issued in Switzerland to a 37-year Swedish citizen who had just taken delivery of his brand new $240,000 Mercedes SLS AMG and was driving home.[21] Police clocked his speed at over 180 mph. His excuse was that the speedometer was faulty. Under Swiss law there is no cap on fines for speeding. Based on his annual income and severity of the speed, authorities set the number of day fine units at 300 and his daily income at $3,600, making the

EXHIBIT 5–5	Example of a Day Fine Unit Scale

Staten Island Day Fine Unit Scale (Selected Offense Categories)

Penal Law Charge*	Type of Offense**	Number of Day Fine Units		
		Discount	PRESUMPTIVE	Premium
120.00 AM	Assault 3: Range of 20–95 DF			
	A. Substantial Injury	81	**95**	109
	Stranger-to-stranger; or where victim is known to assailant, he/she is weaker, vulnerable			
	B. Minor Injury	59	**70**	81
	Stranger-to-stranger; or where victim is known to assailant, he/she is weaker, vulnerable; or altercations involving use of a weapon			
	C. Substantial Injury	38	**45**	52
	Altercations among acquaintances; brawls			
	D. Minor Injury	17	**20**	23
	Altercations among acquaintances; brawls			
110/120.00 BM	Attempted Assault 3: Range of 15–45 DF			
	A. Substantial Injury	38	**45**	52
	Stranger-to-stranger; or where victim is known to assailant, he/she is weaker, vulnerable			
	B. Minor Injury	30	**35**	40
	Stranger-to-stranger; or where victim is known to assailant, he/she is weaker, vulnerable; or altercations involving use of a weapon			
	C. Substantial Injury	17	**20**	23
	Altercations among acquaintances; brawls			
	D. Minor Injury	13	**15**	17
	Altercations among acquaintances; brawls			

* AM = Class A misdemeanor; BM = Class B misdemeanor.
** DF = Day fines.
Source: Bureau of Justice Assistance.

total fine $1,080,000.00 (300 fine units × $3,600 daily income—calculating day fines is discussed below and shown in Exhibits 5–5 and 5–6).

A day fine system has two parts: (1) an offense units scale that ranks offenses by severity and (2) a valuation scale for determining the dollar amount per unit.

The first step in setting a day fine is to determine the number of fine units to be imposed. A portion of the unit scale used in a Staten Island, New York, day fine experiment is shown in Exhibit 5–5. The number of offense units ranges from a low of 5 to a high of 120 for the most serious misdemeanors handled by the court. For example, the presumptive number of units for the offense of assault with minor injury and aggravating factors is 70; the range is from 59 to 81 units. The presumptive number is the starting point. Negotiation and consideration of individual circumstances may raise or lower the number. There is no magic in the unit scale established. The unit scale will vary from place to place. For example, in Sweden, the range is from 1 to 120 units. In Germany the range is 1 to 360 units. What is important is to establish a scale broad enough to cover the full range of offenses handled by the courts that will use structured fines.

Once the unit scale is established, the second step is to create a valuation table. The purpose of the valuation table is to establish the dollar amount of each fine. A portion of the valuation table used in the Staten Island

EXHIBIT 5–6   Example of a Day Fine Valuation Table

Staten Island, New York, Valuation Table Dollar Value of One Day Fine Unit, by Net Daily Income and Number of Dependents

Net Daily Income ($)	Number of Dependents (Including Self)							
	1	2	3	4	5	6	7	8
3		1.05	0.83	0.68	0.53	0.45	0.37	0.30
4	1.70	1.40	1.10	0.90	0.70	0.60	0.50	0.40
5	2.13	1.75	1.38	1.13	0.88	0.75	0.62	0.50
6	2.55	2.10	1.65	1.35	1.05	0.90	0.75	0.60
7	2.98	2.45	1.93	1.58	1.23	1.05	0.87	0.70
8	3.40	2.80	2.20	1.80	1.40	1.20	1.00	0.80
9	3.83	3.15	2.48	2.03	1.58	1.35	1.12	0.90
10	4.25	3.50	2.75	2.25	1.75	1.50	1.25	1.00
11	4.68	3.85	3.03	2.47	1.93	1.65	1.37	1.10
12	5.10	4.20	3.30	2.70	2.10	1.80	1.50	1.20
13	5.53	4.55	3.58	2.93	2.28	1.95	1.62	1.30
14	7.85	4.90	3.85	3.15	2.45	2.10	1.75	1.40
15	8.42	5.25	4.13	3.38	2.63	2.25	1.87	1.50

Source: Bureau of Justice Assistance.

experiment is shown in Exhibit 5–6. Net daily incomes run down the left side, and numbers of dependents run across the top. Net daily income is the person's income (minus fixed expenses for family and housing obligations) divided by the number of days in a payment period. Staten Island planners also adjusted the net daily income downward to account for subsistence needs, family responsibilities, and incomes below the poverty line.

Suppose a defendant convicted of assault, with minor injury and aggravating factors, has a net daily income of $15 and supports four people, including herself. Find the row for her net daily income. Move across the row to the column for the number of dependents. The figure there is the value of one structured fine unit for that defendant. Multiply the number of fine units to be imposed (70) by the value of a single fine unit (3.38). The product, $236.60, is the amount of the day fine to be imposed.

Even though day fines have been tried experimentally in some areas of the United States including Arizona, Connecticut, Iowa, New York, Oregon, and Wisconsin, there has been little evidence-based research on the effectiveness of fines in reducing recidivism rates. The Washington State Institute for Public Policy wrote that day fine programs need additional research and development before we can conclude that they do or do not work.[22] However, because the use of fines could reduce the costs of courts and corrections and because day fines address problems of inequality, fines are a promising intermediate sanction. At present, most Western justice systems, except the United States, rely heavily on financial penalties. In the 21st century, U.S. jurisdictions are likely to continue their experiments with monetary penalties and to assign them greater importance. Exhibit 5–7 outlines the pros and cons of day fines. Which arguments do you see as the most compelling?

community service   CO5-5

A sentence to serve a specified number of hours working in unpaid positions with nonprofit or tax-supported agencies. Also known as fine of time.

Community Service   **Community service** is a sentence to serve a specified number of hours working in unpaid positions with nonprofit or tax-supported agencies. Community service is punishment that takes away a person's time and energy and is sometimes called a *fine of time*.

EXHIBIT 5−7   Pros and Cons of Day Fines

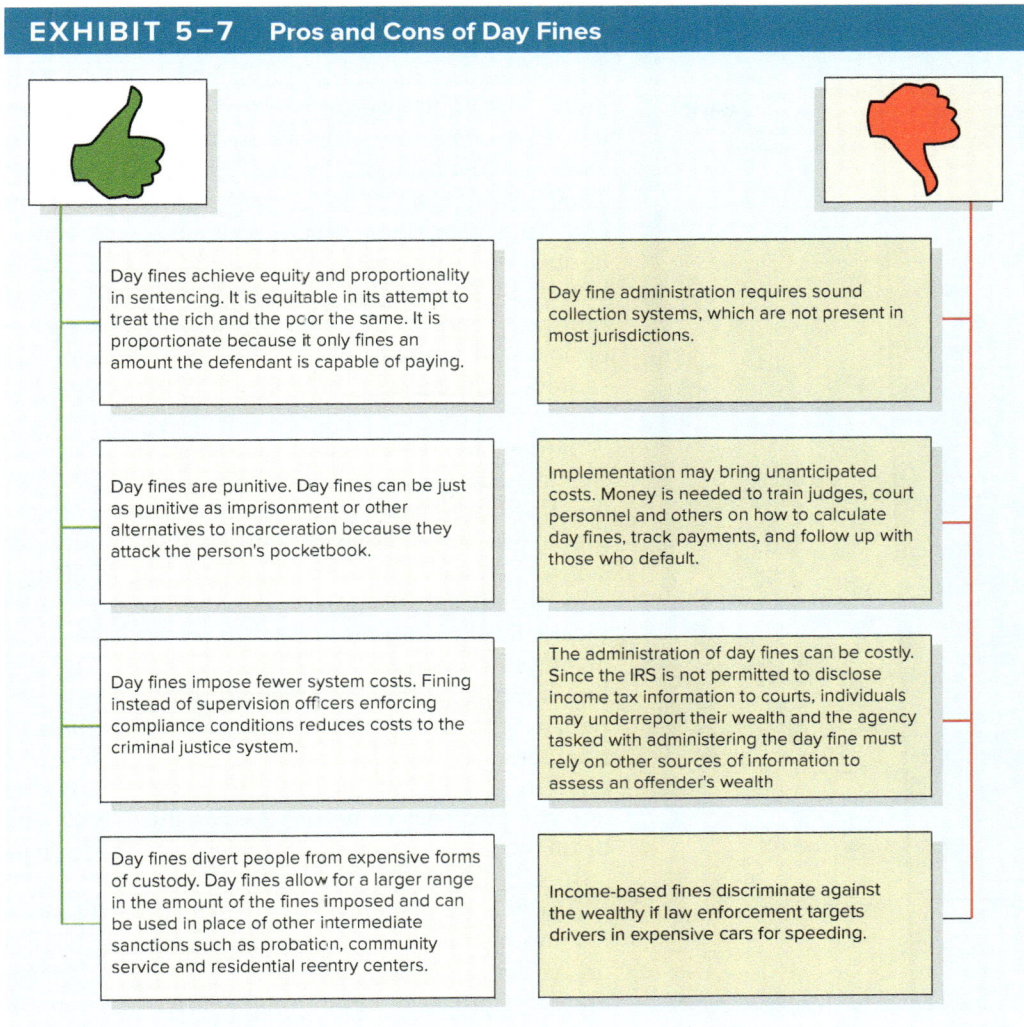

Day fines achieve equity and proportionality in sentencing. It is equitable in its attempt to treat the rich and the poor the same. It is proportionate because it only fines an amount the defendant is capable of paying.

Day fine administration requires sound collection systems, which are not present in most jurisdictions.

Day fines are punitive. Day fines can be just as punitive as imprisonment or other alternatives to incarceration because they attack the person's pocketbook.

Implementation may bring unanticipated costs. Money is needed to train judges, court personnel and others on how to calculate day fines, track payments, and follow up with those who default.

Day fines impose fewer system costs. Fining instead of supervision officers enforcing compliance conditions reduces costs to the criminal justice system.

The administration of day fines can be costly. Since the IRS is not permitted to disclose income tax information to courts, individuals may underreport their wealth and the agency tasked with administering the day fine must rely on other sources of information to assess an offender's wealth

Day fines divert people from expensive forms of custody. Day fines allow for a larger range in the amount of the fines imposed and can be used in place of other intermediate sanctions such as probation, community service and residential reentry centers.

Income-based fines discriminate against the wealthy if law enforcement targets drivers in expensive cars for speeding.

Community service as a criminal sanction began in the United States in 1966 in Alameda County, California. Municipal judges there devised a community service sentencing program for women who violated traffic and parking laws. Too poor to pay fines, these women were likely to be sentenced to jail. But putting them behind bars imposed a hardship on their families. Community service orders (CSOs) increased sentencing options, punished the individuals, lightened the suffering of innocent families, avoided the cost of imprisonment, and provided valuable services to the community. As Alameda judges gained experience with the new sentencing option, they broadened the program to include adults, juveniles, and persons convicted of crimes more serious than traffic or parking violations.

The Alameda County community service program received international attention. England and Wales developed pilot projects in the 1970s, using community service as a midlevel sanction between probation and prison and as an alternative to prison sentences up to six months. By 1975, community service had become a central feature of English sentencing. The approach swept throughout Europe, Australia, New Zealand, and Canada.

Vitalii Sediuk was convicted of misdemeanor battery and pled no contest. He was sentenced to 36 months of probation; fined $220; ordered to stay 500 yards away from red carpets, Hollywood premiers, and award shows; and given 20 days of community service cleaning up Griffin Park in Los Angeles for punching Brad Pitt as the actor signed autographs for his fans. At the time of the Pitt attack, Sediuk was already on probation for crashing the stage at the Grammy Awards as Adele was presented with an award by Jennifer Lopez and Pitbull. What do you think? Is community service "fluff," or can it be fashioned as a serious criminal sanction?
David Buchan/Getty Images

day reporting center (DRC)

A nonresidential facility to which a person under correctional supervision reports every day or several days a week for supervision and programming.

Community service can be an intermediate sanction by itself or be used with other penalties and requirements, including substance abuse treatment, restitution, or probation. Individuals sentenced to community service are usually assigned to work for government or private nonprofit agencies. They restore historic buildings; maintain parks and construct campsites; clean roadways and county fairgrounds; remove snow from around public buildings; perform land and river reclamation; and renovate schools and nursing homes. The service options are limited only by the imagination of the sentencing judge and the availability of personnel to ensure that the sentence is completed.

States like Washington, Georgia, and Texas are making extensive use of community service. At least one-third of persons convicted of a felony in Washington receive sentences that include community service. Washington State sentencing guidelines also permit substitution of community service for incarceration at a rate of 8 hours of work for 1 day of incarceration, with a limit of 30 days. Washington State also is breaking new ground in sentencing reform with the idea of *interchangeable sentences* for nonviolent or not very violent crimes against strangers. The actual sentence depends on the individual and the purposes to be served. For those with little or no income, community service may substitute for a fine.

There is no evidence-based corrections literature examining the effectiveness of community service on reducing criminal activity. What we find instead are descriptions of community service programs in use across the United States. Before it can be concluded that community service does or does not reduce criminal activity, strong research designs are needed. Until then, the jury is still out on community service.

Day Reporting Centers One particular intermediate sanction that has gained notable attention over the past two decades is the day reporting center. **Day reporting centers (DRCs)** are nonresidential facilities that require persons on probation or parole to report to a physical location on a regular basis to participate in various rehabilitation-related activities. DRCs were first introduced in Great Britain in the late 1960s. The first DRC in the United States was established by the Hampden County Sheriff's Department in Springfield, Massachusetts, in 1986. Ten years later, a National Institute of Justice survey identified 114 DRCs in 22 states.[23]

DRCs have three primary goals: (1) enhance supervision and surveillance, (2) provide treatment directly or through collaboration with community treatment programs, and (3) reduce jail and prison crowding.

DRCs differ in their implementation and the justice-involved populations they serve. Some serve persons with severe mental illness.[24] Others serve

Courtesy of Tim Czaja

Timothy Czaja

Director of Berkeley County Community Corrections
Martinsburg, WV

Tim Czaja has been serving as the Director of Berkley County Community Corrections since August of 2016. His responsibilities include the oversight of the Berkeley County Day Report Center, the Berkeley County Home Confinement Office, and the Berkeley County Recovery Resource Center. These are alternative sentencing programs for persons whose legal issues are a direct result of substance abuse. Each of these programs has grown significantly in Berkeley County and has resulted in millions of dollars being saved by decreasing the jail bill.

Tim entered into the field of addictions treatment after overcoming demons in his own life. He struggled with heroin addiction as a young man and was in and out of treatment programs for about 7 years. At age 24, he entered a long-term faith-based treatment program called Teen Challenge. This is where his life changed for good. "I know first-hand that true freedom from addiction is possible," Czaja said. He attributes his freedom from addiction to his relationship with Christ. He went on to earn a Bachelor's Degree in Psychology from the University of Valley Forge. He worked as a Treatment Specialist in Dauphin County Prison in Harrisburg, PA for 8 years. This is where most of his experience in corrections came from. He facilitated a Therapeutic Community for Violent Offenders in the prison called MENDS, Men Establishing New Directions. The large majority of these men all had their own substance abuse problems and Czaja gained great experience working with these men during this period of time.

Czaja's own experience with the hopelessness of addiction and his recovery journey are what drives him to continue to grow these Community Corrections programs in his hometown of Martinsburg, WV. "I've worked with countless individuals over the years whose lives are enslaved to addiction. Not one of them likes their condition. They desperately want to be free, they just don't know how to get there. Our programs provide them an opportunity to learn to live a lifestyle of recovery and to be reunited with their true selves, and their families. It is extremely rewarding work."

> *I know first-hand that true freedom from addiction is possible.*

persons who violate parole.[25] Some are faith-based.[26] Most, like the adjacent photo of the Berkeley DRC in Martinsburg, West Virginia, are public.[27]

In most DRCs clients are required to pass through phases. Phase I, "intensive supervision," requires participants to check in seven days a week and to take a drug test once a week. Phase II, "intermediate supervision," requires participants to check in five days a week and to take a drug test twice per month. Phase III, "regular supervision," requires participants to check in three days a week and to take a drug test once per month. The aftercare phase requires participants to check in once a month with no drug testing requirements. All participants are given a breathalyzer test each time they report to the DRC.

DRCs typically offer numerous services to address a client's needs, and they strictly supervise clients in a setting that is more secure than probation but less inhibiting than incarceration. DRCs commonly require clients to obey a curfew, perform community service, and undergo routine drug testing. They differ from other intermediate sanctions by a marked

A peer recovery support group meets at the Berkeley County Day Report Center in Martinsburg, West Virginia. Peer recovery support as the word "peer" implies is designed and delivered by people who have experienced both substance use disorder and recovery. Because they are designed and delivered by peers who have been successful in the recovery process, they embody a powerful message of hope, as well as a wealth of experiential knowledge. The group meeting is facilitated by a trained peer support specialist, to talk with one another about their experiences, struggles, and challenges. The support group becomes an anchor as persons recover from their illnesses and develop skills to live more effectively in their communities. What do we know about DRCs' effectiveness in reducing recidivism?
Timothy Czaja

concentration on rehabilitation. Staff assess client needs and either provide in-house programming and treatment for substance abuse, education, vocational training, and mental health treatment or contract with community providers. DRCs have an aura of rigor that appeals to those wanting punishment and control of persons who commit crime, and it appeals to those advocating more access to treatment. While DRCs may differ in the type of individuals they serve and whether they are publicly or privately operated, they all have three common threads: frequent reporting, available programming, and accountability.

Compared to some of the other intermediate sanctions, there is limited research on the effectiveness of DRCs. Furthermore, depending on what question is asked, the results are mixed.

A recent posting on CrimeSolutions.gov that merged the findings of several well-controlled treatment studies to calculate an overall outcome of recidivism found that DRCs do not differ from other traditional supervision options in terms of a reduction in recidivism.[28]

However, when questions are asked about whether DRCs are effective with special populations, e.g., persons with a mental illness, there is strong evidence that participants with a diagnosed mental illness who successfully complete a DRC program are 40 percent less likely to be reconvicted after discharge.[29] Researchers hypothesized that a reduction in their criminogenic needs during the course of treatment had a significant effect on their post-discharge behavior.

Today, we find only one evaluation of a DRC that CrimeSolutions.gov rated as "Promising." The Community Reporting Engagement Support and Training (CREST) Center in New Haven, Connecticut, is a DRC that serves persons on probation with severe mental illness. Participants were 40 percent less likely to be reconvicted after discharge from the program but not after program admission. That difference highlights the importance that remaining in treatment has on resolving an individual's criminogenic risk factors and improving program outcomes. While "Promising," research replications are required before CrimeSolutions.gov elevates the program to a "policy" level and rates it as "Effective." What we know about the effectiveness of DRCs today is this: The jury is still out.

Home Confinement and Remote-Location Monitoring Technologies that probation and parole officers use to monitor remotely the physical location of a person under community supervision is known as **remote-location monitoring.** Remote-location monitoring is used in the pretrial stage as a condition of release through the courts or a bail bond agreement as the individual awaits their trial. It is also imposed at sentencing as a condition of probation, or after release from jail or prison as a condition of parole or community monitoring.

There is no exact accounting on the number of persons under remote-location, but almost ten years ago the PEW Charitable Trusts estimated that more than 125,000 people were under remote-location monitoring. Since then this number is believed to have increased to over 150,000, especially during the COVID-19 pandemic when more people were placed on monitors to decrease jail and prison populations.

In theory, remote-location monitoring satisfies three correctional goals. First, it incapacitates the person by restricting them to a single location. Second, remote-location monitoring is punitive because it forces the person to stay home when not at work, school, counseling, or community service. And third, it contributes to rehabilitation by allowing the individual to remain with their family and continue employment, education, or vocational training.

Remote-location monitoring uses technological systems such as EM, global positioning systems (GPSs), voice verification, and other tracking systems to verify a person's physical location, either periodically or continuously, 24 hours a day. Common electronic monitoring devices and their uses are shown in Exhibit 5–8.

The advantages and disadvantages of electronic monitoring are shown in Exhibit 5–9. One of the major arguments against electronic monitoring is cost. We pointed out in Chapter 4 that incarceration costs anywhere between $30,000 and $70,000 a year depending upon the level of security. In contrast, the cost of electronic monitoring devices is between $1,000 and $14,000 a year depending upon the person's offense, risk level, and the type of device. Even though the cost of electronic monitoring is cheaper than incarceration, the cost is shouldered by people who are least positioned to pay.[30] Opponents argue that some of the devices can be so expensive that some people must choose between paying rent or their electronic monitoring fees, raising significant problems for people who have to wear the device for years.

In response to criticism that the individual must pay for their monitoring, California and Oregon passed legislation prohibiting local governments from charging EM fees. Although private monitoring companies in both states can still charge participants EM fees.

Across the United States, we find that six states (HI, NH, NM, NY, OR, and VT) and the District of Columbia removed authorizing language in state codes but did not prohibit it. The rest (43 states) have statutes authorizing fees for EM for pretrial or post-sentencing. Twenty-nine states authorize electronic monitoring fees for both pretrial and post-sentencing. A sample of the states authorizing fees for EM is shown in Exhibit 5–10.

It is relatively easy to find reports claiming that home confinement with remote-location monitoring is effective. For example, the federal Bureau of Prisons tracked 11,000 persons who were released from federal prison during COVID-19 and placed on home confinement with electronic monitoring. Each person was required to wear an ankle monitor with GPS tracking, stay home except when given permission to leave for things such as work or doctor's appointments, and remain drug- and crime-free. According to the

CO5-7

remote-location monitoring

Technologies, including global positioning system (GPS) devices and electronic monitoring (EM), that probation and parole officers use to monitor remotely the physical location of a person under correctional supervision.

EXHIBIT 5–8 Common Electronic Monitoring Devices

Some of the common electronic monitoring devices and their uses.

Guy Corbishley/Alamy Stock Photo

Secure Continuous Remote Alcohol Monitoring (SCRAM) Monitors — Tests the wearer's sweat for alcohol content

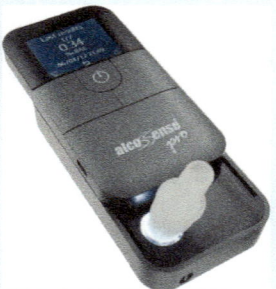

Hugh Threlfall/Alamy Stock Photo

Breathalyzer Monitors — Test a person while at home for alcohol content

PA Images/Alamy Stock Photo

Ignition Interlocks — A device installed in a vehicle that prevents the engine from starting if it detects alcohol.

Ilene MacDonald/Alamy Stock Photo

Global Positioning System — Monitors that transmit specific geographical coordinates of the wearer on a continuous basis, enabling round-the-clock location monitoring.

Rolf Vennenbernd/dpa picture alliance/ Alamy Stock Photo

Radio Frequency — Monitors which inform the monitoring organization about the general whereabouts of the wearer in relation to a home base unit. RF is similar to an invisible fence in that it alerts the monitoring agency when a person isn't at the location but does not indicate where the person may be.

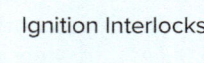

EXHIBIT 5-9   **Pros and Cons of Electronic Monitoring**

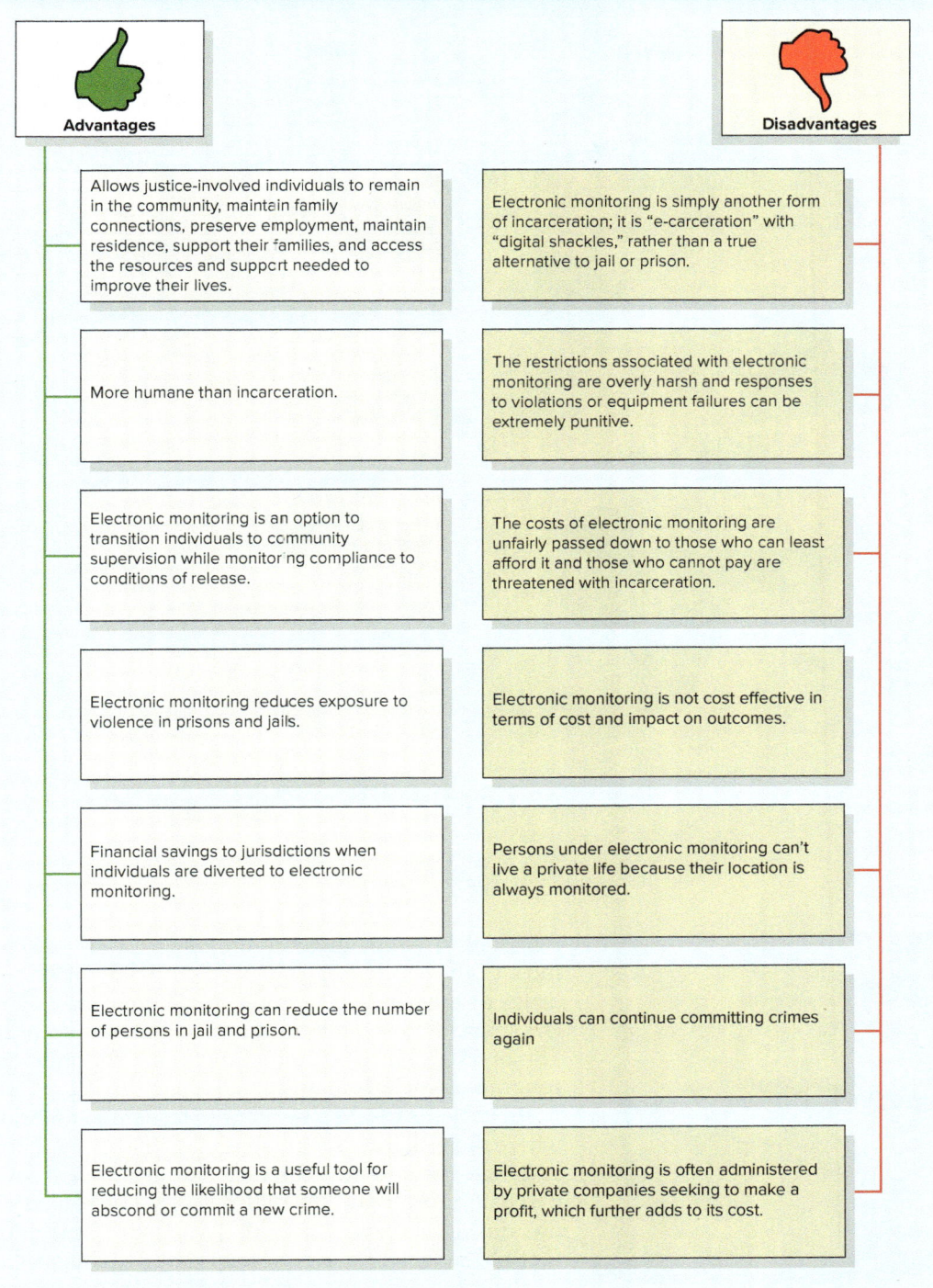

Advantages	Disadvantages
Allows justice-involved individuals to remain in the community, maintain family connections, preserve employment, maintain residence, support their families, and access the resources and support needed to improve their lives.	Electronic monitoring is simply another form of incarceration; it is "e-carceration" with "digital shackles," rather than a true alternative to jail or prison.
More humane than incarceration.	The restrictions associated with electronic monitoring are overly harsh and responses to violations or equipment failures can be extremely punitive.
Electronic monitoring is an option to transition individuals to community supervision while monitoring compliance to conditions of release.	The costs of electronic monitoring are unfairly passed down to those who can least afford it and those who cannot pay are threatened with incarceration.
Electronic monitoring reduces exposure to violence in prisons and jails.	Electronic monitoring is not cost effective in terms of cost and impact on outcomes.
Financial savings to jurisdictions when individuals are diverted to electronic monitoring.	Persons under electronic monitoring can't live a private life because their location is always monitored.
Electronic monitoring can reduce the number of persons in jail and prison.	Individuals can continue committing crimes again
Electronic monitoring is a useful tool for reducing the likelihood that someone will abscond or commit a new crime.	Electronic monitoring is often administered by private companies seeking to make a profit, which further adds to its cost.

EXHIBIT 5–10   Pretrial and Post-sentencing Electronic Monitoring Fees

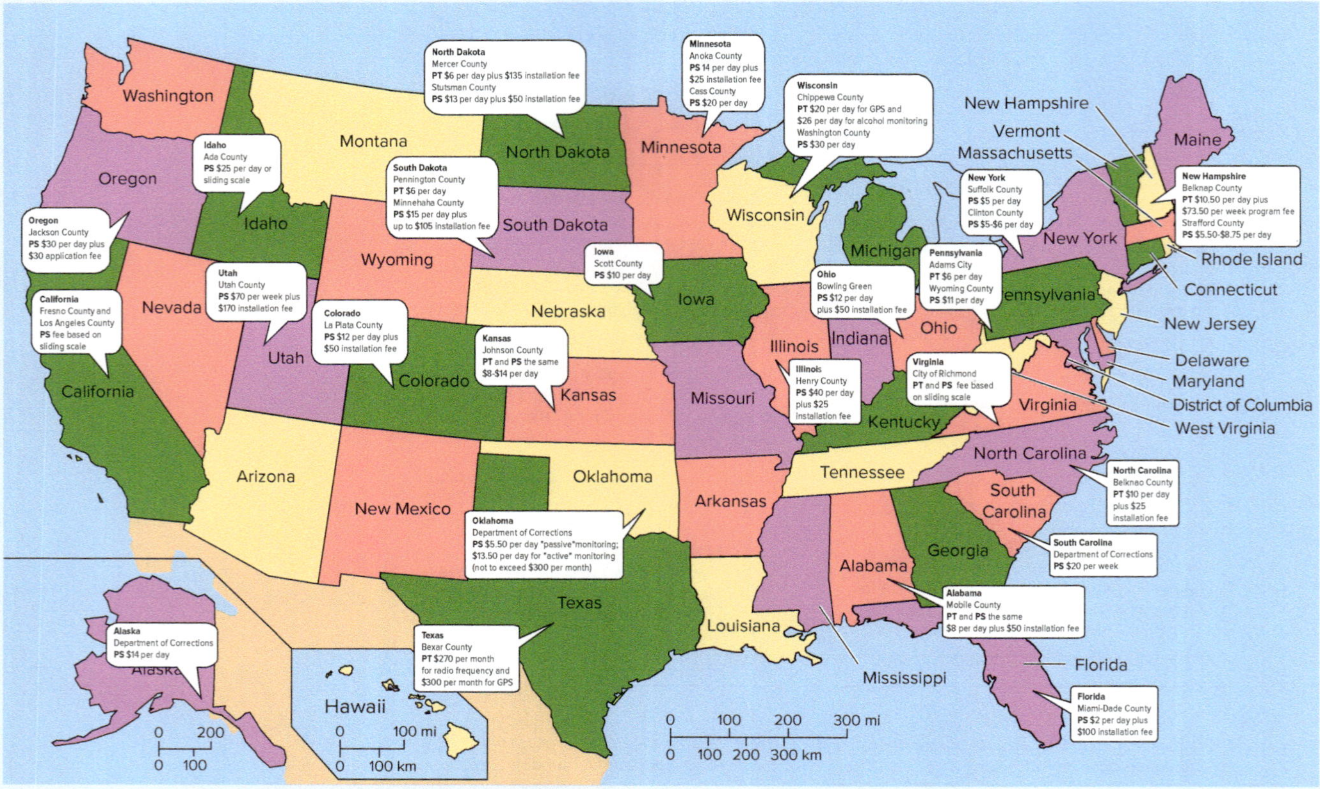

North Dakota
Mercer County
PT $6 per day plus $135 installation fee
Stutsman County
PS $13 per day plus $50 installation fee

Minnesota
Anoka County
PS 14 per day plus $25 installation fee
Cass County
PS $20 per day

Wisconsin
Chippewa County
PT $20 per day for GPS and $26 per day for alcohol monitoring
Washington County
PS $30 per day

Idaho
Ada County
PS $25 per day or sliding scale

South Dakota
Pennington County
PT $6 per day
Minnehaha County
PS $15 per day plus up to $105 installation fee

New York
Suffolk County
PS $5 per day
Clinton County
PS $5–$6 per day

New Hampshire
Belknap County
PT $10.50 per day plus $73.50 per week program fee
Strafford County
PS $5.50–$8.75 per day

Oregon
Jackson County
PS $30 per day plus $30 application fee

Iowa
Scott County
PS $10 per day

Pennsylvania
Adams City
PT $6 per day
Wyoming County
PS $11 per day

Ohio
Bowling Green
PS $12 per day plus $50 installation fee

California
Fresno County and Los Angeles County
PS fee based on sliding scale

Utah
Utah County
PS $70 per week plus $170 installation fee

Colorado
La Plata County
PS $12 per day plus $50 installation fee

Kansas
Johnson County
PT and **PS** the same $8–$14 per day

Illinois
Henry County
PS $40 per day plus $25 installation fee

Virginia
City of Richmond
PT and **PS** fee based on sliding scale

Oklahoma
Department of Corrections
PS $5.50 per day "passive" monitoring; $13.50 per day for "active" monitoring (not to exceed $300 per month)

North Carolina
Belknap County
PT $10 per day plus $25 installation fee

South Carolina
Department of Corrections
PS $20 per week

Alabama
Mobile County
PT and **PS** the same $8 per day plus $50 installation fee

Alaska
Department of Corrections
PS $14 per day

Texas
Bexar County
PT $270 per month for radio frequency and $300 per month for GPS

Florida
Miami-Dade County
PS $2 per day plus $100 installation fee

PT - Electronic monitoring fee imposed at the pretrial stage
PS - Electronic monitoring fee imposed at the post-sentencing stage

Source: Adapted from Fines and Fees Justice Center, Electronic Monitoring Fee: A 50-State Survey of the Costs Assessed to People on E-Supervision, https://finesandfeesjusticecenter.org.

A probation officer sets up an exclusion zone in red for a person who is territory-restricted. What are the pros and cons of remote location monitoring as a probationary strategy?
picture alliance/Contributor/Getty Images

BOP, only 17 individuals committed new crimes and most of those offenses were for possessing or selling drugs or other minor offenses. Only one was violent (an aggravated assault), and none were sex offenses. The BOP has since expanded the home confinement program to include almost 50,000 persons.[31]

Proponents of EM also point to research in Florida where more than 5,000 persons classified as medium- and high-risk and monitored electronically were compared to more than 266,000 persons not placed on EM during a six-year period. The report concluded that EM reduced the risk of failure by 31 percent.[32]

However, when we examine the body of literature on remote-location monitoring more closely, we find two things. First, the methods used in these studies do not meet the threshold of scientific rigor. Very few employ the gold standard of research—randomly assign subjects to remote-location monitoring programs (the experimental group) and others to programs-as-usual (the control group). And even if randomization is employed, most studies do not focus on the different kinds of remote-location monitoring, meaning which type of monitoring was used, how did it operate, how reliable was the equipment (down time, location failures, errors, tampering), and ways in which remote-location monitoring is linked to other forms of community supervision and treatment. Without scientific rigor, it is questionable whether the available research can be a guide for policymakers on important questions, beginning with, "Is remote-location monitoring effective?"

And second, the studies focus only on whether remote-location monitoring suppresses an individual's criminal behavior rather than changes it. The positive results just noted in the study of federal home confinement and electronic monitoring in Florida may simply be the result of the extra surveillance offered by remote-location monitoring. The majority of studies on remote-location monitoring do not examine the therapeutic aspects of correctional programs that are known to reduce criminal activity. Changes in cognitive skills of thinking, reasoning, empathy, and problem solving are seldom subject to the same evaluation that control and surveillance are. After reviewing thousands of studies on correctional interventions, management policies, and treatment and rehabilitation programs, Dr. Doris MacKenzie, adjunct Senior Scientist in Criminology at Pennsylvania State University, wrote, "Restraining individuals in the community by increasing surveillance and control over their activities does not reduce their criminal activities."[33] "[E]ffective correctional programs must focus on changing the individual."[34] Unless remote-location monitoring is coupled with other wraparound services such as employment readiness, cognitive behavioral therapy, and substance abuse treatment, and without measuring its effectiveness on reducing criminal activity, reporting only on control and surveillance leads to the conclusion that remote-location monitoring does not work.

Residential Reentry Centers A **residential reentry center (RRC)** is a correctional setting where people leaving prison or jail (or sometimes as a condition of probation or parole) are required to live before being fully released into the community. In these settings individuals live in a group environment under a set of rules and requirements and, depending upon the individual's needs, seek employment, attend school or vocational training, and participate in treatment programming. The objectives of RRCs are community protection and reintegration of the individual into community life. Community protection is achieved by setting curfews; administering drug or polygraph tests; confirming that when residents leave the center they go directly to work, school, or treatment; and providing a medium-security correctional setting. Reintegration is achieved by giving residents opportunities to learn and use legitimate skills, thereby reducing their reliance on criminal behavior. Using the risk-needs-responsivity principle discussed in Chapter 4, staff members determine the obstacles to each resident's reintegration; plan a program to overcome those obstacles; and provide a supportive environment to help the resident test, use, and refine the skills needed.

The benefits of RRCs for persons under supervision, their communities, and the criminal justice system are many. RRCs benefit persons under supervision by providing them with the basic necessities of food, clothing, and shelter while they find housing and employment. RRCs also offer residents emotional support to deal with the pressures of readjustment and help them obtain community resources. Benefits to the community include a moderately secure correctional setting in which residents' behavior is monitored and controlled, as well as an expectation that opportunities for persons on supervision to get on their feet will reduce postrelease adjustment problems and criminal behavior. For the criminal justice system, an RRC offers a

CO5-8

residential reentry center (RRC)

A correctional setting where people leaving prison or jail (or sometimes as a condition of probation or parole) are required to live before being fully released into the community.

low-cost housing alternative to incarceration. An RRC can control persons under supervision in the community at less cost than building and operating more secure facilities. It may also serve as a condition of community supervision and an option for dealing with persons who violate probation and parole.

Initially, such centers were called *halfway houses* and were for individuals who either were about to be released from an institution or were in the first stages of return to the community. However, as the number of halfway houses grew and new client groups were added, the umbrella term *residential reentry center* was adopted. Some RRCs specialize in a type of client or treatment—for example, in drug and alcohol abuse, persons charged with a violent or a sex crime, women, abused women, or persons on prerelease from federal prison.

In 2012, the Bureau of Justice Statistics reported there were 527 state, local, and federal RRCs across the United States, with an average daily population of almost 52,000. Today the federal government maintains 186 active RRC contracts with an average daily capacity of 7,742 residents.[35] The average length of stay is 6 1/2 months. But much less information exists on how many state and locally contracted RRCs there are today. The reason we know more about federal than state and locally operated RRCs has to do with the contracting process. Federal contracting is relatively standardized and transparent. State contracting processes, on the other hand, vary widely; contract information is controlled; and authorization is required for access. Furthermore, the majority of RRCs in the United States are operated by private companies and they release no publicly available data on their RRC populations.

Another difficulty in estimating the number of persons that RRCs serve is that many residents are already counted in the publications of persons under correctional supervision in jail and prison and on probation and parole published annually by the U.S. Department of Justice, Bureau of Justice Statistics.

Research on RRCs has produced mixed but mostly positive results. A statewide study of 3,000 persons released from halfway houses in Colorado and tracked for 24 months found that 69 percent had no arrest within 24 months.[36] Of those who recidivated, the majority were drug or alcohol related. Less than 4 percent were for violent offenses.

A study of Ohio's 38 RRCs found that RRCs were most effective with persons considered high-risk and who violate parole. The study found that the most effective RRCs provided the greatest number of services targeting criminogenic needs, offered cognitive behavioral treatment, and engaged in roleplaying and practicing of newly learned skills.[37]

On the other hand, a study of over 3,500 persons released from work release in Minnesota found that while the risk of reoffending for a new crime was low and residents found employment, work release residents were at a higher risk of being returned to prison for violating the conditions of their community supervision.[38]

An evaluation of a work release program for women in Illinois found that the length of time spent in work release programming is related to higher earnings and a higher probability of being employed after incarceration as well as during the time in work release. Women who dropped out of the program received fewer job offers and earned less.[39]

The importance of completing a program and reducing one's criminogenic needs in order to lower the chances of recidivism cannot be overstated. Persons who complete RRC programming are almost twice as likely to successfully complete their community supervision and they are almost half as likely to recidivate compared to clients who do not complete programming within one year of discharge.[40]

Recently CrimeSolutions.gov combined the data from nine independent program evaluations of halfway houses to find common results and identify overall trends. Across the board persons who transitioned back into the community via halfway houses are significantly less likely to recidivate, compared with individuals released on standard parole or released from incarceration with services and supervision in the community.[41] Based on the combined results, the Department of Justice's National Institute of Justice rated the practice of halfway houses as "Promising" for reducing the recidivism of persons who transition back into the community through halfway houses.

Correctional Boot Camps In 1983, in an effort to alleviate prison crowding and reduce recidivism, the departments of corrections in Oklahoma and Georgia opened the first adult correctional boot camps modeled after military boot camps. The belief was that criminal behavior deserves a harsh response commensurate with the harm it caused. Furthermore, behavioral change will occur only when bad behavior is punished and correct behavior is taught through harsh discipline.

Correctional **Boot camp (BC)** is a short institutional term of confinement, usually followed by probation, that includes a physical regimen designed to develop self-discipline, respect for authority, responsibility, and a sense of accomplishment. According to the NIJ, four characteristics distinguish boot camps from other correctional programs.

correctional boot camp (BC)

A short institutional term of confinement that includes a physical regimen designed to develop self-discipline, respect for authority, responsibility, and a sense of accomplishment.

1. military drill and ceremony;
2. a rigorous daily schedule of hard labor and physical training;
3. separation of boot camp participants from the general prison population; and
4. the idea that boot camps are an alternative to long-term confinement.

However, after almost four decades of the BC movement, its use is on the decline. Boot camps were promoted as a means of reducing recidivism but research from diverse jurisdictions and populations have reached the same discouraging conclusion: Boot camps have not proven effective in reducing recidivism, nor have positive attitude changes resulted in reduced recidivism.[42]

Boot camps were also promoted as a means of reducing mass incarceration and corrections costs. However, most boot camps did not reduce prison crowding because the programs were designed for offenders who would otherwise be on probation, not those who would have received prison terms.[43] In a multisite evaluation of five boot camps, MacKenzie and her colleagues found that only two programs appeared to save prison beds. The remaining three increased the need for prison beds.[44]

The Federal Bureau of Prisons ended its boot camps in 2005, and most states shifted their camps toward the "evidence-based" rehabilitative models discussed in this and other chapters. In 2013, after an exhaustive review of boot camp evaluations, the National Institute of Justice's CrimeSolutions.gov rated boot camps as having "no effects" and no reduction in recidivism. One analyst wrote, "If an offender can't read [or] write and is drug-involved, sending him to a 90-day boot camp that does not address his job or literacy needs will only have a short-term effect, if any, on his behavior."[45]

COMMUNITY CORRECTIONS   CO5-10

In Chapter 1, you learned that the correctional system can be either institutional or community. The intermediate sanctions discussed in this chapter, probation (Chapter 4), and parole (Chapter 8) are examples of community

community corrections

A philosophy of correctional treatment that embraces (1) decentralization of authority, (2) citizen participation, (3) redefinition of the population of individuals for whom incarceration is most appropriate, and (4) emphasis on rehabilitation through community programs.

corrections. Community corrections supervises people who are either awaiting trial or have been sentenced by the court but are living in the community. More than two-thirds of all individuals under correctional supervision live in the community on either probation, parole or an intermediate sanction.

We define **community corrections** as a philosophy of correctional treatment that embraces (1) decentralization of authority from state to local levels; (2) citizen participation in program planning, design, implementation, and evaluation; (3) redefinition of the population of individuals for whom incarceration is most appropriate; and (4) emphasis on rehabilitation through community programs.

Today, all of the major components of the criminal justice system have alliances with the community. The field is experiencing many changes, including the following:

- *community policing*—a law enforcement strategy to get residents involved in making their neighborhoods safer by focusing on crime prevention, nonemergency services, public accountability, and decentralized decision making that includes the public;
- *community-based prosecution*—a prosecution strategy that uses a combination of criminal and civil tactics and the legal expertise, resources, and clout of the prosecuting attorney's office to find innovative solutions to a neighborhood's specific problems;
- *community-based defender services*—a defender strategy that provides continuity in representation of individuals who are indigent and helps with personal and family problems that can lead to legal troubles; and
- *community courts*—a judicial strategy of hearing a criminal case in the community that is most affected by the case and including that community in case disposition.

The American Correctional Association's policy statement on community corrections is shown in Exhibit 5-13. The policy advances the importance of a graduated continuum of intermediate sanctions and services like those first shown in Exhibit 5-1. How important are evidence-based practices to the success of communty corrections?

CO5-11

Community Corrections Acts

community corrections acts (CCAs)

State laws that give economic grants to local communities to establish community corrections goals and policies and to develop and operate community corrections programs.

This spirit of correctional collaboration and community partnership has led states to pass **community corrections acts (CCAs)**. CCAs are state laws that give economic grants to local communities to build a policy framework of science-based supervision with the focus of reducing the prison population and getting better outcomes for people on community supervision. Under a typical CCA, the state provides local agencies the funds to create or expand intermediate sanctions and, in return, the state benefits by avoiding the costs of incarceration. The funding supports a spectrum of evidence-based practices such as ISP and drug and other problem-solving courts. As community corrections programs expand, recall the problem of "net-widening" discussed earlier in this chapter. It is important that new programs do not increase social control over individuals who do not need it.

In 1973, Minnesota was the first state to enact a CCA. Colorado and Oregon followed enacting CCA in 1976 and 1978, respectively. Today, most states have a CCA or similar structure in place.

EXHIBIT 5-11   American Correctional Association

Public Correctional Policy on Community Corrections

Introduction:

Community corrections are comprised of residential and nonresidential programs that are a critical component of the public safety continuum that supervises individuals under the legal authority in the community. These programs are proven to reduce crime and victimization and should be used for both juveniles and adults for reentry from postincarceration and, when appropriate, to divert non-violent offenders from incarceration.

The effective use of community corrections programs should be utilized to provide programming and treatment of offenders to protect the public, reduce recidivism and to reserve jail and prison space for those individuals deemed to be the highest risk to public safety.

To be successful, community corrections programs must promote public safety and a continuum of care that responds to the needs of victims, offenders and the community. These programs enable offenders to work and pay taxes, make restitution, meet court obligations, maintain family ties and develop and/or maintain critical support systems with the community.

These programs should include a collaborative, comprehensive planning process for the development of effective policies and services.

Policy Statement:

Community corrections programs shall require offenders, based upon a validated risk and needs assessment, to participate in certain activities and/or programs that are specifically directed toward reducing their risk to the community. Those responsible for community corrections programs, services and supervision should:

A. Seek statutory authority and adequate funding for community programs and services as part of a comprehensive corrections strategy;

B. Embrace and fully utilize a validated risk and needs assessment and base offender programming on criminogenic needs established by the assessment. Further dosages of programming and/or treatment should match the identified risk and needs established by the assessment;

C. Implement and maintain evidence-informed practices and approaches when developing all programming and curricula. These programming and curricula shall encourage behavior change for offenders by offering incentives for behavioral change while also holding offenders accountable;

D. Deliver all programming and curricula with fidelity by establishing an effective quality improvement plan.

E. Communicate with the public about the benefits of community programs and services, the criteria used to select individuals for these programs, and the requirements for successful completion;

F. Recognize that public acceptance of community corrections is enhanced by the provision of identifiable needs of victims and victim services, community service and conciliation programs.

G. Mobilize the participation of a well-informed constituency, including citizen advisory boards and broad-based coalitions, to address community corrections issues;

H. Participate in collaborative, comprehensive planning efforts that provide a framework to assess community needs and develop a system wide plan for services; and

I. Ensure the integrity and accountability of community programs by establishing a reliable system for monitoring and measuring performance and outcomes in accordance with accepted standards of professional practices and sound evaluation methodology.

Simply having correctional programs in a community does not mean that a community corrections program exists. Consistent goals, consistent approaches, and the use of science-based practices to achieving those goals are the backbone of successful community corrections. Community corrections legislation can help accomplish that consistency.

REVIEW AND APPLICATIONS

SUMMARY

1 *Intermediate sanctions* is the term given to the range of new sentencing options developed to fill the gap between traditional probation and traditional jail or prison sentences, better match the severity of punishment to the seriousness of the crime, reduce institutional crowding, and control correctional costs. Punishments typically identified as intermediate sanctions include intensive supervision probation (ISP), drug courts, fines, community service, day reporting centers, remote-location monitoring, residential reentry centers, and correctional boot camps.

2 *Intensive supervision probation* (ISP) is supervision in the community through strict enforcement of conditions and frequent reporting to a probation officer with a reduced caseload.

3 *Drug courts* are specialized court docket programs to help people who have alcohol and other drug dependency problems.

4 A *day fine* is a financial penalty scaled both to the person's income and the seriousness of the crime.

5 *Community service* is a sentence to serve a specified number of hours working in unpaid positions with nonprofit or tax-supported agencies.

6 A *day reporting center* (DRC) is a nonresidential facility to which a person under correctional supervision reports each day to file a daily schedule with a supervision officer, showing how each hour will be spent.

7 *Remote-location monitoring* refers to technologies that probation and parole officers use to monitor remotely the physical location of a person under correctional supervision. For example, home-based electronic monitoring (EM) is often used by officers to monitor remotely individuals who are restricted to their homes.

8 *Residential reentry centers* (RRCs) are correctional settings where people leaving prison or jail (or sometimes as a condition of probation or parole) are required to live before being fully released into the community.

9 *Correctional boot camp* is a short institutional term, usually followed by probation, that includes a physical regimen designed to develop self-discipline, respect for authority, responsibility, and a sense of accomplishment.

10 *Community corrections* is a philosophy of correctional treatment that embraces decentralization of authority from state to local levels; citizen participation in program planning, design, implementation, and evaluation; redefinition of the population of persons for whom incarceration is most appropriate; and emphasis on rehabilitation through community programs.

11 *Community corrections acts* (CCAs) are state laws that give economic grants to local communities to establish community corrections goals and policies and to develop and operate science-based community corrections programs. CCAs decentralize services and engage communities in the process of reintegrating individuals by transferring correctional responsibility from the state to the community and by providing financial incentives for communities to manage more of their own correctional cases.

KEY TERMS

QUESTIONS FOR REVIEW

1 Explain intermediate sanctions and describe their purpose.

2 Differentiate between intensive supervision probation and regular probation.

3 Explain what problem-solving courts have in common and how they are different.

4 Explain the principles behind day fines.

5 Why is community service sometimes called a "fine of time"?

6 What are the features of a day reporting center?

7 For which justice-involved individuals do you believe remote-location monitoring is most beneficial?

8 What criteria would you use to assess the effectiveness of residential reentry centers?

9 Explain the rating CrimeSolutions.gov gave to correctional boot camp

10 Discuss the importance of community involvement in community corrections.

11 How do community corrections acts implement the philosophy of community corrections?

THINKING CRITICALLY ABOUT CORRECTIONS

Fines

Criminal justice policymakers may not be convinced that day fines are a meaningful alternative to probation or incarceration. What could you say to convince them otherwise?

Day Reporting Centers

The evidence is mixed on whether day reporting centers have any impact on reducing criminal activity. Recognizing that it takes time, money, and talent to build an adequate body of scientifically rigorous research, explain to a group of legislators why they should not pull the plug on day reporting centers. What will you tell them is lacking in the literature before they can make an informed policy decision?

ON-THE-JOB DECISION MAKING

Why Community Service?

Your state legislature recently passed a bill authorizing community service, in addition to other penalties, for all but the most serious Class A felonies. Part of the bill requires each probation department to send one or more probation officers to a workshop to prepare for implementing the bill. The chief probation officer asks you to attend the workshop. Before the workshop, you are asked to consider this issue in advance: How can you link community service to the harm caused by the offense? Why is it that apologies and restitution are always linked to the harm, but community service is rarely so connected? How can your agency avoid assigning hours of labor arbitrarily (oftentimes defined in terms of personal preference or convenience; for example, the individual likes working with children or lives near a particular service agency, such as a food bank) and instead make sure that community service labor is linked to the identified harm of the crime and make amends to the victim and/or affected community? What will you say?

Are Drug Courts Working?

Imagine that you are Herbert M. Klein, founder of the nation's first drug court in Miami, Florida, in 1989. Experience tells you that drug courts provide closer, more comprehensive supervision and much more frequent drug testing and monitoring than other forms of community supervision. Now almost 35 years later the President's Commission on Combating Drug Addiction and the Opioid Crisis has called for the establishment of drug courts in each of the 93 federal districts. How would you respond?

ENDNOTES

1. U.S. Department of Justice, Office of Public Affairs, *Former NFL Player Sentenced to Prison for Nationwide Health Care Fraud Scheme* (Washington, DC: U.S. Department of Justice, Office of Public Affairs, Wednesday, February 9, 2022); John Keim, "Clinton Portis Sentenced to 6 Months in Prison, 6 Months' Home Confinement for Role in Scheme to Defraud Health Care Benefit Program," *ESPN*, January 6, 2022, espn.com (accessed January 7, 2022).

2. See, for example, "Changing Public Attitudes Toward the Criminal Justice System," www.soros.org/initiatives/usprograms/focus/justice/articles_publications/publications/hartpoll_20020201 (accessed October 28, 2022); Marc Mauer, Race to Incarcerate (New York: Free Press, 2006), p. 13; Frank T. Cullen and Brenda A. Vose, "Public Support for Early Intervention: Is Child Saving a Habit of the Heart?" *Victims and Offenders*, vol. 2, no. 2 (2007), pp. 109–124; "The UConnPoll: Prison Crowding," University of Connecticut, Center for Survey Research and Analysis, March 8, 2004.

3. William H. DiMascio, *Seeking Justice: Crime and Punishment in America* (New York: Edna McConnell Clark Foundation, 1997), p. 43.

4. Pew Center on the States, "Public Attitudes on Crime and Punishment," www.pewcenteronthestates.org, September 2010 (accessed October 28, 2022); Pew Center on the States, "Public Opinion on Sentencing and Corrections Policy in America," www.pewcenteronthestates.org, March 2012 (October 28, 2022); Lincoln B. Sloas and Mariemilia Larrea, "Rethinking Sanctioning for Offenders with Mental Health Issues: A Balanced Justice Approach," *American Journal of Criminal Justice*, (2021). https://doi.org/10.1007/s12103-021-09620-1.

5. Betsy A. Fulton, Susan Stone, and Paul Gendreau, *Restructuring Intensive Supervision Programs: Applying What Works* (Lexington, KY: American Probation and Parole Association, 1994).

6. Doris Layton MacKenzie, "Evidence-Based Corrections: Identifying What Works," *Crime & Delinquency*, vol. 46, no. 4 (October 2000), pp. 457–472.

7. Doris Layton MacKenzie, *What Works in Corrections: Reducing the Criminal Activities of Offenders and Delinquents* (New York: Cambridge University Press, 2006), p. 322; and Steve Aos, Marna Miller, and Elizabeth Drake, *Evidence-Based Public Policy Options to Reduce Future Prison Construction, Criminal Justice Costs, and Crime Rates* (Olympia, WA: State Institute for Public Policy, 2006), p. 6.

8. Joan Petersilia, Arthur J. Lurigio, and James M. Byrne, "Introduction," in James M. Byrne, Arthur J. Lurigio, and Joan Petersilia (eds.), *Smart Sentencing: The Emergence of Intermediate Sanctions* (Newbury Park, CA: Sage, 1992), pp. ix–x; Elizabeth Deschenes, Susan Turner, and Joan Petersilia, *Intensive Community Supervision in Minnesota: A Dual Experiment in Prison Diversion and Enhanced Supervised Release* (Washington, DC: National Institute of Justice, 1995); Joan Petersilia and Susan Turner, *Evaluating Intensive Supervision Probation/Parole: Results of a Nationwide Experiment* (Washington, DC: National Institute of Justice, May 1993).

9. Steve Aos, Marna Miller, and Elizabeth Drake, *Evidence-Based Public Policy Options to Reduce Future Prison Construction, Criminal Justice Costs, and Crime Rates* (Olympia, WA: State Institute for Public Policy, 2006).

10. "Washington State Researchers Rates What Works in Treatment," *Criminal Justice Newsletter*, September 1, 2006, p. 2.

11. See http://crimesolutions.gov (accessed December 19, 2018).

12. Bureau of Justice Assistance, *Justice Today Podcast, National Drug Court Month*, https://bja.ojp.gov/podcast/national-drug-court-month, June 1, 2022 (accessed October 29, 2022).

13. Kimberly Kaiser, "An Evaluation of Successful Program Completion Across Types of Problem-Solving Courts," *Justice Evaluation Journal*, vol. 3, no. 1 (2020), pp. 54–68.

14. National Institute of Justice, *NIJ's Courts Research: Examining Alternatives to Incarceration for Veterans and Other Policy Innovation* (Washington, DC: U.S. Department of Justice, National Institute of Justice, November 1, 2021); Peter Dujardin, "Hampton's First Behavioral Health Docket, An Alternative Court Program, Helps Turn Lives Around," www.pilotonline.com, January 30, 2022 (accessed October 1, 2022); Caitlin J. Taylor, "Mentee and Mentor Perceptions of a Mentoring Court for High-Risk Probationers," *Probation Journal*, vol. 67, no. 3 (2020), pp. 214–227; Caitlin J. Taylor, "Does Mentoring Work with High-Risk Adult Probationers?: The Implementation and Outcomes of an Adult Mentoring Court, *American Journal of Criminal Justice* (2022). https://doi.org/10.1007/s12103-022-09670-z; Bureau of Justice Assistance, *Fact Sheet: 2019 Innovations in Supervision Initiative: Community Corrections Collaborations to Reduce Violent Crime and Recidivism* (Washington, DC: U.S. Department of Justice, Bureau of Justice Assistance, March 2021); David Purdum, "Mercy Rule: Judge Aims to Get Gambling Addicts 'Out of Chaos' Rather Than Send Them to Prison," www.espn.com, March 16, 2021

(accessed August 15, 2022); Cheryl Moss, "Nevada's First Gambling Treatment Diversion Court," www.nvbar.org, September 2019 (accessed August 15, 2022).

15. Shelli B. Rossman, John K. Roman, Janine M. Zweig, Michael Rempel, and Christine H. Lindquist, *The Multi-Site Adult Drug Court Evaluation: Executive Summary* (Washington, DC: Urban Institute, June 2011).

16. Kevin T. Wolff, Laura M. Baber, Christine A. Dozier, and Roberto Cordeiro, "Assessing the Efficacy of Alternatives to Incarceration Within Seven Federal Districts," *Justice Evaluation Journal*, vol. 3, no. 3 (2020), pp. 27–53.

17. Aos, Miller, and Drake, *Evidence-Based Public Policy Options*, 2006.

18. "Drug Courts Unavailable to Most," *Corrections Today*, vol. 71, no. 6 (December 2009), p. 16; and Sam Hananel, "Drug Courts Successful for Few Who Get It," *The Washington Post*, November 30, 2009, www.washingtonpost. com (accessed October 31, 2022).

19. Beth A. Colgan, *Addressing Modern Debtors' Prisons with Graduated Economic Sanctions That Depend on Ability to Pay* (Washington, DC: Hamilton Project, March 2019).

20. Bureau of Justice Assistance, *How to Use Structured Fines (Day Fines) as an Intermediate Sanction* (Washington, DC: Department of Justice, November 1996).

21. "$1 Million Speeding Fine in Switzerland for Swedish SLS Owner," https://www.motor1.com, August 13, 2010 (accessed November 1, 2022).

22. Aos, Miller, and Drake, *Evidence-Based Public Policy Options*, p. 9, 2006.

23. Dale G. Parent et al., *Day Reporting Centers* (Washington, DC: National Institute of Justice, 1995).

24. W. Amory Carr, Amy Nicole Baker and James J. Cassidy, "Reducing Criminal Recidvism with an Enhanced Day Reporting Center for Probationers with Mental Illness," *Journal of Offender Rehabilitation*, vol. 55, no. 2 (2016), pp. 95–112.

25. Douglas J. Boyle, Laura M. Ragusa-Salerno, Jennifer L. Lanterman and Andrea Fleisch Marcus, "An Evaluation of Day Reporting Centers for Parolees," *Criminology & Public Policy*, vol. 12, no. 1 (2013), pp. 119–143.

26. Misty Buck, "First Day Reporting Center in Miami-Dade County Opens," June 9, 2021, https://communitynewspapers .com (accessed September 15, 2021).

27. Jenni Vincent, "Berkeley Day Report Center Building Dedication Set for April 17," April 7, 2021, https:// www.heraldmailmedia.com (accessed September 15, 2021).

28. Jennifer S. Wong, Jessica Bouchard, Chelsey Lee and Kelsy Gushue, "Examining the Effects of Reporting Centers on Recidivism: A Meta-Analysis," *Journal of Offender Rehabilitation*, vol. 58, no. 3 (2019), pp. 240–260.

29. W. Amory Carr, Amy Nicole Baker, and James J. Cassidy, "Reducing Criminal Recidivism With an Enhanced Day Reporting Center for Probationers With Mental Illness," *Journal of Offender Rehabilitation*, vol. 55, no. 2 (2016), pp. 95–112.

30. The Crime Report Staff, "Electronic Monitoring 'Sets People Up to Fail': Study, *The Crime Report*, September 24, 2021, https://thecrimereport.org/ (accessed October 15, 2021); James Kilgore, *Understanding E-Carceration* (New York: The New Press, 2022); Andrea Cipriano, "Ankle Monitors Tether Wearers to the Carceral System: Study," *The Crime Report*, July 6, 2021, https://thecrimereport. org/ (access July, 6, 2021).

31. Billy Sinclair, "Home Confinement: A Safe Alternative to Mass Incarceration," The Crime Report, December 29, 2022, thecrimereport.org (accessed December 28, 2022); Molly Gill, "Opinion: Thousands Were Released From Prison During COVID. The Results Are Shocking," *The Washington Post*, September 29, 2022, washingtonpost. com (access December 29, 2022).

32. William Bales, Karen Mann, Thomas Blomberg, Gerry Gaes, Kelle Barrick, Karla Dhungana, and Brian McManus, *A Quantitative and Qualitative Assessment of Electronic Monitoring* (Washington, DC: U.S. Department of Justice, National Institute of Justice, January 2011).

33. Doris MacKenzie, *What Works in Corrections*, p. 322.

34. Ibid., p. 335; see also William D. Burrell and Robert S. Gable, "From B. F. Skinner to Spiderman to Martha Stewart: The Past, Present and Future of Electronic Monitoring of Offenders," *Journal of Offender Rehabilitation*, vol. 46, no. 3/4 (2008), pp. 101–118.

35. Roxanne Daniel and Wendy Sawyer, *What You Should Know About Halfway Houses* (Northampton, MA: Prison Poilicy Initiative, 2020); see also the federal Bureau of Prisons website, bop.gov (accessed January 24, 2023).

36. Division of Criminal Justice, Office of Research and Statistics, *Executive Summary: 2000 Community Corrections Study Results* (Denver: State of Colorado, Division of Criminal Justice, Office of Research and Statistics, March 22, 2001), www.cdpsweb.state.co.us/ors/docs .htm (accessed November 1, 2022).

37. Christopher T. Lowenkamp and Edward J. Latessa, "Developing Successful Reentry Programs: Lessons Learned from the 'What Works' Research," *Corrections Today*, vol. 67, no. 2 (April 2005), pp. 72–77; and "Halfway Houses Seen as Way to Cut Prison Costs in Ohio," www.cleveland.com/metro (accessed November 1, 2022).

38. Grant Duwe, "An Outcome Evaluation of a Prison Work Release Program: Estimating Its Effects on Recidivism, Employment, and Cost," *Criminal Justice Policy Review*, vol. 26, no 6 (2015), pp. 531–554.

39. Haeil Jung and Robert J. LaLonde, "Prison Work-Release Programs and Women's Labor Market Outcomes," *The Prison Journal*, vol. 99, no. 5 (2019), pp. 535–558.

40. S.E. Costanza, Stephen M. Cox, and John C. Kilburn, "The Impact of Halfway Houses on Parole Success and Recidivism," *Journal of Sociological Research*, vol. 6, no. 2 (2015), 39–55.

41. National Institute of Justice, Practice Profile: *Halfway Houses*, September 3, 2019, https://crimesolutions.ojp.gov, (accessed November 8, 2022).

42. Doris L. MacKenzie and J. W. Shaw, "The Impact of Shock Incarceration on Technical Violations and New Criminal Activities," *Justice Quarterly*, vol. 10, no. 3 (1993), pp. 463–486; Dionne T. Wright Dionne T. Wright and G. Larry Mays, "Correctional Boot Camps, Attitudes, and Recidivism: The Oklahoma Experience," *Journal of Offender Rehabilitation*, vol. 28, no. 1/2 (1998), pp. 71–87; Jeanne B. Stinchcomb and W. Clinton Terry III, "Predicting the Likelihood of Rearrest Among Shock Incarceration Graduates: Moving Beyond Another Nail in the Boot Camp Coffin," *Crime & Delinquency*, vol. 47, no. 2 (April 2001), pp. 221–242.

43. W. J. Dickey, *Evaluating Boot Camp Prisons* (Washington, DC: National Institute of Justice, 1994); Peter Katel and Melinda Liu, "The Bust in Boot Camps," *Newsweek*, February 21, 1994, p. 26; Parent, "Boot Camps Failing to Achieve Goals."

44. Doris L. MacKenzie and Claire Souryal, *Multi-Site Evaluation of Shock Incarceration: Executive Summary* (Washington, DC: National Institute of Justice, 1994); see also Doris L. MacKenzie and A. Piquero, "The Impact of Shock Incarceration Programs on Prison Crowding," *Crime & Delinquency*, vol. 40 (1994), pp. 222–249.

45. Merry Morash and Lila Rucker, "Critical Look at the Idea of Boot Camp as Correctional Reform," *Crime & Delinquency*, vol. 36 (1990), pp. 204–222; DiMascio, Seeking Justice, p. 41.

Institutional Corrections

Part Three examines jail, prison, and parole. These three correctional components supervise more than 2.6 million persons every day.

How much have persons in jail and facilities changed since the country's first jail opened in Philadelphia in 1773? Today, jails are adapting new technology and architectural designs to their purposes. However, concerns are still being raised over jail as the first step in mass incarceration, the lack of services for women, the overrepresentation of minorities and persons who are mentally ill, pay-to-stay jails, privatization, reentry, and jail standards.

Prisons also first developed in Pennsylvania. In 1790, a wing of the Walnut Street Jail was devoted to long-term incarceration and served as a model for the world's first prison, the Eastern State Penitentiary, in 1829. As you will learn in Chapter 6, the architecture of jails and prisons changed over the years from linear to podular. Supervision approaches also changed from indirect to direct.

Each day, almost 1,500 people will leave prison. How prepared are they to reenter society? Did they receive the educational and vocational preparation and drug treatment they need to minimize their likelihood of reoffending? This chapter offers you the evidence to make that decision.

Sheriff Paula S. Dance, Pitt County Sheriff's Office, Greenville, North Carolina

Howard Humphries/Pitt County Sheriff's Office

[6]

JAILS
Front Door to Corrections

Julie Jacobson/AP Image

 *The mental illness leads to them committing these crimes and there's really no place else for them to go, so they come here. This is not a hospital. This is a jail. You do the best you can.*

—Lt. Ryan Snyder, Champagne County Jail, Illinois

In November 2021, U.S. District Court Judge Robert B. Kugler sentenced Richard Tobin, 20, from Brooklawn, New Jersey, to one year and one day in federal prison followed by three years of supervised release for his role in conspiring with members of a white supremacist hate group intending to instill fear, threaten and intimidate African-Americans and Jewish Americans by vandalizing minority-owned properties in September 2019.[1] Tobin admitted his role in a white supremacist group called "The Base." He instructed members to post propaganda flyers and break windows and slash tires belonging to African Americans and Jewish Americans. Members of the hate group then vandalized synagogues in Racine, Wisconsin, and Hancock, Michigan, by spray-painting them with hate symbols. The Michigan place of worship, Temple Jacob, was defaced with a swastika.

In 2019, when Richard Tobin was 18 years old, he was arrested and charged with conspiring with members of the neo-Nazi group, "The Base," to vandalize properties owned by African-Americans and Jewish Americans. Tobin planned and directed other members to spray-paint antisemitic graffiti on the back side of Congregation Shaarey Tefilla's garbage shed in Carmel, Indiana. Tobin dubbed the plot "Kristallnacht" after the 1938 night of terror in Nazi Germany in which synagogues and Jewish businesses were destroyed and nearly one hundred Jews were murdered. Tobin was sentenced to one year and one day in federal prison followed by three years of supervised release. How can corrections change the way individuals like Tobin view minorities and people of color?
Justin Mack/IndyStar/Imagn Content Services, LLC

If "a year and a day" sounds familiar, it should. A year and a day is the minimum incarceration sentence in a state or federal prison facility for persons convicted of felonies. Misdemeanors, on the other hand, are considered less serious than felonies and are punishable by confinement for one year or less and often in a county jail. In addition, depending on the jurisdiction, persons can only obtain early release from prison for good behavior while incarcerated if their sentence is longer than a year. Hence a year and a day might save a person about 50 days before the full sentence would have ended.

Is Tobin's sentence fair? (Refer back to Chapter 3 and the issues related to fairness in sentencing.) What meaning do you give to "a year and a day?" Why does it matter if someone serves 366 days in state or federal prison or 365 days in county jail? What do you think the research would show?

In this chapter you will learn about the history of jails in the United States and how they impact the problem of mass incarceration. You will learn how jail populations are different from prison populations and how jails have changed in design and management. We also discuss what's happening with reforming the "cash bail system" or what some call "checkbook justice." And we focus on the important work being done in the area of evidence-based jail reentry.

JAILS IN HISTORY

CO6-1

It is believed that King Henry II of England ordered the first jail built in 1166. The purpose of that jail was to detain persons until they could be brought before a court, tried, and sentenced. From that beginning, jails spread throughout Europe but changed in scope and size over time.

First Jail in the United States

The first jail in the United States was the Walnut Street Jail in Philadelphia, built in 1773. The jail housed together all persons without regard to sex, age, or offense. Following the jail's opening, conditions quickly deteriorated.

According to some, the jail became a "promiscuous scene of unrestricted intercourse, universal riot, and debauchery."[2] The Philadelphia Quakers had wanted the Walnut Street Jail to be a place where individuals reformed themselves through reflection and remorse. Unfortunately that never happened.

In 1798 a fire destroyed the workshops at Walnut Street Jail. The destruction brought about disillusionment and idleness. Rising costs crippled the jail's budget. Disciplinary problems rose with overcrowding, and escape and violence increased. The number of persons in jail who were destitute and had nowhere else to go soared, as did the incidence of disease. Political conflicts also broke out between the religious Quakers and the non-Quaker prison board members. On October 5, 1835, the Walnut Street Jail closed. The people in jail convicted of state crimes were transferred to the new Eastern State Penitentiary in Philadelphia, the first institution of its kind in the world (see Chapter 7). Persons charged with county offenses and those awaiting trial were transferred to a new county jail.

By the close of the 19th century, most cities across the United States had jails and, as was customary since the end of the American Revolution, the jail was run by the elected local sheriff.

Today there are 3,116 jail facilities and three-quarters are under the jurisdiction of an elected sheriff. The rest are municipal jails, regional jails, and private jails.

However because of the close link between jail administration and election politics, experts differ on whether jail management should be a function of an elected law enforcement official or a separate branch of municipal government administered by a professional agency head. The argument is a lot of correctional work takes place in jail (e.g., probation officers conduct pre-sentence reports, external service providers offer treatment on a wide range of issues, programs are evaluated, grants are sought after, and evidence-based practices are considered and adopted) therefore jail administration requires specialized knowledge, skills, and training in management and rehabilitation that are not normally found in law enforcement.

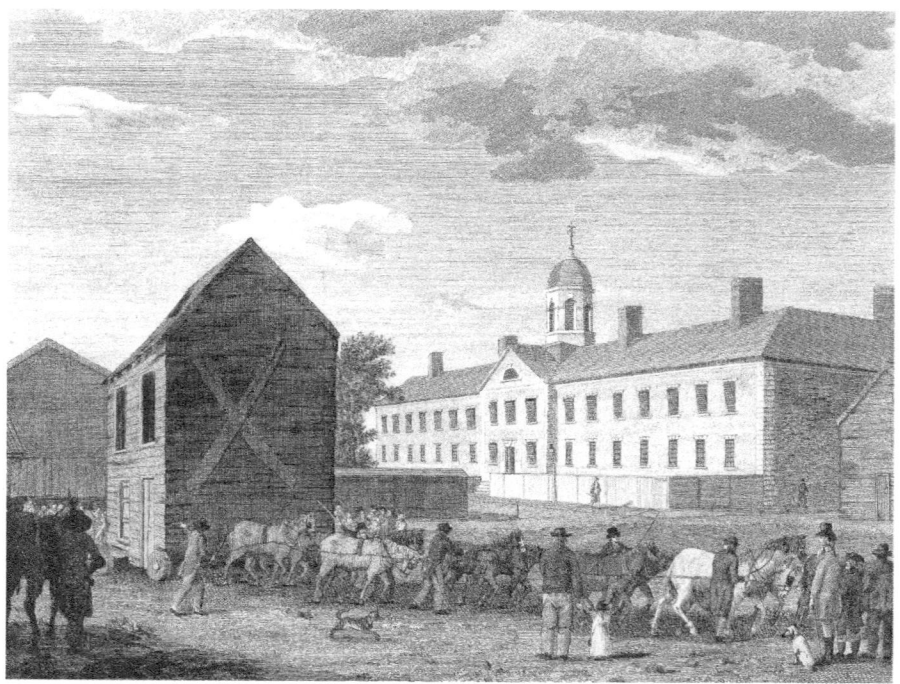

The Walnut Street Jail, started in Philadelphia in 1773, originally housed together all persons without regard to sex, age, or offense. Following its redesignation as a penitentiary in 1790, it housed only persons convicted of felonies. Which religious group's principles influenced correctional institutions in Pennsylvania?

Photo by Encyclopedia Britannica/UIG/Getty Images

Architecture and Management of Persons in Jail   **CO6-2**

Jails have progressed through three phases of architectural design. Each design is based on a particular philosophy of jail management and control of people in jail.

First-Generation Jails First-generation jails were built in a linear design that dates back to the 18th century, when prison and jail design was shifting from single-cell and religious emphasis to congregate housing and secular administration.

In a typical **first-generation jail,** people in jail live in multiple-occupancy cells or dormitories. The cells line corridors that are arranged like spokes. Staff supervision is sporadic or intermittent; staff must patrol the corridors to observe people in their cells. Contact between people in jail and the jail staff is minimal unless there is an incident to which staff must react (see Exhibit 6–1).

The design of such linear jails reflects the assumption that people in jail are violent and destructive and will assault staff, destroy jail property, and try to escape. The facility is designed to prevent these behaviors. Heavy metal bars separate staff from jail residents. Reinforced metal beds, sinks, and toilets are bolted to the ground or wall. Reinforced concrete and razor wire surround the facility.

The biggest problem with first-generation jails is the inability of an officer to see what is going on in more than one or two cells at a time. That limitation gave rise to the second-generation jails of the 1960s.

Second-Generation Jails Second-generation jails emerged in the 1960s to replace old, rundown linear jails and provide officers the opportunity to observe as much of the housing area as possible from a single vantage point.

Second-generation jails adopted a different philosophical approach to construction and management of people in jail. In a **second-generation jail,** staff remain in a secure control booth overlooking housing areas, called

first-generation jail

Jail with multiple-occupancy cells or dormitories that line corridors arranged like spokes. Staff supervision is intermittent; staff must patrol the corridors to observe people in their cells.

second-generation jail

Jail where staff remain in a secure control booth surrounded by housing areas called *pods* and surveillance is remote. *Also known as* podular remote-supervision facilities.

EXHIBIT 6–1   First-Generation Jail—Intermittent Supervision

 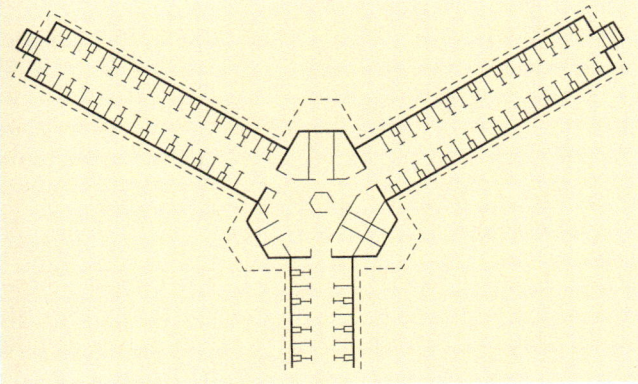

Cells line corridors in first-generation jails. Unable to observe all housing areas from one location, prison and jail staff must patrol living areas to provide supervision. What are the consequences of first-generation jails?

Nagel Photography/Shutterstock

EXHIBIT 6–2   Second-Generation Jail—Remote Supervision

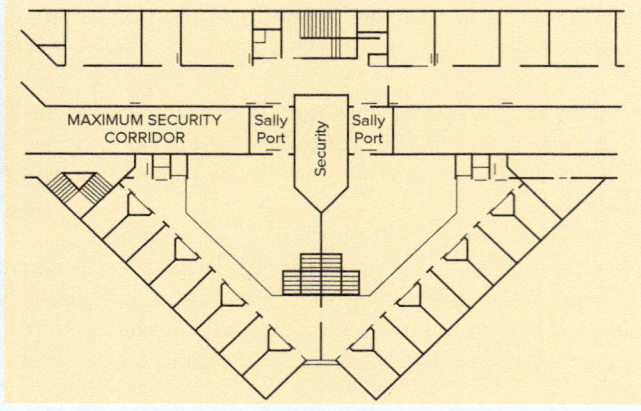

MAXIMUM SECURITY CORRIDOR — Sally Port — Security — Sally Port

Living areas are divided into pods, or modules, in which cells are clustered around dayrooms that are under remote observation by staff in a secure control room. What are the consequences of second-generation jails?
Charlie Riedel/AP Photo

pods (see Exhibit 6–2). Although visual supervision increases in such jails, observation is remote, and verbal interaction between staff and jail residents is even less frequent than in first-generation jails. Property destruction is minimized because steel and cement continue to define the living areas. Second-generation jails have been termed **podular remote-supervision facilities.**

Although staff can observe activity in common areas, or *dayrooms,* they are unable to respond quickly to problems or even to interact effectively because of the intervening security control booth. In both the first- and second-generation jails, the biggest problem is that staff and people in jail are separated. As David Parrish, former detention commander for the Hillsborough County Sheriff's Department (Tampa, Florida) put it, "Staff managed the hallways and control rooms, generally about 10 percent of the facility, while people in jail ran the housing areas, roughly 90 percent."[3]

third-generation jail (also *direct-supervision jail*)

A jail where residents are housed in small groups, or pods, staffed 24 hours a day by specifically trained officers. Officers interact with residents to help change behavior. Bars and metal doors are absent, reducing noise and dehumanization. *Also known as* direct-supervision jail.

Third-Generation Jails **Third-generation jails,** also known as **direct-supervision jails,** emerged in 1974 when the Federal Bureau of Prisons opened three Metropolitan Correctional Centers (MCCs) in three cities: New York, Chicago, and San Diego. These three federal facilities were the first jails planned and designed to be operated under the principles of unit management, which later became known as *direct supervision* (see Exhibit 6–3 for a list of the nine principles of direct supervision). The housing unit design of such jails is podular. Cells are arranged around a common area, or dayroom. There is no secure control booth for the supervising officer, and there are no physical barriers between the officer and the residents. Furnishings are used to reduce inmate stress caused by crowding, excessive noise, lack of privacy, and isolation from the outside world. Bars and metal doors are absent, reducing noise and the dehumanization common in first- and second-generation jails. Direct supervision places a single deputy directly in a "housing pod" with between 32 and 64 people. The officer may have a desk or table for paperwork, but it is in the open dayroom area.

EXHIBIT 6–3   Nine Principles of Direct Supervision

1. **Effective control.** Staff firmly establish their authority over all space and activities in the unit.

2. **Effective supervision.** Continuous supervision is maintained by the unit officers.

3. **Competent staff.** Correctional standards guide recruitment.

4. **Staff and inmate safety.** Performance-based data are collected.

5. **Manageable and cost-effective operations.** There are more architectural choices, commercial-grade furnishings, and equipment options.

6. **Effective communication.** Direct communication exists between residents and officers, officers and supervisors.

7. **Classification and orientation.** Know with whom you are dealing; intense supervision is maintained for the first 12 to 72 hours.

8. **Justice and fairness.** Unit officers exercise primary informal discipline.

9. **Ownership of operations.** Policy decisions are guided by a team approach.

In a third-generation jail, the management style is direct supervision. An officer is stationed in the pod with the residents, much like a teacher in a classroom. The officer moves about the pod and interacts with the residents to manage their behavior. Advocates of direct supervision tell us that when correctional officers are in the housing space with residents, talking with them, listening to them, listening to what's going on, anticipating problems, and dealing with them proactively, residents will have a better chance of leading productive lives after they finish their sentence. The nine principles of direct supervision are shown in Exhibit 6–3. Today, an estimated 10 to 20 percent of the nation's 3,116 local jails use direct supervision.

EXHIBIT 6–4   Third-Generation Jail—Direct Supervision

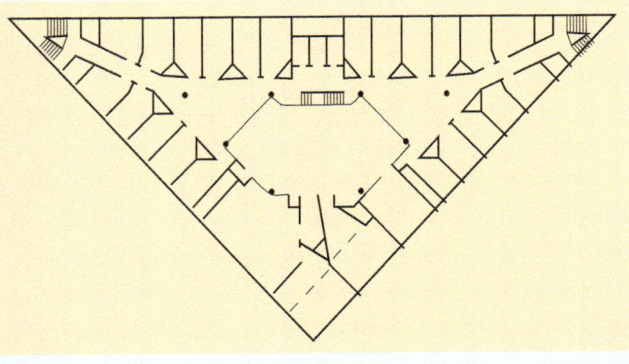

Cells are grouped in housing units, or pods. Each pod has a central dayroom. Prison staff are stationed inside the housing unit to encourage direct interaction between themselves and residents. What are the consequences of direct-supervision jails?

Stephen Osman/Los Angeles Times/Getty Image

CO6-3   # PURPOSE OF JAILS

Jails

What are the differences between jails and prisons? What is bail, and how is it used? What is the "jail separation mandate"?

jails

Locally operated correctional facilities that confine people before or after conviction.

total admission

The total number of people admitted to jail each year.

average daily population (ADP)

The sum of the number of people held in a jail or prison each day for a year, divided by the total number of days in the year.

Almost 40 percent of the nation's jails like the one pictured are small (less than 50 cells), hold only 4 percent of the jail population. Most small jails were built in the early part of the 20th century. What management style does this jail suggest?

Dr. Gary Bayens

Except for six states that run combined jail/prison systems (Alaska, Connecticut, Delaware, Hawaii, Rhode Island, and Vermont), **jails** are locally operated correctional facilities that confine people before or after conviction. Jails are different from prisons (the subject of Chapter 7) in a number of ways that you will learn about as you read. The fundamental difference between jail and prison is the nature of their populations.[4]

Total admission is the total number of persons admitted to jail each year. At the start of 2021, jails reported almost 9 million admissions, down from 10.3 million a year earlier due to the release of people from jail during the COVID-19 pandemic.[5] That translates into almost 25,000 people released from jails each day, a small minority of whom are "frequent fliers" and responsible for one-half to three-fourths of all admissions to jail. In Chicago, for example, 21 percent of the individuals admitted to jail between 2007 and 2011 accounted for 50 percent of all admissions. In New York City, the situation is similar. From 2008 through midyear 2013, almost 500 people were admitted to jail 18 times or more, accounting for more than 10,000 jail admissions and 300,00 days in jail.[6]

The **average daily population (ADP),** on the other hand, is the sum of the number of people in a jail or prison each day for a year divided by the total number of days in the year. Whereas some 9 million people are admitted to jail each year (most for short periods of time), the daily jail population is 658,100. For prisons, however, the numbers are reversed. Fewer persons are admitted to prison each year than are admitted to jail (346,461 compared to 9 million), but the average daily prison population is higher than jail (1,215,821 and 658,100, respectively). Put another way, although prisons hold about twice the number of people on any given day than jails do, jails have almost 26 times the number of annual admissions. The annual number of jail bookings is much larger than a one-day jail population count. For prisons, however, a one-day prison count is larger than the number of persons admitted to prison each year. The changing nature of jail populations raises significant issues and problems that form the core of this chapter.

People sentenced to jail usually have a sentence of 1 year or less. The estimated average time they spend in jail is 28 days. Seventy percent are released within 3 days; 13 percent are estimated to stay longer than two months, 7 percent longer than four months, and 4 percent longer than six months. The majority of the nation's jail population today (almost 70 percent) are pretrial detainees—persons awaiting court action on a current charge or held in jail for other reasons, a topic we return to later in this chapter. Ten years ago only 60 percent of the people in jail were pretrial detainees and had not been convicted of any crime. The increase from 60 to almost 70 percent in the number of persons in jail today who are unconvicted raises a number of concerns ranging from how do jails guarantee the unconvicted their legal rights? Is the increase in the number of pretrial detainees contributing to mass incarceration? Are there alternatives to pretrial detention? We explore these issues in this chapter.

EXHIBIT 6-5 **American Jail Association**

We will lead, educate, and support American jail professionals to enhance public safety.

Source: Copyright ©American Jail Association. Reprinted with permission.

Jails also incarcerate persons in a wide variety of other categories. Jails are used to do the following:

CO6-4

- hold persons who are sentenced to jail facilities and usually have a sentence of one year or less
- receive individuals pending arraignment and hold them as they await trial, conviction, or sentencing
- readmit persons who violate probation, parole, and bail bond violators and absconders
- detain juveniles pending their transfer to juvenile authorities
- hold persons with mental illness pending their movement to appropriate mental health facilities
- hold individuals for the military, for protective custody, as witnesses for courts, and for contempt of court
- release persons to the community on completion of sentence
- transfer people to federal, state, or other authorities
- house individuals for federal, state, or other authorities due to crowding of their facilities
- operate community-based programs as alternatives to incarceration

The American Jail Association mission statement is shown in Exhibit 6-5.

JAIL POPULATION AND FACILITY CHARACTERISTICS

CO6-5

Who is in jail? Why are they there? What do we know about the operation and administration of jail facilities? To these and related questions we now turn our attention.

Population Characteristics

The characteristics of people in jail have changed little over the past two decades. The most recent census of people in jail shows that 87 percent are men, over half are under 35 years old, almost half are white, 70 percent are unconvicted as we learned, and almost 80 percent are in jail on felony charges.[7] These characteristics differ from the general population in several ways. People in jail are younger and disproportionately minority. (see Exhibit 6-6).

The Department of Justice's Bureau of Justice Statistics reports the number of persons held in jail on the last weekday every June. In 2020, that number was almost 600,000. One year earlier it was almost 735,000. The jail population dropped to mitigate the spread of COVID-19 in correctional facilities, where physical distancing and other public health measures were challenging to implement. Police issued citations in lieu of arrests, prosecutors declined to charge people for "low-level" offenses, courts used more bail options, and jail administrators released more people detained pretrial as well as those serving short sentences for nonviolent offenses.

However by 2022 the number of persons in jail custody increased to 663,000, a significant change of almost 11 percent from the reduced jail population observed two years earlier. As COVID restrictions began to recede, the criminal justice system scaled back the initiatives made during the pandemic. Some have asked what happened to persons who were not sent to jail during the pandemic. Unfortunately that evidence-based data is not yet available. There are however important questions to answer about the impact of those initiatives and the outcomes for individuals who were not sent to jail during the pandemic. Did these measures, such as issuing citations instead of arrests or implementing bail reforms, achieve their intended goals or did they create new challenges? Assessing their impact on public safety, recidivism rates, and individual outcomes is essential in making informed decisions about future of criminal justice policies and practices. How would you evaluate the effectiveness of those criminal justice initiatives?

Jail populations, like prison populations, vary from region to region and state to state. Because of differences in population, however, population counts don't let us compare jurisdictions. Rates of jail incarceration, expressed as the number of persons in jail per 100,000 U.S. residents, provide a more meaningful and useful analysis of trends in incarceration. With rate data, we can compare changes over time and jurisdictions with different

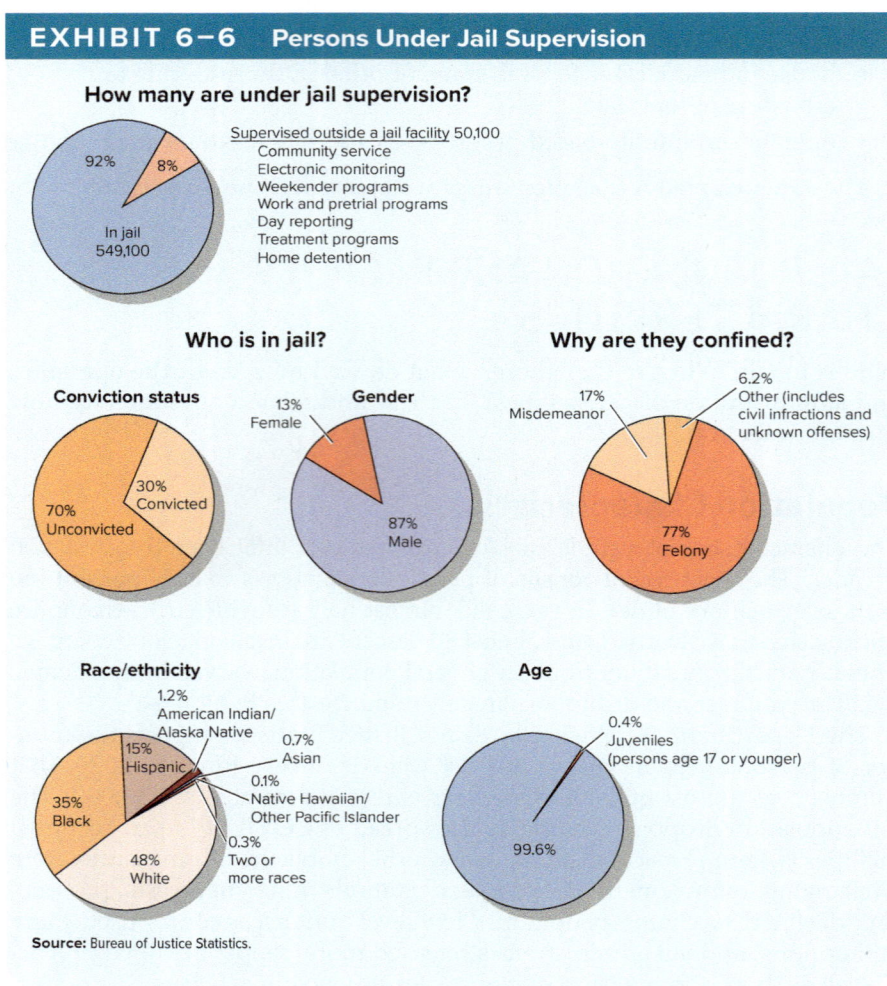

EXHIBIT 6–6   Persons Under Jail Supervision

How many are under jail supervision?

92%   8%
In jail 549,100

Supervised outside a jail facility 50,100
Community service
Electronic monitoring
Weekender programs
Work and pretrial programs
Day reporting
Treatment programs
Home detention

Who is in jail?

Conviction status

30% Convicted
70% Unconvicted

Gender

13% Female
87% Male

Why are they confined?

17% Misdemeanor
6.2% Other (includes civil infractions and unknown offenses)
77% Felony

Race/ethnicity

1.2% American Indian/Alaska Native
0.7% Asian
0.1% Native Hawaiian/Other Pacific Islander
0.3% Two or more races
15% Hispanic
35% Black
48% White

Age

0.4% Juveniles (persons age 17 or younger)
99.6%

Source: Bureau of Justice Statistics.

jail populations. Data on jail rates give policy makers the information they need to decide if their programs and policies are working.

Consider Ohio and Indiana, for example. They share a common border. They are similar in some respects but different in others. Even though Ohio's population of almost 12 million is close to double Indiana's 7 million, the adult population in both states is similar—23 percent. Both states also have similar jail populations: 20,580 people in jail in Ohio and 20,430 people in jail in Indiana. Both states also have similar crime rates: 2,349 crimes per 100,000 adult population in Ohio and 2,342 crimes per 100,000 adult population in Indiana. However Indiana's rate of jail incarceration is more than one-third the rate of Ohio's (303 vs. 176). In simple terms this means that even though both states have similar adult and jail populations, Ohio uses jail much less often. It also tells us that jail incarceration rates are influenced more by political decisions than by population or levels of crime rates. Exhibit 6–7 shows jail incarceration rates across the states.

In spite of all their differences and even if some portion of the 9 million admissions to jail each year is admitted more than once, jails are in a unique position to help persons resume life in the community. Policymakers recognize that because people in jail have shorter lengths of stay than people incarcerated in state or federal prison, the community location of most jail

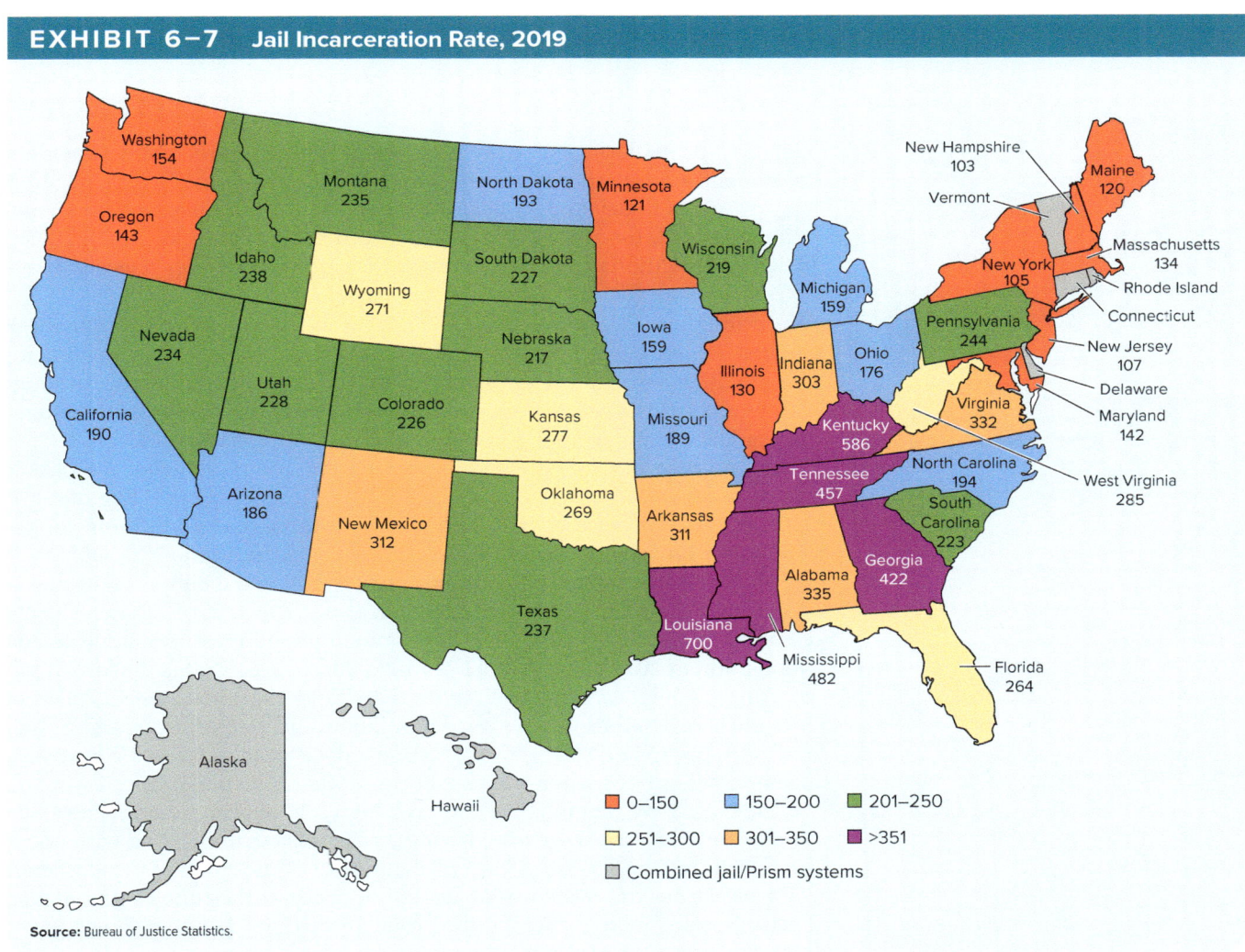

EXHIBIT 6–7   Jail Incarceration Rate, 2019

Legend:
- 0–150
- 150–200
- 201–250
- 251–300
- 301–350
- >351
- Combined jail/Prism systems

Source: Bureau of Justice Statistics.

RELIABLE RESEARCH. REAL RESULTS.

Enter your keyword(s)   Search Site   Advanced Search

Home | Help | Contact Us | Site Map | Glossary

EVIDENCE-BASED CORRECTIONS

Allegheny County Jail-Based Reentry Specialist Program

The Allegheny County Jail-Based Reentry Specialist Program was established in 2010 and sought to reduce recidivism and improve inmates' transition into the community by coordinating the reentry services the inmates received in jail and in the community. The program operates in two phases. Phase 1 provides inmates with in-jail programming and services to prepare them for release. Phase 2 provides inmates with up to 12 months of supportive services in the community.

The program includes males and females who had been sentenced to a minimum of 6 months in jail and were returning to the county upon release. The inmates were also those categorized as medium- to high-risk offenders.

Researchers found that the Allegheny County Jail-Based Reentry Specialist Program had a statistically significant impact on the probability of future arrests. Program participants had a 10 percent chance of rearrest, compared with a 34 percent chance for the comparison group.

The Allegheny County Jail-Based Reentry Specialist program is rated *Effective*.

Source: Adapted from Bureau of Justice Statistics.

facilities means less time away from family, friends, treatment providers, faith institutions, and other social supports. They also realize that jails have opportunities to develop strategies to reduce the criminalization of persons with mental illness and substance use disorders and respond with evidence-based interventions and reentry programs prior to and after release.

Women in Jail   There has been an upsurge in the number of women incarcerated in the United States, explained, in part, by guideline sentencing under which sex is not regarded as an appropriate consideration. Although women have historically been treated more leniently than men at sentencing, guideline sentencing has tended to limit or end this practice.

The number of women in jail has more than quintupled over the past 30 years, from 19,000 in 1985, to a high of over 115,000 in 2018. Beginning in June 2019, however, local jails experienced a large decline in their population due primarily to the COVID-19 pandemic. The number of women in jail dropped from almost 111,000 in 2019 to under 70,000 in 2020 due to declining admissions and expedited releases.[8] The rate of women's incarceration in jail also declined from 66 women per 100,000 U.S. adult female population in 2019 to a low of 42 per 100,000 in 2020. That is the lowest rate of women's jail incarceration in more than 25 years. In the post-COVID era, it is unclear whether women's jail admission and rate of incarceration will return to pre-COVID levels or correctional decision makers will continue to use non-jail options when they are appropriate for justice-involved women.

The typical woman in jail is poor, is a high school dropout with low skills, has held mainly low-wage jobs, is young (25 to 29), is unmarried with one to three children, and belongs to a racial minority. Almost half of the women in jail were under the influence of alcohol or drugs at the time of the offense. Forty-six percent had members of their immediate families sentenced to incarceration. Two of every 10 grew up in a home where one or both parents

EXHIBIT 6–8   Ten Facts About Women in Jails

1. Women are a lower public safety risk than men.

2. Women's pathways to crime are different than men's.

3. Women's participation in crime is related to their connections with others.

4. Women have histories of victimization and trauma.

5. Women's programs have been developed through the lens of managing men.

6. Classification systems have not been validated for women.

7. Women need gender-informed risk assessment tools that more accurately identify women's risks and needs.

8. Women respond more favorably when staff adhere to evidence-based, gender-responsive principles.

9. Women's transition and reentry from jail to the community are challenging because of their overwhelming needs as mothers, less evidence of employment history, and greater levels of poverty.

10. Women's technical violations stem from unmet survival needs such as meeting financial obligations, finding gainful employment, and finding safe housing.

abused drugs, alcohol, or both. And more than one-half of the women (55 percent) had been physically or sexually abused before age 18. Other facts about women in jails is shown in Exhibit 6–8.

Some scholars believe that many women in jail do not pose a threat to public safety but are jailed because they do not have the financial resources to make bail, which makes our discussion of the problems with monetary bail discussed later in this chapter even more salient for this group of offenders. Over 80 percent are charged with nonviolent traffic, property, drug, or public-order offenses.[9]

Women in jail have high needs for education, job training, health care, mental health care, alcohol and drug abuse counseling, and parenting skills development. Properly classifying women according to their risks and needs is beyond the scope of most jails in the United States.[10] The National Institute of Justice surveyed 54 jails and found that the same classification instrument was used for both women and men in 50 jails. The survey found no effort to gauge women's different needs, circumstances, and risk profiles.[11] As a result, a number of female-specific classification instruments have been developed for justice-involved women, but with little exception, there are no peer-reviewed, published assessments of them.[12]

The National Institute of Corrections released a report to help jail and prison administrators more effectively work with the women in their care.[13] According to NIC, four factors influence women's involvement in crime. Understanding these factors in combination with one another will help jail administrators consider how to adjust policies and procedures and how to assess and improve services to women in their care. They are:

1. **Pathways perspective.** Women in jail have histories of sexual and/or physical abuse, substance abuse, and mental illness. Typically they are unskilled, earn low incomes, have sporadic work histories, and are single parents. As such, it is imperative to utilize the growing body of evidence-based literature concerning women's criminality and their needs to help jail staff respond appropriately.

2. **Relational theory and female development.** Relational theory describes the different ways women and men develop. An important difference suggested by the research is that women develop a sense of self and self-worth when their actions arise out of, and lead back into, connections with others even if this means establishing dysfunctional relationships. Many women are drawn into criminal activity because of their relationships with others. Knowing this explains why jail staff often perceive that communicating with women in jail is more difficult and time-consuming than communicating with men in jail.

3. **Trauma theory.** Trauma is the injury done by violence and abuse, and it is largely unrecognized by the women themselves. Mental health services that understand past trauma and its effect on current behavior are needed to respond to trauma.

4. **Addiction theory.** When substance abuse treatment programs for women are combined with additional pathway factors (mental illness, trauma, abuse), jail-based treatment is successful.

Jail administrators can do three things to address the critical issues that women face in jail:[14]

1. Provide jail staff with training to understand the differences between women and men in jail, the implications of gender-responsive research, and information on trauma-informed care.

2. Provide jail staff with access to current studies of effective jail programs for women and promising approaches to achieving successful outcomes.

3. Provide jail staff with skill-based training focused on effective communication, motivational interviewing, case management, and coaching—all concentrated on working with women in jail.

Race and Jail Populations Whites comprise 70 percent of the U.S. population and 48 percent of the jail population. Hispanics comprise 19 percent of the U.S. population and Black or African American, 13 percent. In jail, their populations are 15 percent and 35 percent, respectively. American Indian/Alaska Native, Asian, and Native Hawaiian/other Pacific Islander account for about 2 percent of the U.S. jail population.

One of the most glaring and troubling observations facing jails is the rate of incarceration for minorities and people of color compared to whites. Although jail incarceration rates for all races are in decline, the Black incarceration rate is still more than three times the rate for white Americans in jail. For every 100,000 Black adults in the U.S. population, 465 are in jail. That is more than three times the rate for white people—133—even though there are more white people than Black people in the United States. The rate for American Indians/Alaska Natives is also double the white rate—274 per 100,000 compared to 133. The rates for whites and Hispanics are similar, 134 and 133, respectively.

Is the disparity at which different races are subject to the criminal justice system explained by legitimate factors, or are minorities and people of color differentially treated without regard to their individual circumstances?

The prevailing thought in criminology is that the opioid crisis, problems with the bail system, racial profiling, and the war on drugs are often-cited reasons for the overrepresentation of minorities. The jail population is heavily influenced by bail decisions, as we will discuss later in this chapter. A number of researchers have found that judges impose higher bail—or are more likely to deny bail altogether—if the defendant is a racial minority.[15]

Minorities and people of color comprise approximately 40 percent of the U.S. population, but they make up more than 50 percent of the jail population. What are the explanations for the overrepresentation of minorities in jail?

Jeff Schrier/The Saginaw News/AP Image

Still another reason is the impact of the war on drugs and on law enforcement strategies of racial profiling. Researchers have argued that the war on drugs has had a particularly detrimental effect on Black males.[16] Across the past two decades, more Black males than white males have been detained for drug offenses. Researchers at the University of Nebraska argue that police are *reactive* in responding to crimes against persons and property but are *proactive* in dealing with drug offenses. "There is evidence," they write, "to suggest that they [police] target minority communities—where drug dealing is more visible and where it is thus easier to make an arrest—and tend to give less attention to drug activities in other neighborhoods."[17]

Mental Illness and Jail Populations Jails have become the largest de facto mental health facility in the United States. Estimates are three times as many persons are in jail diagnosed with a **serious mental illness** (SMI) than there are in psychiatric hospitals in the U.S., 150,000 compared to 52,000.[18] Twenty to 26 percent of the jail population compared to 4.2 percent of the general population suffers from a SMI.[19]

The National Institute of Mental Health defines SMI as a mental, behavioral, or emotional disorder resulting in serious functional impairment, which substantially interferes with or limits one or more major life activities.[20] These disorders include schizophrenia and other psychotic disorders, bipolar disorder, severe forms of depression, and anxiety disorders. And whether or not persons in jail with a mental illness receive treatment varies significantly depending on various factors, including the state or jurisdiction, as well as the specific policies and practices of the correctional facilities in question. Many jails struggle to provide adequate mental health treatment due to budget constraints, overcrowding, and a lack of trained staff. As a result, a substantial number of persons in jail – as many as three in five - do not receive the appropriate mental health care they need.[21]

A look at a few jails in the United States gives us a sense of the scope of the problem.[22] The Orange County Jail in Florida (the fourth-largest jail in Florida with an ADP of 2,400) reports that 4 out of 10 persons in jail suffer from a mental illness. Roughly a third of the people confined in Chicago's Cook County Jail (ADP of 6,000) suffer from a mental illness. Over 50 percent of the 10,000 persons confined in New York's main jail complex on

Twenty to 26 percent of the jail population compared to 4.2 percent of the general population suffers from a serious mental illness. Women residents at the Pinellas County facility (Clearwater, Florida) struggling with PTSD, loss of their children, and other problems meet with a clinical counselor every Thursday to talk while they make gifts for their children. Why are persons with mental illness not fit individuals for retribution and punishment?
Pat Sullivan/AP Image

Amanda Gallegos, clinical mental health counselor, is the second appointed mental health provider to run the Cook County, Illinois, jail, which is the nation's second largest jail. How would you advise Ms. Gallegos to reduce the number of persons in jail with mental illness?
Courtesy of Amanda Gallegos, and the Cook County Sheriff's Office

Rikers Island have a mental health diagnosis. And the Los Angeles County Jail with an ADP of 15,000 also reports that 4 out of 10 persons in jail suffer from a mental illness. Researchers with the Rand Corporation studied the backgrounds of the persons in the LA County Jail with a mental health diagnosis and reported that 61 percent could be safely diverted into community-based treatment programs like those discussed in Chapter 5. They also reported that another 7 percent could be considered potentially appropriate and 32 percent could be considered not appropriate.

Despite the large number of persons in jail with mental illness, these individuals are not often fit subjects for retribution or punishment. Jails are not therapeutic environments. Because of the constant noise, bright lights, and an ever changing population, jails do not offer rest or relief for people with mental illness. James Gondles, former executive director of the American Correctional Association, said, "The notion that the prospect of incarceration will deter an individual with a mental illness from committing a crime does not apply to a population that cannot fully comprehend the consequences of its actions, especially in cases where crime is a direct result of illness."[23]

Over the years, the nation's sheriffs have also said that jails are not equipped to meet the complex needs of persons living with mental illness and asked county and general hospitals to accept them as patients. The sheriffs spelled out six factors as to why jails should not be used for such people:

1. The mentally ill person has usually committed no crime.
2. County jails are overcrowded.
3. Small county sheriffs' officers are not specially trained for the proper handling and care of a mental patient.
4. Many jails do not have proper or adequate detention rooms for the mentally ill.
5. Detention in the county jail is unfair to the patient as well as to the corrections officers.

6. Psychiatrists agree that a patient originally detained in a jail is much more difficult to treat and readjust, and incarceration can contribute to the further decompensation of many people with mental illness.[24]

Throughout the United States and other nations worldwide, a well-known strategy to reduce the number of persons with mental illness from going to jail is the adoption of Crisis Intervention Teams (CIT).[25] CIT is a police-based first responder program that has become nationally known as the "Memphis Model" of pre-arrest jail diversion for those in a mental illness crisis. Selected police officers receive up to 40 hours of training in mental illness and ways to de-escalate crises involving those exhibiting signs of mental disorder. Instead of arresting people who commit low-level crimes—such as disorderly conduct, public urination, or trespassing—and taking them to jail, officers can take them to community mental health centers or sobering centers. Currently, out of the 18,000 law enforcement agencies in the United States, CIT programs operate in nearly 3,000.

In addition to CIT as a way to respond to persons for a low-level offense, other police agencies are experimenting with "**deflection**," moving a person away from the justice system and toward community behavioral health and social services without ever being arrested and processed into the criminal justice system.[26] Whereas CIT uses specially selected and trained police officers, deflection makes every law enforcement officer a potential pathway to behavioral intervention services, drug treatment, mental health treatment, and social services when called for. Over 600 police department across the United States are using some type of deflection. The benefits of CIT and deflection are shown in Exhibit 6–9.

deflection

Moving a person away from the justice system and toward community behavioral health and social services without ever being arrested and processed into the criminal justice system.

Juveniles and Jail Populations   Over the past 50 years, there has been a dramatic reversal in the theory and practice of punishing juveniles. When Congress passed the Juvenile Justice and Delinquency Prevention Act of 1974, it mandated four things:

1. Young people charged with offenses that would not be a crime if committed by an adult (e.g., running away, truance, and underage drinking) may not be held in secure confinement.

2. Juveniles generally may not be held in jails and lockups in which adults are confined.

3. When juveniles are temporarily detained in the same facilities as adults, they must have no "sight or sound" contact with adults serving time.

4. Reduce the disproportionate number of minority youth who come into contact with the juvenile justice system.

EXHIBIT 6–9   Benefits of CIT and Deflection

- ✓ Immediacy of response
- ✓ Increased officer safety
- ✓ Reduced officer/citizen injuries
- ✓ Increased jail diversion
- ✓ Increased chance for consumer to connect to mental health system
- ✓ Increased officer confidence in calls
- ✓ Reduced liability
- ✓ Reduced unnecessary arrests or use of force
- ✓ Avoidance of costs to criminal justice system
- ✓ Positive perception of program
- ✓ Linkages to long-term services promoting recovery for the individual

However, policy changes do not happen overnight and juveniles continue to be held in jail and as adults. In 2000, 2.5 million persons under the age of 18 were arrested, 7,600 were sent to jail, and 80 percent were held as adults. In 2020, 425,000 juveniles were arrested, 2,300 were sent to jail, and almost 9 out of 10 were held as adults.[27]

While the number of juveniles in jail and held as adults has declined, jailing juveniles continues to be criticized for a number of reasons. Holding juveniles in adult jails places young people at greater risk of being physically, sexually, and mentally abused by adults. Juvenile girls are especially vulnerable to sexual assault. Juveniles in adult jail are almost eight times more likely to commit suicide than are those in juvenile detention centers. One explanation is that juveniles are held in isolated parts of adult jails where they receive less staff support and supervision. Another is that jail staff are not trained to recognize depression in juveniles.

Momentum for change grew, and in 2018, Congress passed the Juvenile Justice Reform Act, a groundbreaking piece of legislation that updated the original law passed in 1974 and its reauthorization in 2002. The 2018 law requires states to end the practice of placing youth who are transferred into adult court in adult jails or lockups and moving them instead to juvenile detention centers within three years. Thus, if a teen is transferred into adult court, he or she cannot enter an adult facility until they turn 18.

The new law also places emphasis on prevention and support for a continuum of evidence-based programs and practices that are trauma informed, reflect the science of adolescent development, and are designed to meet the needs of at-risk youth and youth who come into contact with the justice system. The law also places a renewed emphasis on racial equity and requires states to collect data on racial and economic disparities and to develop a plan to reduce them.

Jail Suicide, Homicide, and Sexual Victimization

Since the Bureau of Justice Statistics started collecting data on jail suicides in 2000 we've learned that suicide is the leading cause of death in local jails and has been every year since 2000. Jail suicides increased 13 percent from 289 in 2000 to 355 in 2019. When compared to the U.S. adult population's suicide rate, the suicide rate in jail is more than double—49 per 100,000 jail suicides compared to 22 per 100,000 adult U.S. resident suicides. Estimates also show that there are 80 suicide attempts for every fatal suicide within a correctional facility.[28]

The majority of jail suicides typically occur within the first week of incarceration. One out of four happens within the first two days of admission. The demographic and criminal justice profile of persons who committed suicide in jail in 2019 is similar to previous years. The majority were most often unmarried non-Hispanic White men with a high school education, aged 24 to 44, and in custody for committing a violent crime. More than one-third had a history of serious mental illness, and 77 percent were never convicted and were still awaiting trial.

The consequences of suicide are lost lives, devastation to families, short- and long-term psychological effects on other people in jail and correctional staff, expensive investigations and litigation, and medical care costs. Kentucky is one state that successfully reduced its jail suicides from 17 to 4 per year by cross-training jail personnel and mental health providers, developing new screening instruments for arresting and booking officers, establishing a telephonic service that allows jail staff to call a licensed mental health professional for risk management consultation 24 hours a day, and establishing a statewide data collection and analysis system.[29]

Homicide in jail is another concern of jail administrators, and here the news has not been good.[30] In 2000, 17 people in jail were murdered. In 2006, the number peaked at 36, decreased to 16 in 2008, and continued to increase every year since, reaching 25 homicides in 2014. Since then, the Department of Justice has not released data on jail homicides.

The literature on jail homicides offers very few insights other than revealing that people charged with kidnapping are the most likely victims, followed by persons charged with violent crimes, property, and then public-order. The majority of jail homicide victims are male, mostly between the ages of 18 and 54, and evenly split between white and Black.

In 2003, Congress passed the Prison Rape Elimination Act. The goal of the act is to eradicate all forms of sexual victimization in jail and prison. The Act requires the U.S. Department of Justice to report on the incidence of rape and other forms of sexual victimization in correctional facilities. Almost 8,000 allegations of sexual victimization were reported by jails in 2016, and 576 were confirmed. In 2018 (the last year for which data are available), allegations increased slightly to approximately 8,600 and 547 were substantiated.[31]

After conducting a series of public hearings, reviewing the data, conducting site visits, and speaking with correctional staff and persons in jail and prison, the Prison Rape Elimination Act's review panel concluded that sexual assaults can be reduced by changing attitudes toward potentially vulnerable populations, including female, lesbian, gay, bisexual, transgender, queer (LGBTQ), and physically frail individuals, paying close attention to institutional design and surveillance; providing education and staff training; improving operational policies and post orders; and monitoring adherence to established policies. In addition, a reliable classification system; improved efforts on the part of first responders, investigators, and prosecutors; and timely victim assistance and health care services can help an agency reduce, if not eliminate, sexual victimization in jail.[32]

Jail Facilities

Occupancy **Rated capacity**, as defined by the Bureau of Justice Statistics, is the number of beds a jail can hold, set by a rating official. Understanding rated capacity in jails is essential for maintaining safety, legal compliance, and the wellbeing of both residents and staff. It also contributes to the effectiveness of rehabilitation programming and responsible resource allocation, all of which are critical aspects of a well-functioning jail.

rated capacity
The maximum number of beds or inmates allocated to each jail facility by a state or local rating official.

The rated capacity of the nation's jails is 913,700 beds. For the past decade jails have added around 3,000 new beds a year.[33] During the COVID pandemic, jail bed occupancy was at about 60 percent. Today the rate is 70 percent, a sign the criminal justice system is returning to pre-pandemic levels of jail incarceration. We also see that overcrowding has worsened. During the pandemic, about 200 jails (or 7 percent of jails) were operating at or above 100 percent of their rated capacity. Today, it's more than 400 (almost 13 percent of jails). Overall these trends suggest a return to pre-COVID policies and practices within the criminal justice system, leading to higher jail occupancy rates and increased jail overcrowding in some areas. What is the rated capacity of your jail?

Private Jails and Jails Under Court Order The last census of the nation's jails published by the U.S. Department of Justice in 2021 reported that 34 of the nation's 3,116 jails were privately operating under contract to local governments.[34] Private jails are located in 12 states: California (2), Colorado (3), Florida (1), Indiana (1), Kansas (1), Louisiana (5), Mississippi (2), New Mexico (2), Ohio (1), Pennsylvania (5), Tennessee (2), and Texas

The Fremont, California, Police Department offers individuals who are serving short sentences on lesser charges an option to pay-to-stay for a one-time fee of $45 and $155 a night to stay in a smaller, quieter facility and avoid going to the county jails. The city expects to make almost $250,000 annually if 16 persons spend two nights a week under the program. What are the advantages and disadvantages of pay-to-stay jails?

Photo by Justin Sullivan/Getty Images

Marian Brown is Sheriff of Dallas County, Texas. Sheriff Brown operates the seventh largest jail in the United States with an ADP of over 6,000 and more than 2,000 employees. Why are staffing issues a major concern of most jails today?

Courtesy of Marian Brown - Sheriff, Dallas County

(9). In Chapter 7 you will that of the nation's 1,161 prisons, 82 are privately operating with governmental agencies.

We also learn from the U.S. Department of Justice that almost 4 percent (175) of the nation's 3,116 jails are under a court order to do or not do something or under a consent decree (a settlement agreement approved by the court) revolving around specific conditions such as crowding, recreation, exercise, staffing, medical facilities, procedures or policies, food services, religious practices, programming, and classification. Are there any privately operated jails in your area? Are any of the jails under court order, and if so, for what?

Jail Size, Budgets, and Fees   The U.S. Department of Justice classifies jail size into seven levels (less than 50 people in jail, 50 to 99, 100 to 249, 250 to 499, 500 to 999, 1,000 to 2,499, and more and 2,500). The largest jails (those with an ADP of 1,000 or more) hold 38 percent of the entire jail population but account for only 4 percent of all jail facilities nationwide.

In comparison, the smallest jails (those with an ADP of less than 50) hold 4 percent of the jail population but account for almost 40 percent of all the jails.[35]

Incarceration is not cheap. Taxpayers spend more than $25 billion annually to support the nation's jails.[36] The Vera Institute of Justice reported that operating budgets are highest in New York at $2.4 billion, and lowest in North Dakota at $4 million.[37] The national average cost of operating jails is approximately $34,000 per person in jail. San Francisco pays about $63,000 a year or about $135 a night. Across the United States, almost 185,000 correctional officers (CO) supervise the nation's jail population of 600,000. One-third of COs are women. On average, one CO supervises four persons in jail. One might reasonably ask if more money and staff makes us any safer.

Recall that we reported in Chapters 4 and 5 that various components of the criminal justice system require persons on probation or an intermediate sanction to pay a supervision fee. Today, at least one-third of county jails across

40 states also charge people in jail fees for a growing number of services, some of which arguably discriminate against the poor and contribute to mass incarceration.[38] Privacy and services in jail come with a price tag. For example:

- The Brown County Jail in Wisconsin charges $6 to see a nurse, $12 to see a doctor, and $20 per day for the jail cell, food, and accommodations.
- The Riverside County Jail in California charges $142 per day for the jail cell, food, and accommodations.
- The Vanderburgh County Jail in Indiana allows families and friends to purchase "a restaurant-quality meal on behalf of their incarcerated loved one" from Aramark Correctional Services. The meal is delivered to the person in jail.
- A number of California jurisdictions in Los Angeles and Orange counties offer "privileges" to persons in **pay-to-stay jails** who pay almost $300 a day for a private cell, bathroom, and shower stall, use of one's cell phone, and food brought in or delivered from the outside. Exhibit 6–10 compares six pay-to-stay jails in southern California in terms of cost per day, number of beds available, amenities, what persons are allowed to bring in, and eligibility criteria.

pay-to-stay jails

Local correctional facilities that allow persons in jail to pay between $100 and $300 a day for extra privileges in accommodation, food, and entertainment.

EXHIBIT 6–10   Comparison of Six Pay-to-Stay Jails

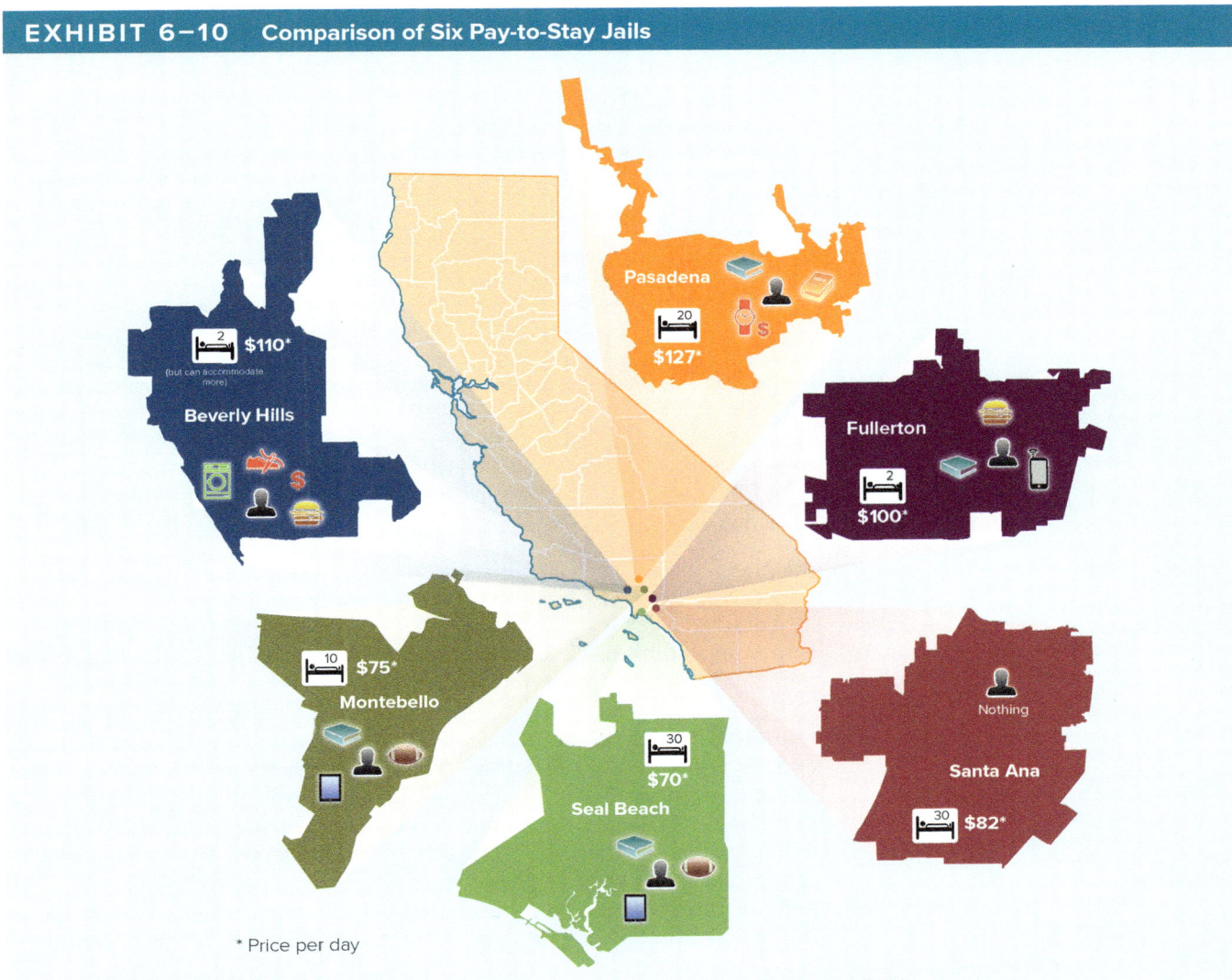

* Price per day

Source: Information for Santa Ana, Seal Beach, Montebello, Pasadena, and Fullerton adapted from "Hard Time Made Easier," *The New York Times*, April 29, 2007.

EXHIBIT 6–11 Arguments Favoring and Opposing Jail Fees and Pay-to-Stay Jail Programs

PRO

- Revenues collected from persons in jail help to offset expensive incarceration budgets.
- Charging individuals for their stay teaches them that if they violate the law, they pay for it.
- Pay-to-stay jail programs act as a deterrent.
- Pay-to-stay jail programs can be part of the rehabilitative process.
- Law-abiding citizens should not be burdened with the cost of incarceration when they never use the service.
- Law-abiding citizens should not be victimized by supporting persons who have the ability to pay.
- Policymakers, judges, and sheriffs can gain the support of the local citizenry by advocating for pay-to-stay programs.
- Pay-to-stay jail programs reduce frivolous requests for services.

CON

- Because the community has chosen to remove certain individuals from society, the society should bear the brunt of the fiscal costs of feeding, housing, and providing medical attention.
- Individuals are already deprived of their freedom by the state; therefore, it is unjust to punish them again by charging them for room, board, and services.
- Persons confined in jail are involuntary consumers and not permitted to forego the punishment of the state or obtain the services elsewhere.
- Shifting the cost to individuals who are confined in jail (80 percent of whom are indigent by most accounts) provides less incentive to policymakers to keep down costs associated with mass incarceration.
- Families with loved ones in jail often become the de facto source of pay-to-stay fees.
- Pay-to-stay jail program is a bad fiscal policy because it withdraws resources from poor families to fund its own operations.
- Pay-to-stay jail fees disproportionately affect indigent populations along with racial and ethnic minorities, all of whom are disproportionately represented among the jail population.
- Pay-to-stay jail fees generate further barriers to successful reentry after jail and encourage a cycle of poverty that is difficult to escape.
- Pay-to-stay jail fees may discourage people from seeking medical attention, leaving jail staff unprotected from communicable diseases.
- It may cost more to administer the fee program than what is generated in revenue.

Arguments favoring and opposing jail fees and pay-to-stay jails are presented in Exhibit 6–11. Considering the demographics of the nation's jail population, which arguments are most persuasive?

We might also ask, if jails had more revenue, would it mean a lower crime rate? The Pew Charitable Trusts looked at how much states spent on jails and its impact on crime rates.[39] They found that some states with lower crime rates spent more of their local budgets on jails than states with higher crime rates and some states with similar crime rates spent widely different amounts. For example, the crime rate in both Missouri and Nevada is 3,500 crimes per 100,000 adult population. However, jail spending is at opposite ends of the spectrum in both states. Less than 1 percent of local spending is spent on jails in Missouri. In Nevada, 3 percent of local spending is spent on jails. There is no clear correlation between state crime rates and jail spending.

JAIL ISSUES

We conclude this chapter by elaborating on three jail issues that are on the forefront of correctional concerns today: bail and pretrial detention, reentry, and jail standards and accreditation.

Bail and Pretrial Detention

CO6-6

Until the 1990s, release on recognizance (one's promise to appear in court) was the most common type of pretrial release. However across the "get-tough-on-crime" era of the 1990s and into the 21st century, its use had declined by one-third, the use of financial pretrial release through commercial bail bonding companies increased proportionally, and the number of persons held in jail who could not afford cash bail quadrupled.[40]

On any given night in the United States, more than half a million people are in jail even though 70 percent have not been convicted of anything and are detained because they can't afford to post bail. What stands in the way of their freedom is money—sometimes a bail amount as low as $250 that they simply cannot afford. The average felony bail set in the United States is $10,000, yet according to the Federal Reserve, about 40 percent of people in the United States could not afford a surprise $400 payment.[41]

How does bail work? Bail amounts are usually set by published schedules based on the offense, normally ranging from $1,000 to $25,000. Persons are required to put down a percentage of the total to secure bail, so they can go home. Too often however the bail amount is set too high for many individuals or their families to afford at which point a commercial bond agent steps in to write a "surety" bond on the individual's behalf. The individual pays a nonrefundable premium—usually 10 percent of the total bond—to the bond company, which will pay the full amount if the person does not appear in court. In some cases, bond agents also require individuals to provide collateral such as the title to a vehicle or home. Some even borrow the money from their bail agent on installment plans, generally with high interest. Under the current system, the bonding company is not required to put up any cash of its own—just a promissory note to the court to pay the full amount if the person fails to appear.

Consider this example: Mr. Holt gets arrested for assault in New York City. The court sets his bail at $1,500. The **bail** bond company needs $150 (10 percent) to post Holt's bail. Holt doesn't have it, so he sits in the Rikers Island detention center for 75 days awaiting trial where it costs about $460 per day to incarcerate one person.[42] Holt pleads guilty and is sentenced to time served and released. Because Mr. Holt did not have $460, taxpayers shelled out a whopping $34,500. The Pretrial Justice Institute estimates that taxpayers spend approximately $38 million per day to jail people like Mr. Holt who are awaiting trial simply because they are too poor to pay bail.

The United States leads the world in the number of **pretrial detainees**—defendants who are held in jail prior to their trial on criminal charges because either no bail is posted, the individual cannot afford the amount, or bail is denied. Of the three reasons, the cash bail practices for persons who

bail

A written obligation with or without collateral security, given to a court to guarantee appearance before the court.

pretrial detainee

A person who is held in jail prior to trial on criminal charges because no bail is posted, the individual cannot afford bail, or bail is denied.

cannot afford bail is a significant contributor to mass incarceration. The U.S. Commission on Civil Rights reported that from 1970 to 2015, there was a 433 percent increase in the number of persons who were detained pretrial.[43] Today, 70 percent (more than 400,000) of persons in jail are detained pretrial, most because they cannot afford bail, what some call "wealth-based detention."

Concerns over Money for Bail   The judicial system depends on monetary bail under the assumption that it protects public safety and ensures that the released individual returns to court. However where data exist measuring public safety from before and after the adoption of pretrial reforms we find that whether the jurisdictions eliminated money bail for some or all charges, began using a validated risk assessment tool, introduced services to remind people of upcoming court dates, or implemented some combination of these reforms, the results were the same: Financial collateral does not ensure an individual's return for their court appearance. Furthermore, releasing people pretrial does not negatively impact public safety.[44] On the contrary, studies have shown that individuals who are detained before their trial tend to receive harsher sentencing outcomes compared to those who remain free until their trial. They are four times as likely to be sentenced to imprisonment and three times as likely to receive longer prison terms.[45]

Other consequences of being held in jail pretrial aren't always so visible, but researchers and others have noticed them.[46] Individuals held in pretrial detention often cannot maintain their appearance as well as those who come to trial from their homes. Jurors who see defendants in restraints and jail attire, may associate these outward characteristics as signs of dangerousness. Additionally, pretrial detention severely restricts a person's ability to collaborate effectively with their attorney in preparing a defense, contacting witnesses, and engaging in other essential activities, often due to limited telephone access. It can also disrupt established medical routines. Children whose parents are detained pretrial may have to move, leading to disruptions in their education. Furthermore, persons detained before trial also lose an estimated $29,000 in income on average over a lifetime compared with persons who were not detained pretrial.[47] Consequently, many argue that the ability to maintain employment, housing, caregiver responsibilities, and other essential aspects of life should be available to all individuals awaiting their court date, ensuring safety without necessitating financial resources as a prerequisite.

Several states and jurisdictions have enacted laws aimed at eliminating cash bail. Nonetheless, these bail reforms have encountered obstacles, with some being temporarily halted due to legal challenges or revised and adjusted. Notably, Illinois became the pioneering state to completely abolish monetary bail in 2023. In Illinois, judges have the authority to determine whether an individual presents a significant community risk that precludes their release or if release can be granted under specific conditions, such as refraining from contact with certain individuals or avoiding specific locations.

In places where money bail is not completely abolished, we find a number of other alternatives including:

- release on recognizance (a promise to return to court)
- conditional release (release with specific conditions, e.g., enroll in programming, education, find employment, etc.)

EXHIBIT 6–12   **National Association of Pretrial Services Agencies (NAPSA) Code of Ethics**

As a pretrial services professional I will:

- Assist the criminal justice system in its dealings with pretrial defendants to the best of my ability and will conduct myself as a professional at all times;
- Respect the dignity of the individual, be they defendants, victims, or fellow criminal justice professionals;
- Respect the dignity and integrity of the court;
- Respect the presumption of innocence of all defendants, until proven guilty beyond a reasonable doubt, and to uphold the fundamental right of every accused person who has been arrested and is facing prosecution under the U.S. criminal justice system;
- Pledge that the information I provide to the court and the decisions I make are as accurate and objective as possible;
- Treat all people equally regardless of race, national origin, disability, age, gender, sexual orientation or religion;
- Protect the confidentiality of all information obtained, except when necessary to prevent serious, foreseeable, and/or imminent harm to a defendant or other identifiable person(s);
- Avoid impropriety or the appearance of impropriety;
- Avoid any conflicts of interest and will not evaluate, supervise and/or provide services to anyone I have an existing relationship with, nor enter into a personal or business relationship with anyone I evaluate, supervise or provide services to;
- Continue to pursue my own professional development and education to further my expertise in the field;
- Promote the growth of pretrial services, as well as encourage and cooperate with research and development in advancing the field;
- Respect and promote the fundamental principles and professional standards which guide pretrial services and will implement these best practices to the extent I am able;
- Refrain from providing legal advice to any pretrial defendants; and lastly,
- Promise to conduct myself as an individual of good character who will act in good faith in making reliable ethical judgments.

- release to a pretrial services agency for supervision and monitoring during the pretrial period
- citations and summonses
- diversion into social programs for people who have mental, emotional, or alcohol-related problems.

Some of the problem-solving courts discussed in Chapter 5 can be tailored as alternatives to money bail. The National Association of Pretrial Services Agencies, a professional association dedicated to promoting pretrial justice and public safety through practices informed by science, supports the professionalization of its members. NAPSA's Code of Ethics is shown in Exhibit 6–12.

We also learned in this chapter and Chapter 4 that evidence-based risk assessment tools can aid the court in making the decision on which type of alternative to money bail is appropriate. Exhibit 6–13 lays out the myths and facts of using risk assessments.

Reentry (Begins at Entry)

CO6-7

In recent decades, professionals in the field of corrections have dedicated significant efforts to addressing the issue of jail **reentry**, the transition persons make from jail (or prison) to the community. Nevertheless, it is evident that this challenge remains formidable. The nation's jails house a substantial population with diverse and pressing needs.

reentry
The transition persons make from jail (or prison) to the community.

EXHIBIT 6–13   Myths and Facts: Using Risk and Need Assessments to Enhance Outcomes and Reduce Disparities in the Criminal Justice System

Myths...	...and facts
1 Professional judgment is more accurate than risk and need assessments when predicting the risk to recidivate.	Actuarial risk and need assessments have consistently been found to be more accurate than professional judgment alone in risk prediction.
2 Risk and need assessments exacerbate racial bias within the criminal justice system.	Risk and need assessments can reduce racial bias in criminal justice decisions if objectively used as designed and are specifically validated in the jurisdictions where they are applied.
3 Eliminating risk and need assessments would help to eliminate racial bias in criminal justice decision making.	Eliminating actuarial risk and need assessments would decrease accuracy in risk prediction and increase bias by relying solely on professional judgment.
4 The use of risk and need assessments increases the likelihood that justice-involved individuals are incarcerated.	Risk and need assessments used to make front-end decisions are typically used to identify and safely divert individuals who are more appropriate for supervision and treatment in the community.
5 Risk and need assessments should be used to make sentencing decisions more punitive.	Actuarial risk and need assessments were designed to predict risk, identify areas of criminogenic need, and guide decisions for treatment, not for punitive purposes.
The bottom line:	Risk and need assessments currently provide the most accurate, objective prediction of the risk to recidivate. While risk and need assessments do not predict with perfect accuracy, they guide practitioners in the field towards the most accurate and equitable decisions available for safely managing justice-involved individuals.

Source: Community Corrections Collaborative Network and National Institute of Corrections.

Unfortunately, many jails provide limited services within their facilities, and even fewer establish meaningful connections to programs and support services in the community for those preparing to reenter society.

On the other hand, the nation's 3,116 jails face a promising moment. Jail reentry is an opportunity to intervene in the lives of the individuals who cycle in and out of jail each year (also known as "frequent fliers"). Jails can be a prevention strategy—meaning they avert future offending and processing through the criminal justice system. However, effective prevention strategies require partnerships between jails and community-based organizations and new ways of doing business. While the three Cs of jail (Care, Custody, and Control) have long been the traditional jail mission, a new mission involves partnerships with community-based agencies. Incorporating reentry into mission statements may help better reflect both the evolving purposes of jails beyond confinement and a commitment to institutionalize reentry services into jail operations.

Reentry from jail requires that jails quickly and efficiently assess the risks and needs of the women and men they house and develop reentry plans for their return to the community. For most, it may be sufficient to provide a reentry handbook or referral list of community-based resources. For others, reentry strategies may involve programming, training, and case management that spans continuity of care from jail to the community.

The National Institute of Corrections and Urban Institute designed the Transition from Jail to Community (TJC) model to support jail reentry. The model focuses on three priority areas:

- screening and assessment for those at the highest risk to recidivate

- implementing an evidence-based process that addresses criminogenic needs (dynamic/changeable risk factors such as substance use) and continues into the community
- implementing a data and performance process that supports reentry

Evaluations of jail-based reentry initiatives at the Suffolk County Jail (Riverhead, NY) and the Davidson County Jail (Nashville, TN) by the Urban Institute and Harvard University's Kennedy School of Government found that jail-based reentry initiatives in partnership with community-based organizations lowered rearrests and return to jail.

In the future, jail reentry is poised to undergo significant transformation, aiming for a more comprehensive and supportive approach. In the short

Career Profile

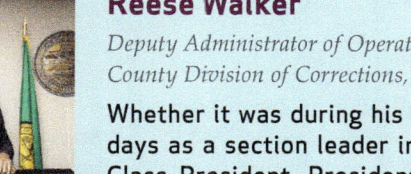

Reese Walker

Reese Walker

Deputy Administrator of Operations/Program Services, Shelby County Division of Corrections, Memphis, TN

Whether it was during his Mississippi Valley State University days as a section leader in the marching band, MVSU Senior Class President, President of the Delta Phi Chapter of Phi Beta Sigma Fraternity Inc., or as President of the Pan Hellenic Council, Reese G. Walker has never taken his position in a leadership role lightly.

After graduating MVSU with a Bachelor of Science in Criminal Justice, Reese joined the Shelby County (TN) Division of Corrections because he wanted a career where he could help others. He also knew that a career in corrections offered job stability, and opportunities for personal growth and professional development. Starting out as a Care and Custody counselor, Reese's commitment to leadership development quickly earned him promotions to Counselor A, Supervisor A, Assistant Watch Commander, Manager of Training, Administrative Captain, and in 2022, Deputy Administrator of Operations/Program Services.

Reese's commitment to corrections earned him several notable awards and achievements including Outstanding Training Class Recruit and President, Employee of the Month, Outstanding Performance Award, Supervisor of the Year, State Trainer of the Year by Tennessee Corrections Institute, Mentor and Senior Mentor of the National Jail Leadership Command Academy, and American Jail Association Certified Jail Manager, Board of Directors and Commissioner on the Jail Manager Certification Commission.

Community service and community leadership are equally important to Reese. He serves his church as a member of the choir and men's ministry. He also engages with Phi Beta Sigma Fraternity and Sigma Beta Club to foster the development of youth into effective lifelong leaders.

For persons considering a career in corrections and a role in corrections leadership, Reese offers these sage words of advice: "I advise anyone looking to advance into correctional leadership to earn certification in their field. I remind my staff that correctional facilities look at certification as a way to assess whether an individual possesses the skills and knowledge required for successful performance in a particular job role. By becoming certified in your field of expertise, and maintaining your competency year after year, you are saying to your employer that you have met standards that have been established and verified by a national accrediting body. It also says that you are dedicated to maintaining quality in your work on a regular basis."

I advise anyone looking to advance into correctional leadership to earn certification in their field...By becoming certified in your field of expertise, and maintaining your competency year after year, you are saying to your employer that you have met standards that have been established and verified by a national accrediting body. It also says that you are dedicated to maintaining quality in your work on a regular basis.

In partnership with Shawsheen Valley Technical High School, the Culinary Arts Program at the Middlesex Jail and House of Correction (Billerica, Massachusetts) prepares persons in jail for careers in food service. At the end of the 12-week course, participants receive a five-year ServSave National Restaurant Association certificate and 12 credits in culinary arts from Middlesex Community College. Elsewhere around the country persons in jail can be certified in Heating Ventilation and Air-Conditioning (HVAC), Amazon's Cloud Certification, auto repair, body work and detailing, computer programming, welding, digital imaging, hospitality management, warehouse operation, and more. What are the pros and cons of teaching persons in jail new vocational skills?

Photo by Pat Greenhouse/The Boston Globe/Getty Images

term, this could entail that individuals leaving jail have essential resources, such as necessary medications, identification documents, a place to live, and a support network in the community, which could include family members, sponsors, or treatment providers, all ready to assist with their reintegration.

In the long run the goals could be even more ambitious. These might include a future where recidivism rates are substantially reduced, relapses into criminal behavior become rare occurrences, and the number of individuals returning to jails, hospitals, and shelters, diminishes significantly. In essence, the future of jail reentry aspires to not only support individuals leaving incarceration but also enhancing the well-being of society as a whole.

CO6-8   Jail Standards, Inspection, and Accreditation

Dr. Ken Kerle, former editor of *American Jails* and probably the most known advocate for improving our nation's jails, wrote, "[J]ail inspection is about as popular in many places as a skunk in the living room and many county officials, including sheriffs, would just as soon avoid it altogether. It is no accident that 12 states today have no jail inspections and 8 states with inspection standards have no enforcement agency to compel compliance."[48]

On the other hand, other states such as Illinois, New York, Ohio, Pennsylvania, and Texas mandate state oversight of county jails. Texas, for example, has the Commission on Jail Standards, an independent state agency with the authority to develop standards, conduct inspections, and fine or close jails if they fail to comply. New York state statute allows the Commission of Corrections' jail investigators to visit any of the state's prisons or county jails at any time and may view any records they deem necessary to complete their duties. They may close any correctional facility if it is unsafe, unsanitary, or inadequate. Any person who does not obey its orders is guilty of a misdemeanor. The American Bar Association agrees with independent oversight and authority to act. It recommends that all federal, state, tribal, and territorial governments create independent bodies with broad authority and access to corrections facilities, including jails.[49]

Jail accreditation is a process through which correctional facilities and agencies can measure themselves against nationally adopted standards and through which they can receive formal recognition and accredited status. Although jails were slow to respond to the standards movement, their response has increased in recent years. The American Correctional Association has accredited over 1,300 jails and prisons including all 122 federal correctional institutions.

There are several reasons jails have been slow to adopt national standards or seek national accreditation. First, accreditation is expensive and time-consuming. Many jails do not have the resources to commit to it. This is especially true for small jails that are already overburdened. Second, jails hold relatively few long-term individuals. Few persons are in a jail long enough to file a successful legal action regarding poor conditions in the jail. Knowing this, some jail administrators may not be willing to undergo the expense and burden of seeking accreditation. Third, some states have their own standards that jails must meet.

There are, however, at least five reasons for jails to have national accreditation:

1. Accreditation indicates that a jail adheres to strict standards to protect the health and safety of staff and residents.
2. Being accredited may help a jail defend itself against lawsuits over conditions of incarceration.
3. In preparing for the accreditation review, the sheriff's office may evaluate all operations, procedures, and policies, leading to better management practices.
4. With accreditation come professional recognition and status, greater appreciation by the community, and a sense of pride in the achievement and in the hard work that went into it.
5. And recently, ACA, in conjunction with the American Jail Association, National Sheriff's Association, National Institute of Corrections, and the Federal Bureau of Prisons, developed a set of core jail standards to establish minimum practices for small and medium-sized facilities. This new option makes certification easier now for small and medium-sized jails.

jail accreditation

Process through which correctional facilities and agencies can measure themselves against nationally adopted standards and through which they can receive formal recognition and accredited status.

REVIEW AND APPLICATIONS

SUMMARY

1 Jails emerged in Europe in the 12th century to detain persons for trial. In the 15th and 16th centuries, the poor and unemployed were detained alongside criminals. The first jail in America was the Walnut Street Jail. Quakers designed it according to their principles of religious reflection and penance. It fell short of reaching its goals and closed in 1835.

2 American jails have progressed through three phases of architecture and management: first-generation jails (linear design and sporadic supervision), second-generation jails (pod design and remote supervision), and third-generation jails (pod design and direct supervision).

3 The *daily* population of jails is lower than that of prisons, but the *annual* total of people incarcerated in jails is higher.

4 There are 3,116 local jails and 80 Indian country jails in the United States. Besides incarcerating people who have sentences of a year or less, jails serve a number of purposes. They hold people awaiting trial, persons who violate the conditions of their probation and parole, adults and juveniles awaiting transfer, and sometimes persons about to be released from prison. Sometimes they operate community-based programs. The jail population is different from the prison population in terms of total admissions and average daily population.

5 Today, almost 600,000 persons are held in the nation's jails. In addition to the confined population, jail authorities also supervise persons in programs outside the jail. An estimated 30 percent of the persons in jail are convicted. Women represent 15 percent of the jail population; nonwhites, 50 percent; and juveniles, 0.4 percent. Almost two-thirds have a mental health problem, and there are more people with mental illness in jail than there are in mental health hospitals. Suicide and heart disease are the top two causes of death in local jails. Thirty-four jails are privatized. The most (nine) are in Texas.

6 Some bail release options require money or property while others do not. Concerns over money bail have given rise to new alternatives.

7 Jail reentry is an opportunity to intervene in the lives of the individuals who cycle in and out of jail each year. The National Institute of Corrections and the Urban Institute created the Transition from Jail to Community (TJC) model to support jail reentry. The model's three priority areas are: screen and assess those at the highest risk to recidivate; implement an evidence-based process that addresses criminogenic needs; and implement a data and performance process that supports reentry.

8 Jail standards, inspection, and accreditation are important for five reasons. First, inspection and accreditation indicate that a jail adheres to strict standards. Second, accreditation may help a jail defend itself against lawsuits over conditions of incarceration. Third, through inspection and accreditation, the sheriff's office may evaluate all jail operations, procedures, and policies, leading to better management practices. Fourth, accreditation generates professional recognition and status, greater appreciation by the community, and a sense of pride. And fifth, the ACA in conjunction with the American Jail Association, National Sheriff's Association, National Institute of Corrections, and the Federal Bureau of Prisons now has a set of core jail standards to establish minimum practices for small and medium-sized facilities. This new option makes certification easier for small and medium-sized jails.

KEY TERMS

first-generation jail, p. 127

second-generation jail, p. 127

third-generation jail, p. 128

jails, p. 130

total admission, p. 130

average daily population (ADP), p. 130

deflection, p. 139

rated capacity, p. 141

pay-to-stay jail, p. 143

bail, p. 145

pretrial detainee, p. 145

reentry, p. 147

jail accreditation, p. 151

QUESTIONS FOR REVIEW

1 Summarize the history of jails.

2 Explain how first-, second-, and third-generation jails differ.

3 Describe how jail populations are different from prison populations.

4 Jails serve a number of purposes. Which do you believe is the most important and why?

5 What can you infer from the jail population and facility characteristics?

6 What is the purpose of bail? Discuss bail release options and the concerns over money bail.

7 Why is reentry from the jail to the community important?

8 What ideas can you add to the arguments for and against jail standards, inspection, and accreditation?

THINKING CRITICALLY ABOUT CORRECTIONS

Persons in Jail with Menal Illness

Explain why persons in jail with mental illness should not be subjects for incarceration as some suggest, and why jails are ill-equipped to meet their needs.

Evidence-Based Practices

Why are evidence-based practices necessary for jails?

ON-THE-JOB DECISION MAKING

Promoting Direct Supervision

You are the administrator of a new county jail with the architecture and philosophy of direct supervision. The new jail replaced a jail built in 1912. Some of the senior staff have begun complaining to you about direct supervision. They say they don't like to interact with the persons they supervise. They talk about "the good old days" when inmates were "on the other side" of the reinforced glass and steel bars. There's even been a letter to the editor in the local newspaper complaining that the new jail doesn't "look like a jail."

1. What could you tell the senior staff about direct-supervision philosophy that might ease their concerns?

2. What strategies might you use to educate the public about the benefits of direct supervision?

Jail Tips for Justice Involved Women

The National Resource Center for Justice Involved Women and the American Jail Association developed a series of eight jail tip sheets to facilitate the implementation of gender-informed approaches with women in jail. Each tip sheet includes a brief overview of the topic, selected evidence-based research findings, and brief action steps that jail leadership and staff can take to enhance gender-responsive practices. Locate the tip sheets at cjinvolvedwomen.org/jail-tip-sheets. After reviewing the tip sheets, assume you are a jail administrator. How would you encourage "buy-in" from your jail staff to follow research-based guidelines and change your facility's culture or norms that are based almost exclusively on gender-neutral operational practices?

ENDNOTES

1. U.S. Department of Justice, Office of Public Affairs, *New Jersey Man Sentenced to One Year and a Day in Prison for Conspiring with White Supremacists to Vandalize Synagogues Across the Country* (Washington, DC: U.S. Department of Justice, Office of Public Affairs, Tuesday, November 16, 2021); Joshua Rhett Miller, "New Jersey White Supremacist Sentenced for Planning Vandalism Attack on Synagogues," *New York Post,* November 17, 2021, www.nypost.com (accessed December 1, 2021).

2. Marilyn D. McShane and Frank P. Williams III (eds.), *Encyclopedia of American Prisons* (New York: Garland, 1996), p. 494.

3. David M. Parrish, "The Evolution of Direct Supervision in the Design and Operation of Jails," *Corrections Today,* www.corrections.com/aca/cortoday/october00/parrish.html (accessed November 26, 2022).

4. Michael O'Toole, "Jails and Prisons: The Numbers Say They Are More Different Than Generally Assumed," *American Jails,* www.corrections.com/aja/mags/articles/toole.html (accessed January 7, 2019); see also Daron Hall, "Jails vs. Prisons," *Corrections Today,* vol. 68, no. 1 (February 2006), p. 8.

5. Todd D. Minton and Zhen Zeng, *Jail Inmates in 2020—Statistical Tables* (Washington, DC: U.S. Department of Justice, Bureau of Justice Statistics, December 2021).

6. Ram Subramanian, Ruth Delaney, Stephen Roberts, Nancy Fishman, and Peggy McGarry, *Incarceration's Front Door: The Misuse of Jails in America* (New York: Vera Institute of Justice, February 2015); Marilyn Chandler Ford, "Frequent Fliers: The High Demand User in Local Corrections," *California Journal of Health Promotion,* vol. 3, no. 2 (2005), pp. 61–71; TCR Staff, "Arrest, Release, Repeat: The Tragic Cycle of American Jails," *The Crime Report,* August, 27, 2019, www.thecrimereport (accessed November 28, 2022).

7. Todd D. Minton and Zhen Zeng, *Jail Inmates in 2020—Statistical Tables.*

8. Todd D. Minton and Zhen Zeng, *Jail Inmates in 2020—Statistical Tables.*

9. Doris J. James, *Profile of Jail Inmates, 2002* (Washington, DC: U.S. Department of Justice, Bureau of Justice Statistics, July 2004); see also Gail Elias and Kenneth Ricci, *Women in Jail: Facility Planning Issues* (Washington, DC: U.S. Department of Justice, National Institute of Corrections, March 1997).

10. Tim Brennan and James Austin, *Women in Jail: Classification Issues* (Washington, DC: U.S. Department of Justice, National Institute of Corrections, March 1997).

11. Merry Morash, Timothy S. Bynum, and Barbara A. Koons, *Women Offenders: Programming Needs and Promising Approaches* (Washington, DC: U.S. Department of Justice, National Institute of Justice, August 1998).

12. Holly Ventura Miller, "Female Re-entry and Gender-responsaive Programming," *Corrections Today* (May/June 2021).

13. Barbara Bloom, Barbara Owen, and Stephanie Covington, *Gender-Responsiveness Strategies Research, Practice, and Guiding Principles for Women Offenders* (Washington, DC: U.S. Department of Justice, National Institute of Corrections, June 2003); Tara Gray, G. Larry Mays, and Mary K. Stohr, "Inmate Needs and Programming in Exclusively Women's Jails," *Prison Journal,* vol. 75, no. 2 (1995), pp. 186–195.

14. Stevyn Fogg, "Female Inmates in Jail Settings: Identifying Challenges and Critical Issues," *American Jails,* vol. 26, no. 6 (January/February 2014), pp. 12–16.

15. Samuel Walker, Cassia Spohn, and Miriam DeLone, "Corrections: A Picture in Black and White," in Tara Gray (ed.), *Exploring Corrections* (Boston: Allyn & Bacon, 2002), pp. 13–24.

16. Michael Tonry, *Malign Neglect* (New York: Oxford University Press, 1995); *Targeting Blacks: Drug Law Enforcement and Race in the United States* (New York: Human Rights Watch, 2008); and Ryan S. King, *Disparity by Geography: The War on Drugs in America's Cities* (Washington, DC: Sentencing Project, 2008).

17. Walker, Spohn, and DeLone, "Corrections," p. 16.

18. Substance Abuse and Mental Health Services Administration, *National Mental Health Services Survey (N-MHSS): 2020. Data on Mental Health Treatment Facilities* (Rockville, MD: Substance Abuse and Mental Health Services Administration, 2021).

19. John S. Shaffer, Joe Russo, Dulani Woods, and Brian A. Jackson, *Managing the Seriously Mentally Ill in Corrections* (Santa Monica, CA: Rand Corporation, 2019).

20. National Institute of Mental Health, "Transforming the Understanding and Treatment of Mental Illnesses," March 2023, www.nimh.nih.gov/health/statistics /mental-illness (accessed June 1, 2023).

21. Sam McCann, *Locking People Up with Mental Health Conditions Doesn't Make Anyone Safer* (New York: Vera, 2022); Doris J. James and Lauren Glaze, *Mental Health Problems of Prison and Jail Inmates* (Washington, DC: Bureau of Justice Statistics, 2006). See also Steven L. Proctor, Norman G. Hoffman and Alyssa Raggio, "Prevalence of Substance Use Disorders and Psychiatric Conditions Among County Jail Inmates: Changes and Stability Over Time," *Criminal Justice and Behavior*, vol. 46, no. 1 (2018), pp. 24-41.

22. Tracy Zampaglione, "New Start: A Blueprint for Managing Mentally Ill Inmates," *American Jails*, vol. 36, no 3 (July/August 2022), pp. 57–60; Sam McCann, *Locking People Up with Mental Health Conditions Doesn't Make Anyone Safer*; Samantha Michaels, "Chicago's Jail is One of the Country's Biggest Mental Health Providers," *Mother Jones*, January 8, 2019, www.motherjones.com (accessed December 3, 2022); Stanley Richards, "What Will It Take to Stop Inmate Jail Deaths?" *The Crime Report*, July 13, 2022, www.thecrimereport.org (accessed December 3, 2022).

23. James A. Gondles, "The Mentally Ill Don't Belong in Jail," *Corrections Today*, vol. 67, no. 2 (April 2005), p. 6.

24. Kenneth E. Kerle, *Exploring Jail Operations* (Hagerstown, MD: American Jail Association, 2003), p. 31.

25. Ken Kerle, "The Mentally Ill and Crisis Intervention Teams: Reflections on Jails and the U.S. Mental Health Challenge," *The Prison Journal*, vol. 96 (January 2016), pp. 153–161.

26. Jac A. Charlier, "The 'Deflection' Surge: Key to Reducing Arrests," *The Crime Report*, March 21, 2017, www .thecrimereport.org (accessed (December 4, 2022); Jac A.

Charlier, "Can We Help Opiod Abusers Without Jailing Them?," *The Crime Report*, January 7, 2019, www .thecrimereport.org (accessed December 4, 2022).

27. Howard J. Snyder, *Juvenile Arrests 2000* (Washington, DC: U.S. Department of Justice, Office of Juvenile Justice and Delinquency Prevention, November 2002); Office of Juvenile Justice and Delinquency Prevention, "Statistical Briefing Book 2020," www.ojjdp.gov (accessed December 4, 2022); Todd Minton and Zhen Zeng, *Jail Inmates in 2020–Statistical Tables*.

28. E. Ann Carson, *Mortality in Local Jails, 2000–2019– Statistical Tables* (Washington DC: U. S. Department of Justice, Bureau of Justice Statistics, December 2021); TCR Staff, "Jail Raises the 'Risk Factor' for Inmate Suicides: Study," *The Crime Report*, February 25, 2022, www.thecrimereport.org (accessed February 25. 2022); Margaret E. Noonan, *Mortality in Local Jails, 2000–2014 Statistical Tables* (Washington, DC: US. Department of Justice, Bureau of Justice Statistics, December 2016); "Jail Suicides Up, Says Federal Report," *The Crime Report*, December 16, 2016, www.thecrimereport.org (accessed January 10, 2019).

29. Connie Milligan and Ray Sabbatine, "From Public Crisis to Innovation—The Mental Health Crisis Network," *American Jails*, vol. 21, no. 6 (January/February 2008), pp. 9–14.

30. Margaret E. Noonan, *Mortality in Local Jails, 2000–2014 Statistical Tables*.

31. *PREA Data Collection Activities, 2018* (Washington, DC: U.S. Department of Justice, Bureau of Justice Statistics, June 2018).

32. G. J. Mazza, *Report on Sexual Victimization in Prisons and Jails: Review Panel on Prison Rape* (Washington, DC: Department of Justice, April 2012).

33. Zhen Zeng, *Jail Inmates in 2021 - Statistical Tables* (Washington, DC: U.S. Department of Justice, Bureau of Justice Statistics, December 2022).

34. Zhen Zeng and Todd D. Minton, *Census of Jails, 2005– 2019–Statistcial Tables* (Washington, DC: U.S. Department of Justice, Bureau of Justice Statistics, October 2021).

35. Todd D. Minton and Zhen Zeng, *Jail Inmates in 2020–Statistical Tables*.

36. PEW Charitable Trusts, "Local Spending on Jails Tops $25 Billion in Latest Nationwide Data," www.pewtrusts .org, January 29, 2021 (accessed December 10, 2022).

37. Nicolas Median Mora, "New York Jails Cost Twice as Much as What the City Says They Cost," *BuzzFeed News*, May 21, 2015, www.buzzfeed.com/nicolasmedinamora /new-york-jails-cost-twice-as-much-as-what-the-city -says-they#.meLG722Wm (accessed December 7, 2022); David J. Simourd and Bryan Brandenburg, "Implementing Rehabilitation into Jails: A Case Example of Success," *American Jails*, vol. 32, no. 3 (November/December 2018), pp. 53–56.

38. Alysia Santo, Victoria Kim and Anna Flagg, "Afraid of Jail? Buy and Upgrade," The Marshall Project, March 9, 2017, www.themarshallproject.org (accessed December 23, 2022); Lauren-Brooke Eisen, *Paying for Your Time: How Charging Inmate Fees Behind Bars May Violate the Excessive Fines Clause* (New York: Brennan Center for Justice, New York University School of Law, July 2014); Izabela Zaluska, "Paying to Stay in Jail: Hidden Fees Turn Inmates Into Debtors," *The Crime Report,* September 19, 2019, www.thecrimereport.org (accessed December 8, 2022).

39. The Pew Charitable Trust, "Local Spending on Jails Tops $25 Billion in Latest Nationwide Data," *American Jails,* vol. 35, no. 2 (May/June2021), pp. 47–53.

40. Prison Policy Initiative, "Pretrial Detention," www .prisonpolicy.org (accessed January 2, 2023).

41. Board of Governors of the Federal Reserve System, *Report on the Economic Well-Being of U.S. Households in 2017* (Washington, DC: Federal Reserve, May 2018).

42. Natasha Lennard, "State Prison Inmate Costs NY as Much as Ivy League Education," *Salon,* October 1, 2013, www.salon.com (accessed January 2, 2023).

43. U.S. Commission on Civil Rights, "The Civil Rights Implications of Cash Bail," January 20, 2022, www.usccr .gov (accessed December 28, 2022).

44. Tiana Herring, "Releasing People Pretrial Doesn't Harm Public Safety," Prison Policy Initiative, November 17, 2020, www.prisonpolicy.org (accessed January 2, 2023); "Monitoring Pretrial Reform in Harris County: Fourth Report of the Court-Appointed Monitor," April 18, 2022, jad.harriscountytx.gov (accessed January 2, 2023); Office of New York City Comptroller Brad Lander, "NYC Bail Trends Since 2019," March 22, 2022, comptroller.nyc.gov (accessed January 2, 2023); Michael R. Jones, *Unsecured Bonds: The Most Effective and Efficient Pretrial Release Option* (Washington, DC: Pretrial Justice Institute, 2013); Arpit Gupta, Christopher Hansman, and Ethan Frenchman, "The Heavy Cost of High Bail: Evidence from Judge Randomization," *The Journal of Legal Studies* vol. 45, no. 2 (2016), pp. 471–516; Aurelie Ouss and Megan Stevenson, "Does Cash Bail Deter Misconduct?" January 1, 2022, http://dx.doi.org/10.2139/ssrn.3335138 (accessed January 2, 2023); and Jake Monaghan, Eric Joseph van Holm, and Chris W. Surprenant, "Get Jailed, Jump Bail? The Impacts of Cash Bail on Failure to Appear and Re-Arrest in Orleans Parish," *American Journal of Criminal Justice,* vol. 57 (2022), pp. 56–74.

45. "Pretrial Criminal Justice Research," Laura and John Arnold Foundation, November 2013, http://www .arnoldfoundation.org/wp-content/uploads/2014/02 /LJAF-Pretrial-CJ-Research-brief_FNL.pdf (accessed January 2, 2023).

46. Melissa Neal, *Bail Fail: Why the U.S. Should End the Practice of Using Money for Bail* (Washington, DC: Justice Policy Institute, 2012), p. 13.

47. Nancy Bilyeau, "Could Eliminating Cash Bail Save the U.S. Billions," *The Crime Report,* March 26, 2021, www .thecrimereport.org (accessed March 26, 2021).

48. Kerle, *Exploring Jail Operations,* p. 128.

49. American Bar Association, "Criminal Justice Section, Report to the House of Delegates," August 21, 2008, www.abanet.org/crimjust/policy/am08104b.pdf-2008-08 -21 (accessed January 3, 2023).

Daniel Russell/Hobbs News-Sun/AP Image

[7] PRISONS TODAY

Change Stations or Warehouses?

CHAPTER OBJECTIVES

After completing this chapter you should be able to do the following:

1 Explain the differences between the Pennsylvania and Auburn prison systems.

2 Outline the ten eras of prison development.

3 Describe the characteristics of persons in prison today and discuss reasons for the incarceration of women, minorities, and people of color.

4 Explain the need for educational and vocational programs in prison.

5 What does the evidence-based literature tell us about the impact of educational and vocational programs in prison?

6 Compare state and federal prison organization and administration.

7 Outline the emergence of solitary confinement and supermax prison and the impacts on staff and people incarcerated.

8 Discuss the impact of technology on corrections.

We habitually underestimate the power of language ... The worst part of repeatedly hearing your negative definition of me is that I begin to believe it myself ... It follows then, that calling me inmate, convict, prisoner, felon, or offender indicates a lack of understanding of who I am, but more importantly what I can be. I can be and am much more than an "ex-con," or an "ex-offender," or an "ex-felon."

Eddie Ellis, 1941–2014. Mr. Ellis spent 25 years in New York maximum-security prisons, including Attica, for a murder he did not commit. Upon his release, he became an activist, author, and co-founder of a think-tank that advocates for the formerly incarcerated.

Jacob Anthony Chansley, 34, of Phoenix, Arizona, the so-called QAnon Shaman was sentenced to 41 months in federal prison for his criminal conduct during the breach of the U.S. Capitol on January 6, 2021, which disrupted a joint session of the U.S. Congress that was in the process of counting the electoral votes related to the 2020 presidential election.[1]

Wearing a Viking hat and carrying a six-foot spear, Chansley was among the first 30 rioters in the building. He was shirtless, wearing a Viking hat with fur and horns, covered in red, white, and blue face paint, and carrying an American flag tied to a pole with a sharp object at the tip and a bullhorn. He entered the Capitol at approximately 2:10 p.m., as the certification proceedings were under way. When he reached the Senate floor he scaled the Senate podium. He sat where Vice President Mike Pence had sat an hour earlier. He took pictures of himself and refused to vacate the seat when asked to do so by law enforcement. Instead, he shouted "Mike Pence is a f----ing traitor" and scratched out a threatening note to the Vice President saying, "it's only a matter of time, justice is coming," before leaving the Chamber at approximately 3:09 p.m.

Before he was sentenced, Chansley told U.S. District Judge Royce Lamberth it was wrong for him to enter the Capitol and that he accepts responsibility for his actions. "I have no excuse," he said. "No excuses whatsoever. My behavior is indefensible."

Jacob Chansley, the so-called QAnon Shaman, was among the first rioters to enter the U.S. Capitol Building on January 6, 2021 intent on disrupting a joint session of Congress that was in the process of counting the electoral votes related to the 2020 presidential election. Chansley scaled the Senate podium, sat in Vice President Mike Pence's chair and wrote Pence a threatening note. Chansley told the Court that he was not thinking about the consequences of his actions. He was sentenced to 41 months in federal prison, three years of supervised release, and ordered to pay $2,000 in restitution. Which evidence-based treatment program can change Chansley's thinking patterns?"
Win McNamee/Staff/Getty Images

Judge Lamberth said Chansley's remorse appeared to be genuine but noted the seriousness of his actions in the Capitol. "What you did was terrible," Lamberth said. "You made yourself the center of the riot."

In addition to serving his sentence at the Federal Correctional Institution (FCI) at Safford, Arizona, Judge Lamberth ordered Chansley to serve three years of supervised release following completion of his prison term and pay $2,000 in restitution. If you were Chansley's case manager at FCI-Safford is there an evidence-based program you would recommend that would further change the way Chansley thinks about his actions?

You'll learn in this chapter that the majority of persons who are incarcerated are in state prisons. Since Chansley's offense was federal he is serving his sentence in a federal prison in Safford, Arizona. We begin the chapter with a brief look at the history of American prisons. Then we discuss who is in prison, the problem with mass incarceration, programs for persons incarcerated, prison organization and management, solitary confinement and supermax prison, and technocorrections.

CO7-1   HISTORY OF PRISONS IN AMERICA

Prisons are relatively modern social institutions, and their development is distinctly American. Until the mid-18th century, fines, banishment from the community, corporal punishment, and execution were the primary forms of punishment. By the latter part of the century, incarceration was championed as a more humane form of punishment. It reflected and fueled a shift from the assumption that someone who commits a crime is inherently criminal to a belief that they were simply not properly trained to resist temptation and corruption. The two prison systems that emerged in the United States—the Pennsylvania system and the Auburn system—were copied throughout the world.

The Pennsylvania and Auburn prison systems developed in the United States at the turn of the 19th century. Pennsylvania Quakers advocated a method of punishment more humane than the public corporal punishment used at the time. The Quakers shifted the emphasis from punishing the body to reforming the mind and soul. Together with an elite group of 18th-century Philadelphians, they ushered in the first **penitentiary,** a place for reform through repentance and rehabilitation. They believed that persons in prison needed to be isolated from one another in silence to repent, to accept God's guidance, and to avoid having a harmful influence on one another. Those incarcerated were not allowed to interact with each other. They did everything alone and not as a group.

Known as the **Pennsylvania system** or the **separate system,** the idea for Eastern State Penitentiary was conceived in 1790 and completed in 1829. The penitentiary was designed for solitary confinement and labor with instruction in labor, morals, and religion.

Overcrowding soon became an issue at Eastern State and the separate system was too expensive to maintain. It also reportedly drove persons insane and further hardened criminal tendencies. Reformers responded with what has been termed the **Auburn system:** regimentation, military-style drill, silence unless conversation was required in workshops, congregate working and eating, separation of those incarcerated into small individual cells at night, harsh discipline, shaved heads, black-and-white striped uniforms, and industrial workshops that contracted with private businesses to help pay for the institution. Prison factories in the 19th century produced shoes, barrels, carpets, engines, boilers, harnesses, clothing, and furniture—goods that could not be produced under the "solitary" system of Pennsylvania or not in quantities sufficient to make a profit. The first prison to use

penitentiary

The earliest form of large-scale incarceration. It punished persons in prison by isolating them so that they could reflect on their misdeeds, repent, and reform.

Pennsylvania system (also separate system)

The first historical phase of prison discipline, involving solitary confinement in silence instead of corporal punishment; conceived by the American Quakers in 1790 and implemented at the Walnut Street Jail.

Auburn system

The second historical phase of prison discipline, implemented at New York's Auburn prison in 1815. It followed the Pennsylvania system and allowed people in prison to work silently together during the day, but they were isolated at night.

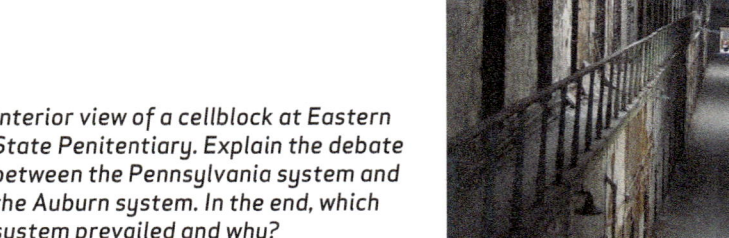

Interior view of a cellblock at Eastern State Penitentiary. Explain the debate between the Pennsylvania system and the Auburn system. In the end, which system prevailed and why?
Courtesy of the Justice Research Association

*The Eastern State Penitentiary, completed in 1829, was designed on the Quakers'
principle of solitary confinement in silence with instruction in labor, morals, and
religion. What name was given to this separate system of prison management?*

Paul Marotta/Getty Images

this system opened in Auburn, New York, in 1819. The Auburn system, congregate by day and separate by night, eventually gave way to congregate cells
at night and removal of the restrictions against talking.

In the United States, the debate over whether the Pennsylvania system
of "solitary and silent" or the Auburn system of "congregate and speaking"
raged on for decades. In the end, the Auburn system won out because the
Auburn model was less expensive to build, and its congregate labor system and factories resulted in higher productivity in the prison and higher
profits for the state. The Pennsylvania system limited the type of work a
person could do; hence, the costs of imprisonment were too high for the
state to bear. In 1913, Eastern State Penitentiary converted to the Auburn
system, ending the great debate. Congregate prisons have been the mode
ever since. Today, however, new voices are calling for a return to long-term
solitary confinement in supermax prisons (something we will discuss later
in this chapter). Prisons in the United States have progressed through at
least ten stages of development (see Exhibit 7–1).

WHO IS IN PRISON TODAY?   CO7-2

In spite of the fact that the U.S. prison population has been decreasing for
the past decade, the United States is still the world's leader in incarceration.
Holding only 5 percent of the world's population, the United States holds
25 percent of the world's prison population and 30 percent of the world's
incarcerated women. A decade ago, over 1.6 million adults were in prison.
Today, that number is slightly more than 1.2 million, a decrease of almost
25 percent.[2]

The U.S. prison population took an unprecedented 15 percent drop
in 2020 and 2021 when the coronavirus hit. State and federal prisons

EXHIBIT 7–1   Stages of Prison History in the United States

Stage	Penitentiary Era	Mass Prison Era	Reformatory Era	Industrial Era	Punitive Era
Years	1790–1825	1825–1876	1876–1890	1890–1935	1935–1945
Goal	Rehabilitation and deterrence	Incapacitation and deterrence	Rehabilitation	Incapacitation	Retribution
Characteristics	Separate and silent. Congregate and silent	Congregate labor and living spaces without silence	Indeterminate sentencing Parole	Public accounts industries Contract labor	Strict punishment and custody
		Contract prison labor		State-use labor Convict lease	U.S. Penitentiary, Alcatraz, CA
				Public works labor	1934 Alcatraz ("Hellcatraz") opens. 1939 Great Depression ends. 1939–1945 World War II begins and ends. 1942–1945 Japanese and Japanese American relocation centers open and close.
Examples of Institutions	Walnut Street Penitentiary, Philadelphia, PA Eastern State Penitentiary, Cherry Hill, PA Auburn Prison, Auburn, NY	Sing Sing Prison, Ossining, NY San Quentin State Prison, San Quentin, CA	Elmira, NY Indiana Reformatory for Women and Girls, Indianapolis, IN	Most major prisons	
Related Events	1819 Auburn Penitentiary, New York, implements congregate, silent system. 1829 Eastern State Penitentiary opens under the Pennsylvania prison model.	1841 John Augustus begins the practice of probation in Massachusetts. 1871 *Ruffin v. Commonwealth* establishes that persons convicted a felony not only forfeit liberty but also are slaves of the state; this provides the legal justification for courts to maintain a "hands-off doctrine." 1913 Eastern State Penitentiary converts to the Auburn prison model.	1876 The first women's prison, the Indiana Reformatory for Women and Girls, opens. 1876 Zebulon Brockway is appointed warden at Elmira Reformatory and initiates first parole system in the United States. 1878 First probation law is passed in Massachusetts.	1891 Federal prison system established. 1899 First juvenile court established in Cook County (Chicago), Illinois. 1914–1918 World War I. 1929 Hawes-Cooper Act is passed to regulate interstate sale of prison-made goods. 1929 Great Depression begins. 1930 Federal Bureau of Prisons is established.	

Carol M. Highsmith/Library of Congress

EXHIBIT 7–1 Stages of Prison History in the United States *(continued)*

Treatment Era	Community-Based Era	Warehousing Era	Just Deserts Era	Criminal Justice Reform
1945–1967	1967–1980	1980–1995	1985–2010	2010–Present
Rehabilitation	Reintegration	Incapacitation	Retribution	Reduce mass incarceration
Medical model Emerging unrest in prisonst	Intermediate sanction: halfway houses, work release centers, group homes, fines, restitution, community service	Sentencing guidelines End of discretionary parole release Serious crowding More prison riots	Just deserts Determinate sentencing Truth in sentencing Three-strikes law Mass incarceration	Data-driven policy Science-based
Patuxent Institution, Jessup, MD	Major prison riots (Attica, NY; Santa Fe, NM)	Most major prisons	Spreading throughout the United States	Prison admission rates drop 33 percent from 2000 to 2021. Broad section of states use risk and needs assessments and focus on people with co-occurring mental illnesses and substance addiction to reduce recidivism.
1950 Federal Youth Corrections Act is passed to create treatment for persons under the age of 22 in the federal system. 1964 *Cooper v. Pate* formally recognizes the constitutional rights of persons in prison. 1967 *In re Gault,* U.S. Supreme Court rules that juveniles are entitled to state-provided counsel and due process guarantees. 1967 President Johnson's Commission on Law Enforcement and Administration of Justice recommends changing the criminal justice system.	1970 Massachusetts becomes first state to close all of its juvenile reform schools. 1974 Robert Martinson's "What Works" is published and is used by politicians as reason to pull resources from prisons. 1976 Maine is first state to abolish discretionary parole board release. 1979 Prison Industry Enhancement (PIE) certification program repeals limitations on interstate commerce in prison-made goods.	1980s President Reagan declares "war on drugs." 1984 Federal Sentencing Reform Act imposes mandatory sentences for specific crimes. 1993 Three-strikes-and-you're-out laws spread across the United States. 1994 Congress passes the Violent Crime Control and Law Enforcement Act, which increases financial incentives for states to put more persons who commit violent offenses in prison.	1994 Federal Bureau of Prisons opens its supermax prison. 1996 Prison Litigation Acts curtailed using the courts as an avenue for improving conditions and created an uptick in the use of prisons and jails. 1999 Number of people incarcerated in the United States exceeds 2 million for the first time. 2007 Evidence-based research and economic recession start to shape correctional practice. 2010 Federal Fair Sentencing Act reduces disparity in sentencing between crack and powder cocaine offenses.	2011 U.S. Supreme Court ruled that overcrowding in California's prisons constituted a violation of the Eighth Amendment and ordered the state to decrease the prison population. 2014 U.S. Sentencing Commission reduces sentencing guidelines for persons convicted of federal drug trafficking. 2016 California voters pass Proposition 57, which increases parole and good behavior opportunities for persons convicted of nonviolent crimes. 2016 Tennessee creates a system of graduated sanctions for violations of community supervision with the aim of reducing the number of people incarcerated. 2018 Fourteen additional states enacted laws ending restricting occupational licensing to improve access to occupational licenses for people with a criminal record. 2018 President Trump signs the First Step Act to reform the federal prison system and reduce recidivism. 2020–2021 Criminal justice agencies adjust policies and procedures to mitigate the spread of COVID-19: fewer persons arrested and prosecuted; trials and sentencing delayed; jail, prison, and probation populations reduced;

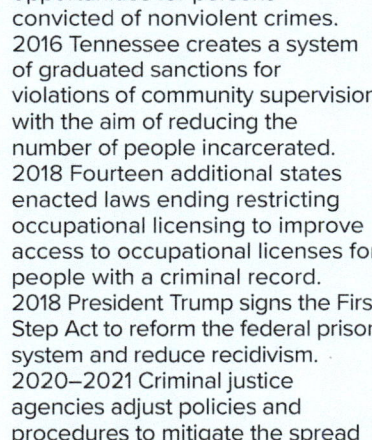

Tracy Harmon/The Pueblo Chieftain via AP

adjusted policies and procedures to mitigate risk and maintain the safety of those incarcerated and the staff. Many prisons enacted early release and home confinement for persons incarcerated for nonviolent offenses and those close to a release date.

However, the dramatic decrease in the prison population was primarily driven by fewer admissions to state and federal prisons. Over 200,000 fewer people were admitted to prison in 2020 than in 2019 because of several reasons. Due to the coronavirus, courts altered their operations hearing 40 percent less cases in 2020 than in 2019, leading to delays in trials and sentencing; fewer persons were transferred from local jails to state and federal prisons; and persons who violated their community supervision—infractions during probation, parole, and postrelease supervision—fell by 31 percent for technical supervision violations and 18 percent for new offense violations for a total of 57,000 fewer persons sent to prison in 2020 than in 2019. The Council of State Governments argued that if states sustained a reduction of 57,000 fewer people incarcerated for supervision violations each year, they could save an estimated $2.7 billion annually—from $990 million saved in California to more than $330,000 saved in Alabama.[3] The savings could be reinvested into strengthening communities and expanding access to community resources. Later in this chapter, we will return to the concept of **justice reinvestment**, a policy of reducing spending on incarceration and reinvesting a portion of those savings into evidence-based strategies for preventing and addressing crime.

justice reinvestment

A criminal justice policy approach of reducing spending on incarceration and reinvesting a portion of those savings into evidence-based strategies for preventing and addressing crime.

In spite of the decrease, however, nationwide, the prison population still looks very different than the nonprison population. White people are underrepresented in prison, while almost every other racial and ethnic group is overrepresented.

In prison today, 33 percent of people are Black. In the U.S. general population, it is 13 percent. In prison, 30 percent are white. But across the United States, 70 percent are white. Hispanics make up 20 percent of the prison population and 19 percent of the U.S. population. Persons who are multiracial make up 11 percent in prison but only 2 percent outside prison. In prison, 2 percent are American Indian/Alaska Native, but across the United States it is 1 percent. And in prison, 1 percent are Asian, Native Hawaiian, and other Pacific Islanders. In the general population, it is 7 percent.[4] Additional characteristics of persons in prison are presented in Exhibit 7–2.

Racial disparity in prison is not new. The fact that these disparities continue to exist, however, means that any criminal justice reform designed to address mass incarceration must also address the racial disparities that imprison a disproportionate number of people of color.

The imprisonment rate—the number of persons under state or federal prison jurisdiction per 100,000 U.S. residents—has also been declining. The imprisonment rate at year-end 2020 (358 per 100,000 U.S. residents) was the lowest since 1992 (330 per 100,000). The imprisonment rate ranged from 55 in the federal prison system and 125 in Massachusetts (the two lowest), to 760 in Louisiana and 767 in Mississippi (the two highest). Prison statistics among the states and the federal government are shown in Exhibit 7–2.

What causes these disparities among states and their prison use? An interesting answer to this question was provided by Bowers and Waltman. Their investigation of felony sentencing in the United States found that the preferences of the public weigh heavily on sentencing decisions. World leaders of the prison administrations of the 46 member countries of the Council of Europe concluded that levels of imprisonment are usually influenced more by political decisions than by levels of crime or rates of crime detection. They also concluded that jurisdictions can choose to have high or low rates of imprisonment and that this choice is reflected in the

EXHIBIT 7–2   Select Prison Statistics Among the States and the Federal Government

Number of Persons Under State and Federal Prison Jurisdiction		Incarceration Rate per 100,000		Number/Incarceration Rate of Women Under Jurisdiction of State and Federal Prisons	
5 Highest		**5 Highest**		**5 Highest**	
Federal	152,156	Mississippi	767	Texas	10,359/614
Texas	135,906	Louisiana	760	Federal	10,192/55
California	100,396	Oklahoma	741	Florida	5,015/466
Florida	81,027	Arkansas	693	Arizona	3,655/661
Georgia	47,141	Texas	614	Ohio	3,628/491
5 Lowest		**5 Lowest**		**5 Lowest**	
Vermont	1,284	Federal	55	Vermont	84
North Dakota	1,401	Massachusetts	125	Rhode Island	89
Maine	1,714	Maine	145	Maine	128
Wyoming	2,087	Rhode Island	156	North Dakota	162
Rhode Island	2,227	Vermont	172	Massachusetts	198

Source: Adapted from E. Ann Carson, Prisoners in 2014 (Washington, DC: U.S. Department of Justice, Bureau of Justice Statistics, September 2015).

sentencing patterns adopted by legislatures.[5] As states grappled with the coronavirus and the economic realities of imprisonment, we can see how political decisions about what constitutes dangerousness or seriousness impacted prison populations and release decisions that would not otherwise have happened. A decade ago, parole violators and persons in prison for nonviolent offenses would have been incarcerated. Yet we know that 57,000 persons who violated their community supervision were not sent to prison. Today's economic problems find legislators and policymakers reducing prison time for persons convicted of drug and nonviolent offenses and establishing programs like California's nonrevocable parole (see Chapter 8). We turn our attention now to learn more about who is in prison and why.

Women and Gender Identity in Prison

CO7-3

The United States Department of Justice's Bureau of Justice Statistics has always reported everyone in a women's prison as female (7 percent) and everyone in a men's prison as male (93 percent). In 2021 for the first time, BJS released data on incarcerated persons' self-reported gender identity. The bureau reported that 0.3 percent of persons in prison identify as transgender and a much smaller portion identify as neither male or female nor transgender.[6] The experiences and unmet needs of transgender people in prison and those who do not identify as female, male, or transgender have not been fully studied. Only recently have data become available on the sexual victimization of LGBTQ+ persons in prison. We investigate it further in Chapter 10.

Women have historically represented a small share of the prison population. However, since 1980, the number of women in prison has been increasing at a rate 50 percent higher than men. In 1980, 13,000 women were in prison. The year before the coronavirus, it was almost 108,000. However, due to the mitigation efforts discussed earlier, to reduce the spread of COVID-19 in prison, in 2020 the number of women in prison declined to 83,800. The downward trend continued into 2021 when close to 83,400 women were in prison (see Exhibit 7–3).

EXHIBIT 7–3 Persons Under the Jurisdiction of State and Federal Prisons

How many persons are under the jurisdiction of state and federal correctional authorities and why?

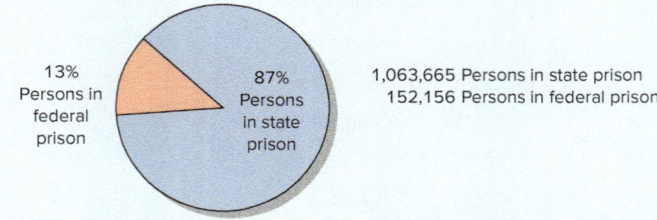

13% Persons in federal prison

87% Persons in state prison

1,063,665 Persons in state prison
152,156 Persons in federal prison

Who is in prison?

Gender

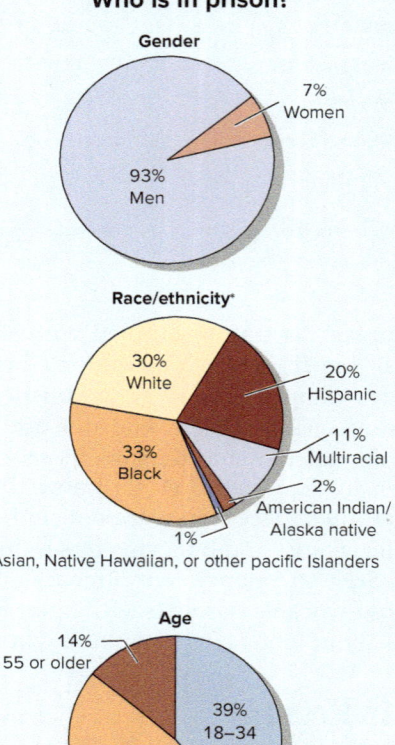

7% Women

93% Men

Race/ethnicity*

30% White

20% Hispanic

33% Black

11% Multiracial

2% American Indian/ Alaska native

1% Asian, Native Hawaiian, or other pacific Islanders

Age

14% 55 or older

39% 18–34

47% 35–54

Why are they in prison?

Persons in state

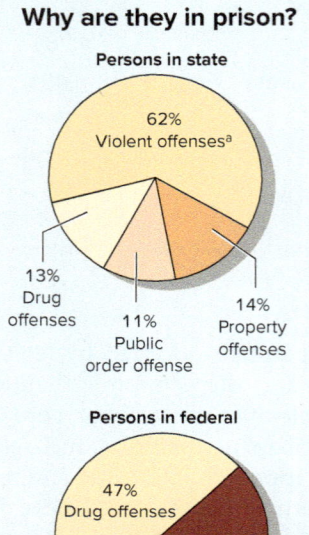

62% Violent offenses[a]

13% Drug offenses

11% Public order offense

14% Property offenses

Persons in federal

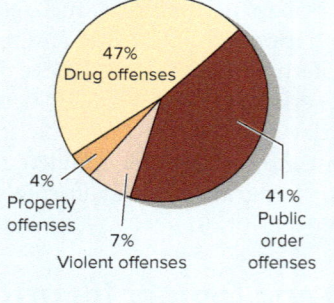

47% Drug offenses

4% Property offenses

7% Violent offenses

41% Public order offenses

Average sentence length and average time served by offense in state prison before release, 2018

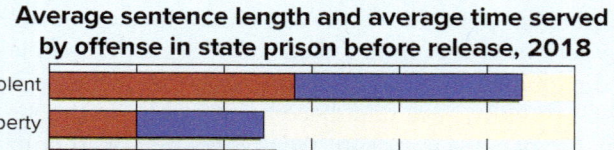
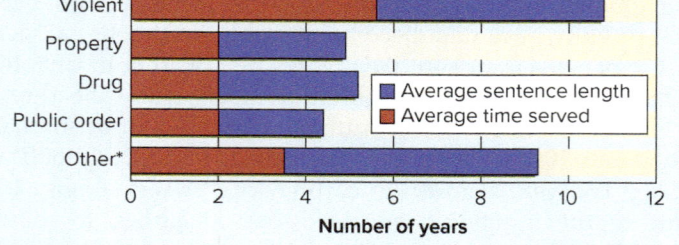

Violent

Property

Drug

Public order

Other*

■ Average sentence length
■ Average time served

0   2   4   6   8   10   12
Number of years

Source: Bureau of Justice Statistics

*Unspecified

Today, the federal prison system, along with Arizona, Florida, and Texas, hold 35 percent of all women in prison. Exhibit 7–2 lists the jurisdictions with the highest and lowest female prison populations.

Beth Richie, department head of criminology, law, and justice at the University of Illinois at Chicago, and Elaine Lord, former superintendent of the Bedford Hills Correctional Facility (New York's maximum-security prison for women), describe the racial/ethnic profile of women in prison as one of the most vivid examples of racial disparity in the United States and prison as the worst environment possible for mothers and women with mental illness.[7] Lord quit her job after 20 years because she stopped believing in the confinement of mentally ill women.

The majority of women in prison are women of color. Two-thirds are Black, Hispanic, or of other non-white ethnic groups. They are also young and poor. Only one-third graduated from high school or earned a GED. Two-thirds have a history of physical or sexual abuse, and 3.5 percent are HIV positive. Over half have a child under the age of 18. Three-fourths suffer from major depression and manic psychotic disorders. Sadly, the corrections literature suggests that, despite the fact that some women do quite well putting their lives back together when they are released from prison, most are likely to return to the same disenfranchised neighborhoods and difficult situations without having received any services to address their underlying problems. If it is true, as the corrections literature suggests, that prior arrest history predicts postprison recidivism, then the outlook for women in prison is bleak: almost 50 percent of women in prison have a history of prior convictions. One-fourth have five or more convictions.

Scholars debate the reasons for the increase in women's incarceration over men's. Some suggest that as women moved into jobs from which they were formerly excluded, they gained the opportunities and skills to commit criminal acts for which they were incarcerated. Others disagree, saying that poverty of young, female, single heads of households has contributed to the increase in women's crime and incarceration, particularly for property and drug offenses. One scholar put it this way: "The war on drugs has translated into a war on women."[8] Others think the criminal justice system is becoming more "gender blind" due to the emergence of "get-tough" attitudes and sentencing policies. Instead of seeing women as weaker and giving them differential, if not preferential treatment, judges and juries now sentence women more harshly whether it's their first drug offense or they have committed crimes against persons or property. The combined effects of harsh drug laws, changing patterns of drug use, and mandatory sentencing policies have led to a significant increase in women's incarceration. Twenty-six percent of women in state prisons and almost 62 percent of women in federal prisons are serving time for nonviolent, drug-related offenses. Quite likely, the reason for the increase in women's incarceration is a product of all these theories. To reduce women's incarceration is to understand and implement programs about women's development, trauma, and addiction discussed in Chapter 6.

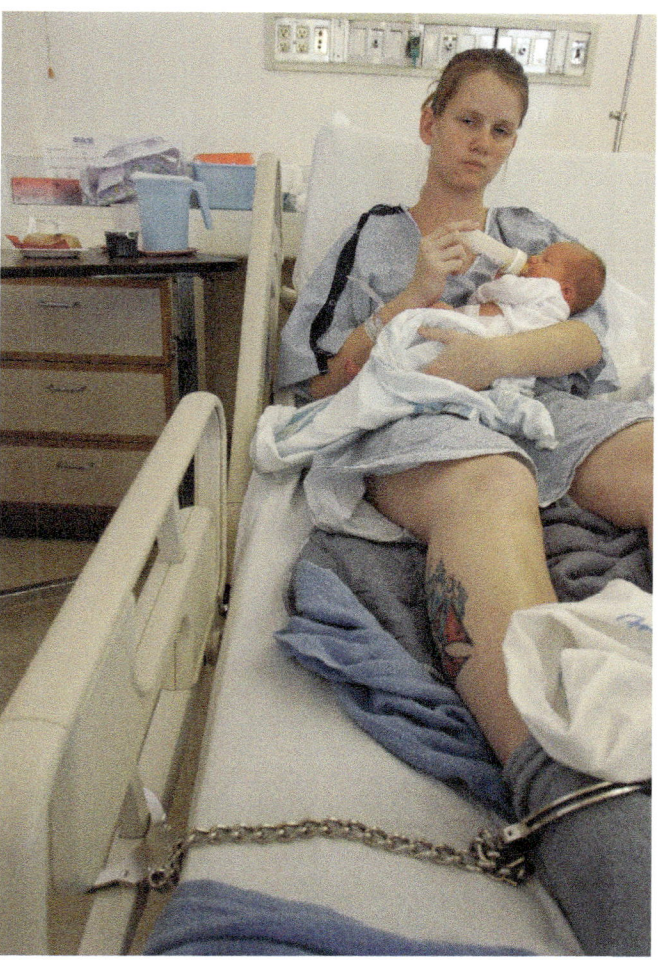

Today, over 83,800 women are under state or federal prison jurisdiction, 35 percent of them in Arizona, Florida, Texas, and federal prisons. Why are women in prison, and what will it take to reduce their incarceration?

Mark Allen Johnson/ZUMAPRESS.com/Newscom

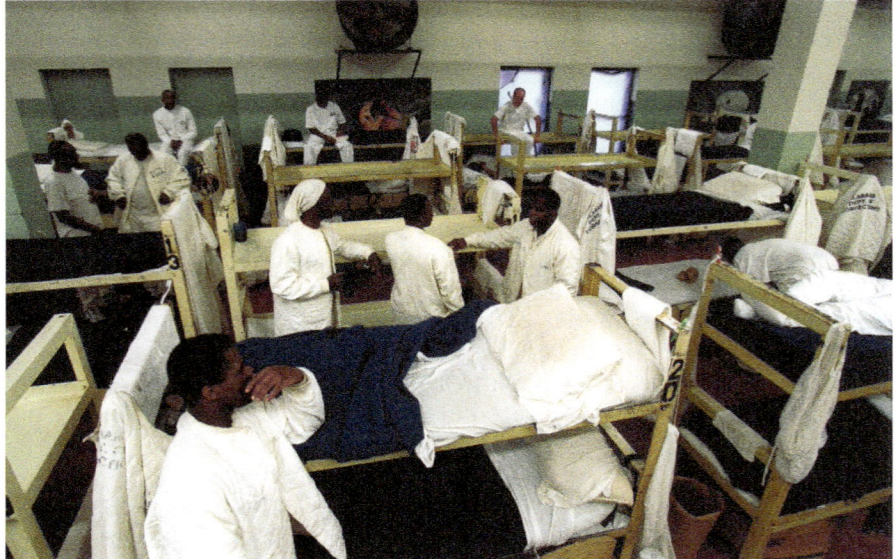

The number of state, federal, and private confinement correctional facilities in the United States is 1,161, of which 1,079 are public and 82 are private. Minorities and people of color make up 70 percent of the prison population. Why is that so?
ZUMA Press, Inc/Alamy Stock Photo

Race and Ethnicity of Persons in Prison

The primary observation to be made about the prison population in the United States is that it looks very different from the non-prison population. Minorities and people of color are strikingly overrepresented. Although minorities and people of color comprise about 30 percent of the U.S. population, they make up 70 percent of the prison population. Conversely, whites are underrepresented: approximately 70 percent of the general population but only 30 percent of the prison population.

We noted earlier that imprisonment rates for all races have been declining steadily for the past 25 years. Overall that is good news, but some races benefit more than others. Exhibit 7–4 shows the rate of imprisonment for white U.S. residents at year-end 2020 is 183 per 100,000. For Black U.S. residents, the rate is almost five times (938 per 100,000) the rate for white residents. For Hispanic residents, it is more than double (446 per 100,000) the rate for white residents. And for American Indian/Alaska Native

EXHIBIT 7–4   **Imprisonment Rates of U.S. Residents Under the Jurisdiction of State and Federal correctional Authorities, per 100,000, by Race or Ethnicity**

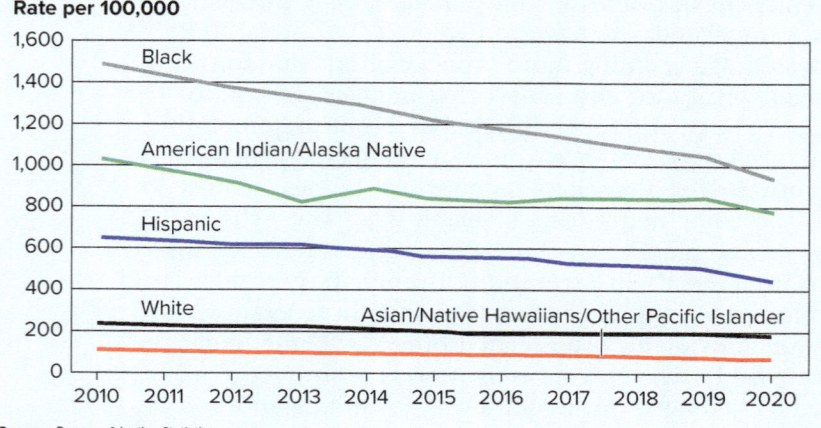

Source: Bureau of Justice Statistics

residents, the rate is more than four times (778 per 100,000) the rate for white residents. Only Asians, Native Hawaiians, and Pacific Islanders have a smaller rate of imprisonment (74 per 100,000) than white residents.

If current trends continue, 1 of every 3 Black males born today can expect to go to prison in his lifetime as can 1 of every 6 Latino males compared to 1 in 17 white males.[9]

As is the case with so many other criminological controversies, there is a debate over the relationship between race and crime. Official prison data suggest that the reason more minorities and people of color are disproportionately in prison and for longer terms is differential crime offending. They point to BJS data that show that almost two-thirds (63 percent) of persons in state prison serving time for a violent offense are minority and people of color. In federal prison, although fewer persons are incarcerated for a violent offense (most are sentenced for drug or public order offenses such as immigration and weapons), 75 percent are minorities and people of color. Recently, two Washington State Supreme Court justices stunned audiences when they said they didn't believe that anyone was in prison because of age, race, disability, and other factors. One of the Justices referred to those who represent the poor as "poverty pimps" and used the words "you people" when stating that Black people commit crimes in their own communities.[10]

Others argue that the higher arrest rates, convictions, and sentences to prison of minorities and people of color are a function of racial profiling and racism in the criminal justice system. After reviewing 32 state-level studies of the decision to incarcerate and of length of sentence imposed, Cassia Spohn, professor of criminology and criminal justice at Arizona State University, concluded that there is ample evidence among these studies that, controlling for other relevant factors, Blacks and Hispanics are more likely to be incarcerated than whites and, in some jurisdictions, receive longer sentences. And others have found gross racial disparities when arrest and incarceration for drug dependence and abuse are examined at the city and county levels.[11]

Still others argue that although discriminatory practices exist, it is improbable that criminal justice bias alone could account for the disproportionate arrest rates of Blacks. They suggest the social problems of unemployment, economic deprivation, social disorganization, and social isolation of the nation's inner cities as additional causes. The inner city, the residence of most of the nation's poor, experiences by far the highest crime rates. While middle-class communities have more resources to work with persons convicted of crime and get them into treatment, those resources are not as readily available in low-income areas, so a drug problem, for example, is more likely to develop into a criminal justice problem.

These levels of racial disparity are causing some states to implement racial impact statements. Policymakers routinely require analysis of the fiscal or environmental impact of proposed new laws, and it has been proposed that legislators do the same before implementing new sentencing laws. Iowa and Connecticut (two states with some of the highest Black-to-white ratios of incarceration) took the lead among the states and enacted racial impact statements.

Age of Persons in Prison

The nation's population is aging, and this is reflected in the prison population. Middle-aged and older inmates make up a growing portion of the prison population. In 2010, 46 percent of the nation's prison population was between 18 and 34 years old, 45 percent were between 35 and 54, and 8 percent were over 55. Today, the representation of 18- to 34-year-olds has decreased to 39 percent, the presence of 35- to 54-year-olds had increased to 47 percent, and the presence of inmates 55 and older had increased to 14 percent (see Exhibit 7–4). In Chapter 12, we'll discuss the issues surrounding persons in prison who are older in more detail.

On the other end of the age range, we find there has been a sustained drop in juvenile incarcerations in adult prison.[12] In 2000, almost 14,000 people under 18 were held in adult prison. In 2010, the number dropped to 2,300. By contrast, today approximately 300 youth are incarcerated in adult prison, a drop of 98 percent over the past 25 years. In 2021, Alabama, Alaska, Colorado, Delaware, Georgia, and Nevada passed legislation and joined half the states and no longer confined persons under 18 in adult prison. For young people to lead productive lives, these new laws use evidence-based programs and practices, and the research on brain development and behavior that shows that under age 18 is not full, mature adulthood.

Most Serious Offense of Persons in Prison

Another characteristic to compare is the most serious offense of which a person was convicted. Today, 62 percent of persons serving time in state prisons are held for violent offenses, up from 53 percent ten years ago. Persons in state prison for property and drug offenses both dropped by 5 percent from 2010 to 2020. In 2010, 19 percent were in state prison for a property offense and 18 percent for a drug offense. Ten years later, it was 14 and 13 percent, respectively. However, the number of persons in state prison for public order offenses (weapons, DUI, and supervision violations, among others) increased from 9 to 11 percent.

The federal prison population, however, looks quite different. Whereas more persons are sentenced to state prison for violent and property offenses and fewer for drug and public order offenses, almost 90 percent of persons in federal prison are charged with drug and public order offenses including immigration, regulatory violations, tax violations, and wildlife and environmental matters, among others. There are far fewer persons in federal prison than in state prison charged with a violent or property crime. Characteristics of persons under the jurisdiction of state and federal prisons are shown in Exhibit 7–3, along with the average sentence length and average time served by offense in state prison in 2018 before release.

PRISON AND OTHER DRIVERS OF MASS INCARCERATION

In Chapter 1 you learned that mass incarceration refers to the overuse of correctional facilities in the United States, particularly prisons, as determined by historical and cross-cultural standards. Mass incarceration has profound consequences: loss of a job or housing, falling behind on bills, losing custody of one's children, receiving a conviction that has collateral consequences such as disenfranchisement and restrictions on occupational licensing after prison, broken communities, no advancement in public safety, and billions spent on crime policy that doesn't work.

The rise in mass incarceration started in the 1970s and continued through the first two decades of the 21st century. It started early in states like Washington and California and later in states like Massachusetts and Minnesota. In 1970, around 328,000 persons were in U.S. jails and prisons. By 2010, that number had grown to more than 2 million. In 2019, the year before the coronavirus pandemic, the adult confinement population reached more than 2.1 million. However, due to the pandemic-related slowdowns in 2020, it dropped to 1.8 million.

For 50 years, reliance on incarceration was mainstream public policy, and we spent billions of dollars to incarcerate millions of people without much consideration of the consequences of our crime policies. We thought we could build our way out of the crime problem. Throughout the era, the U.S. Department of Justice funded new construction as a way to reduce crime. Investment in prison and jail construction and expansion was so widespread and intensive that the era was also known as the prison boom. It was, in the words of the National Research Council, "historically unprecedented and internationally unique" without the promised impact on public safety.[13]

As a result of the recession in 2000 and the subsequent financial crisis of 2008, continued incarceration growth became unjustifiable in many states. National and statewide polls tapping public attitudes about treatment over incarceration and growing awareness that locking people up in huge numbers had, at best, a marginal impact and, at worst, a corrosive impact on society, gave policymakers and legislators breathing room to pass legislation to reduce prison populations during this time of fiscal crisis.

However, because the criminal justice system is an amalgamation of thousands of city, county, and state systems that operate differently (even when bound by the same laws), some jurisdictions have shown considerable reform in reducing incarceration, while others have been slow to respond.

The criminal justice reform era also made clear that "what you see is what you solve." So instead of focusing only on prison data to reduce mass incarceration, researchers and policymakers directed our attention to the front end—where four community supervision and jail practices drive prison populations and mass incarceration. They ask us to imagine the impact it would have if only a small fraction of each of these correctional populations were sentenced differently and jurisdictions found ways to function without so much reliance on correctional control.

1. **Jail admission data.** Nine to ten million persons are admitted to jail each year. Imagine the reduction in mass incarceration if a small fraction were diverted/deflected to social services for mental health and substance abuse treatment?

2. **Pretrial jail population.** Imagine the reduction in mass incarceration if only a fraction of the two-thirds of the jail population that have not been convicted were offered alternatives to money bail.

3. **Sentenced jail population.** Imagine the reduction in mass incarceration if only a small fraction of the one-third of persons in jail who have been convicted were sentenced to intermediate sanctions.

4. **Prison admissions.** Pandemic-related slowdowns brought almost a 40 percent drop in the number of adults sentenced to prison from 2019 to 2020, from 577,000 to 346,500. However 30 percent of the prison population is there because they violated the conditions of their community supervision (whether probation or parole). Although the Department of Justice does not specify what percent are incarcerated for a new offense or a technical violation, we pointed out earlier that most violations are the result of technical infractions, not new offenses. Imagine the reduction in mass incarceration if persons were not incarcerated for violating a technical condition of their community supervision.

Reducing mass incarceration is complicated, and progress across and within states is uneven at best. What we have tried to show is that there's more to understanding and unpacking mass incarceration than focusing on prison data alone. Five myths about ways to end mass incarceration

Career Profile

Courtesy of Courtney McCoy

Courtney C. McCoy

Corrections Sergeant, Lancaster County Department of Corrections, Lincoln, Nebraska

Sergeant Courtney McCoy was born in Vallejo, California, prior to moving to the Lincoln, Nebraska area for college. McCoy has a family history in law enforcement and criminal justice, including a father and grandfather who had careers in law enforcement, retiring as a police corporal and sergeant, respectively, and a mother who works as a police and fire dispatcher. McCoy began her career in the criminal justice field as an evidence technician prior to hiring on with the Lancaster County Department of Corrections as a correctional officer. McCoy was then promoted to the rank of sergeant.

McCoy has served roles as a correctional officer including intake and release, housing unit officer (to include male units and female units), special management housing officer, and supervision of inmate work details. McCoy was also assigned as the Training Coach for her shift in which she was tasked with the training of new staff. As a sergeant, McCoy has supervised shift operations and is presently assigned as the Grievance Investigator under the department's Security Manager. McCoy is a departmental Use of Force instructor, Emergency Management Procedures instructor, NCIC trainer, and Grievance and Response to Inmate Sexual Assault trainer. McCoy has also taught classes at the Nebraska Basic Corrections Officer Training in report writing and cell searches. She is a 2022 graduate of the Lancaster County Leadership Academy.

McCoy has an academic background to include a Bachelor of Science in Biology from Concordia University, Nebraska, and a Master of Science in Forensic Science from Nebraska Wesleyan University. She is currently pursuing her Doctor of Criminal Justice from Saint Leo University. McCoy's diverse family and academic background have led her to understand and appreciate the value that collaboration between stakeholders has in the field of corrections. The importance of cooperation between governmental and nongovernmental organizations is a powerful tool to improve the field of corrections not only for those within the custody of the system but also for those choosing to serve within this capacity. She would encourage those interested in pursuing a career in corrections to never underestimate the power and importance of collaboration and to never stop seeking training and education.

> *Education and training can only augment the experience that you will gain on the job.*

followed by the facts are shown in Exhibit 7–5. Data-driven policies that also consider jail admissions, the pretrial jail population, the sentenced jail population, prison admissions, and community supervision are needed so that legislatures and policymakers can reverse the effects of mass incarceration.

EDUCATIONAL PROGRAMMING AND VOCATIONAL TRAINING IN PRISON

Correctional education and vocational training have been the cornerstones of prison programming since the start of the rehabilitative era discussed earlier in this chapter. The objective of these programs is to improve behavior, both before and after release from prison. Today there is evidence-based research supporting the success rates for correctional programming.

Prison Industries

Why are prison industries important? What impact did the Ashurst-Sumners Act have on prison industries?

EXHIBIT 7–5   Five Myths About Mass Incarceration

Here are five common myths about ways to end mass incarceration followed by the facts. What do you think?

1. **Myth:** Releasing persons sentenced for drug offenses will end mass incarceration.

Fact: Releasing persons sentenced for nonviolent drug offenses will not end mass incarceration because more persons are in prison for violent and property crimes than for drug offenses alone. This means new criminal justice reforms will have to do more than release persons sentenced for drug offenses. Reforms such as justice reinvestment, discussed in this chapter, will benefit not only people in prison for drug offenses but also all persons at risk for any type of incarceration.

2. **Myth:** Eliminating privatization will end mass incarceration.

Fact: Of the nation's 1,161 adult confinement facilities, 1,079 are public and 82 are private. The latter hold 8 percent (100,200) of the nation's total prison population of 1.2 million.

Privatization is not the root of incarceration problems. Nevertheless, because the industry lobbies state and federal policymakers to use their services, some argue that their lobbying efforts maintain high levels of incarceration. On the surface, the argument may be appealing, but appearance is not the same as evidence. Too often myths repeated are taken as fact when in reality we should look beyond the surface to the evidence. We should argue for more accountability and better results from providers of both public and private correctional facilities, whether that's in building and operating entire correctional systems or in delivering subcontracts for food, health, education and vocational programming, and telephone calls.

3. **Myth:** Eliminating prison factories will end mass incarceration.

Fact: Prison factories are not the source of most prison jobs, nor do they stand in the way of ending mass incarceration. Less than 1 percent of people in prison are employed by private companies through the federal PIE program, which allows private companies to operate within correctional facilities to provide job training and pay prevailing wages. We return to a discussion of work in prison later in this chapter.

Instead, the majority of people in prison perform institutional work assignments where they do the laundry, repair and maintain the institution's heating and air conditioning, and assist in food preparation and service, and are paid on average 52 cents an hour. Several states pay nothing (see Exhibit 7-7). Instead of eliminating prison jobs and partnerships with private companies under the PIE program, meaningful prison work programs that pay prevailing wages and carry over to employment opportunities after release are needed. Nobody expects prison work to be highly remunerative; however, forcing people in prison to work for pennies a day is counterproductive to rehabilitation.

4. **Myth:** Expanding community supervision will reduce mass incarceration.

Fact: Probation, parole, and pretrial supervision are court-ordered sanctions that keep people in the community under supervision in lieu of incarceration. In many instances, persons under community supervision are required to fulfill certain conditions of their supervision (e.g., payment of fines, fees or court costs, participation in treatment programs) and adhere to specific rules of conduct. Failure to comply can result in incarceration. Sometimes the conditions are so onerous they create the very problems they were designed to avert in the first place. Long periods of supervision, intensive monitoring, rigid requirements, and remote surveillance result in failures for violating the technical conditions of supervision such as breaking curfew, failure to pay fees or court costs, and missing appointments. In 2020, almost 10 percent (or 140,000) adults on probation were returned to incarceration with either a new sentence or under their current sentence. Another 19 percent of adults (or almost 71,400) were returned to incarceration from parole with either a new sentence or revoking their parole. Opponents of mass incarceration argue that until community supervision practices are reformed, probation, parole, and pretrial supervision have no chance of breaking the cycle of mass incarceration.

5. **Myth:** Persons convicted of violent crimes are too dangerous to be released.

Fact: Opponents of mass incarceration argue that, in light of how history has taught us to question past policies, it is time to use that same lens to question our current responses to persons convicted of a violent crime. Science shows us that persons convicted of a violent offense are less likely to recidivate than persons convicted of property and drug offenses, yet they spend years and decades in prisons and face long if not lifetime postrelease supervision, which increases their chances of returning to prison for a technical violation.

The federal Bureau of Justice Statistics data on recidivism of persons released from state prisons in 2008 and followed for ten years found that 77 percent of persons released from state prison after serving time for a violent offense were arrested for any offense compared to 87 percent of persons released after serving time for property offenses, 81 percent after serving time for drug offenses, and 82 percent who served time for public order offenses. Furthermore, persons released from state prison after serving time for property, drug, or public order offenses were as likely to commit a violent offense in postrelease as persons initially sentenced for a violent offense.

Source: Adapted from Prison Policy Initiative, *Mass Incarceration: The Whole Pie 2022* (Northampton, MA, 2022) with updates by the authors.

But what does success mean? According to one of the best reviews of the current evidence of the effectiveness of adult correctional programming by Aos and his colleagues at the Washington State Institute for Public Policy, it means reducing recidivism by 5 to 15 percent.[14]

Space does not permit us to evaluate each and every correctional program. Instead, Exhibit 7–6 covers some of the more typical correctional programs found in state and federal prisons that have been evaluated and address the main characteristics, traits, problems, or issues of an individual that directly relate to the individual's likelihood to reoffend and commit another crime. Broadly speaking, cognitive behavioral therapy (CBT) has proven to be the most effective in reducing prison misconduct and deceasing recidivism. It also has one of the highest returns on investment. Social support programming helps individuals maintain, develop, or enhance prosocial sources of support such as prison visitation and faith-based programming. They too have shown success in deceasing misconduct, reducing recidivism, and potential cost-effectiveness. Our discussion here centers around two correctional programs—education and vocational training—known to exist in almost every state and federal prison.

CO7-4 Educational Programming

The majority of people in prison cannot read or write well enough to function in society. Among persons incarcerated in federal and state prisons, two out of three (62 percent) do not have a high school diploma or a GED, compared to 19 percent of the general population.[15] The education gap means persons in prison have fewer marketable job skills and earn lower wages.

A survey of prison education programs published by the U.S. Department of Justice in November 2021 reported on the type of prison education programs available across the United States, the number of facilities that offer the program, and the percent of persons enrolled. In all categories, the percents are higher today than they were when the last census of prison programming was published in 2008.[16] While the number of programs and enrollments are increasing, there is still considerable room for improvement to reduce recidivism, increase wages and higher rates of employment after release from prison, and reduce violence behind bars, leading to safer conditions for staff and those incarcerated. According to the Bureau of Justice Statistics:

- 88 percent of the nation's 1,161 confinement facilities offered the GED with 87 percent of persons enrolled.
- 84 percent offered lower basic adult education (first to fourth grade) with 94 percent of individuals participating.
- 81 percent offered upper basic adult education (fifth to eighth grade) with 91 percent of individuals participating.
- 72 percent offered vocational training with 84 percent of persons enrolled.
- 54 percent offered special education with 63 percent enrolled.
- 49 percent offer college courses with 58 percent enrolled.
- 38 percent offer English as a Second Language (ESL) with 13 percent enrolled.

If, as we will show below, corrections-based education programs are effective, why aren't more persons enrolled? There are several reasons. First, correctional educators face substantial hurdles in delivering effective

EXHIBIT 7–6   Impact of Correctional Programming on Prisoners: Pre- and Postrelease Outcomes

	Prison Misconduct: Failure to follow institutional rules and regulations	**Postrelease Employment:** Institutional programming designed to improve postrelease employment outcomes	**Recidivism:** A return to criminal behavior resulting in either rearrest, reconviction, resentencing to prison for new offense, and return to prison for technical violation	**Cost-Benefit:** Monetary benefit to society through costs avoided from the prevention of crime
Educational Programming	Results are mixed. Overall the evidence suggests that postsecondary educational programming may yield better outcomes.	Both secondary and postsecondary educational programming have yielded positive results.	Although there have been exceptions, the evidence suggests that educational programming, especially postsecondary education, reduces recidivism.	Research suggests that educational programming produces a relatively high return on investment.
Employment Programming	Employment programming, particularly prison labor, has generally been found to reduce prison misconduct.	Employment programming has typically improved postrelease employment outcomes.	The results have varied by type of program. Prison labor has not consistently been found to lower recidivism and work release produces, at best, a modest reduction. The most promising findings have been for employment programming that provides a continuum of service delivery.	Existing research suggests that employment programming produces a solid return on investment
Cognitive Behavioral Therapy (CBT)	CBT programs have been found to have the best outcomes for prison misconduct.	No evidence is available.	CBT programs have produced relatively strong results in reducing recidivism.	CBT programs have been found to provide some of the highest return on investments for correctional programming.
Chemical Dependency (CD) Treatment	Very little evidence exists, although one study found that prison-based drug treatment increased misconduct.	No evidence is available, although CD treatment has been found to be successful in preventing relapse.	Results generally show that prison-based CD treatment is successful in reducing recidivism, especially if the treatment provides a continuum of care, uses a therapeutic community, and is delivered within a cognitive-behavioral framework.	Existing research reveals relatively strong return on investment outcomes for prison-based CD treatment, especially for outpatient/ nonintensive programs.
Sex Offender Treatment	No evidence is available.	No evidence is available.	The evidence indicates that, in general, treatment for persons who commit sex crimes significantly lowers sexual recidivism.	Existing research suggests that treatment for persons who commit sex crimes provides a moderate return on investment.

EXHIBIT 7–6   Impact of Correctional Programming on Prisoners: Pre- and Postrelease Outcomes (continued)

Social Support Programming	Existing research has generally found that prison visitation decreases misconduct.	No evidence is available.	The evidence indicates that social support programming is successful in lowering recidivism.	Little evidence currently exists, although a few evaluations of programs that provide social support suggest that they deliver a return on investment.
Mental Health Programming	No evidence is available.	No evidence is available.	Existing research has found that mental health interventions do not reduce recidivism when the programming targets mental health symptoms. There is, however, some evidence indicating that these interventions can lower reoffending if they also target known criminogenic needs.	Little evidence exists, although evaluations of Washington's program for the dangerous mentally ill has produced strong returns on investment outcomes.
Domestic Violence Programming	No evidence is available.	No evidence is available.	Existing research has found that domestic violence interventions (e.g., separating the parties for a "cooling off" period) do not reduce recidivism.	Little evidence currently exists, although Washington State found that DV programs actually cost, rather than save, taxpayer dollars.

Source: National Institute of Justice.

instruction. Persons in prison did not enter prison to attend classes. The ability of many of them is hampered by a lack of basic reading and computational skills. Too often persons in prison do not see the importance of gaining an education, and many have a history of educational failure. They also tend not enroll in programs or participate in classes with the same enthusiasm as the noninstitutionalized population. Even negative peer pressure can discourage inmates from joining programs.

Second, research has also shown a link between learning disabilities and criminal behavior. An estimated 30 to 50 percent of persons in prison have a learning disability, compared with 5 to 15 percent of the U.S. adult population.[17]

And, third, we know that educational programming has not been a high priority in correctional budgeting, particularly due to the beginning of the warehousing era in the 1980s. The bulk of correctional spending is on custody and security. In 2021, the budget for the Federal Bureau of Prisons was $9.3 billion. Two-thirds was spent on institutional security, management and administration, and contracting.

However, can educational programming change behavior so that persons leaving prison contribute constructively to society and cost less than incarceration? The answer is a resounding, "Yes, it can."

Rand Corporation published the results of the largest study to date measuring the effectiveness of correctional education on recidivism and employment.[18] It found that persons who participated in correctional education programs—remedial education to develop reading and math

skills, GED preparation, postsecondary education, or vocational training—were 43 percent less likely to return to prison within three years of release in comparison to those who did not participate, and that participating in secondary degree programs produced a 30 percent decrease in recidivism. The researchers also found that persons who participated in academic or vocational education programs had a 13 percent better chance of finding employment than those who did not. And those who participated specifically in vocational training programs (including welding, computing, culinary arts, construction trades, and auto mechanics) were 28 percent more likely to be employed after release from prison than those who did not participate. Attending education classes in prison has also been associated with improved social climate and communication and reduced problems with disciplinary infractions. The RAND findings also suggest that prison education programs are cost effective. The direct costs of providing education in prison are approximately $1,400 to $1,744 per individual per year, with re-incarceration costing $8,700 to $9,700 *less* for each person who received their education as compared to those who did not. The study also makes it clear that while the results consistently demonstrate the benefits of prison education programs, there is not yet enough evidence to determine which programs performed the best. The authors write, "Our findings suggest that we no longer need to debate whether correctional education works. But we need more research to tease out which parts of these programs work best."[19]

Until recently, access to higher education in prison was limited. During the "get-tough" era of the 1990s, Congress passed the Violent Crime Control and Law Enforcement Act in 1994. The act barred persons in prison from receiving Pell grants for college studies. The argument was that incarcerated individuals were taking away funds from other students who were not serving time in prison. In reality eligible incarcerated individuals used less than 1 percent of funds from the Pell Grant's total annual spending.

Yet with time, the U.S. Department of Education undertook an experiment in 2016 to make Pell grants available to incarcerated students under the Second Chance Pell *Pilot* Program. From 2016 to 2021, almost 800 incarcerated Pell recipients earned bachelor's degrees. Another 8,000 earned certificates, postsecondary diplomas, and graduate degrees. The success of those educational programs in promoting positive self-worth and development, preparing for postrelease jobs and successful re-entry, racial equity (especially among people of color who disproportionately make up the prison population), public safety, safety inside prison, and economic savings moved Congress to repeal the ban altogether in 2020. Pell grants are scheduled to be widely available for all academically eligible incarcerated people to enroll in college-level courses in the 2023–2024 academic year.

Participation in education programs is also an opportunity to earn good time credits (also called *earned time* or gained time). In most jurisdictions people in prison can earn time off their sentences by participating in or completing treatment

Persons in prison at the Fremont Correctional Facility in Cañon City, Colorado, learn new career skills in renewable energy fields. They attend class five hours a day and do homework from a textbook in their cells. Persons who pass the program earn certificates and 20 college credits. What is the illiteracy rate among the incarcerated population compared to that of the general population? Why are there so few persons enrolled in education classes?

Andy Cross/The Denver Post via Getty Images

Twenty-eight men of the Mississippi State Penitentiary receive their associate and bachelor of arts degrees from the New Orleans Baptist Theological Seminary's Christian Ministry program. Why are prison education and vocational training programs important?

Rogelio V. Solis/AP Images

CO7-5

programs, educational courses, or vocational training. In Nevada, for example, people in prison can earn 10 days per month for participation in an education program and an additional 60, 90, or 120 days for obtaining a certificate, diploma, or degree, respectively. Arkansas awards persons in prison 90 days off their sentence for completing either their GED or a vocational certificate. Persons incarcerated in federal prison can earn 10 days off their projected release date for every 30 days of successful participation in evidence-based recidivism reduction programs and activities.

Vocational Training, Prison Industries, and Prison Work Assignments

Vocational training is the acquisition of practical skills, attitudes, understanding, and knowledge necessary for effective employment in specific occupations. Its primary purpose is to increase the economic value of a person's experience and skills, enabling them to realize their potential as productive members of society.

Vocational training in prison has its supporters because poor job skills are related to the problems people face after release from prison. Program completion and certification signals to potential employers the individual's seriousness in moving forward, which, in part, may compensate for the offending behavior.

However the same argument that was used to bar incarcerated persons from receiving Pell grants—no social benefits for persons in prison beyond the bare minimum—has also been used to strip away vocational training, exercise equipment, movies, and the like. Before discussing vocational skill-building programs and prison industries around the country and sharing what is known about "what works," we describe the current landscape of prison work assignments across the United States.

Men incarcerated at Folsom State Prison in California learn to inspect, maintain, and repair cars and light trucks and pursue postincarceration employment as automotive service technicians and mechanics. The auto mechanics industry provides mechanical and electrical repair and maintenance work for cars, trucks, vans, and trailers. According to the U.S. Department of Labor, Bureau of Labor Statistics, the employment outlook for automotive service technicians and mechanics is projected to grow 2 percent from 2022 to 2032. What are the benefits of prison industries for persons who are incarcerated, their families, and victims while in prison and after release; for the institution; for the business community; and for taxpayers?

Hector Amezcua/Sacramento Bee/MCT via Getty Images

Prison Work Assignments In federal and state prisons, people who are incarcerated are required to work if they are medically able. Prison jobs include working in food service, grounds-keeping, plumbing, electrical, laundry, HVAC, and other tasks that offset operational expenses. Others may perform road, park, or other public maintenance work outside of the facility. The average prison wage is 52 cents an hour.[20]

Some argue prison work programs are an opportunity to increase individuals' postrelease employment opportunities. Too often, however, these work programs teach low-skilled positions characterized by the kind of low-wage earning potential that makes it difficult for formerly incarcerated workers to achieve financial security.

Prison Industries Prison industries, on the other hand, are designed to place incarcerated workers in a realistic work environment, provide job skills, pay the prevailing local wage for similar work, and enable them to acquire marketable skills to increase their potential for successful rehabilitation, meaningful employment upon release, and contribute as a tax-paying citizen. Prison industries also have the potential to keep persons in prison constructively involved which is proven to decrease violence. Each state oversees its own prison industry initiative, and the federal system runs a separate program.

Federal Prison Industries (FPI), better known under the trade name **UNICOR**, is the largest complex of prison industries across the nation producing a wide variety of goods and services. FPI employs close to 20,000 persons under the custody of federal correctional authorities in 80 federal prisons. Workers spend their days in warehouses within their prison complexes that look like typical factories and earn between 23 cents an hour to $1.15 an hour. Among the products FPI produces are cable assemblies and wire harnesses for tactical aircraft, ground vehicles, smart weapons, and secure communications systems; solar panels; eyewear and optics; vehicle uplift, remanufacturing, and fleet services for the Army, Navy, and Marine Corps, and all Homeland Security border patrol vehicles; furniture systems; and signage.

Federal Prison Industries (FPI)

A federal, paid prison work program and self-supporting corporation.

UNICOR

The trade name of Federal Prison Industries. UNICOR provides, among other things, cable assemblies, solar panels, and vehicle and fleet services for the Army, Navy, Marine Corps, and Homeland Security.

With few exceptions, FPI is restricted to selling its products to the federal government. The exception to this is goods produced through the Prison Industry Enhancement Certification Program (PIECP) that Congress created in 1979 to allow the interstate and foreign sale of goods produced by incarcerated persons. Private corporations like Semah Tronix (manufacturer of wire harnesses), Electrex Inc. (manufacturer of electrical systems), Landus Cooperative (provider of agronomy services), Graphic Edge (producer of sportswear), Jelt (producer of sustainable clothing), Prison Blues (producer of denim clothing), Craig Industries (manufacturer of insulated building panels), and hundreds more have partnered with federal and state-governed public and private prisons to produce goods certified under PIECP. In year-end 2019, over 5,000 incarcerated persons worked in over 200 prison factories nationwide.

PIECP certification requires that state correctional agencies meet certain criteria—including that incarcerated workers receive local "prevailing wages." However, PIECP programs nationwide are accused of ignoring or openly violating the "prevailing wage" requirement in order to generate more profit.[21] In Florida, for example, Prison Rehabilitative Industries and Diversified Enterprises (PRIDE) requires incarcerated workers to complete an initial 480-hour training course followed by three more training periods with reduced pay for years before earning prevailing wages. PIECP also allows prison industry programs to deduct up to 80 percent of a worker's total earnings for taxes, room and board, and restitution. Critics argue that incarcerated workers are exploited captive labor earning on average 52 cents

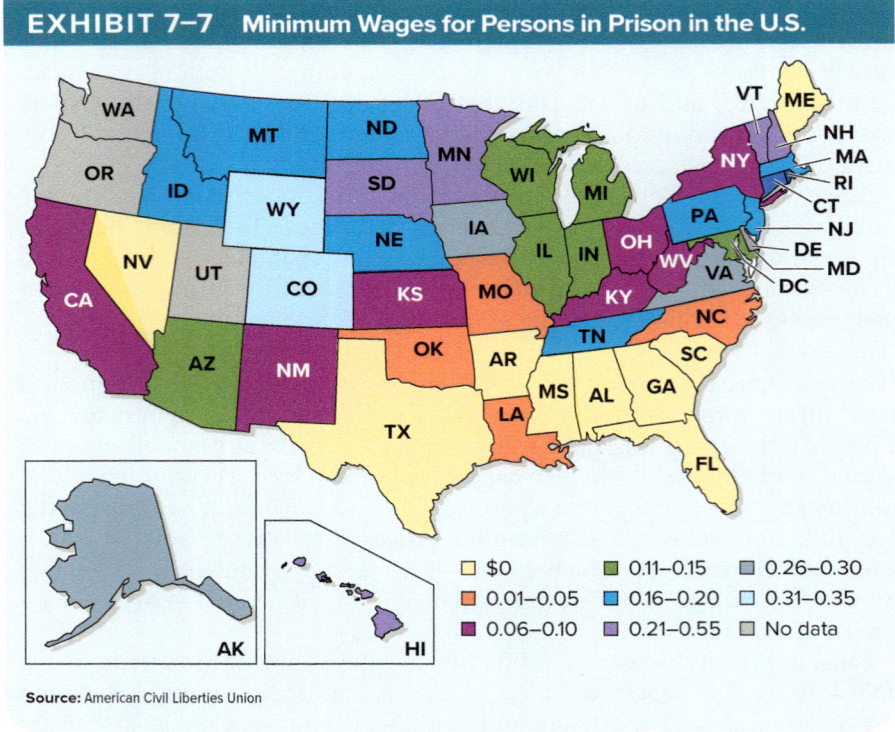

EXHIBIT 7–7 Minimum Wages for Persons in Prison in the U.S.

Legend:
- $0
- 0.01–0.05
- 0.06–0.10
- 0.11–0.15
- 0.16–0.20
- 0.21–0.55
- 0.26–0.30
- 0.31–0.35
- No data

Source: American Civil Liberties Union

an hour while producing over $2 billion in goods and over $9 billion worth of prison maintenance services.[22] Exhibit 7–7 shows minimum wages for incarcerated workers across the United States. What do you believe? Should incarcerated workers be paid for their labor? If not, why? If so, should they receive minimum wage or prevailing wage? Consider the link between employment, successful reentry, and recidivism in your decision.

Vocational Training Earlier we explained what vocational training is and its purpose. There is no reliable estimate on the number of prison-based vocational training programs separate from prison work assignments and prison factories. BJS combines prison industries and vocational training in its count of prison work programs. Space allows us only to present several examples of vocational programs that work.

Women and men confined in two Arizona prisons are able to earn their commercial driver's license (CDL).[23] Since the program began, nearly 100 of the participants have earned their commercial driver's license (CDL) and are working in the trucking and crane operator industry.

Another popular vocational training program found in Western prisons is wildland firefighting. Since the program began in Colorado in 2002, more than 2,500 persons completed the same extensive training as any other state or local firefighters to become a member of the Colorado's Wildland Inmate Fire Team (SWIFT). A new law passed in 2022 is designed to help more SWIFT members find jobs as full-time firefighters. The bill encourages the state's Division of Fire Prevention and Control to give hiring preference to formerly incarcerated people with firefighting experience and start a peer mentor program for those hired by the state agency so they can develop professional skills.[24]

Vocational training is also expanding in the fields of software development and computer coding. The Bureau of Labor Statistics (BLS) reports that the 2020 median annual salary for web developers and digital designers was $77,200.[25]

The Last Mile (TLM) is a non-profit organization that provides in-prison technology education and postincarceration mentorship for individuals nearing the end of their sentence.[26] Since its founding in 2010, TLM has served almost 1,000 women and men incarcerated in 16 prisons in seven states (California, Indiana, Kansas, Oklahoma, Michigan, Montana, North Dakota).

The TLM coding program requires a high school diploma or GED and takes 12 months to complete. Participants are provided Apple products and Google Chromebooks. The course curriculum includes web development fundamentals, such as HTML, CSS, JavaScript, jQuery, and Bootstrap. In addition, there is a reentry mentorship program for career development (assistance with resume writing, interview prep, and soft skill building), job placement support (connections to apprenticeship and employment opportunities, as well job search assistance), and access to TLM's network of alumni who share and discuss common obstacles and goals in the reentry process, particularly relating to career development.

Syd Heller, TLM executive director, told participants at the start of the web development program at the Montana State Prison in Deer Lodge in October 2022, "The web development industry is more receptive to nontraditional education. I don't care where you're from, if you can write code, you can work at Google."[27] TLM program graduates are employed by Zoom, Dropbox, and Slack, among others.

Although there are exceptions, the general conclusion about prison industries and vocational training is they work. The National Institute of Justice examined all the available literature on prison industries and vocational training and found that persons who participated in prison-based vocational training programs and prison industries like those presented here were significantly less likely to recidivate and more likely to be gainfully employed after release compared with persons who had not participated.[28]

However, prison work assignments in food service, grounds-keeping, plumbing, electrical, laundry, HVAC, and other tasks that offset operational expenses, as well as performing road, park, or other public maintenance work outside the facility, are low-skilled positions not known to reduce recidivism or increase individuals' postrelease employment opportunities. Prison work assignments keep persons busy during the day and decrease idleness. There may be other health and skill-learning benefits correctional administrators point to. However, to the larger question of do prison work assignments reduce recidivism and increase postprison employment, there is no evidence that they do. The work is done because persons in prison are required by law to work.

Many state correctional systems channel prison labor into industrial and commercial programs. One such program is the Prison Blues® brand of jeans, T-shirts, work shirts, and yard coats manufactured by Oregon Corrections Enterprises, a division of the Oregon Department of Corrections. What benefits do such work programs provide?

Matt Joyce/AP Images

PRISON ORGANIZATION AND ADMINISTRATION

CO7-6

All 50 states and the BOP operate prisons. In addition, four local jurisdictions in the United States operate prison systems: Cook County (Chicago), Illinois; Philadelphia; New York City; and Washington, D.C. Across the U.S., there are 122 federal confinement facilities and 1,039 state confinement facilities. (Private confinement facilities, discussed later in this chapter, operate under contract to state or federal correctional authorities and are included in those counts.)

State Prison Systems

Organization and Administration   The administration of state prisons is a function of the executive branch of government. The governor appoints the director of corrections, who in turn appoints the wardens of the state prisons. A change in governors often means a change in state prison leadership and administration.

The organization of most state prison systems involves a central authority, based in the state capital. Local communities, private contractors, or the state itself may provide prison services (from treatment and education to maintenance and repair). Still, for legal control and for maintaining an equitable distribution of resources, a centralized model has been maintained while in other areas of corrections (e.g., community corrections and probation), services are often decentralized.

Size and Cost   State departments of corrections vary in size. The smallest are North and South Dakota. The North Dakota Department of Corrections and Rehabilitation has an annual budget of $110 million and employs almost 1,000 persons. The South Dakota Department of Corrections has an annual budget of $130 million and employs almost 800 people. The largest is California's with over 62,000 authorized positions and an annual operating budget of $8.6 billion.[29]

An estimated 442,000 people work in adult prisons. About one-half are corrections officers. In 2022, the average annual salary for a corrections officer was $50,000, according to data from the Bureau of Labor Statistics.[30] Almost 75 percent of correctional officers are male. Nineteen percent of all correctional facility staff are Black, and 7 percent are Hispanic.

In 2000, the United States spent about $36 billion on corrections. Today, state spending on corrections is over $107 billion.[31] Corrections is the fourth-largest category of states' spending following education, Medicaid, and transportation. The vast majority of funds that go to state corrections systems—9 of every 10 dollars—goes to prisons. Some ask if the money spent on state corrections encroaches on funds for higher education because the money has to come from somewhere. Jennifer Gonnerman, a staff writer for the *New Yorker,* wrote, "When parents get a tuition bill for their kids' college education, I always think they should get a little note that says tuition went up $200 last year because we decided to build two new prisons. Then we can all decide whether we think that's a good use of our money or not."[32] Others have said, "Every additional dollar spent on prisons, of course is one dollar less that can go to preparing for the next hurricane, educating young people, providing health care to the elderly, or repairing roads and bridges."[33]

States spend, on average, approximately $33,274 a year to incarcerate one individual.[34] Incarceration cost per person ranges from a low of $14,780 in Alabama to a high of $69,355 in California. Eight states (Alaska, California, Connecticut, Massachusetts, New Jersey, New York, Rhode Island, Vermont) spend over $50,000 per incarcerated person. In 18 states—mostly southern states—the cost is less than $25,000. Five states with the most expensive cost per person incarcerated are shown in Exhibit 7–8.

States have closed or announced closures for nearly 300 prisons and have invested a portion of the estimated savings in infrastructure and civic institutions such as substance abuse treatment, housing, education, and jobs located in high-risk neighborhoods, a practice known as the Justice Reinvestment Initiative (JRI).[35]

EXHIBIT 7–8 Five States with the Most Expensive Cost Per Person Incarcerated

Average Annual	Cost Per Person Incarcerated
California	$69,355
New York	$64,642
New Jersey	$62,159
Connecticut	$61,603
Vermont	$57,615

Source: Christian Henrichson and Ruth Delaney, *The Price of Prisons: Examining State Spending Trends, 2010–2015* (New York: Vera Institute of Justice, May 2017).

JRI is funded by BJS and the Pew Charitable Trusts. It is data-driven approach that ensures that policymaking is based on a comprehensive analysis of criminal justice data and the latest research about what works to reduce crime and that is tailored to the needs of the local jurisdiction. The approaches vary, but the laws generally aim to reduce the flow of people into prison, limit their time behind bars, streamline release procedures, and strengthen community supervision. Exhibit 7–9 details how several states have used JRI to improve community supervision.

Federal Bureau of Prisons

The Federal Bureau of Prisons (BOP) is a separate correctional agency apart from state departments of corrections. The BOP is operated by the federal government and incarcerates persons convicted of breaking federal laws. In contrast, state prisons are operated by state governments and incarcerate people convicted of breaking state laws.

Organization and Administration Before the 1890s, the federal government did not operate its own prisons. Instead, the Department of Justice paid state prisons and county jails to house people convicted of federal crimes. The public outcry over the convict lease system, however, motivated the passage of a federal law prohibiting the leasing of people under federal correctional authority. Many state prisons and county jails subsequently became reluctant to incarcerate people convicted of federal crimes because it was not economically advantageous to incarcerate people they could not lease. Moreover, the expansion of federal law enforcement activities and the enactment of new federal laws in the late 19th century led to an increase in the prosecution of federal lawbreakers and overcrowding in the prisons where they were held. With a growing population of people convicted of federal crimes and the growing reluctance of nonfederal prisons to house them, the federal government had no choice but to build prisons of its own.

In 1891 Congress passed the Three Prisons Act which authorized the establishment of three federal penitentiaries: Atlanta (Georgia), Leavenworth (Kansas), and McNeil Island (Washington). Forty years later—1930—Congress established the Bureau of Prisons within the Department of Justice and charged it with the "management and regulation of all Federal penal and correctional institutions." Eleven federal prisons were in operation at that time.

The director of the BOP is appointed by the U.S. Attorney General. Ms. Colette Peters was appointed director in August 2022. She is the second woman to hold the position. The new director faces a number of challenges

EXHIBIT 7–9 Justice Reinvestment Initiative in Six States

Louisiana

Concentrate Supervision Resources on Individuals at the Highest Risk to Reoffend

In 2017, Louisiana enacted JRI legislation to:

- reduce probation and parole officers' caseloads
- adopt evidence-based practices
- prioritize prison space for people convicted of serious offenses
- allow community supervision officers to focus on people at the highest risk to recidivate
- reduce the maximum probation term for nonviolent offenses from five to three years
- incentivize compliance with supervision and establish an earned compliance credit system
- expand probation eligibility by extending the use of intermediate sanctions
- $12.2 million saved in 2018—double the original projected savings

Massachusetts

Expand Access to Community-Based Behavioral Health Treatment

In 2018, Massachusetts enacted JRI legislation to:

- incentivize good behavior in prison
- divert people to treatment and programming
- strengthen community supervision
- allocate more supervision services to persons at the highest risk to reoffend
- align community supervision with best practices
- expand behavioral health programs for persons with serious mental illnesses and/or substance use disorders

Mississippi

Strengthen Responses to Supervision Violations and Require the Use of Evidence-Based Practices

In 2014, Mississippi enacted JRI legislation to:

- use risk and needs assessments to focus resources on persons at the highest risk to reoffend
- adopt graduated sanctions to address violations
- incentivize compliance with supervision and establish an earned compliance credit system
- adopt evidence-based practices and train parole board members and community supervision officers
- by 2018 the number of people who successfully completed probation increased 10 percent

Missouri

Strengthen Gender-Responsive Approaches to Supervision

In 2018, Missouri enacted JRI legislation to:

- open a female-only, trauma-recovery center
- implement gender-responsive approaches to supervision, case management, and programming
- implement cognitive behavioral intervention programs
- increase evidence-based practices
- improve community supervision outcomes
- reduce prison admissions due to revocations
- implement a risk and needs assessment
- incentivize compliance with supervision and establish an earned compliance credit system

Nebraska

Identify Effective Ways to Use Funding to Improve Community Supervision

In 2015, Nebraska enacted JRI legislation to:

- require probation rather than incarceration for persons convicted of nonviolent offenses
- ensure postrelease supervision for individuals released from prison
- strengthen parole
- hire additional supervision officers
- expand community-based treatment
- by 2018, people released to parole or post-release supervision grew to 74 percent, an increase of 39 percent compared to 2015

Wyoming

Provide Judges with More Tools to Determine Probation Term Lengths

In 2019, Wyoming enacted JRI legislation to:

- reduce recidivism
- increase community-based behavioral health treatment
- promote the use of early discharge
- reduce the number of people who are revoked from supervision
- focus resources where they provide the most public safety benefit
- provide judges with data to determine the period of probation
- use unsupervised probation where appropriate
- impose fines
- incentivize compliance with supervision and establish an earned compliance credit system
- train supervision officers on evidence-based practices

Source: Adapted from Justice Center, The Council of State Governments, *The Justice Reinvestment Initiative Improves Community Supervision* (New York: Justice Center, The Council of State Governments, May 2021).

including aging buildings, mounting cost of medical care (especially for the elderly—a topic we return to in Chapter 12), failure to implement criminal justice reform, and lack of transparency.

In March 2023 the Government Accountability Office announced that the BOP had failed to implement a risk and need assessment (RNA) system—part of the criminal justice reforms ordered under the First Step Act of 2018.[36] Recognizing that 45 percent of people released from federal prison are rearrested or return to federal prison within three years of their release, the First Step Act includes certain requirements for the Department of Justice and BOP to help reduce recidivism among individuals incarcerated in federal prisons.

The act requires the Attorney General to develop a risk and need assessment system to be used by the BOP to assess the recidivism risk of all incarcerated people in federal prisons, and to place these individuals in evidence-based recidivism reduction programs and activities that may help reduce this risk. BOP staff are to use the risk and need assessment system to determine the type and amount of programming appropriate for each incarcerated person and to assign recommended programming based on the incarcerated person's specific need.

Additionally, the First Step Act allows eligible incarcerated people who successfully complete evidence-based recidivism reduction programs and activities to earn time credits that reduce the amount of time they spend in federal prison. For every 30 days of successful participation in the program or activity, a person in federal prison earns 10 days off their projected release date. Exhibit 7–10 is an example of an incarcerated person that the BOP has determined eligible to earn time credits and a low risk of recidivism.

However, what the GAO found was the BOP does not have readily available, complete, or accurate data to determine if risk-need assessments are completed on time, nor did the BOP have a mechanism to track an

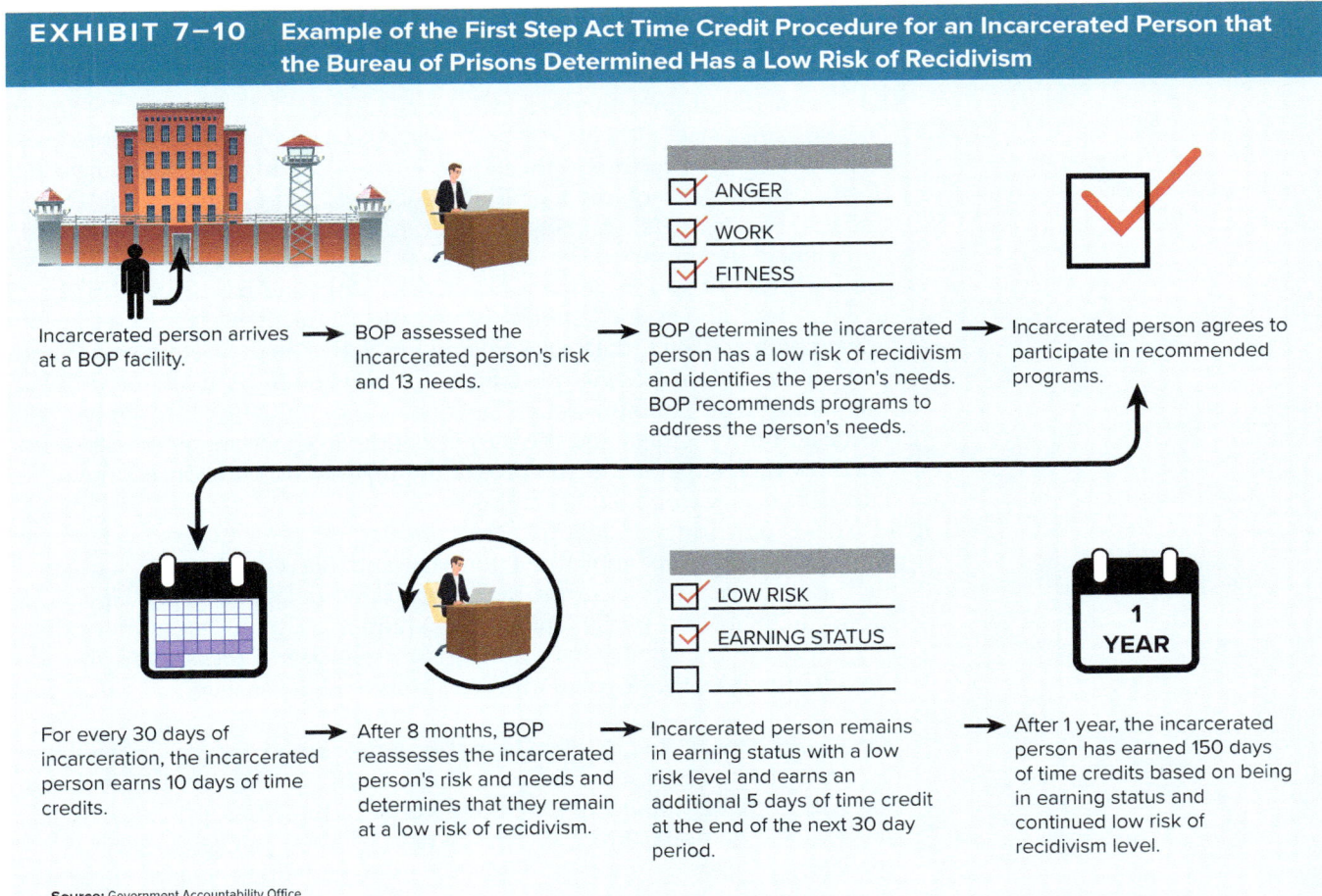

EXHIBIT 7–10   Example of the First Step Act Time Credit Procedure for an Incarcerated Person that the Bureau of Prisons Determined Has a Low Risk of Recidivism

ANGER
WORK
FITNESS

Incarcerated person arrives at a BOP facility.

BOP assessed the Incarcerated person's risk and 13 needs.

BOP determines the incarcerated person has a low risk of recidivism and identifies the person's needs. BOP recommends programs to address the person's needs.

Incarcerated person agrees to participate in recommended programs.

LOW RISK
EARNING STATUS

1 YEAR

For every 30 days of incarceration, the incarcerated person earns 10 days of time credits.

After 8 months, BOP reassesses the incarcerated person's risk and needs and determines that they remain at a low risk of recidivism.

Incarcerated person remains in earning status with a low risk level and earns an additional 5 days of time credit at the end of the next 30 day period.

After 1 year, the incarcerated person has earned 150 days of time credits based on being in earning status and continued low risk of recidivism level.

Source: Government Accountability Office

individual's participation in evidence-based recidivism reduction programs which is necessary to earn time credits. As a result, the GAO found that some people in federal prison lost their time credits and were incarcerated longer than they should have been.

To address these shortcomings, the GAO recommended and the BOP agreed to:

1. collect and maintain complete and accurate data
2. conduct risk and need assessments in accordance with the First Step Act
3. document the results of risk and need assessments and take corrective action as needed
4. set quantifiable goals for evaluating evidence-based recidivism reduction programs
5. evaluate evidence-based recidivism reduction programs
6. monitor on an on-going basis whether the BOP offers a sufficient amount of evidence-based recidivism reduction programs to meet the need of the incarcerated population

Two years earlier, a report by the National Institute of Justice found that the vast majority of correctional systems across the U.S. use RNAs.[37] However according to the report, most RNAs have not lived up to the promise of identifying how likely a person is to commit another crime or violate the rules of jails, prisons, or community supervision. The authors argue that most of the RNAs are outdated, inefficient, and ineffective, the same problem the GAO found in the BOP two years later.

As more correctional agencies are required by law to collect and use data to guide postsentencing decisions that align with promoting public safety and preventing reoffending, the NIJ report proposes that the RNA tool should be designed and implemented with four fundamental principles in mind: *fairness, efficiency, effectiveness,* and *communication.* These four principles call our attention to important issues when designing and implementing RNAs. "Fairness" requires that RNA tools yield more equitable outcomes and that efforts are taken to eliminate or minimize potential sources of bias. "Efficiency" is improved by adopting automated and computer-assisted scoring processes to increase reliability, validity, and assessment capacity to save time and reduce subjective scoring. "Effectiveness" means using advances in statistics, data science, and predictive analytics to monitor and assess outcomes of offender programming based on RNA assessments. And the principle of "communication" means helping individuals under correctional authority understand the purpose of the RNA assessment, its results, and how their supervision and programming is tailored to address the need and risks underlying their offending.

These four principles address the concerns expressed by the GAO over the BOP's failure to implement the risk and need assessment legislated by the First Step Act. And for the incarcerated person, the principles call attention to how the design and implementation of RNAs can monitor their participation in evidence-based recidivism reduction programs so they do not lose the time they earned off their projected release date.

Size and Costs Today 158,844 persons are under federal correctional authority (down from the peak of 219,298 in 2013). The decrease is due to legislative changes and the First Step Act of 2018, which provides eligible individuals the opportunity to earn 10 days off their projected release date for every 30 days of successful participation in evidence-based programs and activities. The bill also envisions but does not require that the savings achieved by reducing the number of persons held in federal institutions will be reinvested in rehabilitative programming available within the BOP, residential reentry centers, or other community settings—what we referred to earlier as justice reinvestment.

The BOP operates 122 federal confinement facilities. Ninety-one percent (145,333) of persons under federal correctional authority are held in either a federal institution or a residential reentry center, also known as half-way houses, to provide assistance to persons nearing release from prison. Almost 14,000 persons are also under home confinement. In 2022, the BOP budget totaled $7.8 billion. The average cost to confine one person in a federal prison is $39,158.

The BOP employs almost 35,000 staff. Twenty-eight percent are female, and 40 percent are nonwhite. Career opportunities with the BOP include positions working directly with persons incarcerated (correctional officer, chaplain, psychologist, teacher, treatment specialist); to health services (dentist, dental hygienist, nurse, physical therapist); institution work supervisors; vocational training specialists; and positions in support and administration (accountant, attorney, human resource specialist, secretary). The bureau also offers a number of student opportunities as volunteers, interns, and programs for students nearing graduation including the attorney general's Honors Program for law students. Consult the Federal BOP website for career opportunities (bop.gov).

Privately Operated Prisons

The issue of correctional privatization was discussed in Chapter 6. The focus here is on the current use of privately operated prison facilities.

Today's trend toward privatization of prisons began in 1984 when President Reagan asked the Grace Commission to study waste and inefficiency in the federal government. What followed was an aggressive movement by federal and state officials who saw privatization as a way to ameliorate overcrowding in public prisons and obtain additional prison beds. At the same time as the private corrections industry emerged in the mid-1980s, about three-quarters of the states were under some sort of federal court

The GEO Group, Inc. is a provider of private correctional, detention, and community reentry services with 102 facilities, encompassing approximately 82,000 beds, and 18,000 employees worldwide. The American Correctional Association awarded GEO's Graceville facility its Innovation in Corrections Award for its enhanced in-custody evidence-based rehabilitation programming integrated with postrelease support services. What are evidence-based principles?
Courtesy of The GEO Group, Inc.

order to reduce the prison population in at least one of their prisons. Cash-strapped states turned to the private sector, which offered to build new prisons more cheaply, build them faster, and operate them better.

Today, of the 1,161 confinement facilities across the United States, 82 are private prisons operating in 27 states and the federal government. Almost 100,000 men and women are held in private prisons, representing 8 percent of the total state and federal prison population.

States vary considerably in their use of private prisons. Forty percent of the private prison population is in five states: Florida (10,810), Texas (9,249), Arizona (7,185), Tennessee (6,984) and Ohio (6,204). While in another 23 states private prisons are not used at all.

In 2019, *Criminology & Public Policy*, one of the most prestigious journals in criminology and criminal justice, published a special issue of 13 articles on privatized corrections.[38] Topics included what we know and the gaps in our knowledge about private corrections, historical analysis, private community corrections, privatized juvenile corrections, cost-effectiveness, public attitudes, international privatization, and the philosophical and ethical consideration that shape the debate about private correctional facilities.

The issue that stands at the center of the debate about private prisons is the belief that administering punishment is an inherent responsibility of the government, not the private sector. Others believe that the goal of privatizing prisons is profit, and, as a result, the private sector will disregard the goals of the justice system of inmate rehabilitation, advocate for longer prison sentences, and keep persons in prison longer than needed.

Research exits to support these and other claims. However, the research is often preliminary, judgmental about privatization in its approach and not of the caliber of an evidence-based approach that we have come to rely on as a correctional benchmark for judging effectiveness. Given the prevalence of private corrections in the United States and internationally, their disappearance is unlikely. Some ask since the trend in corrections today is to develop good performance measures, why not incentivize private prisons to improve as they do in the United Kingdom and France—reform the model rather than end the experiment. More data, not less, would breathe fresh air into the debate surrounding private prisons.

Prison Security Levels

Prisons are classified by the level of security they provide. Most local, state, and federal jurisdictions use minimum-, medium-, and maximum-security classifications.[39] **Minimum-security institutions** confine persons for both short and long periods. It allows as much freedom of movement and as many privileges and amenities as are consistent with the facility's goals while following procedures to avoid escape, violence, and disturbance. Minimum-security institutions have dormitory housing, a relatively low staff-to-incarceree ratio, and limited or no perimeter fencing. These institutions are work and program oriented. Some persons leave the institution for programming in the community. These institutions are sometimes referred to as **open institutions** because no fences or walls surround them. Approximately 16 percent (208,000) of the U.S. state and federal prison population are confined in one of 287 minimum-security prisons.

Persons incarcerated in **medium-security prisons** are considered less dangerous than those in maximum-security prisons and may serve short or long sentences. Medium-security prisons impose fewer controls on the incarcerated population and visitors' freedom of movement than do maximum-security facilities. Medium-security facilities have strengthened perimeters (often double fences with electronic detection systems), mostly

---

minimum-security institution

A facility that confines people who are the least dangerous for both short and long periods. It allows as much freedom of movement and as many privileges and amenities as are consistent with the goals of the facility. It may have dormitory housing, and the staff-to-incarceree ratio is relatively low.

open institution

A minimum-security facility that has no fences or walls surrounding it.

medium-security prison

A prison that confines individuals considered less dangerous than those in maximum security, for both short and long periods. It places fewer controls on the incarcerated population's and visitors' freedom of movement than does a maximum-security facility. It has barred cells and a fortified perimeter. The staff-to-incarceree ratio is generally lower than that in a maximum-security facility, and the level of amenities and privileges is slightly higher.

Minimum-security prisons confine persons considered the least dangerous. They are sometimes referred to as open institutions because they have limited or no perimeter fencing surrounding them. How do minimum-security prisons differ from medium- and maximum-security prisons?

ZUMA Press, Inc/Alamy Stock Photo

cell-type housing, a wide variety of work and treatment programs, an even higher staff-to-incarceree ratio than minimum-security institutions, and even greater internal controls. Across the United States, 41.7 percent (approximately 545,100) of the prison population is incarcerated in 1 of 451 medium-security correctional facilities.

A **maximum- or close/high-security prison** is designed, organized, and staffed to confine persons considered the most violent and dangerous for long periods. It imposes strict controls on the movement of incarcerated persons and their visitors, and custody and security are constant concerns. The prison has a highly secure perimeter with watchtowers and high walls. Persons live in single- or multiple-occupancy barred cells. The staff-to-incarcerated people ratio is high, routines are highly regimented, and there are frequent counts of the incarcerated population throughout the day. Programs, amenities, and privileges are few. The BOP operates 17 maximum-security facilities. Approximately 42.3 percent (roughly 549,000) of the incarcerated population in the United States are in maximum-security facilities.

maximum- or close/high-security prison

A prison designed, organized, and staffed to confine individuals considered the most dangerous individuals for long periods. It has a highly secure perimeter, barred cells, and a high staff-to-incarceree ratio. It imposes strict controls on the movement of the incarcerated population and visitors, and it offers few programs, amenities, or privileges.

Medium-security prisons incarcerate persons considered less dangerous than those in maximum-security prisons. They impose fewer controls on the incarcerated population's freedom of movement and place more emphasis on treatment and work programs. How do medium-security prisons differ from minimum- and maximum-security prisons?

Stephanie Zollshan/The Berkshire Eagle/AP Image

Crime SOLUTIONS.gov

RELIABLE RESEARCH. REAL RESULTS.

Enter your keyword(s)   Search Site   Advanced Search

Home | Help | Contact Us | Site Map | Glossary

EVIDENCE-BASED CORRECTIONS

Rehabilitation Programs for Adult Offenders

Rehabilitation programs are designed to reduce recidivism among adults who have been convicted of an offense by improving their behaviors, skills, mental health, social functioning, and access to education and employment. Most programs are delivered within correctional settings while the person completes his or her sentence, or in community settings (i.e., probation or parole-based programs).

Rehabilitation programs do not generally follow a common, well-defined treatment protocol. Instead, interventions and services may vary significantly by program. All programs address at least one of the risk factors commonly associated with offending (such as mental health status, substance use, education level, or employment status). More commonly, however, rehabilitation programs combine multiple services: for example, a drug court program that provides an individual not only with substance abuse treatment, but also with individual counseling and vocational training.

The general types of treatment services provided by rehabilitation programs include group work; cognitive behavioral therapy (CBT); counseling (group, individual, mentoring); academic work (GED or college classes); employment-related (work-release, job placement, vocational training); supportive residential (therapeutic community, halfway house); drug court or other specialized court; multimodal, mixed treatments; intensive supervision (reduced probation or parole); or restorative interventions (mediation, reparations, community service, victim-offender conferencing).

Researchers reviewed the evidence from meta-analyses about the effects of rehabilitation programs on recidivism and found a statistically significant reduction in recidivism indicating that adult offenders who participated in rehabilitation programs demonstrated reductions in offending, compared with control groups who did not participate.

The Rehabilitation Programs for Adult Offenders practice is rated *Effective*.

Source: Adapted from Bureau of Justice Statistics

Maximum-security prisons confine persons considered the most violent and dangerous for long periods. They are surrounded by high walls and gun towers. How do maximum-security prisons differ from minimum- and medium-security prisons?

Brett Coomer/AP Images

The Federal Bureau of Prisons and several states also have confinement facilities with special missions, such as the treatment of persons with serious or chronic medical problems or the confinement of individuals considered extremely dangerous, violent, or escape-prone. One such institution is the BOP's Administrative Maximum (ADX) facility in Florence Colorado, built to confine persons who pose the greatest risk to staff, other incarcerated persons, and the public. These facilities are also referred to as supermax prisons and are considered next.

Solitary Confinement and Supermax Prisons

CO7-7

Prison systems have always needed a way to deal with individuals whose violent behavior makes it impossible for them to live with the general prison population. Generally, such measures involve separating those individuals and are called *segregation* or *solitary confinement.* Persons who are dangerous or chronically violent, have caused injury or death while incarcerated, have escaped or attempted to escape from a high-security correctional facility, have incited or attempted to incite disruption in a correctional facility, belong to a **security threat group (STG),** or have preyed on weaker persons are removed from the general population. STGs like the Latin Kings, Bloods, Crips, Mexican Mafia, Aryan Brotherhood, and Gangster Disciples number around 200,000 (or 16 percent) of the nation's 1.2 million prison population.[40]

security threat groups
The current term for prison gangs that describes how they negatively impact the security of prison operations.

Earlier in this chapter, you learned that, in 1829, the Eastern State Penitentiary in Cherry Hill, Pennsylvania, was built on the principle of solitary confinement. However, in 1913 the Pennsylvania legislature dropped "solitary" from sentencing statutes, and housing arrangements at Eastern State became congregate. From that point forward, specialized housing units were developed for individuals in prison considered the most dangerous, most violent, most prone to escape, and a threat to the operation of the institution.

The Federal BOP returned to the idea of controlling the most violent and disruptive individuals in indefinite solitary confinement when it opened Alcatraz in 1934. Alcatraz, which had a capacity of 275, did not offer any treatment program; its sole purpose was to incarcerate and punish what the federal prison system deemed the most desperate and worst of the federal prison population.

By 1963, Alcatraz was judged an expensive failure and was closed. For the next 10 years, prison officials used the *dispersal model*—individuals who caused problems were sent to other institutions. Prison officials hoped that dispersal among populations of generally law-abiding individuals would dilute the influence of those who caused trouble, but they soon learned that dispersing individuals who were chronically violent and otherwise dangerous across dozens of prisons led to having dozens of problem facilities.

The BOP reverted to the *concentration model*—all problem individuals would be confined together in a separate facility, arguing that it was necessary for prison safety and order. In 1994, the BOP opened its first **supermax housing** facility at Florence, Colorado, a hundred miles southwest of Denver. Officially known as the United States Penitentiary Florence Administrative Maximum (ADMAX; also known as ADX Florence), the so-called Alcatraz of the Rockies confines over 300 persons that federal correctional authorities believe are the most dangerous, violent, escape-prone, and security threat group (STG) federal prison leaders who pose a serious, ongoing threat to public safety and national security. Persons incarcerated at ADX Florence

supermax housing
A freestanding facility, or a distinct unit within a facility, that provides for management and secure control of persons who have been officially designated as exhibiting violent or serious and disruptive behavior while incarcerated.

At the federal supermax prison in Florence, Colorado, three mirrored-glass gun towers define the maximum-security level of heightened confinement. It is officially known as the United States Penitentiary Florence Administrative Maximum (ADMAX). What are the pros and cons of such facilities?

Pueblo Chieftain, Chris McLean/AP Image

are given a higher, more controlled level of custody than a maximum-security prison and are kept in isolation for 22 hours a day. There is only one federal supermax prison, but there are numerous maximum security state prisons or prisons with maximum security units within them, also known as segregation, lockdown, or solitary confinement. In 2021, researchers at Yale law school investigated solitary confinement and estimated that the number of persons in supermax-like conditions across the United States at between 40,000 and 50,000, down from 100,000 less than ten years ago.[41]

Inside ADX Florence is H Unit, the most restricted area where persons are subject to Special Administrative Measures (SAMs). Individuals under SAM restrictions aren't allowed to talk to the media because of concerns they might send coded messages to criminal or terrorist organizations. The only contacts they are permitted on the outside consist of a few government-approved family members and their attorneys—all of whom are sworn not to divulge anything the individual communicated to them, under threat of facing prosecution themselves. Mail, phone calls, media consumption, and family visits are all tightly restricted and monitored. The FBI and BOP have translators who listen to every call and review every letter, whether it's in English, Arabic, or Swahili. An estimated 40 to 50 individuals are under SAMs restrictions. Among them are Dzhokhar Tsarnaev, Boston Marathon bomber; Zacarias Moussaoui, confessed 9/11 conspirator; Olympic Park bomber Eric Rudolph; Oklahoma City bombing conspirator Terry Nichols; would-be "shoe bomber" Richard Reid; and 1993 World Trade Center bombing conspirator Ramzi Yousef.

Criminologists, psychiatrists, lawyers, and the courts who have studied the effects of long-term solitary confinement report evidence of acute sensory deprivation, paranoid delusion belief systems, irrational fears of violence, resentment, little ability to control rage, and mental breakdowns. The few studies that examined the impact of solitary confinement on recidivism have shown mixed results, no increase in recidivism for persons released from solitary confinement in Washington, but recidivism did increase for persons convicted of violent offenses and released from solitary confinement in Florida.[42] Researchers also discovered that the risk of recidivism is also higher if persons are released directly to the community from solitary confinement compared to those who spend some time in the general prison

Lizzie Himmel/Contributor/Getty Images

population between solitary confinement and release to the community.

Conditions of solitary confinement and prolonged isolation also present extraordinary challenges for staff. When there is little interaction except in control situations, the adversarial nature of the relationships tends to be one of dominance and, in return, resistance on both sides. Stuart Grassian, a physician and expert on prison control units, believes that people who work in facilities with supermax conditions may lose their capacity to be shocked by the kinds of things they see. "It may put money in your pocket," Dr. Grassian notes, "but over time it destroys you psychologically and brings out rage and sadism and violence and brutality."[43]

Even though many believe that supermax-like conditions should be abolished altogether, the move to limit its use to an absolute minimum is occurring within the larger movement of mass incarceration. The Yale law school study on solitary confinement referenced earlier found that three states—Delaware, North Dakota, and Vermont—have eliminated solitary confinement. Other states have embraced the Nelson Mandella Rules adopted by the United Nations in 2015 and limited the use of solitary confinement to 15 days. To date, Colorado is the only state to ban the practice of holding persons in segregated isolation for longer than 15 days. Maine and other states have reduced their solitary confinement populations by not using it to punish persons for disciplinary infractions and instead using it only for safety reasons that endanger staff or other persons. Solitary confinement at the Maine State Prison in Warren, Maine, dropped from 139 to 16 after staff stopped using solitary confinement as the default punishment for institutional violations. Maine and other states that use solitary confinement are relying on behavior management, an increase in treatment, and more frequent assessments. Some of the main arguments supporting and opposing solitary confinement are shown in Exhibit 7–11.

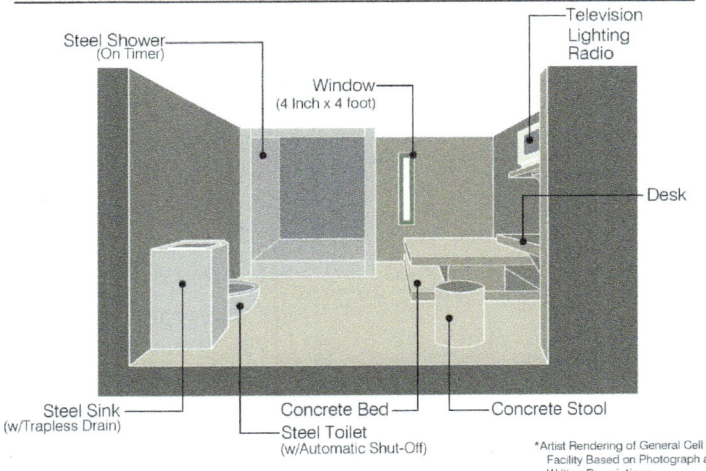

SUPERMAX CELL DIAGRAM

*Artist Rendering of General Cell In Facility Based on Photograph and Written Descriptions.

Steel Shower (On Timer)
Window (4 Inch x 4 foot)
Television
Lighting
Radio
Desk
Steel Sink (w/Trapless Drain)
Concrete Bed
Steel Toilet (w/Automatic Shut-Off)
Concrete Stool

Each bed, desk, stool, and bookcase at the federal supermax prison in Florence, Colorado, are made of reinforced concrete and anchored in place. Each 7- by 12-foot cell has a shower stall with flood-proof plumbing. Cells are staggered so that persons cannot make eye contact with one another. Each cell has a double-entry door: an interior barred cage door backed up by a windowed steel door that prevents voice contact. However, cells in H Unit are 75 square feet, slightly smaller than the typical ADMAX cell because of the absence of a shower. Persons confined in H Unit are escorted to a shower several days a week unless lockdowns or staffing issues disrupt the routine. What kind of persons should/should not be held in supermax-like conditions?

Jonathon Ortiz-Smykla, www.LuckyBandanaDesigns.com

Advantages	Disadvantages
Higher security protocols ensure the safety of the rest of the prison population.	Deteriorates personality and causes mental health disorders.
Option to discipline negative behavior.	Damages physical health.
Form of rehabilitation. Helps persons reflect on what they did wrong.	Violates basic human rights, as stated in international human rights treaties.
Acts as a general deterrent to discourage others.	Does not rehabilitate without human interaction. Goal is to let time pass.
Protects the outside public from serious threats.	Loss of freedom resorts to self-destructive behavior.
Morally appropriate and supported by laws of the United States.	Cannot motivate behavior if fundamental physiological and safety needs are not met.
Satisfies the interests of victims and members of society to see persons punished.	Surveillance 24/7 offers little to no privacy.
When all else fails, solitary confinement is the last resort to correct negative behavior.	Ignores what other jurisdictions are doing to scale back solitary confinement.

CO7-8 # TECHNOCORRECTIONS

We conclude this chapter with an introduction to the role of technology in corrections. Correctional facilities have been using advanced technologies for security and communications monitoring, case management, and data collection, analysis, and sharing for decades. What's new are the ways that technology can be expanded to provide a more safe and secure correctional environment for staff and residents, and promote rehabilitation.

Contraband Cell Phones and Drugs

contraband

Any item that represents a serious threat to the safety and security of the institution.

Contraband is any item that represents a serious threat to the safety and security of the correctional institution, staff, incarcerated population, and the general public. The major forms of prison contraband are cell phones and drugs. They are smuggled in within objects or body cavities, brought in by visitors and accomplices, carried in by correctional employees, thrown over or dropped by drones, or delivered via consumables. While the courts continue to crack down on corrections officers and visitors who smuggle contraband into correctional institutions,[44] contraband drone deliveries present new challenges. In May 2022, 42-year-old Bryant Leray Henderson flew a drone from the parking lot of Wyatt High School in Fort Worth, Texas to a federal BOP medical facility one-half mile away, but the drone crashed inside the prison ground. Henderson strapped four 10-inch by 11-inch packages to the undercarriage of a DJI Inspire 2 Model T650A drone with methamphetamine, cellular telephones, MP3 players, and pressed THC. He faces up to 20 years in federal prison.

Contraband cell phones is an ongoing challenge that prison officials have been facing for years. Cell phones can be used to plan escape attempts, manage criminal enterprises such as extorting money or distributing drugs, intimidate or arrange for the murder of victims, witnesses, or public safety officers, use as currency to barter with other incarcerated individuals, or record and post videos or pictures that compromise the safety and security of the institution. In 2017, South Carolina officials confiscated one phone for every three persons in prison. In 2019 prison officials in California seized over 12,000 cell phones—almost one cell phone for every ten persons incarcerated. Oklahoma officials found one phone for every six incarcerated individuals, and Mississippi prisons seized 1,800 cell phones—approximately one phone for every ten persons in prison.[45]

Correctional authorities have tried a number of options for detecting and disabling contraband cell phones. Point-of-entry physical searching along with x-ray technologies is used to identify and locate concealed items before

Most states now use videoconferencing for legal hearings. Here, Dylann Roof appears via a video uplink from jail for his bond hearing in North Charleston, South Carolina. In federal court, Roof was charged with nine counts of using a firearm to commit murder, 12 hate crime charges, and 12 counts of violating a person's freedom of religion in the shooting deaths at Emanuel African Methodist Church in Charleston on June 17, 2015. Roof was sentenced to nine consecutive sentences of life without parole after formally pleading guilty to state murder charges. How does courtroom videoconferencing serve the interests of the defendant, courtroom personnel, and the community?

Photo by Grace Beahm-Pool/Getty Images

entering the facility, although they are not always reliable. To compensate, a number of facilities are using radiofrequency detection (RFD). RFD systems are portable, lightweight hand-held devices that enable correctional staff to locate a cell phone or the ferromagnetic materials which are the components of cell phones whether concealed on a person or in a body cavity.

Other detection technologies are managed access system, cell phone grabbing, and micro-jamming. Managed access systems block phone numbers to or from devices that have not been pre-approved. The Mississippi State Penitentiary at Parchman, MS blocked almost 117,000 illegal call attempts *each* month from August 2010 through July 2012 using a managed access system.[46]

Cell phone grabbing uses GPS and a permanently installed device at an institution to identify the geographical location of contraband cell phones. Micro-jamming disables contraband cell phones by transmitting a stronger signal than the cell phone on the same frequency so that the two signals cancel one another out. It tricks the cell phone to react as if no signal was received (called *spoofing*). So far however every detection system has disadvantages related to cost and potential interference with the federal Communications Act of 1934 that prohibits the manufacture, importation, marketing, sale, or operation of jamming or spoofing devices because they would "bleed" over into the public broadcast area.

In addition to controlling contraband cell phones, there's a prevalence of contraband drugs in prison. California prison authorities alone confiscated 592 ounces of heroin and 1,200 ounces of marijuana in 2019. The year before, almost 1,000 persons overdosed in prison in California.

Correctional authorities are working to control the flow of contraband drugs smuggled through the mail into an institution. Drugs can be sprayed onto paper, incorporated into ink, hidden under stamps, and inconspicuously concealed with a piece of correspondence. Chatham County (GA) Sheriff John Wilcher said his staff has intercepted letters and envelopes addressed to persons in prison laced with fentanyl, a synthetic and inexpensive opioid that is 50 to 100 times more potent than morphine.[47] "They soak the paper in fentanyl and they take it out and dry it and then they write a letter on it and send it to the jail and then [the inmates] would take and tear it off and sell it like chewing gum and people would get it and get high on it," Sheriff Wilcher said. Without knowing what other compounds are in contraband drugs, persons risk becoming violent, overdosing or dying.

To control the flow of contraband drugs entering through the mailroom, a number of jurisdictions are experimenting with digitized mail processing. Under this model, friends and families of persons in prison are instructed to send personal mail not to a correctional facility, but to a contracted vendor at an outside location. The vendor receives the mail, screens it for compliance with the institution's regulations, electronically scans it, and uploads it to the prison's system for the person to read either on a secure tablet or a prison kiosk. Legal documents are the exception. Unlike personal mail, legal mail is protected by attorney-client privilege. Staff are permitted to open legal mail to check for contraband but only in the presence of the recipient, and then handed to them. However corrections officials have found instances of fake legal documents laced with strips of Suboxone, a drug designed to help people get off heroine.

In addition to understanding how drugs are smuggled through the mail and how digitization of mail can stop it, controlling contraband drugs from entering prison is important for another reason. Choosing to keep contraband drugs from entering prison speaks to the corrections agency's commitment to substance abuse treatment. Were contraband drugs left unchecked, they would undermine an institution's rehabilitative efforts for persons who want to overcome their addiction. Recall the data in Exhibit 7–4—almost

210,000 persons are in prison for drug offenses, while others sentenced for violent, property or public order offenses also have co-occurring disorders of which substance use is oftentimes a part. The evidence-based literature shows that drug treatment works. It can reduce recidivism if it provides a continuum of care for the person after they are released from prison back in to the community, uses a therapeutic community approach while the person is incarcerated, and is delivered within a cognitive-behavioral framework. Controlling contraband drugs from entering prison promotes the institution's efforts at drug treatment.

Videoconferencing and Video Visitation

In-person prison visitation, whether by family members, friends, attorneys, health care providers, treatment specialists, ministers, and others has always been challenging. The geographical distance between prisons and visitors, transportation costs, lodging, child care, possible lost wages for time off, and the difficulty working through prison security procedures helped fuel the growth in video conferencing and video visitation.

When the coronavirus pandemic halted in-person visitation for almost everyone, correctional authorities turned to video conferencing and video visiting. Most states now use video conferencing for legal hearings, tele-health, educational programming, and staff development. It is an option for all incarcerated persons especially those who are not permitted contact visits to engage with visitors. It reduces the cost associated with transporting persons from prison to courtrooms or medical offices, although new costs accrue from the introduction of video conferencing hardware and software. And it improves security by reducing movement and the flow of contraband.

Video visitation for family and friends is also rapidly expanding in prisons across the United States. We know from traditional in-person visiting that incarcerated individuals have better outcomes when they receive visits from family and supportive community members.[48] Visitation can maintain and strengthen family bonds and parent–child relationships. It can facilitate planning and support for release, help with housing and employment, increase the individual's motivation to participate in prison programming, and reduce behavioral infractions compared to those who do not receive visits. Whether video visiting results in the same outcomes, only time will tell.

The limited research that exists on video visitation also raises questions that have yet to be answered. Video visiting is not for all families and friends. Some may not be able to travel to a video-visiting site in their communities or at a facility. Some may not own a computer or have access to the Internet. Based on experience, some are dissatisfied with video systems that present technical problems, and poor video and audio quality. Technology is confusing for people who lack computer skills or have visual and/or hearing impairments. Setting up a video visiting account can be confusing and expensive. And for too many, fees are charged that may be unaffordable. A hybrid approach, that offers both video and in-person visiting affords families and friends the options that work best for them.

Artificial Intelligence in Correctional Institutions

In simplest terms, artificial intelligence (AI) refers to the general ability of computers to mimic human intelligence to enable problem-solving. Apple's Siri, Google Now, Amazon's Alexa, and Microsoft's Cortana are examples of AI that we use every day to solve problems, place phone calls, create

Prison medical staff videoconference with an offsite physician about an incarcerated person's physical health. Advances in technology have helped make prisons and jails safer and more secure, while facilitating innovations such as telemedicine. What promises might tomorrow's technologies hold for correctional institutions?

F. Carter Smith/Contributor/Getty Images

schedules, locate something on the web, act as a security device, transcribe and translate foreign languages, interact with digital assistants for physical and mental health care, get first aid, find restaurants, check credit card balances, start the car, turn lights and appliances on and off, control the thermostat, check the pet's litter box, and other commands too many to mention.

In corrections, AI technologies are working to assist or augment the correctional staff's ability to make data-driven decisions. AI applications are used in prison to monitor communication, location, and biometrics; detect contraband; create risk and needs assessment; and increase educational and treatment programming.

Monitoring Communication In 2019, the RAND Corporation surveyed a panel of corrections experts on the most pressing safety and security concerns in prison.[49] Controlling contraband was Number 1 (a problem we discussed earlier). Attack on an institution's infrastructure (e.g., a prison's power grid) was Number 2. And Number 3 was the unmonitored telephone communication of persons in prisons. Attacks on a prison's infrastructure is technical and we refer the reader to the RAND study for further discussion. Here we raise the issue of unmonitored telephone communications as a security threat everywhere.

Robert Hood, former warden at ADX Florence "supermax" federal facility said prisons lack the staffing to monitor every single call. "In the three prisons where I was warden, it was pretty much reactive: a very small percentage of inmate calls was monitored and it was done after the fact, when there was a crime or alleged crime, that you'd get on your phone monitoring equipment and try and hunt down what occurred," he said.[50] After a hearing on contraband cell phone use in federal prisons, the U.S. House of Representatives called on the Department of Justice to explore AI technology to monitor the phone calls of persons in federal prisons as part of DOJ's spending bill.

AI systems flag phone calls in near real time that contain conversations indicating violence or criminal behavior, keywords, code words, local slang, suspicious language, or phrases that signal criminal intent enabling staff to take action. Its software identifies discussions among people in prison and their outside conversation partners focusing on weapons, contraband, threats to other incarcerated individuals, gangs, homicides, assaults, or suicide.

Advocacy groups for persons in prison and their families argue that relying on AI to interpret communications opens up the system to mistakes, misunderstandings, and racial bias. Researchers at Stanford and Georgetown found that Amazon's automatic speech recognition software had an error rate for Black speakers that was nearly twice as high as for white speakers.[51] Several state and local facilities, including Alabama and Georgia, already use the technology.

Location Services and Biometrics We also see how AI is used in location services and **biometrics** (the methods used to verify a person's identity based on their unique physiological and behavioral characteristics). Fitbit-like trackers incorporate GPS and location-based services. Common biometrics are fingerprint, facial and voice recognition, and iris and retina recognition. Biometrics is considered a secure method of authentication because it relies on characteristics that are hard to duplicate.

biometrics
The automated identification or verification of human identity through measurable physiological and behavioral traits.

Detecting Contraband Earlier we discussed how digitizing mail is reducing the flow of contraband into prisons. Machine vision and image analysis like those used at airports identify and locate concealed contraband before entering the facility. Other agencies are investing in a combination of biometrics, facial identification, and mail digitization to prevent contraband from entering.

Risk and Needs Assessment In Chapter 4 we introduced the concept and practice of risk and needs assessment (RNA) to identify how likely a person is to commit another crime or violate the rules of prison, jail, or community supervision. AI technologies scan mass datasets on people who have committed similar crimes and create categories that show the statistical likelihood that certain kinds of behavior may happen—including recidivism. Supporters point to the potential of AI-driven RNAs to reduce human bias in decision-making. A large body of social science evidence shows that objective, reliable, and valid RNAs are more accurate in assessing risk than human judgments alone. Opponents argue that RNAs are biased against minorities and people of color because they are based partly on criminal records where biases in the deployment of police, arrest, policies, charging decisions, pretrial decisions, and sentencing practices have been uncovered.

Programming AI can also play an important and promising role in institutional programming for successful reentry. Outside prison we find AI applications in every level of education from elementary school to graduate school. Chatbots, self-directed learning, automated assessments, personalized learning paths, writing assignments, digital learning scorecards, natural language processing, and course analytics to monitor student learning are helping students and supporting teachers.

Inside prison however we do not find the same concern for AI technology in education and treatment that we find for addressing other threats to institutional security. The corrections experts who completed the RAND survey mentioned earlier did not prioritize a person's lack of education and marketable skills as a current or emerging threat to institutional security. This is unfortunate for several reasons. Almost 62 percent of persons in prison (compared to 19 percent of the general population) do not have a high school diploma or GED. We also know that at least 95 percent of persons in prison will one day be released. We see the consequences of missed educational and treatment opportunities in the fact that two-thirds of persons released from prison are rearrested within 3 years and 70 percent are rearrested within 5 years.[52]

Prisons are charged with keeping individuals safe and reducing internal and external threats to security. At the same time, prisons are also charged with preparing those under correctional authority for successful, law-abiding lives after release. A comprehensive AI security system focuses not only on how to control internal and external threats but also on AI technologies in education and treatment. Best practices and guidance are needed to help institutions understand that access to AI technology for programming not only mitigates the odds of recidivism but also reduces threats to the institution's security.

REVIEW AND APPLICATIONS

SUMMARY

1 The Pennsylvania and Auburn prison systems emerged in the United States at the turn of the 19th century. The Pennsylvania system isolated persons in prison from one another to avoid harmful influences and to give individuals reflection time so that they might repent. The Auburn system allowed incarcerated persons to work together during the day under strict silence. At night, however, they were isolated in small sleeping cells. With time, sleeping cells became congregate, and restrictions against talking were removed.

2 There have been ten eras in U.S. prison history:
- Penitentiary era (1790–1825)
- Mass prison era (1825–1876)

- Reformatory era (1876–1890)
- Industrial era (1890–1935)
- Punitive era (1935–1945)
- Treatment era (1945–1967)
- Community-based era (1967–1980)
- Warehousing era (1980–1995)
- Just deserts era (1985–2010)
- Criminal Justice Reform era (2010–present)

3 Today, 1,063,665 people are under the jurisdiction of state correctional authorities, and 152,156 are under the jurisdiction of the federal prison system. Seven percent of the prison population are female, 30 percent are white, 33 percent are Black, 20 percent are Hispanic, 11 percent are multiracial, 2 percent are American Indian/Alaska Native, and 1 percent is Asian, Native Hawaiian, or Pacific Islander. Reasons for the increase in women in prison include women's presence in the U.S. labor market, which has brought about increased opportunities for crime; the increased poverty of young, female, single heads of households, which means that more women are turning to crime to support themselves and their families; changes in the criminal justice system, which no longer affords women differential treatment; and the combined effects of harsh drug laws, changing patterns of drug use, and mandatory sentencing policies. Reasons for the increase in minorities and people of color in prison include an increase in criminal activity that results in incarceration; racial profiling and racism by the criminal justice system; and the prevalence of social conditions that exist in the nation's inner cities, which is where most minorities and people of color in the United States regardless of race live, and the fact that large urban areas have the highest violence rates.

4 Among federal and state inmates, about 62 percent do not have a high school diploma or a GED compared to 19 percent of the general population. Evidence-based literature shows that corrections-based educational programs are effective in reducing crime.

5 The evidence-based literature on education and employment programming shows that persons who participated in correctional education programs or vocational training—were 43 percent less likely to return to prison within three years of release in comparison to those who did not participate and that participating in secondary degree programs produced a 30 percent decrease in recidivism. The researchers also found that persons who participated in academic or vocational education programs had a 13 percent better chance of finding employment than those who did not.

6 All 50 states, the Federal Bureau of Prisons (BOP), and four local jurisdictions operate correctional institutions. State prison administration, a function of the executive branch of government, is most often organized around a central authority operating from the state capital. There are three levels of prison security: minimum, for persons deemed the least dangerous; medium, for those considered less dangerous serving long or short sentences; and maximum, for those considered most dangerous serving long sentences.

7 A supermax housing facility is a method for managing and controlling individuals who have been officially designated as violent or who exhibit serious and disruptive behavior while incarcerated. Some experts who have studied the effects of long-term solitary confinement report evidence of acute sensory deprivation, paranoid delusion belief systems, irrational fears of violence, resentment, little ability to control rage, and mental breakdowns. Supermax prisons also present extraordinary challenges for staff.

8 Technology is used in corrections to control contraband cell phones and drugs, offer more videoconferencing and video visitation, monitor communication, assess risk and needs, and deliver programming.

KEY TERMS

penitentiary, p. 158

Pennsylvania system, p. 158

Auburn system, p. 158

justice reinvestment, p. 162

Federal Prison Industries (FPI), p. 177

UNICOR, p. 177

minimum-security institution, p. 186

open institution, p. 186

medium-security prison, p. 186

maximum- or close/high-security prison, p. 187

security threat groups, p. 189

supermax housing, p. 189

contraband, p. 192

biometrics, p. 195

QUESTIONS FOR REVIEW

1 Explain the differences between the Pennsylvania and Auburn prison systems.

2 Summarize the eras of prison development.

3 What can you infer from the characteristics of those in prison today and the reasons for the incarceration of women, minorities, and people of color?

4 What ideas can you add to the reasons for offering education for the incarcerated population?

5 Discuss the impact of the evidence-based literature on prison employment programming.

6 Compare and contrast how state and federal prisons are organized and administered.

7 Summarize the emergence of supermax housing and its impact on staff and the prison population.

8 Debate the pros and cons of using technology in corrections.

THINKING CRITICALLY ABOUT CORRECTIONS

Reducing Mass Incarceration

Some argue that public safety is undermined when we waste space and money on imprisoning persons who violate the "technical" conditions of their community supervision or commit low-level offenses, especially when these offenses are the result of mental illness, drug addiction, or first-time offenses. Reserving prison space for those who truly pose significant threats to public safety would help reduce mass incarceration. How would you defend these reforms to persons who believe they should be incarcerated?

Postsecondary Education in Prison

According to a 2018 study by the Department of Justice, participating in a postsecondary education program while incarcerated lowers the likelihood that a person returns to prison by 43 percent. Beginning in the 2023–2024 academic year, persons in prison will once again be eligible for Pell Grants to pay for college costs under certain conditions. It is estimated that 500,000 persons in prison may be eligible. Members of the public complain that incarcerated people should not get a free education. What do you think and why?

ON-THE-JOB DECISION MAKING

Technocorrections

Correctional institutions use technology to control contraband, videoconferencing and video visitation, managing communications, location and biometrics, assessing a person's risks and needs, and programming. If you were a warden making your first investment into using technology, where would you use technology?

Advancing Prison Education Programming

As the newly appointed director of prison education programming, you remember two things from your undergraduate corrections course: First, few persons participate in prison education programs; second, while literacy alone will not prevent crime, it is one of the many skills needed to function well as a responsible and law-abiding adult in our society.

Your warden would like to create a model prison education program and asks you (1) what can be done with little or no budget increase to encourage more individuals to participate in prison education and (2) how will you know whether your strategies have been effective? What will you tell the warden?

ENDNOTES

1. U.S. Department of Justice, U.S. Attorney's Office, District of Columbia, *Arizona Man Sentenced to 41 Months in Prison on Felony Charge in Jan. 6 Capitol Breach* (Washington, DC: U.S. Department of Justice, U.S. Attorney's Office, District of Columbia, November 17, 2021); Dan Mangan, "QAnon Shaman Jacob Chansley Appeals Sentence, Seeks to Avoid Guilty Plea in Jan. 6 Capitol Riot Case," CNBC, November 30, 2021, www.cnbc.com (accessed December 5, 2021).

2. E. Ann Carson, *Prisoners in 2020—Statistical Tables* (Washington, DC: U.S. Department of Justice, December 2021); E. Ann Carson, *Prisoners in 2021—Statistical Tables* (Washington, DC: U.S. Department of Justice, December 2022).

3. Council of State Governments, *More Community, Less Confinement* (New York: Council of State Governments, 2023).

4. Ann Carson, *Prisoners in 2020—Statistical Tables* and *USA Facts*, July 2022, www.googleleadservices.com (accessed January 9, 2023).

5. Andrew Coyle, "The Use and Abuse of Prison Around the World," *Corrections Today* (December 2004), pp. 64–67; see also David A. Bowers and Jerold L. Waltman, "Do More Conservative States Impose Harsher Felony Sentences? An Exploratory Analysis of 32 States," *Criminal Justice Review*, vol. 18, no. 1 (Spring 1993), pp. 61–70.

6. Lauren G. Beatty and Tracy L. Snell, *Profile of Prison Inmates, 2016* (Washington, DC: U.S. Department of Justice, Bureau of Justice Statistics, December 2021).

7. Beth R. Richie, "Challenges Incarcerated Women Face as They Return to Their Communities: Findings from Life History Interviews," *Crime & Delinquency*, vol. 47, no. 3 (July 2001), pp. 368–389; and Elaine A. Lord, "The Challenges of Mentally Ill Offenders in Prison," *Criminal Justice and Behavior*, vol. 35, no. 8 (August 2008), pp. 928–942.

8. Meda Chesney-Lind, "Putting the Breaks on the Building Binge," *Corrections Today*, vol. 54, no. 6 (August 1992), p. 30.

9. Mauer, "Addressing Racial Disparities in Incarceration," *The Prison Journal*, vol. 91, no. 3 (2011), pp. 87–101.

10. Steve Miletich, "Two State Supreme Court Justices Stun Some Listeners with Race Comments," *The Seattle Times*, October 22, 2010, seattletimes.nwsource.com (accessed January 13, 2023).

11. Cassia Spohn, Thirty Years of Sentencing Reform: *The Quest for a Racially Neutral Sentencing Process* (Washington, DC: U.S. Department of Justice, National Institute of Justice, 2000); Phillip Beatty, Amanda Petteruti, and Jason Ziedenberg, *The Vortex: The Concentrated Racial Impact of Drug Imprisonment and the Characteristics of Punitive Counties* (Washington, DC: Justice Policy Institute, 2007); Ryan S. King, *Disparity by Geography: The War on Drugs in America's Cities* (Washington, DC: Sentencing Project, May 2008).

12. The Sentencing Project, "Despite Progress, Thousands of Youth Remain Locked in Adult Facilities," January 11, 2023, www.sentencingproject.org (accessed January 11, 2023).

13. The Sentencing Project, "Despite Progress, Thousands of Youth Remain Locked in Adult Facilities," January 11, 2023, www.sentencingproject.org (accessed January 11, 2023).

14. Steve Aos, Marna Miller, and Elizabeth Drake, *Evidence-Based Public Policy Options to Reduce Future Prison Construction, Criminal Justice Costs, and Crime Rates* (Olympia, WA: State Institute for Public Policy, 2006); National Research Council, *The Growth of Incarceration in the United States: Exploring Causes and Consequences* (Washington, DC: National Research Council, 2014).

15. Lauren G. Beatty and Tracy L. Snell, *Profile of Prison Inmates, 2016* (Washington, DC: U.S. Department of Justice, Bureau of Justice Statistics, December 2021); United States Census Bureau, "High School Completion Rate Is Highest in U.S. History," December 14, 2017, census.gov (accessed January 16, 2023).

16. Laura M. Maruschak and Emily D. Buehler, *Census of State and Federal Adult Correctional Facilities, 2019* (Washington, DC: U.S. Department of Justice, Bureau of Justice Statistics, November 2021) and James J. Stephan, *Census of State and Federal Correctional Facilities, 2019* (Washington, DC: U.S. Department of Justice, Bureau of Justice Statistics, October 2008).

17. Anne F. Parkinson and Stephen J. Steurer, "Overcoming the Obstacles in Effective Correctional Instruction," *Corrections Today*, vol. 66, no. 2 (April 2004), pp. 88–91.

18. Lois M. Davis, Robert Bozick, Jennifer L. Steele, Jessica Saunders, and Jeremy N. V. Miles, *Evaluating the Effectiveness of Correctional Education* (Santa Monica, CA: Rand Corporation, 2013).

19. RAND Corporation, "Education and Vocational Training in Prison Reduces Recidivism, Improves Job Outlook," August 23, 2013, www.rand.org (accessed January 10, 2023).

20. Beth Schwartzapfel and Lawrence Batrley, "What People Really Make (and Spend) Behind Bars," *National Public Radio*, August 16, 2022, www.npr.org (accessed January 16, 2023). and Charlotte Plantive, "US Makes Billions from Prison Labor as Inmates Earn Pennies: Rights Group," *Barrons*, June 15, 2022, barrons.com (accessed January 16, 2023). See also Lauren G. Beatty and Tracy L. Snell, *Work Assignments Reported by Prisoners, 2016* (Washington, DC: United States Department of Justice, Bureau of Justice Statistics, April 2023).

21. Corporate Accountability Lab, "Private Companies Producing With Us: Prison Labor in 2020," August 2020, corpaccountabilitylab.org (accessed January 17, 2023).

22. ACLU, *Captive Labor: Exploitation of Incarcerated Workers* (New York: ACLU, June 2022).

23. Arizona Department of Transportation, "Successful Interagency Program Helps Former Inmates Find Jobs as Truckdrivers," February 2, 2022, www.azdot.gov (accessed January 19, 2023) and Marc Thompson, "ADOT Helping Former Inmates Get Their CDL License, Jobs," February 2, 2022, www.abc15.com (accessed January 19, 2023).

24. Olivia Prentzel and Jennifer Brown, "Colorado Prison Inmates Fight Wildfires While They're Serving Time, But Can't Get Hired When They Get Out," *The Colorado Sun*, June 22, 2021, www.coloradosun.com (accessed June 27, 2021) and Helen H. Richardson, "Colorado's Prison Firefighters Have a Bridge to Permanent Employment Under New Law," *The Denver Post*, April 15, 2021, www.denverpost.com (accessed April 19, 2021).

25. U.S. Bureau of Labor Statistics, Occupational Outlook Handbook, "Web Developers and Digital Designers," September 14, 2022, www.bls.gov (accessed January 20, 2023).

26. Seaborn Larson, "State Prison Coding Program Officially Online," *Independent Record*, October 25, 2022, www.helenair.com (accessed October 26, 2022).

27. Seaborn Larson, "State Prison Coding Program Officially Online," *Independent Record*, October 25, 2022, www.helenair.com (accessed October 26, 2022).

28. National Institute of Justice, "Practice Profile: Correctional Work Industries," June 9, 2014, www.crimesolutions.gov (accessed September 10, 2022); National Institute of Justice, "Program Profile: Prison Industry Enhancement Certificate Program," March 28, 2016, www.crimesolutions.gov (accessed September 10, 2022); National Institute of Justice, "Practice Profile: Corrections-Based Vocational Training Programs" May 14, 2014, www.crimesolutions.gov (accessed September 10, 2022).

29. Excerpted from California and South Dakota's departments of corrections Web sites (accessed January 21, 2023).

30. U.S. Bureau of Labor Statistics, "Occupational Employment and Wage Statistics—Correctional Officers and Bailiffs," September 6, 2023, www.bls.gov (accessed September 21, 2023); see also U.S. Bureau of Justice

Statistics, "Justice Expenditure and Employment Tool (JEET)," www.bjs.ojp.gov (accessed January 21, 2023).

31. U.S. Bureau of Justice Statistics, "Justice Expenditure and Employment Tool (JEET)," www.bjs.ojp.gov (accessed January 21, 2023).

32. Jennifer Gonnerman, "An Expert Analyzes the Prison Population Boom," *Village Voice,* February 22, 2000, p. 56; and Pew Center on the States, *One in 31: The Long Reach in American Corrections* (New York: Pew Charitable Trusts, March 2009), p. 20.

33. Pew Charitable Trusts, *Public Safety, Public Spending: Forecasting America's Prison Population 2007–2011* (Philadelphia: Pew Charitable Trusts, 2007).

34. Christian Henrichson and Ruth Delaney, *The Price of Prisons: Examining State Spending Trends, 2010–2015* (New York: Vera Institute of Justice, May 2017).

35. Nicole D. Porter, Repurposing: *New Beginnings for Closed Prisons* (Washington, DC: Sentencing Project, December 2016); Urban Institute, *Reforming Sentencing and Corrections Policy* (Washington, DC: Urban Institute, 2016); Aaron Kalischer-Coggins, "How to Free an Entire Prison and Help It Find New Life as a Farm," *The Hill,* October 15, 2021, www.thehill.com (accessed October 23, 2021).

36. United States Government Accountability Office, *Federal Prisons, Bureau of Prisons Should Improve Efforts to Implement its Risk and Needs Assessment System* (Washington, DC: United States Government Accountability Office, March 2023).

37. Kristofer Bret Bucklen, Grant Duwe and Faye S. Taxman, *Guidelines for Post-Sentencing Risk Assessment* (Washington, DC: United States Department of Justice, National Institute of Justice, 2021).

38. Special Issue: Private Corrections, *Criminology & Public Policy,* vol. 18 (2019), pp. 209-505. https://doi.org/10.1111/1745-9133.12387

39. Laura M. Maruschak and Emily D. Buehler, *Census of State and Federal Adult Correctional Facilities,* 2019—Statistical Tables.

40. Billy Sinclair, "How Racist Prison Culture Infects Mainstream Politics," *The Crime Report,* October 17, 2022, www.thecrimereport.org (accessed October 17, 2022).

41. Correctional Leaders Association and The Arthur Liman Center for Public Interest Law at Yale Law School, *Time-in-Cell: A 2021 Snapshot of Restrictive Housing Based on a Nationwide Survey of U.S. Prison Systems* (New Haven, CT: Yale Law School, August 2022)

42. D. Lovell, L. C. Johnson, and K. C. Cain, "Recidivism of Supermax Priosners in Washington State," *Crime* and *Delinquency,* vol. 53, no. 4 (2007), pp. 633–656; D. P. Mears and W. D. Bales, "Supermax Incarceration and Recidivism," *Criminology,* vol. 47, no 4. (2009), pp. 1131–1166; and Valerie A. Clark and Grant Duwe, " From Solitary to the Streets: The Effect of Restrictive Housing on Recidivism," *Corrections: Policy, Practice and Research* (2018), https://doi.org/10.1080/23774657.2017.1416318.

43. As quoted in Corey Weinstein, "Even Dogs Confined to Cages for Long Periods of Time Go Berserk," in John P. May and Khalid R. Pitts (eds.), *Building Violence: How America's Rush to Incarcerate Creates More Violence* (Thousand Oaks, CA: Sage, 1999), p. 122.

44. Audrey Nielsen, "Courts Crack Down on Correction Officers Smuggling Contraband in Jails," *The Crime Report,* November 4, 2022, www.thecrimereport.com (accessed November 21, 2022). See also Bryce Peterson, Megan Kizzort, KiDeuk Kim, and Rochisha Shukla, "Prison Contraband: Prevalence, Impacts, and Interdiction Strategies," *Corrections: Policy, Practice and Research* (2021), https://doi.org/10.1080/23774657.2021.1906356.

45. M.N. Parsons, K. Lissy, M. Camello, M. Dix, T. Craig, M. Planty, and J.D. Roper-Miller, *Detecting and Managing Cell Phone Contraband: An Overview of Technologies for Managing Contraband Cell Phone Presence and Use in Correctional Facilities* (Washington, DC: U.S. Department of Justice, Office of Justice Programs, September 2021). See also Megan Cassidy, "Overdoses in California Prisons Up 113% in Three Years - Nearly 1,000 Incidents in 2018," *San Francisco Chronicle,* May 5, 2019, www.sfchronicle.com (accessed September 10, 2023) and E. Ann Carson, *Prisoners in 2019* (Washington, DC: United States Department of Justice, Bureau of Justice Statistics, October 2020).

46. Eric Grommon, Jeremy G. Carter, Fred Frantz, and Phil Harris, *A Case Study of Mississippi State Penitentiary's Managed Access Technology* (Washington, DC: U.S. Department of Justice, National Institute of Justice, August 2015).

47. As quoted in Katie Nussbaum, "Paper Letters Soaked in Drugs Leads Jail to Digitize Mail," *The Savannah Morning News,* September 7, 2021, savannahnow.com (accessed September 7, 2021). See also Megan Cassidy, "Overdoses in California Prisons Up 113% in Three Years - Nearly 1,000 Incidents in 2018."

48. David Patrick Connor and Richard Tewksbury, "Prison Inmates and Their Visitors: An Examination of Inmate Characteristics and Visitor Types," *The Prison Journal,* vol. 95, no.2 (2015), pp. 159–177.

49. Joe Russo, Dulani Woods, John S. Shaffer, and Brian A. Jackson, *Countering Threats to Correctional Institution Security: Identifying Innovation Needs to Address Current and Emerging Concerns.* (Santa Monica, CA: RAND Corporation, 2019). https://www.rand.org/pubs/research_reports/RR2933.html.

50. As quoted in Chris Francescani, "US Prisons and Jails Using AI to Mass-Monitor Millions of Inmate Calls," *ABC NEWS,* October 24, 2019, www.abcnews.go.com (accessed January 25, 2023).

51. David Sherfinski and Avi Asher-Schapiro, "U.S. Prisons Mull AI to Analyze Inmate Phone Calls," *Reuters,* August 9, 2021, www.reuters.com (accessed January 28, 2023).

52. Matthew R. Durose and Leonardo Antenangeli, *Recidivism of Prisoners Released in 34 States in 2012: A 5-Year Follow-Up Period, 2012–2017* (Washington, DC: U.S. Department of Justice, Bureau of Justice Statistics, July 2021) and Leonardo Antenangeli and Matthew R. Durose, *Recidivism of Prisoners Released in 34 States in 2008: A 10-Year Follow-Up Period, 2008–2018* (Washington, DC: U.S. Department of Justice, Bureau of Justice Statistics, September 2021).

PAROLE

Early Release and Reentry

[8]

David R. Frazier/Science Source

CHAPTER OBJECTIVES

After completing this chapter you should be able to do the following:

1. Present a brief history of parole development in the United States.

2. Explain who is on parole.

3. Discuss the reentry issues persons face on parole.

4. Explain what a parole-releasing authority is and what happens at a parole hearing.

5. Summarize current issues in parole.

Whether it is safe, secure housing, employment, or food on the table, supporting formerly incarcerated people in accessing tools to reach their potential makes our communities safer and stronger.

— Attorney General Merrick B. Garland

The U.S. Parole Commission (USPC) was established in May 1976. The USPC is a semiautonomous agency within the U.S. Department of Justice and decides parole cases involving persons in federal and District of Columbia (DC) correctional facilities, persons under the jurisdiction of military correctional authorities who are in Bureau of Prisons (BOP) custody, transfer treaty cases (U.S. citizens transferred from foreign custody to the United States pursuant to a transfer treaty), and persons on state probation or parole in the Federal Witness Protection Program.

At one time, the USPC was a much larger commission than it is today; it was scaled back in the 1980s following landmark changes in sentencing laws after Congress passed the Comprehensive Crime Control Act, which made major changes to federal sentencing and parole policies by replacing indeterminate sentences with determinate sentencing guidelines and abolishing parole and replacing it with "supervised release."

Today, the acting chairwoman of the USPC is Patricia K. Cushwa. Ms. Cushwa was nominated to the USPC and confirmed by the U.S. Senate in November 2004. Prior to her appointment, Ms. Cushwa served 12 years on the Maryland Parole Commission, seven of those years as Chair. She was named acting chairwoman of the USPC on August 5, 2018.

Patricia K. Cushwa became acting chairwoman of the United States Parole Commission on August 5, 2018. What sentencing laws changed in the 1980s that reversed the scope and function of the USPC?
Department of Justice

The major functions of the USPC are to:

- manage a person's risk on parole in the community;
- monitor a person's compliance with the terms and conditions governing behavior while on parole or on mandatory or supervised release;
- issue warrants for violation of supervision;
- determine probable cause for the revocation process;
- revoke parole or mandatory or supervised release;
- make parole release decisions;
- authorize methods of release and conditions under which release occurs;
- release from supervision those individuals who no longer pose a risk to public safety; and
- promulgate rules, regulations, and guidelines for the exercise of the USPC's authority and the implementation of a national parole policy.

PAROLE AS PART OF THE CRIMINAL JUSTICE SYSTEM

parole

The conditional release of a person from prison, prior to completion of the imposed sentence, under the supervision of a parole officer.

discretionary release

Early release based on the paroling authority's assessment of eligibility.

mandatory release

Early release after a time period specified by law.

Parole is the conditional release of a person from prison, prior to completion of the imposed sentence, and under the supervision of a parole officer. Responsibility for the parole decision passes from the courts to the corrections system. Parole is granted by authorities in the correctional system.

Release on parole may be mandatory or discretionary. **Discretionary release** exists when a parole board has authority to conditionally release a person based on a statutory or administrative determination of eligibility. **Mandatory release** is early release after a specific period of time as specified by law.

In those states that permit discretionary release, state laws give correctional officials the authority to change, within certain limits, the *length* of a sentence. Correctional officials may also change the *conditions* under which persons are supervised—for example, they may release individuals from prison to supervision in the community or to an outside facility. The American Correctional Association—recognized as a worldwide authority in corrections—published a policy statement on discretionary parole to guide and determine present and future decisions of the Association (see Exhibit 8–1).

Parole and Reentry

What is parole? Differentiate between mandatory and discretionary parole board release. How can risk assessments help with successful reentry strategies?

Historical Overview

CO8-1

Parole has its roots in an 18th-century English penal practice—indentured servitude. Judges transferred custody of physically fit men and women convicted of a felony to independent contractors, paying those contractors a fee to transport the individuals to the American colonies and sell their services for the duration of their sentences to the highest bidder. This practice was similar to today's parole in that the indentured servant had to comply with certain conditions to remain in supervised "freedom." This practice was discontinued with the beginning of the American Revolutionary War in 1775 because the persons transported from England were joining colonial forces against England.

EXHIBIT 8–1   American Correctional Association

Policy Statement on Discretionary Parole

Parole is the discretionary release of an individual from confinement to serve the remainder of the sentence pursuant to specified terms and conditions of supervision in the community. Parole is a fundamental function of the correctional process as the public is best protected by a supervised transition from institutional to community reintegration. The discretionary granting of parole and its revocation are the responsibilities of the paroling authority. Supervision is provided by a designated agency that monitors compliance with all of the specified terms and conditions of release through a case management process. Parole offers economic advantages by maximizing opportunities for persons leaving prison to become productive, law-abiding citizens.

Policy Statement:

The paroling authority should function under separate and independent decision-making to fully represent the views of all stakeholders. Paroling authorities should seek a balance in weighing the public interest, victim interest, and the readiness of the person leaving prison to reenter society under a structured program of supervisory management and control. Paroling authorities should be equipped with resources and technologies for tracking and administering investigative, supervisory, and research functions. Laws and administrative regulations governing the granting of parole, its revocation, case supervision practices, and discharge procedures should incorporate standards of due process and administrative fairness. To achieve the maximum benefits of parole supervision, full advantage should be taken of community-based resources to offer employment, training needs, continuing health care, and other related services.

The parole system should:

A. Establish procedures to provide an objective decision-making process, incorporating standards of due process and fundamental fairness in granting of parole that will address, at a minimum, the risk to public safety, impact on—and views of—the victim, and information about the offense and the individual being considered for early release;

B. Provide access to community services to meet the individual's risks and needs consistent with realistic objectives for promoting law-abiding behavior;

C. Ensure that supervision requirements will not exceed the minimum needed to adhere to the terms and conditions of parole and are consistent with public safety;

D. Provide a case management system to allocate supervisory resources through a standardized classification process, report progress, and monitor supervision and treatment plans;

E. Provide for the timely and accurate transmittal of status reports to the paroling authority for use in decision making with respect to revocation, modification, or discharge of parole cases;

F. Establish programs for sharing information, ideas, and experiences with other agencies and the public;

G. Involve the public, victims, and victims' families in the parole process;

H. Evaluate program efficiency, effectiveness, and overall accountability; and

I. Be sensitive to and provide for gender differences and special needs that may affect supervision processes.

Source: American Correctional Association, Alexandria, VA.

From 1775 through 1856, persons who were convicted of serious offenses in England were sent to Australia as punishment. Those who committed more felonies in Australia were transported to England's most punitive prison on Norfolk Island, 1,000 miles off the east coast of Australia.

In 1840, British Navy Captain Alexander Maconochie was appointed superintendent of the penal colony. Maconochie favored indeterminate sentences rather than fixed sentences. He recommended and in part implemented a marks system to measure a person's progress toward release from prison, and he urged a system of graduated release and aftercare to resettle them in the community.

Macanochie developed a "ticket of leave" system, which moved individuals through stages: imprisonment, conditional release, and complete restoration of liberty. Persons moved from one stage to the next by earning "marks" for improved conduct, frugality, and good work habits.

Although Maconochie had control over island tickets of leave, he could not control a graduated return to society in England. Maconochie's ideas did not blend well with the official English position on punishment, which was rooted in deterrence and relied on the infliction of suffering. He was removed in 1844, and the penal colony at Norfolk Island lapsed into a period of extraordinary brutality before it closed in 1856. Maconochie is referred to as the founder of parole.

In 1854, Sir Walter Crofton, director of the Irish prison system, implemented a system that was based on Maconochie's ticket of leave system. Crofton's version required that upon conditional release, a formerly confined individual must do the following:

1. Report immediately to the constabulary on arrival and once a week thereafter.
2. Abstain from any violation of the law.
3. Refrain from habitually associating with notoriously bad characters.
4. Refrain from leading an idle and dissolute life without means of obtaining an honest living.
5. Produce the ticket of leave when asked to do so by a magistrate or police officer.
6. Not change locality without reporting to the constabulary.[1]

Those who did not comply with these conditions were reimprisoned. Crofton's system of conditional release is considered the forerunner of modern American parole.

Early American Parole Development The first legislation authorizing parole in the United States was enacted in Massachusetts in 1837. The first U.S. correctional institution to implement an extensive parole program was the Elmira Reformatory in New York, which opened in 1876 (see Chapter 7).

By 1889, 12 states had implemented parole. Federal legislation authorizing parole was enacted in 1910. By 1944, all 48 states had enacted parole legislation. Prior to statehood in 1959, the concept of parole saw its beginning in Hawaii in 1909. When the United States purchased Alaska from Russia in 1867, the federal Bureau of Prisons exercised correctional jurisdiction over the territory, and federal parole legislation prevailed.

Parole Development in the Early 20th Century The 1920s and early 1930s were a turbulent period in the United States. During Prohibition, organized crime increased, street gang warfare escalated, and the media provided obsessive coverage of persons charged with crime and their

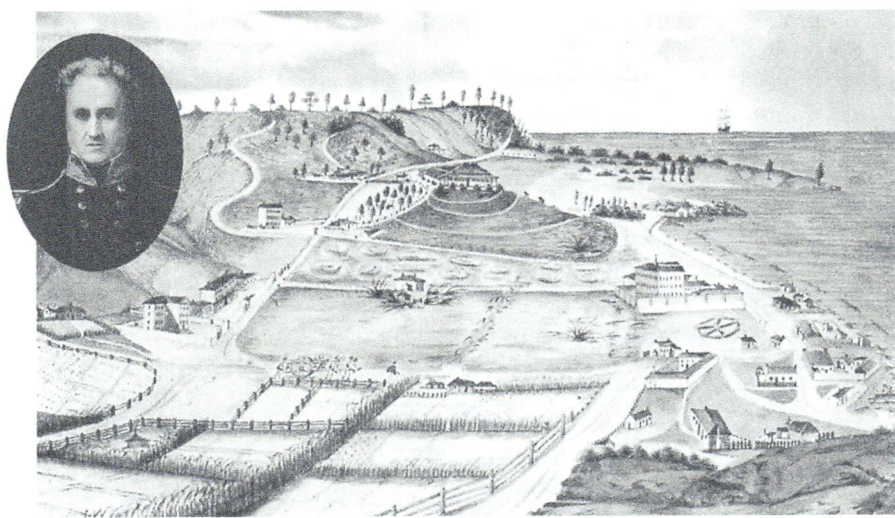

Captain Alexander Maconochie, who became superintendent of the British penal colony on Norfolk Island, Australia, in 1840, implemented a "ticket of leave" system to ease the transition from custody to freedom. Later, Sir Walter Crofton, director of the Irish prison system, implemented a system based on Maconochie's ideas. How did their systems influence current parole practices?

Portrait by E.V. Rippingille, 1836.

Thomas Seller, The National Library of Australia, 1835.

activities. Prison riots erupted in response to idleness in prison and arbitrary rules and punishment. Prisons and parole systems were accused of failing to rehabilitate persons in prison.

In response to the turmoil, in 1929, President Herbert Hoover appointed then-Attorney General George Wickersham to conduct the first national study of crime and law enforcement in the United States. The commission produced 14 volumes and advocated uniformity in state parole practices. It recommended that states establish centralized policymaking boards to write standards and guidelines for parole practices.[2] The commission wrote that the elements of a good parole system are the following:

1. indeterminate sentence law permitting the individual to be released (conditionally) at the time when they are most likely to make a successful transition back to society;

2. provision of quality release preparation—in the institution—for the person who is reentering the community;

3. familiarity by the parole officer with the home and environmental conditions before the individual leaves the institution; and

4. sufficient staffing levels to ensure an adequate number of parole officers.[3]

The Wickersham Commission reported that parole was logical because it was an inexpensive way to supervise individuals in the community. Moreover, the commission reported, the **person on parole** earns money whereas the person in prison cannot support themselves and cannot contribute financially to their family.

Despite the fact that all states had enacted parole legislation, by the mid-1940s, opposition to it was strong. The attitude that parole boards were turning hardened criminals loose on society sparked a series of angry attacks through national and state commissions, investigatory hearings, editorials and cartoons, press releases, and books.[4] Opponents claimed that parole had a dismal performance record, its goals were never realized, parole board members and parole officers were poorly trained, and parole hearings were little more than hastily conducted, almost unthinking interviews.

In spite of the gap between its goals and reality, parole fulfilled important functions for officials in the criminal justice system. Wardens supported parole because the possibility of earning parole served as an incentive for persons in prison to obey the rules, making it easier to keep peace. Wardens also

person on parole (also formerly incarcerated)

A person who is conditionally released from incarceration to community supervision.

used parole to control prison overcrowding by keeping the number of people being released on parole about equal to the number of new admissions to prison. Legislators supported parole because it cost less than incarceration. District attorneys supported parole because they felt it helped with plea bargaining. Without parole, district attorneys argued, there was little motivation for defendants, particularly those facing long prison sentences, to plead guilty to lesser crimes. District attorneys also supported parole because persons on parole could be returned to prison without new trial proceedings.

Together, these groups made a claim to the public that parole actually extended state control because the formerly incarcerated were supervised. Eventually, the public accepted the claim that parole was a tough punishment and that abolishing it would end state control over dangerous persons.

Parole Development in the Late 20th Century Opposition to parole resurfaced in the 1960s and 1970s, this time as part of a larger political debate about crime, the purposes of sanctioning, and the appropriateness of the unlimited discretion afforded various sectors of the criminal justice system (paroling authorities in particular). During this period, the debate on correctional policy addressed both the assumptions of the rehabilitative ideal and the results of indeterminate sentencing and parole.

In the 1970s, research indicated that prison rehabilitation programs had few positive benefits. The formerly incarcerated were not rehabilitated, as parole advocates had claimed.[5] This position was supported on all sides of the political spectrum, including by those who believed that prisons "coddled" dangerous criminals and by those who questioned the ethics of coercing incarcerated individuals into submitting to unwanted treatment as a condition of release.[6] These research findings led to many of the sentencing reforms of the 1970s and 1980s and helped usher in the warehousing and just deserts eras shown in Chapter 7. During a time when supporting parole represented a "soft" stance on crime and when crime rates and recidivism were up, the public did not want persons released on parole.

In 1987, the American Probation and Parole Association voiced its support of parole and objected to efforts to abolish it. Nevertheless, in that same year, six states abolished discretionary parole board release. By the year 2000, 16 states and the federal government had abolished it, and another four states had abolished it for certain violent offenses or other crimes against a person, a topic we return to later in this chapter. The APPA position statement on parole is presented in Exhibit 8–2.

EXHIBIT 8–2   American Probation and Parole Association

Position Statement on Parole

The mission of parole is to prepare, select, and assist offenders who, after a reasonable period of incarceration, could benefit from an early release while, at the same time, ensuring an appropriate level of public protection through conditions of parole and provision of supervision services. This is accomplished by:

- assisting the parole authority in decision making and the enforcement of parole conditions;
- providing prerelease and postrelease services and programs that will support offenders in successfully reintegrating into the community; and
- working cooperatively with all sectors of the criminal justice system to ensure the development and attainment of mutual objectives.

Source: Reprinted with permission of American Probation and Parole Association.

CHARACTERISTICS OF PERSONS ON PAROLE CO8-2

The incarceration of 1.2 million adults in state and federal prisons has given many people a sense of safety and security. However, the majority of the population is also unconcerned—or unaware—that at least 97 percent of those who enter prisons eventually return to the community, and most do so in about two and one-half years.

Over 1,500 persons leave prison every day. About one in four leaves prison with no postrelease supervision because of changes in sentencing legislation that allow some individuals to "max out" (serve their full sentences) and leave prison with no postcustody supervision as discussed previously. The majority, however, are released to community supervision with conditions.

Who Is on Parole?

According to the most recent data released by the Bureau of Justice Statistics, whereas the U.S. probation population decreased almost 27 percent from 2005 to 2020, the opposite is true for parole. The U.S. parole population increased almost 10 percent over the same time period from 784,400 to 878,900.[7] One in every 299 U.S. adults is on parole. Eighty-seven percent are under state parole jurisdiction; the rest are under federal parole. What do you think it says about mass incarceration if fewer persons are on probation than on parole today than in 2005?

The number of people leaving prison is expected to swell even more in the next few years as a result of the U.S. Sentencing Commission's 2014 Reduction of Drug Sentences Act and the 2018 First Step Act's changes in federal sentencing laws, which aimed to reduce disparities in sentencing for like crimes. An estimated 30,000 persons in federal prison are expected to qualify for reductions of about two years, on average, as the new guidelines are applied retroactively. Preference is given to individuals who participate in evidence-based programming—prison work, job training, or education. To qualify, persons also have to show that they had no disciplinary infractions while incarcerated. Some will go directly into society, but most will transfer to either a halfway house for five or six months, to the custody of another state or county, or to home supervision.

The basic demographics of adults on parole have not changed much over the past 20 years. The typical adult on parole is a white, non-Hispanic male on discretionary parole and under active parole supervision for more than one year. The median age is 34, with an 11th-grade education. Women make up 10 percent of the parole population (see Exhibit 8–3). The region with the highest number of persons on parole is the South, followed by the West, Northeast, and Midwest.

Not all who are sent to prison are released on parole. Those who are convicted of the most serious offenses (those who have life sentences or who face the death penalty) or who have disciplinary problems while incarcerated generally are not paroled. Instead, they live out their lives in prison or are released when they have served their entire sentences.

Exhibit 8–4 defines parole populations among the states. Texas had the largest number of adults on parole, followed by California and the federal government. Arkansas had the highest rate of parole supervision, followed by Pennsylvania and Oregon, which means they used parole more than any other jurisdiction. Maine used parole the least.

Reentry CO8-3

We said earlier that reentry is the transition persons make from a correctional facility to the community. Reentry has occurred since the Walnut Street Jail opened in 1773. However, the scale of reentry is larger today than ever before,

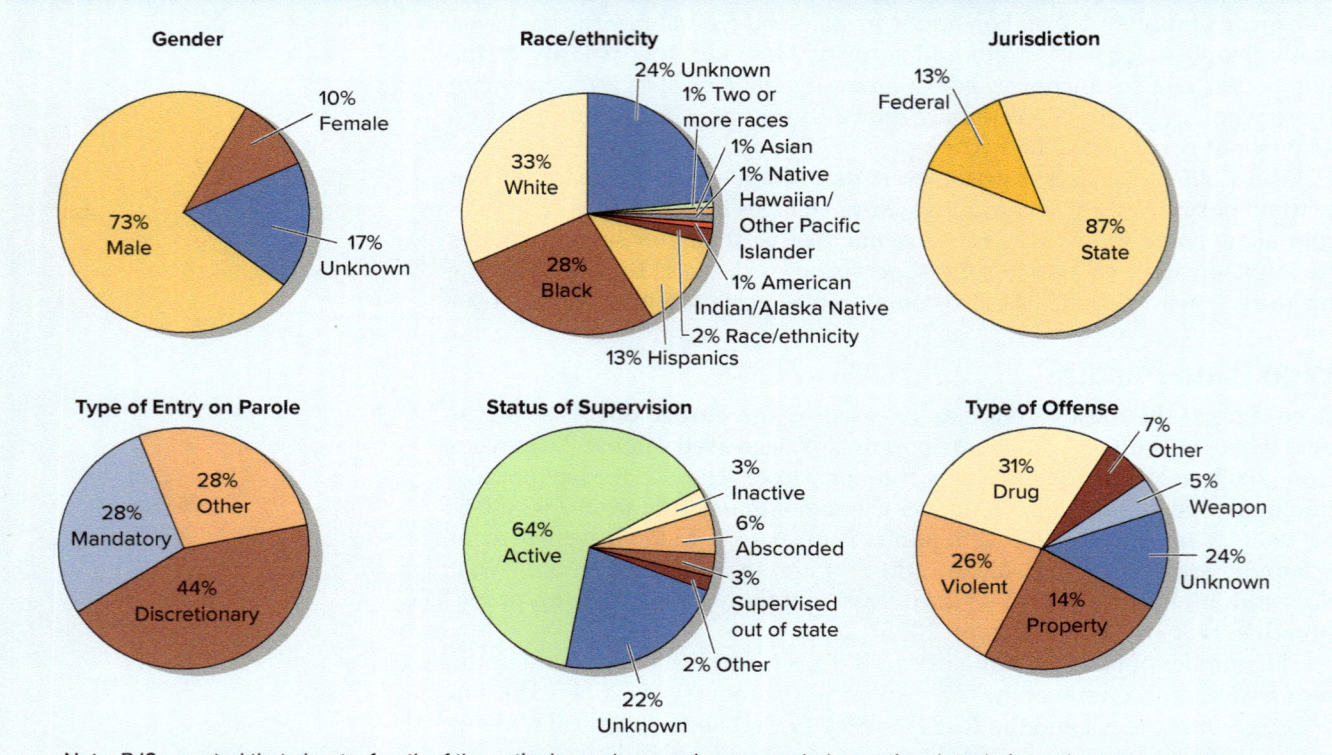

EXHIBIT 8–3   Selected Characteristics of Adults on Parole

Note: BJS reported that about a fourth of the nation's parole agencies suspended reporting data during at least one quarter of the 2020 COVID pandemic, thus accounting for the high percentages of "unknown" in the data above.

Source: Bureau of Justice Statistics.

EXHIBIT 8–4   Parole Populations and Rates of Supervision Across the United States

Five Jurisdictions with the Largest Parole Populations	Number Supervised	Five Jurisdictions with the Highest Rates of Supervision	People Supervised per 100,000 Adult U.S. Residents	Five Jurisdictions with the Lowest Rates of Supervision	People Supervised per 100,000 Adult U.S. Residents
Texas	110,437	Arkansas	1,106	Maine	2
California	110,340	Pennsylvania	868	Florida	24
Federal	107,922	Oregon	702	Massachusetts	24
Pennsylvania	88,263	Louisiana	605	Virginia	30
New York	43,979	South Dakota	543	Federal	42

Source: Adapted from Danielle Kaeble, Laura M. Maruschak, and Thomas P. Bonczar, Probation and Parole in the United States, 2014 (Washington, DC: U.S. Department of Justice, Bureau of Justice Statistics, November 2015).

and we face enormous challenges in managing the reentry of persons leaving prison. Virtually every person incarcerated in a jail in the United States, and approximately 97 percent of everyone in prison, will eventually be released. And when they walk out of prison, here's some of what they face:

- Their job prospects are dim.
- Their unemployment rate is five times higher than it is among the general population—27 versus 3.7 percent in 2022.

- Their chances of finding a place to live are bleak—on average about 10 percent are homeless immediately following their release from prison.
- Their health is poor.
- Their incidence of serious mental illness is two to four times greater than it is among the general population.
- Fewer than half have a job lined up before leaving prison.
- Three-fourths still have a substance abuse problem.
- More than 70 percent with serious mental illnesses also have a substance use disorder.
- More than 80 percent have a physical or mental disability.
- Almost one in five has hepatitis C.
- More than half have dependent children who rely on them for financial support.
- Two of every five lack a high school diploma or its equivalent.
- Only one-third participated in educational programs while incarcerated, and even fewer participated in vocational training.

They soon learn that they are back in society but they are not completely free. They face not only the legal consequences of their incarceration such as a record of conviction, fines, and conditions of release, but they also face collateral consequences that make it more difficult to reintegrate into society and increase the chances that they will recidivate. Two out of three will be back in prison within three years. Seven out of ten will be reincarcerated within five years, and eight out of ten will be back in prison within 10 years.[8]

In Chapter 7 we discussed reasons for an individual's reincarceration and learned that over 30 percent are sent back to prison, not because they committed a new crime, but because they violated the technical conditions of their supervision, including unpaid fines and fees. Imagine the reduction in mass incarceration if states followed California's lead and passed "non-revocable" parole legislation, a topic we turn to later in this chapter.

Collateral Consequences No matter which state they live in, each person released from prison will face collateral consequences or restrictions because they are labeled a "convicted felon."[9] **Collateral consequences** are legal and regulatory restrictions that limit or prohibit people convicted of crimes from accessing housing, public benefits, employment, business and occupational licensing, most government jobs, civil rights including voting, public office and jury service, firearms ownership, educational opportunities, and more.

collateral consequences

Legal and regulatory restrictions imposed by law as a result of a conviction.

Collateral consequences are not part of a person's criminal punishment. They are civil in nature and imposed without the involvement of courts. They are difficult to identify because they are scattered throughout state and federal statutory and regulatory codes, in civil service codes, in trade and occupation codes, and elsewhere. According to the National Inventory of Collateral Consequences of Conviction, a person leaving prison today faces an average of 750 state consequences and 950 federal consequences.[10]

Nationally, almost 75 percent of all collateral consequences affect employment opportunities due to increases in state regulatory powers over occupations, professions, and employment. In the mid-20th century, less than 5 percent of jobs required a state-issued license. Today nearly one in four jobs in the United States requires a government-issued license and it's predominately in fields and industries where employment growth, salary, and professional development are relatively high but outside the reach of persons

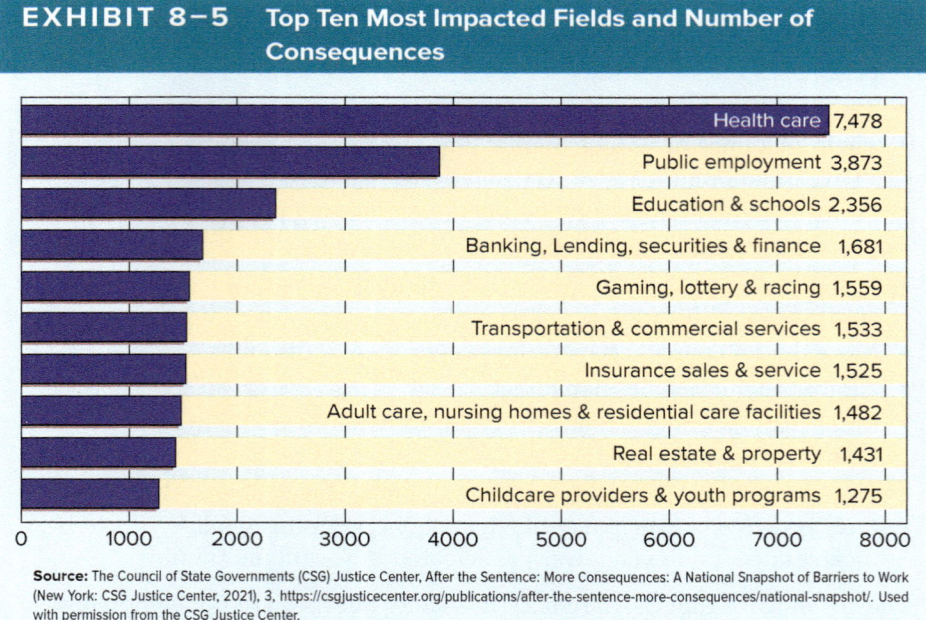

EXHIBIT 8–5   Top Ten Most Impacted Fields and Number of Consequences

Field	Number
Health care	7,478
Public employment	3,873
Education & schools	2,356
Banking, Lending, securities & finance	1,681
Gaming, lottery & racing	1,559
Transportation & commercial services	1,533
Insurance sales & service	1,525
Adult care, nursing homes & residential care facilities	1,482
Real estate & property	1,431
Childcare providers & youth programs	1,275

Source: The Council of State Governments (CSG) Justice Center, After the Sentence: More Consequences: A National Snapshot of Barriers to Work (New York: CSG Justice Center, 2021), 3, https://csgjusticecenter.org/publications/after-the-sentence-more-consequences/national-snapshot/. Used with permission from the CSG Justice Center.

leaving prison. Exhibit 8–5 is a list of the top ten employment fields with the most restrictions. Yet many people with a criminal record are prohibited from receiving occupational licenses or discouraged from seeking jobs in licensed fields.

Employment alone, however, is no magic bullet and will not lead to significant reductions in recidivism unless we go beyond simply getting jobs for persons on parole. To help persons leaving prison avoid illegal activity and succeed in their jobs, it is just as important to address criminogenic factors—underlying thinking and behavior patterns about crime and work that relate to an individual's likelihood to reoffend and commit another crime. As shown in Chapter 7, Exhibit 7–6, there is a large body of evidence-based research that demonstrates that cognitive behavioral therapy (CBT) is the most effective treatment in addressing antisocial thinking and behavior and reducing prison misconduct and postrelease recidivism. Employment programs that do not pay attention to this research run the risk of being ineffective.

Several studies have shown that judges, parole officers, and persons on parole have different ideas of what it takes to stay out of trouble. Individuals leaving prison and persons on parole rate financially based issues such as limited employment opportunities, the ability to pay court fines and fees, low wages, inability to return to former employment, and poor credit rating as their top postrelease challenge to abide by the law.[11] Judges and parole officers, on the other hand, score personal challenges as the most pressing reentry challenges such as lack of motivation, poor work ethic, blaming others, temptation to reoffend, and associating with the wrong kind of peers.

What this tells us is that there is a disconnect between the perceived reentry challenges for judges, parole officers, and persons on parole. Judges and parole officers see defendants as "cases" and relate them to previous patterns and classifications. Individuals on parole, on the other hand, see themselves differently. They see collateral consequences such as employment preventing them from successful reentry. In all likelihood, what is needed is a combination of both—programs that emphasize changing criminal thinking patterns and breaking down the collateral consequences that prevent formerly incarcerated persons to succeed after release from prison.

Reentry problems are magnified for women leaving prison, especially minority and women of color. Nearly two-thirds of the women confined in state and federal prisons are Black, Hispanic, or of other nonwhite ethnic groups. Women in prison have a high rate of prior sexual or physical abuse, high rates of positive-HIV status and other sexually transmitted diseases, and high alcohol, drug use, and addiction rates at the time of arrest. "In most of their communities," writes Beth Richie of the University of Illinois at Chicago, "there are few services and very limited resources available to assist women in the process of reentry."[12]

The situation is even more grim when we look at the reentry problems for Black women.[13] Current reentry systems do not consider their unique needs in the areas of family and health care. We reported in Chapter 7 that over half of imprisoned women have a child under the age of 18. However, Black children are more likely than white or Hispanic children to have a parent who is incarcerated. They are also more likely to be in foster care and remain there longer than white or Hispanic children. Compounding the problem is a generation of Black men who are not present in the community to assist with childcare and provide an income for the family. Reentry services have not accounted for the additional challenges that Black women face but that white and Hispanic women do not. Although the challenges facing Black women leaving prison are daunting, in recent years the United States has witnessed a surge of policy interest and innovation in response to these realities.

In March 2022, the Collateral Consequences Resource Center published the results of a national survey of laws and reforms in each state surrounding voting, records of conviction, employment, and licensing opportunities. The Center created a reported card for each state on how it handles reentry barriers in each of these categories and a national ranking of the 50 states and the federal BOP. Space does not permit us to cover each state. Illinois ranked number one because of reforms to reduce collateral consequences followed by Connecticut, California, Colorado, and Delaware. On the flip side, Montana, South Dakota, Alaska, Florida, and the federal BOP received the lowest rankings because they have the fewest regulations or laws offering reentry aid. Read what several governors are saying about the importance of reentry and second chances in Exhibit 8–6.

EXHIBIT 8–6   What Are Governors Saying About Reentry and Second Chances?

Reentry means success for a 25-year-old mentee I met at a specialized program for the emerging adult population, called the TRUE Unit, while visiting a prison in my first month in office. He is in final stages of our mentor program and told me he had to come to prison to get an education. It's a sad reality, but if we can take this unfortunate moment for people like him and turn it into an opportunity, we all will benefit.

Connecticut Governor Ned Lamont

Reentry is about ensuring enhanced public safety, a good quality of life, and the opportunity for enjoying the benefits of citizenship for Ohioans that have paid their debt to society. I believe that everyone—no matter where they were born or who their parents are—deserves the chance to succeed, to get a good-paying job, to raise a family, and to be secure in their future.

Ohio Governor Mike DeWine

A successful transition from prison means someone is liberated from past choices and able to take the things they've learned and apply them to a new chapter of their life, becoming productive and healthy in their new neighborhood.

North Dakota Governor Doug Burgum

Source: National Reentry Resource Center.

Federal Reentry Legislation The federal government's involvement in reentry programs occurs through grant funding to state, local, and tribal jurisdictions, nonprofit organizations, and the reentry programs developed by the U.S. Probation and Pretrial Services for persons under supervised release from federal prison.

Several pieces of federal reentry legislation have impacted not only persons under federal supervised release but also provided millions of dollars to state, local, and tribal initiatives to:

1. strengthen support for comprehensive reentry programming;
2. expand efforts to reduce substance addiction;
3. implement evidence-based educational practices;
4. allow nonprofit organizations to receive funding for career training and substance addiction services; and
5. put new accountability measures in place, making sure tax dollars are spent responsibly.

In 2003, the Department of Justice resurrected rehabilitation as a goal of correctional policy by funding all 50 states, the District of Columbia, and the U.S. Virgin Islands to develop and implement programs to facilitate the reentry of individuals convicted of "serious and violent offenses." The Serious and Violent Offender Reentry Initiative (SVORI) was the first federal reentry-specific undertaking not only because it invested more than $100 million in local communities to develop and implement reentry programs, but because it was the first to focus on addressing the multiple challenges that persons sentenced for serious and violent offenses face leaving prison.

Building on the positive findings of SVORI, the Second Chance Act was signed into law by President George W. Bush on April 9, 2008. The Act authorizes federal agencies to invest in local communities to support reentry initiatives focusing on employment, housing, substance abuse and mental health treatment, and family and child services to reduce recidivism and increase public safety.

The act also supports research and evaluation of programs and policies that promote successful reentry and reduce recidivism. Additionally, it establishes a National Reentry Resource Center to provide information and assistance to states, localities, and tribes on reentry issues.

The most recent piece of federal legislation affecting parole is the First Step Act signed into law by President Donald Trump on December 21, 2018. The law aims to reduce recidivism, reform sentencing laws, and improve the conditions of confinement in federal prisons.

The First Step Act includes several key provisions, including:

1. Sentencing reform: The law reforms certain mandatory minimum sentencing laws for nonviolent drug offenses and expands the "safety valve" provision that allows judges to use their discretion to sentence below the mandatory minimums.
2. Good time credit: The law increases the amount of good time credit that persons can earn while incarcerated, which can be used to reduce their sentence and potentially earn early release.
3. Compassionate release: The law expands eligibility for compassionate release for elderly and terminally ill people in prison.
4. Prison reform: The law includes provisions to improve prison conditions, including the requirement that person be placed in facilities that are within 500 driving miles of their families, the prohibition of

shackling pregnant women, and the requirement of menstrual products for women in prison.

5. Reentry programs: The law provides for the expansion of evidence-based recidivism reduction programs, such as job training, education, and substance abuse treatment programs, to help individuals successfully reintegrate into society after their release.

The First Step Act is seen as an important step toward reforming the criminal justice system in the United States and has been praised by both Democrats and Republicans for its bipartisan approach to criminal justice reform.

Fair Chance Licensing Across the country, states are also taking steps to advance fair chance licensing policies, laws, or regulations that aim to reduce barriers to employment for individuals with criminal records by removing questions about criminal history from occupational licensing applications or delaying such inquiries until later in the hiring process. The goal is to expand access to licensure for qualified workers with records of conviction and make it easier for them to enter licensed occupations, which often require a government-issued license or certification to practice. At least 44 states have adopted fair chance licensing.

Fair chance licensing policies vary by jurisdiction, but they generally fall into one of two categories:

1. Ban the box: Research affirms that a conviction record reduces the likelihood of a job callback or offer by nearly 50 percent.[14] But, if people on parole can get to the interview stage, they have a good chance of being hired. In response, the public sector, nonprofit organizations, and private corporations have been equally busy in addressing reentry issues. Recognizing that between 70 million and 100 million Americans—or as many as one in three adults—have a criminal record that can limit their job opportunities or shut them out of work altogether and more than a quarter of the formerly incarcerated people are unemployed, 37 states, the District of Columbia, over 150 cities and counties, and hundreds of private companies have adopted a ban-the-box ("fair chance") policy.

    General Motors, Coca-Cola, Target, Walmart, Home Depot, Koch Industries, Starbucks, Facebook, and Bed, Bath & Beyond have removed arrest history and conviction questions from their initial job applications.[15] (See Exhibit 8–7 for the states that ban the box for public-sector employment.) The new law allows employers to judge applicants on their qualifications first, without the stigma of a record. The law removes barriers to employment of people with criminal records by prohibiting employers from requiring disclosure of past convictions and arrest history on initial applications, information that often ends any realistic job prospects for persons on parole. Employers are asked to make individualized assessments instead of blanket exclusions and consider the age of the offense and its relevance to the job. Employers can ask about criminal backgrounds and run background checks after determining that an applicant meets minimum job qualifications. However the new reforms do not apply to police, schoolteachers, or other government jobs working with children, the elderly, or persons with disabilities. When Minneapolis banned the box in 2007, more than 50 percent of job seekers with criminal convictions, whose records were previously marked as a "concern," were hired for public employment in the first year. And in Durham, North Carolina, 96 percent of those with criminal records applying for city jobs were recommended for hire.

EXHIBIT 8−7   States That Have Passed "Ban-the-Box" as of February 2023

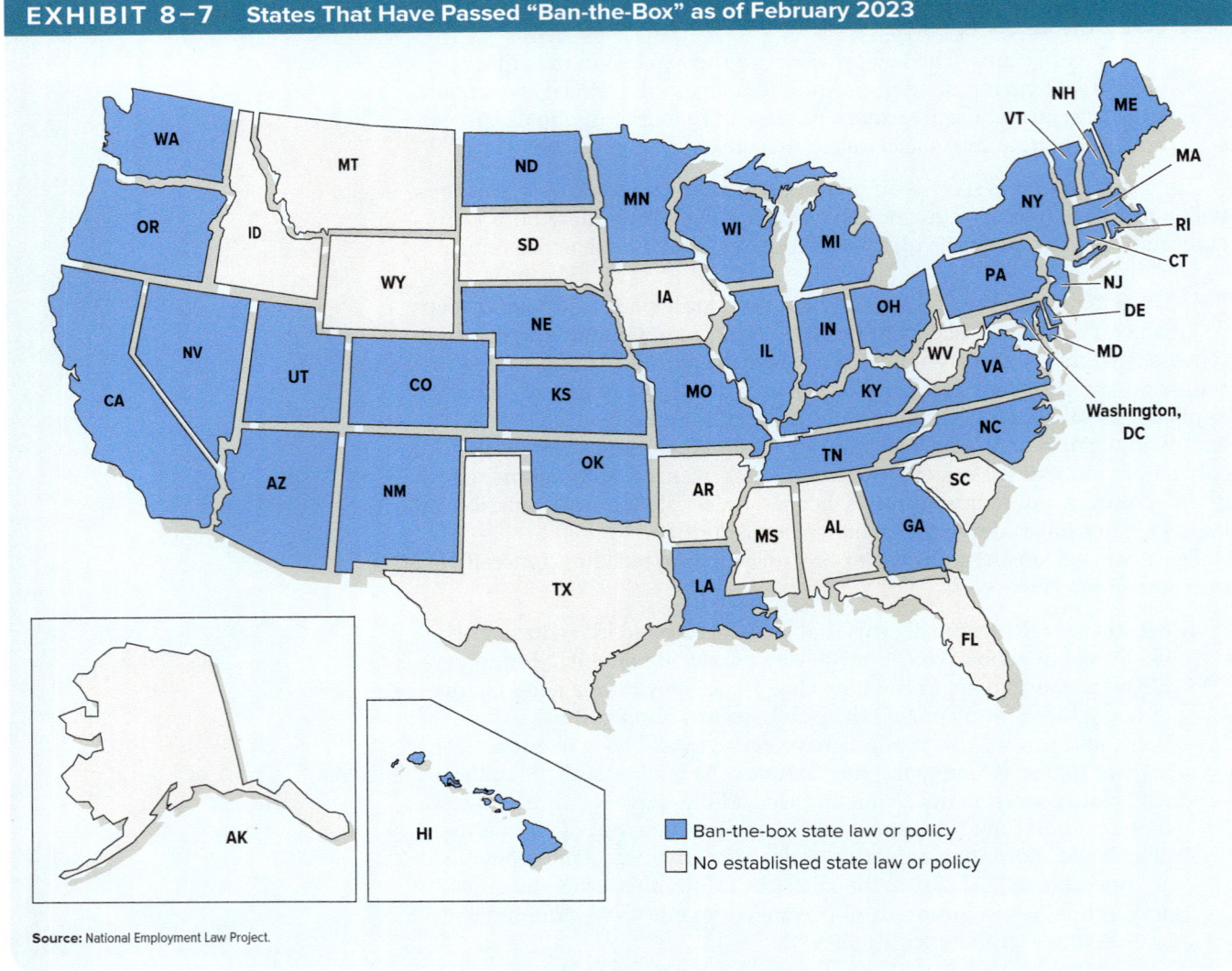

Ban-the-box state law or policy
No established state law or policy

Source: National Employment Law Project.

Ban the box is also applicable to colleges and universities where we find that two-thirds of the nation's almost 4,700 postsecondary two- and four-year colleges and universities collect criminal history information from all applicants. Persons who check "yes" to questions about criminal history are generally required to provide detailed explanation and supporting documentation, and their applications are reviewed by special admissions panels. Also troubling is the fact that some schools that ask for criminal histories have some criminal history-related automatic bar to admission.

Opponents to ban the box charge that unless postsecondary institutions collect criminal history information, there will be more crime on campus. They argue that a previous record of conviction is something that admission committees and employers deserve to know when they are choosing applicants to interview or enroll on campus. On the other hand, advocates of ban the box argue that colleges and universities are in a unique position to help remove barriers that prevent persons with criminal records from pursuing higher education.

They argue that education is the key to finding successful employment. Where does your college or university stand?

New research also shows that ban-the-box has unintentional negative consequences. Ban-the-box laws may inadvertently harm young Black men seeking jobs. Researchers found that when employers can neither access nor inquire about an applicant's criminal history, they instead discriminate more broadly against demographic groups they believe are more likely to have a criminal record. In ban-the-box jurisdictions, employers are less likely to interview young, low-skilled Black men because those groups are more likely to include persons on parole. They instead focus on hiring groups made up of men they believe are less likely to have gone to prison.

2. Individualized assessment: This policy allows licensing authorities to consider an applicant's criminal history, but only after an individualized assessment has been conducted to determine if the conviction is directly related to the occupation in question. This assessment considers factors such as the nature of the offense, the time since the offense occurred, and the applicant's rehabilitation efforts.

   Fair chance licensing policies are becoming increasingly common in the United States, with many states and localities enacting laws or regulations that limit the use of criminal history information in licensing decisions. These policies have been shown to increase employment opportunities for people with criminal records and reduce recidivism by providing a path to stable employment.

Examples of how states are working to reduce licensing barriers include:

   Arizona expanded the factors licensing boards must consider when evaluating a record of conviction to include time since the commission of the offense and evidence of rehabilitation. The state also barred consideration of juvenile records and nonviolent misdemeanors and sealed, expunged, or dismissed convictions in licensing decisions.

   Illinois requires licensing bodies to provide written notice of the reasons for a conviction-based denial, mandated online publication of a list of all the potential barriers to licensure imposed by state law, and expanded reporting provisions to require boards to collect and publish information on the number of conviction-based denials and the types of convictions that resulted in them.

   Ohio created one of the most comprehensive fair chance licensing laws in the nation. The 2019 law incorporates nearly all national best practices, including placing limits on the age of convictions that can be considered, prohibiting denial absent a "direct relationship" between a conviction and the licensed activity, and providing robust procedural protections.

   Vermont enacted standards for considering whether to deny a license based on the history of illegal activity, including the relationship between the crime and profession, evidence of rehabilitation, and passage of time since the commission of the offense.

paroling-releasing authority (also parole board or parole commission)

A person or correctional agency that has the authority to grant parole, revoke parole, and discharge from parole.

THE PAROLE-RELEASING AUTHORITY

Forty-eight states, the District of Columbia, and the federal government each have a **parole-releasing authority**, the government agency or body responsible for making decisions about whether or not to grant parole, as well as postrelease supervision by community corrections officers, parole officers, or probation officers. In the federal system, U.S. probation officers supervise persons released early from their prison sentences on parole or mandatory release by the U.S. Parole Commission.

The nature of parole-releasing authority among the states varies widely depending on the jurisdiction, but it too is usually a state agency that has the authority to grant, revoke, and discharge from parole as well as set the conditions of release. For jurisdictions with determinate sentencing and no discretion for the timing of release, the paroling authority may still determine conditions of release.

The Parole Board

A parole board is a group of individuals who are responsible for making decisions about the early release of persons who are serving a sentence in a correctional institution.

Parole boards vary in size from three members (Alabama and Hawaii) to 10 or more (Michigan and Utah, 10 each; New Jersey and Ohio, 12 each; Illinois, 15; Texas, 18; and New York, 19). The average number of members serving on parole boards is 7.

Each state has different professional qualifications for parole board members. In the majority of states, appointment to a paroling authority is made by the governor. The president of the United States appoints three members to the U.S. Parole Commission. In 28 states, the District of Columbia, and the federal government, paroling authorities are composed solely of full-time members. Only eight states (Colorado, Indiana, Massachusetts, Nevada, New York, Pennsylvania, Rhode Island, and West Virginia) specifically require a bachelor's degree. Thirty-one states do not specify any educational requirements.[16]

There is no question that paroling authorities exert a significant influence on the nation's parole policy. The board's preference to err on the side of caution and deny parole rather take a chance of releasing someone who might reoffend is risk aversion, largely stemming from being a political appointee. Although parole hearings are open to the public, they lack transparency and are out of public view, and attendance usually requires written prior approval. Furthermore, there is no research on whether the work experience, education, and training of parole authority members affect recidivism or parole-decision making. We may see the public face of a parole hearing, but there is no reliable information on its internal workings. Failure to understand risk aversion, the politics of parole, and the panoply of qualifications for parole authority members cannot be overstated.

When a person becomes eligible for parole, the parole board reviews the individual's case and decides whether to release them from prison before the completion of their sentence. The board considers a variety of factors, such as the individual's behavior while in prison, their likelihood of committing additional crimes if released, and the seriousness of the offense they were convicted of. If the parole board grants parole, the individual is typically required to adhere to certain conditions, such as regular meetings with a parole officer, drug testing, and curfews. Failure to comply with these conditions can result in the revocation of parole and a return to prison.

Parole is not guaranteed and is granted only to those individuals who demonstrate that they are a low risk to reoffend and have demonstrated good behavior and rehabilitation while incarcerated.

A parole board meets to consider a release candidate. While discretionary release by parole boards was at one time very common, it has been eliminated in many jurisdictions. Does parole provide individuals with an effective opportunity to reintegrate into society?
DAMIAN DOVARGANES/Getty Images

The Parole Hearing

A parole hearing is a formal proceeding where a parole board reviews the case of an incarcerated individual to determine whether they are eligible for early release on parole. The purpose of a parole hearing is to assess the risk that the individual poses to the community and to determine whether they are suitable for release from prison before the completion of their sentence.

During a parole hearing, the individual has the opportunity to present evidence and arguments in support of their case for parole. This may include evidence of good behavior, participation in educational or rehabilitative programs, and support from family and friends. The person may also be questioned by members of the parole board about their offense, their behavior in prison, and their plans for the future if released.

Parole Hearings are generally attended by victims, the applicant, the institutional representative, and hearing examiners or parole board members. A two-year study of 5,000 parole hearings in Colorado found that the parole board heard too many cases to allow for individualized treatment.[17] The time for a typical parole hearing was 10 to 15 minutes. Unusual cases take longer.

The final decision to grant or deny parole is based on both eligibility guidelines and the interview. If parole is granted, a contract that defines the release plan is executed, and the person is given a release date.

If parole is denied, the common reasons are "not enough time served," "too much of a safety risk," "poor disciplinary record," "need to see movement to lower security and success there," and "lack of satisfactory parole program" (proposed home, work, or treatment in the community). In that case, the individual remains in prison, and a date is set for the next review. The waiting period between hearings depends on the jurisdiction and the offense.

For example, in 2022, California Governor Gavin Newsom rejected California's Board of Parole's recommendation to release Patricia Krenwinkel, a former follower of Charles Manson and convicted of seven counts of first-degree murder in 1969. The governor said that despite her young age at the time of the killings, her positive behavior in prison, and her current age, she continued to pose an unreasonable risk of danger to public safety because her lack of insight into her crimes has not reduced her risk for future dangerousness.

The Conditions of Parole

The conditions of parole are requirements that an individual must comply with to remain free in the community under supervision after being released from prison. Sometimes the rules are established by law, but more often they are established by the parole board. Some common conditions of parole include the following:

1. Regular meetings with a parole officer: An individual on parole is typically required to meet regularly with a parole officer who will monitor their compliance with the conditions of parole and provide guidance and support.

2. Prohibition on drug and alcohol use: An individual on parole may be required to abstain from using drugs and alcohol and may be subject to random drug testing.

3. Curfew: An individual on parole may be required to adhere to a curfew, which restricts their movements outside of their approved residence during specific hours.

4. Employment: An individual on parole may be required to obtain and maintain employment and may be required to seek permission from their parole officer before changing jobs.

5. Restrictions on travel: An individual on parole may be required to obtain permission from their parole officer before traveling outside a certain geographic area.

6. Attendance at counseling or treatment programs: An individual on parole may be required to attend counseling or treatment programs to address substance abuse or other issues.

7. Electronic monitoring: An individual on parole may be required to wear an electronic monitoring device to track their movements and ensure compliance with the conditions of parole.

The standard conditions of parole in Alaska are shown in Exhibit 8–8. It's important to note that failure to comply with the conditions of parole can result in revocation and a return to prison.

We wrote earlier that almost one-third of the 350,000 persons admitted to prison in 2020 and one-third of the 421,000 admitted in 2021 were due to violations of the conditions of supervision.[18] New York taxpayers spend almost $700 million a year to incarcerate people for technical violations such as missing a court hearing, being out past curfew, or failing a drug test.[19] Imagine the reduction in mass incarceration and what $700 million would do in justice reinvestment if jurisdictions followed California's lead in nonrevocable parole (discussed next) and persons were not reincarcerated for technical violations.

The Types of Parole

At the beginning of this chapter, you learned that release on parole may be mandatory or discretionary.

Discretionary Parole Discretionary parole is release from incarceration based on the board's decision of eligibility. In 1977, parole boards granted discretionary parole seven out of 10 times. However discretionary release

EXHIBIT 8–8 **Sample State Conditions of Parole**

State of Alaska

Standard Conditions of Parole

The following standard conditions of parole apply to all prisoners released on mandatory or discretionary parole, in accordance with AS 33.16.150(a).

1. REPORT UPON RELEASE: I will report in person no later than the next working day after my release to the parole officer located at the PAROLE OFFICE and receive further reporting instructions. I will reside at _____.

2. MAINTAIN EMPLOYMENT/TRAINING/TREATMENT: I will make a diligent effort to maintain steady employment and support my legal dependents. I will not voluntarily change or terminate employment without receiving permission from my parole officer to do so. If discharged or if employment is terminated (temporarily or permanently) for any reason, I will notify my parole officer the next working day. If I am involved in an education, training, or treatment program, I will continue active participation in the program unless I receive permission from my parole officer to quit. If I am released, removed, or terminated from the program for any reason, I will notify my parole officer the next working day.

3. REPORT MONTHLY: I will report to my parole officer at least monthly in the manner prescribed by my parole officer. I will follow any other reporting instructions established by my parole officer.

4. OBEY LAWS/ORDERS: I will obey all state, federal, and local laws, ordinances, orders, and court orders.

5. PERMISSION BEFORE CHANGING RESIDENCE: I will obtain permission from my parole officer before changing my residence. Remaining away from my approved residence for 24 hours or more constitutes a change in residence for the purpose of this condition.

6. TRAVEL PERMIT BEFORE TRAVEL OUTSIDE ALASKA: I will obtain the prior written permission of my parole officer in the form of an interstate travel agreement before leaving the state of Alaska. Failure to abide by the conditions of the travel agreement is a violation of my order of parole.

7. NO FIREARMS/WEAPONS: I will not own, possess, have in my custody, handle, purchase, or transport any firearm, ammunition, or explosives. I may not carry any deadly weapon on my person except a pocket knife with a 3" or shorter blade. Carrying any other weapon on my person such as a hunting knife, axe, club, etc., is a violation of my order of parole. I will contact the Alaska Board of Parole if I have any questions about the use of firearms, ammunition, or weapons.

8. NO DRUGS: I will not use, possess, handle, purchase, give, or administer any narcotic, hallucinogenic (including marijuana/THC), stimulant, depressant, amphetamine, barbiturate, or prescription drug not specifically prescribed by a licensed medical person.

9. REPORT POLICE CONTACT: I will report to my parole officer, no later than the next working day, any contact with a law enforcement officer.

10. DO NOT WORK AS AN INFORMANT: I will not enter into any agreement or other arrangement with any law enforcement agency which will place me in the position of violating any law or any condition of my parole. I understand the Department of Corrections and Parole Board policy prohibits me from working as an informant.

11. NO CONTACT WITH PRISONERS OR FELONS: I may not telephone, correspond with, or visit any person confined in a prison, penitentiary, correctional institution or camp, jail, halfway house, work release center, community residential center, restitution center, juvenile correctional center, etc. Contact with a felon during the course of employment or during corrections-related treatment is not prohibited if approved by my parole officer. Any other knowing contact with a felon is prohibited unless approved by my parole officer. I will notify my parole officer the next working day if I have contact with a prisoner or felon.

12. CANNOT LEAVE AREA: I will receive permission from my parole officer before leaving the area of the state to which my case is assigned. My parole officer will advise me in writing of limits of the area to which I have been assigned.

13. OBEY ALL ORDERS/SPECIAL CONDITIONS: I will obey any special instructions, rules, or order given to me by the Alaska Board of Parole or by my parole officer. I will follow any special conditions imposed by the Alaska Board of Parole or my parole officer.

Source: State of Alaska Board of Parole.

RELIABLE RESEARCH. REAL RESULTS.

Enter your keyword(s)   Search Site   Advanced Search

Home | Help | Contact Us | Site Map | Glossary

EVIDENCE-BASED CORRECTIONS

Harlem (NY) Parole Reentry Court

The Harlem (NY) Parole Reentry Court is a problem-solving court that assists individuals in the transition from life in prison to life in the community. The goal is to build a support system for persons leaving prison and reduce their likelihood of recidivism. The target population for the program is persons returning to Upper Manhattan, one of the poorest neighborhoods in New York City.

As with other problem-solving courts, the Harlem reentry court is a collaborative team effort involving a judge, case managers, parole officers, and social service providers. The reentry court program takes, on average, six to nine months to complete, and has five core elements:

- Prelease planning: Case managers meet in prison with persons before they return to Upper Manhattan. The goal is to determine immediate problems or areas of concern and provide service needs upon release.

- Active judicial oversight: The judge and the team monitor an individual's progress, assist with solutions, and provide positive reinforcement or a negative sanction if needed. A formal contract is created and signed by the team and the participant that outlines specific goals and objectives for areas such as treatment, employment, and housing.

- Coordination of support services: Linking persons with social services is one of the highest priorities of the reentry court. Drug treatment and employment are often the most needed services. Services are also available for housing, health care, and mental health treatment. Recognizing the important role that family support systems have in a person's successful return home, the program also works with families to increase stability in the home.

- Graduated sanctions: In lieu of revoking a person's parole for something minor, the reentry court uses a system of graduated sanctions to punish persons who violate the conditions of their freedom. These can include increased appearances before the judge, delayed promotion through the program, increased drug treatment and testing, tighter curfews, and electronic monitoring.

- Incentives for success: Participants receive incentives for achieving goals such as obtaining employment or completing a treatment program. These include judicial recognition, certificates of accomplishment, relaxation of restrictions, small gifts such as pens or journals, and public ceremonies to mark milestones. There is a formal public graduation ceremony following the completion of the program.

Researchers used the gold standard of a randomized control trial to study the impact of reentry court. After three years they found that reentry court participants had statistically significant reductions in rates of reconvictions and parole revocations, increases in the numbers of months employed, and a greater likelihood of receiving a high school diploma or GED, compared with the parole-as-usual group. However, there were no statistically significant differences in the rate of rearrests or substance use.

The practice of the Harlem (NY) Reentry Court is rated *Promising* for reducing recidivism.

Source: Adapted from Bureau of Justice Statistics.

declined in the just-deserts era of the 1980s. Three decades later as mandatory minimum sentences and three-strikes laws were rolled back discretionary parole re-emerged in the criminal justice reform era (see Exhibit 8-9). While there appears to be an increase in the percentage of persons released on discretionary parole, more recent data show that parole boards heard one-third fewer cases in 2022 than in 2019, and released 41 percent fewer people in 2022 than in 2019. Depending on how it is used, discretionary parole can be a driver of mass incarceration or a valuable tool in the effort to combat it. Its success hinges on thoughtful and equitable implementation.

Proponents of discretionary parole board release such as the American Correctional Association (see Exhibit 8-1) argue that parole boards serve

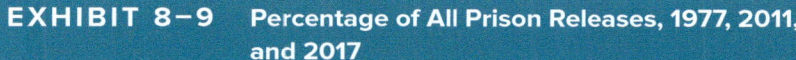

EXHIBIT 8−9   Percentage of All Prison Releases, 1977, 2011, and 2017

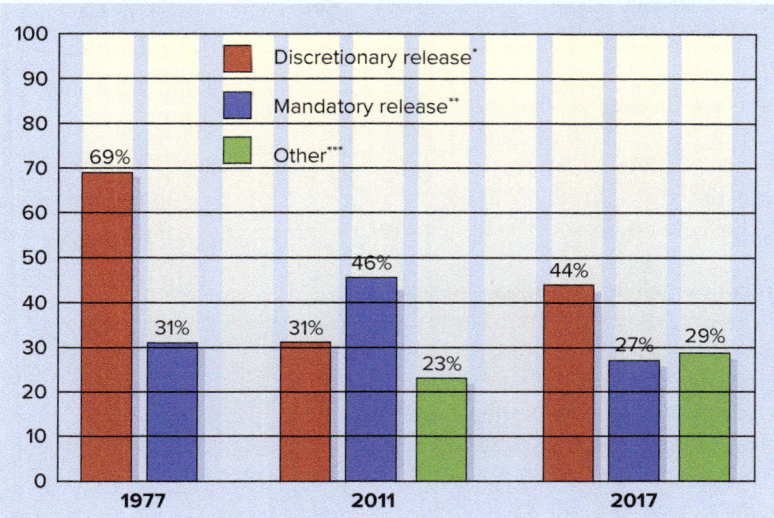

* Discretionary release applies to persons who entered parole as the result of a parole board decision.
** Mandatory release applies to persons who entered parole because of determinate sentencing statutes, good time provisions, or emergency release.
*** Other includes reinstatements (persons returned to parole after serving time in prison because of a parole violation), term of supervised release (persons sentenced by a judge to a fixed period of incarceration), other (persons who were transferred from another state, placed on supervised release from jail, released to a drug transition program, released from a boot camp, conditional medical or mental health release to parole, absconders, and others), and unknown.

Source: Bureau of Justice Statistics.

a salutary function by requiring persons incarcerated to focus their efforts on successful reentry from prison to the community. Without the prospect of discretionary release, individuals in prison have fewer incentives for engaging in good behavior or participating in rehabilitative programs and prison administrators have fewer mechanisms for relieving institutional crowding.

Mandatory Parole Mandatory parole, on the other hand, is granted automatically to persons who have served a certain portion of their sentence, usually a predetermined percentage of the sentence. For example, Minnesota uses determinate sentencing. Under this system, there is no parole board and no time off for good behavior. Individuals serve two-thirds of their sentence in prison and the remaining one-third on supervised release. The decision to grant mandatory parole is not based on the discretion of a parole board but rather on the completion of a set portion of the sentence.

The nature of supervised release and the conditions imposed are similar to parole. However while "parole" operates in lieu of the remainder of an unexpired prison term, "supervised release" begins only after a person has completed their full sentence minus good time credits.

Nonrevocable Parole In January 2010, the California legislature introduced a new type of release from prison called **nonrevocable parole (NRP)**.[20] NRP is a type of unsupervised parole that, unlike regular parole, cannot be revoked

nonrevocable parole (NRP)

A prison release option in California for persons convicted of nonviolent, nonsexual and low level offenses that cannot be revoked for technical violations.

Nakishaw Zambrana

Nakishaw Bishop Zambrana

Deputy Corrections Officer, Corrections Court Security Division, Palm Beach County Sheriff's Office, West Palm Beach, FL

Nakishaw Bishop Zambrana is a Deputy Corrections Officer with the Palm Beach County Sheriff's Office. She serves in the Corrections Court Security Division where her duties and responsibilities include the transportation of high-risk persons in jail to their court appearances in the 15th Judicial Circuit in and for Palm Beach County.

Officer Zambrana started her career in corrections, helping individuals enroll in a drug program. From that initial experience, she knew at the age of 20 that she wanted to become a Corrections Officer. After completing the academy, she worked six years with a private corrections agency before joining the Palm Beach County Sheriff's Office in 2004 as a corrections deputy. She worked for the Detention Security Division for 15 years before transferring to the Corrections Court Security Division.

Officer Zambrana has earned several notable awards for her work in corrections. In 2020, the Palm Beach County Sheriff's Office named her Corrections Deputy of the Year for demonstrating exemplary service in the line of duty. In 2021, Deputy Zambrana was awarded the Medal of Honor from Corrections USA, a professional association of the nation's corrections officers. While off-duty she witnessed a domestic battery suspect assaulting a victim and another deputy sheriff. She immediately rushed to the victim and officer's assistance and the two deputies restrained the suspect. Sergeant Daniel Mercier wrote in his letter of commendation, "Deputy Zambrana's courage, dedication and willingness to 'engage' exemplifies a selfless spirit and the caring character of a person who puts the safety of others before her own. She is a true reflection of the reputation of our great agency and an asset to the community she has sworn to serve. Deputy Zambrana never hesitated and never gave up."

Officer Zambrana's valor and selflessness are seen in the quote she lives by: "Faith is stepping out into the darkness not knowing if you will be given something solid to stand on or you will be taught to fly."

> *Faith is stepping out into the darkness not knowing if you will be given something solid to stand on or you will be taught to fly.*

Every day in the United States over 1,500 persons are released from prison. How many are granted discretionary release? Mandatory release? Which release is better and why?

Gerardo Mora/Getty Images

for technical violations. Persons are returned to prison only if they are arrested for a new offense, convicted, and sentenced to a term of incarceration.

Only persons convicted of nonviolent, nonsexual, and low-level crimes who have been assessed and determined not to be a serious risk to the public are eligible for NRP. In addition, they must have demonstrated acceptable behavior in prison and must have made progress with any substance abuse issues. Persons allowed NRP are no longer under the jurisdiction of the California Department of Corrections and Rehabilitation, and they do not report to a parole officer. They are discharged from NRP after one year.

In the first year of operation, some 6,500 prisoners received NRP at an estimated cost savings of $100 million to California taxpayers. It is too early to tell what impact NRP will have, but if it costs less than regular parole and does not contribute to an increase in serious and violent crime, chances are other states will consider adopting it.

ISSUES IN PAROLE AND REENTRY

CO8-5

This chapter concludes with a discussion of several important issues in parole and reentry, including felony disenfranchisement and voting rights, reentry courts, successful reintegration programs involving victims, the abolition of parole, reentry and community policing, and community-focused parole.

Felony Disenfranchisement and Voting

Felony disenfranchisement is the practice of depriving individuals with felony convictions of their right to vote, serve on a jury, hold public office, and restricts the issuance of professional licenses. Earlier we addressed the scope of collateral consequences. Here, we focus only on a person's right to vote.

Currently, an estimated 4.6 million people (representing 2 percent of the voting age population) in the United States cannot vote because they have a felony conviction on their record. State laws banning people with felony convictions from voting exist in 48 states. Only two states—Maine and Vermont (as well as the District of Columbia and the Commonwealth of Puerto Rico)—have no restrictions and allow persons convicted of a felony to vote while incarcerated or on parole or probation. As shown in Exhibit 8–10, 26 states

Parole: The Good and the Bad
What are the advantages and disadvantages of parole?

felony disenfranchisement

The practice of depriving individuals with felony convictions of their right to vote, serve on a jury, hold public office, and restricts the issuance of professional licenses.

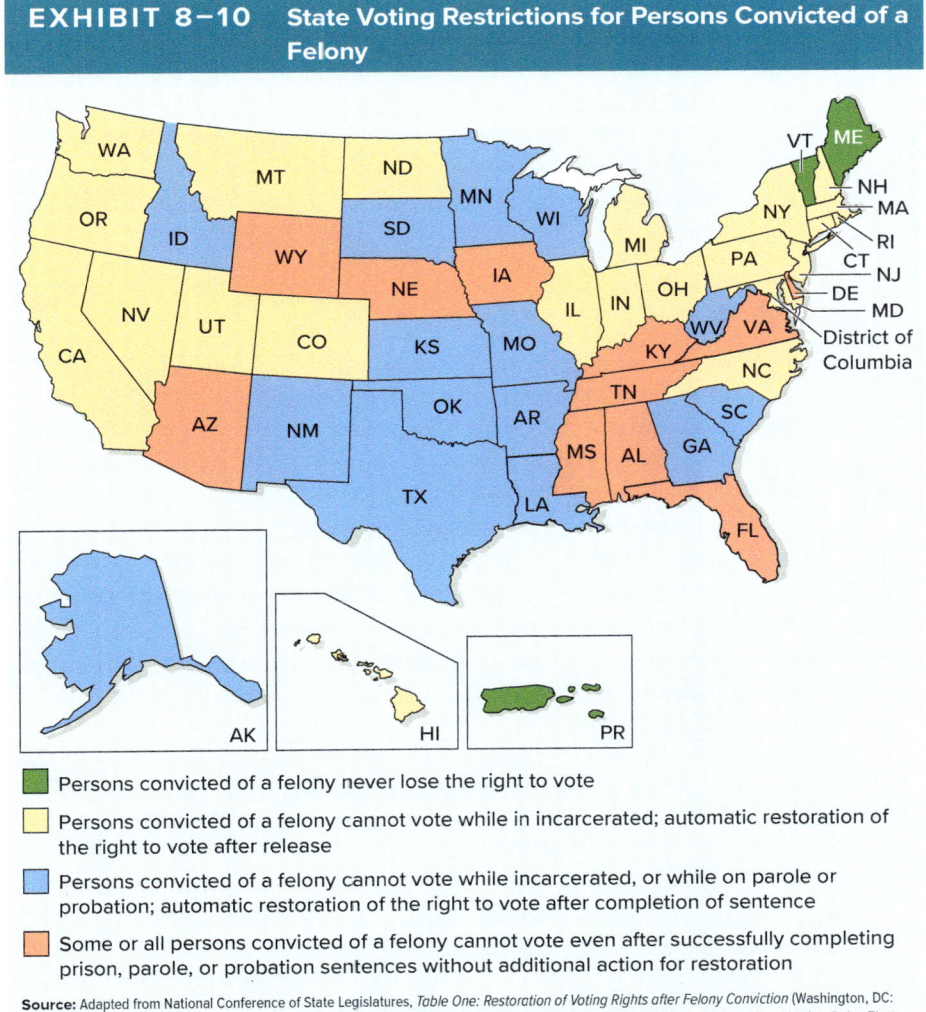

EXHIBIT 8–10 State Voting Restrictions for Persons Convicted of a Felony

■ Persons convicted of a felony never lose the right to vote

■ Persons convicted of a felony cannot vote while in incarcerated; automatic restoration of the right to vote after release

■ Persons convicted of a felony cannot vote while incarcerated, or while on parole or probation; automatic restoration of the right to vote after completion of sentence

■ Some or all persons convicted of a felony cannot vote even after successfully completing prison, parole, or probation sentences without additional action for restoration

Source: Adapted from National Conference of State Legislatures, *Table One: Restoration of Voting Rights after Felony Conviction* (Washington, DC: National Conference of State Legislatures, February 2023) and U.S. Department of Justice, Civil Rights Division, *Guide to State Voting Rules That Apply after a Criminal Conviction* (Washington, DC: U.S. Department of Justice, Civil Rights Division, June 2022).

Maine, Vermont, District of Columbia and the Commonwealth of Puerto Rico do not place any restrictions on the right to vote for people with felony convictions. Missy Shea of the Vermont Secretary of State's office helps at Marble Valley Regional Correctional Facility in Rutland with the voter registration process. An estimated 4.6 million people in the United States have lost their voting rights as a result of a felony conviction. What are the arguments for and against felony disenfranchisement?

Toby Talbot/AP Images

deny voting rights to people convicted of a felony while incarcerated, or while on parole or probation, and 11 states deny voting rights to all persons who successfully complete their prison, parole, or probation sentences. In some of these states there may be a postsentencing waiting period or additional action required for restoration.[21]

We present the arguments for and against felon disenfranchisement next. As you read them, remember that they have not been scientifically proven. They sound rational on the surface, but social science research has yet to validate them.

There are at least five arguments in support of felon disenfranchisement.

1. Persons convicted of a felony should be denied the right to vote as a matter of principle because they committed a serious crime.
2. States have the right to deny persons convicted of a felony the right to vote as added punishment, just as they have the right to restrict individuals from certain occupations.
3. Felon disenfranchisement reinforces the idea that criminal behavior is not acceptable in society. By taking away their right to vote, it sends a message to others that criminal behavior is unacceptable and will be punished.
4. Supporters of felon disenfranchisement believe that allowing convicted felons to vote could lead to election fraud or compromise the integrity of the voting system.
5. Article 1, Section 2 of the U.S. Constitution gives the matter of voting rights to the states.

On the other hand, there are a number of arguments against felon disenfranchisement.

1. Disenfranchisement laws are unfair to minorities and people of color, and to the 70 percent of the jail population because they are unconvicted and are not currently serving a sentence for a felony conviction. One in 19 Black persons of voting age in the United States are disenfranchised, a rate 3.5 times that of non-Blacks.
2. Disenfranchisement laws are not an effective form of punishment because most persons convicted of a felony did not vote before incarceration.
3. Removal of the right to vote inhibits reintegration and prevents individuals from feeling fully integrated into society.
4. Disenfranchisement denies individuals the ability to fully participate in the democratic process, which can be seen as inconsistent with democratic principles.
5. Disenfranchisement is counterproductive to reducing recidivism and prevents individuals from feeling fully invested in their community.

John Timoney, former Miami police chief and commissioner of the Philadelphia police department, put it this way:

I do not think we should give criminals an excuse for not reforming themselves because they are bitter about having had one of their most important rights—the right to vote—taken away. I think it is better to remove any obstacles that stand in the way of offenders resuming a healthy, full, productive life. . . . My sense is, once you've cleared the four walls of the jail, your right to vote should be restored."[22]

Do you agree with the chief that, once persons finish their incarceration, their right to vote should be restored?

Reentry Court

In Chapter 5 you learned about problem-solving courts and the drug court model that inspired the development of other specialty courts. One of the latest specialty courts to emerge is **reentry court**—programs that employ the authority of the court to combine supervision with treatment and rehabilitation for persons leaving prison to reduce relapse and recidivism for their successful reentry. As with most other types of problem-solving courts, reentry courts operate with a team approach, typically involving a judge, probation officers, prosecutor, public defender, treatment providers, and law enforcement.

The reentry team marshals the resources necessary to support the individual's reintegration by working with the participant and the team to find solutions to the problems each person faces when they first leave prison. The team provides close supervision, links to social services, and intensive case management.

The U.S. Department of Justice proposes that a reentry court have five core elements: prerelease planning, active judicial oversight, coordination of support services, graduated sanctions, and incentives for success. These five core elements are spelled out in the profile of the Harlem (NY) parole reentry court featured in this chapter.

In spite of the fact that there is limited evidence of the effectiveness of reentry courts, their numbers are expanding. There are approximately 40 federal reentry courts and over 60 state reentry court programs.[23] Chances are these estimates are low because not all reentry courts are evaluated or written about.

What is clear is that there are few independent and peer-reviewed evaluations on the effectiveness of reentry courts. So far the only reentry court to meet the research standards to be included in the National Institute of Justice's clearinghouse on "what works" is the Harlem (NY) reentry court highlighted in this chapter. Outside that review though, research on six reentry courts in California, eight adult reentry courts across the United States, one reentry court in Indiana, and eight federal reentry courts have produced mixed results. Some show reductions in reconvictions and revocations, while others do not. Some show a statistically significant impact on recidivism, while others do not.[24] More rigorous evaluations of reentry court programs are needed before the National Institute of Justice elevates reentry court from a program to a practice and answers the question, "How effective is reentry court *on average* across many evaluations"?

Researchers who study reentry court outcomes are also asking if recidivism should be the only appropriate measure to monitor, a question we first raised in Chapter 4. The problem-solving court literature recognizes other outcome measures that are more germane to their mission and goals, such as treatment retention rates, a reduction in crime severity, education and employment attainment, sobriety, stable housing, or compliance with program requirements. Lawson, Grommon, and Ray put it this way: "If recidivism indicators are the only measure by which reentry courts are judged, the emphasis on rehabilitation and encouraging therapeutic progress in reentry is obscured."[25]

Reintegration Involving Victims

Successful reintegration programs also involve victims.[26] Victims and victim organizations can assist in the reintegration of individuals leaving prison by providing parole board members and parole officers with relevant

The Honorable M. Casey Rodgers, U.S. District Court, Northern District of Florida, congratulates graduates of the Robert A. Dennis Jr. Reentry Court. Reentry courts are problem-solving courts that help people leaving prison make a successful adjustment back to their communities. What are the core elements of reentry court that facilitate an individual's successful return to the community?

M. Casey Rodgers, Chief Judge, Northern District of Florida

reentry court

A problem-solving court that helps people leaving prison makes a successful adjustment back to their communities.

information, offering their experience and expertise, and encouraging accountability.

Most states give victims the right to (1) be notified about parole proceedings, (2) be heard on matters relating to the possibility of parole, (3) be present at parole proceedings, and (4) receive restitution as a condition of parole. These rights are designed to ensure that the views of victims are taken into account before decisions about parole are made and to help victims prepare themselves for the person's release. Victim input can highlight the need for strict supervision or special conditions such as restitution orders, order of protection, or mandated treatment in order to discourage reoffending and encourage reintegration.

Programs involving victims operate in a number of ways. Some encourage victims to volunteer relevant information to parole officers. For example, in stalking cases, victims can tell parole officers whether the individual released from prison is in areas where they are not supposed to be. Other programs encourage the victim and the person being considered for parole to meet and talk about the impact of the crime and generate remorse in the hope that they can change offending behavior in the future. Whether the program features a one-on-one conversation or a victim talking to an audience of incarcerated individuals, the aim is to convey the consequences of their actions in terms of the victims' pain and suffering.

Abolish Parole

Earlier in this chapter, we discussed the strong opposition to parole in the 1930s and that opponents wanted to abolish it. They argued that parole boards were turning persons convicted of serious crimes loose on society, parole had a dismal performance record, its goals were never realized, parole board members and parole officers were poorly trained, and parole hearings were little more than hastily conducted, almost unthinking interviews. In spite of the gap between goals and this 1930s reality, parole fulfilled important functions for wardens, legislators, and district attorneys, as discussed earlier in this chapter.

The movement to abolish parole boards resurfaced in the 1970s when the concept of "just deserts"—the idea that persons convicted of crime deserve punishment for what they do to society—was being discussed.[27] Advocates argued that abolishing parole would increase community safety by getting tough on persons who commit crime in a time of increasing crime rates and the public's fear of crime.

However, states did not do away with parole altogether; they restructured it. As the data in Exhibit 8–11 show, 16 states and the federal government have abolished discretionary release from prison by a parole board for all incarcerated people. Another four states abolished it for certain violent offenses or other crimes against a person. In these states, postrelease supervision still exists and is referred to as mandatory supervised release, controlled release, or community control. Parole boards still have discretion over persons who were sentenced for crimes committed prior to the effective date of the law.

Why did some states abolish discretionary release from prison by a parole board? There are several reasons.

First, indeterminate sentencing gave parole boards almost unlimited discretion to decide when to release an individual from prison. Studies showed that instead of achieving rehabilitation, parole boards' decisions were influenced as much by a person's race, socioeconomic status, and place of conviction, as they were by the characteristics of the crime. Mounting evidence of extralegal factors affecting parole boards' decisions fueled the movement to abolish parole.

Second, eliminating parole appeared to be tough on crime. Third, parole boards' lack of openness in the decision-making process, in which they made their decisions on a case-by-case basis without a written set of policies and procedures, prompted criticism. Today, 30 states allow public access to the individual votes of parole board members and 19 do not (Minnesota does not have a parole board).[28] And, fourth, state politicians were able to convince the public that parole was the cause of the rising crime problem and abolishing parole was the answer.

Today parole restoration bills are being discussed in Florida, Illinois, Maine and Virginia, states that abolished it 30 to 40 years ago. Proponents of parole restoration argue that eliminating parole led to crowded prisons, escalating medical costs for the incarcerated elderly, and inequities in sentencing that disproportionately affected minorities and people of color. However victim groups argue that the possibility of releasing persons before their incarceration expires would force them to relive their traumatic experiences. If parole is restored can evidence-based practices help?

Reentry and Community Policing

Reentry isn't just for corrections anymore for two reasons. First, the large number of persons being released each year from state and federal prisons over the past two decades into neighborhoods that lack services and support systems is more than community corrections officers can handle. There has not been a sufficient increase in the number of community supervision officers for the population they serve.

Second, in spite of all the efforts being made at reforming corrections, most persons leave prison unprepared for successful reentry. Not enough incarcerated persons are receiving education or vocational training. Not enough correctional institutions offer evidence-based programming and not enough persons avail themselves to programming while incarcerated. Unless that changes, individuals leaving prisons are not prepared to lead productive, law-abiding lives.

Joint supervision of persons leaving prison by teams of police and parole officers is the most common way that police contribute to reentry efforts.[29] Team supervision usually takes the form of police accompaniment on parole home visits, parole ride-alongs on police patrols, and parole involvement in policing activities, such as attending community meetings and staffing neighborhood substations. The team approach sends the message that community corrections is not soft on crime. Researchers have noted a number of benefits to police–parole partnerships:[30]

1. Police can offer additional protection and legitimate authority to the parole officer.
2. Police generally possess more advanced telecommunications devices and a greater street presence.

EXHIBIT 8–11	Jurisdictions That Abolished Parole

For All Incarcerated People	For Certain Violent Offenses
Arizona	Alaska
California*	Louisiana
Delaware	New York
Florida**	Tennessee
Illinois	
Indiana	
Kansas***	
Maine	
Minnesota	
Mississippi	
North Carolina	
Ohio****	
Oregon	
Virginia	
Washington	
Wisconsin	
Federal Government	

*In 1976 the Uniform Determinate Sentencing Act abolished discretionary parole for all offenses except some violent crimes with a long sentence or a sentence to life.
**In 1995 parole eligibility was abolished for offenses with a life sentence and a 25-year mandatory term.
***Excludes a few offenses, primarily first-degree murder and intentional second-degree murder.
****Excludes murder and aggravated murder.

Source: Bureau of Justice Statistics.

EXHIBIT 8–12 Reentry and Community Policing

Las Vegas (Nevada) Metropolitan Police Department (LVMPD) identified homelessness as a major issue in one of its largest police districts, and found that individuals in need of services were not being connected with existing resources available to them. In response, LVMPD staff designed and implemented a pilot reentry initiative that focuses on people booked into the county jail who have no home where they can return upon release. During the period of this project, LVMPD staff gathered and coordinated relevant stakeholders, implemented a screening process during booking at the jail, and arranged a collaborative reentry process that places program participants in housing and connects them to necessary services.

Washington, D.C. Metropolitan Police Department (MPD) coordinated with officers from CSOSA (Court Services & Offender Supervision Agency) to conduct home visits to people under CSOSA supervision. Building on this effort, specific police districts extended this practice to include people recently released from the metropolitan area correctional facilities and identified as most at risk of reoffending. In one particular district, MPD staff formalized an existing relationship with a local social service provider, and leveraged this relationship to connect this high-risk population to services.

Muskegon County (Michigan) Sheriff's Department (MCSD) struggled with an overpopulated jail. A significant portion of the jail population comprises people incarcerated for their first offense. To decrease the jail population and increase public safety, MCSD staff designed a reentry program for persons in jail for the first time to limit the time they serve in jail and connect them to community services.

White Plains (New York) Police Department (WPPD) implemented the White Plains Reentry Initiative in 2004. This program focused on people leaving the Westchester County Penitentiary (WCP), and helped them reenter the White Plains community and develop an ongoing support system in the community. The initiative coordinated with a variety of partners—including professionals from the public school district, community mental health providers, and other service providers—who attended monthly panel meetings in WCP, meeting with people scheduled to be released in the next 30 days to the City of White Plains. At these sessions, the reentry partners provided overviews of each agency's services and a WPPD officer discussed possible repercussions for reoffending. As a learning site, WPPD focused its efforts on improving communication among stakeholders through monthly case conference meetings and the development of a web-based database of reentry participants.

Source: U.S. Department of Justice, Office of Community Oriented Policing Services.

3. Police can serve as additional eyes on the street for the parole officer.
4. Police are generally very familiar with the community and potential threats.
5. Police knowledge of hotspots for crime and gang activity can be valuable to parole officers.
6. Persons on parole may take their supervision conditions more seriously and display greater respect for the parole officer when they witness the coordination between police and parole.

Exhibit 8–12 offers a brief summary of four law enforcement agencies' challenges and progress in establishing reentry programs.

Community-Focused Parole

Earlier we said that communities that provide persons leaving prison the services and environment to transition successfully into the community will also protect themselves from further harm. Community policing and reentry is one strategy.

Another is community-focused parole, a process of engaging the community so the community engages parole.[31] The process requires at least three changes to current parole practice.

The first is to capture a mission statement that the public understands. Some parole agencies are adopting public safety in addition to reform of individuals leaving prison as a definition of their services. By raising their profile in the community as agencies that deliver public safety and highlighting that in their mission statement, parole agencies could decentralize parole officers into local neighborhoods (perhaps utilizing neighborhood

Joint supervision by teams of community police officers and supervision officers is the most common way that police currently contribute to the reentry efforts of the formerly incarcerated. Explain the argument for involving community policing in reentry.

Kari Rene Hall/Los Angeles Times/Getty Images

police substations) and form collaborative partnerships with police and others similar to what community police do with local businesses, residents, government agencies, and other stakeholders to solve underlying crime problems and prevent future offending.

A second change is visibility. Unless the work of parole is made visible to the community, it will not result in the service being valued or supported. For many citizens, the thought of someone from prison returning to society is met with fear. However, scientifically conducted public opinion polls show that the public supports job training, treatment, and education for persons who need it or want it. Media relations can help create a positive image and increase visibility regarding the work of parole. Other examples are participating in local events and using a highly visible community service work program that involves nonprofit organizations.

The third change—building partnerships—is central to any community-oriented initiative. Strategies that raise an agency's profile and elicit support are critical to the development of a community-focused parole service. Appearances on local news shows, articles in local newspapers, meetings with neighborhood associations, and sponsoring of local events such as Relay for Life are ways that parole agencies show they care about the community and that they can educate it about strategies in place to support and supervise persons returning to their communities.

The literature on community-oriented policing has found that proactive crime prevention strategies can yield long-term crime reduction benefits. It stands to reason that community-focused parole can also have a positive impact on community safety.

REVIEW AND APPLICATIONS

SUMMARY

1 Early English judges spared the lives of persons convicted of a felony by exiling them first to the American Colonies and then to Australia as indentured servants. Captain Alexander Maconochie, superintendent of the British penal colony on Norfolk Island, devised a "ticket of leave" system that moved incarcerated people through stages. Sir Walter Crofton used some of Maconochie's ideas for his early release system in Ireland. The first legislation authorizing parole in the United States was enacted in Massachusetts in 1837. The Elmira Reformatory in New York was the first U.S. correctional institution to implement an extensive parole program.

2 The U.S. parole population has increased almost every year since 2000. Today, 878,900 persons are on parole. That's one in every 299 U.S. adults. Eighty-seven percent are under state parole. The typical adult on parole is a white, non-Hispanic male, on discretionary parole and under active parole supervision for more than one year. His median age is 34, and he has an 11th-grade education. Women make up 10 percent of the parole population. The region with the highest number of persons on parole is the South, followed by the West, Northeast, and Midwest.

3 Persons on parole face not only the legal consequences of their incarceration such as a record of conviction, fines, and conditions of release, but they also face collateral consequences that limit or prohibit them from accessing housing, public benefits, employment, business and occupational licensing, most government jobs, civil rights including voting, public office and jury service, firearms ownership, educational opportunities, and more.

4 A parole releasing authority is the agency that has the authority to grant parole, revoke parole, and discharge from parole. Parole hearings are attended by the person under consideration for parole, the victim, and institutional representatives. The parole board reviews the case to determine whether the individual is eligible for early release. The individual has the opportunity to present evidence and arguments in support of their case. This may include evidence of good behavior, participation in educational or rehabilitative programs, and support from family and friends. The person may also be questioned by members of the parole board about their offense, their behavior in prison, and their plans for the future if released. Victims are also allowed to address the parole board and speak about the impact the offense has had on their lives.

5 This chapter discussed six current issues in parole: felony disenfranchisement and voting, reentry court, reintegration involving victims, abolition of parole, community policing and reentry, and community-focused parole. Maine, Vermont, District of Columbia, and the Commonwealth of Puerto Rico do not place any restrictions on the right to vote for people with felony convictions. Reentry court requires the persons leaving parole to make regular court appearances for progress assessment. Reintegration involving victims encourages victims to educate the person(s) who harmed them about the impact of the crime and generate remorse in the hope that they can change offending behavior in the future. Today, 16 states and the federal government have abolished parole for all incarcerated people. Another four states have abolished parole for certain violent offenses or other crimes against a person. In community policing and reentry, we find joint supervision of persons on parole by teams of police and parole officers. The goal of community-focused parole is to engage the community so that the community engages parole.

KEY TERMS

parole, p. 202	person on parole, p. 205	nonrevocable parole (NRP), p. 221
discretionary release, p. 202	collateral consequences, p. 209	felony disenfranchisement, p. 223
mandatory release, p. 202	parole-releasing authority, p. 215	reentry court, p. 225

QUESTIONS FOR REVIEW

1 Explain the history of parole development in the United States.

2 What can you infer from the characteristics of the persons on parole?

3 Explain the differences between the legal and collateral consequences of reentry.

4 Point out what a parole-releasing authority is, what it does, and why.

5 Assess each of the current issues in parole and reentry for their ability to reduce mass incarceration.

THINKING CRITICALLY ABOUT CORRECTIONS

Reentry and Cognitive Transformation

Individual-level change is required before opportunities for work, reuniting families, and providing housing make a difference in the lives of many people in prison. This change is referred to cognitive transformation. How can parole agencies help individuals leaving prison achieve cognitive transformation and successful reentry?

Abolish Parole

Advocates of parole in states that abolished it argue for a middle ground—persons with lengthy prison sentences should be given a chance at redemption and considered for early release after serving 20 or 25 years in prison. If that were the case, what would keep parole board members from sliding backward and using extra-legal factors such as sex, race, education, and substance use that fueled the movement to abolish parole in the first place?

ON-THE-JOB DECISION MAKING

Nonrevocable Parole

To help your state reduce prison crowding and the money it spends on prisons, your parole agency decides it is going to study California's nonrevocable parole (NRP) law and urge your state legislature to adopt something similar. Research NRP online and the eligibility criteria. Are there criteria you believe should be added to the list or possibly deleted?

Defend your position to a legislative subcommittee on criminal justice.

Collateral Consequences

Several states are enacting fair chance licensing laws to determine if a person's conviction is directly related to the occupation in question. What criteria should be used for these individualized assessments?

ENDNOTES

1. Charles L. Newman, *Sourcebook on Probation, Parole and Pardons*, 3rd ed. (Springfield, IL: Charles C Thomas, 1970), pp. 30–31; see also Norval Morris, *Maconochie's Gentlemen: The Story of Norfolk Island and the Roots of Modern Prison Reform* (New York: Oxford University Press, 2002).

2. G. W. Wickersham, *Reports of the United States National Commission on Law Observance and Enforcement: Wickersham Commission, Report on Penal Institutions, Probation and Parole* (Washington, DC: U.S. Government Printing Office, 1930–1931), p. 324.

3. Ibid., p. 325.

4. David J. Rothman, *Conscience and Convenience: The Asylum and Its Alternatives in Progressive America* (Boston: Little Brown, 1980), pp. 159–161.

5. Douglas R. Lipton, Robert Martinson, and Judith Wilks, *The Effectiveness of Correctional Treatment: A Survey of Treatment Evaluation Studies* (New York: Praeger, 1975).

6. Peggy McGarry, *Handbook for New Parole Board Members* (Philadelphia: Center for Effective Public Policy, 1989), p. 4.

7. Danielle Kaeble, *Probation and Parole in the United States, 2020* (Washington, DC: U.S. Department of Justice, Bureau of Justice Statistics, December 2021).

8. Leonardo Antenangeli and Matthew Durose, *Recidivism of Prisoners Released in 24 States in 2008: A 10-Year Follow-Up Period (2008–2018)* (Washington, DC: U.S. Department of Justice, Bureau of Justice Statistics, September 2021) and Matthew Durose and Leonardo Antenangeli, *Recidivism of Prisoners Released in 34 States in 2012: A 5-Year Follow-Up Period (2012–2017)* (Washington, DC: U.S. Department of Justice, Bureau of Justice Statistics, July 2021).

9. Justice Center, Council of State Governments, *After the Sentence, More Consequences: A National Report of Barriers to Work* (New York Justice Center, Council of State Governments, 2021).

10. Ibid.

11. Kyle C. Ward, Robert P. Stallings, and Paul M. Hawkins, "Comparing the Perceptions of Reentry Challenges: An Examination of Pennsylvania Magisterial District Judges, Probation/Parole Officers, and Inmates," *Corrections: Policy, Practice and Research,* doi.or/10.1080/23774657.2019.1579685. See also Demelza Baer, Avinash Bhati, Lisa Brooks, Jennifer Castro, Nancy La Vigne, Kamala Mallik-Kane, Rebecca Naser, Jenny Osborne, Caterina Roman, John Roman, Shelli Rossman, Amy Solomon, Christy Visher, and Laura Winterfield, *Understanding the Challenges of Prisoner Reentry: Research Findings from the Urban Institute's Prisoner Reentry Portfolio* (Washington, DC: Urban Institute, 2006).

12. Beth E. Richie, "Challenges Incarcerated Women Face as They Return to Their Communities: Findings from Life History Interviews," *Crime & Delinquency*, vol. 47, no. 3 (July 2001), p. 370.

13. Geneva Brown, *The Intersectionality of Race, Gender, and Reentry: Challenges for African-American Women* (Washington, DC: American Constitution Society, November 2010); Lisa M. Carter, "All They Do Is See the Charge: Reentry Barriers and Correctional Programming Needs of Women Returning to Society After Incarceration," *Corrections: Policy, Practice and Research,* doi.org/10.1080/23774657.2017.1399096.

14. Devah Pager, "The Mark of a Criminal Record," *American Journal of Sociology,* vol. 108, no. 5 (March 2003), pp. 937–975, as cited in Michelle Natividad Rodriguez, "'Ban the Box' Is a Fair Chance for Workers with Records," National Employment Law Project, March 1, 2016, http://www.nelp.org/content/uploads/Ban-the-Box-Fair-Chance-Fact-Sheet.pdf (accessed February 20, 2019).

15. *Back to Business: How Hiring Formerly Incarcerated Job Seekers Benefits Your Company* (New York: American Civil Liberties Union, 2017); Jesse Kelley, "Ban the Box for Colleges, Too," *The Crime Report,* January 10, 2019, www.thecrimereport.org (accessed February 14, 2023); Jennifer L. Dolac and Benjamin Hansen, "Does "Ban-the-Box" Help or Hurt Low-Skilled Workers? Statistical Discrimination and Employment Outcomes When Criminal Histories are Hidden," *National Bureau of Economic Research, Working Paper 22469,* July 2016, www.nber.org/papers/w22469 (accessed February 14, 2023); Amanda Y. Agan and Sonja B. Starr, "Ban the Box, Criminal Records, and Statistical Discrimination: A Field Experiment," *University of Michigan Law & Econ Research Paper No. 16-012,* June 15, 2016.

16. Mario A. Paparozzi and Joel M. Caplan, "A Profile of Paroling Authorities in America: The Strange Bedfellows of Politics and Professionalism," *The Prison Journal,* vol. 89, no. 4 (2009), pp. 401–425.

17. Mary West-Smith, Mark R. Pogrebin, and Eric D. Poole, "Denial of Parole: An Inmate Perspective," *Federal Probation,* vol. 63, no. 2 (December 2000).

18. E. Ann Carson, *Prisoners in 2020–Statistical Tables* (Washington, DC: United States Department of Justice, Bureau of Justice Statistics, December 2021) and E. Ann Carson, *Prisoners in 2021–Statistical Tables* (Washington, DC: United States Department of Justice, Bureau of Justice Statistics, December 2022).

19. TCR Staff, "The $680M Cost of NY Reincarceration: 'Technical' Violations of Parole," *The Crime Report,* March 11, 2021, www.thecrimereport.com (accessed May 4, 2021).

20. "Non-Revocable Parole," California Department of Corrections and Rehabilitation, www.cdcr.ca.gov (accessed February 20, 2023); Sam Stanton, "Critics Say New California Parole Policy Is Costly, Dangerous," *The Sacramento Bee,* April 12, 2010, www.sacbee.com (accessed February 20, 2023); and John Wilkens, "Inmates Released Under New Law," *The San Diego Union Tribune,* January 26, 2010, www.signonsandiego.com (accessed February 20, 2023).

21. Christophefr Uggen, Ryan Larson, Sarah Shannon and Robert Stewart, *Locked Out 2022: Estimates of People Denied Voting Rights* (Washington DC: The Sentencing Project, 2022).

22. John F. Timoney, "Two More Issues for President Obama, with Implications for Justice and Race," *Subject to Debate: A Newsletter of the Police Executive Research Forum,* vol. 22, no. 11 (November 2008), p. 2.

23. Barbara Meierhoefer, "Judge-Involved Supervision Programs in the Federal Courts: Summary of Findings from the Survey of Chief United States Probation Officers," *Federal Probation,* vol. 75, no. 1 (December 2016), pp. 37–46; and National Drug Court Resource Center, *Treatment Courts Across the United States*: 2020 (University of North Carolina, Wilmington, NC: National Drug Court Resource Center, 2020).

24. Matthew S. Crow and John Ortiz Smykla, "The Effect of Reentry Court Participation on Post-Release Supervision Outcomes and Re-Arrest." Department of Criminology and Criminal Justice, University of West Florida, June 2019; A. Farrell and K. Wunderlich, *Evaluation of the Court-Assisted Recovery Effort (C.A.R.E.) Program* (United States District Court for the District of Massachusetts, 2009); Stephen E. Vance, "Judge-Involved Supervision Programs in the Federal System: Background and Research." *Federal Probation,* vol. 81, no. 1 (2017), pp. 15–23; Daniel W. Close, Kevin Alltucker and Melissa Aubin, The District of Oregon Reentry Court: Evaluation, Policy Recommendations, and Replication Strategies. Available at https://www.ussc.gov/sites/default/files/pdf/training/annual-national-training-seminar/2009/008c_Reen-

try_Court_Doc.pdf (Accessed February 7, 2023); David Rauma, *Evaluation of a Federal Reentry Program Model* (Washington, DC: Federal Judicial Center, 2016); Zachary Hamilton, *Do Reentry Courts Reduce Recidivism: Results from the Harlem Parole Reentry Court* (New York: Center for Court Innovation, 2010); Zachary Hamilton, "Adapting to Bad News: Lessons from the Harlem Parole Reentry Court," *Journal of Offender Rehabilitation*, vol. 50 (2011), pp. 385–410; Caitlin J. Taylor, *Program Evaluation of the Federal Reentry Court in the Eastern District of Pennsylvania* (Philadelphia, PA: La Salle University, Department of Sociology and Criminal Justice, 2016); and Spencer G. Lawson, Eric Grommon, and Bradley Ray, "Does Reentry Court Completion Affect Recidivism Three Years After Exit? Results from a Retrospective Cohot Study," *Corrections, Policy, Practice and Research*, vol. 6, no. 4 (2021): pp. 288–304.

25. Bradley Ray, "Does Reentry Court Completion Affect Recidivism Three Years After Exit? Results from a Retrospective Cohort Study," pp. 300–301.

26. Susan Herman and Cressida Wasserman, "A Role for Victims in Offender Reentry," *Crime & Delinquency*, vol. 47, no. 3 (July 2001), pp. 428–445.

27. Andrew von Hirsch, *Doing Justice: The Choice of Punishments, Report of the Committee for the Study of Incarceration* (New York: Hill and Wang, 1976).

28. Boston Herald, "Where States Stand on Parole Votes," *Boston Herald*, November 17, 2018, www.bostonherald.com (accessed February 24, 2023).

29. La Vigne et al., *Prisoner Reentry and Community Policing, Strategies for Enhancing Public Safety*, p. 16.

30. Justin Jones and Edward Flynn, "Cops and Corrections: Reentry Collaborations for Public Safety," *Corrections Today*, vol. 70, no. 2 (April 2008), pp. 26–29; and Ashbel T. Wall II and Tracy Z. Poole, "Partnerships with Local Law Enforcement and Community Agencies: A Critical Component to Successful Prison Reentry Initiatives," *Corrections Today*, vol. 70, no. 2 (April 2008), pp. 30–37; Adam K. Matz and Bitna Kim, "A National Survey of Chief Probation/Parole Officers' Perceived Interest in and Impact of Partnerships with Police," *Corrections: Policy, Practice and Research*, (2017), doi:10.1080/23774657.2017.131004.

31. Donald G. Evans, "Community-Focused Parole," *Corrections Today*, vol. 68, no. 7 (December 2006), pp. 90–91.

The Prison World

Part Four explores life inside prison for residents and staff, the legal challenges surrounding their roles and responsibilities and the special needs of residents who are elderly, infected with HIV or AIDS, or mentally or physically challenged.

Custodial staff are most directly involved in the daily work of managing the resident population. The extent to which correctional officers share beliefs, values, and behaviors is largely a function of the correctional officer subculture and each individual's personality.

People who are held in prison also develop a subculture that helps them adjust to the self-doubt, reduced self-esteem, and deprivations they experience as a result of confinement. Inmate subculture is also based on the life experiences that residents bring with them when they enter confinement. One question that we try to answer concerns why men's prisoner subculture encourages isolation but women's prisoner subculture encourages relationships.

For a century, people held in prison were considered civilly dead, and prisons operated entirely without court intervention. However, in 1970, the U.S. Supreme Court declared that if states were going to operate prisons, they would have to do so according to the dictates of the Constitution. Since then, people in prison have reclaimed many of their conditional rights under the U.S. Constitution. But today, changes in state and federal statutes have slowed the pace of prisoners' rights cases, and the U.S. Supreme Court seems to have become less sympathetic to the civil rights claims of people in prison.

Residents with special needs—those who are elderly; suffer from HIV, AIDS, or other chronic diseases; or are mentally or physically challenged—present significant problems for correctional managers. Special needs residents may be more prone to violence and disruption. They frequently require close monitoring to reduce the risk of suicide, and they may tax scarce medical resources and become targets of abuse by other residents.

The preprison drug use and sexual activity of many people in confinement has brought HIV, AIDS, and tuberculosis into jails and prisons. Managing these problems requires training in early detection, treatment, classification, staff education, and adequate funding. These problems are compounded by the fact that many residents have co-occurring physical and mental health problems.

Linda Davidson/The Washington Post/Getty Images

[9]

THE STAFF WORLD

Managing the Resident Population

CHAPTER OBJECTIVES

After completing this chapter you should be able to do the following:

1 List the staff roles within the organizational hierarchy of correctional institutions.

2 Identify the types of power available to correctional officers, and list and describe the most common correctional officer personality types.

3 List and describe the seven correctional officer job assignments.

4 Identify five significant correctional staff issues.

5 Detail the nature of workplace corruption among correctional personnel, and explain its causes.

6 Explain the impact that terrorism is having on prisons and on the operation of correctional institutions today.

> *Corrections is not a business where only one sex, race, religion, or type of person can succeed. It takes men and women of all races, religions, and color to create a dynamic and effective workforce to manage diverse inmates and solve the problems we face.*
>
> —Dora Schriro, former Missouri director of corrections

Recently, the Pew Charitable Trusts, a highly regarded nonprofit organization that researches American social issues, sounded a warning saying that "many states face a dire shortage" of correctional officers.[1] The Trust cited New Mexico as "one of several states ... trying to solve a dire shortage and high turnover in state correctional officers this year by proposing pay increases or starting new training academies." It found that many other states—including Michigan, Kansas, Nebraska, Missouri, West Virginia, North Carolina, Texas, and Oklahoma—are working hard to hire and retain more correctional officers. It is important to find a solution because, as the Trust notes, "Understaffed prisons result in long hours, fatigue and stress for guards, and canceled recreational and social programs for people held in prisons, such as family visits—all of which can lead to potentially dangerous situations."[2]

A state correctional officer at work. Why is there a shortage of correctional staff in many states? What can be done to address the issue?
Portland Press Herald/Getty Images

THE STAFF HIERARCHY

CO9-1

Practically speaking, a prison of any size has a number of different staff roles—each with its own unique set of tasks. **Roles** are the normal patterns of behavior expected of those holding particular social positions. **Staff roles** are the patterns of behavior expected of correctional staff members in particular jobs. Eventually, many people internalize the expectations others have of them, and such expectations can play an important part in their self-perceptions.

Today's correctional staff members have four main goals:

1. to provide for the security of the community by incarcerating those who break the law;
2. to promote the smooth and effective functioning of the institution;
3. to ensure that incarceration is secure but humane; and
4. to give residents the opportunity to develop a positive lifestyle while incarcerated and to gain the personal and employment skills they need for a positive lifestyle after release.[3]

Prison staff are organized into a hierarchy, or multilevel categorization, according to responsibilities. An institution's hierarchy generally has a warden or superintendent at the top and correctional officers at a lower level. A typical correctional staff hierarchy includes:

- administrative staff (wardens, superintendents, assistant superintendents, and others charged with operating the institution and its programs and with setting policy);
- clerical personnel (record keepers and administrative assistants);

roles

The normal patterns of behavior expected of those holding particular social positions.

staff roles

The normal patterns of behavior expected of correctional staff members in particular jobs.

- program staff (psychologists, psychiatrists, medical doctors, nurses, medical aides, teachers, counselors, caseworkers, and ministers— many of whom contract with the institution to provide services);
- custodial staff (majors, captains, lieutenants, sergeants, and correctional officers charged primarily with maintaining order and security);
- service and maintenance staff (kitchen supervisors, physical plant personnel, and many outside contractors); and
- volunteers (prison ministry, speakers, and other volunteers in corrections).

Organizational charts graphically represent the staff structure and the chain of command within an institution. An organizational chart for a typical medium-to-large correctional institution is shown in Exhibit 9–1. **Custodial staff** are most directly involved in managing the resident population through daily contact with people in prison. Their role is to control residents within the institution. **Program staff,** on the other hand, are concerned with encouraging residents to participate in educational, vocational, and treatment programs. Custodial staff, who make up more than 60 percent of prison personnel, are generally organized in

custodial staff

Those staff members most directly involved in managing the resident population.

program staff

Those staff members concerned with encouraging residents to participate in educational, vocational, and treatment programs.

EXHIBIT 9–1   Organizational Chart of a Typical Midsize or Large Correctional Institution

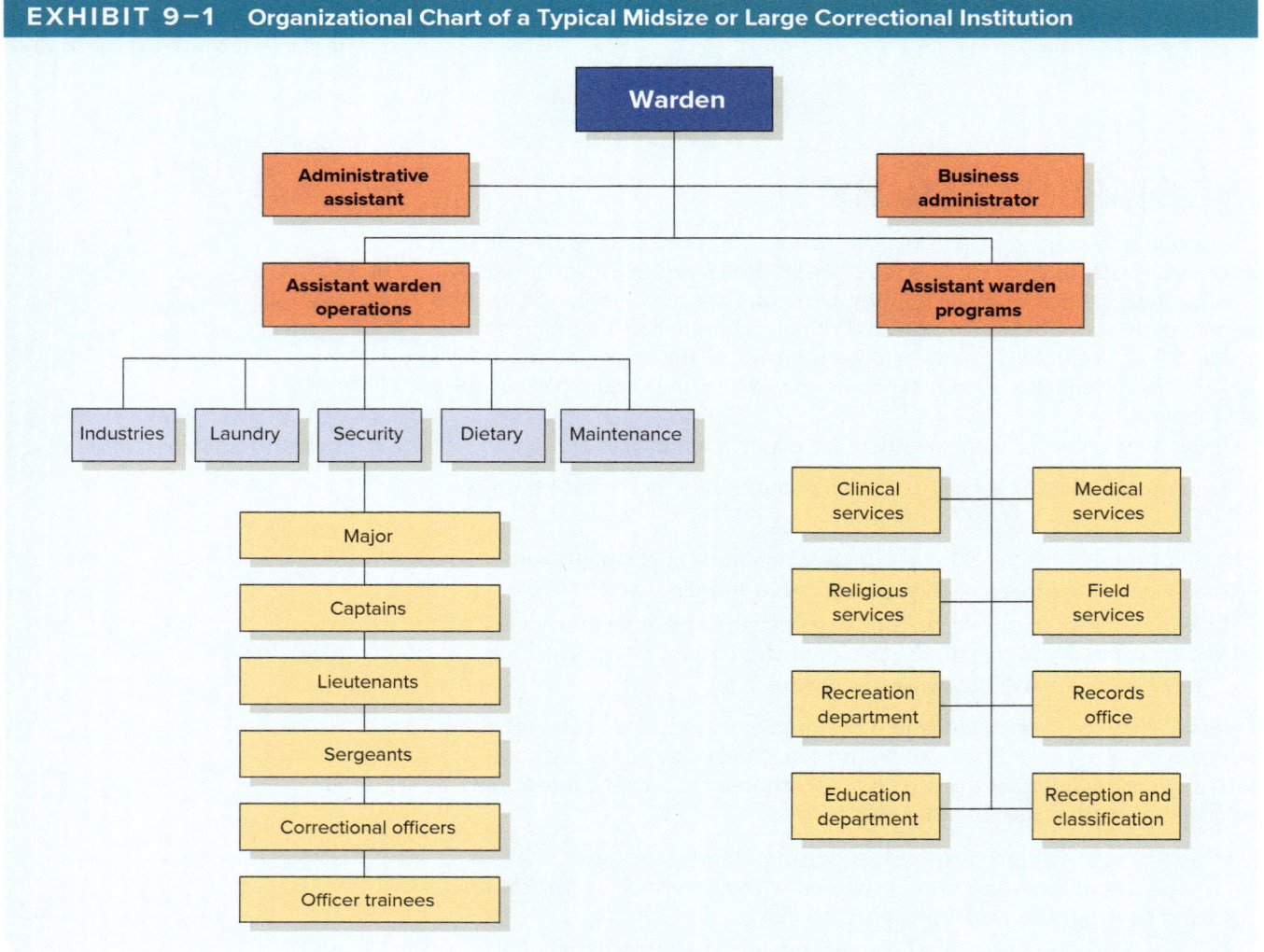

Securing a person in prison in preparation for a trip back to his cell. Correctional officers need to elicit clients' cooperation to effectively carry out their custodial duties. What are some techniques officers might use?

Andrew Lichtenstein/Corbis/Getty Images

a military-style hierarchy, from assistant or deputy warden down to correctional officer. Program staff generally operate through a separate organizational structure and have little in common with custodial staff.

To a great extent, prison management involves managing relationships—among employees, between employees and residents, and among residents. Prisons are unique in that most of the people held in them are forced to live there according to the terms of their sentence; and they really do not want to be there. Such a situation presents tremendous challenges. The people on the front lines dealing around the clock with such challenges are the correctional officers.

THE CORRECTIONAL OFFICER— THE CRUCIAL PROFESSIONAL

Although security is still the major concern, correctional officers today are expected to perform a variety of other tasks. As Joe Russo, the corrections technology lead at the Justice Technology Information Center (an NIJ-funded program), says:

> Corrections is fundamentally a "people profession," where interpersonal skills and effective face-to-face interactions are keys to effectiveness. Staff, both within institutions and in community supervision, must protect the public from individuals accused or convicted of crimes. At the same time, staff must prepare those under correctional control for successful, law-abiding lives in the community and support these individuals through the reentry process. The task facing corrections staff, then, is complex. Staff are in a unique position to have a significant impact not only on the lives and prospects of the incarcerated individuals with whom they interact but also on the larger communities where these individuals reside or where they will return.[4]

Bases of Power

CO9-2

Correctional officers rely on a variety of strategies to manage resident behavior. After surveying correctional officers in five prisons, John Hepburn identified five types of officers' power, according to the bases on which they rest: legitimate power, coercive power, reward power, expert power, and referent power.

Persons in custody from the California Department of Corrections and Rehabilitation prepare to join a firefighting team during the height of California wildfires. People in custody earn gain time, or reductions in their sentence, for performing work that contributes to the public good. Who do you think is most likely to volunteer?
DAVID MCNEW/AFP/Getty Images

gain time

Time taken off of a person's sentence for participating in certain positive activities such as going to school, learning a trade, and working in prison.

Legitimate Power Correctional officers have power by virtue of their positions within the organization. That is, they have formal authority to command. As Hepburn says, "The prison guard has the right to exercise control over [residents] by virtue of the structural relationship between the position of the guard and the position of the [resident]."[5]

Coercive Power Residents' beliefs that a correctional officer can and will punish disobedience give the officer coercive power. Many correctional officers use coercive power as a primary method of control.

Reward Power Correctional officers dispense both formal and informal rewards to induce cooperation among residents. Formal rewards include assignment of desirable jobs, housing, and other resident privileges. Correctional officers are also in a position to influence parole decisions and to assign good-time credit and **gain time** to residents. Informal rewards correctional officers use include granting special favors and overlooking minor infractions of rules.

Expert Power Expert power results from residents' perceptions that certain correctional officers have valuable skills. For example, residents seeking treatment may value treatment-oriented officers. Residents who need help with ongoing interpersonal conflicts may value officers who have conflict-resolution skills. Such officers may be able to exert influence on residents who want their help.

Referent Power Referent power flows from "persuasive diplomacy." Officers who win the respect and admiration of the people who are held in prisons—that is, officers who are fair and not abusive—may achieve a kind of natural leadership position over people.

In a now-classic study, Gresham Sykes wrote that correctional officers' power can be corrupted through inappropriate relationships with those whom they supervise.[6] Friendships with residents as well as indebtedness to them can corrupt. According to Sykes, staff members who get too close to residents and establish friendships are likely to find their "friends" asking for

special favors. Similarly, officers who accept help from residents may one day find that it is "payback time." In difficult or dangerous situations, help may be difficult to decline. In such cases, staff members must be careful not to let any perceived indebtedness to residents influence their future behavior.

The Staff Subculture

Prison life is characterized by duality. An enormous gap separates those who work in prisons from those who live in them. This gap has a number of dimensions. One is that staff members officially control the institution and enforce the rules by which residents live. Other formal and informal differences exist, including differences in background, values, and culture. Primarily, however, the relationship between correctional officers and residents can be described as one of structured conflict.[7]

Structured conflict is a term that highlights the tensions between prison staff members and residents that arise out of the correctional setting. In one sense, the prison is one large society in which the worlds of residents and staff bump up against one another. In another sense, however, the two groups keep their distance from each other—a distance imposed by both formal and informal rules. Conflict arises because staff members have control over the lives of residents, and residents often have little say over important aspects of their own lives. The conflict is structured because it occurs within the confines of an organized institution and because, to some extent, it follows the rules—formal and informal—that govern institutional life.

Both worlds—resident and staff—have their own cultures. Those cultures are generally called *subcultures* to indicate that both are contained within and surrounded by a larger culture. One writer has defined **subculture** as the beliefs, values, behavior, and material objects shared by a particular group of people within a larger society.[8] That is the definition we will use. The subcultures of residents and correctional officers exist simultaneously in any prison institution. The beliefs, values, and behavior that make up the **staff subculture** differ greatly from those of the resident subculture. Additionally, staff members possess material objects of control, such as keys, vehicles, weapons, and security systems.

Kauffman has identified a distinct correctional officer subculture within prisons.[9] Those beliefs, values, and behaviors set correctional officers apart

Staff Subculture

What are some important aspects of the code followed by most correctional staff members? Why does the code exist?

structured conflict

The tensions between prison staff members and residents that arise out of the correctional setting.

subculture

The beliefs, values, behavior, and material objects shared by a particular group of people within a larger society.

staff subculture

The beliefs, values, and behavior of staff. They differ greatly from those of the resident subculture.

from other prison staff and from residents. Their beliefs and values form an "officer code," which includes the following:

- Always go to the aid of an officer in distress.
- Do not "lug" (bring in for resident use) drugs or other contraband.
- Do not rat on other officers.
- Never make a fellow officer look bad in front of residents.
- Always support an officer in a dispute with a resident.
- Always support officer sanctions against residents.
- Do not be a "white hat" or a "goody two-shoes."
- Maintain officer solidarity in dealings with all outside groups.
- Show positive concern for fellow officers.

Correctional Officers' Characteristics and Pay

Many people believe that working in corrections is not financially rewarding unless an employee can rise to supervisory positions. Numbers from the Bureau of Labor Statistics, however, show otherwise. Mid-2020 average annual salaries for correctional officers (COs) in California were $81,170, and in New York they were $71,160.[10] Entry-level salaries, however, are lower, with California having a starting salary for COs of $42,000. New York's starting salary is $45,000. Some states do pay less than the two just mentioned, bringing the average annual salary of a correctional officer to around $47,920. Starting pay for a correctional officer trainee with the federal Bureau of Prisons is $44,000. That figure, however, does not include overtime pay—which can be considerable. Many correctional officers earn six figure incomes because of the number of hours they work. Recently, for example, the top-earning correctional officer in Pennsylvania made $232,562—putting him among the 30 highest paid state employees for that year! Similarly, all states reward academic credentials, and correctional officers with associates, bachelor's and master's degrees earn more than those without. The pay for correctional officers varies depending on things like location, years of experience, level of education, and whether the correctional employer is state, federal, local, or private. Supervisory personnel can earn far more than line officers, while those who receive overtime pay can more than double their base salary. When considering a job in corrections, it is important to realize that most employers offer significant benefits, including medical, dental, and vision insurance; sick and vacation leave; paid holidays; recruitment incentives; retention pay differentials; bilingual pay; education incentives; physical fitness incentive pay; and various employer/employee-funded retirement plans.

In terms of ethnicity, the American Correctional Association (ACA) says that most correctional personnel at state and local levels are white males. Two-thirds of female custodial and administrative staff members are white. Thirty-two percent of corrections personnel at the state level are members of minority groups.[11] Of these, most are Black. See Exhibit 9–2 for the demographic characteristics of staff members working for the federal Bureau of Prisons.

Although Blacks comprise only 12.6 percent of the U.S. population, they account for 21 percent of the correctional workforce. Hispanics are underrepresented (accounting for 16.3 percent of the country's population and just 12 percent of the correctional workforce), as are other minorities (5 percent of the population, 4 percent of correctional staff). Whites, who comprise 66% of the population are slightly underrepresented.

The federal BOP employs approximately 35,921 personnel in its prisons, and about 28 percent of them are women.[12] About 21 percent of correctional

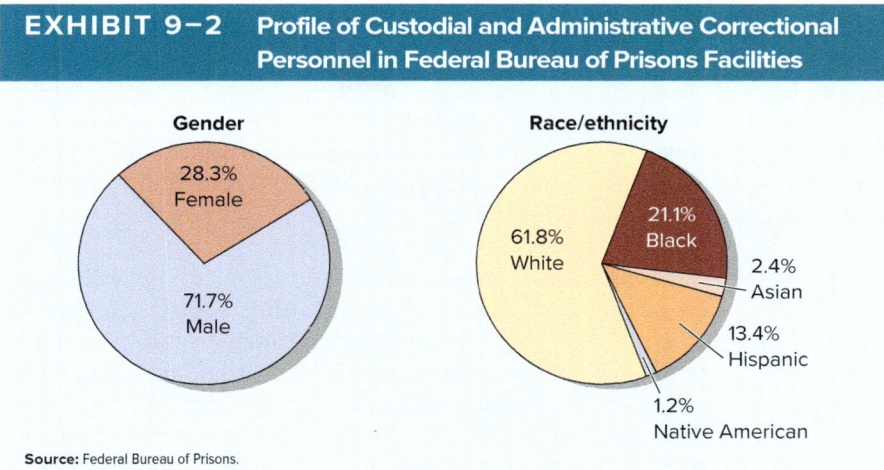

EXHIBIT 9–2 Profile of Custodial and Administrative Correctional Personnel in Federal Bureau of Prisons Facilities

Gender

28.3% Female

71.7% Male

Race/ethnicity

61.8% White

21.1% Black

2.4% Asian

13.4% Hispanic

1.2% Native American

Source: Federal Bureau of Prisons.

staff members in federal institutions are Black. In juvenile facilities, females make up slightly more than 42 percent of the correctional workforce.

The ACA also says that approximately 13 percent of all correctional staff positions are supervisory (i.e., above the level of sergeant). Females hold 16 percent of all supervisory positions but fewer positions at the level of warden or superintendent.[13]

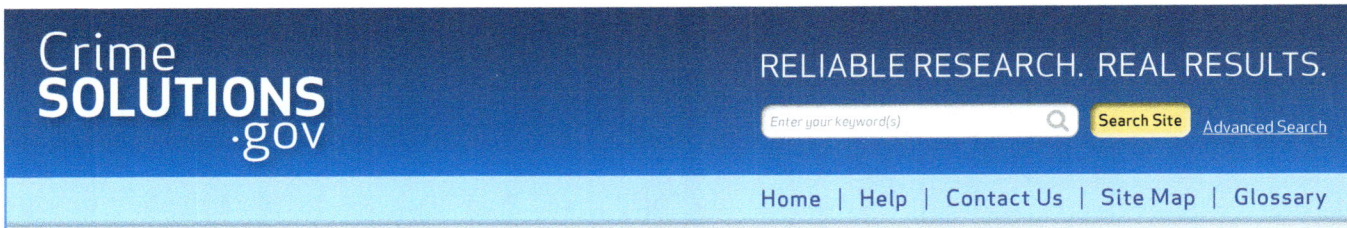

Crime SOLUTIONS.gov

RELIABLE RESEARCH. REAL RESULTS.

Enter your keyword(s)   Search Site   Advanced Search

Home | Help | Contact Us | Site Map | Glossary

EVIDENCE-BASED CORRECTIONS

Staff Training Aimed at Reducing Rearrest (STARR)

Staff Training Aimed at Reducing Rearrest (STARR) is a training program for federal community supervision officers providing direct service to clients (i.e., offenders under supervision). Its overall goal is to reduce clients' failure rates and recidivism by training officers to use behaviorally based skills during client interactions. STARR teaches officers about a structured cognitive–behavioral supervision approach that seeks to address dynamic risk factors of clients by improving one-on-one officer–client interactions.

The STARR curriculum was developed with the risk–need–responsivity (RNR) model, which has three core principles:

1. *Risk principle:* The level of services should be matched to the level of the offender. High-risk offenders should receive more intensive services; low-risk offenders should receive minimal services.

2. *Need principle:* Target criminogenic needs with services—that is, target those factors that are associated with criminal behavior. Such factors might include substance abuse, pro-criminal attitudes, criminal associates, and the like. Do not target other, non-criminogenic factors (such as emotional distress, self-esteem issues) unless they act as a barrier to changing criminogenic factors.

3. *Responsivity principle:* The ability and learning style of the offender should determine the style and mode of intervention. Research has shown the general effectiveness of using social learning and cognitive–behavioral style interventions.

Officers in STARR participate in 3½-day classroom training sessions. The training sessions include a discussion of the theory and research supporting the development of the STARR curriculum (including the RNR model), a demonstration of each skill, exercises, and an opportunity for officers to practice each skill and receive feedback. The program is rated "promising."

Source: Adapted from the Bureau of Justice Statistics.

correctional officer personalities

The distinctive personal characteristics of correctional officers, including behavioral, emotional, and social traits.

Correctional Officer Personalities

The staff subculture contributes to the development of **correctional officer personalities.** Those personalities reflect the personal characteristics of the officers as well as their modes of adaptation to their jobs and institutional conditions, the requirements of staff subculture, and institutional expectations. We will next explore the common personality types that have been identified among correctional officers.[14]

The Dictator The dictator likes to give orders and seems to enjoy the feeling of power that comes from ordering around other people who are in prison. Correctional officers with dictator personalities are often strongly disliked by residents and may face special difficulties if taken hostage during a prison uprising. Some dictator officers cross the line by personally degrading residents under their charge through the use of profanity or racist language or by displays of religious and ethnic intolerance. Certain aspects of the dictator personality may lead to illicit and illegal activities by forcing residents to provide sexual and other favors.

The Friend The correctional officer who tries to befriend residents is often a quiet, retiring, but kind individual who believes that close friendships with residents will make it easier to control them and the work environment. Residents, however, usually try to capitalize on friendships by asking for special treatment, contraband, and the like.

The Merchant Merchant-personality correctional officers (also called *rogue officers* or *rotten apples*) set themselves up as commodity providers to the resident population. If a resident needs something not easily obtained in prison, the merchant will usually procure it—at a cost. Often such behavior is a violation of institutional rules, and it can lead to serious violations of the law as the merchant correctional officer smuggles contraband into the institution for the "right price." We will discuss correctional officer corruption in more detail later in this chapter.

The Turnkey Turnkey officers do little beyond the basic requirements of their position. A turnkey usually interacts little with other officers and does the minimum necessary to get through the workday. Unmotivated and bored, the turnkey may be seeking other employment. Some turnkey officers have become disillusioned with their jobs. Others are close to retirement.

The Climber The correctional officer who is a climber is set on advancement. He or she may want to be warden or superintendent one day and is probably seeking rapid promotion. Climbers are often diligent officers who perform their jobs well and respect the corrections profession. Climbers who look down on other officers, however, or attempt to look good by making coworkers look bad, can cause many problems within the institution.

The Reformer The reformer constantly finds problems with the way the institution is run or with existing policies and rules. He or she always seems to know better than anyone else and frequently complains about working conditions or supervisors.

The Do-Gooder The do-gooder is another type of reformer—one with a personal agenda. A devoutly religious do-gooder may try to convert other correctional officers and residents to his or her faith. Other do-gooders actively seek to counsel residents, using personal techniques and philosophies that are not integrated into the prison's official treatment program.

Although the personalities described here may be exaggerated, their variety suggests that correctional officer personalities result from many influences, including:

- general life experiences;
- biological propensities;
- upbringing;
- staff subculture;
- working conditions; and
- institutional expectations and rules.

Tom Hanks as a correctional officer in The Green Mile. This chapter describes a variety of correctional officer personality types. Which do you think is the most common? The least?

Ralph Nelson/KRT/Newscom

Problem Correctional Officers

One type of correctional officer that we did not mention in the preceding discussion is the **problem correctional officer**. Problem officers are those who have an unusually large number of grievances filed against them or those with whom other staff have difficulty working.

In one New York civil case, the state agreed to pay a resident $300,000 after a corrections officer squeezed the testicles of a person who was confined so hard that he lost control of his bowels.[15] The judge in that case said afterward that there were "red flags all over the employment history" of the correctional officer and noted that the officer had been accused of abuse by numerous residents over the years.

Corrections technology helps in the identification of problem officers through the use of computer-based performance management systems (PMIS).[16] According to the National Institute of Justice, a PMIS performs three critical functions. First, it identifies any officers who may be at risk for poor performance or misconduct. Second, it provides the opportunity for counseling, training, or other interventions to assist the officer. Finally, it monitors the officers' behavior and performance to gauge the success of the interventions.

A PMIS uses mathematical algorithms to identify at-risk officers. These algorithms consider a number of possible indicators of performance or conduct issues, such as absenteeism, complaints from the public, excessive use-of-force incident reports, and number of citations written. They may also assess discriminatory or racially biased language used by an officer and can even go so far as to count the number of swear words an officer uses in interaction with residents (although that kind of data is not easily available today, it will be in the near future, especially when most officers are equipped with cameras or other recording devices while on duty). Research suggests, however, that the factors monitored and the thresholds for flagging problem officers vary among departments.

A National Institute of Justice (NIJ) study identified the following potential indicators for problem corrections staff. They are applicable even when a PMIS system is not in use:

- Internal affairs incidents related to dishonesty, unprovoked physical violence, use of sick leave, lack of promptness, or carelessness
- The rate at which an officer receives human resource performance reviews identifying a need for improvement
- The rate at which an officer completes trainings

problem correctional officer

A correctional officer who exhibits problem behavior, as indicated by high rates of resident complaints and use-of-force incidents, and by other evidence.

Although law enforcement agencies use early intervention systems widely, corrections agencies have yet to do so. In any case, it is thought that the earlier an at-risk officer is identified, the better the chance of a successful outcome.

CO9-3   CORRECTIONAL OFFICER JOB ASSIGNMENTS

Seven different correctional officer roles or job assignments have been identified.[17] They are classified by their location within the institution, the duties required, and the nature of the contact with residents. The seven types are as follows:

block officers

Those responsible for supervising residents in housing areas.

1. **Block officers** are responsible for supervising residents in housing areas. Housing areas include dormitories, cell blocks, modular living units, and even tents in some overcrowded prisons. Safety and security are the primary concerns of block officers. Conducting counts, ensuring the orderly movement of residents, inspecting personal property, overseeing resident activity, and searching residents are all part of the block officer's job. Block officers also lock and unlock cells and handle problems that arise within the living area. Block officers are greatly outnumbered by the residents they supervise. Hence, if disturbances occur, block officers usually withdraw quickly to defensible positions within the institution.

work detail supervisors

Those who oversee the work of individual residents and work crews.

2. **Work detail supervisors** oversee the work of individual residents and work crews assigned to jobs within the institution or outside it. Jobs assigned to residents may include laundry, kitchen, and farm duties as well as yard work and building maintenance. Work detail supervisors must also keep track of supplies and tools and maintain inventories of materials. Prison buildings are sometimes constructed almost exclusively with the use of resident labor—creating the need for large work details comprised of residents. On such large projects, supervising officers usually work in conjunction with outside contractors.

industrial shop and school officers

Those who ensure efficient use of training and educational resources within the prison.

3. **Industrial shop and school officers** work to ensure efficient use of training and educational resources within the prison. Such resources include workshops, schools, classroom facilities, and associated equipment and tools. These officers oversee residents who are learning trades, such as welding, woodworking, or automobile mechanics or who are attending academic classes. Ensuring that students are present and on time for classes to begin, protecting the school and vocational instructors, and securing the tools and facilities used in instruction are all part of the job of these officers. The officers work with civilian instructors, teachers, and counselors.

yard officers

Those who supervise residents in the prison yard.

4. **Yard officers** supervise residents in the prison yard. They also oversee residents who are (a) moving from place to place, (b) eating, or (c) involved in recreational activities. Like other officers, yard officers are primarily concerned with security and order maintenance.

administrative officers

Those who control keys and weapons and sometimes oversee visitation.

5. **Administrative officers** are assigned to staff activities within the institution's management center. They control keys and weapons. Some administrative officers oversee visitation. As a result, they have more contact with the public than other officers do. Many administrative officers have little, if any, contact with residents.

perimeter security officers (also *wall post officers*)

Those assigned to security (or gun) towers, wall posts, and perimeter patrols. These officers are charged with preventing escapes and detecting and preventing intrusions. *Also known as* wall post officers.

6. **Perimeter security officers** (also called **wall post officers**) are assigned to security (or gun) towers, wall posts, and perimeter patrols. They are charged with preventing escapes and detecting and preventing intrusions (such as packages of drugs or weapons thrown over fences or walls from outside). Perimeter security can become a routine job because it involves little interaction with other officers or residents

and because relatively few escape attempts occur. Newer institutions depend more heavily on technological innovations to maintain secure perimeters, requiring fewer officers for day-long perimeter observation.

7. **Relief officers** are experienced correctional officers who know and can perform almost any custody role in the institution. They are used to temporarily replace officers who are sick or on vacation or to meet staffing shortages.

relief officers

Experienced correctional officers who know and can perform almost any custody role within the institution, used to temporarily replace officers who are sick or on vacation or to meet staffing shortages.

CORRECTIONAL STAFF ISSUES

CO9-4

Gender and Staffing

On a pleasant Sunday morning a few years ago, a high-custody female resident at the Chillicothe (Missouri) Correctional Center was sitting in a dormitory, drinking her morning coffee. Having a good time, surrounded by friends, the woman began laughing. Soon, however, the laughter turned to choking. Unable to breathe, she turned blue. Correctional officer Lisa Albin rushed to her side and found her hanging onto her bed, unable to speak. Albin remained calm as she applied the Heimlich maneuver to the resident. After three attempts, the trapped coffee cleared the resident's windpipe and she began breathing again. After the incident, the resident wrote a letter of thanks to the superintendent, saying, "If it had not been for Mrs. Albin I could have very well died in that room. She literally saved my life and I will be forever grateful to her and for the training she received."[18]

Literature and films almost invariably portray correctional officers as "tobacco-chewin', reflective sunglasses-wearin', chain-gang-runnin', good ol' boys."[19] Today's officer generally defies this stereotype, and women working in corrections have helped erode this otherwise persistent myth. See Exhibit 9–3 for the ACA policy on women in corrections.

Like most women working in male-dominated professions, female correctional officers face special problems and barriers—many of which are rooted in sexism. Prisons are nontraditional workplaces for women. As a consequence, female correctional officers—especially those working in men's prisons—often find themselves in an unusual situation. As one author explains it, "On the one hand, to be female is to be different, an outsider. On the

---

EXHIBIT 9–3   American Correctional Association

Public Correctional Policy on Employment of Women in Corrections

The American Correctional Association affirms the value of all employees and supports equal employment opportunities for women in adult and juvenile correctional agencies. To encourage the employment of women in corrections, correctional agencies shall:

- ensure that recruitment, selection, and promotional opportunities for women are open and fair;
- provide women employees with equal opportunities and assignments that provide career development and promotional opportunities;
- provide all levels of staff with appropriate training on developing mutually respectful, effective, and cooperative working relationships between male and female correctional personnel;
- provide all levels of staff with appropriate education, training, and support in cross-gender supervision; and
- conduct regular monitoring and evaluation of affirmative action practices and be proactive in achieving corrective actions.

Source: Reprinted with permission of the American Correctional Association, Alexandria, VA.

Tracy Andrus

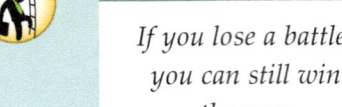

Dr. Tracy Andrus

Director, Lee P. Brown Criminal Justice Institute
Wiley College—Home of the Great Debaters
Marshall, Texas

If you lose a battle, you can still win the war.

Tracy Andrus understands the criminal justice system not only from a theoretical perspective but from practical experience. He was sentenced to 57 years in the Louisiana and Texas Correctional Institutions for felony theft, check kiting, and theft of services. He ended up serving a total of three years because of the concurrent nature of the sentences he received.

Once released from prison in 1994, Andrus entered college at Louisiana College where he earned his associate's and bachelor's degrees in criminal justice. He then enrolled in the University of Louisiana Monroe in 2000 and graduated with his master's degree in criminology. In 1995, Andrus became the first African-American in the United States to earn a Ph.D. in juvenile justice. He went on to earn his doctorate from Prairie View A&M University.

Recently, he has achieved the rank of associate professor at Wiley College in Texas and has served as the director of the Lee P. Brown Criminal Justice Institute at the college for over 17 years. Wiley College offers associate's and bachelor's degrees in three Louisiana Penal Institutions including Davis Wade Correctional Center where Andrus was previously incarcerated for three years.

Andrus is a published author of seven books including the top seller *From Prisoner to PhD, My Eleven Year Journey.* Andrus was elected as president of the Southwestern Association of Criminal Justice Regional Conference in 2008-2009.

Andrus is very active in the community where he serves as the executive director of the Tracy Andrus Foundation, to assist returning citizens and the homeless with food, shelter, and vocational services. He also offers diversion and reentry services to juveniles and adult offenders. Andrus is the pastor of Edwards Chapel BC in Marshall, Texas, and is married to Dr. Sonya Burnett-Andrus who is a principal with the Marshall Independent School District. Andrus is the father of Desmond and Tracy Jr. Andrus' only daughter Heather Dawn Mouton was killed in 2018 by her husband in Crowley, Louisiana. Through protest and advocacy, the state of Louisiana passed Heather's Law in 2019. Governor John Bel Edwards Signed SB36 into law, which became known as Heather's Law.

Andrus' advice to anyone is that even if you lose a battle, you can still win the war. Don't ever give up! There are a lot of people who will help you if you show them that you are trying to improve your condition. He preaches that education is the great equalizer. "Education," he says, "levels the playing field regardless of what side of the tracks you are born on!"

other hand, female guards have much in common with and are sympathetic to their male peers as a result of their shared job experience."[20]

According to studies, female correctional officers typically say that they perform their job with a less aggressive style than men.[21] This difference in style seems due mostly to differences in life experiences and to physical limitations associated with women's size and strength. Life experiences prepare many women for helping roles rather than aggressive ones. As a consequence, women are more likely to rely heavily on verbal skills and intuition. Female correctional officers use communication rather than threats or force to gain resident cooperation. They tend to talk out problems. Studies have also found that female correctional officers rely more heavily than male correctional officers on established disciplinary rules when problems arise. Male staff members, on the other hand, have been found to be more likely to bully or threaten residents to resolve problems.

According to research, 55 percent of female officers indicate that their primary reason for taking a job in corrections is an interest in human service work or in rehabilitation.[22] In striking contrast, only 20 percent of male officers give this as their primary reason for working in corrections.

Perhaps as a result of such attitudes, gender makes a dramatic difference in the number of assaults on correctional officers. One national survey of maximum-security prisons in 48 states, the District of Columbia, and the federal BOP showed that female officers were assaulted only about one-fourth as often as male officers.[23]

A female CO watches residents playing a game of checkers. Female correctional officers competently perform day-to-day custodial tasks. Are there any areas of a male prison that female correctional officers should be barred from supervising?

Thinkstock Images/Getty Images

Although female correctional officers may take a different approach to their work, the skills they use complement those of male staff members. As one expert writes, "Women may humanize the workplace in small ways by establishing less aggressive relationships with inmates."[24]

Studies also show that male officers, by and large, believe that female officers competently perform day-to-day custodial tasks. Most male staff members are "pro-woman," meaning that they applaud women in the corrections profession.[25] Some male correctional officers express concerns about women's ability to provide adequate backup in a crisis, however. It is important to note that the need to use force in prison is relatively rare and that officers generally do not respond to dangerous situations alone. Nonetheless, some female correctional officers report that in emergencies, some male officers adopt a protective, chivalrous attitude toward them. Women generally report that they resent such "special treatment" because it makes them feel more like a liability than an asset in an emergency.

Another issue concerning women in today's workplace is personal and sexual harassment. Studies show that few female correctional officers personally experience unwanted touching or other forms of sexual harassment. The forms of harassment women most commonly experience are physical (nonsexual) assaults, threats, unfounded graphic sexual rumors about them, and demeaning remarks from peers, residents, and supervisors.[26]

In short, women working as correctional officers in a prison or jail setting have the same duties and responsibilities as their male counterparts, including maintaining security and order, supervising residents, and enforcing rules and regulations. However, the acceptance of women in these roles by male officers has historically been a subject of concern. In some cases, female officers may face gender-based discrimination or harassment from male coworkers. Nevertheless, over time, as the number of women in correctional positions has increased, the acceptance of female officers by male officers has generally improved, and many departments now have policies and programs in place to address gender-based discrimination and harassment. However, it is important to note that challenges may still persist in some work environments and the acceptance of female officers by male colleagues may vary depending on the specific workplace culture and individual attitudes.

Stress

In all occupational categories, employers estimate that more than 25 percent of all reported sick time is due to stress.[27] **Stress**—tension in a person's body

stress

Tension in a person's body or mind, resulting from physical, chemical, or emotional factors.

or mind resulting from physical, chemical, or emotional factors—appears to be more commonplace in prison work than in many other jobs.

Correctional officers frequently deny that they are under stress, fearing that admitting to feelings of stress might be interpreted unfavorably. One correctional lieutenant, an 11-year veteran, reported repeatedly observing new correctional employees succumbing to the effects of stress by becoming depressed or turning to alcohol for relief. Although she wanted to intervene, she said she "couldn't" because "no one in law enforcement is allowed to show any emotion or signs of weakness."[28]

This kind of attitude is consistent with prevailing correctional culture, which has traditionally supported dysfunctional behaviors to the point where they have become self-sustaining and self-reinforcing. New recruits are especially vulnerable through unhealthy indoctrination into the negative aspects of correctional staff culture as they assimilate into the affected workplace.[29]

In misguided attempts to deal with the effects of stress, many COs resort to self-medication or other tactics to deal with feelings that they may not readily admit, even to themselves. Unfortunately, such ineffective methods do not alleviate the pressure and may instead make it worse.

Stress among correctional officers has a number of sources. Feelings of powerlessness, meaninglessness, social isolation, and self-estrangement all contribute to stress. Some authors have identified job alienation as the major source of stress among COs.[30] Correctional officers rarely participate in setting the rules they work under and the policies they enforce; as a result, they may feel alienated from those policies and rules and from those who create them.

One recent report found that the most significant stressors faced by correctional officers include (in order of declining significance):[31]

- job dangerousness,
- job pay,
- conflict with supervisors,
- conflict with peers,
- role conflict,
- job satisfaction, and
- pressure due to gender.

Exhibit 9–4 shows this list graphically.

Symptoms of stress can be psychological, behavioral, or physical. Psychological symptoms of stress include anxiety, irritability, mood swings, sadness or depression, low self-esteem, emotional withdrawal, and hypersensitivity (to others and to what others say). Behavioral symptoms of stress include an inability to make decisions, increased interpersonal conflict, blocked creativity and judgment, poor memory, lowered productivity, and difficulty concentrating. The physical symptoms of stress include insomnia, headaches, backaches, gastrointestinal disturbances, fatigue, high blood pressure, and frequent illnesses.

Poorer job performance and exhaustion are the results of stress. When stress reaches an unbearable level, burnout can occur. Burnout, a severe reaction to stress, is "a state of physical and emotional depletion that results from the conditions of one's occupation."[32]

Studies have shown that a person's ability to tolerate stress depends on the frequency, severity, and types of stressors confronted.[33] Stress tolerance also depends on a number of personal aspects, including past experiences, personal values and attitudes, sense of control, personality, residual stress level, and general state of health.

EXHIBIT 9–4 Major Sources of Correctional Officer Stress

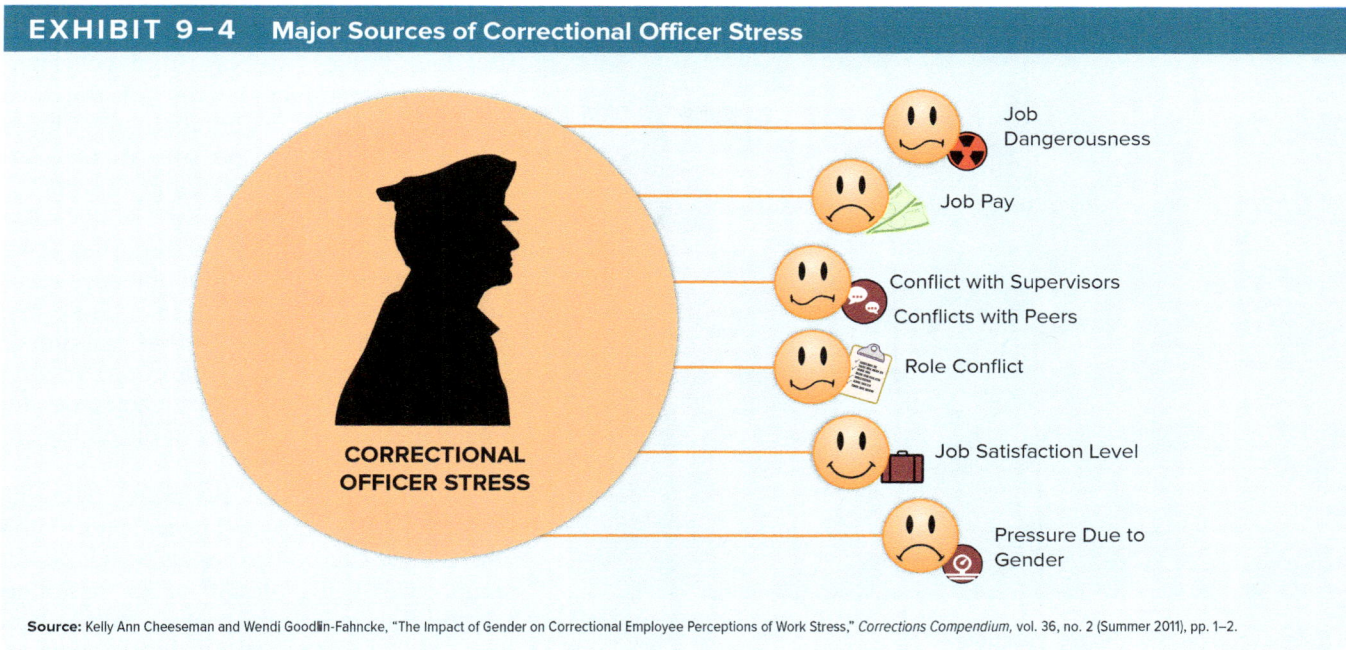

Source: Kelly Ann Cheeseman and Wendi Goodlin-Fahncke, "The Impact of Gender on Correctional Employee Perceptions of Work Stress," *Corrections Compendium*, vol. 36, no. 2 (Summer 2011), pp. 1–2.

Authorities suggest a number of techniques for avoiding or reducing job stress. Among them are the following:[34]

1. Communicate openly. Tell people how you feel.
2. Learn not to harbor resentment, not to gossip, and to complain less often.
3. Learn to feel confident in your skills, your values and beliefs, and yourself.
4. Develop a support system. Close friends, pets, social activities, and a happy extended family can all help alleviate stress.
5. Be a good and conscientious worker, but don't become a workaholic.
6. Learn to manage your time, and do not procrastinate.
7. Make it a habit to get a good night's sleep.
8. Exercise regularly.
9. Watch your diet. Avoid excessive fat, sugars, salt, red meat, and caffeine.
10. Learn some relaxation exercises such as self-affirmation, mental imaging, deep breathing, stretching, massage, or yoga.
11. Try to have fun. Laughter can combat stress quite effectively.
12. Spend time cultivating self-understanding. Analyze your feelings and your problems—and recognize your accomplishments.
13. Set goals and make plans. Both bring order and direction to your life.

One especially effective strategy for coping with job stress is to develop clear and favorable role definitions. According to J. T. Dignam and colleagues:

Officers who have more opportunities for receiving assistance and goal clarification from supervisors and coworkers [are] less likely to experience role ambiguity than those for whom such support is not available or. Further, the risk of burnout or other deleterious consequences of occupational stress may be reduced for those who are 'insulated' by social support.[35]

Stress may be an unhappy outcome of the correctional officer's job. How does on-the-job stress arise in the correctional officer's role? How might it be reduced?

Sue Ogrocki/AP Images

Similarly, another group of researchers found that "support from colleagues or supervisors may be one of the most important factors ameliorating stress in the workplace."[36] The same researchers also found that when correctional officers felt "rewarding companionship" with fellow correctional officers, they reported fewer stressful events (even when objective measures showed an actual rise in such events). Most researchers agree that candidates need more extensive and thorough training to prepare them for the psychological and sociological consequences of becoming correctional officers.

Finally, the Desert Waters Correctional Outreach (DWCO—an organization that focuses on the occupational, personal, and family well-being of staff of all disciplines within the corrections profession) has been working with the National Institute of Corrections to develop solutions to workplace stress. DWCO notes that successful "interventions involve gradually 'deprogramming' and 'reprogramming' staff's thinking, beliefs, and behaviors in response to challenging corrections workplace experiences, situations, and circumstances." DWCO says that "through an agency's efforts, current and future staff can learn to adapt successfully to occupational stressors" but notes that improvements in workplace culture can be "a slow and laborious—but deeply critical process."[37]

Staff Safety

Staff safety is a major stressor for individual correctional officers and a primary management concern for correctional administrators. Safety planning must include consideration of the following elements (adapted, in part, from studies of staff safety needs in both juvenile[38] and adult[39] institutions):

- a functionally designed physical plant that limits resident movement and incorporates technologically advanced security systems, perimeter barriers, and rooms, doors, and locks;
- a behavior management system that establishes clear guidelines for acceptable behavior, reward systems to reinforce expected behavior, and disciplinary systems to discourage unacceptable behavior;
- appropriate staff and resident relationships (in particular, staff must be aware of and prepared to respond to the dangers posed by prison gangs);
- policies and procedures, published in a manual and distributed to staff and supervisors, that support consistent implementation of rules and regulations and prevent the risk of staff letdowns resulting from excessive routine;
- shift scheduling that ensures a mutually supportive balance of senior and junior staff because a sound mix of age and experience facilitates the achievement of resident control while providing opportunities for on-the-job development of junior officers by senior officers;
- effective supervision at every level;

- comprehensive staff training that ensures all correctional officers and their supervisors know every rule, regulation, policy, and procedure that affects their particular job (if, as the saying goes, knowledge is power, such training is key to empowering the staff to maintain a controlled, safe environment); and
- development of and training for a sound action plan that addresses all contingencies.

In addition to advocating thorough planning as just outlined, Stewart and Brown[40] urge continuing research to identify what works, what doesn't work, and emerging trends in staff safety. In particular, they recommend development of a safety program tailored to the needs of correctional officers nationwide. It should be modeled, they suggest, on safety programs designed for police officers, probation officers, and other officers in law enforcement.

Job Satisfaction

High levels of stress reduce the satisfaction correctional officers get from their jobs. In a sad indictment of the corrections field, one study found that correctional officers were significantly different from most other groups of correctional employees. "They showed the lowest levels of organizational commitment, possessed the highest levels of skepticism about organizational change, were the least positive about careers in corrections and the rehabilitation of offenders, possessed the lowest levels of job satisfaction, were the least involved in their jobs, and were described as having the poorest work habits and overall job performance."[41] In a separate study, correctional supervisors and managers were found to have much higher levels of job satisfaction and professionalism.[42]

One reason for the difference in job satisfaction between supervisory personnel and those on the front lines of corrections work is that correctional officers often feel alienated from policymaking.[43] As one writer puts it, "When looking at the atmosphere and environment of a state or federal prison, it would seem obvious what correction personnel like least about working there: surveys of personnel who resign or quit show that their biggest problems are with supervisory personnel rather than inmates."[44]

Correctional officers' job satisfaction appears to be tied to the amount of influence they feel they have over administrative decisions and policies. Officers who feel they have some control over the institution and over their jobs seem much more satisfied than officers who believe they have no control. Hence, it appears that correctional officers' job satisfaction can be greatly enhanced by caring administrators who involve the officers in policymaking.

For some correctional officers, the perception that their profession suffers a generally poor public image[45] further reduces their job satisfaction. Compared to local and state police officers and agents of the various federal law enforcement organizations, correctional officers may be viewed as the "poor relations" of the law enforcement family. As one researcher wrote, "Most people do not know of a child who says, I want to be a correctional officer when I grow up."[46]

Media portrayals of correctional officers exacerbate the situation. Movies and television often depict COs as lowly qualified "guards" (considered a derogatory title; "guards work at Macy's and banks")[47] whose primary function seems to be abusing residents. Correctional officers "believe they are seen as brutes, only a shade better than the people behind bars."[48] Consequently, COs have a difficult time overcoming these images as they attempt

A correctional recruit participates in self-defense training. Training can enhance professionalism. As more and more prison staff develop a professional perspective, the structural organization of prisons and interactions among staff and people held in prison may significantly change. What kinds of training may help correctional officers adjust to a changing environment?

The News Tribune, Bruce Kellman/AP Photo

to convey the significance and professional demands of their positions to civic leaders and the public.[49]

There is evidence, however, that job satisfaction among correctional officers is rising. The rise may be partly due to increasing awareness of what correctional officers find most important in the work environment. Recent studies have identified the most important determinants of job satisfaction among correctional officers as (1) working conditions, (2) the level of work-related stress, (3) the quality of working relationships with fellow officers, and (4) length of service.[50]

In one early study, treatment-oriented correctional staff reported far higher levels of job satisfaction than did custody-oriented staff.[51] The study was of survey data collected from 428 Arizona correctional service officers (CSOs) and 118 correctional program officers (CPOs). Job satisfaction was significantly greater among the human-services-oriented CPOs than among the traditional-custody-oriented CSOs. The findings suggest that additional attention should be given to enhancing and enriching the duties of correctional officers, extending their control over and involvement in residents' activities, and redefining their roles more as service workers than as control agents.

Determinants of job satisfaction appear to differ for male and female correctional officers. One study found that the quality of working relationships with other officers, the amount of stress experienced at work, the length of service as a correctional officer, and educational level were all positively related to job satisfaction for males.[52] Women officers, on the other hand, appeared to place more emphasis on the quality of working relationships with all other correctional officers (not just the ones with whom they worked) and tended to be happier in prisons at lower security levels. Other studies have related higher job satisfaction among white female officers to the officers' positive evaluation of the quality of supervision. In other words, white female correctional officers tend to be happier in prisons that they believe are well run.[53]

Professionalism

A common difference between a professional and a nonprofessional is that a professional learns every aspect of the job whereas a nonprofessional avoids the learning process and often considers it a waste of time. Professionals seek to prevent mistakes at all costs, but if they occur, the professional does not let them slide; nonprofessionals tend to ignore or hide them. A professional tries to be great, whereas a nonprofessional just tries to get by at what he or she does.

Professionalism is commitment to a set of agreed-upon values aimed at improving the organization while maintaining the highest standards of excellence and dissemination of knowledge.[54] In addition to having knowledge and skills, professionals must present humanistic qualities: selflessness, responsibility and accountability, leadership, excellence, integrity, honesty, empathy, and respect for coworkers and residents.

Professional correctional organizations that operate at the national level, such as the ACA (discussed in Chapter 1), have qualified and well trained employees, well run professional development departments, and well developed standards of conduct. Such organizations provide the support needed for operating agencies and individual correctional facilities to achieve fairness in handling residents and correctional personnel while documenting and addressing issues that may arise in resident and employee conduct. These organizations also help to define common sets of values that establish the tone and climate for day-to-day operations in correctional facilities.

The vision provided by professional organizations helps build confidence that employees will be professional and will have integrity, respect, the ability to engage in teamwork, the motivation for continued learning, and commitment to the profession.

According to William Sondervan, former commissioner of the Maryland Division of Corrections and previous director of professional development for the ACA, professionalism in corrections is vitally important to the integrity, safety, and security of correctional agencies and institutions.[55] Corrections professionalism, says Sondervan, requires that any correctional organization establish or clarify the following three elements:

- **Purpose.** The reason for an organization's existence
- **Mission.** What is done to support the organization's purpose
- **Vision.** The planned future direction of the organization

Together, says Sondervan, purpose, mission, and vision provide a roadmap for the development of professionalism within an organization.

Exhibit 9–5 depicts the formal mission, vision, and goals of the federal Bureau of Prisons, and Exhibit 9–6 lists the values and beliefs that support the Bureau's mission and vision statements.

Although the development of an appropriate mission statement is vital at the organizational level, the development of a sense of personal ethics is crucial to daily on-the-job success.

Officer Corruption

CO9-5

A few years ago, 24 members of the violent Black Guerrilla Family prison gang were arrested in Maryland following a seven-month-long investigation into the smuggling of contraband into Baltimore-area prisons.[56] Four of those arrested were state correctional officers. Using bribes, threats, and promised favors, leaders of the gang were able to coerce the officers into smuggling

purpose

The reason for an organization's existence.

mission

That which is done to support an organization's purpose.

vision

The planned future direction of an organization.

EXHIBIT 9−5   Federal Bureau of Prisons Mission and Vision Statement

Mission

It is the mission of the Federal Bureau of Prisons to protect society by confining offenders in the controlled environments of prisons and community-based facilities that are safe, humane, cost-efficient, and appropriately secure, and that provide work and other self-improvement opportunities to assist offenders in becoming law-abiding citizens.

Vision

The Federal Bureau of Prisons, judged by any standard, is widely and consistently regarded as a model of outstanding public administration, and as the best value provider of efficient, safe and humane correctional services and programs in America.

This vision will be realized when the public is safe; prisons are safe; inmates successfully reenter society; we are a good steward of public funds; our staff are exceptional; our staff are treated equally; our staff are respected; our staff are safe; our staff have superior judgment; [and] our staff are happy.

Source: Federal Bureau of Prisons.

EXHIBIT 9–6   Federal Bureau of Prisons Core Values

Accountability	We are responsible and transparent to the public, ourselves, and to those in our care and custody by the standards we establish, the actions we take, and the duties we perform.
Integrity	We are true to our ethical standards in all circumstances.
Respect	We foster an inclusive environment where the viewpoints of employees, the public, and those in our care and custody are considered and valued.
Compassion	We will strive to understand one another's circumstances and act with empathy and by we, we mean each other as colleagues and corrections professionals and also compassion for those in our care and custody.
Correctional Excellence	We demonstrate leadership in our corrections field through our practices and values.

Source: https://www.bop.gov/about/agency/agency_pillars.jsp

contraband to imprisoned associates and extorting money from other residents. The favored prisoners feasted on salmon, shrimp, and other delicacies while smoking expensive cigars and drinking premium vodka. Using smuggled cell phones, they were able to arrange for attacks on witnesses and rival gang members living outside the prison. One of the corrupt officers, a woman who played a central role in facilitating the gang's illegal activities, is reported to have provided sexual favors for people in prison in return for money.

In another incident that apparently stemmed from correctional officer corruption, 76-year-old convicted mass murderer Charles Manson was caught with a mobile phone in his prison cell at California's Corcoran State Prison in February 2011. It was the second time in two years that officers had confiscated a phone from Manson during a cell search. Manson, who was serving a life sentence, was convicted in the 1969 murders of seven people, including pregnant actress Sharon Tate. Manson died in a prison hospital in 2017.

The California Department of Corrections and Rehabilitation says that almost 5,000 illicit cell phones were discovered during cell searches in state prisons between January 1, 2019, and June 30, 2022.[57] According to experts, prison employees are the main source of smuggled phones that end up in the hands of residents. One California state inspector general's report detailed the story of how a single CO made $150,000 a year smuggling phones to people in prison. Although his activities were eventually discovered and he was fired, he was not criminally prosecuted because it is not against the law in California to take cell phones into prisons—even though it is a violation of prison rules for people in prison to possess them.

Joyce Mitchell, 51, a former supervisor in the tailor shop at Clinton Correctional Facility in Dannemora, N.Y., stands alongside her attorney before a judge in the Plattsburgh City Court in New York in 2015. Mitchell was sentenced to more than two years in prison for helping two convicted murderers escape the facility where she worked. How can the manipulation of correctional workers by people who are incarcerated be prevented?

G.N. Miller-Pool/Getty Images

Other forms of correctional officer corruption and job malfeasance include the misuse of confidential information, drinking and abusing drugs while on duty, sleeping on duty, unnecessary roughness or brutality against residents, racism, and filing false disciplinary reports on residents. A small number of sadistic people may even be attracted to working in corrections because they think it will provide them the opportunity to physically abuse others. Preemployment personality inventories, background checks, and face-to-face preemployment interviews are all crucial in preventing such people from obtaining positions of authority in correctional facilities.

Contributing to the problem of corruption among correctional staff is low pay—especially in some jurisdictions. "If someone is desperate to make ends meet and someone offers them $2,100 to smuggle in a cell phone, it's a hell of a temptation," says Brian Olsen, executive director of a Texas labor union that represents Texas correctional officers.[58]

While all examples used in this chapter come from state correctional agencies, a look at statistics seems to show that corruption among federal correctional personnel is relatively rare. A recent Congressional report by the U.S. Department of Justice's (DOJ) Office of the Inspector General (OIG), for example, found only 238 likely cases of criminal misconduct by BOP employees.[59] Given that the number of persons employed by the BOP is approximately 39,000, BOP misconduct levels appear to be among the lowest in government.

Fraternization with Clients

On September 28, 2015, former prison employee Joyce E. Mitchell was sentenced to spend at least two years and four months in prison.[60] Mitchell, 51, had made national headlines following the escape of two convicted killers from a maximum-security prison in northern New York. The escape had been facilitated by Mitchell, who had apparently become romantically involved with one of the men and used her position as a supervisor in the prison's tailor shop to provide the escapees with hacksaws, replacement blades, and screwdrivers. In her defense, Mitchell argued that the convicts had exploited her emotional instability and that she feared for the safety of her family if she didn't help the men escape.

Some psychologists point out that "inmates have lived a lifestyle of lying, and using people and manipulating others is a way of life" for them. Not only do many people in prison attempt to manipulate staff members, but they also work at controlling and deceiving fellow residents. While it is important for correctional officers to always be aware of the potential for client manipulation, it helps to know that some manipulation schemes are short term (like the effort to move a contraband cell phone from one imprisoned individual to another), and some are long term (like the escape that involved Joyce Mitchell) and take a long time to come to completion.[61]

One long-time correctional officer says that COs must always remember that "no correctional client is your friend," and offers these guidelines to help others falling prey to manipulation by the residents:[62]

1. Be an active part of your correctional team.
2. Be suspicious, question, and verify every client action or request.
3. Follow institutional rules, policies, and procedures.
4. Monitor and document client remarks, gestures, and actions.
5. Communicate openly and often with supervisors and other employees.
6. Know your job and get further education.
7. Learn to say "No."

CO9-6 # THE IMPACT OF TERRORISM ON CORRECTIONS

Prisoner Radicalization

Why are some residents more likely to be recruited by terrorists than others?

In 2022, 45-year-old Kevin James (aka Ahmed Binyamin Alasiri) was sentenced to 188 months in federal prison for the sale of four pounds of methamphetamine while he was on supervised release.[63] James had been released from prison only three years earlier, after serving 16 years for terrorism. Earlier, in 2007, he plead guilty to conspiracy to wage war against the United States and had also been accused of plotting terrorist attacks on Jewish and military targets throughout California. Among those targets were Los Angeles International Airport, the Israeli Consulate, and Army recruiting centers. Jame's 2022 sentence included 24 months for violating the terms of his release, but that time was to run currently with the 188-month term.

Those who investigated James, who was no stranger to prison, found that he had formed an Islamic terrorist group in California's Tehachapi Prison back in 1997. While serving a 10-year sentence for robbery in the 1990s, James joined the Nation of Islam—a traditional American Islamic faith. Soon, however, he became engaged with a fringe group of Sunni Muslims at Tehachapi. The group, known as *Jamiyyat Ui Islam Is Saheeh* (the Assembly of Authentic Islam, or JIS), operates today throughout prisons in California where it is known as a radical Islamist prison gang, or STG. JIS advocates attacks on enemies of the Islamic faith, the U.S. government, Jews, "infidels," and supporters of Israel.

Eventually, James took control of JIS and began distributing a handwritten manifesto known as the JIS Protocol in which he justified the killing of infidels. Following transfer to the maximum-security California State Prison in Sacramento, James recruited more residents to join JIS and used those soon-to-be paroled to recruit additional members outside of prison. Using smuggled letters and phone calls, James communicated his plans for terrorist attacks to recruits on the outside.

Mark Hamm, a criminal justice professor who studied the case of Kevin James, notes that "prisoner radicalization grows in the secretive underground of inmate subcultures through prison gangs and extremist interpretations of religious doctrines that inspire ideologies of intolerance, hatred and violence."[64] Hamm also learned that "prisoners are radicalized through a process of one-on-one proselytizing by charismatic leaders." Especially vulnerable, says Hamm, are people in prison who no longer have contact with their families and are angry and embittered by their circumstances. "I discovered," says Hamm, "that charismatic leadership was more important than other commonly cited factors associated with prisoner radicalization."[65]

Because of their marginal social status, people in prison may be particularly vulnerable to recruitment by terrorist organizations. According to Chip Ellis, research and program coordinator for the National Memorial Institute for the Prevention of Terrorism: "Prisoners are a captive audience, and they usually have a diminished sense of self or a need for identity and protection. They're usually a disenchanted or disenfranchised group of people, [and] terrorists can sometimes capitalize on that situation."[66] Ellis points out that people in prison can be radicalized in a variety of ways, including exposure to extremist literature and other radical residents as well as through anti-U.S. sermons delivered during religious services.

The FBI says that al-Qaeda continues to actively recruit followers inside American correctional institutions. Islamic terrorists are keenly aware of the 9,600 Muslims held in the federal prison system and see them as potential converts. "These terrorists seek to exploit our freedom to exercise religion to their advantage by using radical forms of Islam to recruit operatives," says FBI counterterrorism chief John Pistole.[67] "Unfortunately," notes Pistole, "U.S. correctional institutions are a valuable venue for such radicalization and recruitment."

Anti-Terrorism Planning

Not only must today's prison administrators be concerned about client involvement in terrorist activities, they must also think about and plan for the impact of the terrorism event within their facilities and within the communities in which their facilities are located. Moreover, incarcerating those who have been convicted of acts of terrorism presents new challenges for correctional administrators. For example, Sheik Omar Abdel-Rahman, spiritual leader for many terrorists, including Osama bin Laden, spent more than 20 years in a U.S. federal penitentiary for conspiring to assassinate former Egyptian president Hosni Mubarak and blow up five New York City landmarks in the 1990s. Speculation that the sheik continued to motivate terrorist acts against the United States while in prison gained credibility when his attorney was sentenced to 28 months in prison in 2006 for passing illegal communications between Abdel-Rahman and an Egyptian-based terrorist organization known as the Islamic Group.[68] Abdel-Rahman died in prison in 2017. Another convicted terrorist, September 11 conspirator Zacarias Moussaoui, also known as the 20th hijacker, is serving a life sentence at the federal administrative maximum facility in Florence, Colorado. Moussaoui's fellow residents, housed on what has come to be known as Bomber's Row, include al-Qaeda shoe bomber Richard Reid; Ramzi Yousef, mastermind of the 1993 World Trade Center bombing; seven of Yousef's accomplices; Ahmed Ressam, who was arrested at the Canadian border with explosives he intended to use to bomb Los Angeles International Airport; four men convicted in the 1998 bombing of U.S. embassies in Africa; and Abdul Hakim Murad, convicted in a 1995 al-Qaeda plan to bomb 12 airplanes during a two-day period.

Jess Maghan, former training director for the New York City Department of Corrections and later director of the Forum for Comparative Corrections and professor of criminal justice at the University of Illinois at Chicago, points out that "the interaction of all people in a prison (staff, officers, and residents) can become important intelligence sources."[69] Moreover, says Maghan, the flow of information between residents and the outside world

A guard tower at a high-security prison. Some argue that prisons are breeding grounds of radicalization and may serve to recruit correctional clients to extremist ideologies. How can prison authorities prevent them from turning to terrorist activity upon release?

Rich Pedroncelli/AP Images

Imprisoned Muslim men at prayer in a Virginia correctional facility. Radicalized residents of any faith can represent a threat to facility security. What connection might exist between radicalized imprisoned people and criminals or terrorist groups on the outside?

Andrew Lichtenstein/Corbis/Getty Images

needs to be monitored in order to detect attack plans—especially when prisons house known terrorist leaders or group members. Covert information, says Maghan, can be passed through legal visits (where people conveying information may have no idea of its significance), sub rosa communications networks in prisons that can support communications between people in prison and the outside world, and prison transportation systems.

A few years ago, the Institute for the Study of Violent Groups at Sam Houston State University charged that Wahhabism—the most radical form of Islam—was being spread in American prisons by clerics approved by the Islamic Society of North America (ISNA). ISNA is one of two organizations that the federal BOP uses to select prison chaplains to serve residents in its facilities.[70] "Proselytizing in prisons," said the institute, "can produce new recruits with American citizenship." An example might be Chicago thug Jose Padilla, aka Abdulla al-Mujahir, who converted to Islam after exposure to Wahhabism while serving time in a Florida jail. Authorities claim Padilla intended to contaminate a U.S. city with a radiological dirty bomb. In 2007, Padilla was convicted of federal terrorism charges. Similarly, convicted shoe bomber Richard Reid converted to radical Islam while in an English prison before planning his attack on an American Airlines flight from Paris to Miami.[71]

A few years after the attacks of 9/11, the Office of the Inspector General of the U.S. Department of Justice released a review of the practices used by the federal BOP in selecting Muslim clergy to minister to people held in the bureau's facilities. The report concluded that the primary threat of radicalization came not from chaplains, contractors, or volunteers but from people already in prison. According to the report, "Inmates from foreign countries politicize Islam and radicalize inmates, who in turn radicalize more inmates when they transfer to other prisons."[72] The report also identified a form of Islam unique to the prison environment called Prison Islam.[73] The report said that Prison Islam is a form of Islam that is used by gangs and radical residents to further unlawful goals. It adapts itself easily to prison values and promotes the interests of the incarcerated. Prison Islam was found to be especially common in institutions where religious services are led by lay *Mullahs* (spiritual leaders, who are often residents)—a practice made necessary by a lack of Muslim chaplains. The report recommended that "the BOP can and should improve its process for selecting, screening, and supervising Muslim religious services providers. We recommend," said the report, that "the BOP take steps to examine all chaplains', religious contractors', and religious volunteers' doctrinal beliefs to screen out anyone who poses a threat to security." Echoing those sentiments is Mark Hamm, who says that the most significant thing that prison administrators can do to undercut terrorist recruitment in prison is to hire chaplains who have been properly vetted. "Without them," says Hamm, "radicalized prisoners are free to operate on their own, independent of religious authority to ensure moderation and tolerance."[74]

When concern about prison terrorism was at its highest, the U.S. Justice Department's OIG released another report—this one critical of BOP mail monitoring procedures, saying that "the threat remains that terrorist and other high-risk residents can use mail and verbal communications to conduct terrorist or criminal activities while incarcerated." The report was based on findings that three convicted terrorists had been able to send 90 letters to Islamic extremists in the Middle East, praising Osama bin Laden. The report noted the fact that the BOP did not have the needed number of translators proficient in Arabic who were able to read resident mail and said that budget restrictions did not allow for the reading of all incoming and outgoing mail.[75]

The threat of a terrorist act being carried out by people held in a prison or jail can be an important consideration in facility planning and management. Of particular concern is the possibility of bioterrorism. A concentrated population such as exists within a prison or jail would be highly susceptible to rapid transmission of the ill effects from such an attack.[76]

Significant recommendations for addressing the terrorist threat within correctional institutions come from Y. N. Baykan, a management specialist with the Maryland Division of Correction. Baykan says that no successful strategies are being used today to control radical Islamist influences in American prisons and suggests the following:[77]

Indonesian terrorist Imam Samudra in prison in Bali, as he was awaiting execution. Samudra was convicted of masterminding terrorist bombings that killed 202 people in 2002 and was sentenced to death by firing squad. While imprisoned, Samudra wrote a jailhouse manifesto on the funding of terrorism through cyberfraud. He was executed in 2008. How might incarcerated terrorists constitute a threat to the facilities in which they are housed? To the rest of society?
ALI KURDI/AP Images

- Prison administrators must realize that the threat of transnational terrorism in American facilities is real.
- Radical Islamic groups should be seen as sophisticated social networks rather than gangs.
- Prison authorities must evaluate existing policies and strategies, looking closely at the roles and backgrounds of chaplains and volunteers and the rules governing religious conversions.
- Meetings of radicals should be closely monitored, as should incoming propaganda.
- Prison staff should be taught to understand political Islam and should use information-management solutions that involve cutting-edge collection, storage, and analysis of data.
- Prison authorities must follow what is happening in other countries and learn from it.
- Threat information should be shared by all stakeholders, including state and federal systems and other law enforcement agencies.

Finally, it should be noted that most Western European countries prioritize changing the mindset of terrorists held in prison and frequently use imams and family members to redirect their lives. Joby Warrick, the Pulitzer Prize–winning author of *Black Flags: The Rise of ISIS*, says that American prisons, unlike their European counterparts, have failed to implement successful intervention programs that could change the thinking of potential terrorists among correctional populations. Because of this failure, Warrick notes, imprisoned U.S. Jihadists could be a "ticking time bomb."[78]

REVIEW AND APPLICATIONS

SUMMARY

1 There is a hierarchy of staff positions from warden (or superintendent) at the top, down to correctional officer and correctional officer trainee. A typical correctional staff includes (1) administrative staff, (2) clerical personnel, (3) program staff, (4) custodial staff, (5) service and maintenance staff, and (6) volunteers.

2 The types of power available to correctional officers are legitimate power, coercive power, reward power, expert power, and referent power. Correctional officer personality types discussed in this chapter are (1) the dictator, (2) the friend, (3) the merchant, (4) the turnkey, (5) the climber, (6) the reformer, and (7) the do-gooder.

3 The seven correctional officer assignments are (1) block officers, (2) work detail supervisors, (3) industrial shop and school officers, (4) yard officers, (5) administrative officers, (6) perimeter security officers (also called *wall post officers*), and (7) relief officers.

4 The five significant correctional staff issues discussed in this chapter are (1) gender-related concerns, (2) correctional officer stress, (3) staff safety, (4) job satisfaction among those working in corrections, and (5) professionalism.

5 Some correctional officers become corrupt, and serious corruption can threaten the security of the institution. Greed, the desire for sexual gratification, and a lack of professionalism can all contribute to corruption among corrections personnel. Problem correctional officers are those who have an unusually large number of resident grievances filed against them or those with whom other staff have difficulty working.

6 Today's prison administrators and corrections personnel must be vigilant against the threat of terrorism and must guard against terrorist activities from within the institution and from outside.

KEY TERMS

roles, p. 237

staff roles, p. 237

custodial staff, p. 238

program staff, p. 238

gain time, p. 240

structured conflict, p. 241

subculture, p. 241

staff subculture, p. 241

correctional officer personalities, p. 244

problem correctional officer, p. 245

block officers, p. 246

work detail supervisors, p. 246

industrial shop and school officers, p. 246

yard officers, p. 246

administrative officers, p. 246

perimeter security officers, p. 246

relief officers, p. 247

stress, p. 249

purpose, p. 255

mission, p. 255

vision, p. 255

QUESTIONS FOR REVIEW

1 What staff roles does the hierarchy of a typical correctional institution include?

2 According to John Hepburn, what are five bases of the power that correctional officers use to gain compliance?

3 What are the seven correctional officer job assignments?

4 What are the five significant correctional staff issues discussed in this chapter?

5 How might correctional officers become corrupt? What kinds of activities might corrupt officers engage in?

6 Briefly explain the impact that terrorism can have on prisons and prison administration.

THINKING CRITICALLY ABOUT CORRECTIONS

Prison Sex Abuse as a Tool of Control?

James Gilligan, M.D., contends that rape in prisons is "an intrinsic and universal part of the punishments that our government metes out to those whom it labels as 'criminal.'"[79] In essence, Gilligan suggests, prison administrators passively but knowingly employ rape as a management tool to control the resident population.

Dr. Gilligan bases his charge on three contentions:

First, the relevant legal authorities, from judges to prosecutors who send people to prison, to the prison officials who administer them, are all aware of the existence, the reality, and the near-universality of rape in the prisons. Indeed, this is one reason that many conscientious judges are extremely reluctant to send anyone to prison except when they feel compelled to, either by the violence of the crime or by laws mandating prison sentences.

Second, the conditions that stimulate such rapes (the enforced deprivation of other sources of self-esteem, respect, power, and sexual gratification) are consciously and deliberately imposed upon the prison population by the legal authorities.

Third, all these authorities tacitly and knowingly tolerate this form of sexual violence, passively delegating to the dominant and most violent residents the power and authority to deliver this form of punishment to the more submissive and nonviolent ones, so that the rapists in this situation are acting as the vicarious enforcers of a form of punishment that the legal system does not itself enforce formally or directly.

Given that rape is universally acknowledged as a crime, Dr. Gilligan's charge is tantamount to an accusation of criminal conspiracy of monumental proportions.

1. Do you believe there is merit to Gilligan's claims?
2. If so, how would you propose addressing this issue?

The Staff Subculture

The staff culture is generally instilled in correctional officer trainees by more experienced officers and by work experiences. Socialization into the staff subculture begins on the first day of academy training or the first day of work (whichever comes first). One of the most important beliefs of the staff subculture is that officers should support one another.

Some people argue that the staff subculture is dangerous because it can sustain improper and even illegal behavior while forcing correctional officers to keep to themselves what they know about such behavior. Others, however, suggest that the staff subculture is a positive element in the correctional world. It is important to correctional officer morale, they claim. They also suggest that it "fills the gaps" in formal training by establishing informal rules to guide staff behavior and decision making in difficult situations. The staff subculture can provide informal "workarounds" when the formal requirements of a correctional officer's position seem unrealistic.

1. Do you think the staff subculture contributes to or detracts from meeting the goals of institutional corrections? Why?
2. Do you think the staff subculture benefits or harms the lives and working environment of correctional officers? Explain.
3. What functions of the staff subculture can you identify? Rate each of those functions as positive or negative for its role in meeting the goals of institutional corrections.

ON-THE-JOB DECISION MAKING

Use of Force

You are an experienced correctional officer assigned to yard duty. As you patrol the prison yard, watching clients milling around and talking, a fellow officer named Renée approaches you. Renée was hired only a week ago, and she has gained a reputation for being inquisitive—asking experienced correctional officers about prison work. Renée walks up and says, "You know, I'm wondering what I should do. Yesterday I saw an officer push an inmate around because the guy didn't do what he asked. I don't know if the person didn't hear what was being said, or if he was just ignoring the officer." Renée looks at the ground. "What am I supposed to do in a situation

like that? Should I have said something right then? Should I talk to the officer privately? Should I suggest to the officer that maybe the person didn't hear him? He knows we aren't supposed to use force on people unless it's really necessary. If I see him do this kind of thing again, should I report him?" Looking up, Renée says, "I know we're supposed to support each other in here. But what would you do?" How would you respond to Renée's questions?

Former CO/Now a Resident

For about four years, Alex Kaminsky was one of your fellow correctional officers at the McClellan Correctional Facility.

During your service together, you developed a friendship close enough to include social occasions outside the job, and your wives became good friends.

Two years ago, Kaminsky was convicted of dealing controlled substances to residents and received a 12- to 20-year sentence. Upon your recent transfer to the Brownley Correctional Facility, you discover that Kaminsky is one of the people incarcerated there. He resides in one of the cell blocks that falls in your area of responsibility and works on the maintenance crew that you supervise.

1. Should you seek assignment to another area of the prison or seek to have Kaminsky transferred out, to prevent the necessity of having contact with him? Explain.

2. If Kaminsky approaches you, should you permit the reestablishment of a relationship that might (or might not) prove beneficial to his rehabilitation?

ENDNOTES

1. Jen Fifield, "Stateline: Many States Face Dire Shortage of Prison Guards," March 1, 2016, https://stateline.org/2016/03/01/many-states-face-dire-shortage-of-prison-guards (accessed October 19, 2023).

2. Ibid.

3. See Sylvia G. McCollum, "Excellence or Mediocrity: Training Correctional Officers and Administrators," *The Keeper's Voice,* vol. 17, no. 4 (Fall 1996).

4. Joe Russo, *Workforce Issues in Corrections* (Washington, D.C.: National Institute of Justice, 2019), https://nij.ojp.gov/topics/articles/workforce-issues-corrections (accessed March 15, 2023).

5. John Hepburn, "The Exercise of Power in Coercive Organizations: A Study of Prison Guards," *Criminology,* vol. 23, no. 1 (1985), pp. 145–164.

6. Gresham Sykes, *The Society of Captives* (Princeton, NJ: Princeton University Press, 1958).

7. See, for example, "Prisons: Correctional Officers," Encyclopedia.com, https://www.encyclopedia.com/law/legal-and-political-magazines/prisons-correctional-officers (accessed July 4, 2023).

8. Adapted from John J. Macionis, *Society: The Basics,* 12th ed. (Hoboken, NJ: Prentice Hall, 2012).

9. Kelsey Kauffman, *Prison Officers and Their World* (Cambridge, MA: Harvard University Press, 1988), pp. 85–86.

10. "Highest Paying States for Correctional Officers and Jailers," *USA Wage,* https://www.usawage.com/high-pay/states-correctional_officers_and_jailers.php (accessed March 5, 2023).

11. American Correctional Association, *Vital Statistics in Corrections* (Lanham, MD: ACA, 2000), p. 143; Laura M. Maruschak and Emily D. Buehler, *Census of State and Federal Correctional Facilities, 2019* (Washington, DC: Bureau of Justice Statistics, 2021).

12. Federal Bureau of Prisons, "Staff Ethnicity/Race," https://www.bop.gov/about/statistics/statistics_staff_ethnicity_race.jsp (accessed March 15, 2023).

13. ACA, *Vital Statistics in Corrections.*

14. Adapted from Frank Schmalleger, *Criminal Justice Today: An Introductory Text for the 21st Century,* 17th ed. (Upper Saddle River, NJ: Prentice Hall, 2024).

15. Tom Robbins, "New York State Prisons Take Steps to Track Complaints About Guards," *The New York Times,* December 20, 2015.

16. Jack Harne, "Identifying At-risk Officers: Can It Be Done in Corrections?," *NIJ Journal,* No. 278 (February 2017), from which some of the information in this section is taken.

17. Lucien X. Lombardo, *Guards Imprisoned: Correctional Officers at Work,* 2nd ed. (Cincinnati, OH: Anderson, 1989).

18. Adapted from Dora B. Schriro, "Women in Prison: Keeping the Peace," *The Keeper's Voice,* vol. 16, no. 2 (Spring 1995).

19. Ibid.

20. M. I. Cadwaladr, "Women Working in a Men's Jail," *FORUM,* vol. 6, no. 1 (1994).

21. Ibid.

22. N. C. Jurik and J. Halemba, "Gender, Working Conditions, and the Job Satisfaction of Women in a Non-Traditional Occupation: Female Correctional Officers in Men's Prisons," *Sociological Quarterly,* vol. 25 (1984), pp. 551–566.

23. Joseph R. Rowan, "Who Is Safer in Male Maximum Security Prisons?" *The Keeper's Voice,* vol. 17, no. 3 (Summer 1996).

24. Ibid.

25. See, for example, R. Ricciardelli and L. McKendy, "Gender and Prison Work: The Experience of Female Provincial Correctional Officers in Canada," *The Prison Journal,* vol. 100, no. 5 (2020), pp. 617–639. https://doi.org/10.1177/0032885520956394

26. Ricciardelli and McKendy, op. cit.

27. Public Service Commission (of Canada), "Stress and Executive Burnout," *FORUM,* vol. 4, no. 1. Some of the material in this section is taken from this work.

28. Shannon Black, "Correctional Employee Stress & Strain," *Corrections Today,* October 2001, p. 99.

29. Caterina Spinaris and Mike Denhof, "Countering Staff Stress—Why and How," *National Jail Exchange*, 2015.

30. Lombardo, *Guards Imprisoned.*

31. Kelly Ann Cheeseman and Wendi Goodin-Fahncke, "The Impact of Gender on Correctional Employee Perceptions of Work Stress," *Corrections Compendium*, vol. 36, no. 2 (Summer 2011), pp. 1–2.

32. Public Service Commission, "Stress and Executive Burnout."

33. For an excellent overview of the literature on correctional officer stress, see Tammy L. Castle and Jamie S. Martin, "Occupational Hazard: Predictors of Stress Among Jail Correctional Officers," *American Journal of Criminal Justice*, vol. 31, no. 1 (Fall 2006), pp. 65–80.

34. "Not Stressed Enough?," *FORUM*, vol. 4, no. 1 (1992). Adapted from C. C. W. Hines and W. C. Wilson, "A No-Nonsense Guide to Being Stressed," *Management Solutions*, October 1986, pp. 27–29.

35. J. T. Dignam, M. Barrera, and S. G. West, "Occupational Stress, Social Support, and Burnout Among Correctional Officers," *American Journal of Community Psychology*, vol. 14, no. 2 (1986), pp. 177–193.

36. M. C. W. Peeters, B. P. Buunk, and W. B. Schaufeli, "Social Interactions and Feelings of Inferiority Among Correctional Officers: A Daily Event-Recording Approach," *Journal of Applied Social Psychology*, vol. 25, no. 12 (1995), pp. 1073–1089.

37. Spinaris and Denhof, "Countering Staff Stress—Why and How."

38. Jessie W. Doyle, "6 Elements That Form a Context for Staff Safety," *Corrections Today*, October 2001, pp. 101–104.

39. Terry L. Stewart and Donald W. Brown, "Focusing on Correctional Staff Safety," *Corrections Today*, October 2001, pp. 90–93.

40. Ibid.

41. David Robinson, Frank Porporino, and Linda Simourd, "Do Different Occupational Groups Vary on Attitudes and Work Adjustment in Corrections?" *Federal Probation*, vol. 60, no. 3 (1996), pp. 45–53.

42. Jennifer C. Buden, Alicia G. Dugan, Sara Namazi, Tania B. Huedo-Medina, Martin G. Cherniack, and Pouran D. Faghri, "Work Characteristics as Predictors of Correctional Supervisors' Health Outcomes," *Journal of Occupational and Environmental Medicine*, vol. 58, no. 9 (September 2016), pp. e325–e334.

43. Lombardo, *Guards Imprisoned.*

44. Martinez, "Corrections Officer."

45. Thomas Gillan, "The Correctional Officer: One of Law Enforcement's Toughest Positions," *Corrections Today*, October 2001, p. 113.

46. Black, "Correctional Employee Stress & Strain," p. 99.

47. Andrew Metz, "Life on the Inside: The Jailers," in Tara Gray (ed.), *Exploring Corrections* (Boston: Allyn & Bacon, 2002), p. 65.

48. Ibid. p. 64.

49. Black, "Correctional Employee Stress & Strain," p. 99.

50. Jennifer C. Buden, et al., op. cit.

51. John R. Hepburn and Paul E. Knepper, "Correctional Officers as Human Services Workers: The Effect on Job Satisfaction," *Justice Quarterly*, vol. 10, no. 2 (1993), pp. 315–337.

52. Stephen Walters, "Gender, Job Satisfaction, and Correctional Officers: A Comparative Analysis," *The Justice Professional*, vol. 7, no. 2 (1993), pp. 23–33.

53. Dana M. Britton, "Perceptions of the Work Environment Among Correctional Officers: Do Race and Sex Matter?" *Criminology*, vol. 35, no. 1 (1997), pp. 85–105.

54. Adapted from William Sondervan, "Professionalism in Corrections," in Frank Schmalleger and John Smykla (eds.), *Corrections in the Twenty-First Century*, 5th ed. (New York: McGraw-Hill, 2011), p. 572.

55. Ibid.

56. Justin Fenton, "Indictments Reveal Prison Crime World," *Baltimore Sun*, April 18, 2009.

57. California Department of Corrections and Rehabilitation, "CDCR's Contraband Interdiction Efforts," https://www.cdcr.ca.gov/contraband-interdiction (accessed March 15, 2023).

58. Mike Ward, "Low Pay May Make Prison Guards Ripe for Smugglers," *American Statesman*, October 24, 2008.

59. U.S. Department of Justice, Office of the Inspector General, *Semiannual Report to Congress: April 1, 2008–September 30, 2008* (Washington, DC: USGPO, 2008).

60. Marc Santora, "Joyce Mitchell, Ex-Prison Employee, Is Sentenced," *The New York Times*, September 28, 2015; Gary F. Cornelius, "Avoiding Inmate Manipulation," *Corrections.com*, February 14, 2011, http://www.correctionsone.com/correctional-psychology/articles/3328579-Avoiding-inmate-manipulation (accessed March 30, 2016).

61. Ibid.

62. Tracy Barnhart, "Inmate Manipulations," *Corrections.com*, June 21, 2009, http://www.corrections.com/tracy_barnhart/?p=298 (accessed March 30, 2016).

63. United States Attorney's Office for the Central District of California, "Convicted Terrorist Sentenced to Over 15 Years in Federal Prison for Selling Pounds of Methamphetamine While on Supervised Release," March 28, 2022, https://www.justice.gov/usao-cdca/pr/convicted-terrorist-sentenced-over-15-years-federal-prison-selling-pounds (accessed April 15, 2023).

64. Mark S. Hamm, "Prisoner Radicalization: Assessing the Threat in U.S. Correctional Institutions," *NIJ Journal* (No. 261), p. 17.

65. Ibid., p. 18.

66. Quoted in Meghan Mandeville, "Information Sharing Becomes Crucial to Battling Terrorism Behind Bars," *Corrections.com*, December 8, 2003, http://database.corrections.com/news/results2.asp?ID_8988 (accessed August 1, 2005).

67. "FBI: Al-Qaida Recruiting in U.S. Prisons," *United Press International Wire Service,* January 7, 2004, http://database.corrections.com/news/results2.asp?ID_9148 (accessed August 1, 2005).

68. "Lawyer Sentenced to 28 Months in Prison on Terrorism Charge," *Court TV News,* October 16, 2006, www.courttv.com/news/2006/1016/cynne_Stewart_ap.html.

69. Jess Maghan, *Intelligence-Led Penology: Management of Crime Information Obtained from Incarcerated Persons,* paper presented at the Investigation of Crime World Conference, 2001, p. 6.

70. Ibid., p. 18.

71. Office of the Inspector General, *A Review of the Federal Bureau of Prisons' Selection of Muslim Religious Services Providers* (Washington, DC: U.S. Department of Justice, 2004).

72. Ibid. p. 8.

73. Ibid.

74. Mark S. Hamm, "Terrorist Recruitment in American Correctional Institutions: An Exploratory Study of Non-Traditional Faith Groups," nonpublished paper, December 2007.

75. U.S. Department of Justice, Office of the Inspector General, *The Federal Bureau of Prisons' Monitoring of Mail for High-Risk Inmates* (Washington, DC: U.S. Government Printing Office, 2006).

76. Keith Martin, "Corrections Prepares for Terrorism," *Corrections Connection News Network,* January 21, 2002, www.corrections.com (accessed July 10, 2005).

77. Y. N. Baykan, "The Emergence of Sunni Islam in America's Prisons," *Corrections Today,* February 2007, pp. 49–51.

78. Quoted in Nancy Bilyeau, "Imprisoned U.S. Jihadists Called a 'Ticking Time Bomb' by U.S. Expert," *The Crime Report,* October 16, 2018, https://thecrimereport.org/2018/10/16/imprisoned-u-s-jihadists-called-a-ticking-time-bomb-by-isis-expert (accessed March 10, 2019).

79. James Gilligan, *Violence: Reflections on a National Epidemic* (New York: Vintage Books, 1997), p. 165.

THE CLIENT WORLD

Living Behind Bars

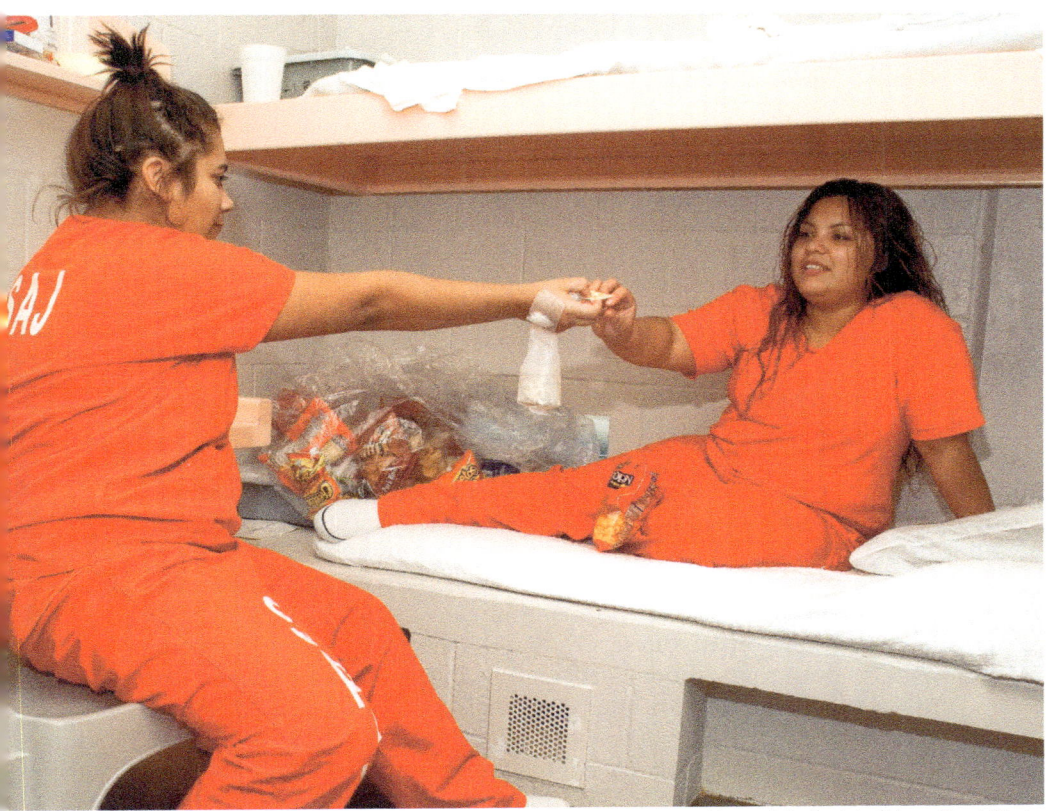

Marmaduke St. John/Alamy Stock Photo

CHAPTER OBJECTIVES

After completing this chapter you should be able to do the following:

1 Explain what total institutions are and describe the subcultures they contain.

2 Know what is meant by the *prison code,* and be able to list some elements of it.

3 Explain what is meant by *prison argot.*

4 List some common roles that men who are incarcerated assume.

5 Describe some major differences between women's and men's prisons.

6 Describe some of the known characteristics of women in prison.

7 Explain how the social structure in women's prisons differs from that in men's prisons.

8 Describe the impact that COVID-19 has had on state and federal prisons.

In prison, those things withheld from and denied to the prisoner become precisely what he wants most of all.

—Eldridge Cleaver, African American author and activist

New York Governor Kathy Hochul, shown shortly before announcing her state's change in the official terminology used to refer to prison inmates. Do you agree that the change is a good one? Why or why not?

Ben Von Klemperer/Shutterstock

In 2022, New York Governor Kathy Hochul announced an official change in vocabulary when referring to people in prison. In the future, Hochul said, imprisoned people would be called "incarcerated individuals" instead of "inmates" or "prisoners." New York State Senator Gustavo Rivera, who sponsored the bill mandating the change, said that "for too long, we as a society have thought of incarcerated individuals as less than people." The change in wording, he said, would humanize the justice system and help it to focus on rehabilitation rather than punishment. The governor added that it would also "reduce harmful stigma against incarcerated people."[1]

This chapter will examine prison life, prison subculture, and the prison experience in general by looking first at men in prison and then at imprisoned women.

TOTAL INSTITUTIONS

As we have already seen, most of the people who are in state prisons are biological males and people of color. They are relatively young and have been incarcerated for a violent offense. A recent Bureau of Justice Statistics (BJS) study examined social, economic, and other characteristics of people in state prisons nationwide.[2] Highlights of that study are shown in Exhibit 10–1.

Prisons and other total institutions are small, self-contained societies with their own social structures, norms, and rules. Although not entirely isolated, people in prison are physically, emotionally, and socially restricted from anything more than minor participation in the surrounding society. As a consequence, they develop their own distinctive lifestyles, roles, and behavioral norms.

In his now-classic work *Asylums,* Erving Goffman used the phrase **total institution** to describe a place where the same people work, eat, sleep, and engage in recreation together day after day.[3] Life within total institutions is closely planned by those in control, and activities are strictly scheduled. Prisons, concentration camps, mental hospitals, and seminaries are all total institutions, said Goffman. They share many of the same characteristics—even though they exist for different purposes and house different kinds of populations. His words were echoed years later by Hans Toch, who noted that "prisons are 24-hour-a-day, year-in-and-year-out environments in which people are sequestered with little outside contact."[4]

Goffman also identified a number of modes of adaptation to prison life by which people who are incarcerated attempt to adjust to the conditions around them. Some people, said Goffman, *convert* to life within institutions, taking on the staff's view of themselves and of institutional society. Others *withdraw.* Still others make attempts at *colonization*—meaning that they strike a balance between values and habits brought from home and those dictated by the social environment of the prison. Finally, some people who are experiencing incarceration *rebel*, rejecting the demands of their

total institution

A place where the same people work, play, eat, sleep, and recreate together on a continuous basis. The term was developed by the sociologist Erving Goffman to describe prisons and other facilities.

EXHIBIT 10−1   **National Profile of People in State and Federal Prisons**

38%
had a high school diploma or its equivalent (state)

59%
had never married (state)

35%
had lived with both parents most of the time while growing up (state)

8%
military veteran (state and federal)

33%
self-identifying as black (state and federal)

96%
self-identified as cisgender (state and federal)

48%
imprisoned for a drug offense (federal)

75%
were U.S. citizens (federal)

14.5%
unhoused in the year prior to arrest (state)

30%
had been incarcerated five or more time prior to current incarceration (state and federal)

56%
incarcerated for a violent crime (state)

48%
serving time for a drug offense (federal)

Source: E. Ann Carson, Prisoners in 2020 (Washington, DC: Bureau of Justice Statistics, 2021); National Prisoner Statistics Program, https://bjs.ojp.gov/data-collection/national-prisoner-statistics-nps-program (accessed October 20, 2023) and Jennifer C. Karberg, "Drug Use and Dependence, State and Federal Prisoners, 2004" (Washington, DC: Bureau of Justice Statistics, 2006).

surroundings and often ending up in trouble with authorities. As Victoria R. Derosia points out in her book *Living Inside Prison Walls,* some people:

> will make it through incarceration relatively unscathed and move on to a better life as a rehabilitated (or habilitated) citizen, while others will repeatedly fail at life outside prison. Offenders will successfully or poorly adjust to prison because of, or in spite of, who they were before incarceration, who they were while in prison, what they chose to do or not to do in prison, and who they want to become once released.[5]

What Is the Prison Subculture?

prison subculture

The habits, customs, mores, values, beliefs, or superstitions of the people incarcerated in correctional institutions; also, the social world of people who are incarcerated. Also known as *resident* subculture.

prisonization

The process by which people who are incarcerated adapt to prison society; the taking on of the ways, mores, customs, and general culture of the penitentiary.

Resident subculture

What are some of the central elements of the resident code?

pains of imprisonment

Major problems that inmates face, such as loss of liberty and personal autonomy, lack of material possessions, loss of heterosexual relationships, and reduced personal security.

Although any prison has its own unique way of life or culture, it is possible to describe a general **prison subculture** that characterizes the lives of people in correctional institutions nationwide. The prison subculture (also called the *resident subculture*) can be defined as "the habits, customs, mores, values, beliefs, or superstitions of the [people] incarcerated in correctional institutions."[6]

People in prison are socialized into prison subculture through a process known as *prisonization.* The concept of **prisonization** was identified by Donald Clemmer in his classic work *The Prison Community.*[7] Clemmer defined *prisonization* as the process by which people who are incarcerated adapt to prison society, and he described it as "the taking on of the ways, mores, customs, and general culture of the penitentiary." When the process of prisonization is complete, Clemmer noted, people who are incarcerated have become "cons."

In a further study of prisonization, Stanton Wheeler examined how people in prison adapted to life at the Washington State Reformatory.[8] Wheeler found that prisonization has greater impact with the passage of time. The prisonization of incarcerated people, said Wheeler, can be described by a *U*-shaped curve. When a person first enters prison, the conventional values of the outside society still hold sway in his or her life. As time passes, however, he or she increasingly adopts the prison lifestyle. Wheeler also found that within the half year before release, most people who are incarcerated begin to demonstrate a renewed appreciation for conventional values.

In *The Society of Captives,*[9] a book that helped establish corrections as a field of study, Gresham Sykes described what he called the **pains of imprisonment.** According to Sykes, newly incarcerated people face major problems including the loss of liberty, a lack of material possessions, deprivation of goods and services, the loss of heterosexual relationships, the loss of personal autonomy, and a reduction in personal security. These deficits, Sykes noted, lead to self-doubts and reduced self-esteem. Prison society compensates for such feelings and reduces the pains of imprisonment for the prison population as a whole. It also meets the personal and social needs induced in incarcerated persons by the pains of imprisonment. In short, said Sykes, inmate society compensates for the losses caused by imprisonment, and it offers varying degrees of comfort to those who successfully adjust to it.

The resident subculture can vary from one institution to another. Variations are due to differences in the organizational structure of prisons. Maximum-security institutions, for example, are decidedly more painful for those held there because security considerations require greater restriction of freedoms and severely limit access to material items. As a result, the subcultures in maximum-security institutions may be much more rigid in their demands on people who are incarcerated than those in less secure institutions.

How Do Prison Subcultures Form?

Early students of prison subcultures, particularly Clemmer and Sykes, believed that such subcultures developed in response to the deprivations in prison life. This perspective is called **deprivation theory.** Shared deprivation gives people held in confinement a basis for solidarity.[10]

A more recent perspective is that an prison subculture does not develop in prison but is brought into prison from the outside world. Known as **importation theory,** this point of view was popularized by John Irwin and Donald R. Cressey.[11] It was further supported by the work of James Jacobs.[12] Importation theory holds that inmate society is shaped by factors outside of prison—specifically, preprison life experiences and socialization patterns. People in prison who lived violent lives on the outside tend to associate with other violent people in prison and often engage in similar behavior in prison.[13]

More realistic is the **integration model,** which acknowledges that both theories have some validity. According to the integration model, people undergo early socialization experiences. In childhood, some people develop leanings toward delinquent and criminal activity, acquiring—from peer groups, parents and other significant adults, television, movies, other mass media, and even computer and video games—values that support law-violating behavior. Those who become incarcerated are also likely to have experienced juvenile court proceedings and may have been institutionalized as juveniles. As a consequence, such people are likely to have acquired many of the values, much of the language, and the general behavioral patterns of deviant or criminal subcultures before entering adult prison.

The integration model also recognizes, however, the effects that the norms and behavioral standards of people incarcerated in a particular prison have on those who are imprisoned. If a person newly admitted to prison has already been socialized into a criminal lifestyle, the transition into inmate subculture is likely to be easy. For some people, however—especially white-collar offenders with little previous exposure to criminal subcultures—the transition can be very difficult. The language, social expectations, and norms of prison society are likely to be foreign to them.

deprivation theory

The belief that prison subcultures develop in response to the deprivations in prison life.

importation theory

The belief that prison subcultures are brought into prison from the outside world.

integration model

A combination of importation theory and deprivation theory. The belief that, in childhood, some people who are in prison have acquired, usually from peers, values that support law-violating behavior but that the norms and standards in prison also affect incarcerated individuals.

MS-13 prison gang members flash hand signs from inside of a cell. In some prisons, inmate subculture is fragmented as people in prison form competing gangs and other groups along ethnic, racial, and geographic lines. How could the differences among such groups affect the order and stability of a prison?
Jan Sochor/Alamy Stock Photo

 **THE PRISON CODE**

prison code

A set of norms and values among prison inmates. It is generally antagonistic to the official administration and rehabilitation programs of the prison.

Central to prison society is a code of behavior for all incarcerated persons. The **prison code** is a set of rules antagonistic to the official administration and rehabilitation programs.[14] Violations of the code result in sanctions imposed by people who are already in prison, ranging from ostracism to homicide. Sykes and Messinger have identified five main elements of the prison code:[15]

1. Don't interfere with the interests of other people. Never rat on a con. Don't have loose lips.
2. Don't lose your head. Don't quarrel with other people. Play it cool. Do your own time.
3. Don't exploit other people. Don't steal. Don't break your word. Pay your debts.
4. Don't whine. Be tough. Be a man.
5. Don't be a sucker. Don't trust the guards or staff. Remember that prison officials are wrong residents and are right.

 **PRISON ARGOT—THE LANGUAGE OF CONFINEMENT**

prison argot

The special language of the prison subculture.

Prison argot is the special language of the inmate subculture. *Argot* is a French word meaning "slang." Prison society has always had its own unique language illustrated by the following argot-laden paragraph:

Career Profile

Craig A. Waleed, Ed.D.

Craig A. Waleed, Ed.D.

Author, Educator, Counselor, Certified Restorative Practices Group Facilitator, Motivational Speaker, Activist, and Formerly Incarcerated Person.

Craig Waleed was incarcerated for eight years in New York State prisons beginning when he was 19. During his incarceration, Waleed earned an Associate of Arts degree in Liberal Arts from Canisius College (Buffalo, New York). Following his release from prison in 1997, Waleed continued pursuing his studies. He eventually earned a Bachelor of Science Degree in Health Sciences with a concentration in Substance Abuse Counseling and a Master of Science Degree in Mental Health Counseling from the State University of New York (SUNY) Brockport College. In 2017, Waleed completed a Doctorate of Education degree from St. John Fisher College in Rochester, New York; his dissertation was entitled *What Aspects of Emotional Intelligence Help Former Prisoners Make Decisions to Desist Crime?*

Dr. Waleed currently works with Disability Rights North Carolina, where he is the Project Manager for Unlock the Box (UTB), and the End Solitary Confinement Campaign Against Solitary Confinement. Dr. Waleed previously served as a Substance Abuse Counselor and Reentry Case Manager for post-incarcerated persons. Dr. Waleed has also engaged with student bodies on several college campuses in New York State and sat on community panels exploring carceral matters. Dr. Waleed was a guest speaker at TEDx SingSing 2020. In addition, he has created and facilitated emotional intelligence training, taught counseling and communication courses in higher education, and is the author of a 2020 autobiography entitled *Prison to Promise: A Chronicle of Healing and Transformation* and host of the podcast *Prison to Promise.*

> *To remain free after release from incarceration or any form of bondage begins with how one thinks.*

The new con, considered fresh meat by the screws and other prisoners, was sent to the cross-bar hotel to do his bit. He soon picked up the reputation through the yard grapevine as a canary-bird. While he was at the big house, the goon squad put him in the freezer for his protection. Eventually, he was released from the ice-box and ordered to make little ones out of big ones until he was released to the free world. Upon release he received $100 in gate money, vowing never to be thrown in the hole or be thought of as a stool-pigeon again.[16]

Prison argot originated partly as a form of secret communication. Gresham Sykes, however, believed that it serves primarily as "an illustrative symbol of the prison community"—or as a way for confined persons to mark themselves as outlaws and social outcasts.[17] Sykes's work brought prison argot to the attention of sociologists and criminologists. Since Sykes's time, other authors have identified a number of words, terms, and acronyms in prison argot. Some of these terms are presented in Exhibit 10–2, and while some are still found in prison language today, many of them now are only of historical interest. Interestingly, rap musicians, some of whom have spent time in prison or deal with prison-related themes, have brought prison argot to a wider audience.

SOCIAL STRUCTURE IN MEN'S PRISONS

Inmate societies, like other societies, have a hierarchy of positions. People in prison assume or are forced into specific social roles, and some people—by virtue of the roles they assume—have more status and power than others.

Early writers often classified incarcerated persons by the crimes they had committed or their criminal histories. Irwin, for example, divided prisoners into such categories as thieves (those with a culture of criminal values), convicts (time doers), square johns (people in prison who are unfamiliar with criminal subcultures), and dope fiends (drug-involved residents).[18]

Other writers have identified **prison roles**, defining them as prison lifestyles or as forms of ongoing social accommodation to prison life. Each role has a position in the pecking order, indicating its status in the prison society.

About a decade ago, Frank Schmalleger developed a typology of male prison roles. It is based on actual social roles found among people in prison, and it uses the prison argot in existence when it was created to name or describe each type. Each type can be viewed as a prison lifestyle either chosen by incarcerated persons or forced on them. Some of the types were previously identified by other writers. Although the terminology used in the typology sounds dated, the types of incarcerated persons it identifies are still characteristic of prison populations today. The 13 types are discussed in the following paragraphs.

The Real Man Real men do their own time, do not complain, and do not cause problems for other residents. They see confinement as a natural consequence of criminal activity and view time spent in prison as an unfortunate cost of doing business. Real men know the inmate code and abide by it. They are well regarded within the institution and rarely run into problems with other people. If they do, they solve their problems on their own. They never seek the help of correctional officers or the prison administration. Although they generally avoid trouble within the institution, they usually continue a life of crime once released.

The Mean Dude Some people in prison are notorious for resorting quickly to physical power. They are quick to fight and, when fighting, give no quarter. They are callous, cold, and uncaring. Mean dudes control those around them through force or the threat of force. The fear they inspire usually gives

Prison Roles

What is prison subculture, and what are some of the central elements of the prison code?

prison roles

Prison lifestyles; also, forms of ongoing social accommodation to prison life.

EXHIBIT 10−2   Historical Prison Argot: The Language of Confinement

Argot in Men's Prisons

ace duce: best friend

all day: a life sentence

back door parole: to die in prison

badge (or bull, hack, "the man," or screw): a correctional officer

ball busters: violent residents

banger (or burner, shank, sticker): a knife

billys: white men

boneyard: conjugal visiting area

booty bandit: an imprisoned sexual predator who preys on weaker residents

bug juice: antidepressant or antipsychotic medications provided by the medical staff

cantones: gang term for prisons

catch a ride: asking a friend to get you high

catch cold: to be killed

cat-J (or J-cat): a prisoner in need of psychological or psychiatric therapy or medication

cellie: cell mate

center men: residents who are close to the staff

chester: child molester

chin check: punching another resident to test him and to see if he'll fight back

chota: a correctional officer

croaker: a physician or a doctor

dancing on the blacktop: being stabbed

diaper sniper: child molester

diddler: a child molester or pedophile

dog: homeboy or friend

fag: a male resident believed to be a natural (preprison) homosexual

fish: a newly arrived resident

four-piece suit: a full set of restraints, including handcuffs, leg irons, and waist chains

gorilla: a resident who uses force to take what he wants from others

got stretched: became angry

grandma's: gang headquarters

hacks: correctional officers

hipsters: young, drug-involved residents

homeboy: a prisoner from one's hometown or neighborhood

in the car: circle of friends

ink: tattoos, tats

jointman: a prison resident who behaves like a correctional officer

kite: a contraband letter

lemon squeezer: a resident who has an unattractive "girlfriend"

lugger: a resident who smuggles contraband into the facility

man walking: phrase used to signal that a guard is coming

merchant (or peddler): one who sells when he should give; or one who sells goods and services to other residents illegally

nimby: not in my back yard

ninja turtles: correctional officers dressed in riot gear

punk: a male resident who is forced into a submissive role during homosexual relations

rabbit: a resident who often tries to escape

rat (or snitch): a resident who squeals (provides information about other residents to the prison administration)

real men: residents who are respected by other residents

road kill: cigarette butts picked up from the roadsides by prisoners working on a highway

seed: the resident's child

shank: a knife

schooled: knowledgeable in the ways of prison life

shakedown: search of a cell or a work area

shu (pronounced shoe): special housing unit

sleeved: covered with tatoos

slinging rock: selling crack

soda: cocaine

stainless-steel ride: lethal injection

toughs: those with a preprison history of violent crimes

tree jumper: rapist

turn out: to rape or make into a punk

veterano: a long-time gang member

wolf: a male resident who assumes an aggressive role during homosexual relations

Argot in Women's Prisons

cherry (or cherrie): a resident not yet introduced to lesbian activities

fay broad: a white resident

femme (or mommy): an inmate who plays a female role during a lesbian relationship

lark: a woman who talks with the staff

safe: the vagina, especially when used for hiding contraband

stud broad (or daddy): a resident who assumes a male role in a same-sex relationship

Source: Gresham Sykes, The Society of Captives (Princeton, NJ; Princeton University Press, 1958): Rose Giallombardo, Society of Women: A Study of Women's Prison (New York: John Wiley, 1966); Richard A. Clowardet al., Theoretical Studies in Social Organization of the Prison (New York: Social Science Research Council, 1960). For a more contemporary listing of prison slang terms, see Reinhold Aman, Hillary Clinton's Pen Pal: A Guide to Life and Lingo in Federal Prison (Santa Rosa, CA: Maledicta Press, 1996); Jerome Washington, Iron House: Stories from the Yard (Ann Arbor, MI: QED Press, 1994); Morrie Camhi, The Prison Experience (Boston:Charles Tuttle, 1989); Harold Long, Survival in Prison (Port Townsend, WA: Loompanics Unlimited, 1990); insideprison.com (accessed March 24, 2009); Mother Jones, "A Glossary of Prison Slang" (July/August 2008), http://motherjones.com/politics/2008/07/glossary-prison-slang (accessed March 10, 2011).

them a great deal of power in prison society. At the very least, other people in prison are likely to leave the mean dude alone.

The Bully A variation of the mean dude is the bully. Bullies use intimidation to get what they want. Unlike mean dudes, they are far more likely to use threats than to use actual physical force. A bully may make his threats in public so that others see the victim's compliance.

The Agitator The agitator, sometimes called a *wise guy*, is constantly trying to stir things up. He responds to the boredom of prison life by causing problems for others. An agitator may point out, for example, how a powerful person in prison society has been wronged by another person or that a person seen talking to a "rat" must be a snitch him/herself.

The Hedonist The hedonist adapts to prison by exploiting the minimal pleasures it offers. Hedonists always seek the easy path, and they plot to win the "cushiest" jobs. They may also stockpile goods to barter for services of various kinds. Hedonists live only in the now with little concern for the future. Their lives revolve around such activities as gambling, drug running, smuggling contraband, and exploiting sexual opportunities.

The Opportunist The opportunist sees prison as an opportunity for personal advancement. He or she takes advantage of the formal self-improvement opportunities of the prison, such as schooling, trade training, and counseling. Others in prison generally dislike opportunists, seeing them as selfish *do-gooders*. Staff members, however, often see opportunists as model residents.

The Retreatist Some people in prison, unable to cope with the realities of prison life, withdraw psychologically from the world around them. Depression, neurosis, and even psychosis may result. Some retreatists attempt to lose themselves in drugs or alcohol. Others attempt suicide. Isolation from the general prison population combined with counseling or psychiatric treatment may offer the best hope for retreatists to survive the prison experience.

The Legalist Legalists are known as *jailhouse lawyers*, or simply *lawyers*, in prison argot. They are usually among the better-educated persons who are confined, although some legalists have little formal education. Legalists fight confinement through the system of laws, rules, and court precedent. Legalists file writs with the courts, seeking hearings on a wide variety of issues. Although many legalists work to better the conditions of their own confinement or to achieve early release, most also file pleas on behalf of other residents.

The Radical Radicals see themselves as political prisoners of an unfair society. They believe that a discriminatory world has denied them the education and skills needed to succeed in a socially acceptable way. Most of the beliefs held by radicals are rationalizations that shift the blame for personal failure onto society. Radicals are likely to be familiar with contemporary countercultural figures.

The Colonist Colonists, also referred to as *convicts*, turn prison into home. Colonists know the ropes of prison, have many "friends" on the inside, and often feel more comfortable in prison than outside it. They may not look forward to leaving prison. Some may even commit additional offenses to extend their stay. Colonists are generally well regarded by other people in prison. Many are old-timers. Colonists have learned to take advantage of the informal opportunity structure in prisons, and they are well versed in the inmate code.

The Religious Religious residents profess a strong religious faith and may attempt to convert both confined people and staff. Religious residents frequently form prayer groups, request special meeting facilities and special diets, and may ask for frequent visits from religious leaders. The religious are often under a great deal of suspicion from all sides, who tend to think they are faking religious commitment to gain special treatment. Those judged sincere in their faith may win early release, removal from death row, or any number of other special considerations.

The Punk The punk is a young imprisoned individual, often physically small, who has been forced into a sexual relationship with an aggressive, well respected resident. Punks are generally "turned out" through rape. A punk usually finds a protector among more powerful imprisoned people. Punks keep their protectors happy by providing them with sexual services.

The Gang-Banger Gang-bangers, or those affiliated with prison gangs, know that there is power in numbers. They depend upon the gang for defense and protection as well as for the procurement of desired goods and services. Gang-bangers are known by their tattoos and hand signs, which indicate gang affiliation and can be read by anyone familiar with prison society. Prison gangs often have links outside prison—leading to continued involvement in crime by those directing them from inside prison and to the creation of channels for the importation of banned items into correctional facilities.

Adapting to Prison Life

People in prison often have a number of opportunities to improve their lives. In 2020, for example, a report by the Crime and Justice Research Alliance found that college-in-prison programs offered some of the most significant life-changing options for people who are incarcerated. The report focused on the Bard Prison Initiative (BPI), which is largely funded by Second Chance Pell Grants and has offered college courses since 1999 to incarcerated students in six New York correctional facilities. Program participants were found to experience a 38% drop in recidivism, and rates of recidivism fell across all racial groups.[19]

Correctional clients at a prayer service at Men's Central Jail in Los Angeles. How does this chapter describe a "religious" type of resident?

Carolyn Cole/Los Angeles Times/Getty Images

In a comprehensive report on the *personal* strategies that people in prison use to adapt to the strains of institutional life, Lindsay Leban and colleagues found considerable variation among coping responses.[20] Leban stresses that the context of an imprisoned person's surroundings, including prison culture, gang membership, length of time served, past victimization history, personal characteristics, and numerous other things shape the choice of coping mechanisms. Nonetheless, she was able to identify three general categories of coping strategies that characterize prison life: behavioral, cognitive, and emotional.

Behavioral strategies include things like direct physical retaliation, escaping from the situation, or seeking help from more powerful residents or from staff. Retaliation was a common strategy, used by 73 percent of the men in the study. *Cognitive strategies* encompass "minimizing the importance of an incident" (i.e., pretending that it never happened or acknowledging that it is of minor significance), empathy (knowing what it must have felt like for the other person), and acceptance of responsibility (feeling like the disturbing event was deserved). *Emotional strategies*, the least commonly used techniques, were attempted by only 10 percent of the people in prison who were studied. Emotional strategies involve keeping busy, sleeping, or trying to block out negative thoughts. Because private time is very limited in correctional facilities, Leban found that people in prison "often tried and failed and eventually used more aggressive coping styles."

She also noted that responses to the strain of prison life were at least partially determined by past experiences and influenced by the prior development of coping techniques. She concluded the study by calling for further research on the relationship between strain and offending, noting that it's not entirely clear when and under what conditions individuals will react to strain with offending behavior.

Sexuality in Men's Prisons

Sexual experiences in prison vary from institution to institution, but the general consensus is that sex practices between residents are widespread. Men often form relationships with each other, and consent is not always a factor when it comes to sexual contact. Sexual coercion is a major concern in prisons, as prisoners may use their personal status or power within the prison subculture to gain access to other residents' bodies. This can lead to feelings of shame or guilt for those who have been coerced into having sex, or it can lead to identity issues if an inmate is unable to satisfactorily define his or her sexuality or gender. In addition, sexual health knowledge and attitudes are often lacking in men's prisons. Many inmates lack basic knowledge about STDs and how they can be transmitted through sexual activity.[21]

The prevalence of sexuality in men's prisons is determined by factors such as time in prison and previous sexual experience. Significantly, prison sexuality can impact inmates' mental health. Men who are incarcerated express their sexuality in a variety of ways, and prison sex consists of sex with others who are incarcerated, staff, and visitors. It may also include penitentiary sex (or rape of other residents), writing sexually explicit letters to girlfriends or family members, and sexual contact with correctional officers or other persons such as visitors. There are also residents who engage in avoidance strategies to reduce sexual abuse and victimization. In particular, rape victims may need to take extra precautions when it comes to engaging in prison sex. Prisoners may also attempt to satisfy their emotional needs

Former Texas prisoner Roderick Johnson, who claims that he was raped hundreds of times after his return to prison on charges of bouncing a $300 check while on parole for breaking and entering. In 2004, a federal lawsuit filed by Johnson, 33, who identifies as bisexual, was allowed to go to trial. It named the head of the Texas Department of Criminal Justice, along with more than a dozen other officials at the James V. Allred Unit in Iowa Park, claiming that they failed to protect him from violent sexual attacks. A federal jury dismissed his claims. What does the Prison Rape Elimination Act mean for residents like Johnson? Use the Internet to learn what happened to the civil suit filed on Johnson's behalf.
Wichita Falls Times Record New/Torin Halsey/AP Images

based on desires through nonsexual activities such as writing letters or participating in sexual fantasies. Employee–resident relationships are clearly prohibited, and any kind of sexual contact between an employee and a resident is considered illegal.[22]

Therefore, it is not surprising that the sexual lives of inmates in prisons are a topic that has been largely overlooked. However, recent research on the topic has suggested a correlation between low sexual satisfaction and poorer mental health among people in prison. Specifically, studies have found that sexually active residents had worse mental health than those who did not have any sexual activity. In addition, one study showed that sexually abstinent groups of residents had better mental health than those who had heterosexual relationships while incarcerated. This suggests that a resident's satisfaction with their incarceration and mental health can be affected by their level of sexual activity. Referring to most authors in the field, having a partner during incarceration can improve a resident's mental health significantly; however, it is important to note that this does not necessarily mean having sex with them, as there are other ways for people in prison to connect emotionally with another person without engaging in physical contact.

Research on sexuality in men's prisons has noted that many participants take part in consensual sex with other residents. There is a high degree of tolerance toward sexual activity in prison culture, although condoms are rarely used. Interviewees have reported a tacit acknowledgment of these activities, but officials in prisons and jails often look the other way.

One British study of a prison sample indicated that most male residents had engaged in consensual homosexual activity.[23] Other studies have also found that many male residents have multiple sexual partners while incarcerated. The study also indicated that one-fourth of the interviewees had engaged in sexual activity while in prison, and the number of partners ranged from one to many.

The majority of the men interviewed reported having sex with other inmates, and more than half of them had sexual relationships with both men and women. Gay and bisexual men were more likely to report having had multiple sexual partners in prison. Although it was less common for self-identified cisgender inmates to report engaging in same-sex sexual activity, it was not unheard of. The study found that friendships between residents often helped their sexual relationships develop, as strong emotional bonds were formed through these friendships. Sex offenders specifically reported that they felt a greater sense of comfort engaging in same-sex sexual activity when they had a close relationship with their partner. Formation of close friendships among prisoners was also commonplace among women prisoners, even though women were less likely to report engaging in any type of sex activity while incarcerated. Overall, the study provides insight into the prevalence and nature of sexuality in men's prisons. It highlighted the fact that same-sex sexual activity is a normal part of life in prison, and many residents form strong emotional bonds through their activities and relationships. In addition, it showed that gay and bisexual men are more likely than self-identified cisgender individuals to engage in same-sex sexual activity while incarcerated.[24]

Sexually active residents in men's prisons often face a unique set of challenges while pursuing sexual relationships. Many of these people self-identify as gay and may be more likely to engage in same-sex relationships than other inmates. Sex offenders stir worry among many inmates, due to negative attitudes toward them. Some enlightened prison administrators have implemented policies that include controlled experimentation with the goal of lessening policy restrictions on same-sex relations among residents. These policies seek to provide a rehabilitative effect for sexually involved residents by lessening tensions caused by the stigma associated with same-sex relationships.

With many prisons now providing clinical sexual health services, HIV/AIDS and other sexually transmitted infections can be prevented through the use of condoms and other preventive measures. Many prison policies also encourage self-expression by tacitly allowing homosexual sex acts; however, these are limited to acts between consenting adults. Advocates believe that providing this type of opportunity will help residents stay psychologically healthy while they are incarcerated, providing a benefit to society by helping prevent the spread of HIV/AIDS in the prison system. In addition, most prisons, including those for men and women, have taken steps to ease access to condoms to prevent any unwanted or unplanned pregnancies or the spread of sexually transmitted diseases among residents.

A sexual health module has been developed to provide sexual health consultations and communication about sexuality-related issues for the men within the prison. This module is delivered by prison nurses and other providers who work closely with young incarcerated men. The module focuses on developing health interventions to reach young men, educate them about safe sexual practices, and deliver sexual health promotion messages. The module also includes a lesson on health promotion activities aimed at improving nurses' skills in delivering sexuality-related communication to young men. Also included is a fatherhood intervention that encourages fathers (or potential fathers) in the prison system to take active roles in their children's lives. This method of reaching out to the younger population within prison is seen as an important way of improving the overall well-being of residents, while also providing them with access to appropriate sexual health care services. By providing these services, prisons are able to improve the sexual healthcare for young men and women within their walls, helping them become more informed about safe sex practices and better equipped for life after their release from prison.[25]

The Prison Rape Elimination Act (PREA)

In 2003, in an effort to learn more about prison rape, Congress mandated the collection of prison rape statistics under the Prison Rape Elimination Act (PREA).[26] The PREA, which also established the federal Prison Rape Commission, calls for an evaluation of issues related to prison rape as well as for the development of national standards to help prevent prison rape.

Tasked by the PREA to gather data on prison rape, the BJS completed the first-ever national Survey of Sexual Victimization (SSV) based on reports of former state prisoners in 2012. The survey, which has been conducted annually ever since, includes information from completed interviews with more than 18,000 people who had been formerly confined and who are still under parole supervision. Survey results published in 2023 show:

- there were 2,886 reported victims of sexual victimization committed by one confined person on another and 2,496 victims of staff-on-resident sexual victimization in adult correctional facilities;
- half of both types of sexual victimization incidents occurred in an area not under video surveillance;
- staff-on-resident sexual victimization was perpetrated by correctional officers or supervision staff in 64 percent of incidents, by maintenance or facility support staff in 13 percent, and by medical or healthcare staff in 10 percent;
- about 67 percent of reported staff sexual misconduct perpetrators were female, and 69 percent of staff sexual harassment perpetrators were male;
- about 25 percent of victims of resident-on-resident nonconsensual sexual acts, and 43 percent of victims of abusive sexual contact were female;

- the victim was given a medical examination in 61 percent of known resident-on-resident nonconsensual sexual act incidents and in 36 percent of alleged abusive sexual contact incidents;
- legal action was ultimately taken against the alleged perpetrator of staff sexual misconduct in more than half of incidents in jails (53%) and in a third of incidents in prisons (33%); and
- the alleged perpetrator of staff sexual misconduct was convicted, pled guilty, was sentenced, or was fined in 20 percent of incidents in jails, three times the share of incidents in prisons (6%).[27]

Official reports by correctional administrators are unlikely to reflect the true incidence of sexual violence. As BJS notes, "due to fear of reprisal from perpetrators, a code of silence among inmates, personal embarrassment, and lack of trust in staff, victims are often reluctant to report incidents to correctional authorities."[28] To circumvent such issues and to gather more reliable information, BJS has implemented a system of self-reports in which data are collected from incarcerated individuals as well as those recently released.

LGBTQ+ Representation in U.S. Prisons

According to the most recent BJS survey of incarcerated persons, an estimated 7.1 percent of jail inmates and 7.9 percent of prison inmates identify as lesbian, gay, bisexual, or other non-binary.[29] Additionally, about 0.2 percent of inmates in both jails and prisons identify as transgender. These numbers have remained largely consistent over time. In both jails and prisons, a higher percentage of inmates who identify as lesbian, gay, bisexual, or others report sexual victimization than heterosexual inmates. In jails, LGBQ+ inmates are approximately seven times more likely to report inmate-on-inmate victimization than heterosexual inmates. In prisons, they are about 10 times more likely. In both jails and prisons, LGBQ+ inmates are two and a half times more likely to report staff sexual misconduct than heterosexual inmates.

Finally, transgender inmates also report higher rates of sexual victimization. More than 15 percent of transgender jail inmates report inmate-on-inmate victimization, 15.8 percent, or staff sexual misconduct, which was reported by 18.3 percent. Again, about 15 percent of transgender prison inmates report staff sexual misconduct; and nearly one-third of transgender prison inmates report inmate-on-inmate sexual victimization.

Drug Use in American Prisons

Despite efforts to prevent drugs from entering prisons and to provide drug treatment programs for incarcerated individuals, illegal drugs continue to be a problem in many prisons throughout the United States.

Many people who are in prison struggle with addiction and may turn to drugs as a way to cope with the stresses of incarceration. Additionally, some people may have been using drugs before they were incarcerated and continue to do so while in prison.

The prison drug problem can have serious consequences, including increased violence and health risks for incarcerated individuals. It can also make it more difficult for people to successfully reintegrate into society after they are released from prison. Moreover, researchers have found that drug use in American prisons is significantly higher than in the general population, with estimates of active substance use ranging from 35 to 90 percent. Numbers like these have had a significant impact on the national drug overdose death rate, which has increased by more than 50 percent since 2000.

Overdose rates are particularly high among state prisoners as overdose deaths account for more than 10 percent of all state prisoner deaths.[30]

According to a new federal data analysis, prison overdose deaths have grown steadily. The rate of overdose death has more than tripled from 0.7 per 100,000 in 2011 to 2.4 per 100,000 in 2018. Alcohol intoxication was found to be the cause of one out of every four emergency room visits for state prisoners, and alcohol remains the most common substance associated with overdose death among state prisoners.[31]

Many prison systems are working to address the issue of drug addiction and drug smuggling in prisons through a variety of approaches, including drug treatment programs, increased security measures, and educational programs for incarcerated individuals.

Treatment programs that focus on reducing substance use among inmates include evidence-based interventions such as cognitive behavioral therapy and medication-assisted treatment for both alcohol and drug use disorders. Additionally, providing support services such as job training or educational programs can help individuals address the underlying issues that may have contributed to their substance abuse while also providing them with the skills they need upon release from prison for successful reentry into society.

Other than alcohol, the most commonly used drugs in correctional settings are opioids, methamphetamine, cocaine, heroin, and marijuana. Drug abuse can lead to other forms of criminal activity within prison walls as well as on the outside when residents are released back into society.

To reduce the drug problem in prison and better manage its population, many correctional centers have implemented training for staff members on how to detect and prevent drug use. The aim is to stop the flow of drugs before they can be used by inmates within prisons.

The United Nations Office on Drugs and Crime (UNODC) recognizes drugs as a major factor in prison violence, overcrowding, and recidivism rates. Correctional residents may have to compete with one another to acquire drugs or be forced into providing favors to access them. Similarly, staff may have to deal with angry outbursts caused by withdrawal symptoms or take on the role of mediator if disputes occur among inmates over the availability of drugs.

A recent study found that a disturbingly large number of inmates—approximately 73 percent—are believed to have an untreated substance abuse issue. This figure is even more concerning given the fact that many inmates will eventually be released back into society with little or no help for their addiction issues. It is difficult for inmates to successfully reintegrate back into society without further assistance from viable treatment providers. Furthermore, reduced tolerance levels after spending time away from drugs can cause newly released individuals to be more susceptible to their effects—sometimes leading to overdoses and overdose-related deaths. Similarly, formerly incarcerated people who use drugs and fail to receive help transitioning to street life may commit drug-related crimes upon release.[32]

Findings suggest that addiction treatment is necessary for nonviolent drug offenders, and comprehensive substance use disorder treatment may be considered for all offenders. Prevention efforts such as drug misuse education and continued research on effective strategies to reduce or eliminate drug use among inmates should also be implemented. Some suggest that prison administrators should invest in programs that are specifically geared toward identifying those at risk for addiction, monitoring those who are already using drugs, providing education about the risks of drug misuse, and offering access to addiction treatment services when necessary.

CO10-5   # WOMEN IN PRISON

In America today, there are far fewer women's prisons than men's prisons, and men in prison outnumber women in prison 12 to 1. However, the number of women in prison has grown faster than that of men. Between 1980 and 2020, the number of incarcerated women increased by more than 475% percent (Exhibit 10–3).

A state usually has one women's prison housing a few hundred women. The size of a women's prison generally depends on the population of the state. Some small states house women in special areas of what are otherwise institutions for men.

Women's prisons are generally quite different from men's. Here's how one writer describes a traditional women's prison:

> Often, there are no gun towers, no armed guards, and no stone walls or fences strung on top with concertina wire. Neatly pruned hedges, well-kept flower gardens, attractive brick buildings, and wide paved walkways greet the visitor's eye at women's prisons in many states. Often these institutions are located in rural, pastoral settings that may suggest tranquility and well-being to the casual observer.[33]

Such rural settings, however, make it hard for women who are in prison to maintain contact with their families who may live far from the correctional facility.

Many prisons for women are built on a cottage plan. Cottages dot the grounds of such institutions, often arranged in pods. A group of six or so cottages constitutes a pod. Each cottage is much like a traditional house, with individual bedrooms; a day room with a television, chairs, couches, and tables; and small personal or shared bathrooms.

Security in women's prisons is generally more relaxed than in men's, and women residents may have more freedom within the institution than their male counterparts. Practically speaking, women—even those in prison—are seen as less dangerous than men and less prone to violence or escape.

Treatment, education, recreation, and other programs in women's prisons have often been criticized as inferior to those in men's prisons. Recent research has uncovered continuing disparities in many areas.[34] For example, men's institutions often have a much wider range of vocational and educational training programs and services and larger and better equipped law libraries. Similarly, exercise facilities—including weight rooms, jogging

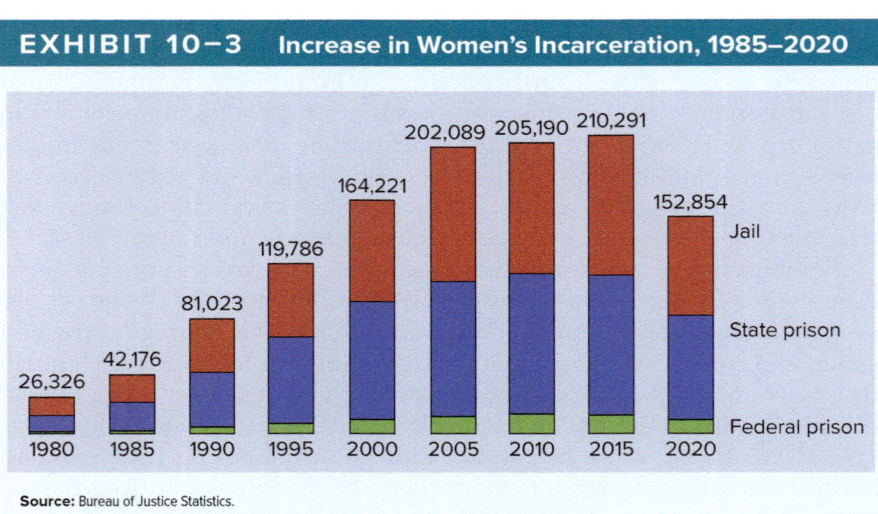

EXHIBIT 10–3   Increase in Women's Incarceration, 1985–2020

26,326   42,176   81,023   119,786   164,221   202,089   205,190   210,291   152,854

1980   1985   1990   1995   2000   2005   2010   2015   2020

Jail

State prison

Federal prison

Source: Bureau of Justice Statistics.

areas, and basketball courts—are often better equipped and larger in men's institutions today than in women's.

Prison administrators have often found it impractical to develop and fund programs at the same level in women's and men's prisons because of differences in interest, participation, and space and the fact that relatively low numbers of women in prison don't allow for the same economies of scale found in men's institutions. Nonetheless, it is important to strive for parity of opportunity as an ideal. The American Correctional Association (ACA), for example, through its Guidelines for Women's Prison Construction and Programming,[35] insists that the same level of services and opportunities be available in women's prisons as in men's prisons in the same jurisdiction.

In some instances, women may be placed in an institution housing residents with a range of security levels. Consequently, women who are low security risks may have less personal freedom than their male counterparts. Women may also not have the opportunity to transfer to a less secure institution as their risk level drops.

However, a 2022 study found that many correctional institutions for women have begun moving in the right direction. The study noted that "given the sharp increase in the population of incarcerated women, as well as the range of trauma and victimization that incarcerated women experience both prior to and during incarceration, development of policies, practices and programs that address women's needs and experiences in trauma-informed ways is crucial."[36] Fifty-nine percent of state departments of corrections (DOCs) were found to have adopted workable practices for incarcerated women. Thirty-seven percent of the states that were surveyed reported using a gender-responsive, validated risk assessment tool that considered women's trauma histories to measure their unique circumstances and mental health needs. Assessment tools that were typically used included the Correctional Offender Management Profiling for Alternative Sanctions (COMPAS) for Women, the Service Planning Instrument for Women (SPIN-W), and the Women's Risk and Needs Assessment (WRNA). Various state correctional systems also reported providing evidence-based programs to address women's trauma, and 44 percent said that they employed more than one evidence-based program to address trauma.

Although there are far fewer women in prison than men, the number of women behind bars is growing steadily. What might account for the increasing number of imprisoned women?
Marmaduke St. John/Alamy Stock Photo

RELIABLE RESEARCH. REAL RESULTS.

Enter your keyword(s)   Search Site   Advanced Search

Home | Help | Contact Us | Site Map | Glossary

EVIDENCE-BASED CORRECTIONS
The "Moving On" Program

"Moving On" is a curriculum-based, gender-responsive intervention program created to address the different cognitive–behavioral needs of incarcerated women. Moving On is delivered in 26 sessions over the course of 12 weeks, with each session lasting 1.5 to 2 hours. Class sizes tend to be small, ranging from 5 to 10 participants (there is a maximum of 10 participants per facilitator). Sessions consist of both group and one-on-one discussions. Program activities include self-assessments, writing exercises, role-playing, and modeling activities. Participation in Moving On is voluntary. The program is offered on a quarterly basis to incarcerated women who are serving the last half of their confinement period.

The program is rated Promising. Participants in Moving On were significantly less likely to be rearrested or reconvicted, compared with the control group. Participating in Moving On lowered the risk of reoffending by 33 percent. It did not, however, not have a significant impact on reincarcerations for a new offense and technical violation revocations.

Source: Adapted from Bureau of Justice Statistics.

In addition, many states reported using proven systems to respond to in-custody victimization of women inmates. Sixty-three percent of states reported providing a toll-free hotline managed by a victim service provider or by an independent entity tasked with investigating reported incidents. Provided services included connections with victim advocates at local victim services agencies and the provision of mental health treatment.[37]

Finally, many states also reported adapting operational and custodial practices (e.g., disciplinary processes, housing practices, body searches, and restraints) in trauma-informed ways to provide women with choices and enhance their sense of safety and trust. Specific examples included having an officer verbally walk women through searches step by step and conducting strip searches with correctional staff who are of the same gender as the individual being searched; having a policy of not restraining pregnant women during specific stages of their pregnancy; and providing an option to have a fully unclothed or half unclothed search. In addition, state officials indicated that staff were trained on de-escalation techniques and methods to work and communicate effectively with women.[38]

CO10-6 CHARACTERISTICS OF WOMEN IN PRISON

Many of our conceptions of women who are in prison derive more from myth than from reality. Recent BJS surveys provide a more realistic picture of female residents.[39] At the start of 2021, women comprised approximately 6.0 percent of all people sentenced to prison in the nation.[40] In the last two decades, the female prison population has grown at a noticeably higher rate than the male prison population. As of January 1, 2021, there were 83,054 women under the jurisdiction of state and federal prison authorities.[41]

Women who are in prison largely resemble male residents in terms of race, ethnic background, and age. However, they are substantially more likely to be serving time for a drug offense and less likely to have been sentenced for a violent crime. Women are also more likely than men to be serving time for larceny or fraud.

Overall, women who are in prison have shorter criminal records than men who are in prison. They generally have shorter maximum sentences than men. Half of all women receive a maximum sentence of 60 months or less, and half of all men are sentenced to 120 months or less.

Significantly, more than 4 in 10 of women who are incarcerated and who respond to BJS surveys report prior physical or sexual abuse. One of the major factors distinguishing men who are in prison from females in prison is that the women have experienced far more sexual and physical abuse than men. Interviews with incarcerated women have found that 70 percent of them report the occurrence of sexual molestation or severe physical abuse in childhood at the hands of parents or adolescent caregivers.[42] Fifty-nine percent report some form of sexual abuse in childhood or adolescence, and 75 percent of those interviewed report having been severely abused by an intimate partner as adults.

Women who are in prison. How do men's and women's prisons differ?
Scott Houston/Alamy Stock Photo

A report by the National Institute of Corrections (NIC) found that women enter correctional institutions through different "pathways" than men. According to the report, most women are typically nonviolent, and their crimes are less threatening to community safety than those committed by male offenders. "Women's most common pathways to crime," said the report, "result from abuse, poverty, and substance abuse"—all of which, according to the report, are interconnected.[43] Exhibit 10–4 is a comparison of selected characteristics of men and women who are in prison.

Offenses of Incarcerated Women

Drug offenses account for the incarceration of a high percentage of the women behind bars. Twenty-six percent of all women in state prisons are serving time on drug charges.[44] Some sources estimate that drug crimes and other crimes indirectly related to drug activities together account for the imprisonment of around 95 percent of women who are in prison today. In short, drug use and abuse, or crimes stimulated by the desire for drugs and drug money are what send most women to prison. This has been true for decades. According to an ACA report, the primary reasons incarcerated women most frequently give for their arrest are (1) trying to pay for drugs, (2) attempts to relieve economic pressures, and (3) poor judgment.[45]

According to the BJS, before arrest, women in prison use more drugs than men and use those drugs more frequently.[46] About 59 percent of imprisoned women used drugs daily in the month before the offense for which they were arrested compared with 56 percent of the men. Women in prison are also more likely than men who are in prison to have used drugs regularly (65 percent versus 62 percent), and to have been under the influence at the time of the offense (36 percent versus 31 percent). Nearly one in four women in prison who were surveyed reported committing the offense to get money to buy drugs compared with one in six males.

EXHIBIT 10−4   Characteristics of Women and Men in State Prisons

Women in Prison

Criminal Offense

37% are in prison for violent offenses.

25% are in prison for drug offenses.

29% are in prison for property offenses.

8% are in prison for public-order offenses.

1% or less are in prison for other offenses.

Criminal History

46% are nonviolent recidivists.

28% have no previous sentence.

26% are violent recidivists.

Family Characteristics

78% have children.

42% lived with both parents most of time growing up.

33% had a parent/guardian who abused alcohol or drugs.

17% were married at the time they committed the offense for which they were incarcerated.

45% have never married.

47% have a family member who had been incarcerated.

Drug and Alcohol Use

59% used drugs daily in the month before the current offense.

36% were under the influence of drugs at the time of the offense.

12% were under the influence of alcohol at the time of the offense.

Men in Prison

Criminal Offense

54% are in prison for violent offenses.

18% are in prison for property offenses.

17% are in prison for drug offenses.

11% are in prison for public-order offenses.

1% or less are in prison for other offenses.

Criminal History

50% are violent recidivists.

31% are nonviolent recidivists.

19% have no previous sentence.

Family Characteristics

64% have children.

43% lived with both parents most of time growing up.

26% had a parent/guardian who abused alcohol or drugs.

18% were married at the time they committed the offense for which they were incarcerated.

56% have never married.

37% have a family member who had been incarcerated.

Drug and Alcohol Use

56% used drugs daily in the month before the current offense.

31% were under the influence of drugs at the time of the offense.

18% were under the influence of alcohol at the time of the offense.

Source: Bureau of Justice Statistics.

Women in prison who used drugs differed from those who did not in the types of crimes they committed. Regardless of the amount of drug use, users were less likely than nonusers to be serving a sentence for a violent offense.

 ## SOCIAL STRUCTURE IN WOMEN'S PRISONS

As might be expected, the social structure and the subcultural norms and expectations in women's prisons are quite different from those in men's prisons. Unfortunately, however, relatively few studies of resident life have been conducted in institutions for women.

One early study of women at the Federal Reformatory for Women in Alderson, West Virginia, was an effort to compare subcultural aspects of women's prisons with those of men's. Rose Giallombardo reached the conclusion that "many of the subcultural features of the institution are imported from the larger society."[47] Giallombardo believed that male and female resident subcultures are actually quite similar except that women's prisons develop "a substitute universe," a world "in which inmates may preserve an identity, which is relevant to life outside the prison."

Giallombardo was unable to find in the women's prison some of the values inherent in a male resident subculture, such as "Do your own time." The resident subculture in a women's prison, she said, tends to encourage relationships rather than isolation. Hence, women are expected to share their problems with other residents and to offer at least some support and encouragement to others. On the other hand, she observed, women in prison tend to see each other as conniving, self-centered, and scheming. Hence, a basic tenet of the resident subculture in a women's prison is, "You can't trust other women."

Giallombardo concluded that the social structure of women's prisons and the social role assumed by each resident are based on three elements:

1. the individual woman's level of personal dependence and her status needs (which are said to be based upon cultural expectations of the female role);
2. the individual's needs arising from incarceration combined with the institution's inability to meet female residents' emotional needs; and
3. needs related to the individual's personality.

A more recent study was of residents in the District of Columbia Women's Reformatory at Occoquan, Virginia.[48] Esther Heffernan identified three roles that women commonly adopt when adjusting to prison. According to Heffernan, women's roles evolve partly from the characteristics the women bring with them to prison and depend partly on the ways the women choose to adapt to prison life. The roles she described are discussed in the following paragraphs.

The Cool Resident Cool women usually have previous records, are in the know, are streetwise, and do not cause trouble for other residents while in prison. Cool women are seen as professional or semiprofessional criminals who work to win the maximum number of prison amenities without endangering their parole or release dates.

The Square Resident Square women are not familiar with criminal lifestyles and have few, if any, criminal experiences other than the one for which they were imprisoned. They tend to hold the values and roles of conventional society.

The Life Resident Life residents are habitual or career offenders and are generally well socialized into lives of crime. They support resident values and subculture. Life residents typically have been in and out of prison from an early age and have developed criminal lifestyles dedicated to meeting their political, economic, familial, and social needs outside conventional society.

More recently, California State University (Fresno) criminologist Barbara Owens studied the culture of imprisoned women at Central California Women's Facility in Chowchilla, California, and found a "prison culture that is itself complex and diverse across numerous dimensions."[49] Owens identified a central component of that culture that she refers to as "the mix."

The *mix*, according to Owens, "is any behavior that can bring trouble and conflict with staff and other prisoners." It consists of fighting, doing drugs, prison-based lesbian activity ("homo-secting," in Owens's terms), and making trouble for the staff. It also involves continuing the kinds of behaviors that brought women to prison. Consequently, the mix is to be avoided by those who want to leave prison and not return. New women coming into the institution, Owens found, were advised to "stay out of the mix." The mix, says Owens, is also a state of mind, a way of thinking like a troublemaker.

One writer, summarizing the results of studies such as those discussed here, found that two primary features distinguish women's prisons from men's prisons:[50]

1. The social roles in women's prisons place greater emphasis on same-sex relations as a mode of adaptation to prison life.
2. The mode of adaptation a female resident selects is best assessed by studying the resident's preinstitutional experiences.

Pseudofamilies and Sexual Liaisons

pseudofamilies

Family-like structures, common in women's prisons, in which residents assume roles similar to those of family members in free society.

A unique feature of women's prisons is pseudofamilies. **Pseudofamilies** are family-like structures, common in women's prisons, in which residents assume roles similar to those of family members in free society. Pseudofamilies appear to provide emotional and social support for the women who belong to them. Courtship, marriage, and kinship ties formed with other women residents provide a means of coping with the rigors of imprisonment. One resident explained pseudofamilies this way: "It just happens. Just like on the outside, you get close to certain people. It's the same in here—but we probably get even closer than a lot of families because of how lonely it is otherwise."[51]

Some authors suggest that pseudofamilies are to women's prisons what gangs are to men's.[52] Men establish social relationships largely through power, and gang structure effectively expresses such relationships. Women relate to one another more expressively and emotionally. Hence, family structures are one of the most effective reflections of women's relationships in prison, just as they are in the wider society. At least one study of prison coping behavior found that women who were new to prison, especially those most in need of support, advice, and assistance in adjusting to the conditions of incarceration, are those most likely to become members of prison pseudofamilies.[53]

The kinship of substitute families plays a major role in the lives of many female residents, who take the relationships very seriously. How might these relationships supplant values such as "do your own time" commonly found in the subculture of men's prisons?

imageBROKER/SuperStock

To a large extent, the social and behavioral patterns of family relationships in prison mirror their traditional counterparts in the community. Families in women's prisons come in all sizes and colors. They can be virtual melting pots of ethnicity and age. A member of a family may be young or old and may be Black, white, or Hispanic. As in families in free society, there are roles for husbands and wives, sisters, brothers, grandmothers, and children. One special role is that of pseudo-mother. Pseudo-mothers are perceived as maternal, supportive, and wise by their pseudo-children. Roles for aunts and uncles do not exist, however.

"Stud broads," in prison argot, assume any male role, including that of husband and brother. Other residents think of them as men. "Men" often assume traditional roles in women's prisons, ordering women around, demanding to be waited on, expecting to have their rooms cleaned and their laundry done, and so forth. Most women who assume masculine roles within prison are said to be "playing" and are sometimes called *players*. Once they leave, they often revert to female roles and assume a female identity. A "femme" or "mommy" is a woman who assumes a female role in a prison family and during lesbian activity.

Most women in prison, including those assuming masculine roles, were generally not gay before entering prison. They resort to lesbian relations within prison because relationships with men are unavailable.

Although gender roles and family relationships within women's prisons appear to have an enduring quality, women can and sometimes do change gender roles. When a woman identifying as a male, for example, reverts to a female identity, she is said to have "dropped her belt." A stud broad who drops her belt may wreak havoc on relationships within her own family and in families related to it.

Special Needs of Women in Prison

Rarely are the special needs of imprisoned women fully recognized—and even less frequently are they addressed. Many of today's prison administrators and correctional officers still treat women as if they were men. Nicole Hahn Rafter, for example, says that many prisons have an attitude akin to "just add women and stir."[54]

A trend-seting report by the NIC called for criminal justice agencies to acknowledge the "many differences between male and female offenders" and for the implementation of gender–responsive programming for treating the problems of imprisoned women. **Gender-responsiveness** can be defined as "creating an environment ... that reflects an understanding of the realities of women's lives and addresses the issues of the women."[55]

Gender-responsive strategies in women's corrections aim to address the specific needs and experiences of women who are confined. These strategies include:

gender-responsiveness
The intentional creation of an environment that reflects an understanding of the realities of women's lives and addresses the special issues of women in correctional settings.

- Trauma-informed care, which means recognizing and addressing the high rates of trauma and abuse experienced by many imprisoned women. Trauma-informed care in women's prisons recognizes the high levels of trauma that many incarcerated women have experienced and seeks to provide a supportive and understanding environment to address the effects of this trauma. This approach emphasizes the importance of safety, choice, and collaboration in all interactions and decisions made with the incarcerated women and seeks to reduce retraumatization and promote healing and recovery.
- Health and wellness programs, which address the unique health needs of women, including reproductive health, mental health, and substance abuse. Examples of health and wellness programs in women's prisons include trauma-focused therapy and counseling; substance abuse treatment and recovery support; exercise and physical activity programs; nutrition education and healthy meal options; chronic disease management and prevention; reproductive and gynecological care; mental health services; yoga, meditation, and stress management classes; art and music therapy; and smoking cessation programs. These programs aim to address the physical, mental, and emotional health needs of incarcerated women and to promote overall well-being and success upon reentry into society.
- Gender-specific programming, which addresses the specific needs and experiences of women, such as parenting classes, job training, and education. Gender-specific programs in women's prisons are designed to address the unique needs and experiences of incarcerated women, including the effects of trauma, family separation, poverty, and other factors that disproportionately affect women. Examples of gender-specific programs include parenting and family reunification services; domestic violence and trauma support groups; job training and employment readiness programs; life skills and personal development courses; gender-responsive substance abuse treatment; women's health and wellness programs; educational and literacy

programs; mentorship and leadership development opportunities; and spirituality and religious support. These programs aim to provide incarcerated women with the tools and resources they need to overcome the challenges they face and to promote successful reentry into society. They may also seek to address the systemic issues that contribute to high rates of incarceration among women, such as poverty, lack of access to education and healthcare, and gender-based violence.

- Alternatives to incarceration: offering alternatives to traditional prison environments, such as community-based programs and halfway houses. Alternatives to incarceration are alternative forms of punishment or rehabilitation for individuals who have been convicted of crimes that seek to reduce the use of imprisonment and address the root causes of criminal behavior. Examples of alternatives to incarceration include community service, probation and parole supervision, electronic monitoring, drug courts and treatment programs, mental health and substance abuse treatment, restorative justice programs, halfway houses and sober living environments, vocational training and job placement programs, education and skill-building programs, and diversion programs—such as pretrial services or drug courts. The goal of these alternatives is to reduce the number of individuals in prison, to provide effective and evidence-based solutions to criminal behavior, and to improve public safety by reducing the likelihood of reoffending. They may also offer cost savings compared to traditional incarceration and provide a better opportunity for rehabilitation and reintegration into society.

- Family-centered approaches, which recognize the importance of maintaining family connections and providing support for women with children. Family-centered approaches in corrections refer to programs and practices that recognize the importance of family support and engagement in promoting the well-being and successful reentry of incarcerated individuals. Examples of family-centered approaches include family reunification services, parenting programs for incarcerated parents, couples and family counseling services, visitation and communication programs, collaboration with community-based organizations to support families, life skills and family financial management courses, resources and support for families during incarceration and reentry, parent–child visiting programs, and opportunities for family engagement. These approaches aim to reduce the negative impacts of incarceration on families and to promote healthy family relationships as a key component of successful reentry and rehabilitation. By supporting families and addressing their needs, family-centered approaches can also improve public safety and reduce the likelihood of recidivism.

Generally speaking, gender-responsive strategies work to reduce women's recidivism, increase positive outcomes for women and their families, and promote gender equality within correctional settings.

A critical difference between men and women in prison, is "the manner in which they communicate." Females who offend are usually much more open, more verbal, more emotional, and more willing to share the intimacies of their lives than men are. Men in prison, like most men in free society, are guarded about the information they share and the manner in which they share it. "For men, information is power. For women, talking helps establish a common ground, a way to relate to others."

Gender-specific training is vital for corrections officers (COs) who work in women's prisons. Proper staff training can head off the development of inappropriate relationships (especially initiated by male staff members), which could lead to sexual misconduct. Moreover, staff members who work with women should receive additional training in negotiating and listening skills.

Recently, a guide to gender-responsive approaches was developed by the Council of State Governments Justice Center in partnership with the National Resource Center on Justice Involved Women. The guide, entitled *Adopting a Gender-Responsive Approach for Women in the Justice System*,[56] addresses unique aspects of managing women in prison and provides correctional personnel with insights into the behaviors, actions, needs, and backgrounds presented by women who offend. The guide also offers gender-responsive case management models that have been created to better respond to women's complex risks and needs and to connect them with resources and treatment to support successful reentry and later recovery in the community.

It is especially important to realize that a woman's children are usually very important to her and that many imprisoned women have children on the outside. Hence, parenting skills should be taught to imprisoned mothers because most will rejoin and be with their children during critical stages in the children's development.

Mothers in Prison

A woman's children are usually very important to her, and many imprisoned women have children who live on the outside. Hence, parenting skills should be taught to imprisoned mothers because most will rejoin and be with their children during critical stages of the children's development.

Data show, however, that almost 50 percent of mothers in prison have never received a visit from their children but that mail, phone calls, and social media links (if permitted) can substantially enhance opportunities for incarcerated mothers to maintain positive connections with their children.[57]

According to a study done by Johns Hopkins University,[58] 4 percent of women who enter state prisons are pregnant, and 800 women give birth each year while in custody.

The ACA[59] recommends that institutions provide counseling for pregnant residents, that "prenatal care" should be offered, and that deliveries should be made at community hospitals. Similarly, the American Public Health Association's standards for health services in correctional institutions say that pregnant residents should be provided with prenatal care, including medical exams and treatment, and that women who are pregnant should be allowed a special program of housing, diet, vitamin supplements, and exercise. The federal First Step Act, signed into law in 2018, eliminated the practice of shackling women residents while they are giving birth.

Once residents give birth, other problems arise—including the critical issue of child placement. Some states still have partial civil death statutes, which mean that people in prison lose many of their civil rights upon incarceration. In such states, women may lose legal custody of their children. Children either become wards of the state or are placed for adoption.

Although there is some historical precedent for allowing women to keep newborns with them in the institutional setting, very few women's prisons permit this practice. Overcrowded prisons lack space for children, and the prison environment is a decidedly undesirable environment for children. A few women's prisons allow women to keep newborns for a brief period. Most, however, arrange for foster care until the mother is able to find relatives to care for the child or is released. Others work with services that put prison-born infants up for adoption. Some facilities make a special effort to keep mother and child together. Even relatively progressive prisons that allow mother–child contact usually do so only for the first year. Recently, however, the state of Minnesota took the lead by passing its Healthy Start Act. The law permits the state's Commissioner of Corrections to place pregnant people, along with those who have recently given birth, in settings that provide an alternative to prison, during their child's first year of life. The purpose of the program is to allow parent and child to bond outside of a facility setting while receiving behavioral counseling, drug treatment, and other services.

Many women are already mothers when they come to prison, and studies show that children of incarcerated parents face profound and complex threats to their emotional, physical, educational, and financial well-being.[60] A 2021 BJS report found that an estimated 57,700 females in state or federal prisons were parents with minor children.[61] Among state prisoners, an estimated three in five white (60%) and Hispanic (62%) females and about one in two Black (50%) females were mothers with minor children. Nearly 7 in 10 Hispanic (67%) females in federal prison were mothers with minor children, compared to about 1 in 2 white (49%) and Black (54%) females. Among minor children of parents in state prison, 1 percent were younger than age 1, about 18 percent were ages 1 to 4, and 48 percent were age 10 or older. An estimated 13 percent of minor children of federal prisoners were age 4 or younger, and 20 percent were ages 15 to 17.

Studies show that children whose parents are incarcerated are at higher risk for increased antisocial behaviors and psychological problems, such as depression. Worry about children affects the physical and emotional well-being of women in prison. Although 78 percent of mothers (and 62 percent of fathers) report having at least monthly contact with their children, only 24 percent of mothers (and 21 percent of fathers) report personal visits from their children at least monthly.[62] A majority of both mothers (54 percent) and fathers (57 percent) report never having had a personal visit with their children since their imprisonment began.

According to BJS, nearly 90 percent of women with children under age 18 have had contact with their children since entering prison. Half of all surveyed women in prison have been visited by their children, four-fifths have corresponded by mail, and three-quarters have talked with children on the telephone. Women in prison with children under age 18 are more likely than those with adult children to make daily telephone calls to their children. For years, phone calls made from prison were costly and difficult for almost any incarcerated person to afford. That changed in 2023 with the passage of the federal Martha Wright-Reed Just and Reasonable Communication Act, which had been billed as a push for "prison phone justice."[63] The bill allows the Federal Communications Commission to take steps to bring down the high cost of telephone calls for incarcerated people.

Understandably, mothers in prison frequently express concern about possible alienation from their children due to the passage of time associated with incarceration. They often worry that their children will develop strong bonds with new caretakers and be unwilling to return to them upon release.[64]

Finally, it is important to note that a number of women's prisons offer programs designed to develop parenting skills among residents. Included are the Program for Caring Parents at the Louisiana Correctional Institute for Women; Project HIP (Helping Incarcerated Parents) at the Maine Correctional Center; and Neil J. Houston House, a program for nonviolent female offenders in Massachusetts.

Incarcerated fathers and their daughters at the Richmond City Jail during a "Date with Dad Night." Officials say that the dance offers a rare chance for fathers and daughters to bond. What are the problems faced by imprisoned parents? By their children?

Marvin Joseph/The Washington Post via Getty Images

One recent study found that 1.47 million American children had a parent in prison.[65] Statistically speaking, 1 of every 43 American children has a parent in prison today, and ethnic variation in the numbers are striking. Although only 1 of every 111 white children has experienced the imprisonment of a parent, 1 of every 15 Black children has had that experience. Moreover, between 1991 and 2007, the number of incarcerated fathers rose 76 percent while the number of incarcerated mothers increased by 122 percent.

The effects of parental incarceration on children can be significant. A number of studies show that the children of incarcerated mothers experience alienation, hostility, anger, significant feelings of abandonment, and overall dysfunction. They are much less likely to succeed in school than their peers and far more likely to involve themselves in gangs, sexual misconduct, sexual abuse, and overall delinquency.[66]

It is noteworthy that men in prison are, for the most part, rarely provided any special assistance for maintaining contact with their children during their incarceration. During the past decade or two, however, administrators in women's institutions across the country have implemented measures to foster stronger bonds between incarcerated mothers and their children. Ranging from the establishment of prison nurseries to the development of special visitation areas, these measures seek to facilitate the continued family contact that appears to be so important to female offenders.

Some institutions have opted to create nurseries on site. At Nebraska's Correctional Center for Women, for example, residents who are due for release before their children are 18 months old may keep the children with them in a specially designated floor of a standard prison building. The mothers are provided parenting and child-care classes, and they work only part-time. While they work, other trained residents provide child care.[67]

Another example of programs designed to facilitate family bonding is the Ohio Reformatory for Women's annual three-day weekend camp, which brings children ages 6 to 12 from all over the state to spend days with their mothers. Originally pioneered at Bedford Hills Correctional Facility, New York's maximum-security prison for women, such camping visits have become more common in other facilities as well. Some states even allow overnight camping trips, both on and off the prison grounds.

Mothers who are incarcerated apply for the program in January each year. Local churches and other community service groups support the program.[68] Selection criteria include a review of the women's disciplinary records during incarceration, and those whose crimes involved their children are prohibited from participating. During the weekend, activities such as storytelling, softball, crafts, and meals facilitate bonding between mother and child. The women return to the prison to sleep at night, but the children "camp out" in sleeping bags at a local church.

Another innovative effort is Florida's "Reading Family Ties: Face to Face" program.[69] Begun in February 2000, it uses high-speed Internet-conferencing technology to permit weekly family visits between incarcerated mothers in two rural institutions and their children in the Miami area. Mothers who are imprisoned may sit before an Internet-linked camera to read to their children. Logistical limitations, of course, are significant, but administrators plan to expand the program to other major cities in Florida.

Perhaps the most family-centered efforts are being tried in California and Illinois. Oakland's Project Pride permits mothers convicted of nonviolent offenses to serve the last portion of their sentences in residential community settings with their preschool-age children. Under the Family Foundations Program in Santa Fe Springs, California, sentencing of convicted mothers with substance abuse histories can include treatment in residential centers where they can live with their children. Similarly, at Illinois's Decatur Correctional Center, infants live in separate rooms with their mothers. Books and toys are plentiful in the unit, and large day rooms are decorated with colorful murals. The program is intended to serve women whose children will be two years old or younger by the time they are released from prison.

Prison programs to help fathers learn better parenting are also on the increase. The National Fatherhood Initiative, for example, started Inside Out Dad in 2004, and it now operates in more than 400 prisons and jails nationwide. The program's goal is to reduce recidivism through better fathering.

Some critics might decry such programs as unjustified coddling of people who are in prison. Few, however, can argue the benefits such programs provide to the children of incarcerated parents. Meanwhile, it remains to be seen whether the programs will serve to sustain family relationships, ease return to the family environment after release, and, ultimately, reduce recidivism rates.

COVID-19'S IMPACT ON STATE AND LOCAL PRISONS

COVID-19 test

A viral or polymerase chain reaction (PCR) test for COVID-19.

COVID-19

Coronavirus disease and the virus causing the disease, i.e., severe acute respiratory syndrome coronavirus 2 (SARS-CoV-2).

From March 2020 to the end of February 2021, state and federal correctional facilities performed 4,816,400 **COVID-19 tests** on persons in prison. Of these tests, 396,300 (8.2%) were positive for **COVID-19**, representing 374,400 infected persons in state and federal prisons.[70]

The infection rate in prisons during this period was 219 per 1,000 individuals confined in state prisons and 298 per 1,000 people held in federal prisons. Almost 2,500 people confined in state and federal prisons died of COVID-19-related causes during the 12-month study period. Put another way, people held in state and federal prisons had a mortality rate of 1.5 COVID-19-related deaths per 1,000 persons during the survey period.

Whites accounted for 44 percent of COVID-19-related deaths in prisons, while Blacks accounted for 34 percent (Exhibit 10–5). Eighty-three percent of COVID-19-related deaths in state and federal prisons occurred in persons aged 55 or older.

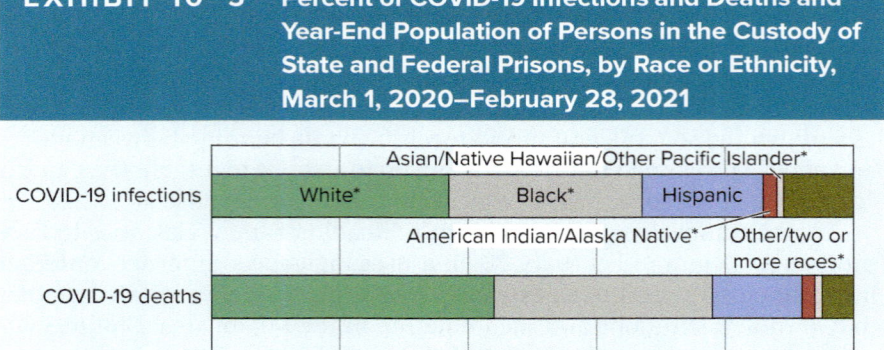

EXHIBIT 10–5   Percent of COVID-19 Infections and Deaths and Year-End Population of Persons in the Custody of State and Federal Prisons, by Race or Ethnicity, March 1, 2020–February 28, 2021

*Excludes persons of Hispanic origin (e.g., "White" refers to non-Hispanic White persons, and "Black" refers to non-Hispanic Black persons).

Source: Bureau of Justice Statistics, National Prisoner Statistics program – Coronavirus Pandemic Supplemental Survey, 2021.

A number of staff members also became infected during the study period, and some of them died. Staff in state correctional facilities had an infection rate of 269 per 1,000, while those working in Federal Bureau of Prisons (BOP) facilities had a rate of 188 per 1,000. From the end of February 2020 to the end of February 2021, a total of 196 correctional staff in state and federal prisons died as a result of COVID-19.

Partially as a result of COVID-19 fears, the U.S. prison population declined by 157,500 persons during the first six months of the COVID-19 study period (through the end of August 2020), and by 58,300 in the last six months of the study period (through the end of February 2021). Twenty-four states released a total of 37,700 persons from prison on an expedited basis (i.e., earlier than scheduled) during the study period in an effort to reduce prison populations densities and thereby lower the risk of COVID-19 transmission.

Every state, with the exception of Louisiana, Tennessee, Alaska, Nebraska, and Idaho, had at least a 10 percent decline in its prison population. States with the largest prison populations (Texas, California, and Florida) and the BOP experienced a combined decrease of 84,100 persons held in confinement. This accounted for 39 percent of the total decline of 215,800 in confinement across the United States from the end of February 2020 to the end of February 2021. The majority of the decrease in the number of those confined occurred between the beginning of February and the end of August 2020 (12% in state DOCs and 10% in the BOP). During these six months, the prison populations of all states and the BOP declined at least 4 percent. Similarly, admissions to prison decreased by 66 percent during the pandemic as more and more diversionary sentences were imposed.

During the COVID epidemic, most prisons adopted strategies to mitigate the risk of transmission, including the quarantine of newly admitted persons, viral testing of individuals prior to release, and suspension of familial and legal visits. In 2022, the Centers for Disease Control and Prevention (CDC) issued guidance on the management of COVID-19 in correctional and detention facilities.[71] Among its recommendations were those pertaining to physical distancing—something not always achievable in correctional facilities. The CDC offered these recommendations:

- Maintain at least 6 feet of distance between all people, even those who do not have symptoms). Physical distancing strategies can be applied on an individual level (e.g., avoiding physical contact), a group level (e.g., canceling group activities where people would be in close contact), and an operational level (e.g., rearranging chairs in the dining hall to increase the distance between them or using protective barriers if space is limited).

- Make a list of possible physical distancing strategies that could be implemented as needed at different stages of transmission intensity. When distancing is not possible, protective barriers may be used in areas such as offices and classrooms. Strategies will need to be tailored to the individual space in the facility and the needs of the residents and staff.

- Consider options to prevent overcrowding (e.g., diverting new intakes to other facilities with available capacity, and encouraging alternatives to incarceration and other decompression strategies where allowable).

- When feasible and consistent with security priorities, encourage staff members to maintain a distance of 6 feet or more from a person with COVID-19 symptoms, while interviewing, escorting, or interacting in other ways. Staff members should always wear recommended PPE when in close contact with a person with COVID-19 symptoms.

- If there are people with COVID-19 inside the facility, prevent unnecessary movement between different parts of the facility and mixing of people from different housing units. For example, maintain consistent duty assignments for staff across shifts to prevent transmission across different facility areas and modify resident work detail assignments so that each detail includes only residents from a single housing unit.
- If possible, designate a room near each housing unit to evaluate residents with COVID-19 symptoms, rather than having them walk through the facility to the medical unit. If this is not feasible, consider staggering sick calls.

REVIEW AND APPLICATIONS

SUMMARY

1 people in prison live their daily lives in what have been described as *total institutions,* and accordance with the dictates of the prison subculture. Prison subculture consists of the customs and beliefs of those incarcerated in correctional institutions. *Deprivation theory* holds that prison subcultures develop in response to the pains of imprisonment. *Importation theory* claims that prison subcultures are brought into prisons from the outside world. The *integration model* uses both theories to explain prison subcultures.

2 An important aspect of the prison subculture is the prison code. The prison code is a set of norms for the behavior of people who are incarcerated Central elements of the code include notions of loyalty (to prison society), control of anger, toughness, and distrust of prison officials. Because the prison code is a part of the prison subculture, it is mostly opposed to official policies.

3 Prison subculture also has its own language, called *prison argot.* Examples of traditional prison argot are "fish" (a new resident), "cellie" (cell mate), and "homeboy" (a resident from one's hometown).

4 Prison roles are different prison lifestyle choices. They include the real man, the mean dude, the bully, the agitator, the hedonist, the opportunist, the retreatist, the legalist, the radical, the colonist, the religious, the punk, and the gang-banger.

5 There are far fewer women's prisons than men's in the United States. Women's prisons often have no gun towers or armed guards and no stone walls or fences topped by barbed wire. They tend to be more attractive and are often built on a cottage plan. Security in most women's prisons is more relaxed than in institutions for men, and women who are in prison may have more freedom within the institution than do male counterparts in their institutions. Other gender-based disparities favoring men who are in prison exist. A lack of funding and inadequate training have been cited to explain why programs available to women who are imprisoned are often not on a par with those available to men who are in prison.

6 Females who are incarcerated largely resemble men who are in prison in terms of race, ethnic background, and age. However, they are substantially more likely to be serving time for drug offenses and less likely to have been sentenced for violent crimes.

7 Although there are many similarities between men's and women's prisons, the social structure and the subcultural norms and expectations of women's prisons differ from those of men's prisons in a number of important ways. One important difference is that the resident subculture in a women's prison tends to encourage relationships rather than isolation. As a consequence, pseudofamilies arise, with fully developed familial relationships and roles.

8 State and federal prisons have recently been impacted by COVID-19. Both correctional staff and clients have experienced COVID infections, with most prisons adopting strategies to mitigate the risk of transmission, including the quarantine of newly admitted persons, viral testing of individuals prior to release, and suspension of familial and legal visits.

KEY TERMS

total institution, p. 268

prison subculture, p. 270

prisonization, p. 270

pains of imprisonment, p. 270

deprivation theory, p. 271

importation theory, p. 271

integration model, p. 271

prison code, p. 272

prison argot, p. 272

prison roles, p. 273

pseudofamilies, p. 288

gender-responsiveness, p. 289

COVID-19 test, p. 294

COVID-19, p. 294

QUESTIONS FOR REVIEW

1 What is *inmate subculture,* and how is it central to understanding society in prisons?

2 What is the *prison code?* What are some of its key features? How does it influence behavior in prisons?

3 What is *prison argot?* Give some examples.

4 Explain what is meant by *prison roles,* and give some examples.

5 In what ways do women's prisons differ from men's prisons?

6 Compare men and women who are incarcerated by their criminal histories, their family characteristics, and the offenses for which they are incarcerated.

7 How does the social structure of women's prisons differ from that in men's prisons? What are *pseudofamilies,* and why are they important to the society of women's prisons?

8 What impact has COVID-19 had on prisons? What strategies have been employed to limit its impact?

THINKING CRITICALLY ABOUT CORRECTIONS

Prison Birth

A woman who gives birth in prison may lose her child to state authorities or may have her parental rights severely restricted. In most cases, the child is removed from the mother who is incarcerated shortly after birth. Do you think this is fair? Why or why not?

Housing Assignments

Not surprisingly, state policies differ significantly on the question of housing assignments for people sent to prison. Some permit them to choose their cell mates while others enforce random cell assignments. What are the advantages and disadvantages of each policy style? Which style do you think is best?

ON-THE-JOB DECISION MAKING

Male Officers in Women's Prisons

You are a correctional officer assigned to a women's prison. Six months ago, the superintendent of your institution ordered an investigation to determine the proper role of male officers within the facility. The investigation centered on charges by a handful of incarcerated women that they had been sexually harassed by male COs. The alleged harassment included requests for sexual favors in return for special privileges, observation of women residents in various states of undress while in their rooms and in shower facilities, and inappropriate touching during cell and facility searches (policy allows only female COs to conduct body searches).

Although the investigation was inconclusive, the activities of male COs have been restricted. They are no longer permitted to have any physical contact with incarcerated persons unless an emergency demands that they restrain or search

them. They have been reassigned to areas of the facility where they cannot view shower and toilet facilities. They are expected to announce their presence in living areas, and they have been ordered to take special classes on staff-resident interaction.

Unfortunately, however, there are not enough female COs for all of the reassignments required by the recent shift in policy. As a result, the routines of female officers are being significantly disrupted. Female officers are being asked to work shifts that are inconvenient for their personal lives (many are mothers or college students and had come to count on predictable shift work). Most female COs also feel that their workload has increased because they have to cover areas of the institution and assume tasks that male officers would previously have handled.

A few female COs have already left for jobs elsewhere, citing difficulties created in the work environment by the new policies. The talk among the correctional staff is that many of the remaining female staff members might also soon leave. If more female COs leave the facility, it will be impossible for those who remain to keep the facility running under the new rules.

1. Did the superintendent make the right decision in limiting the activities of male COs? Why or why not?
2. Might there be other ways to resolve the issues raised by the investigation into sexual harassment? If so, what might they be?

Same-Sex Relationships

You are a chaplain working in a large state-run correctional facility. You take pride in your reputation among the people held there as a fair and reasonable counselor who treats them with courtesy and respect and never judges them for past transgressions or present problems.

Ronald, a resident whom you know well, comes to you with a special request. He wants to marry Lawrence, another person being held in confinement, and he wants you to perform the ceremony in private. He also tells you that he knows that the "marriage" will have no legitimacy on the outside but says that the ceremony will be deeply moving for him and for Lawrence. Ronald's incarceration record is sterling. His disciplinary record shows no infractions, and there are numerous positive signs regarding the obvious sincerity of his efforts to rehabilitate himself in preparation for his return to free society.

You are concerned that Ronald may actually be cisgender and that his relationship with Lawrence might arise more from the pains of imprisonment than from any innate sexual orientation or gender identity. You are uncertain what prison regulations might say about such a ceremony, but you suspect that, were you to inquire, the ceremony would be officially disallowed. Additionally, church elders in your denomination have condemned same-sex marriages like the one you are being asked to perform. Still, you think that Ronald is well-meaning in his efforts to form a more stable relationship with Lawrence, and you believe that such a relationship can help him adjust to the stresses of prison life.

1. What do you do? Is this an issue that you need time to think about, or do you answer right away?
2. Would you counsel Ronald in order to better assess his "true" sexual orientation?
3. Is his "true" sexual orientation even an important consideration?
4. Would you further consider counseling Ronald and Lawrence, individually and jointly, regarding their desire to formalize their relationship?
5. Would you take the issue to the prison superintendent?

ENDNOTES

1. "New York Replaces 'Inmates' with 'Incarcerated individuals'", *The Crime Report,* August 9, 2022, https://thecrimereport.org/2022/08/09/new-york-replaces-inmates-with-incaceratedindividuals (accessed March 10, 2023).
2. Lauren G. Beatty and Tracy L. Snell, *Profile of Prison Inmates, 2016* (Washington, DC: U.S. Department of Justice, December 2021).
3. Erving Goffman, *Asylums: Essays on the Social Situation of Mental Patients and Other Inmates* (Garden City, NY: Anchor Books, 1961).
4. Hans Toch, *Living in Prison: The Ecology of Survival,* reprinted (Washington, DC: American Psychological Association, 1996), p. xv.
5. Victoria R. DeRosia, *Living Inside Prison Walls: Adjustment Behavior* (Westport, CT: Praeger, 1998).
6. "Inmate Subculture," in Virgil L. Williams (ed.), *Dictionary of American Penology: An Introductory Guide* (Westport, CT: Greenwood, 1979).
7. Donald Clemmer, *The Prison Community* (Boston: Holt, Rinehart & Winston, 1940).
8. Stanton Wheeler, "Socialization in Correctional Communities," *American Sociological Review,* vol. 26 (October 1961), pp. 697–712.
9. Gresham M. Sykes, *The Society of Captives: A Study of a Maximum Security Prison* (Princeton, NJ: Princeton University Press, 1958).
10. Stephen C. Light, *Inmate Assaults on Staff: Challenges to Authority in a Large State Prison System,* dissertation, State University of New York at Albany (Ann Arbor, MI: University Microfilms International, 1987).
11. John Irwin and Donald R. Cressey, "Thieves, Convicts and the Inmate Culture," *Social Problems,* vol. 10 (Fall 1962), pp. 142–155.
12. James Jacobs, *Stateville: The Penitentiary in Mass Society* (Chicago: University of Chicago Press, 1977).
13. Miles D. Harer and Darrell J. Steffensmeier, "Race and Prison Violence," *Criminology,* vol. 34, no. 3 (1996), pp. 323–355.
14. John M. Wilson and Jon D. Snodgrass, "The Prison Code in a Therapeutic Community," *Journal of Criminal Law, Criminology, and Police Science,* vol. 60, no. 4 (1969), pp. 472–478.
15. Gresham M. Sykes and Sheldon L. Messinger, "The Inmate Social System," in Richard A. Cloward et al. (eds.), *Theoretical Studies in Social Organization of the Prison* (New York: Social Science Research Council, 1960), pp. 5–19.

16. Peter M. Wittenberg, "Language and Communication in Prison," *Federal Probation,* vol. 60, no. 4 (1996), pp. 45–50.

17. Sykes, *The Society of Captives.*

18. John Irwin, *The Felon* (Englewood Cliffs, NJ: Prentice Hall, 1970).

19. Matthew G.T. Denney and Robert Tynes, "The Effects of College in Prison and Policy Implications," *Justice Quarterly,* Vol 38, No. 7 (2021), pp. 1542–1566.

20. Lindsay Leban, Stephanie M. Cardwell, Heith Copes, and Timothy Brezina, "Adapting to Prison Life: A Qualitative Examination of the Coping Process Among Incarcerated Offenders," *Justice Quarterly,* 2016, http://dx.doi.org/10.1080/07418825.2015.1012096 (accessed March 1, 2023).

21. Christopher Hensley and Richard Tewksbury, "Inmate-to-Inmate Prison Sexuality: A Review of Empirical Studies." *Trauma, Violence, & Abuse,* vol. 3, no. 3 (2002), pp. 226–243. doi:10.1177/15248380020033005 (accessed March 22, 2023).

22. R. J. Carecedo, et al., "Heterosexual Romantic Relationships Inside of Prison: Partner Status as Predictor of Loneliness, Sexual Satisfaction, and Quality of Life," *International Journal of Offender Therapy and Comparative Criminology,* vol. 55, no. 6 (2011), pp. 898–924. doi:10.1177/0306624x10373593

23. The Howard League for Penal Reform, "Former Prisoners Share Their Experiences of Sex in Prison" (no date), https://howardleague.org/news/prisonersexperiencesofsexinprison (accessed April 2, 2023).

24. "Women Prisoners Coerced into Sex with Staff," February 26, 2014, *The BBC,* https://www.bbc.com/news/uk-26324570 (accessed April 2, 2023).

25. Michelle Templeton et al., "Developing a Sexual Health Promotion Intervention with Young Men in Prisons: A Rights-Based Participatory Approach," JMIR Research Protocol, vol. 8, no. 4 (2019).

26. Pub. L. No. 108–79.

27. Emily D. Buehler, "Substantiated Incidents of Sexual Victimization Reported by Adult Correctional Authorities, 2016–2018" (Washington, DC: Bureau of Justice Statistics, 2023), https://bjs.ojp.gov/sites/g/files/xyckuh236/files/media/document/sisvraca1618.pdf (accessed May 5, 2023).

28. Allen J. Beck and Timothy A. Hughes, *Sexual Violence Reported by Correctional Authorities, 2004* (Washington, DC: Bureau of Justice Statistics, 2005).

29. Bureau of Justice Statistics, "Sexual Orientation and Gender Identity Measures in BJS Survey Data Collections," BJS Webinar, September 29, 2022.

30. National Institute on Drug Abuse, "Criminal Justice Drug Facts," June 2020, https://nida.nih.gov/download/23025/criminal-justice-drugfacts.pdf (accessed June 10, 2023).

31. Beth Schwartzappel and Jimmy Jenkins, "Inside the Nation's Overdoes Crisis in Prisons and Jails," *The Marshall Project,* 2021, https://www.themarshallproject.org/2021/07/15/inside-the-nation-s-overdose-crisis-in-prisons-and-jails (accessed June 10, 2023).

32. Recovery First Treatment Center, "Drug Addiction in Prison," 2022, https://recoveryfirst.org/blog/treatment/drug-addiction-in-prison (accessed June 10, 2023).

33. Phyllis J. Baunach, "Critical Problems of Women in Prison," in Imogene L. Moyer (ed.), *The Changing Roles of Women in the Criminal Justice System* (Prospect Heights, IL: Waveland Press, 1985), pp. 95–110.

34. See Wendy Sawyer, "The Gender Divide: Tracking Women's State Prison Growth," Prison Policy Initiative, January 9, 2018, https://www.prisonpolicy.org/reports/women_overtime.html (accessed October 20, 2023).

35. American Correctional Association, *Standards for Adult Correctional Institutions* (Lanham, MD: ACA, 1990).

36. Much of the material in this paragraph and the two that follow have been adapted from Yunsoo Park, "Addressing Trauma in Women's Prisons," National Institute of Justice, May 11, 2022.

37. Ibid.

38. Ibid.

39. E. Ann Carson, *Prisoners in 2020* (Washington, DC: U.S. Department of Justice, 2021).

40. E. Ann Carson, *Prisoners in 2020* (Washington, DC: U.S. Department of Justice, 2021).

41. E. Ann Carson, *Prisoners in 2020* (Washington, DC: U.S. Department of Justice, 2021).

42. Angela Browne, Brenda Miller, and Eugene Maguin, "Prevalence and Severity of Lifetime Physical and Sexual Victimization Among Incarcerated Women," *International Journal of Law and Psychiatry,* vol. 22, no. 3–4 (1999), pp. 301–322.

43. Bloom et al., *Gender-Responsive Strategies: Research, Practice, and Guiding Principles for Women Offenders* (Washington, DC: National Institute of Corrections, 2003).

44. Carson, *Prisoners in 2020.*

45. American Correctional Association, *Female Offenders: Meeting Needs of a Neglected Population* (Laurel, MD: ACA, 1993).

46. Tracy Snell, *Women in Prison* (Washington, DC: Bureau of Justice Statistics, 1994).

47. Rose Giallombardo, *Society of Women: A Study of a Women's Prison* (New York: John Wiley, 1966).

48. Esther Heffernan, *Making It in Prison: The Square, the Cool, and the Life* (New York: Wiley-Interscience, 1972).

49. Barbara Owens, "The Mix: The Culture of Imprisoned Women," in Mary K. Stohr and Craig Hemmens (eds.), *The Inmate Prison Experience* (Upper Saddle River, NJ: Prentice Hall, 2004), pp. 152–172.

50. Williams, "Inmate Subculture," p. 109.

51. Kathryn Watterson, *Women in Prison: Inside the Concrete Tomb,* 2nd ed. (Boston: Northeastern University Press, 1996), p. 291.

52. See, for example, Julia Dillavou, Derek A. Kreager, Theodore Greenfelder, and Yiwen Zhan, "Mothers Inside and Out? Pseudo-Families and Motherhood in a Woman's Prison," *Crime and Delinquency,* April 2022, pp. 1–23.

53. Doris Layton MacKenzie, James Robinson, and Carol Campbell, "Long-Term Incarceration of Female Offenders: Prison Adjustment and Coping," *Criminal Justice and Behavior,* vol. 16, no. 2 (1989), pp. 223–238.

54. Nicole Hahn Rafter, *Partial Justice: Women, Prisons and Social Control* (New Brunswick, NJ: Transaction, 1990).

55. Barbara Bloom and Stephanie Covington, *Gendered Justice: Programming for Women in Correctional Settings,* paper presented at the American Society of Criminology annual meeting, San Francisco, November 2000, p. 11.

56. Office of Justice Programs, *Adopting a Gender-responsive Approach for Women in the Justice System: A Resource Guide,* Washington, D.C., 2021.

57. Susan Cranford and Rose Williams, "Critical Issues in Managing Female Offenders," *Corrections Today,* vol. 60, no. 7 (December 1998), pp. 130–135.

58. John Hopkins Medicine, "First of Its Kind Statistics on Pregnant Women in U.S. Prisons," March 21, 2019, https://www.hopkinsmedicine.org/news/newsroom/news-releases/first-of-its-kind-statistics-on-pregnant-women-in-us-prisons (accessed March 10, 2023).

59. American Correctional Association, *Standards for Adult Correctional Institutions,* 3rd ed. (ACA, January 1990).

60. Eric Martin, "Hidden Consequences: The Impact of Incarceration on Dependent Children," *National Institute of Justice Journal,* No. 278 (March 2017).

61. Laura M. Maruschak, et al, *Parents in Prison and Their Minor Children* (Washington, DC: Bureau of Justice Statistics, 2021).

62. National Institute of Corrections, *Services for Families of Prison Inmates* (Washington, DC: NIC, 2002), p. 3.

63. S. 1541, The Martha Wright-Reed Just and Reasonable Communications Act of 2022.

64. Maruschak, *Parents in Prison and Their Minor Children,* op. cit.

65. L. Wright and C. Seymour, *Working with Children and Families Separated by Incarceration: A Handbook for Child Welfare Agencies* (Washington, DC: Child Welfare League of America, 2000).

66. Kelsey Kauffman, "Mothers in Prison," *Corrections Today* (February 2001), pp. 62–65.

67. Christopher J. Mumola, *Incarcerated Parents and Their Children,* Bureau of Justice Statistics Special Report (Washington, DC: Bureau of Justice Statistics, August 2000), p. 1.

68. Suzanne Hoholik, "Weekend Camp Lets Mother, Kids Bond," *The Columbus Dispatch,* July 22, 2000, pp. A1–A2.

69. Rini Bartlett, "Helping Inmate Moms Keep in Touch," *Correctional Compass* (Tallahassee, FL: Department of Corrections, February 2001), www.dc.state.fl.us/pub/compass/0102/page07.html (accessed June 2, 2007).

70. Bureau of Justice Statistics, E. Ann Carson, Melissa Nadel, and Gerry Gaes, Impact of COVID-19 on State and Federal Prisons, March 2020-[en dash]February 2021, https://bjs.ojp.gov/content/pub/pdf/icsfp2021.pdf (accessed March 10, 2023).

71. Centers for Disease Control and *Prevention, Interim Guidance on Management of Coronavirus Disease 2019 (COVID-19) in Correctional and Detention Facilities* (Washington, DC; CDC, 2022).

THE LEGAL WORLD

The Rights of Confined Persons

[11]

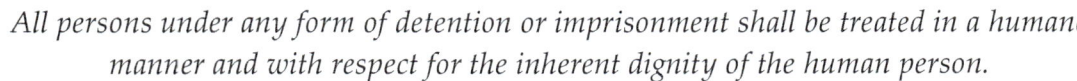

Hisham F. Ibrahim/Getty Images

CHAPTER OBJECTIVES

After completing this chapter you should be able to do the following:

1 Explain what is meant by the *hands-off doctrine.*

2 Identify the key legal sources of the rights of incarcerated persons.

3 List the five ways in which people who are in prison can challenge their conditions of confinement.

4 Describe the major changes that took place during the prisoners' rights era.

5 List and explain the four amendments to the U.S. Constitution on which most claims made by incarcerated persons are based.

6 Explain how the development of rights for females who are incarcerated has differed from that of rights for males in prison.

7 Describe the doctrine of sovereign immunity, and explain how some limited court protections shield correctional officers today from certain types of civil lawsuits.

All persons under any form of detention or imprisonment shall be treated in a humane manner and with respect for the inherent dignity of the human person.

—*United Nations General Assembly Resolution 43/173, December 9, 1988*

In 2023, federal district judge Roslyn O. Silver ordered the Arizona Department of Corrections, Rehabilitation, and Reentry to make "substantial" changes to its facility and staffing operations after finding that Arizona prison conditions constitute an "unconstitutional substantial risk of serious harm" to people in state custody. The case, *Jensen* v. *Shinn*, built on other lawsuits brought against the department on charges that it had failed to provide adequate medical and mental health care, and that it had sustained unconstitutional conditions through the use of solitary confinement. Judge Silver's decision built on a 2014 case in which Arizona prison officials had been ordered to improve the system. Later hearings found those same officials in contempt of the order; and another found that the department had "knowingly created documents in a false or misleading manner" about claimed improvements at facilities under its control.

Commenting on the court's order, Arizona governor Kathe Hobbs said, "The system is broken and will require a committed, long-term plan for implementing fair standards to improve the health and safety conditions for correctional officers and incarcerated individuals."[1] In rendering her decision, Judge Silver was drawing upon a legal tradition recognizing the rights of inmates that began in the United States more than 50 years earlier.

Arizona State Prison Complex—Yuma, one of a number of facilities in the Arizona prison system. In 2023, a federal district court judge found that the Arizona Department of Corrections, Rehabilitation, and Reentry had created and maintained conditions in its facilities that were unconstitutional, and thereby created a substantial risk of serious harm to people held in its custody. Why do judges have such power over prisons?
Arizona Department of Corrections Rehabilitation & Reentry

CO11-1

THE HANDS-OFF DOCTRINE

In 1871, more than 150 years before the Arizona order was issued, a Virginia judge declared the following:

> A convicted felon … punished by confinement in the penitentiary instead of with death … is in a state of penal servitude to the State. He has, as a consequence of his crime, not only forfeited his liberty, but all his personal rights except those which the law in its humanity accords to him. He is for the time being the slave of the State. He is *civiliter mortuus;* and his estate, if he has any, is administered like that of a dead man. The Bill of Rights is a declaration of general principles to govern a society of freemen, and not of convicted felons and men civilly dead.[2]

In the case of *Ruffin* v. *Commonwealth,* the judge was voicing what had long been believed: that people who were confined had no rights. It was this kind of thinking that long supported a "hands-off" approach to prisoners' rights. If people held in confinement were really civilly dead, the federal government and the federal courts certainly had no cause to tell the states how to run their prisons.

Under the **hands-off doctrine,** U.S. courts for many decades avoided intervening in prison management. The doctrine was based on two rationales: (1) that under the *separation of powers* inherent in the U.S. Constitution, the judicial branch of government should not interfere with the running of correctional facilities by the executive branch and (2) that judges should leave correctional administration to correctional experts. For a very long time in our nation's history, states ran their prisons as they saw fit. People in prison were thought of as "nonpersons," and rights pertained only to persons. Pleas from people held in confinement based on allegations of deprivations of their rights were ignored.

hands-off doctrine

A historical policy of the American courts not to intervene in prison management. Courts tended to follow the doctrine until the late 1960s.

The hands-off doctrine and the philosophy of the prisoner as a slave of the state began to change in the mid-1900s. Public attitudes about punishment versus rehabilitation changed, and more and more people became aware that those held in prison had *no* rights. As a result, the courts began to scrutinize the correctional enterprise in America.

Decline of the Hands-Off Doctrine

The 1941 case of *Ex parte Hull* began a dismantling of the hands-off doctrine. Prior to *Hull,* it had been common for corrections personnel to screen inmate mail, including petitions for writs of *habeas corpus* that had been authored by confined people. Corrections officials often confiscated the petitions, claiming they were improperly prepared and not fit to submit to court. In *Hull,* the Supreme Court ruled that no state or its officers may interfere with the right of a person in confinement to apply to a federal court for a writ of *habeas corpus.* Thus, court officials, not corrections officials, have the authority to decide whether such petitions are prepared correctly.

Although this seemed like a small step at the time, it would facilitate a major leap in prisoners' rights. Three years later, in *Coffin* v. *Reichard* (1944), the Sixth Circuit Court of Appeals extended *habeas corpus* hearings to consider the conditions of confinement. Even more important, the *Coffin* case was the first in which a federal appellate court ruled that people who are confined do not automatically lose their civil rights when in prison.[3] In the words of the Court, a person in confinement "retains all the rights of an ordinary citizen except those expressly, or by necessary implication, taken from him by law."

Another important development occurred in 1961 with the Supreme Court's ruling in *Monroe* v. *Pape.* Prior to *Pape,* it was believed that the phrase "under color of state law" in the Civil Rights Act of 1871 meant that a Section 1983 suit could involve only actions authorized by state law. In *Pape,* however, the Court held that for activities to take place *under color* of state law, they did not have to be *authorized* by state law. The statute, said the Court, had been intended to protect against "misuse of power, possessed by virtue of state law and made possible only because the wrongdoer is clothed with the authority of state law."

San Quentin State Prison in Marin County, California. Opened in 1852, it is one of the state's oldest and best-known correctional institutions. Under the hands-off doctrine, American courts long refused to intervene in prison management. When did the hands-off doctrine end?
Justin Sullivan/Getty Images

Officials "clothed with the authority of state law" seemed to include state corrections officials. Thus, state corrections officials who violated a resident's constitutional rights while performing their duties could be held liable for their actions in federal court regardless of whether state law or policy supported those actions.[4]

A third important case establishing the rights of confined persons to access the courts was *Cooper* v. *Pate* (1964). In *Cooper,* a federal circuit court clarified the *Pape* decision, indicating that people held in confinement could sue a warden or another correctional official under Title 42 of the U.S. Code, Section 1983, based on the protections of the Civil Rights Act of 1871.

Commenting on the importance of *Cooper,* one observer noted:

> Just by opening a forum in which prisoners' grievances could be heard, the federal courts destroyed the custodian's absolute power and the prisoners' isolation from the larger society. The litigation itself heightened prisoners' consciousness and politicized them.[5]

With access to the courts now established, cases challenging nearly every aspect of corrections were soon filed. The courts, primarily the federal district courts, began to review the complaints of people who were confined and intervene on their behalf.

The hands-off era is said to have ended in 1970 when a federal district court declared in *Holt* v. *Sarver* the entire Arkansas prison system "so inhumane as to be a violation of the Eighth Amendment bar on cruel and unusual punishment."[6] At the time, Robert Sarver, the Arkansas commissioner of corrections, admitted that "the physical facilities at both [prison units named in the suit] were inadequate and in a total state of disrepair that could only be described as deplorable." Additionally, he testified that residents with trustee status, some of them serving life or long-term sentences, constituted 99 percent of the security force of the state's prison system.

Commissioner Sarver continued, testifying that "trustees sell desirable jobs to prisoners and also traffic in food, liquor, and drugs. Prisoners frequently become intoxicated and unruly. The prisoners sleep in dormitories. Prisoners are frequently attacked and raped in the dormitories, and injuries and deaths have resulted. Sleep and rest are seriously disrupted. No adequate means exist to protect the prisoners from assaults. There is no satisfactory means of keeping guns, knives, and other weapons away from the prison population."[7]

The *Holt* court declared in 1970:

> The obligation ... to eliminate existing unconstitutionalities does not depend upon what the Legislature may do or upon what the Governor may do... . If Arkansas is going to operate a Penitentiary System, it is going to have to be a system that is countenanced by the Constitution of the United States.[8]

Litigation initiated by people in confinement had brought sad conditions to light, and the court had intervened to institute reforms for confined persons in Arkansas.

The case of Holt v. Sarver brought the hands-off era to a close and opened a new era of rights for incarcerated persons. What were the issues involved in that case?

Comstock/Stockbyte/Getty Images

prisoners' rights · CO11-2

Constitutional guarantees of free speech, religious practice, due process, and other private and personal rights as well as constitutional protections against cruel and unusual punishments made applicable to prison inmates by the federal courts.

THE RIGHTS OF INCARCERATED PEOPLE

Legal Foundations

Prisoners' rights have four legal foundations: the U.S. Constitution, federal statutes, state constitutions, and state statutes. Most court cases involving the rights of incarcerated people have involved rights claimed under the U.S. Constitution, even though state constitutions generally parallel the U.S. Constitution and sometimes confer additional rights. State legislatures and Congress can also confer additional rights to those who are incarcerated.

The U.S. Constitution The U.S. Constitution is the supreme law of our land. At the heart of any discussion of prisoners' rights lies one question: What does the Constitution have to say? As scholars began to search the Constitution, they could find no requirement that people who are incarcerated give up all of their rights as U.S. citizens (and human beings) after conviction.

It is important to remember, however, that **constitutional rights** are not absolute. Does freedom of speech mean that you have a protected right to stand up in a crowded theater and yell "Fire"? It does not (at least not unless there *is* a fire). That is because the panic that would follow such an exclamation would probably cause injuries and would needlessly put members of the public at risk of harm. Hence, the courts have held that, although freedom of speech is guaranteed by the Constitution, it is not an absolute right; in other words, there are limits to it (*Schenck* v. *United States,* 1919).

So the central issue raised by those interested in the rights of incarcerated people seems to be the degree to which a person retains constitutional rights when convicted of a criminal offense and sentenced to prison. Addressing that issue has become a job of the courts. The positions on it depend upon the courts' interpretation of the U.S. Constitution, state constitutions, and federal and state laws. Generally speaking, the courts have recognized four legitimate **institutional needs** that justify some restrictions on the constitutional rights of people in confinement:

1. maintenance of institutional *order;*
2. maintenance of institutional *security;*
3. *safety* of prison residents and staff; and
4. *rehabilitation* of inmates.

According to the courts, *order* refers to calm and discipline within the institution, *security* is the control of individuals and objects entering or leaving the institution, *safety* means avoidance of physical harm, and *rehabilitation* refers to practices necessary for the health, well-being, and treatment of those who are incarcerated.[9]

Federal Statutes Laws passed by Congress can confer certain rights on inmates in federal prisons. In addition, Congress has passed a number of laws that affect the running of state prisons. The Civil Rights Act of 1871, for example, was enacted after the Civil War to discourage lawless activities by state officials. Section 1983 of that act reads as follows:

> Every person who, under color of any statute, ordinance, regulation, custom, or usage, of any State or Territory, subjects, or causes to be subjected, any citizen of the United States or other person within the jurisdiction thereof to the deprivation of any rights, privileges, or immunities secured by the Constitution and laws, shall be liable to the party injured in an action at law, suit in equity, or other proper proceeding for redress.

This section imposes **civil liability** (but not criminal blame) on any person who deprives another of rights guaranteed by the U.S. Constitution. The Civil Rights Act of 1871 allows people held in state prisons to challenge conditions of their imprisonment in federal court. Most law suits brought under this act allege deprivation of constitutional rights. Another important piece of legislation is the Civil Rights of Institutionalized Persons Act (CRIPA),[10] which is discussed in more detail in Chapter 12.

Prisoner Rights

What is the "hands off" approach to the civil rights of prisoners? How common is the hands off approach today?

constitutional rights

The personal and due process rights guaranteed to individuals by the U.S. Constitution and its amendments, especially the first 10 amendments, known as the Bill of Rights. Constitutional rights are the basis of most inmate rights.

institutional needs

Prison administration interests recognized by the courts as justifying some restrictions on the constitutional rights of people in prison. Those interests are maintenance of institutional *order,* maintenance of institutional *security, safety* of prison inmates and staff, and *rehabilitation* of inmates.

civil liability

A legal obligation to another person to do, pay, or make good something.

State Constitutions Most state constitutions are patterned after the U.S. Constitution. However, state constitutions tend to be longer and more detailed than the U.S. Constitution and may contain specific provisions regarding corrections. State constitutions generally do not give prisoners more rights than are granted by the U.S. Constitution except in a few states such as California and Oregon. People held in confinement in such states may challenge the conditions of their confinement in state court under the state's constitutional provision.

State Statutes Unlike the federal government, state governments all have inherent police power, which allows them to pass laws to protect the health, safety, and welfare of their citizens. A state legislature can pass statutes to grant specific rights beyond those conferred by the state constitution. Often such legislation specifies duties of corrections officials or standards of treatment for people held in confiement. Prisoners who can show failure of officials to fulfill state statutory obligations may collect money damages or obtain a court order compelling officials to comply with the law.

Mechanisms for Securing the Rights of People Who Are Incarcerated

CO11-3

People in prison today have five ways to challenge the legality of their confinement, associated prison conditions, and the practices of correctional officials: (1) a state *habeas corpus* action, (2) a federal *habeas corpus* action after state remedies have been exhausted, (3) a state tort lawsuit, (4) a federal civil rights lawsuit, and (5) a petition for injunctive relief.[11]

Writ of *Habeas Corpus* A **writ of *habeas corpus*** is an order from a court to produce a prisoner in court so that the court can determine whether the person is being legally detained. *Habeas corpus* is Latin for "you have the body." The person being confined or someone acting on his or her behalf files a *habeas corpus* petition asking a court to determine the lawfulness of the imprisonment. The petition for the writ is merely a procedural tool. If a writ is issued, it has no bearing on any issues to be reviewed. It guarantees only a hearing on those issues.

People held in state and federal prisons may file *habeas corpus* petitions in federal courts. Those in state prisons, however, must exhaust available state *habeas corpus* remedies. In 2021, people held in confinement in *federal* courts filed 9,805 *habeas corpus* actions.[12]

A writ of habeas corpus is a court order requiring that a person who is incarcerated be brought before the court so that the court can determine whether the person is being legally detained. What is required of a person held in state prison who wants to bring a habeas corpus action in federal court?
Hemera/Getty Images

writ of *habeas corpus*

An order that directs the detaining authority to bring the person who is being detained before a judge, who will determine the lawfulness of the imprisonment.

Tort Action in State Court People held in state prisons can file a tort action in state court. A **tort** is a civil wrong, a wrongful act, or a wrongful breach of duty, other than a breach of contract, whether intentional or accidental, from which injury to another occurs. In tort actions, inmates commonly claim that a correctional employee, such as the warden or a correctional officer, or the correctional facility itself failed to perform a duty required by law regarding the inmate. Compensation for damages is the most common objective. Tort suits often allege such deficiencies as negligence, gross or wanton negligence, or intentional wrong.

Federal Civil Rights Lawsuit People held in federal or state prisons can file suit in federal court alleging civil rights violations by corrections officials. Most of these suits challenge the conditions of confinement, under Section 1983 of the Civil Rights Act of 1871, which is now part of Title 42 of the U.S. Code. Lawsuits may claim that officials have deprived people in confinement of their constitutional rights, such as adequate medical treatment, protection against excessive force by correctional officers or violence from other residents, due process in disciplinary hearings, and access to law libraries. According to the Bureau of Justice Statistics, 1 of 10 civil cases filed in U.S. district courts is *Section 1983 litigation,* as it is commonly called.

When such suits seek monetary damages from federal agents for violation of constitutional rights, they are often referred to as *Bivens* actions, recalling the 1971 case in which the U.S. Supreme Court articulated the right of people held in confinement to sue. In subsequent rulings (e.g., *FDIC v. Meyer,* 1994), the Court specified that "a *Bivens* action may only be maintained against an individual," not the federal agency by which he or she is employed, and it declined to extend the damage action authority of *Bivens* to permit suits against private entities operating correctional facilities under federal contract (*Correctional Services Corporation, Petitioner* v. *John E. Malesko,* 2001).

If confined individuals are successful in their civil suits, in state or federal courts, the courts can award three types of damages. **Nominal damages** are small amounts of money that may be awarded when the person suing has sustained no actual damages, but there is clear evidence that their rights have been violated.

Compensatory damages are payments for actual losses, which may include out-of-pocket expenses the confined person incurred in filing the suit, other forms of monetary or material loss, and pain, suffering, and mental anguish. Some years ago, for example, a federal appeals court sustained an award of $9,300 against a warden and a correctional commissioner. The amount was calculated by awarding $25 per confined individual for each day he had spent in solitary confinement (a total of 372 days for all the those who sued) under conditions the court found cruel and unusual (*Sostre* v. *McGinnis,* 1971).

Punitive damages are awarded to punish the wrongdoer when the wrongful act was intentional and malicious or was done with reckless disregard for the rights of the person who is confined.

Request for Injunctive Relief An **injunction** is a judicial order to do or refrain from doing a particular act. A request for an injunction might claim adverse effects of a health, safety, or sanitation procedure and might involve the entire correctional facility. It is important for anyone working in corrections to realize that a lack of funds cannot justify failure to comply with an injunction (*Smith* v. *Sullivan,* 1977).

The Criminal Court System There is a dual court system in the United States; the federal and state court systems coexist (see Exhibit 11–1). The federal court system is nationwide with one or more federal courts in each state. These courts coexist with state court systems. Whether a defendant is tried in a federal court or a state court depends on which court has jurisdiction over the particular case.

The **jurisdiction** of a court is the power or authority of the court to act with respect to a case before it. The acts involved in the case must have taken place or had an effect in the geographic territory of the court, or a statute must give the court jurisdiction.

tort

A civil wrong, a wrongful act, or a wrongful breach of duty, other than a breach of contract, whether intentional or accidental, from which injury to another occurs.

nominal damages

Small amounts of money a court may award when inmates have sustained no actual damages, but there is clear evidence that their rights have been violated.

compensatory damages

Money a court may award as payment for actual losses suffered by a plaintiff, including out-of-pocket expenses incurred in filing the suit, other forms of monetary or material loss, and pain, suffering, and mental anguish.

punitive damages

Money a court may award to punish a wrongdoer when a wrongful act was intentional and malicious or was done with reckless disregard for the rights of the victim.

injunction

A judicial order to do or refrain from doing a particular act.

jurisdiction

The power, right, or authority of a court to interpret and apply the law.

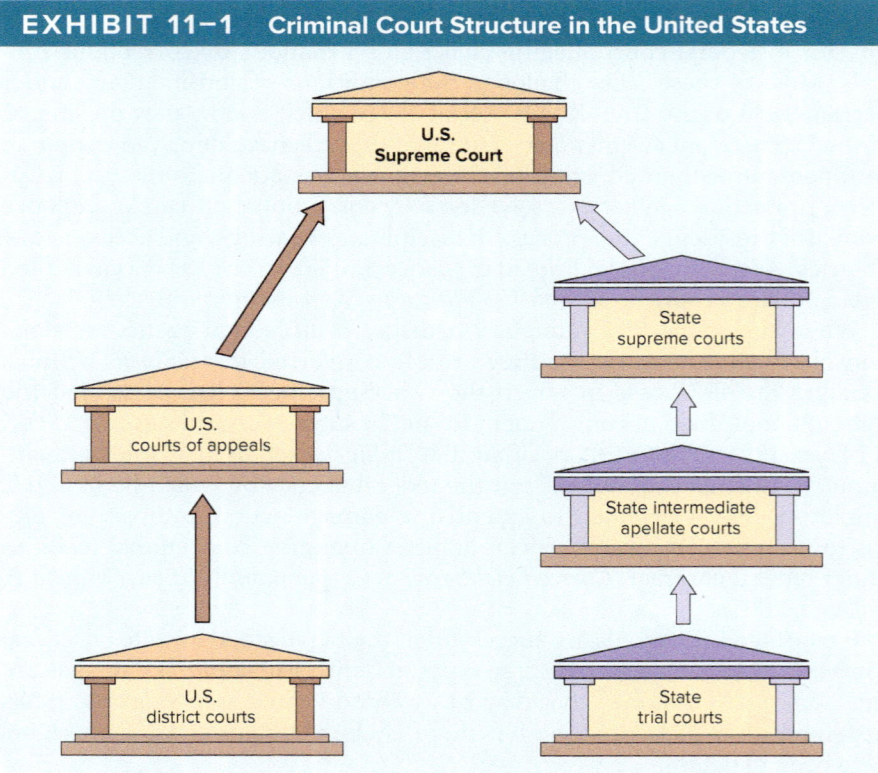

EXHIBIT 11–1   Criminal Court Structure in the United States

District courts are the trial courts of the federal system. They have original jurisdiction over cases charging defendants with violations of federal criminal laws. Each state has at least one U.S. district court, and some, like New York and California, have as many as four. There are also federal district courts in Puerto Rico, the District of Columbia, and the U.S. territories. There are currently 11 U.S. courts of appeals arranged by circuit, a District of Columbia circuit, and one federal circuit (see Exhibit 11–2).

Each state has its own court system. Most state court structures are similar to the federal court structure—with trial courts, intermediate appellate courts, and a top appellate court. In most states, the trial courts are organized by county.

Although federal offenses are prosecuted in federal court and state offenses are prosecuted in state courts, the federal courts have supervisory jurisdiction over the administration of criminal justice in the state courts. The U.S. Supreme Court has ruled that constitutional requirements for criminal procedure in federal courts also apply to the states. Violation of these constitutional requirements can be the subject of both state appeals and federal suits by people in confinement.

Grievance Procedures

Grievance procedures are formal institutional processes for hearing the complaints of people held in prison. Grievance procedures, which typically employ internal hearing boards, are the method most frequently used by people held in confinement to enforce the protections afforded to them by law. Most grievances concern discipline, program assignments, medical issues, personal property, and complaints against staff members. Only about 1 in 12 grievances is approved or results in some action being taken by prison administrators to correct the problem.

EXHIBIT 11–2 Geographic Boundaries of the U.S. Courts of Appeals and U.S. District Courts

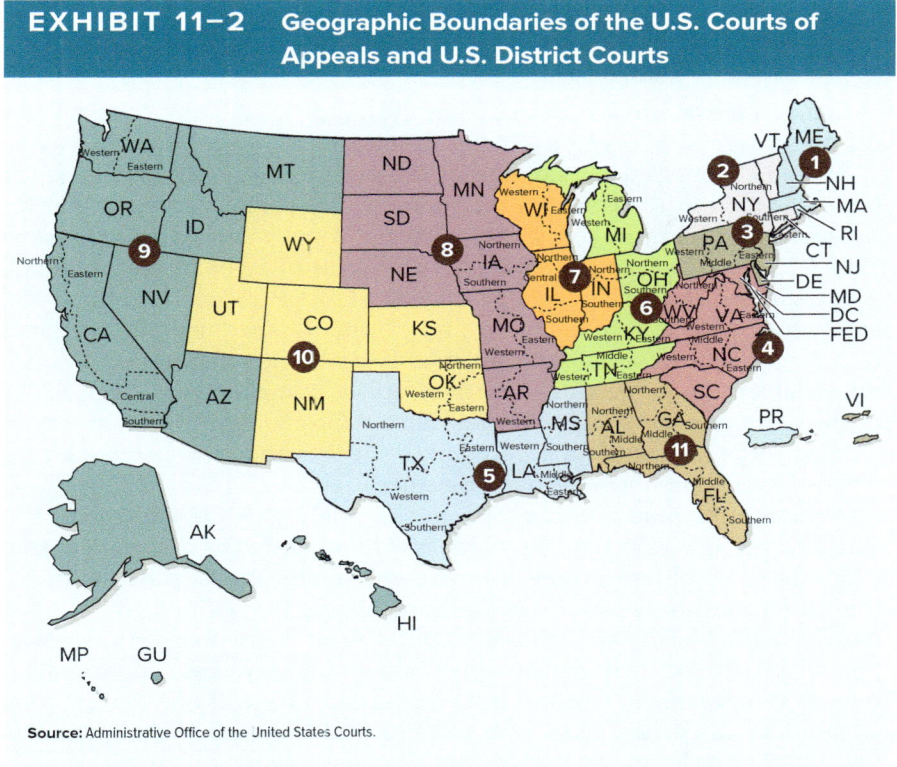

The creation of formal mechanisms for the hearing of grievances was encouraged by the comptroller general of the United States following the riot at New York's Attica Prison. The comptroller's report published in 1977[13] listed a number of reasons for establishing grievance mechanisms, including (1) promoting justice and fairness, (2) providing opportunities to voice complaints, (3) reducing the number of court cases filed, (4) assisting correctional administrators in the identification of institutional problems, and (5) reducing violence.

Today most correctional systems use a three-step process for resolving grievances. First, a staff member or committee in each institution receives complaints, investigates them, and makes decisions. Second, if a person is dissatisfied with that decision, the case may be appealed to the warden. Third, if the person is still dissatisfied, the complaint may be given to the state's commissioner of corrections or the state's corrections board. This three-step procedure satisfies the requirements for U.S. Department of Justice certification.

THE PRISONERS' RIGHTS ERA (1970–1991) `CO11-4`

Before the 1960s, the constitutional rights of people held in confinement were rarely acknowledged. In 1964, for example, the U.S. Supreme Court refused to hear a claim of religious rights violations brought by a Muslim prisoner in New York's correctional system. In that case, *Sostre* v. *McGinnis*, Martin Sostre, a Nation of Islam member, filed a lawsuit claiming that he was denied the opportunity to practice his religion and that prison officials placed him in solitary confinement as a result of his requests to do so. Prior to the case reaching the Supreme Court, the U.S. Court of Appeals for the Second Circuit held, "It is not the business of the Federal Courts to work out a set of rules and regulations to govern the practices of religion in state prisons." Shortly thereafter, the U.S. Supreme Court voiced its agreement, refusing to hear Sostre's petition.

Soon things started to change, however, and what some have called a prisoners' rights era began to emerge around 1970.

As one writer of the period noted, "The prisoners' rights movement must be understood in the context of a 'fundamental democratization' that has transformed American society since World War II, and particularly since 1960."[14] Over the past 55 years, an increasing number of once-marginal groups, including Black people, Hispanics, LGBTQ+ people, and those who are economically disenfranchised and physically and mentally marginalized, have acquired social recognition and legal rights that were previously unavailable to those outside the American social mainstream. Seen in this context, the prisoners' rights era was but a natural outgrowth of an encompassing social movement that recognized the existence and potential legitimacy of a wide number of group grievances.

Although the phrase *prisoners' rights era* might give the impression that confined persons won virtually every case brought during that period, such is not the case. Although they did win some significant court battles, it was the turnaround in legal attitudes toward people in confinement that was most remarkable. As we shall see, courts went from practically ignoring prison systems to practically running them. It might be more appropriate to refer to the period as the court involvement era. We will now review some of the most important cases won *and* lost by those held in confinement—presented in order of the constitutional amendments on which they were based.

CO11-5

When we speak of the rights of confined persons, we are generally speaking of the rights found in four of the amendments to the U.S. Constitution. Three of these—the First (free expression), Fourth (privacy), and Eighth Amendments (cruel and unusual punishment)—are part of the Bill of Rights (the first 10 amendments to the Constitution). The fourth is the Fourteenth Amendment (deprivation of life, liberty, and property). Keep in mind that what we call *inmates' rights* today are largely the result of federal court decisions that have interpreted constitutional guarantees and applied them to prisons and prison conditions. Often such a case sets a **precedent,** serving as an example or authority for future cases. Rulings in cases that find violations of the rights of the confined must be implemented by the administrators of affected correctional systems and institutions. (See Exhibit 11–3 for more U.S. Supreme Court cases involving the rights of people in confinement.)

precedent

A previous judicial decision that judges should consider in deciding future cases.

First Amendment

> Congress shall make no law respecting an establishment of religion, or prohibiting the free exercise thereof; or abridging the freedom of speech, or of the press; or the right of the people peaceably to assemble, and to petition the government for a redress of grievances.

First Amendment guarantees are important to members of a free society. It is no surprise, then, that some of the early prisoners' rights cases concerned free speech rights. For example, in 1974, in *Pell* v. *Procunier,* four California prison inmates and three journalists challenged the constitutionality of regulation 415.071 of the California Department of Corrections and Rehabilitation (CDCR). That regulation specified that "press and other media interviews with specific individual inmates will not be permitted." The rule had been imposed after a violent prison episode that corrections authorities

EXHIBIT 11–3		Selected U.S. Supreme Court Cases Involving the Rights of People in Confinement

Case Name	Year	Decision
Ramirez v. *Collier*	2021	A condemned prisoner may have a pastor pray and lay hands on him/her during execution if requested.
Murphy v. *Collier*	2019	A Buddhist inmate facing execution in Texas was permitted to have a Buddhist religious advisor present in the execution room because state law permitted members of other religions to have clergy of their choice present during executions.
Holt v. *Hobbs*	2015	People in confinement are permitted to grow half-inch beards in accordance with religious beliefs.
Millbrook v. *U.S.*	2013	Federal correctional agencies are generally shielded against civil lawsuits seeking monetary damages for the acts or omissions of their employees.
Florence v. *Burlington County*	2012	Officials may strip-search persons who have been arrested and taken to a detention facility even though the arrest is for a minor offense, in order to insure the safety and security of the jail or detention.
Howes v. *Fields*	2012	People in confinement who are facing questioning by law enforcement officers while incarcerated need not be advised of their *Miranda* rights.
Brown v. *Plata* (Eighth Amendment)	2011	Found that seriously overcrowded conditions in California prisons are a violation of the Eighth Amendment's ban on cruel and unusual punishment.
U.S. v. *Georgia*	2006	Under the Americans with Disabilities Act, a state may be liable for rights deprivations suffered by people who are disabled and held in its prisons.
Johnson v. *California*	2005	The decision invalidated the California Department of Corrections and Rehabilitation's unwritten policy of racially segregating confined persons in double cells each time they entered a new correctional facility.
Wilkinson v. *Austin*	2005	The Court upheld an Ohio policy allowing the most dangerous offenders to be held in "supermax" cells following several levels of review prior to transfer.
Overton v. *Bazzetta*	2003	The decision upheld the Michigan Department of Corrections' visitation regulation that denies most visits to residents who commit two substance abuse violations while incarcerated.
Porter v. *Nussle* (Eighth Amendment)	2002	The "exhaustion requirement" of the Prison Litigation Reform Act of 1995 (PLRA) applies to all suits about prison life, whether they involve general circumstances or particular episodes and whether they allege excessive force or some other wrong.
Hope v. *Pelzer* (Eighth Amendment)	2002	The Court found an Eighth Amendment violation in the case of a confined person who was subjected to unnecessary pain, humiliation, and risk of physical harm.
Booth v. *Churner* (Eighth Amendment)	2001	The decision upheld a requirement under the PLRA that state people who are confined must "exhaust such administrative remedies as are available" before filing a suit over prison conditions.
Lewis v. *Casey*	1996	Earlier cases do not guarantee the wherewithal to file any and every type of legal claim. All that is required is that people in confinement "be provided with the tools to attack their sentences."
Sandin v. *Conner* (Fourteenth Amendment)	1995	Perhaps signaling an end to the prisoners' rights era, this case rejected the argument that disciplining confined persons is a deprivation of constitutional due process rights.
Wilson v. *Seiter* (Eighth Amendment)	1991	The case clarified the totality of conditions notion, saying that some conditions of confinement "in combination" may violate the rights of persons in confinement when each would not do so alone.

EXHIBIT 11–3   Selected U.S. Supreme Court Cases Involving the Rights of People in Confinement *(continued)*

Case Name	Year	Decision
Washington v. *Harper* (Eighth Amendment)	1990	A resident who is a danger to self or others as a result of psychological issues may be treated with psychoactive drugs against his or her will.
Turner v. *Safley* (First Amendment)	1987	A Missouri ban on correspondence between people in confinement was upheld as "reasonably related to legitimate penological interests."
O'Lone v. *Estate of Shabazz* (First Amendment)	1987	A person's right to practice religion was not violated by prison officials who refused to alter his work schedule so that he could attend Friday afternoon services.
Whitley v. *Albers* (Eighth Amendment)	1986	The shooting and wounding of a resident was not a violation of that resident's rights, because "the shooting was part and parcel of a good-faith effort to restore prison security."
Ponte v. *Real*	1985	People in prison have certain rights in disciplinary hearings.
Hudson v. *Palmer* (Fourth Amendment)	1984	A person who is imprisoned has no reasonable expectation of privacy in his or her prison cell that entitles him or her to protections against "unreasonable searches."
Block v. *Rutherford* (First Amendment)	1984	State regulations may prohibit inmate union meetings and use of mail to deliver union information within the prison. People in confinement do not have a right to be present during searches of cells.
Rhodes v. *Chapman* (Eighth Amendment)	1981	Double-celling of residents is not cruel and unusual punishment unless it involves the wanton and unnecessary infliction of pain or conditions grossly disproportionate to the severity of the crime committed.
Ruiz v. *Estelle* (Eighth Amendment)	1980	The Court found unconstitutional conditions in the Texas prison system— including overcrowding, understaffing, brutality, and substandard medical care.
Cooper v. *Morin*	1980	Neither inconvenience nor cost is an acceptable excuse for treating female residents differently from male residents.
Jones v. *North Carolina Prisoners' Labor Union, Inc.* (First Amendment)	1977	Residents have no inherent right to publish newspapers or newsletters for use by other residents.
Bounds v. *Smith*	1977	The case resulted in the creation of law libraries in many prisons.
Estelle v. *Gamble* (Eighth Amendment)	1976	Prison officials have a duty to provide proper medical care for residents.
Wolff v. *McDonnell* (Fourteenth Amendment)	1974	Sanctions cannot be levied against residents without appropriate due process.
Procunier v. *Martinez* (First Amendment)	1974	Censorship of the mail of those held in confinement is acceptable only when necessary to protect legitimate governmental interests.
Pell v. *Procunier* (First Amendment)	1974	People in prison retain First Amendment rights that are not inconsistent with their status as prisoners or with the legitimate penological objectives of the corrections system.
Cruz v. *Beto* (First Amendment)	1972	People who are incarcerated have to be given a "reasonable opportunity" to pursue their religious faiths. Also, visits can be banned if such visits constitute threats to security.
Johnson v. *Avery*	1968	People held in prison have a right to consult "jailhouse lawyers" when trained legal assistance is not available.
Sostre v. *McGinnis*	1964	The Court refused to hear a Muslim resident's petition concerning religious rights in New York prisons, thereby declining to impose any broad-based federal constitutional limits on a resident's confinement.
Monroe v. *Pape*	1961	Individuals deprived of their rights by state officers acting under color of state law have a right to bring action in federal court.

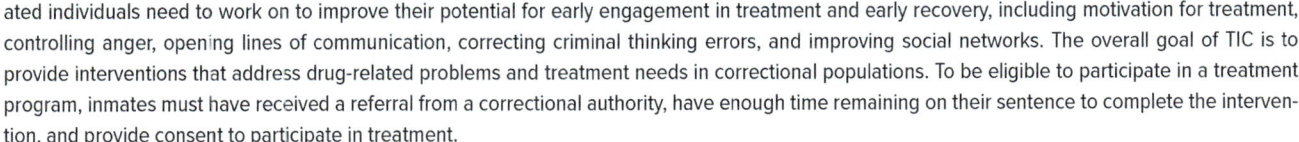

Crime
SOLUTIONS
.gov

RELIABLE RESEARCH. REAL RESULTS.

Enter your keyword(s)   🔍   Search Site   Advanced Search

Home | Help | Contact Us | Site Map | Glossary

EVIDENCE-BASED CORRECTIONS

Targeted Interventions for Corrections (TIC)

Targeted Interventions for Corrections (TIC) consists of six brief life-skill interventions to be used in a variety of correctional-based settings. The interventions address the core aspects of addiction treatment and recovery. They focus on what incarcerated individuals need to work on to improve their potential for early engagement in treatment and early recovery, including motivation for treatment, controlling anger, opening lines of communication, correcting criminal thinking errors, and improving social networks. The overall goal of TIC is to provide interventions that address drug-related problems and treatment needs in correctional populations. To be eligible to participate in a treatment program, inmates must have received a referral from a correctional authority, have enough time remaining on their sentence to complete the intervention, and provide consent to participate in treatment.

The program is rated Promising. TIC participants were found to significantly change their attitudes more favorably than control participants did. The treatment group average change was 4.0 percent, compared with 1.5 percent for the control group. TIC was found to make a statistically significant impact on psychosocial functioning of treatment participants compared with control-group participants. Psychological functioning included measures of decision making, self-esteem, depression, anxiety, and efficacy.

Source: Adapted from the Bureau of Justice Statistics.

attributed at least in part to a former policy of free face-to-face resident–press interviews. Such interviews had apparently resulted in a relatively small number of residents gaining disproportionate notoriety and influence with other residents.

The U.S. Supreme Court held that "in light of the alternative channels of communication that are open to the inmate appellees, [regulation] 415.071 does not constitute a violation of their rights of free speech." Significantly, the Court went on to say, "A prison inmate retains those first amendment rights that are not inconsistent with his status as prisoner or with the *legitimate penological objectives* of the corrections system" (emphasis added). **Legitimate penological objectives** are the permissible aims of a correctional institution. They include the realistic concerns that correctional officers and administrators have for the integrity and security of the correctional institution and the safety of staff and residents. The *Pell* ruling established a **balancing test** that the Supreme Court would continue to use, weighing the rights claimed by people in prison against the legitimate needs of prisons.

Freedom of Speech and Expression Visits to residents by friends and loved ones are forms of expression. But prison visits are not an absolute right. In *Cruz* v. *Beto* (1972), the Supreme Court ruled that all visits can be banned if they threaten security. Although *Cruz* involved short-term confinement facilities, the ruling has also been applied to prisons.

Another form of expression is correspondence. As a result of various court cases, prison officials can (and generally do) impose restrictions on resident mail. People in confinement don't receive mail directly from the hands of postal carriers but from correctional officers. They place their outgoing mail not in U.S. Postal Service mailboxes but in containers provided by the correctional institution.

legitimate penological objectives

The realistic concerns that correctional officers and administrators have for the integrity and security of the correctional institution and the safety of staff and inmates.

balancing test

A method the U.S. Supreme Court uses to decide prisoners' rights cases, weighing the rights claimed by people in prison against the legitimate needs of prisons.

Corrections officials often read such mail—both incoming and outgoing—in an effort to uncover escape plans. Reading resident mail, however, is different from censoring it. In 1974, in *Procunier* v. *Martinez,* the U.S. Supreme Court held that the censoring of inmate mail is acceptable only when necessary to protect legitimate government interests. The case turned upon First Amendment guarantees of free speech.

Under a 1979 federal appeals court decision, in *McNamara* v. *Moody,* prison officials may not prohibit residents from writing vulgar letters or those that make disparaging remarks about the prison staff. Similarly, although correctional administrators have a legitimate interest in curbing residents' deviant sexual behavior, courts have held that viewing nudity is not deviant sexual behavior. Hence, prison officials may not ban mailed nude pictures of residents' wives or girlfriends (*Peppering* v. *Crist,* 1981), although restrictions against posting them on cell walls have generally been upheld. Similarly, officials may not prevent residents from receiving, by mail direct from publishers, publications depicting nudity unless those publications depict deviant sexual behavior (*Mallery* v. *Lewis,* 1983).

In 1989, in the case of *Thornburgh* v. *Abbott,* in an effort to clear up questions raised by lower court rulings concerning mailed publications, the U.S. Supreme Court ruled as follows:

> Publications which may be rejected by a warden include but are not limited to publications which meet one of the following criteria: (1) it depicts or describes procedures for the construction or use of weapons, ammunition, bombs, or incendiary devices; (2) it depicts, encourages, or describes methods of escape from correctional facilities or contains blueprints, drawings, or similar descriptions of Bureau of Prisons institutions; (3) it depicts or describes procedures for the brewing of alcoholic beverages or the manufacture of drugs; (4) it is written in code; (5) it depicts, describes, or encourages activities which may lead to the use of physical violence or group disruption; (6) it encourages or instructs in the commission of criminal activities; (7) it is sexually explicit material which by its nature or content poses a threat to the security, good order, or discipline of the institution or facilitates criminal activity.

Unless at least one of these standards is met, restrictions on the receipt of published materials—especially magazines and newspapers that do not threaten prison security—are generally not allowed. In the 2006 U.S. Supreme Court case of *Beard* v. *Banks,* however, the justices held that Pennsylvania prison officials could legitimately prohibit the state's most violent inmates from having access to newspapers, magazines, and photographs. Prison officials had argued that the policy helped motivate better behavior on the part of particularly difficult prisoners. The Court agreed, noting that "prison officials have imposed the deprivation only upon those with serious prison-behavior problems; and those officials, relying on their professional judgment, reached an experience-based conclusion that the policies help to further legitimate prison objectives."

Similarly, in the case of *Turner* v. *Safley* (1987), the Supreme Court upheld a Missouri ban on correspondence among residents. Such a regulation is valid, the Court said, if it is "reasonably related to legitimate penological interests." *Turner* established that officials had to show only that a regulation was reasonably *related* to a legitimate penological interest. No clear-cut damage to legitimate penological interests had to be shown.

The U.S. Supreme Court sided with corrections officials in its 1977 decision in *Jones* v. *North Carolina Prisoners' Labor Union, Inc.* In *Jones,* the Court upheld regulations established by the North Carolina Department of Correction that prohibited prisoners from soliciting other residents to join the union and barred union meetings and bulk mailings

A prison sally port. The rights of detained persons are not absolute but are limited by legitimate penological objectives. What does the phrase legitimate penological objectives mean?
Courtesy of the Justice Research Association

concerning the union from outside sources. Citing *Pell* v. *Procunier,* the Court went on to say, "The prohibition on inmate-to-inmate solicitation does not unduly abridge inmates' free speech rights. If the prison officials are otherwise entitled to control organized union activity within the confines of a prison, the solicitation ban is not impermissible under the First Amendment, for such a prohibition is both reasonable and necessary."

Freedom of Religion Lawsuits involving religious practices in prison have been numerous for at least 40 years. In 1962, for example, in *Fulwood* v. *Clemmer,* the court of appeals for the District of Columbia ruled that the Black Muslim faith must be recognized as a religion and held that officials may not restrict members of that faith from holding services.

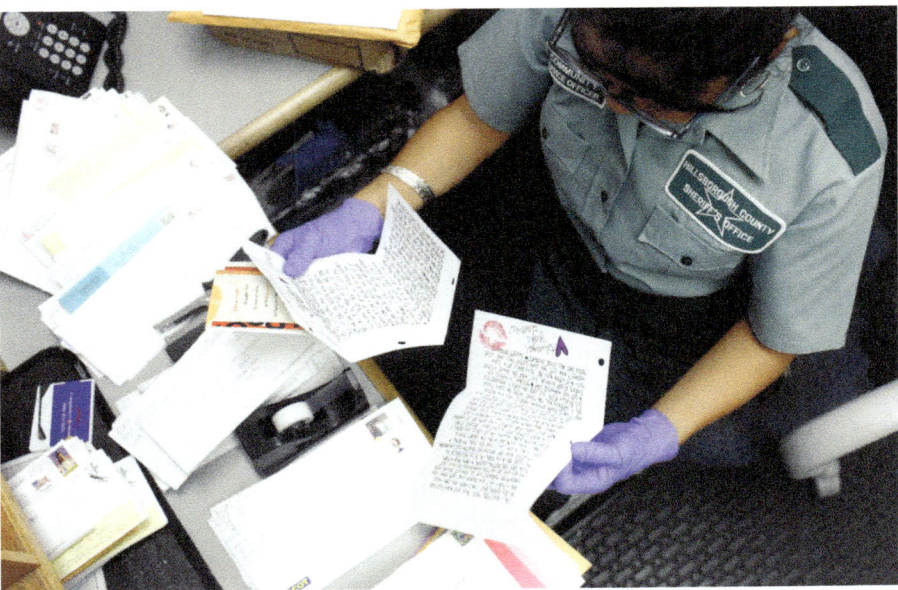

In 1970, the U.S. Supreme Court refused to hear an appeal from Jack Gittlemacker, a resident who wanted the state of Pennsylvania to provide him with a clergyman of his faith. The Court held that although states must give residents the opportunity to practice their religions, they are not required to provide clergy for that purpose.

In *Cruz* v. *Beto* (mentioned earlier), the Supreme Court also decided that people in prison had to be given a "reasonable opportunity" to pursue their religious faiths. Later federal court decisions expanded this decision, requiring officials to provide such a "reasonable opportunity" even to residents whose religious faiths were not traditional.

People who are incarcerated have limited rights to send and receive mail. Restrictions on their mail focus on maintaining institutional security. Judicial interpretations of which constitutional amendment have led to the rights of confined people to send and receive mail?
Eve Edelheit/Tampa Bay Times/ZUMAPRESS.com/ Alamy Stock Photo

In 1975, the U.S. Court of Appeals for the Second Circuit ruled in *Kahane* v. *Carlson* that an Orthodox Jewish resident has the right to a kosher diet unless the government can show good cause for not providing it. Similarly, the courts have held that "Muslims' request for one full-course pork-free meal once a day and coffee three times daily is essentially a plea for a modest degree of official deference to their religious obligations" (*Barnett* v. *Rodgers,* 1969).

On the other hand, courts have determined that some religious demands need not be met. In the 1986 Fifth Circuit Court of Appeals case of *Udey* v. *Kastner,* for example, a person who was a Muslim inmate had requested raw milk, distilled water, and organic fruits, juices, vegetables, and meats. The special diet was so costly that a federal court allowed the prison to deny the resident's request.

In 2000, the Religious Land Use and Institutionalized Persons Act (RLUIPA) became law. RLUIPA says, "No government shall impose a substantial burden on the religious exercise of a person residing in or confined to an institution even if the burden results from a rule of general applicability unless the government demonstrates that imposition of the burden on that person (1) is in furtherance of a compelling governmental interest; and (2) is the least restrictive means of furthering that compelling governmental interest." Because RLUIPA is a federal law, it is especially relevant to prison programs and activities that are at least partially supported with federal monies. In the case of *Benning* v. *State,* the Eleventh Circuit Court of Appeals found in favor of a person who was imprisoned in Georgia who claimed that RLUIPA supported his right as a "Torah observant Jew" to eat only kosher food and wear a yarmulke (or skullcap) at all times. In 2005, in the case of *Cutter* v. *Wilkinson,* the U.S. Supreme Court ruled in favor of past and present Ohio residents who claimed that the state's correctional system failed to accommodate their nonmainstream religious practices. Finally, in 2015, again citing RLUIPA, the Court found in favor of a Muslim Arkansas inmate who wanted to grow a half-inch beard in accordance with his religious beliefs. The Court was not persuaded by arguments made by the Arkansas Department of Correction that beards could be used to conceal contraband. In that case, *Holt* v. *Hobbs* (2015), the justices wrote that the argument made by the department of correction was not compelling, "especially given the difficulty of hiding contraband in such a short beard."

Finally, in 2019, the U.S. Supreme Court overturned a stay of execution that had been granted by a lower court on religious grounds. Dominique Ray, 42, was executed in Alabama after the Court held that he was not entitled to have his Islamic spiritual advisor in the execution chamber when he was put to death. State officials had argued that only prison employees should be allowed into the chamber and offered to allow the prison Christian chaplain to be at Ray's side. Ray, however, refused the offer. In that same year, however, in the case of *Murphy* v. *Collier,* the Court held that a Buddhist inmate facing execution in Texas was permitted to have a Buddhist religious advisor present in the execution room because state law permitted members of other religions to have clergy of their choice present during their executions.

Fourth Amendment

The right of the people to be secure in their persons, houses, papers, and effects, against unreasonable searches and seizures, shall not be violated, and no Warrants shall issue, but upon probable cause, supported by Oath or affirmation, and particularly describing the place to be searched, and the persons or things to be seized.

The right to privacy is at the heart of the Fourth Amendment. Clearly, unreasonable searches without warrants are unconstitutional. Does this mean that a person who is in prison has a right to privacy in his or her cell? When is it reasonable to search a cell without a warrant? Some suggest that the needs of institutional security prohibit privacy for people in prison. Others argue that a prison cell is the equivalent of a person's house. Over the years, the courts have been fairly consistent in deciding that the privacy rights implied in this amendment must be greatly reduced in prisons to maintain institutional security.

In *United States* v. *Hitchcock* (1972), person held in confinement claimed that his Fourth Amendment rights had been violated by a warrantless search and seizure of documents in his prison cell. Previously, courts had generally held that "constitutionally protected" places—such as homes, motel rooms, safe-deposit boxes, and certain places of business—could not be searched without a warrant. In *Hitchcock,* however, the U.S. Court of Appeals for the Ninth Circuit created a new standard: "first, that a person have exhibited an actual (subjective) expectation of privacy and second, that the expectation be one that society is prepared to recognize as reasonable." The court concluded that, although Hitchcock plainly expected to keep his documents private, his expectation was not reasonable. In the words of the court:

> It is obvious that a jail shares none of the attributes of privacy of a home, an automobile, an office, or a hotel room. In prison, official surveillance has traditionally been the order of the day. ... [Hence], we do not feel that it is reasonable for a prisoner to consider his cell private.

Correctional officers searching a cell. People in confinement do not retain the right to privacy in their cells or possessions because institutional interests of safety and security supersede constitutional guarantees of privacy. Under which amendment to the Constitution does the right to be free from unreasonable searches and seizures fall?

Portland Press Herald/Getty Images

In *Hudson* v. *Palmer* (1984), a person who was confined in Virginia claimed a correctional officer had unreasonably destroyed some of his permitted personal property during a search of his cell. The resident also claimed that under the Fourth Amendment, the cell search was illegal. Echoing *Hitchcock,* the U.S. Supreme Court ruled that "a prisoner has no reasonable expectation of privacy in his prison cell entitling him to the protection of the Fourth Amendment against unreasonable searches." Similarly, in *Block* v. *Rutherford* (1984), the Court ruled that residents do not have the right to be present during searches of their cells.

In 1985, the Ninth Circuit Court of Appeals decided a case involving inmates at San Quentin State Prison (*Grummett* v. *Rushen*). The inmates had brought a class action lawsuit against prison administrators, objecting to the policy of allowing female correctional officers to view nude or partly clothed male inmates. Women officers, complained the inmates, could see male inmates while they were dressing, showering, being strip-searched, or using toilet facilities. Such viewing, said the inmates, violated privacy rights guaranteed by the U.S. Constitution.

At the time of the suit, approximately 113 of the 720 correctional officers at San Quentin were female. Both female and male correctional officers were assigned to patrol the cell block tiers and gun rails. Both were also assigned to supervise showering from the tiers and from the gun rails, but only male officers were permitted to accompany inmates to the shower cells and lock them inside to disrobe and shower. Female officers were allowed to conduct pat-down searches that included the groin area.

The court found that prison officials had "struck an acceptable balance among the inmates' privacy interests, the institution's security requirements, and the female guards' employment rights." According to the court:

> The female guards are restricted in their contact with the inmates, and the record clearly demonstrates that at all times they have conducted themselves in a professional manner, and have treated the inmates with respect and dignity. ... Routine pat-down searches, which include the groin area, and which are otherwise justified by security needs, do not violate the Fourteenth Amendment because a correctional officer of the opposite gender conducts such a search.

Eighth Amendment

> Excessive bail shall not be required, nor excessive fines imposed, nor cruel and unusual punishments inflicted.

cruel and unusual punishment

A penalty that is grossly disproportionate to the offense or that violates today's broad and idealistic concepts of dignity, civilized standards, humanity, and decency (*Estelle* v. *Gamble*, 1976, and *Hutto* v. *Finney*, 1978). In the area of capital punishment, cruel and unusual punishments are those that involve torture, a lingering death, or unnecessary pain.

Many prisoners' rights cases turn upon the issue of **cruel and unusual punishment.** Defining such punishment is not easy. A working definition, however, might be "punishments that are grossly disproportionate to the offense as well as those that transgress today's broad and idealistic concepts of dignity, civilized standards, humanity, and decency."[15] Cases concerning constitutional prohibition of cruel and unusual punishment have centered on prisoners' need for decent conditions of confinement. In the 2011 U.S. Supreme Court case of *Brown* v. *Plata*, for example, overcrowded conditions in California prisons were found to have violated the Eighth Amendment by making it impossible for adequate health care to be delivered to most inmates. In *Plata,* the court ordered California to aggressively reduce its prison population by releasing as many as 58,000 inmates over the next two years. Inmates' rights cases involving the Eighth Amendment cover areas as diverse as medical care, prison conditions, physical insecurity, psychological stress, and capital punishment. (See Chapter 3 for a discussion of capital punishment and related court cases.)

Medical Care In 2012, federal Judge Mark Wolf of the District of Massachusetts ordered the Massachusetts Department of Correction to provide a man held in confinement, Michelle Kosilek, with sex change surgery.[16] Kosilek, the judge noted, had twice tried to kill himself and even attempted to castrate himself—proving, in the judge's opinion, a need for immediate medical intervention. In 2014, the First Circuit Court ruled against Kosilek, and the U.S. Supreme Court refused to hear his appeal. Kosilek is serving a life sentence for the murder of his wife.

The history of inmates' rights in the health care area can be traced to the 1970 case of *Holt* v. *Sarver* in which a federal district court declared the entire Arkansas prison system inhumane and found that it was in violation of the Constitution's Eighth Amendment's ban on cruel and unusual punishment.

In a related case, medical personnel in state prisons had given people in their care injections of apomorphine without their consent in a program of "aversive stimuli." The drug caused vomiting, which lasted from 15 minutes to an hour. The state justified it as "Pavlovian conditioning." The federal courts, however, soon prohibited the practice (*Knecht* v. *Gillman,* 1973).

Another decision, that of *Estelle* v. *Gamble* (1976), spelled out the duty of prison officials to provide residents with medical care. The Court held that prison officials could not lawfully demonstrate **deliberate indifference** to the medical needs of people in prison. In the words of the Court, "Deliberate indifference to serious medical needs of prisoners constitutes the 'unnecessary and wanton infliction of pain' proscribed by the Eighth Amendment." A serious medical condition is one that "causes pain, discomfort, or threat to good health" (*Rufo* v. *Inmates of Suffolk County Jail,* 1992). The mental health needs of people in prison are governed by the same constitutional standard of deliberate indifference as those described in court opinions dealing with the physical health of inmates.[17]

deliberate indifference

Intentional and willful indifference. Within the field of correctional practice, the term refers to calculated inattention to unconstitutional conditions of confinement.

Prison Conditions The 1976 federal court case of *Pugh* v. *Locke* introduced the **totality of conditions** standard. That standard, said the court, is to be used in evaluating whether prison conditions are cruel and unusual. The *Pugh* court held that "prison conditions [in Alabama] are so debilitating that they necessarily deprive residents of any opportunity to rehabilitate themselves or even maintain skills already possessed." The totality of conditions approach was also applied in a 1977 federal case, *Battle* v. *Anderson,* in which officials in overcrowded Oklahoma prisons had forced people in their care to sleep in garages, barbershops, libraries, and stairwells. Oklahoma prison administrators were found to be in violation of the cruel and unusual punishment clause of the U.S. Constitution.

totality of conditions

A standard to be used in evaluating whether prison conditions are cruel and unusual.

The U.S. Supreme Court ruled on the use of solitary confinement in *Hutto* v. *Finney* (1978). The Court held that confinement in Arkansas's segregation (solitary confinement) cells for more than 30 days was cruel and unusual punishment. It then went on to exhort lower courts to consider the totality of the conditions of confinement in future Eighth Amendment cases. Where appropriate, it said, a court should specify the changes needed to remedy the constitutional violation.

In the 1991 case of *Wilson* v. *Seiter,* the U.S. Supreme Court clarified the totality of conditions standard. The Court noted:

Some conditions of confinement may establish an Eighth Amendment violation "in combination" when each would not do so alone, but only when they have a mutually enforcing effect that produces the deprivation of a single, identifiable human need such as food, warmth, or exercise—for example, a

A confined person in the Nebraska State Penitentiary at Lincoln receives health care. A number of Eighth Amendment cases have established that prison officials have a duty to provide adequate medical care to people in their charge. How does the concept of "deliberate indifference" relate to that requirement?

Mikael Karlsson/Alamy Images

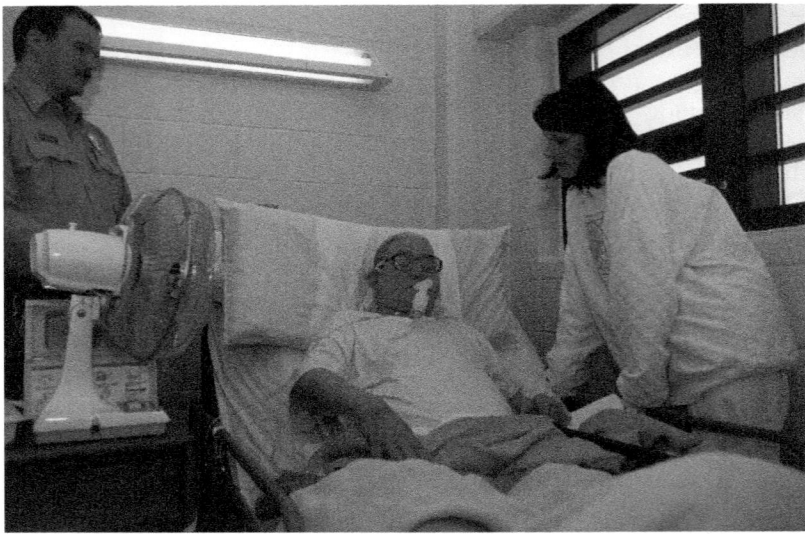

low cell temperature at night combined with a failure to issue blankets. ... To say that some prison conditions may interact in this fashion is a far cry from saying that all prison conditions are a seamless web for Eighth Amendment purposes. Nothing so [shapeless] as "overall conditions" can rise to the level of cruel and unusual punishment when no specific deprivation of a single human need exists.

Several rulings have addressed claims that overcrowding is cruel and unusual punishment. A U.S. Supreme Court case, *Rhodes* v. *Chapman* (1981), decided the issue of double-celling (housing two people in a cell designed for one) in long-term correctional facilities. In response to rising prison populations, Ohio authorities had begun double-celling. There was no evidence that Ohio authorities had wantonly inflicted pain through the practice, and double-celling had not resulted in food deprivation, a lower quality of medical care, or a decrease in sanitation standards. For those reasons, the Court denied the claim.

In *Rhodes,* the Court also emphasized that the Eighth Amendment prohibition of cruel and unusual punishment is a fluid concept that "must draw its meaning from the evolving standards of decency that mark the progress of a maturing society." In other words, what is considered cruel and unusual changes as society evolves.

In 1982, the U.S. Court of Appeals for the Seventh Circuit ruled, in *Smith* v. *Fairman,* that double-celling in a short-term facility (a jail) was not cruel and unusual punishment. The court said that government officials did not intend to punish residents by double-celling. The double-celling was innocent overcrowding required by circumstances.

Many conditions of confinement that violate Eighth Amendment rights can be remedied by changes in prison rules, by special training for correctional personnel, or by educational programs for people in prison. The remedies can be implemented through everyday administrative policies in the prison once court petitions filed by those in confinement have brought violations to light. Relief of overcrowding, however, is not always within the power of prison administrators. Prison officials have little control over the sizes of their prisons or the numbers of residents the courts assign to them. New prison facilities are expensive and take time to build.

Fourteenth Amendment

No State shall make or enforce any law which shall abridge the privileges or immunities of citizens of the United States; nor shall any State deprive any person of life, liberty, or property, without due process of law; nor deny to any person within its jurisdiction the equal protection of the laws.

When the Constitution and the Bill of Rights became law, the people of many states thought the document applied only to federal courts and to federal law. This attitude prevailed at least until the end of the Civil War. After the war, to clarify the status of the newly freed slaves and to apply the Bill of Rights to state actions, the Fourteenth Amendment was passed. The just-quoted portion of the Fourteenth Amendment is relevant to our discussion.

Most cases involving the rights of people in prison and the Fourteenth Amendment deal with issues of **due process.** Due process requires that laws and legal procedures be reasonable and that they be applied fairly and equally. The right to due process is a right to be fairly heard before being deprived of life or liberty.

By 1987, long after the hands-off doctrine had eroded, U.S. Supreme Court justice Sandra Day O'Connor summarized the thrust of earlier opinions, holding that "prison walls do not form a barrier separating prison inmates from the protections of the Constitution" (*Turner* v. *Safley*). Without access to the courts, O'Connor said, people who are in prison have no due process opportunities.

To bring their cases to court, however, people in prison need access to legal materials, and many of them need legal assistance. What if one person understands how to file cases with the court, but a second resident does not? Does the second resident have a right to enlist the aid of the first? "Yes," said the U.S. Supreme Court in *Johnson* v. *Avery* (1968). People held in prison have a right to consult "jailhouse lawyers" (other residents knowledgeable in the law) when trained legal advisers are not available.

The case of *Wolff* v. *McDonnell* (1974) expanded the concept of due process by applying it to disciplinary actions within prisons. Prior to *Wolff,* prison administrators had the discretion to discipline residents who broke prison rules. Disciplinary procedures were often tied to vague or nonexistent rules of conduct and were exercised without challenge. A resident might be assigned to solitary confinement or might have good-time credits reduced because of misconduct. Because the person was physically confined and lacked outside communication, there was no opportunity to challenge the charge. The *Wolff* Court concluded that sanctions (disciplinary actions) could not be levied against people in prison without appropriate due process, saying,

> [The state of Nebraska] asserts that the procedure for disciplining prison inmates for serious misconduct is a matter of policy raising no constitutional issue. If the position implies that prisoners in state institutions are wholly without the protection of the Constitution and the Due Process Clause, it is plainly untenable. Lawful imprisonment necessarily makes unavailable many rights and privileges of the ordinary citizen, a retraction justified by the consideration underlying our penal system. ... But though his rights may be diminished by the needs and exigencies of the institutional environment, a prisoner is not wholly stripped of constitutional protections when he is imprisoned for a crime.

The *Wolff* Court imposed minimal due process requirements on prison disciplinary proceedings that could lead to solitary confinement or reduction of good-time credits. The requirements included (1) advance notice by

The Eighth Amendment's prohibition of cruel and unusual punishment has been tied to the need for decent conditions of confinement. In determining whether conditions such as overcrowding and inadequate diet constitute a denial of such protection, courts have used the concept of totality of conditions. What is meant by the totality of conditions?

Daytona Beach News-Journal/Nigel Cook/AP Images

due process

A right guaranteed by the Fifth, Sixth, and Fourteenth Amendments to the U.S. Constitution and generally understood, in legal contexts, to mean the expected course of legal proceedings according to the rules and forms established for the protection of persons' rights.

People in prison must be allowed access to the courts and assistance in preparing their cases. To meet that requirement, most states stock law libraries in each correctional institution. Under which clause of the Fourteenth Amendment does access to the courts for incarcerated people fall?

Giles Clarke/Contributor/Getty Images

means of a written statement of the claimed violation, (2) a written statement by an impartial fact finder of the evidence relied on and the reasons for imposing punishment, and (3) an opportunity to testify and call witnesses unless the fact finder concluded such proceedings would undermine institutional security.

In 1976, confined persons lost three due process appeals. First, in *Baxter* v. *Palmigiano,* the Supreme Court decided that due process for a resident in a disciplinary hearing does not include a right to counsel even when the consequences are potentially "serious." In a second opinion issued that year (*Meacham* v. *Fano*), the Court held that people in confinement have no right to be in any particular prison and therefore have no due process protections before being transferred from one prison to another. A third case (*Stone* v. *Powell*) denied people held in confinement the right in most instances to seek federal review of state court Fourth Amendment search-and-seizure decisions.

The right of confined persons to legal materials was formally recognized in 1977 in the U.S. Supreme Court decision in *Bounds* v. *Smith.* In *Bounds,* the Court held,

> The fundamental constitutional right of access to the courts requires prison authorities to assist inmates in the preparation and filing of meaningful legal papers by providing prisoners with adequate law libraries or adequate assistance from persons trained in the law.

As a result of the *Bounds* decision, law libraries were created in prisons across the nation. Although adequately funded law libraries have been lacking in many prisons, the Internet age has made it possible to employ computers that can replace books, law journals, and printed statutes with up-to-date digital information. In particular, access to legal research services like LexisNexis and Westlaw can ensure that people in prison they have an opportunity to read the latest court decisions. The federal Bureau of Prisons, for example, now uses a TRULINCS computer system that allows inmates to research federal law. TRULINCS, provided by LexisNexis, does not allow Internet access, so computers in the system must receive periodic manual updates.

As we saw in Chapter 9, one challenge facing corrections personnel is to find safe, humane ways to manage resident populations. Residents often have grievances regarding conditions of confinement or disciplinary actions for infractions. Those grievances must be dealt with to maintain the safety and security of the institution. The Supreme Court's decision in *Jones* v. *North Carolina Prisoners' Labor Union, Inc.* (1977) required prisons to establish and maintain formal opportunities for the airing of grievances. *Ponte* v. *Real* (1985) required prison officials to explain to residents why their requests to have witnesses appear on their behalf at disciplinary hearings were denied.

The due process clause protects against unlawful deprivation of life or liberty. When an imprisoned person sued for damages for injuries (*Daniels* v. *Williams,* 1986), the Supreme Court ruled that people in prison could sue for damages in federal court only if officials had inflicted injury intentionally. According to the Court, "The due process clause is simply not implicated by a negligent act of an official causing unintended loss or injury to life, liberty, or property."

A 2001 ruling by a panel of federal judges in the case of *Gerber* v. *Hickman* addressed a unique claim of unlawful deprivation of life. Gerber wanted to impregnate his wife. He was, however, serving a life sentence in a California Department of Corrections and Rehabilitation (CDCR) prison, and CDCR regulations prohibit conjugal visits for people serving terms of life. Consequently, the Gerbers could not employ the usual method for creating the child they desired.

Undeterred, Gerber sought permission to artificially inseminate his wife. CDCR officials denied his request, citing the facts that (1) impregnating his wife was not medically necessary for Gerber's physical well-being and (2) Gerber had failed to show that denial of the request would violate his constitutional rights.

In a civil suit, however, Gerber alleged that the CDCR regulation violated the due process clause by denying him his constitutional right to procreate. The suit was dismissed in federal district court. Gerber then appealed to the U.S. Court of Appeals for the Ninth Circuit where a three-judge panel initially held "that the right to procreate survives incarceration." The panel reversed the district court's dismissal and reinstated Gerber's claim, mandating further review of the case. Upon review, however, the full Ninth Circuit Court of Appeals ruled that people in prison do not have a constitutional right to fatherhood. The appellate court's majority opinion cited the 1984 U.S. Supreme Court case of *Hudson* v. *Palmer* (mentioned earlier in this chapter), which held that "while persons imprisoned ... enjoy many protections of the Constitution, it is also clear that imprisonment carries with it the ... loss of many significant rights."

As we have seen, people held in federal and state prisons can file suits in federal court alleging civil rights violations by corrections officials. In 1988, the U.S. Supreme Court (in *West* v. *Atkins*) decided that private citizens who contracted to do work for prisons could be sued for civil rights violations committed against imprisoned people. The Court found that such contractors were acting "under color of state law," as required by Section 1983 of the Civil Rights Act of 1871.

As a result of Supreme Court decisions, most prisons now have rules that provide for necessary due process when residents appear before disciplinary committees. The makeup of disciplinary committees varies among institutions. The committees may include both imprisoned people and free citizens.

End of the Prisoners' Rights Era

By the late 1980s, the prisoners' rights era was drawing to a close. Following a change in the composition of the Supreme Court, the justices sitting on the Court had become less sympathetic to civil rights claims by people in prison. As discussed earlier, the 1986 case of *Daniels* v. *Williams* helped establish the notion that due process requirements were intended to prevent abuses of power by correctional officials, not to protect against mere carelessness. Furthermore, judicial and legislative officials began to realize that people in prison frequently abused what had previously been seen as their right of access to the courts. As state costs of defending against **frivolous lawsuits** by imprisoned people began to grow, federal courts began to take a new look at prisoners' rights.

Examples of abuse of the court system by people who are in prison abound. One person sued the state of Florida because he got only one bread roll with dinner. He sued two more times because he did not get a salad with lunch and because prison-provided TV dinners did not come with

frivolous lawsuits

Lawsuits with no foundation in fact. They are generally brought for publicity, political, or other reasons not related to law.

Evan Touchette

Evan Touchette

Unit Manager, Intensive Mental Health Unit, Maine State Prison

Evan M. Touchette is the unit manager for the Intensive Mental Health Unit (IMHU) at the Maine State Prison. The purpose of the IMHU is to help residents with major mental illness receive treatment for their mental health under the least restrictive conditions necessary, while working toward the reduction of criminogenic risk factors that may have impacted placement in a correctional setting. The unit seeks to improve the quality of life of residents through psychiatric treatment and intervention and prepare residents for return to less restrictive settings including transition into the mental health system when possible and appropriate. Evan's role is unique within the correctional system as it requires willingness to be part of an interdisciplinary team; be a member and participant in treatment planning; provide a safe space for staff and residents to work together through a collaboration of psychotherapy, activity therapies, and psychopharmacology; and understand the way mental illness and/or dual diagnosis impact a resident's ability to function within a correctional environment and the world at large.

Evan started his career in corrections in 2013 when he was just 19 years old. His timing was fortuitous because corrections was beginning to shift both culturally and philosophically. What had been a consistent approach to corrections for more than a century was slowly beginning to shift toward one that was more modern and humanistic. Evan has worked in all areas at the state's largest prison. He often found himself working in the most dangerous housing units, which exposed him to violent encounters, the possibility of serious self-injury, and even homicide. He regularly found himself first on the scene.

In 2014 Maine took a hard look at its practices and decided it was time for reform. Reduction of restrictive housing and the development of the IMHU was the first step toward Maine's long journey to safely reduce the number of residents housed in restrictive housing to under 1 percent of its total population. Evan was part of a department-wide initiative that dissected, reimagined, and recreated the state's use of force policies. Evan helped draft, implement, and train over 15 use-of-force policies. From cell extractions to the use of chemical agents, he was heavily involved in the process. From there, Evan was promoted to sargent where he supervised the medium unit at the state's prison. During his time as sargent, some major changes took place that Evan was expected to lead. Maine had completely normalized access to Medication Assisted Treatment for substance use disorders, rolled out a tablet program that gave residents more access to loved ones in the community, and expanded access to educational opportunities for residents. Evan was then promoted to unit manager. He has been a unit manager for over two years, and his responsibilities have increased. He now oversees the administrative control unit, which houses the state's most dangerous residents.

Evan aspires to change the status quo in corrections. Never settling for anything less-than-perfect effort, Evan and his team have created an area where staff and residents can feel safe and cared for while advancing the mission of the department. He follows the theme of "making our communities safer by reducing harm, through supportive intervention, empowering change and restoring lives."

> *Make our communities safer by reducing harm, through supportive intervention.*

drinks. He sued yet again because his cell was not equipped with a television. Another resident claimed prison officials were denying him freedom of religion. His religion, he said, required him to attend prison chapel services in the nude. Still another resident, afraid that he could get pregnant through homosexual relations, sued because prison officials would not give him birth control pills.

As early as 1977, the U.S. Supreme Court refused to hear an appeal from Henry William Theriault, founder of the Church of the New Song (or CONS).[18] Theriault, an inmate at the federal penitentiary in Atlanta, had a mail-order divinity degree. Members of CONS celebrated communion every Friday night. They claimed that prison officials must supply them with steak and Harvey's Bristol Cream sherry for the practice. Although "Bishop Theriault" admitted that he had originally created CONS to mock other religions, he claimed that he became a serious believer as the religion developed and acquired more followers. The U.S. Supreme Court dismissed that argument and held that the First Amendment does not protect so-called religions that are obvious shams.

The Cases One of the important cases setting the stage for a review of the claimed rights of people in prison was that of *Turner* v. *Safley,* decided in 1987. In *Turner,* the U.S. Supreme Court established a four-pronged test for determining the reasonableness of prison regulations. In order for a prison regulation to be acceptable, said the Court, there must first be a "valid, rational connection" between the prison regulation and the "legitimate governmental interest" offered to justify it. A second factor relevant in determining the reasonableness of a prison restriction, especially one that limits otherwise established rights, is whether alternative means of exercising that right remain available to people who are confined. If they do, then the restriction is more acceptable. A third consideration is the impact that accommodating an asserted constitutional right would have on officers and residents and on the allocation of scarce prison resources. If accommodation makes the job of correctional officers more dangerous or if it is unduly expensive, then it need not be granted. Finally, the fourth prong holds that people in prison have no recourse if there are no readily available alternatives that might permit exercise of claimed rights without compromising penological goals. In other words, if people in prison or their attorneys cannot suggest a workable alternative to meet an asserted right, then accommodations need not be made.

In *Wilson* v. *Seiter* (1991), the U.S. Supreme Court sided with prison officials in a way uncharacteristic of the previous two decades. In *Wilson,* the Court found that overcrowding, excessive noise, insufficient locker space, and similar conditions did not violate the Constitution if the intent of prison officials was not malicious. The Court ruled that the actions of officials did not meet the "deliberate indifference" standard defined in *Estelle* v. *Gamble* (1976).

After *Wilson,* people in prison won very few new precedent-setting cases. The courts either reversed themselves or tightened the conditions under which imprisoned people could win favorable decisions. Decisions supporting freedom of religion had been among the earliest and most complete victories during the prisoners' rights era. Even in that area, however, things began to change. The courts held that crucifixes and rosaries could legally be denied to inmates because of their possible use as weapons (*Mark* v. *Nix,* 1993, and *Escobar* v. *Landwehr,* 1993). Although some jurisdictions had previously allowed certain Native American religious items within prisons

(*Sample* v. *Borg,* 1987), the courts now ruled that prohibiting ceremonial pipes, medicine bags, and eagle claws did *not* violate the First Amendment rights of Native American inmates (*Bettis* v. *Delo,* 1994).

In the 1992 Supreme Court case of *Hudson* v. *McMillan,* the "deliberate indifference" standard was interpreted as requiring both actual knowledge *and* disregard of the risk of harm to inmates or others. This tighter definition allowed federal courts to side more easily with state prison officials in cases in which people in prison claimed there was deliberate indifference. In 1994, in the case of *Farmer* v. *Brennan,* the Supreme Court ruled that even when a person held in captivity is harmed and even when prison officials knew that the risk of harm existed, officials cannot be held liable if they took appropriate steps to mitigate that risk.

If there was any question that the prisoners' rights era had ended, that question was settled in 1995 by the case of *Sandin* v. *Conner.* In *Sandin,* the Supreme Court rejected the argument that, by disciplining people in prison, a state deprived them of their constitutional right not to be deprived of liberty without due process. "The time has come to return to those due process principles that were correctly established and applied in earlier times," said the Court. A year later, the decision in *Lewis* v. *Casey* overturned portions of *Bounds* v. *Smith.* The *Bounds* case had been instrumental in establishing law libraries in prisons. The Court in *Lewis* held, however, that "*Bounds* does not guarantee inmates the wherewithal to file any and every type of legal claim but requires only that they be provided with the tools to attack their sentences."

In *Edwards* v. *Balisok* (1997), the Supreme Court made it even harder to successfully challenge prison disciplinary convictions. The Court held that people who are imprisoned cannot sue for monetary damages under Section 1983 of the U.S. Code for loss of good-time credits until they are able to sue successfully in state court to have their disciplinary conviction set aside.

In 2003, in the case of *Overton* v. *Bazzetta,* the Court upheld visitation regulations established by the Michigan Department of Corrections that denied most visits to people in prison who had committed two substance abuse violations while incarcerated. In its ruling, the Court said that "the regulations bear a rational relation to legitimate penological interests [sufficient] to sustain them." Wording taken directly from the Court's opinion is shown in Exhibit 11–4. It provides a summary of the factors used by the courts to decide whether prison regulations meet constitutional requirements.

In a somewhat different kind of case, the U.S. Supreme Court found that federal correctional officers are "law enforcement officers" within the meaning of federal law—and that they are therefore immune from claims alleging injury or loss of property "caused by negligence or a wrongful act or omission" when acting within their scope of employment. The case, *Ali* v. *Federal Bureau of Prisons,*[19] involved a federal prisoner who claimed that some of his personal belongings had disappeared when he was transferred between facilities.

Finally, in two cases from 2012, the Supreme Court sided with correctional officials in limiting the rights of people in prison. In the first case, *Howes* v. *Fields* (2012), the Court found that people who are in prison and who face questioning by law enforcement officers while they are incarcerated need not be advised of their *Miranda* rights prior to the start of interrogation. In the second case, *Florence* v. *Burlington County* (2012), the Court ruled that officials had the power to strip-search persons who had been arrested prior to admission to a jail or other detention facility even if the

EXHIBIT 11–4 *Overton v. Bazzetta* (2003)

Responding to concerns about prison security problems caused by the increasing number of visitors to Michigan's prisons and about substance abuse among inmates, the Michigan Department of Corrections (MDOC) promulgated new regulations limiting prison visitation. ...

The fact that the regulations bear a rational relation to legitimate penological interests suffices to sustain them regardless of whether respondents have a constitutional right of association that has survived incarceration. This Court accords substantial deference to the professional judgment of prison administrators, who bear a significant responsibility for defining a corrections system's legitimate goals and determining the most appropriate means to accomplish them. The regulations satisfy each of four factors used to decide whether a prison regulation affecting a constitutional right that survives incarceration withstands constitutional challenge.

First, the regulations bear a rational relationship to a legitimate penological interest. The restrictions on children's visitation are related to MDOC's valid interests in maintaining internal security and protecting child visitors from exposure to sexual or other misconduct or from accidental injury. They promote internal security, perhaps the most legitimate penological goal, by reducing the total number of visitors and by limiting disruption caused by children. It is also reasonable to ensure that the visiting child is accompanied and supervised by adults charged with protecting the child's best interests. Prohibiting visitation by former inmates bears a self-evident connection to the State's interest in maintaining prison security and preventing future crime. Restricting visitation for inmates with two substance-abuse violations serves the legitimate goal of deterring drug and alcohol use within prison.

Second, respondents have alternative means of exercising their asserted right of association with those prohibited from visiting. They can send messages through those who are permitted to visit, and can communicate by letter and telephone. Visitation alternatives need not be ideal; they need only be available.

Third, accommodating the associational right would have a considerable impact on guards, other inmates, the allocation of prison resources, and the safety of visitors by causing a significant reallocation of the prison system's financial resources and by impairing corrections officers ability to protect all those inside a prison's walls.

Finally, [complainants] have suggested no alternatives that fully accommodate the asserted right while not imposing more than a [minimum] cost to the valid penological goals.

Source: *Overton v. Bazzetta*, 539 U.S. 126 (2003), Syllabus.

offense for which they were arrested was a minor one. In that case, Justice Kennedy, writing for the majority, noted that "maintaining safety and order at detention centers requires the expertise of correctional officials, who must have substantial discretion to devise reasonable solutions to problems." He went on to write that "the term 'jail' is used here in a broad sense to include prisons and other detention facilities."

The Legal Mechanisms Changes in state and federal statutes have also slowed the pace of prisoners' rights cases. In 1980, Congress modified the Civil Rights of Institutionalized Persons Act.[20] Following modification, it requires people held in state prisons to exhaust all state remedies before filing a petition for a writ of *habeas corpus* in federal court. In effect, a person in state prison must give the state an opportunity to correct alleged violations of its prisoners' federal rights (*Duncan* v. *Henry*, 1995). Inmates in federal prisons may still file *habeas corpus* petitions directly in federal court. In their petitions, people held in federal prisons are now required to show (1) that they were deprived of some right to which they were entitled despite the confinement and (2) that the deprivation of this right made the imprisonment more burdensome.

The Prison Litigation Reform Act of 1995[21] (PLRA) was another legislative response to the ballooning number of civil rights lawsuits filed by people in prisons. It restricts the filing of lawsuits in federal courts by:

1. requiring people held in state prisons to exhaust all local administrative remedies prior to filing suit in federal court;

2. requiring people in prison to pay federal filing fees unless they can claim pauper status;[22]

3. limiting awards of attorneys' fees in successful lawsuits;

4. requiring judges to screen all lawsuits brought by those imprisoned, and immediately dismiss those they find frivolous;

5. revoking good-time credit toward early release if imprisoned people file malicious lawsuits;

6. barring people in prison from suing the federal government for mental or emotional injury unless there is an accompanying physical injury;

7. allowing court orders to go no further than necessary to correct the individual's civil rights problem;

8. requiring some court orders to be renewed every two years or be lifted; and

9. ensuring that no single judge can order the release of people from federal prison for overcrowding.

In May 2001, the U.S. Supreme Court further restricted resident options under the PLRA. The ruling mandates that residents in correctional facilities must complete prison administrative processes that could provide some relief before suing over prison conditions even if that relief would *not include a monetary payment* (*Booth* v. *Churner*, 2001).

A 2005 study of the PLRA's effectiveness conducted by the National Council for State Courts (NCSC), found that the PLRA "achieved its intended effects" and significantly lowered the number of frivolous filings in federal courts.[23]

CO11-6 CONFINED WOMEN AND THE COURTS

The prisoners' rights movement has been largely a male phenomenon. While males held in confinement were petitioning the courts for expansion of their rights, females being held frequently had to resort to the courts simply to gain rights that males already had.

The Cases

One early state case, *Barefield* v. *Leach* (1974), demonstrated that the opportunities and programs for women in prison were clearly inferior to those for males. In that case, a court in New Mexico spelled out one standard for equal treatment of males and females held in prison. The court said that the equal-protection clause of the Constitution requires equal treatment of male and female residents but not identical treatment. *Barefield,* however, was a state case—not binding on other states or the federal government.

In 1977, in *State, ex rel. Olson* v. *Maxwell,* the Supreme Court of North Dakota ruled that a lack of funds was not an acceptable justification for unequal treatment of male and female persons held in prison. Although this decision also came in a state court case, it would later be cited as a legal authority in a similar federal court case.

Correctional clients dressed in cap and gown are honored at a GED graduation ceremony in a California prison. Many claims of incarcerated women have focused on the failure of correctional institutions to provide them with educational opportunities and medical care comparable to those provided to men who are in prison. The equal-protection clause of which amendment guarantees imprisoned women the same conditions of as men who are incarcerated?
Marmaduke St. John/Alamy Stock Photo

In *Glover* v. *Johnson* (1979), a U.S. district court case, a group of female prisoners in the Michigan system filed a class action lawsuit claiming that they were denied access to the courts and constitutional rights to equal protection. The imprisoned women demanded educational and vocational opportunities comparable to those for males. At trial, a prison teacher testified that, although men were allowed to take shop courses, women were taught remedial courses at a junior high school level because the attitude of those in charge was, "Keep it simple, these are only women." The court found that "the educational opportunities available to women prisoners in Michigan were substantially inferior to those available to male prisoners." Consequently, the court ordered a plan to provide higher education and vocational training for female residents in the Michigan prison system. *Glover* was a turning point in equal treatment for women in prison. Since 1979, women in prison have continued to win the majority of cases seeking equal treatment and the elimination of gender bias.

In the 1980 case of *Cooper* v. *Morin,* the U.S. Supreme Court accepted neither inconvenience nor cost as an excuse for treating women in jail differently from males. Women at a county jail in New York had alleged that inadequate medical attention in jail violated their civil rights. Later that same year, a federal district court rejected Virginia's claims that services for women in prison could not be provided at the same level as those for males because of cost-effectiveness issues (*Bukhari* v. *Hutto,* 1980). Virginia authorities said that the much smaller number of women in prison raised the cost of providing each woman with services. The appellate court ordered the state of Virginia to provide equitable services for inmates, regardless of gender.

An action challenging the denial of equal protection and the conditions of confinement in the Kentucky Correctional Institution for Women was the basis of *Canterino* v. *Wilson,* decided in U.S. district court in 1982. The district court held that the "levels system" used to allocate privileges to women in prison, a system not applied to males, violated both the equal-protection rights and the due process rights of imprisoned women. The court also held that females in Kentucky's prisons must have the same opportunities as men for vocational education, training, recreation, and outdoor activity.

In 1982, in *McMurray* v. *Phelps,* a district court in Louisiana ordered an end to the unequal treatment of females in that state's jails. (Recall that the federal courts have supervisory jurisdiction over state courts.) The next year, the Seventh Circuit Court of Appeals found that strip searches of female misdemeanants awaiting bond in a Chicago lockup were unreasonable under the Fourth Amendment (*Mary Beth G.* v. *City of Chicago,* 1983). In addition, the court found that a policy of subjecting female arrestees to strip searches while subjecting similarly situated males only to hand searches violated the equal-protection clause of the Constitution.

In 1994, in a class action suit brought by women in prison, a federal district court held the District of Columbia Department of Corrections liable under the Eighth Amendment for inadequate gynecological examinations and testing, inadequate testing for sexually transmitted diseases, inadequate health education, inadequate prenatal care, and an inadequate overall prenatal protocol (*Women Prisoners of the District of Columbia Department of Corrections* v. *District of Columbia,* 1994).

Court oversight of OB-GYN services at the District of Columbia Department of Corrections ended in 2004, following an agreement in which the department promised to continue to provide adequate services for women in prison. The agreement ended 33 years of court oversight of the DC department—involving a total of 15 class action lawsuits filed by people in prison or their representatives during that time.[24]

Also in 2004, U.S. district judge Myron Thompson approved a settlement in a class action lawsuit centered on concerns about medical care and general conditions at three Alabama women's prisons. Thompson said that the settlement, which required lowering the number of prisoners held at three locations, would not make the facilities "comfortable or pleasant" but would "afford class members the basic necessities mandated by the United States Constitution."[25] Affected were the Julia Tutwiler Prison for Women, the Tutwiler Annex, and the Birmingham Work Release Facility—all operated by the Alabama Department of Corrections. The lawsuit, filed by the Southern Center for Human Rights, had complained of "intensely overcrowded" and "unbearably hot and poorly ventilated dormitories." Tutwiler Prison had been built in the 1940s to hold no more than 364 residents but was filled with more than 1,000 people at the time of the lawsuit. Under the agreement, the population was lowered to 700 by sending some people to prisons in Louisiana and by releasing others under community supervision.

CO11-7 CORRECTIONAL OFFICER CIVIL LIABILITY AND LAWSUITS BROUGHT BY CONFINED PEOPLE

doctrine of sovereign immunity

A historical legal doctrine that held that a governing body or its representatives could not be sued because it made the law and therefore could not be bound by it.

Until recently, the **doctrine of sovereign immunity** barred legal actions against state and local governments. The doctrine of sovereign immunity held that a governing body or its representatives could not be sued because it made the law and therefore could not be bound by it. Consequently, federal and state correctional facilities and their officers, acting in their official capacity, were generally held to be immune from lawsuits.

Today, however, immunity is a much more complex issue. Some states have officially abandoned any claims of immunity through legislative action. New York State, for example, has declared that public agencies are equally as liable as private agencies for violations of constitutional rights. Other states, such as California, have enacted statutory provisions that define and limit governmental liability.[26] A number of state immunity statutes have been struck down by court decision. In general, states are moving in the direction of setting dollar limits on liability and adopting federal immunity principles, including "good faith" and "reasonable belief" rules, to protect individual officers.

At the federal level, the concept of sovereign immunity is embodied in the Federal Tort Claims Act (FTCA),[27] which grants broad immunity to certain federal government agencies—especially law enforcement agencies—when their employees act negligently within the scope of their employment. In the 2008 U.S. Supreme Court case of *Ali* v. *Federal Bureau of Prisons,* the Court held that federal correctional officers are law enforcement officers for purposes of civil litigation and found that the BOP was immune to the type of suit that had been brought against it. In *Ali,* a person in a federal prison filed suit against the BOP under the FTCA,[28] which authorizes "claims against the United States for money damages ... for injury or loss of property ... caused by the negligent or wrongful act or omission of any employee in the government while acting within the scope of his office or employment." In denying Ali's claim, the Court found that the law specifically provides immunity for federal law enforcement officers and determined that federal corrections personnel are "law enforcement officers" within the meaning of the law. In the 2013 case of *Millbrook* v. *U.S.,*[29] the Court reaffirmed its earlier finding that federal correctional officers are law enforcement officers whose agencies are protected against suits under the FTCA for acts or omissions that arise within the scope of their employment.

Individual officers (as opposed to the agencies for which they work), however, are not necessarily protected under federal or state law. Nonetheless, federal courts have generally shielded correctional officers from "constitutional lawsuits if reasonable officers believe their actions to be lawful in light of clearly established law and the information the officers possess." In doing so, the Court has recognized a form of qualified immunity as a defense, "which shields public officials from actions for damages unless their conduct was unreasonable in light of clearly established law."[30] According to the Court, "[T]he qualified immunity doctrine's central objective is to protect public officials from undue interference with their duties and from potentially disabling threats of liability."[31]

REVIEW AND APPLICATIONS

SUMMARY

1 The hands-off doctrine was a working philosophy of the courts in this country until 1970. It allowed corrections officials to run prisons without court intervention. The hands-off doctrine existed because courts were reluctant to interfere with activities of the executive branch and because judges realized that they were not experts in corrections.

2 The key legal sources of prisoners' rights are the U.S. Constitution, federal statutes, state constitutions, and state statutes.

3 People in confinement can challenge the legality of their confinement, associated prison conditions, and the practices of correctional officials through (1) a state *habeas corpus* action, (2) a federal *habeas corpus* action, (3) a state tort lawsuit, (4) a federal civil rights lawsuit, and (5) an injunction to obtain relief.

4 During the prisoners' rights era (1970–1991), people who were confined won many court cases based on claims that conditions of their confinement violated their constitutional rights. Court decisions affected the rights of confined people to freedom of expression, including free speech; personal communications; access to the courts and legal services; religion; assembly and association; the voicing of grievances about disciplinary procedures; protection from personal and cell searches; health care, including diet and exercise; protection from violence; adequate physical conditions of confinement; and rehabilitation.

5 Most claims made by people in confinement focus on denial of constitutional rights guaranteed by the First (freedom of expression and religion), Fourth (freedom from unlawful search and seizure), Eighth (freedom from cruel and unusual punishment), and Fourteenth (due process and equal protection of the law) Amendments.

6 The prisoners' rights movement has been largely a male phenomenon. More recently, confined women have had to petition the courts to gain rights that men in confinement already had.

7 In times past, the doctrine of sovereign immunity shielded federal, state, and local governments from lawsuits. More recently, however, correctional agencies—at least on the federal level—have been protected by federal law from certain civil suits stemming from the negligent actions of their employees. Individual officers are also shielded by court precedent to the extent that their actions are reasonable in light of clearly established law.

KEY TERMS

hands-off doctrine, p. 302

prisoners' rights, p. 304

constitutional rights, p. 305

institutional needs, p. 305

civil liability, p. 305

writ of *habeas corpus*, p. 306

tort, p. 307

nominal damages, p. 307

compensatory damages, p. 307

punitive damages, p. 307

injunction, p. 307

jurisdiction, p. 307

precedent, p. 310

legitimate penological objectives, p. 313

balancing test, p. 313

cruel and unusual punishment, p. 318

deliberate indifference, p. 319

totality of conditions, p. 319

due process, p. 321

frivolous lawsuits, p. 323

doctrine of sovereign immunity, p. 330

QUESTIONS FOR REVIEW

1 Why was the hands-off doctrine so named? What was the basis for the doctrine?

2 What are the key legal sources of prisoners' rights?

3 What are the legal mechanisms through which people who are held in confinement can challenge the legality of their confinement and associated prison conditions?

4 What rights were won by confined individuals during what this text calls the *prisoners' rights era?*

5 What constitutional amendments are most often cited by people in confinement who were claiming rights? What claimed rights are associated with each of these amendments?

6 Do the rights accorded men who are incarcerated correspond to the rights of women in confinement? Why or why not?

7 What is the doctrine of sovereign immunity? To what extent are today's correctional officers shielded from civil lawsuits brought by inmates?

THINKING CRITICALLY ABOUT CORRECTIONS

Freedom of Nonverbal Expression

The right to freedom of nonverbal expression is said to be implied in the First Amendment. Hence, how people wear their hair and how they dress are expressions that some believe are protected by the First Amendment.

1. Might there be modes of dress that interfere with a correctional institution's legitimate goals?

2. If so, what might they be?

Checks and Balance

On January 11, 2003, in a dramatic legal move shortly before leaving office, former Illinois governor George Ryan commuted the sentences of every one of the 167 people held on death row in that state. Four of the sentences were reduced to 40-year terms; the remaining 163 sentences were commuted to life in prison. Governor Ryan based his action on his determination of inherent arbitrariness and unfairness in the application of capital punishment and on the high risk of executing an innocent person.

Although the scope of his action was unusual, the commutations typify the power placed in the hands of each state's chief executive. Essentially, this means that, within the respective states and based solely on personal opinion, a single individual is empowered to overturn sentencing decisions and attendant legal rulings on those decisions made at any level up to and including the nation's most powerful court, the U.S. Supreme Court.

1. Should this be the case?
2. Does the lack of a legal mechanism to counter a governor's decision regarding a pardon or a commutation violate the principle of checks and balances so intricately woven into America's state and federal governmental structures?

ON-THE-JOB DECISION MAKING

Inmate Communications

You are a prison administrator. The prison where you work has a rule that incarcerated people may write letters in English only. This rule seems sensible. After all, if correctional clients could write in languages not understood by correctional officers, they could discuss plans to escape, riot, or smuggle drugs or weapons into the prison. The courts allow the censoring of outgoing mail; what good is that power if corrections personnel cannot read the mail?

You realize, however, that people who cannot write in English will have difficulty communicating with the outside world and with their families. Those unable to write in English will not even be able to write to their attorneys. You also wonder what might happen if a person who is incarcerated can write in English but his parents can read only a foreign language. If the person and his parents cannot afford long-distance phone calls, they will not be able to communicate with each other at all. You begin to consider how the English-only rule might be changed to facilitate wholesome communications while still preventing communications that might endanger the safety of the institution and the correctional population.

1. Can the English-only rule be amended to meet the client needs discussed here while still being consistent with legitimate institutional concerns? If so, how?
2. Does a person who is institutionalized have a constitutionally protected right to communicate with his or her parents?
3. What if that right conflicts with prison policy?

Law Libraries

The Supreme Court's ruling in *Bounds* v. *Smith* (1977) led to the establishment of law libraries for use by persons held in correctional facilities throughout the nation. Numerous subsequent civil suits resulted in follow-on rulings mandating the need to maintain these libraries with up-to-date reference materials in serviceable condition.

You are an advisor on correctional issues on the staff of your state's attorney general. In the past few weeks, she has repeatedly complained that these rulings impose excessive financial demands on the state's already nearly impoverished correctional system. In particular, she says, routine vandalism by people in prison who tear pages from law books and take the pages back to their cells—or simply discard them—is especially costly. It also creates a circumstance in which another person in confinement could threaten another civil suit upon finding a book to be "unserviceable" when attempting to use it, a threat to which the system can respond only by immediately purchasing a replacement book.

This, the attorney general says, typifies a cycle that causes an extraordinary drain on limited financial resources. She rants about the "ludicrous" fact that the reference material in her own office is so out of date as to be virtually unusable, but she cannot fix the problem because she spends that portion of her budget on repeatedly restoring the prison law libraries in the various institutions throughout the state.

The attorney general has tasked you to resolve this issue.

1. What will you do?
2. Might advances in information technology be the key to a solution? If so, what new problems might they bring?

ENDNOTES

1. Audrey Nielsen, "Federal Judge Orders Arizona Prison Overhaul Due to Unconstitutional Conditions," *The Crime Report*, January 11, 2023, https://thecrimereport.org/2023/01/11/federal-judge-orders-arizona-prison-overhaul-due-to-unconstitutional-conditions (accessed March 20, 2023), from which much of the information in this opening story is taken.

2. *Ruffin* v. *Commonwealth*, 62, Va. 790, 1871.

3. Frances Cole, "The Impact of *Bell v. Wolfish* Upon Prisoners' Rights," *Journal of Crime and Justice*, vol. 10 (1987), pp. 47–70.

4. D. J. Gottlieb, "The Legacy of *Wolfish* and *Chapman*: Some Thoughts About 'Big Prison Case' Litigation in the 1980s," in I. D. Robbins (ed.), *Prisoners and the Law* (New York: Clark Boardman, 1985).

5. James B. Jacobs, *New Perspectives on Prisons and Imprisonment* (Ithaca, NY: Cornell University Press, 1983).

6. *Holt* v. *Sarver*, 442 F.2d 304 (1971).

7. Ibid.

8. *Holt* v. *Sarver*, 309 F.Supp. 362 (E.D.Ark.1970), aff'd, 442 F.2d 304 (8th Cir. 1971).

9. Todd Clear and George F. Cole, *American Corrections*, 4th ed. (New York: Wadsworth, 1997).

10. Civil Rights of Institutionalized Persons Act, 42 U.S.C. § 1997 et seq. (1976 ed., Supp. IV), as modified 1980. (Current through P.L. 104–150, approved June 3, 1996.)

11. R. Hawkins and G. P. Alpert, *American Prison Systems: Punishment and Justice* (Englewood Cliffs, NJ: Prentice Hall, 1989).

12. Administrative Office of the United States Courts, "U.S. Courts of Appeals—Judicial Caselaod Profile," https://www.uscourts.gov/sites/default/files/fcms_na_appprofile0331.2022.pdf (accessed February 15, 2023).

13. *Report of the Comptroller General of the United States: Grievance Mechanisms in State Correctional Institutions and Large-City Jails* (Washington, DC: U.S. Government Printing Office, June 17, 1977), Appendix I.

14. James B. Jacobs, "The Prisoners' Rights Movement and Its Impacts," in Edward J. Latessa, Alexander Holsinger, James W. Marquart, and Jonathan R. Sorensen (eds.), *Correctional Contexts: Contemporary and Classical Readings*, 2nd ed. (Los Angeles: Roxbury, 2001), p. 211. Reprinted from James B. Jacobs, *Crime and Justice*, vol. II (Chicago: University of Chicago Press, 1980).

15. See *Estelle* v. *Gamble*, 429 U.S. 97 (1976), and *Hutto v. Finney*, 437 U.S. 678 (1978).

16. Sheri Qualters, "Federal Judge Orders Sex-Reassignment Surgery for Mass. Prisoner," *Law Journal*, September 4, 2012.

17. American Civil Liberties Union, *ACLU Position Paper: Prisoners' Rights* https://www.aclu.org/sites/default/files/field_document/prisonerrights.pdf (accessed March 2, 2023).

18. In 1977, Theriault's appeal to the U.S. Supreme Court was denied (see 434 U.S. 953, November 14, 1977).

19. *Ali* v. *Federal Bureau of Prisons*, 552 U.S. 214 (2008).

20. In Section 1997e, Congress created a specific, limited exhaustion requirement for adult prisoners bringing actions pursuant to section 1983.

21. Prison Litigation Reform Act, Pub. L. No. 104-134, § 801-10, 110 Stat. 1321 (1995).

22. If a prisoner wishes to proceed as an indigent on appeal, the prisoner must file in the district court, with the notice of appeal, a motion for leave to proceed as an indigent, a certified copy of a prison trust account statement, and Form 4 from the Appendix of Forms found in the *Federal Rules of Appellate Procedure*.

23. Fred L. Cheesman, Brian J. Ostrom, and Roger A. Hanson, *A Tale of Two Laws Revisited: Investigating the Impact of the Prison Litigation Reform Act and the Antiterrorism and Effective Death Penalty Act* (Williamsburg, VA: National Center for State Courts, 2005).

24. "Court Intervention Ends for D.C. DOC," *Corrections Today*, December 2004, p. 12.

25. "Judge Approves Settlement in Alabama Prison Lawsuit," *Corrections Journal*, August 9, 2004, p. 1.

26. California Government Code, Section 818.

27. Federal Tort Claims Act, U.S. Code, Title 28, Section 1346(b), 2671–2680.

28. U.S.C. Section 1346(b)(1).

29. *Milbrook* v. *U.S.*, 569 U.S. 50 (2013).

30. *Elder* v. *Holloway*, 510 U.S. 510 (1994).

31. Ibid.

SPECIAL POPULATIONS

People in Prison with Substance Use Disorders, HIV/AIDS, Mental Illness, and the Elderly

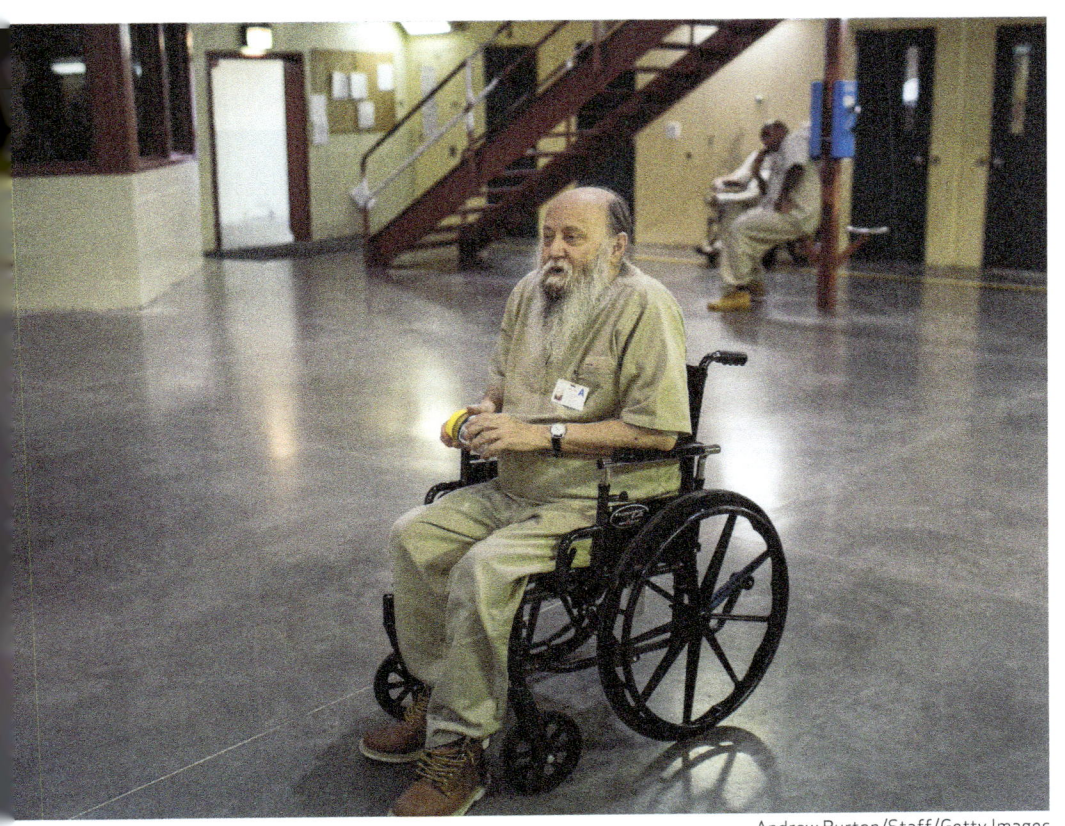

Andrew Burton/Staff/Getty Images

CHAPTER OBJECTIVES

After completing this chapter you should be able to do the following:

1 Define the term *incarcerated people with special needs.*

2 Report on the special treatment and care of persons in prison with special needs.

3 Summarize who is in prison with a substance use disorder, why treatment is important, and what works.

4 Outline the challenges that persons with HIV/AIDS confront in prison.

5 Debate the issues surrounding the incarceration of persons with mental illness.

6 Summarize the health, cost, and recidivism issues associated with persons in prison who are elderly and how states are responding.

I cannot think of a more challenging or needful segment of our work than our involvement with special populations.

—Thomas Patterson, former director, Utah Department of Corrections

Forty years ago, there were almost 9,000 persons in state and federal prison who were age 55 and older. Today, that number is more than 261,000. Experts project that by 2030 this number will be more than 400,000, amounting to more than one-third of the incarcerated population in the United States—enough to fill the Louisiana Superdome more than three times. What are the special needs of the elderly in prison?

SHARON GEKOSKI-KIMMEL/KRT/Newscom

On October 28, 2021, the U.S. Department of Justice Civil Rights Division reached a settlement with the Vermont Department of Corrections (VDOC) to remedy conditions in state prisons that fail to comply with the Americans with Disabilities Act (ADA) of 1990.[1]

The Civil Rights Division received complaints from persons incarcerated in the VDOC alleging the following:

- VDOC fails to provide facilities that are accessible to persons with mobility issues that substantially limit one or more major life activities, including walking and standing.

- VDOC fails to provide effective communication for persons with hearing loss and thereby denies them participation in educational, vocational, religious, and other programs on the basis of their disabilities.

- VDOC has a policy that provides incarcerated persons with hearing loss only one hearing aid, when two are prescribed, and fails to make timely repairs, thereby preventing them from participating fully in counseling, educational, recreational, religious, and social programs.

- VDOC facilities have architectural barriers that prevent them from attending religious services.

- VDOC fails to make reasonable modifications to its policies, practices, and procedures to assign them to a lower bunk where necessary to provide access.

As a result of the investigation, the VDOC agreed to:

- make structural changes to prison buildings and facilities to comply with the ADA Standards for Accessible Design;

- implement a process that begins at intake and continues throughout incarceration to identify and accommodate persons with disabilities;

- develop individualized communication assessments and plans setting out the auxiliary aids and services necessary to ensure effective communication for persons with hearing loss;

- identify and remediate physical barriers to access for persons with mobility issues to ensure access to accessible prison cells and work assignments;

- provide training on the ADA to correctional staff and management responsible for evaluating or making decisions about requests for accommodations;

- engage in compliance reporting and monitoring with the Justice Department; and

- pay $80,000 to compensate current and former incarcerated persons who were harmed.

Incarcerated individuals with special needs are those who exhibit unique physical, mental, social, and programmatic needs that distinguish them from other residents and to whom jail and prison management and staff have to respond to in nontraditional and innovative ways. These special populations suffer from mental illness; chemical dependency (drug or alcohol); communicable diseases (especially HIV/AIDS and tuberculosis); chronic diseases (e.g., diabetes, heart disease, seizures, and detoxification); the general problems of people who are elderly; the special concern of managing young females in correctional settings; the problems that arise when juveniles are housed in adult institutions; and the issues arising from sexual identity, victimization, persons who are transgender, and the management of persons in prison for sexual offenses.

Space does not allow us to discuss all of these special populations. This chapter reviews the management and care of the four largest groups of people in prison with special needs: those with substance use disorders (SUDs), HIV and AIDS, mental illness, and the elderly.

INCARCERATED PEOPLE WITH SPECIAL NEEDS

CO12-1

Persons in prison with special needs present operational and administrative problems for correctional staff—it is often difficult for the staff to know what they are observing or, once they recognize a person's special needs, how to address the situation. Thomas Patterson, former executive director of the Utah Department of Corrections, once said that more and more special populations are the norm rather than the exception.[2] He went on to say that if we add persons in prison for sex offenses and drugs to the mix of special populations, upward of 80 percent of the prison population would require attention to the challenges they present inside prisons and jails.[3] "To turn a blind eye on special populations is to neglect ethical and humane obligations and more rapidly spin the turnstile of recidivism."[4]

A statewide research study on jail management in New Mexico found that the incarcerated population with special needs requires extra attention from staff.[5] For example, they must be watched closely for possible suicide. Almost 9 of 10 disrupt normal jail activities; 7 of 10 require an excess of scarce medical resources; 4 of 10 engage in acts of violence; and almost 3 of 10 are susceptible to bullying by other individuals who are incarcerated.

CO12-2

The Bureau of Justice Statistics reports that nationwide about 40 percent of state prison populations, and 50 percent of women's state prison populations, have needs that require specialized services from correctional staff.[6] From vision-related (12 percent) to hearing (10 percent) and ambulatory (12 percent) disabilities, people in prison have higher rates of special needs compared to the general U.S. population (see Exhibit 12–1).

The data also show that multiracial and native people in state prisons had higher rates of nearly every type of disability, followed by white people. Black, Hispanic, and Asian incarcerated people reported lower-than-average rates of disabilities.

Incarcerated individuals with special needs

Incarcerated individuals who exhibit unique physical, mental, social, and programmatic needs that distinguish them from other residents and to whom jail and prison management and staff have to respond in nontraditional and innovative ways.

The American Correctional Association (ACA) urges correctional agencies to develop and adopt procedures for the early identification of the special needs population, to provide the services that respond to those needs, and to monitor and evaluate the delivery of services in both community and institutional settings (see Exhibit 12-2).

Persons in Prison with a Substance Use Disorder (SUD)

Alcohol and other drug problems are the common denominator for most persons in prison. Almost one-half (49 percent) of the state prison population and one-third (32 percent) of the federal prison population meet the medical criteria for SUD published by the American Psychiatric Association. By comparison, SUD in the U.S. general population aged 12 or older is 17 percent.[7]

EXHIBIT 12−1   People with Disabilities in Prison and the U.S. Population

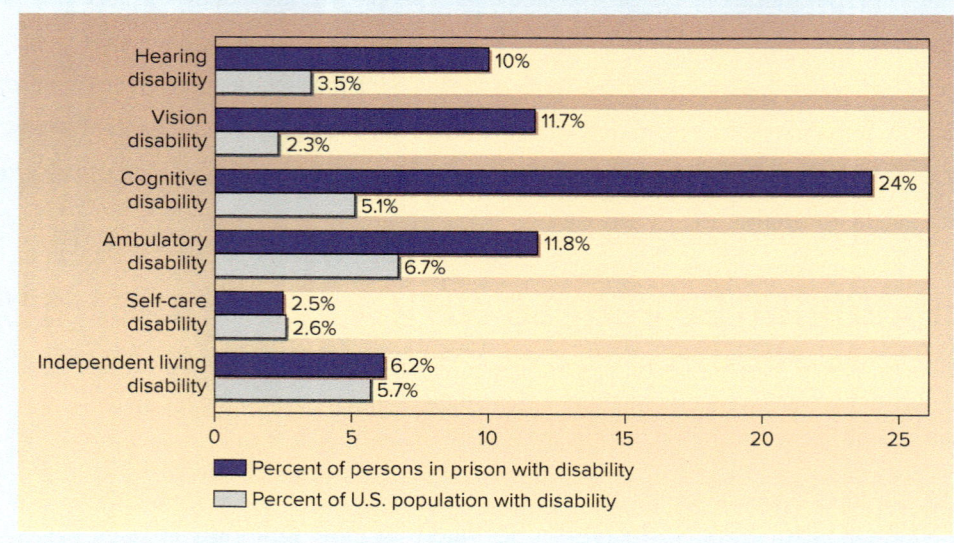

Source: Bureau of Justice Statistics

EXHIBIT 12−2   American Correctional Association

Public Correctional Policy on Offenders with Special Needs

Introduction:

The provision of humane and gender-responsive programs and services for the accused and adjudicated requires addressing the special needs of juvenile, youthful and adult offenders. To meet this goal, correctional agencies should develop and adopt procedures for the early identification of offenders with special needs. Agencies should provide the services that respond to these needs and monitor and evaluate the delivery of services in both confined and community settings.

Policy Statement:

Correctional systems must assure provision of specialized services, programs and conditions of confinement to meet the special needs of offenders. To achieve this, correctional systems should:

A. Identify the juvenile, youthful and adult offenders who require special care or programs including:

- Offenders with psychological needs, developmental disabilities, psychiatric disorders, behavioral disorders, disabling conditions, neurological impairments, and substance abuse disorders;
- Offenders who have acute or chronic medical conditions, are physically disabled or terminally ill;
- Older offenders;
- Offenders with social and/or educational deficiencies, learning disabilities, or language barriers;
- Offenders with special security or supervision needs;
- Sex offenders;
- Female offenders; and
- Transgender offenders.

B. Provide services and programs in a manner consistent with professional standards and nationally accepted exemplary practices. Such services and programs may be provided within the correctional agency itself, by referral to another agency that has the necessary specialized resources, or by contracting with private or volunteer agencies or individuals that meet professional standards;

C. Provide appropriately trained, licensed and/or certified, staff, contractors and volunteers for the delivery of, care, programs, and services and provide incentives to attend the continuing education and training necessary to maintain credentials and state-of-the-art, knowledge and mastery-level skills;

D. Maintain professionally appropriate records of all delivered services and programs;

E. Conduct evaluations of service delivery adherence to program standards, while also evaluating the effectiveness of the services, with regular feedback to administrators and service providers for continuous quality improvement; and

F. Provide leadership and advocacy for legislative and public support to obtain the resources needed to meet these special needs.

BJS also informs us that half of the people in state prisons had a SUD in the year before they went to prison, but only 1 in 10 received any clinical treatment in the community such as professional counseling, participation in residential programming, or received a maintenance drug. And once they went to prison even fewer—only 11 percent—received treatment for SUD, and few of those receive evidence-based care, including access to pharmacological care and the availability of trained staff. Simply offering treatment does not mean that treatment is available to all who need it, nor does it speak to the quality of care.[8]

As this and other chapters point out, we know how to reduce mass incarceration, the cost of imprisonment and the crimes committed by persons with SUD. It begins with acknowledging the fact that addiction is a disease for which evidence-based treatment and prevention programs exist. However, the barriers to action include the setting of mandatory sentences that eliminate the possibilities of alternative sanctions such as drug courts or parole, the lack of a clear mandate to provide treatment, the economic interests in prison expansion, politicians who are more concerned with being reelected and fear being labeled "soft on crime" by opponents, and the failure of public policy to reflect the science of addiction and changing public attitudes about addiction and justice.

However as we pointed out in Chapters 3 and 7, a number of states (and the federal government) have either reversed mandatory sentencing or are considering doing so. Everywhere there are examples of evidence-based practices informing correctional policy. And the public thinks treatment is good. An ABC news poll found that two-thirds of Americans support state laws requiring treatment—not incarceration for persons convicted of a first or second drug offense.[9]

That public support, along with the surge in the number of persons in prison with SUD, and the overwhelming evidence showing that addiction is a treatable disease of the brain for which evidence-based treatment exists are reasons that voters in California and other states have opted to allow persons convicted of nonviolent drug offenses to serve their time in a drug treatment program rather than jail.

Drug Treatment Programs Why should persons with SUD receive drug treatment? There are two powerful reasons.[10]

First, people who use drugs spend over $150 billion a year on illegal drugs such as cocaine, heroin, marijuana, and methamphetamine.[11] A large proportion of spending and drug use comes from a small share of people who use illegal drugs on a daily or near-daily basis. Any reduction in their drug use will decrease the demand for illegal drugs.

Second, we now know from the evidence-based literature that drug abuse treatment improves outcomes for persons with SUD, and has beneficial effects for public health and safety. Ample evidence over the past two decades has consistently shown that cognitive behavioral therapy (CBT) is an effective intervention in the treatment of SUD in a correctional facility even if the motivation for entering treatment is coerced.[12]

Almost one-half of the state prison population and one-third of the federal prison population meet the medical criteria for SUD, but only 11 percent receive any treatment while incarcerated. What should prisons do to control the revolving door of persons with SUD in and out of prison?

Marvin Joseph/The Washington Post/Getty Images

CBT, you'll recall from Chapter 7, addresses antisocial and dysfunctional thinking patterns that support criminal behavior. In-prison CBT programs have been found to have the best outcomes for reducing prison misconduct, produce strong results in reducing recidivism, and provide some of the highest returns on investments for correctional programming.[13] In addition, participation in CBT is associated with enhanced mental and physical health.

Other correctional institutions respond to SUD by offering a "therapeutic community," a residential environment separated from the general prison

Many persons enter prison addicted to illegal drugs. Although there's evidence that cognitive-based drug and alcohol treatment in prison reduces recidivism, only 11 percent of persons in prison who need substance abuse treatment actually receive it. Should correctional facilities be required to provide cognitive-based substance abuse treatment? What are the benefits of cognitive-based substance abuse treatment?

Marmaduke St. John/Alamy Stock Photo

population and where residents participate in intensive self-help and peer group counseling, drug abuse education and treatment, and professional counseling. The National Institute of Justice rated therapeutic communities an *effective* practice in reducing recidivism.

Medications are also used to treat SUD. Methadone, buprenorphine, and naltrexone are beneficial for the treatment of heroin addiction and naltrexone and topiramate for the treatment of alcoholism. However, very few correctional facilities offer pharmacological treatment. Self-help programs such as Alcoholics Anonymous or SMART Recovery can also be valuable adjuncts to formal drug treatment.

What Works? The Fundamentals of Effective Drug Treatment After reviewing all the research that had been published on the treatment of SUD for the past 40 years, researchers with the National Institute of Justice identified 13 principles that constitute effective drug treatment:[14]

1. Drug addiction is a brain disease that affects behavior and the brain's anatomy and chemistry, and these changes can last for months or years after the individual has stopped using drugs.
2. Effective drug abuse treatment engages participants in a therapeutic process, retains them in treatment for an appropriate length of time, and helps them learn to maintain abstinence over time.
3. Effective drug abuse treatment must last long enough (referred to as "dosage") to produce stable behavioral changes.
4. A comprehensive assessment of the nature and extent of an individual's drug problems and mental health evaluation is the first step in effective drug abuse treatment.
5. Tailoring services to fit the needs of the individual is an important part of effective drug abuse treatment because individuals differ in terms of age, gender, ethnicity, problem severity, recovery stage, and level of supervision needed.
6. Effective drug abuse treatment programs carefully monitor drug use through urinalysis or other objective methods because individuals trying to recover from drug addiction may experience a relapse, or return, to drug use.

7. Effective drug abuse treatment programs target cognitions (thoughts and feelings that are associated with criminal behavior). These include believing that one is entitled to have things one's own way; feeling that one's criminal behavior is justified; failing to be responsible for one's actions; and constantly failing to anticipate or appreciate the consequences of one's behavior.

8. Effective drug abuse treatment programs incorporate treatment planning and treatment providers are aware of correctional supervision requirements as treatment goals.

9. Effective drug abuse treatment programs recognize that continuity of care helps persons deal with problems after release from prison such as learning to handle situations that could lead to relapse, learning how to live drug free in the community, and developing a drug-free peer support network.

10. Effective drug abuse treatment programs recognize that a balance of rewards and sanctions encourages prosocial behavior and treatment participation.

11. Effective drug abuse treatment programs recognize that persons with co-occurring drug abuse and mental health problems require an integrated approach that combines drug abuse treatment with psychiatric treatment, including the use of medication to address depression, anxiety, and other mental health problems.

12. Effective drug abuse treatment programs recognize that medications are an important part of treatment and can be instrumental in enabling persons with co-occurring mental health problems to function successfully in society.

13. Effective drug abuse treatment programs understand that rates of infectious diseases such as tuberculosis and HIV/AIDS are higher in the SUD incarcerated population, and those under community correctional supervision than in the general population.

Persons in Prison with HIV and AIDS

HIV is the acronym for **human immunodeficiency virus,** which is any of a group of retroviruses that infect and destroy T cells, which help the immune system fight off infections. When enough of a person's T cells have been destroyed by HIV, the diagnosis is **AIDS, or acquired immunodeficiency syndrome,** the last stage of HIV infection. The AIDS virus attacks the body's natural immune system, making it unable to fight off diseases. In this state, a person is highly vulnerable to life-threatening conditions, which people with healthy immune systems can fight off easily.

Corrections professionals are concerned with treating communicable diseases in the prison population for at least four reasons:

1. Sexually transmitted diseases can be spread to other persons in prison.

2. Correctional employees and prison visitors are at risk of becoming infected if appropriate precautions are not implemented.

3. Almost 1,500 persons are released every day from prison. Unless they are effectively treated, they may transmit their diseases into the community, threatening public health.

4. Unless persons are treated in prison, they burden community health care systems.[15]

HIV (human immunodeficiency virus)

A group of retroviruses that infect and destroy helper T cells of the immune system, causing the marked reduction in their numbers that is diagnostic of AIDS.

AIDS (acquired immunodeficiency syndrome)

A term that applies to the most advanced stages of HIV where a weakened immune system can no longer protect against life-threatening infections and cancers.

CO12-4

EVIDENCE-BASED CORRECTIONS

Motivational Interviewing for Substance Abuse

Motivational interviewing (MI) is an evidence-based conversational counseling approach that employs a specific form of reflective listening—viewing an individual's reluctance to change as a normal part of the human process rather than as a mode of defensiveness—to help people who are ambivalent about changing their behavior find the motivation to make a positive behavior change. When provided to those who abuse substances, the long-term goal is to help them reduce or stop using drugs and alcohol.

Substance abuse generally refers to the overindulgence in and dependence on a drug or other substance (e.g., alcohol) that leads to detrimental effects on an individual's physical and mental health or the welfare of others. MI targets a wide range of problem behaviors, such as smoking, gambling, or eating disorders.

Researchers examined multiple studies that compared individuals who received MI with individuals who received no treatment at follow-up periods between 6 and 12 months. The results showed that individuals in the MI treatment groups significantly reduced their use of substances compared to those in the no-treatment control groups.

The practice of motivational interviewing for substance abuse is rated *Effective*.

Source: Adapted from Bureau of Justice Statistics.

Recently, the Bureau of Justice Statistics reported on HIV in prison.[16] At year-end 2020, an estimated 12,000 persons in the custody of state and federal correctional institutions were known to be living with HIV (see Exhibit 12–3). HIV in prison peaked in 1998 at 26,000. Since then, there have been 22 consecutive years of declining HIV infections among incarcerated populations. AIDS-related deaths in prison also declined from a peak of 955 in 1994 to 17 in 2019 (the last year BJS collected data on death from AIDS).

Treating HIV in prison is difficult for at least five reasons.[17] The first is the issue of privacy. People infected with HIV usually do not want to disclose their condition. The therapeutic regimen often involves taking multiple drugs several times a day, and going to the prison medication line often compromises a person's privacy and increases the risk of stigmatization. Stigmatization can range from isolation and shunning to more overt forms of abuse.

A second reason involves the frequency of taking medication and the prison routine. Some drugs must be taken with food and others in a fasting state. As the therapeutic regimen increases to five or six times a day, it strains the routine of most prisons to dispense medication frequently and to provide food as required.

The third reason is distrust of the medical and legal system. Not surprisingly, many people in prison do not trust the legal and health care systems. This may be especially true for women, minorities, and people of color who have a documented history of being experimented on without consent and being denied appropriate legal and medical care.

The fourth reason is fear of side effects. The HIV drug regimen is known to make patients feel worse than they already do. Consequently, an incarcerated individual is less likely to adhere to the strict dosages and timing.

EXHIBIT 12–3   **HIV and AIDS in Correctional Institutions, 1991–2020**

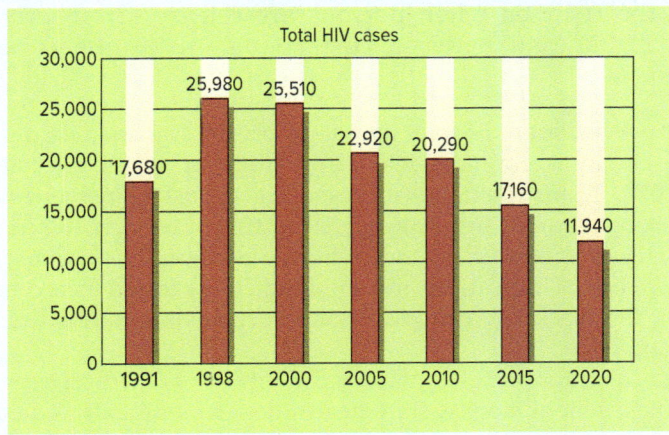

Total HIV cases

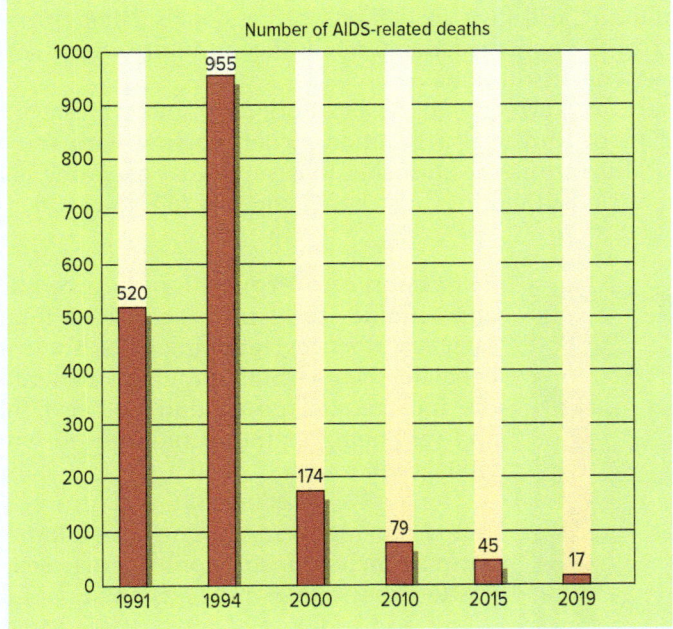

Number of AIDS-related deaths

Source: Bureau of Justice Statistics

The final reason is that the courts have rejected the idea that the level and quality of health care available to persons in prison must be the same as is available to society at large. Instead, the courts have embraced the **principle of less eligibility**—no social benefits for persons in prison beyond the bare minimum.[18] We showed in Chapter 7 that the same argument was used to bar incarcerated persons from receiving Pell grants, vocational training, exercise equipment, treatment, and more. Thus, incarcerated individuals are denied access to medical specialists, timely delivery of medical services, technologically advanced diagnostic techniques, the latest medication and drug therapies, up-to-date surgical procedures, and second opinions.

Overcoming these obstacles will not be easy. If a person receives HIV drug therapy before prison but cannot obtain the same medications when

principle of less eligibility

The concept that persons in prison receive no social benefits beyond the bare minimum.

incarcerated or when they are released, it's not only their health that is affected but everyone around them. The key is developing trust between HIV-infected individuals and the prison health care team, extending the regimen when persons are released from prison, and building collaboration between correctional institutions and public health agencies.

HIV Testing Practices Federal and state prison systems test persons for HIV during the intake process, while in custody, or during discharge planning. In 2020, 16 jurisdictions (representing almost 41 percent of admissions to prison) reported mandatory HIV testing at intake; 48 jurisdictions offered an HIV test while in custody whether requested by the incarcerated individual or clinical indication; and 31 jurisdictions tested incarcerated persons during the discharge process. Some jurisdictions offered more than one testing practice.[19]

Today's corrections professionals need a network of medical experts—university medical school faculty, state health department staff, federal health officials, and local health care providers—to consult about HIV and AIDS. Such consultation will give corrections professionals reliable information and familiarize the noncorrectional medical community with the problems facing correctional institutions.

The American Correctional Association recommends that all correctional staff adopt universal precautions when dealing with the confined population. This means the staff should assume that everyone is carrying the virus because, without testing, there is no way to know who is infected and who is not.[20]

HIV/AIDS is a serious problem for our nation's correctional facilities. To overcome the taboo that prevents at-risk people from testing themselves for HIV, the Reverend Jesse Jackson took an HIV test with persons confined in the Cook County (Chicago) jail. Should persons with HIV in jail or prison be treated any differently? Should they be isolated?

Tim Boyle/Getty Images

Education and Prevention Incarceration offers opportunities to learn basic disease information, safer sex practices, tattooing risks, and triggers for behavior relapse. Such programs benefit not only the incarcerated population but also the health and well-being of the community to which individuals will return.

The types of education and prevention programs provided vary among correctional systems but may include instructor-led programs, pretest/posttest counseling, multisession prevention counseling, and audiovisual and written materials.

Another method of reducing high-risk behavior among incarcerated populations is peer-led counseling. In addition to providing information about HIV in formal settings, the informal interactions that incarcerated peer educators have with others in prison offers opportunities for ongoing dialogue about HIV. Peer-led counseling is also cost-effective because most peer educators are volunteers and therefore provide HIV education to others at no additional cost to the correctional facility.

A little bit of charm and persuasion also works. When the Reverend Jesse Jackson visited the Cook County Jail in Chicago, he along with 177 persons in jail and 25 ministers, took a two-minute HIV test.[21] "We're here to save your lives," Reverend Jackson told the jail population. He talked with them about the psychological barrier, the "taboo," that prevents at-risk people from testing themselves for HIV. He said:

Regardless of the results, people who take the test can't lose. Those who test negative should view themselves as lucky—they can get out of the way of AIDS through their knowledge, behavior, and commitment. HIV-positive detainees, on the other hand, can take solace in the fact that early detection leads to correction.

Persons in Prison with Mental Illness

CO12-5

Mental health is fundamental to a person's overall health, indispensable to personal well-being, and instrumental in leading a balanced and productive life. In previous chapters we showed that every day, our nation's prisons and jails face the challenge of dealing with persons with special needs who are not only suffering from schizophrenia, bipolar disorders, and major depression, among other illnesses, but also from co-occurring substance abuse and dependence disorders and require close monitoring, medication, and other services.

Persons in Prison with Mental Illness
Why are there more persons with mental illness in jail and prison than in mental health hospitals? What can be done to alleviate the problem?

As special needs individuals, people who are mentally ill do not do well in confinement. They are perceived as disruptive, unpredictable, and sometimes dangerous. They are stigmatized, neglected, and easy prey for assaults and robberies. The stress of incarceration can worsen their symptoms, leading to acute psychiatric disturbances, including harm to self or others, and adjustment and disciplinary problems such as refusal to leave one's cell or destruction of property. Behaviors that are characteristic of mental illness such as neglecting personal hygiene, ignoring orders, screaming, and banging against walls oftentimes are met with discipline, which can mean being placed in isolation where the conditions worsen.

Over half of people in state and federal prisons have mental health problems.[22] This is twice the prevalence of mental illness in the U.S. adult population. Of those incarcerated, only one in four has received any professional help in prison. Some corrections professionals like Evan Touchette, Unit Manager for the Intensive Mental Health Unit at the Maine State Prison, whose career profile is featured in Chapter 11, are working to change the status quo and advance the quality of mental health treatment in prison.

We learned in Chapter 6 that our correctional institutions have become de facto mental health providers at a great cost to the well-being of people with mental health disorders. As state mental hospitals closed during the treatment and community-based eras of corrections development in the 1950s (see Exhibit 7–1), state mental hospital patients were released to their communities that were expected to provide medication and community-based treatment and support in lieu of civil incarceration. When the community resources dried up or were not provided, the problem shifted to criminal justice and correctional facilities became de facto mental health providers. Persons with mental illness were put in jail where mental health treatment to support recovery and successful return to the community was inadequate to meet their needs

Incarcerating people with mental illness also costs more. Washington state estimates that it costs more than $100,000 to confine a persons with mental illness, compared with $30,000 for others. Why? In part because they stay longer, are less likely to make bail, and become chronic rule breakers.

There are more people with a mental illness in U.S. jails and prisons than there are in mental hospitals, but correctional officers are not therapists and correctional facilities are not mental hospitals. Why are so many people who have a mental illness in U.S. jails and prisons, and what are the innovative strategies for keeping people with a mental illness out of correctional facilities?

Charles Rex Arbogast-File/AP Images

Treatment Advocacy Center, a nonprofit advocacy group, reported that the average length of stay for most persons in Florida's Orange County (Orlando) jail is 26 days, but people with a mental illness are there for 51 days on average. The average stay at New York's Rikers Island Jail is 42 days, but people with a mental illness are there for an average of 215 days.[23]

Suggesting that jails and prisons replace mental hospitals overstates their treatment capacity and the function of these facilities—the mental health care required is far beyond what jails and prisons are equipped to offer. Correctional officers are not therapists and jails and prisons are not mental hospitals. Corrections personnel are not trained to facilitate mental health treatment and, according to Dr. David Satcher, former U.S. Surgeon General, "they should not have to."[24]

Innovative Alternatives There are many successful and innovative ways to divert persons with a mental illness from the criminal justice system. Three innovative strategies are presented here.

Crisis Intervention Teams The Memphis Police Crisis Intervention Team (CIT) has won widespread national acclaim for the cooperative relationships that have developed between the Memphis police department and the mental health system. Memphis police officers, dispatchers, and other key police personnel receive intensive CIT training about the signs and symptoms of serious mental illnesses, crisis intervention and de-escalation techniques, and community mental health resources and options. A specialized mental health triage unit at the University of Memphis medical center was created to respond specifically to individuals referred by the police. So far there have been fewer arrests, better treatment outcomes, and reduced officer injuries.[25] CIT has been emulated in more than 50 communities across the United States, and other communities have developed alternative law enforcement–mental health partnerships.

Mental Health Court A second innovative strategy for keeping people with mental illness out of jail and prison is mental health court, an intermediate sanction first discussed in Chapter 5. The term *mental health court* refers to a specialized docket for defendants with mental illness that provides the opportunity to participate in court-supervised treatment. A court team, composed of a judge, court personnel, and treatment providers, defines the terms of participation, provides ongoing status assessments with individualized sanctions and rewards, and determines resolution of cases upon successful completion of court-ordered treatment plans.[26]

Two rationales underlie mental health courts: (1) to protect the public by addressing the mental illness that contributes to the criminal act, thereby reducing recidivism, and (2) to recognize that criminal sanctions, whether intended as punishments or deterrents, are neither effective nor morally appropriate when mental illness is a significant cause of the criminal act.

The literature on whether mental health courts reduce recidivism is mixed.[27] Some studies show mental health courts reduce new arrests and days spent incarcerated. However, other studies show no difference between mental health courts and traditional courts. Before mental health courts can be considered an evidence-based practice, more research using experimental designs, representative samples, and longer time frames is needed.

Assertive Community Treatment A third strategy to keep people with a mental illness from returning to jail or prison is the Assertive Community Treatment (ACT) Program. ACT is an evidence-based practice that improves

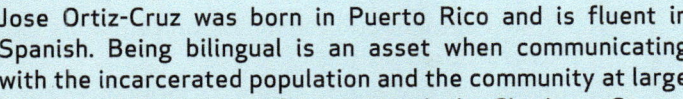

Career Profile

Jose M. Ortiz-Cruz

Sergeant, Charlotte County Sheriff's Office, Punta Gorda, Florida

Jose Ortiz-Cruz was born in Puerto Rico and is fluent in Spanish. Being bilingual is an asset when communicating with the incarcerated population and the community at large and conducting his duties. Ortiz-Cruz is a Sergeant with the Charlotte County Sheriff's Office.

Jose Ortiz-Cruz

Ortiz-Cruz's current assignment is to coordinate, assist, and help with programming in the 960-bed Charoltte County Jail. Current programs include: education (GED, parenting, discharge planning), substance abuse (AA, NA), groups (anger management, batterer's intervention, Charlotte County mental health, dual diagnostics), and miscellaneous activities (religious services, chaplaincy services, leisure reading, recreational games, hydroponics program, aquaculture/fish farm program, and Fresh Start faith-based program).

Ortiz-Cruz also works with the public by assisting in community projects and participating with Habitat for Humanity house dedications, where flowers are donated from the jail's flower program. In five years, Ortiz-Cruz would like to be in a supervisory role with the detention bureau.

His advice to those interested in working in corrections? "Work hard, seek improvement every day, surround yourself with positive successful people, learn from them the positives and negatives of the career, and do not be afraid to fail."

> *Work hard, seek improvement every day, surround yourself with positive successful people, learn from them the positives and negatives of the career, and do not be afraid to fail.*

outcomes for people with severe mental illness who are most at-risk of homelessness, psychiatric crisis and hospitalization, and involvement in the criminal justice system following their release from a correctional facility.[28] ACT is one of the oldest and most widely researched evidence-based models of integrated community care for people with serious and persistent mental illness. ACT is a preventive approach to mental health services that helps people avoid incarceration and further hospitalization.

ACT programs consist of teams of social service professionals who provide a broad and integrated range of services to individuals diverted from jails or reentering communities following release from prison with severe and persistent mental illnesses. The services include medication and medication management, housing assistance, case management, substance abuse treatment, vocational supports, and mobile crisis management. ACT programs are found across the United States as well as in the United Kingdom and Australia.[29]

The American Association for Community Psychiatrists developed a list of nine recommendations to keep people with mental illness out of jail:[30]

1. Improve access to community mental health and substance use disorder services to improve early diagnosis and optimal treatment of individuals suffering from mental health and addictive disorders.
2. Create diversion programs and community-based alternatives to arrest and incarceration.
3. Improve jail and prison conditions that have negative effects on people with mental illness.
4. Improve screening and treatment of mental health and addictive disorders.

5. Establish evidence-based programs to reintegrate people with mental illness into the community following release.

6. Provide organizational support, create oversight bodies, and educate the public about persons with mental illness in the criminal justice system.

7. Allow treatment and rehabilitation programs to have a dominant role in correctional settings.

8. Advocate for an end to solitary confinement because research shows that having a mental illness is associated with a significant increase in the likelihood of being placed in restrictive housing.

9. Advocate for the elimination of racial disparities within and outside the criminal justice system.

Persons in Prison Who Are Elderly

Persons in Prison Who Are Geriatric
What impact does the geriatric prison population have on the administration of prisons?

Another issue being addressed by correctional administrators across the nation is the rising tide of incarcerated people who are elderly, what some are calling the "silver tsunami" of corrections, the issue we turn to next in this chapter.

The Aging of the Prison Population Most of us imagine the incarcerated population as young and aggressive. However, *people who are elderly* and *passive* describe a significant portion of the prison population.

There is no consensus on what constitutes "elderly" with respect to the justice-involved population. While an age of 65 is considered the elderly threshold in community settings, government agencies, researchers, and policy-makers often use 50 or 55 as the elderly cut-off for justice-involved people. They believe that the physiological age of a person in prison is higher than their chronological age because of the impact of unhealthy lifestyle choices, prison lifestyle, the stress of staying safe behind bars, accelerated aging due to substance abuse, and limited access to medical care.

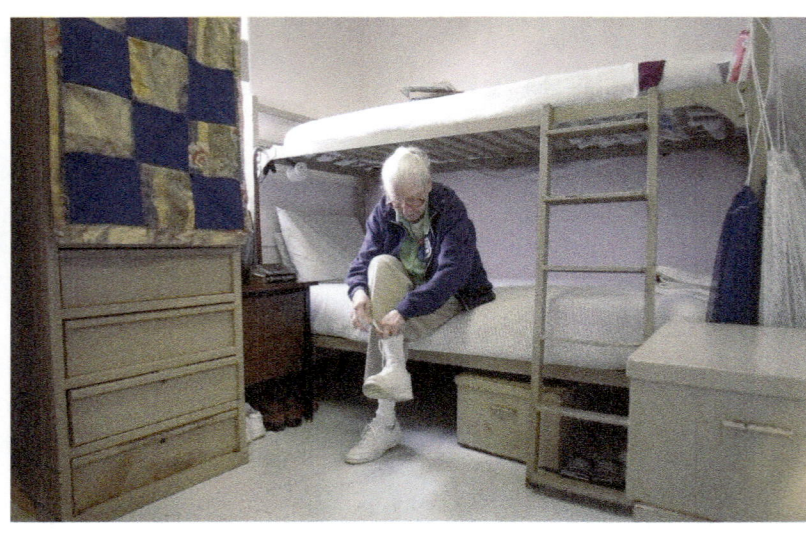

Today, 261,260 persons over the age of 50 are in prison.[31] Men aged 50 or older represent 23 percent and women aged 50 or older are 16 percent—enough to fill the Louisiana Superdome more than three

Serving a sentence for aggravated murder, Betty Tewell ties her shoes on her bunk at the Ohio Reformatory for Women in Marysville, Ohio. The Ohio Department of Rehabilitation and Correction predicts that by 2025, a quarter of its population will be 55 or older. Currently, they make up 10 percent of the state's 43,000 prison population. What are the options states are looking at to save money and respond to the needs of the elderly who pose no threat outside prison?
Amy Sancetta/AP Images

times. Corrections experts predict that the number of older adults in prison will surpass 400,000 by 2030, largely due to the fact that many people are serving sentences that will carry them into their elder years.[32] In 2000, 3 percent of the prison population was age 55 or older. Today, it's 22 percent. In a few more years, it is estimated to be almost 33 percent. In 2016, for the first time, the percent of adults aged 55 and older in prison surpassed the number of young adults ages 18–24 (see Exhibit 12–4).

Two factors contributed to the graying of the prison population: a larger proportion of people serving long-term sentences (more specifically life without the possibility of parole) for persons convicted of violent offenses, and more older people are sent to prison. The mean sentence length for persons in state prison older than 55 was 82 months in 2014 (the last year for which data

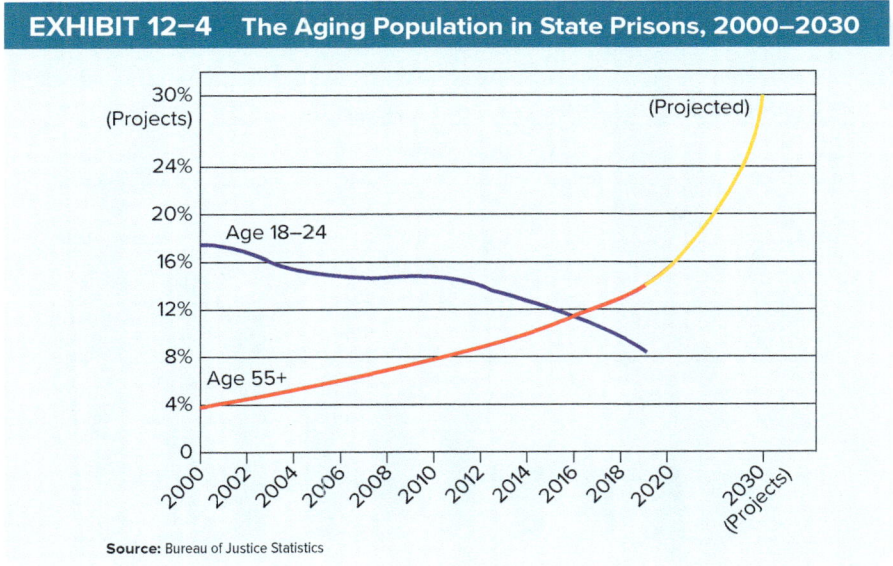

EXHIBIT 12–4   The Aging Population in State Prisons, 2000–2030

Source: Bureau of Justice Statistics

are available), higher than that of 18- to 39-year-olds (69 months) and that of 40- to 54-year-olds (71 months).[33]

Geriatric Care Units in Prison Researchers in California found that almost 70 percent of the women in prison who are elderly said that at least one prison activity was very difficult for them.[34]

- 61 percent said that they had been given jobs that were too difficult to perform, including janitorial and yard crew work.
- 59 percent reported difficulties hearing orders.
- 57 percent said that it was very difficult for them to drop to the floor for alarms.
- 40 percent who were assigned to upper bunks said that it was very difficult for them to climb on and off a top bunk.
- 35 percent said that it was very difficult for them to stand in line for head counts.

Incarcerating older persons with pronounced dementia who are unable to follow rules or may not remember why they are incarcerated or who have impaired eyesight, physical disabilities, cancer, arthritis, diabetes, heart disease, hypertension, or Alzheimer's has serious implications for correctional policymakers, administrators, and staff. Exhibit 12–5 shows the prevalence of disabilities of older people in state and federal prisons.

In 1990 Congress passed the **Americans with Disabilities Act.** The act prohibits discrimination and ensures equal opportunities for persons with disabilities in employment, state and local government services, and public accommodations. In 1998, the U.S. Supreme Court ruled unanimously that ADA covers correctional institutions and the people confined in them. Since then, correctional facilities have been designing **geriatric units**—special intensive care units dedicated to the care of the critically ill elderly with special needs—that are accessible with ramps, good lighting, subtle grades, few stairs, reduced distances, geriatric chairs and beds, walk-in bathtubs, elevators, walkers, wheelchairs, handrails, more crafts and leisure activities, and staff trained in gerontological issues. In 2021, BJS estimated that 5 percent

CO12-6

Americans with Disabilities Act (ADA)

Public Law 101-336, enacted July 26, 1990, which prohibits discrimination and ensures equal opportunity for people with disabilities in employment, state and local government services, public accommodations, commercial facilities, and transportation. It also mandates the establishment of TDD/telephone relay services.

geriatric units

Special intensive care units dedicated to the care of critically ill elderly with special needs.

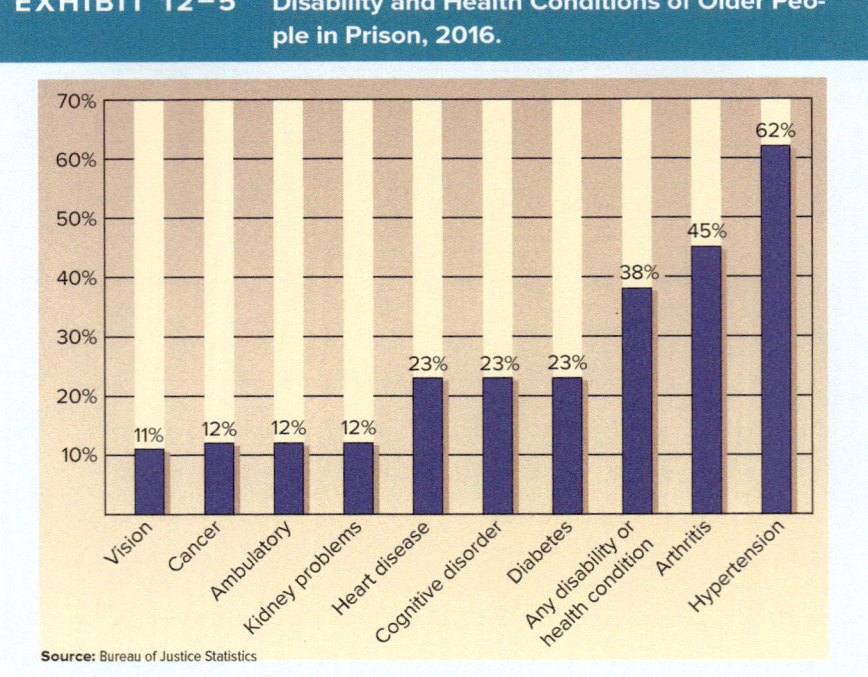

EXHIBIT 12–5 Disability and Health Conditions of Older People in Prison, 2016.

Vision 11%
Cancer 12%
Ambulatory 12%
Kidney problems 12%
Heart disease 23%
Cognitive disorder 23%
Diabetes 23%
Any disability or health condition 38%
Arthritis 45%
Hypertension 62%

Source: Bureau of Justice Statistics

(approximately 60) of the nation's 1,161 prisons have a geriatric unit and more are being built as the number of the elderly in the U.S. incarcerated population increases.[35]

The Federal Bureau of Prisons opened its first memory care unit for persons suffering from dementia in July 2019 at its facility in Devens, Massachusetts. The unit is staffed by incarcerated individuals who are certified nursing assistants and have completed the Massachusetts nursing assistant course and meet state requirements for certification. The staff nurse educators are certified as certified correctional personnel dementia trainers (CCPDT), and the correctional officers are certified as certified dementia trained correctional personnel (CDTCP), after completion of the Alzheimer's disease and

Darren McCollester/Getty Images

dementia care curriculum developed specifically for correctional facilities by the National Council of Certified Dementia Practitioners. There is no count on the number of new memory care and assisted living units in state prisons, but it is clear that more of them will be needed to house people with cognitive problems.

Prison Hospice Programs The increase in persons in prison who are elderly is driving a higher number of deaths. Before the onset of AIDS and the increased elderly population, few individuals died while incarcerated. In 2000, 1.4 million persons were in prison and almost 1,000 of age 55 or older died in prison.[36] Twenty years later, the prison population declined to 1.2 million, but the number of persons 55 or older who died in prison jumped threefold to almost 2,700.[37]

Deaths in prison occur more frequently now, and correctional administrators are taking measures to address the unique problems associated with helping persons in prison who are terminally ill through their passing. A **hospice** is an interdisciplinary, comfort-oriented care facility that helps patients who are seriously ill die with dignity and humanity in an environment that facilitates mental and spiritual preparation for the natural process of dying. Hospice programs provide a wide array of services, including pain management, spiritual support, and psychological counseling as well as grief counseling for bereaved families. To date, there are approximately 75 prison hospice programs in the United States.[38]

One of the nation's best-known prison hospice programs is the one at the Louisiana State Penitentiary (LSP) at Angola. Angola's hospice unit opened in 1998, and two years later it was honored with the American Hospital Association's Circle of Life Award. Of its nearly 6,300 confined population, more than 90 percent are expected to die while incarcerated.[39]

A fundamental part of hospice care at LSP Angola is the emphasis on family. Angola trains incarcerated persons to serve as hospice volunteers. Each incarcerated patient is allowed to designate two other confined persons from Angola's general incarcerated population as "family," and within the constraints of security, these individuals are treated like the elderly person's biological family members. Angola's staff provides whatever considerations are possible within the constraints of security to ensure that the patient's final days are as meaningful as possible for all involved.

In addition to prison hospice programs, we find that compassionate, medical, or geriatric release laws exist in most states, but they are rarely if ever used because of restrictive eligibility criteria, "political considerations" related to public safety policy, and a lengthy review process. Twenty years ago, the U.S. Sentencing Commission granted over 40 percent of the motions it received from persons in federal prison for compassionate release. Today it is less than 15 percent.[40]

The advocacy group, Families Against Mandatory Minimums, graded the states on their compassionate release policies.[41] Their findings parallel the use

hospice

An interdisciplinary, comfort-oriented care facility that helps seriously ill patients die with dignity and humanity in an environment that facilitates mental and spiritual preparation for the natural process of dying.

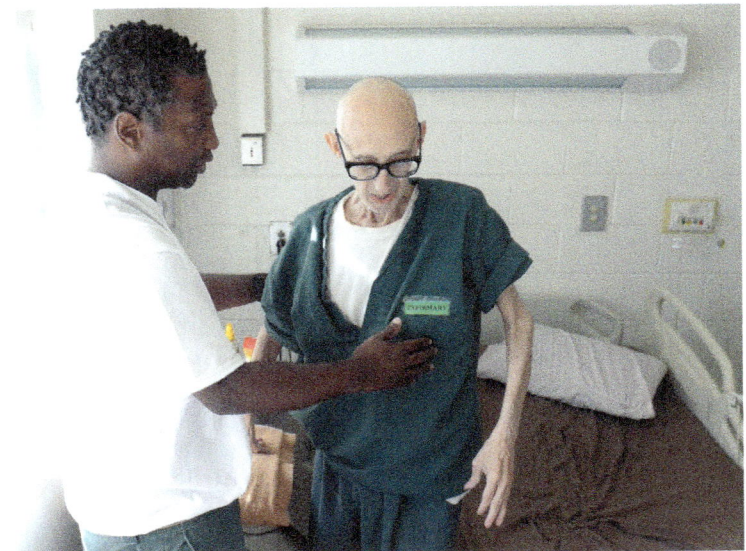

Men who are incarcerated at the Louisiana State Penitentiary at Angola volunteer to act as "family" members to incarcerated hospice patients. Within the constraints of security, they are treated like the patient's biological family member. What are the pros and cons of correctional hospice programs?
RJ Sangosti/The Denver Post/Getty Images

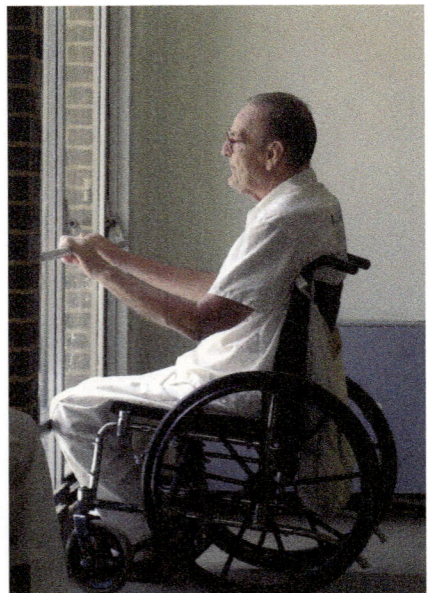

Get-tough-on-crime policies have led to an increased number of persons in prison serving longer periods of time behind bars. The Colorado Territorial Correctional Facility in Cañon City includes a 32-bed infirmary for persons who are elderly with cancer, heart disease, diabetes, and respiratory problems and highlights the public health costs associated with the elderly. What are some of the special needs of incarcerated persons who are geriatric?

Dave Martin/AP Image

of compassionate release in the federal system. Although nearly every state has some form of compassionate release in place, they seldom use them. Five jurisdictions earned the grade of "A" (Colorado, District of Columbia, Illinois, Massachusetts, Rhode Island), one earned a "B" (Minnesota), two earned a "C" (North Carolina, New Jersey), nine earned a "D" (Alabama, California, Idaho, Louisiana, New Mexico, New York, Oklahoma, Texas, and Vermont), and the remainder of states—34—earned an "F."

These forms of release are not without their critics, however. Some argue it's like a shell game and there is no real cost savings: You shift the expense of medical care from one state agency to another, mostly Medicaid, which is funded partly by federal money. Even though the expense of medical care transfers from one state agency to another, hospitals, community health centers, nursing homes, and hospices are better equipped to assist the elderly. Most prisons lack the long-term care we associate with geriatric facilities. Still others are troubled by the fact that convicted criminals are released into adult care homes in the community used by the rest of the population.

Cost and Recidivism Issues The economic consequences of incarcerating the elderly are huge, and across time states will be required to spend more money on the elderly because they will need more drugs and advanced medical care. The estimated national cost per year to confine a person age 50 and older is nearly $70,000, compared with an average of about $34,000 for a younger person.[42] If a 50-year-old person in prison lives to 80, this figure is projected to be $2,048,100. Taxpayers are spending almost $16 billion each year to incarcerate the elderly. The federal Affordable Care Act offers state policymakers who elect to expand their Medicaid programs' eligibility a way to reduce state spending on prison health care. And, as we pointed out earlier, even though the expense of medical care transfers from one state agency to another, hospitals, community health centers, nursing homes, and hospices are better equipped to assist the elderly than incarceration.

It is doubtful that, when mandatory sentencing laws, three-strikes laws, and truth-in-sentencing laws were enacted, the economic impact of incarcerating people who are elderly for long periods of time was actually considered. Unless legislatures give courts and prison administrators more leeway to interchange prison sentences of the elderly with community sentences, states will continue to find themselves in economic crises as they attempt to provide for the 33 percent of the population that is projected to be elderly by the year 2030.

It is also likely that when laws regarding mandatory sentencing, three strikes, and truth in sentencing were enacted, legislatures ignored the evidence-based literature in two areas. First, the data show that the increasing population of aging individuals is not due to any "elderly crime wave" but to individuals entering prison at a younger age and staying there until they are old—often for not so serious crimes. These people are caught in the net of the newer habitual offender and mandatory minimum laws and are given punishments of 20 years or more for low-level and drug offenses. In Texas, 65 percent of people in prison age 50 and older are incarcerated for nonviolent drug, property, and other crimes.[43] In North Carolina, 26 percent of persons age 50 and older are in prison under habitual offender laws or for drug crimes. Another 14 percent are in prison for fraud, larceny, burglary, breaking and entering, and traffic and public order violations.

Second, recidivism drops dramatically with age. For example, only 7 percent of the people who were released from prisons in New York at ages 50 to 64 returned within three years, mostly for technical violations such as missing a meeting with a parole officer, having a positive drug test, or having contact with a victim. That number dropped to 4 percent for persons aged 65 and older. In Virginia, only 1.3 percent age 55 and older returned to prison. And the recidivism rate for persons over 50 leaving federal prison is less than half that of persons under the age of 50 (21 percent compared to 53 percent).[44] The research is clear: There is minimal negative impact on public safety from releasing older people from prison. Where do you stand on the graying of America's prison population?

REVIEW AND APPLICATIONS

SUMMARY

1 Incarcerated people with special needs are those who exhibit unique physical, mental, social, and programmatic needs that distinguish them from other individuals and to whom jail and prison management and staff have to respond in non-traditional and innovative ways.

2 Incarcerated individuals with special needs present unique management concerns because they are typically more violent and prone to be disruptive, require close monitoring as suicide risks, tax scarce medical resources, and are often targets of abuse by other individuals who are incarcerated.

3 Almost one-half (49 percent) of the state prison population and one-third (32 percent) of the federal prison population have a substance use disorder (SUD). A large proportion of drug use comes from the small share of people who use illegal drugs. Any reduction in their drug use will decrease the demand for illegal drugs. The evidence-based literature shows that drug abuse treatment improves outcomes for persons with SUD and has beneficial effects for public health and safety. NIJ identified 13 principles that constitute effective drug treatment.

4 Special difficulties related to HIV/AIDS among prison populations include privacy issues, disruption of the prison routine due to the frequency of taking medication, distrust of the medical and legal systems, fear of side effects, and the legal dilemma embodied in the principle of less eligibility.

5 Over half of people in state and federal prison have mental health problems. Incarceration can worsen their symptoms. Crisis Intervention Teams, Mental Health Court, and Assertive Community Treatment programs are innovative ways to divert persons with a mental health problem from the criminal justiuce system.

6 Persons in prison age 55 or older suffer from the same mental and physical disabilities and health conditions as do adults age 55 or older in the U.S. general population: vision, cancer, ambulatory, heart, cognitive, diabetes, arthritis, and hypertension. The cost of their healthcare to taxpayers is almost $16 billion per year. Research shows that recidivism drops with age and there is minimal negative impact on public safety from releasing older people from prison. Compassionate, medical, and geriatric release are also options to reduce the number of elderly who are incarcerated and pose no threat to public safety.

KEY TERMS

incarcerated people with special needs, p. 337

HIV (human immunodeficiency virus), p. 341

AIDS (acquired immunodeficiency syndrome), p. 341

principle of less eligibility, p. 343

Americans with Disabilities Act (ADA), p. 349

geriatric unit, p. 349

hospice, p. 351

QUESTIONS FOR REVIEW

1 What describes an incarcerated person with special needs?

2 Summarize the management concerns that incarcerated people with special-needs have for corrections officials.

3 What can drug abuse treatment accomplish?

4 What would it take to design a system that makes it easier to treat HIV in prison?

5 What explains why there are so many people in prison with a mental illness and what are the options to divert persons with mental illness from the criminal justice system?

6 What options are available to lessen the health, cost, and recidivism issues associated with incarceration of the elderly?

THINKING CRITICALLY ABOUT CORRECTIONS

Geriatric Care in Prison

Corrections departments are spending upward of $16 billion each year of taxpayers' money to confine and care for the physical and mental health of the elderly prison population. Assume the same or a similar amount was spent to meet their needs if they were in community treatment programs outside prison. Which is more important and why—it's going to cost the same, so for the sake of public safety, keep them incarcerated, or, it's going to cost the same and research shows there is minimal negative impact on public safety from releasing older people from prison?

The Principle of Less Eligibility

According to the principle of less eligibility, the conditions of prison life must be kept lower than those of the poorest workers on the outside. What are the consequences of this line of reasoning on release from prison and recidivism?

ON-THE-JOB DECISION MAKING

Correctional Training in HIV/AIDS Gets Interrupted

You are the warden of a state prison and on record as a supporter of the principle of less eligibility. Walter Edmunds is one of your most dependable correctional officers. Mature, calm, and unfailingly professional, Edmunds can be counted on in every crisis. You have come to rely on his leadership as a positive element among the correctional staff. Unfortunately, Edmunds has a young son dying of AIDS, which he contracted through a blood transfusion during an appendectomy.

Yesterday your medical staff conducted training for your correctional officers on procedures for working with persons suffering from HIV and AIDS. About 10 minutes into the training session, Edmunds apologized for interrupting and then asked why the persons in his prison are receiving top-notch medical treatment for free that ordinary law-abiding citizens can't afford.

From that single question, things quickly deteriorated, and Edmunds became increasingly agitated. Before long, the training room was in turmoil as Edmunds's questions and angry comments whipped up the sympathy and anger of his fellow correctional officers.

The medical officer called for a break and bolted to your office. By the time he finished relating the incident, one of your correctional lieutenants appeared to report that the unionized correctional staff was in an uproar and threatening to walk off the job. How would you handle this situation? Once you contained the situation, what would you say to Edmunds?

Partnering for Mental Health

May is Mental Health Awareness Month. Twenty-two percent (an estimated 58 million) adults age 18 or older in the United States live with a form of mental illness. Almost one-half of the adult prison population (roughly 500,000) also suffers from some form of mental illness. Work with your staff and design a public service announcement that draws attention to the problems persons with mental illness face in prison and why confinement is not the answer.

ENDNOTES

1. U.S. Department of Justice, Office of Public Affairs, *Justice Department Reaches Agreement with Vermont Department of Corrections to Improve Access for Inmates with Disabilities* (Washington, DC: U.S. Department of Justice, Office of Public Affairs, October 28, 2021).

2. Thomas E. Patterson, "Addressing Special Populations in Corrections," *Corrections Today*, vol. 74, no. 4 (August/September, 2012), p. 10.

3. Ibid., p. 10.

4. Ibid., p. 10.

5. G. Larry Mays and Daniel L. Judiscak, "Special Needs Inmates in New Mexico Jails," *American Jails*, vol. 10, no. 2 (1996), pp. 32–41.

6. U.S. Department of Justice, Bureau of Justice Statistics, *Survey of Prison Inmates, United States, 2016* (Ann Arbor, MI: Inter-university Consortium for Political and Social Research [distributor], 2021-09-15. https://doi.org/10.3886/ICPSR37692.v4).

7. Laura M. Maruschak, Jennifer Bronson and Mariel Alper, *Alcohol and Drug Use and Treatment Reported by Prisoners* (Washington, DC: U.S. Department of Justice, Bureau of Justice Statistics, July 2021) and U.S. Department of Health and Human Services, Substance Abuse and Mental Health Services Administration, *SAMSHA Announces National Survey on Drug Use and Health (NSDUH) Results Detailing Mental Illness and Substance Use Levels in 2021,* January 4, 2023, hhs.gov (accessed March 6, 2023).

8. National Center on Addiction and Substance Abuse, *Behind Bars II: Substance Abuse and America's Prison Population* (New York: National Center on Addiction and Substance Abuse, Columbia University, February 2010).

9. Kate Miltner, "Treatment over Jail Time Poll: Most Favor Efforts to Combat Addiction over Punishment," abcnews.com (accessed March 6, 2023).

10. Jeremy Travis, *Framing the National Agenda: A Research and Policy Perspective.* Speech to National Corrections Conference on Substance Abuse, April 23, 1997.

11. Rand Corporation, "Americans' Spending on Illegal Drugs Nears $150 Billion Annually; Appears to Rival What Is Spent on Alcohol," August 20, 2019, rand.org (accessed March 6, 2023).

12. M. D. Anglin and Y. Haer, "Treatment of Drug Abuse," in Michael Tonry and James Q. Wilson (eds.), *Drugs and Crime: Crime and Justice: A Review of Research,* vol. 13 (Chicago: University of Chicago Press, 1990), pp. 393–460; D. N. Nurco, T. W. Kislock, and T. E. Hanlon, "The Nature and Status of Drug Abuse Treatment," *Maryland Medical Journal*, vol. 43 (January 1994), pp. 51–57; Doris Layton MacKenzie, *What Works in Corrections: Reducing the Criminal Activities of Criminals and Delinquents* (New York: Cambridge University Press, 2006); James A. Inciardi, Steven S. Martin, Clifford A. Butzin, Robert M. Hooper, and Lana D. Harrison, "An Effective Model of Prison-Based Treatment for Drug-Involved Offenders, *Journal of Drug Issues*, vol. 27, no. 2 (1997), pp. 261–278; and Frank S. Pearson and Douglas S. Lipton, "A Meta-Analytic Review of the Effectiveness of Corrections-Based Treatments for Drug Abuse," *Prison Journal*, vol. 79, no. 4 (1999), pp. 384–410.

13. Grant Duwe, *The Use and Impact of Correctional Programming for Inmates on Pre- and Post-Release Outcomes* (Washington, DC: U.S. Department of Justice, Bureau of Justice Statistics, June 2017) and James M. Byrne, "The Effectiveness of Prison Programming: A Review of the Research Literature Examining the Impact of Federal, State, and Local Inmate Programming on Post-Release Recidivism," *Federal Probation*, vol. 84, no. 1 (2019), pp. 3–20; Center for Substance Abuse Treatment, *NTIES: The National Treatment Improvement Study—Final Report* (Rockville, MD: U.S. Department of Health and Human Services, Substance Abuse and Mental Health Services Administration, 1997).

14. National Institute on Drug Abuse, *Principles of Drug Abuse Treatment for Criminal Justice Populations—A Research-Based Guide* (Washington, DC: U.S. Department of Health and Human Services, 2006).

15. National Commission on Correctional Health Care, *The Health Status of Soon-to-Be-Released Inmates: A Report to Congress,* Vol. I (Washington, DC: U.S. Department of Justice, September 2004), p. ix.

16. Laura M. Maruschak, *HIV in Prisons, 2020–Statistical Tables* (Washington, DC: U.S. Department of Justice, Bureau of Justice Statistics, May 2022).

17. *Management of the HIV-Positive Prisoner* (New York: World Health CME, n.d.).

18. Michael S. Vaughn and Leo Carroll, "Separate and Unequal: Prison Versus Free-World Medical Care," *Justice Quarterly*, vol. 15, no. 1 (March 1998), pp. 3–40.

19. Laura M. Maruschak, *HIV in Prisons, 2020–Statistical Tables.*

20. American Correctional Association, *Managing Special Needs Offenders* (Lanham, MD: American Correctional Association, 2004).

21. Jaime Shimkus, "Side by Side, Ministers and Detainees Test for HIV Infection," *CorrectCare*, Fall 2001, p. 16.

22. Laura M. Maruschak and Jennifer Bronson, *Indicators of Mental Health Problems Reported by Prisoners* (Washington, DC: U.S. Department of Justice, Bureau of Justice Statistics, June 2021).

23. Stephanie Mencimer, "There Are 10 Times More Mentally Ill People Behind Bars Than in State Hospitals," *MotherJones*, April 8, 2014 (accessed February 10, 2019).

24. As quoted in Phillip Comey, "Health Care and Prisons: Considering the Connection," *On the Line* (Lanham: MD. American Correctional Association, November 2005), p. 1.

25. Randy M. Bourn et al., "Police Perspectives on Responding to Mentally Ill People in Crisis: Perceptions of Program Effectiveness," *Behavioral Sciences and the Law*, vol. 16, no. 4 (1998), pp. 393–402.

26. "Mental Health Courts," Council of State Governments. https://csgjusticecenter.org/mental-health-court-project/ (accessed March 9, 2023).

27. Laura N. Honegger, "Does the Evidence Support the Case for Mental Health Courts? A Review of the Literature," *Law and Human Behavior*, vol. 39, no. 5 (October 2015), pp. 478–488.

28. See for example, http://store.samhsa.gov/list/series?name=Evidence-Based-Practices-KITs (accessed February 10, 2019); Kim T. Mueser, William C. Torrey, David Lynde, Patricia Singer, and Robert E. Drake, "Implementing Evidence-Based Practices for People with Severe Mental Illness," *Behavior Modification*, vol. 27, no. 3 (July 2003), pp. 387–411.

29. Koen Westen, Patrick Boyle, and Hans Kroon, "An Observational Comparison of FACT and ACT in the Netherlands and the US," *BMC Psychiatry*, vol. 22, no. 1 (May 2022) doi: 10.1186/s12888-022-03927-x. PMID: 35505332; PMCID: PMC9063161; and Arlin Cunic, "The Basics of Assertive Community Treatment," verywellmind.com, April 7, 2020 (accessed March 7, 2023).

30. American Association for Community Psychiatrists, *Position Paper on Mental Health and Incarcerated Populations*, communitypsychiatry.org (accessed March 7, 2023).

31. E. Ann Carson, *Prisoners in 2020—Statistical Tables* (Washington, DC: U.S. Department of Justice, Bureau of Justice Statistics, December 2021).

32. KiDeuk Kim and Bryce Peterson, *Aging Behind Bars: Trends and Implications of Graying Prisoners in the Federal Prison System* (Washington, DC: Urban Institute, 2014).

33. Inimal M. Chettiar, W.C. Bunting, and Geoffrey Schotter, *At America's Expense: The Mass Incarceration of the Elderly* (New York: American Civil Liberties Union, June 2012).

34. Ronald H. Aday, "Golden Years Behind Bars: Special Programs and Facilities for Elderly Inmates," *Federal Probation*, vol. 58, no. 2 (June 1994), pp. 47–54; Brie A. Williams et al., "Being Old and Doing Time: Functional Impairment and Adverse Experiences of Geriatric Female Prisoners," *Journal of the American Geriatric Society*, vol. 54, no. 2 (April 2006), pp. 702–707.

35. Laura M. Maruschak and Emily D. Buehler, *Census of State and Federal Adult Correctional Facilities, 2019—Statistical Tables* (Washington, DC: U.S. Department of Justice, Bureau of Justice Statistics, November 2021).

36. Margaret Noonan, Harley Rohloff, and Scott Ginder, *Mortality in Local Jails and State Prisons, 2000–2013—Statistical Tables* (Washington, DC: U.S. Department of Justice, Bureau of Justice Statistics, August 2015).

37. E. Ann Carson, *Mortality in State and Federal Prisons, 2001–2019—Statistical Tables* (Washington, DC: U.S. Department of Justice, Bureau of Justice Statistics, December 2021).

38. Sue Coyle, "End-of-Life Care in Prison," *Social Work Today*, vol. 18, no. 6 (2018), p. 16.

39. Michael J. Osofeky, Philip J. Zimbardo, and Burl Cain, "Revolutionizing Prison Hospice: The Interdisciplinary Approach of the Louisiana State Penitentiary at Angola," *Corrections Compendium*, vol. 29, no. 4 (2004), pp. 5–7; Emma Quail, "Prisons Get Grayer, But Efforts to Release the Dying Lag," *City Limits*, August 6, 2013, www.citylimits.org (accessed March 13, 2023).

40. U.S. Sentencing Commission, *Compassionate Release Data Report, Calendar Years 2020–2021* (Washington, DC: U.S. Sentencing Commission, September 2021).

41. Families against Mandatory Minimums, *Grading the States: The State Compassionate Release Report Card Project* (Washington DC: Families against Mandatory Minimums, October 2022).

42. American Civil Liberties Union, *At America's Expense: The Mass Incarceration of the Elderly*, p. ii.

43. Ibid., p. ii.

44. U.S. Sentencing Commission, *Older Offenders in the Federal System* (Washington, DC: U.S. Sentencing Commission, July 2022).

GLOSSARY

Numbers in parentheses indicate the pages on which the terms are defined.

A

absconding   Fleeing the jurisdiction in which the individual is required to stay without the permission of the PO. (88)

jail accreditation   The process through which correctional facilities and agencies can measure themselves against nationally adopted standards and through which they can receive formal recognition and accredited status. (151)

adjudication   The process by which a court arrives at a final decision in a case; or the second stage of the juvenile justice process in which the court decides whether the individual is formally responsible for (guilty of) the alleged offense. (12)

administrative officers   Those who control keys and weapons and sometimes oversee visitation. (246)

aggravating circumstances   Factors that may increase the culpability of the individual. (52)

AIDS (acquired immunodeficiency syndrome)   A term that applies to the most advanced stages of HIV where a weakened immune system can no longer protect against life-threatening infections and cancers. (341)

Americans with Disabilities Act (ADA)   Public Law 101-334, enacted July 26, 1990, which prohibits discrimination and ensures equal opportunity for people with disabilities in employment, state and local government services, public accommodations, commercial facilities, and transportation. It also mandates the establishment of TDD/telephone relay services. (349)

arraignment   An appearance in court prior to trial in a criminal proceeding. (12)

Auburn system   The second historical phase of prison discipline, implemented at New York's Auburn prison in 1815. It followed the Pennsylvania system and allowed people in prison to work silently together during the day, but they were isolated at night. (158)

average daily population (ADP)   The sum of the number of people held in a jail or prison each day for a year, divided by the total number of days in the year. (130)

B

bail   A written obligation with or without collateral security, given to a court to guarantee appearance before the court. (145)

balancing test   A method the U.S. Supreme Court uses to weigh the rights claimed by people in prison against the legitimate needs of prisons. (313)

bifurcated trial   Two separate hearings for different issues in a trial, one for guilt and the other for punishment. (52)

biometrics   The automated identification or verification of human identity through measurable physiological and behavioral traits. (195)

block officers   Those responsible for supervising residents in housing areas. (246)

correctional boot camp   A short institutional term of confinement that includes a physical regimen designed to develop self-discipline, respect for authority, responsibility, and a sense of accomplishment. (115)

C

capital crime   A crime for which the death penalty may be imposed but need not necessarily be. (47)

capital punishment   Lawful imposition of the death penalty. (46)

carceral state   The social conditions that exist when government power is used to incapacitate, incarcerate, detain, or otherwise limit the physical freedom of vast numbers of people, extending beyond that necessary to ensure a safe and just society. (4)

case investigation   The first major role of probation officers, consisting of interviewing the defendant and preparing the presentence report (PSR). (80)

caseload size   The number of people on a probation officer's caseload. (84)

certification   A credentialing process, usually involving testing and career development assessment, through which the skills, knowledge, and abilities of correctional personnel can be formally recognized. (28)

citation   A type of nonfinancial pretrial release similar to a traffic ticket. It binds the defendant to appear in court on a future date. (154)

civil liability   A legal obligation to another person to do, pay, or make good something. (305)

clemency   Kindness, mercy, forgiveness, or leniency, usually relating to criminal acts. (56)

collateral consequences   Legal and regulatory restrictions imposed by law as a result of a conviction. (209)

community corrections   A philosophy of correctional treatment that embraces (1) decentralization of authority, (2) citizen participation, (3) redefinition of the population of individuals for whom incarceration is most appropriate, and (4) emphasis on rehabilitation through community programs. (15, 117)

community corrections acts (CCAs)   State laws that give economic grants to local communities to establish community corrections goals and policies and to develop and operate community corrections programs. (117)

community service   A sentence to serve a specified number of hours working in unpaid positions with nonprofit or tax-supported agencies. *Also known as* fine of time. (104)

compensatory damages   Money a court may award as payment for actual losses suffered by a plaintiff, including out-of-pocket expenses incurred in filing the suit, other forms of monetary or material loss, and pain, suffering, and mental anguish. (307)

concurrent sentences   Sentences served together. (45)

conditional release   Pretrial release under minimum or moderately restrictive conditions with little monitoring or compliance. It includes ROR, supervised pretrial release, and third-party release. (151)

constitutional rights   The personal and due process rights guaranteed to individuals by the U.S. Constitution and its amendments, especially the first 10 amendments, known as the Bill of Rights. Constitutional rights are the basis of most inmate rights. (305)

contraband   Any item that represents a serious threat to the safety and security of the institution. (192)

correctional clients   Persons in prison, on probation or parole, individuals assigned to alternative sentencing programs, and those held in jails. (9)

correctional officer personalities   The distinctive personal characteristics of correctional officers, including behavioral, emotional, and social traits. (244)

correctional supervision   A term that refers to all persons under the supervision of adult correctional systems and includes those who are supervised in the community under the authority of probation or parole agencies and those held in state and federal prisons or local jails. (3)

corrections   The supervision of persons arrested for, convicted of, or sentenced for criminal offenses. (14)

corrections professional   A dedicated person of high moral character and personal integrity who is employed in the field of corrections and takes professionalism to heart. (27)

cost-benefit analysis   A systematic process used to calculate the costs of a program relative to its benefits. Programs showing the largest benefit per unit of expenditure are seen as the most effective. (21)

COVID-19   Coronavirus disease and the virus causing the disease, i.e., severe acute respiratory syndrome coronavirus 2 (SARS-CoV-2). (294)

COVID-19 test   A viral or polymerase chain reaction (PCR) test for COVID-19. (294)

crime   A violation of the criminal law. (3)

crime rate   The number of major crimes reported for each unit of population. (3–4, 6, 171)

criminal justice   The process of achieving justice through the application of the criminal law and through the workings of the criminal justice system. Also, the study of the field of criminal justice. (10)

criminal justice system   The collection of all the agencies that perform criminal justice functions, whether these are operations or administration or technical support. The basic divisions of the criminal justice system are police, courts, and corrections. (10)

cruel and unusual punishment   A penalty that is grossly disproportionate to the offense or that violates today's broad and idealistic concepts of dignity, civilized standards, humanity, and decency (*Estelle* v. *Gamble,* 1976, and *Hutto* v. *Finney,* 1978). In the area of capital punishment, cruel and unusual punishments are those that involve torture, a lingering death, or unnecessary pain. (318)

custodial staff   Those staff members most directly involved in managing the resident population. (238)

D

day fine   A financial penalty scaled both to the person's income and to the seriousness of the crime. (102)

day reporting center (DRC)   A nonresidential facility to which a person under correctional supervision reports every day or several days a week for supervision and programming. (106)

death penalty   The punishment of execution, imposed on a person who had been legally convicted of a capital crime. (45, 48–59)

death row   A prison area housing persons who have been sentenced to death. (48, 51, 53–59)

deflection   Moving a person away from the justice system and toward community behavioral health and social services without ever being arrested and processed into the criminal justice system. (139)

deliberate indifference   Intentional and willful indifference. Within the field of correctional practice, the term refers to calculated inattention to unconstitutional conditions of confinement. (319)

deprivation theory   The belief that prison subcultures develop in response to the deprivations in prison life. (271)

deserts   See **just deserts.** (37)

deterrence   The discouragement or prevention of crimes through the fear of punishment. (38)

direct-supervision jail   See **third-generation jail.** (128)

discretionary release   Early release based on the paroling authority's assessment of eligibility. (202)

doctrine of sovereign immunity   A historical legal doctrine that held that a governing body or its representatives could not be sued because it made the law and therefore could not be bound by it. (330)

drug court   A specialized court to help people who have alcohol and other drug dependency problems. *Also known as* accountability court or problem-solving court. (98)

due process   A right guaranteed by the Fifth, Sixth, and Fourteenth Amendments to the U.S. Constitution and generally understood, in legal contexts, to mean the expected course of legal proceedings according to the rules and forms established for the protection of persons' rights. (321)

E

earned discharge   A probation reform measure that allows individuals to earn time off for complying with the conditions of their sentences. (79)

equity   A sentencing principle which holds that similar crimes and defendants who are similar should be treated alike, and that sentences should be guided by established, regularly applied standards or guidelines. (62)

evidence-based corrections (EBC)   The application of social scientific techniques to the study of everyday corrections procedures for the purpose of increasing effectiveness and enhancing the efficient use of available resources. *Also known as* evidence-based penology. (21)

evidence-based practice (EBP)   The implementation of programs that have been studied and found to be effective. (21)

exonerate   To clear of blame. (46)

F

fair sentencing Sentencing practices that incorporate fairness for both victims and offenders. *Fairness* is said to be achieved by implementing principles of proportionality, equity, social debt, and truth in sentencing. (61)

Federal Prison Industries (FPI) A federal, paid prison work program and self-supporting corporation. (177)

felony A serious criminal offense; specifically, one punishable by death or by incarceration in a prison facility for more than a year. (8)

felony disenfranchisement The practice of depriving individuals with felony convictions of their right to vote, serve on a jury, and hold public office and restricting the issuance of professional licenses. (223)

fine A financial penalty used as a criminal sanction. (101)

first-generation jail Jail with multiple-occupancy cells or dormitories that line corridors arranged like spokes. Staff supervision is intermittent; staff must patrol the corridors to observe people in their cells. (127)

formerly incarcerated A person who is conditionally released from prison to community supervision.

frivolous lawsuits Lawsuits with no foundation in fact. They are generally brought for publicity, political, or other reasons not related to law. (323)

G

gain time Time taken off of a person's sentence for participating in certain positive activities such as going to school, learning a trade, and working in prison. (240)

gender-responsiveness The intentional creation of an environment that reflects an understanding of the realities of women's lives and addresses the special issues of women in correctional settings. (289)

general deterrence The use of the example of individual punishment to dissuade others from committing crimes. (38)

geriatric units special intensive care units dedicated to the management of critically ill elderly with special needs. (349)

guided discretion Decision making bounded by general guidelines, rules, or laws. (52)

H

hands-off doctrine A historical policy of the American courts not to intervene in prison management. Courts tended to follow the doctrine until the late 1960s. (302)

HIV (human immunodeficiency virus) A group of retroviruses that infect and destroy helper T cells of the immune system, causing the marked reduction in their numbers that is diagnostic of AIDS. (341)

hospice An interdisciplinary, comfort-oriented care facility that helps seriously ill patients die with dignity and humanity in an environment that facilitates mental and spiritual preparation for the natural process of dying. (351)

I

importation theory The belief that prison subcultures are brought into prison from the outside world. (271)

incapacitation The use of imprisonment or other means to reduce a convicted person's capability to commit future offenses. (39)

incarcerated people with special needs People in prison who exhibit unique physical, mental, social, and programmatic needs that distinguish them from other residents and to whom jail and prison management and staff have to respond nontraditionally and innovatively. (336)

individualization A sentencing principle which holds that unique circumstances and attributes of each case and each person entering the criminal justice system should inform sentences as well as the rehabilitation programs, treatment, and services provided. (62)

industrial shop and school officers Those who ensure efficient use of training and educational resources within the prison. (246)

infraction A minor violation of state statute or local ordinance punishable by a fine or other penalty, or by a specified, usually very short term of incarceration. (9)

injunction A judicial order to do or refrain from doing a particular act. (307)

institutional corrections A term that refers to persons housed in secure correctional facilities. (14)

institutional needs Prison administration interests recognized by the courts as justifying some restrictions on the constitutional rights of people in prison. Those interests are maintenance of institutional *order,* maintenance of institutional *security, safety* of prison inmates and staff, and *rehabilitation* of inmates. (305)

integration model A combination of importation theory and deprivation theory. The belief that, in childhood, some people who are in prison have acquired, usually from peers, values that support law-violating behavior but that the norms and standards in prison also affect incarcerated individuals. (271)

intensive supervision probation (ISP) Supervision in the community under strict conditions, by means of frequent reporting to a probation officer whose caseload is generally limited to 30 persons. (97)

intermediate sanctions New punishment options developed to fill the gap between traditional probation and traditional jail or prison sentences and to better match the severity of punishment to the seriousness of the crime. (94)

J

jail accreditation Process through which correctional facilities and agencies can measure themselves against nationally adopted standards and through which they can receive formal recognition and accredited status. (151)

jails Locally operated correctional facilities that confine people before or after conviction. (130)

jurisdiction The power, right, or authority of a court to interpret and apply the law. (307)

just deserts Punishment deserved. A just deserts perspective on criminal sentencing holds that people who violate the criminal law are morally blameworthy and are therefore *deserving* of punishment. (37)

justice reinvestment The practice of reducing spending on prisons and investing a portion of the savings into infrastructure and civic institutions located in high-risk neighborhoods. (193)

L

legitimate penological objectives The realistic concerns that correctional officers and administrators have for the integrity and security of the correctional institution and the safety of staff and persons incarcerated. (313)

low-security prison A prison that confines persons considered more dangerous than those in minimum-security facilities but less dangerous than those confined in medium-security facilities. It has double-fenced perimeters, mostly dormitory or cubicle housing, and strong work and program components. The staff-to-resident ratio in these institutions is higher than in minimum-security facilities. *Also known as* Federal Correctional Institution (FCI). (197)

M

mandatory death penalty A death sentence that the legislature has required to be imposed upon people convicted of certain offenses. (52)

mandatory release Early release after a time period specified by law. (202)

mass incarceration The overuse of correctional facilities, particularly prisons, in the United States as determined by historical and cross-cultural standards. We live in an era of mass incarceration. (4)

maximum- or close/high-security prison A prison designed, organized, and staffed to confine individuals considered the most dangerous individuals for long periods. It has a highly secure perimeter, barred cells, and a high staff-to-incarceree ratio. It imposes strict controls on the movement of the incarcerated population and visitors, and it offers few programs, amenities, or privileges. (187)

medium-security prison A prison that confines individuals considered less dangerous than those in maximum security, for both short and long periods. It places fewer controls on the incarcerated population's and visitors' freedom of movement than does a maximum-security facility. It has barred cells and a fortified perimeter. The staff-to-incarceree ratio is generally lower than that in a maximum-security facility, and the level of amenities and privileges is slightly higher. (186)

minimum-security institution A facility that confines people who are the least dangerous for both short and long periods. It allows as much freedom of movement and as many privileges and amenities as are consistent with the goals of the facility. It may have dormitory housing, and the staff-to-incarceree ratio is relatively low. (186)

misdemeanor A relatively minor violation of the criminal law, such as petty theft or simple assault, punishable by confinement for one year or less. (9)

mission That which is done to support an organization's purpose. (255)

mitigating circumstances Factors that, although not justifying or excusing an action, may reduce the culpability of the individual. (52)

N

new offense violation Arrest and prosecution for the commission of a new crime. (88)

net widening The risk of new reforms expanding social control over individuals more than the program had originally intended. (96)

nolo contendere A plea of "no contest." A no-contest plea may be used by a defendant who does not wish to contest conviction. Because the plea does not admit guilt, however, it cannot provide the basis for later civil suits. (12)

nominal damages Small amounts of money a court may award when incarcerated persons have sustained no actual damages, but there is clear evidence that their rights have been violated. (307)

noninstitutional corrections That aspect of the correctional enterprise that includes "pardon, probation, and parole activities, correctional administration not directly connectable to institutions, and miscellaneous [activities] not directly related to institutional care." *Also known as* community corrections. (15)

nonrevocable parole (NRP) A type of unsupervised parole that cannot be revoked for technical violations; the person does not report to a parole officer. (221)

O

open institution A minimum-security facility that has no fences or walls surrounding it. (186)

operational capacity The number of inmates that a facility's staff, existing programs, and services can accommodate.

P

pains of imprisonment Major problems that incarcerated people face, such as loss of liberty and personal autonomy, lack of material possessions, loss of heterosexual relationships, and reduced personal security. (270)

pardon An executive act that removes both punishment and guilt. (13, 16, 17)

parole The conditional release of a person from prison, prior to completion of the imposed sentence, under the supervision of a parole officer. (202)

parole-releasing authority A person or correctional agency that has the authority to grant parole, revoke parole, and discharge from parole. *Also known as* parole board or parole commission. (215)

parsimony Sentences should be the least necessary in a given situation to attain its end. Imposition of a sentence more severe than is necessary is harmful. (63)

pay-to-stay jails Local correctional facilities that allow persons in jail to pay between $100 and $300 a day for extra privileges in accommodation, food, and entertainment. (143)

penitentiary The earliest form of large-scale incarceration. It punished persons in prison by isolating them so that they could reflect on their misdeeds, repent, and reform. (158)

Pennsylvania system The first confinement in silence instead of corporal punishment; conceived by the American Quakers in 1790 and implemented at the Walnut Street Jail. *Also known as* separation system. (158)

perimeter security officers Those assigned to security (or gun) towers, wall posts, and perimeter patrols. These officers are charged with preventing escapes and detecting and preventing intrusions. *Also known as* wall post officers. (246)

pleasure-pain principle The idea that actions are motivated primarily by a desire to experience pleasure and avoid pain. (38)

precedent A previous judicial decision that judges should consider in deciding future cases. (310)

pretrial detainee A person who is held in jail prior to trial on criminal charges because no bail is posted, the individual cannot afford bail, or bail is denied. (145)

principle of less eligibility   The requirement that persons in prison receive no social benefits beyond the bare minimum. (343)

prison   A state or federal confinement facility that has custodial authority over adults sentenced to confinement. (3)

prison argot   The special language of the prison subculture. (272)

prison code   A set of norms and values among incarcerated persons. It is generally antagonistic to the official administration and rehabilitation programs of the prison. (272)

prison roles   Prison lifestyles; also, forms of ongoing social accommodation to prison life. *Also known as* resident roles. (273)

prison subculture   The habits, customs, mores, values, beliefs, or superstitions of people incarcerated in correctional institutions; also the social world or people who are incarcerated. Also known as resident subculture. (270)

prisoner subculture   See **prison subculture.** (270)

prisoners' rights   Constitutional guarantees of free speech, religious practice, due process, and other private and personal rights as well as constitutional protections against cruel and unusual punishments made applicable to people in prison by the federal courts. (304)

prisonization   The process by which people who are incarcerated adapt to prison society; the taking on of the ways, mores, customs, and general culture of the penitentiary. (270)

privatization   A contract process that shifts public functions, responsibilities, and capital assets, in whole or in part, from the public sector to the private sector. (156)

probation   The conditional release of a person convicted of crime into the community, under the supervision of a probation officer. It is conditional because it can be revoked if certain conditions are not met. (70)

problem correctional officer   A correctional officer who exhibits problem behavior, as indicated by high rates of resident complaints and use-of-force incidents, and by other evidence. (245)

problem-solving courts   Relatively new intermediate sanctions that target serious problems underlying criminal conduct. Also known as *specialty courts, treatment courts, and accountability courts*). (98)

procedural justice   The idea that how individuals regard the justice system is tied more to the perceived fairness of the process and how they were treated rather than to the perceived fairness of the outcome. (81)

profession   An occupation granted high social status by virtue of the personal integrity of its members. (24)

professional associations   Organized groups of like-minded individuals who work to enhance the professional status of members of their occupational group. (27)

program staff   Those staff members concerned with encouraging residents to participate in educational, vocational, and treatment programs. (238)

property crime   Burglary, larceny-theft, motor vehicle theft, and arson as reported by the FBI's Uniform Crime Reporting Program.

proportionality   A sentencing principle which holds that the severity of punishment should match the seriousness of the crime for which the sentence is imposed. (62)

pseudofamilies   Family-like structures, common in women's prisons, in which residents assume roles similar to those of family members in free society. (288)

punitive damages   Money a court may award to punish a wrongdoer when a wrongful act was intentional and malicious or was done with reckless disregard for the rights of the victim. (307)

purpose   The reason for an organization's existence. (255)

R

racism   The systemic oppression of a racial group to the social, economic, and political advantage of another. (30)

rated capacity   The maximum number of beds a jail can hold, set by a rating official. (141)

recidivism   The repetition of criminal behavior; generally defined as *rearrest*. It is the primary outcome measure for probation as it is for all corrections programs. (76)

reentry   The transition persons make from jail (or prison) to the community. (147)

reentry court   A problem-solving court that helps people leaving prison makes a successful adjustment back to their communities. (225)

rehabilitation   The changing of criminal lifestyles into law-abiding ones by "correcting" the behavior of people who have been convicted of criminal offenses through treatment, education, and training. *Also known as* reformation. (39)

reintegration   The process of making the individual a productive member of the community. (40)

release on bail   The release of a person upon that person's financial guarantee to appear in court. (151)

release on recognizance (ROR)   Pretrial release on the defendant's promise to appear for trial. It requires no cash guarantee. (151–152, 154)

relief officers   Experienced correctional officers who know and can perform almost any custody role within the institution, used to temporarily replace officers who are sick or on vacation or to meet staffing shortages. (247)

remote-location monitoring   Technologies, including global positioning system (GPS) devices and electronic monitoring (EM), that probation and parole officers use to monitor remotely the physical location of a person under correctional supervision. (109)

resident subculture   *See* prison subculture. (270)

residential reentry center (RRC)   A correctional setting where people leaving prison or jail (or sometimes as a condition of probation or parole) are required to live before being fully released into the community. (113)

restoration   The process of returning to their previous condition all those involved in or affected by crime—including victims, offenders, and society. (41)

restorative justice   A systematic response to wrongdoing that emphasizes healing the wounds of victims, offenders, and communities caused or revealed by crime. (41)

retribution   A sentencing goal that involves retaliation against a criminal perpetrator. (37)

revenge   Punishment as vengeance; an emotional response to real or imagined injury or insult. (37)

revocation   The formal termination of an individual's conditional freedom. (87)

revocation hearing   A due process hearing that must be conducted to determine whether the conditions of probation have been violated before probation can be revoked and the individual removed from the community. (86)

risk and needs assessments (RNA)   Tools to identify how likely a person is to commit another crime or violate the rules of prison, jail, or community supervision once they have been convicted and/or sentenced. (76)

risk-needs-responsivity (RNR) model   A risk and needs assessment which states that the risks and needs of the person under correctional supervision should determine the strategies appropriate for addressing the person's criminogenic factors. (77)

roles   The normal patterns of behavior expected of those holding particular social positions. (237)

S

salient factor score (SFS)   A scale, developed from a risk-screening instrument, used to predict parole outcome.

second-generation jail   Jail where staff remain in a secure control booth surrounded by housing areas called pods and surveillance is remote. *Also known as* podular remote-supervision facilities. (127)

security threat groups   The current term for prison gangs that describes how they negatively impact the security of prison operations. (189)

sentence   The penalty a court imposes on a person convicted of a crime. (36)

sentencing   The imposition of a criminal sanction by a sentencing authority, such as a judge. (36)

serious error   Error that substantially undermines the reliability of the guilt finding or death sentence imposed at trial. (54)

social diversity   Differences between individuals and groups in the same society, including differences based on culture, race, religion, ethnicity, age, gender identity, and disabilities. (32)

social justice   An ideal that embraces all aspects of civilized life and is linked to fundamental notions of fairness and to cultural beliefs about right and wrong. (4)

social order   The smooth functioning of social institutions, the existence of positive and productive relations among individual members of society, and the orderly functioning of society as a whole. (36)

specific deterrence   The deterrence of the individual being punished from committing additional crimes. (38)

special master   A person appointed by the court to act as its representative to oversee remedy of a violation and provide regular progress reports.

staff roles   The normal patterns of behavior expected of correctional staff members in particular jobs. (237)

staff subculture   The beliefs, values, and behavior of staff. They differ greatly from those of the resident subculture. (241)

stress   Tension in a person's body or mind, resulting from physical, chemical, or emotional factors. (249)

structured conflict   The tensions between prison staff members and residents that arise out of the correctional setting. (241)

subculture   The beliefs, values, behavior, and material objects shared by a particular group of people within a larger society. (241)

supermax housing   A freestanding facility, or a distinct unit within a facility, that provides for management and secure control of persons who have been officially designated as exhibiting violent or serious and disruptive behavior while incarcerated. (189)

supervision   The second major role of probation officers, consisting of resource mediation, surveillance, and enforcement. (81)

sustainable justice   Criminal laws and criminal justice institutions, policies, and practices that achieve justice in the present without compromising the ability of future generations to have the benefits of a just society. (7)

T

technical violation   Actions that would not otherwise be considered a crime but become punishable due to the conditions of supervision. (88)

third-generation jail   A jail where residents are housed in small groups, or pods, staffed 24 hours a day by specifically trained officers. Officers interact with residents to help change behavior. Bars and metal doors are absent, reducing noise and dehumanization. *Also known* as direct-supervision jail. (128)

three-strikes laws   Three-strikes laws impose mandatory prison sentences, generally a life sentence, on those convicted of an offense if they have been previously convicted of two prior serious criminal offenses. (39)

tort   A civil wrong, a wrongful act, or a wrongful breach of duty, other than a breach of contract, whether intentional or accidental, from which injury to another occurs. (307)

total admission   The total number of people admitted to jail each year. (130)

total institution   A place where the same people work, play, eat, sleep, and recreate together on a continuous basis. The term was developed by the sociologist Erving Goffman to describe prisons and other facilities. (268)

totality of conditions   A standard to be used in evaluating whether prison conditions are cruel and unusual. (319)

truth in sentencing (TIS)   The sentencing principle that requires a person who has been convicted to serve a substantial portion of the sentence and reduces the discrepancy between the sentence imposed and actual time spent in prison. (39)

U

UNICOR   The trade name of Federal Prison Industries. UNICOR provides, among other things, cable assemblies, solar panels, and vehicle and fleet services for the Army, Navy, Marine Corps, and Homeland Security. (177)

V

victim-impact statement   A description of the harm and suffering that a crime has caused victims and survivors. (41)

victims' rights   The fundamental rights of victims to be represented equitably throughout the criminal justice process. (43)

violent crime   Interpersonal crime that involves the use of force by individuals or results in injury or death to victims. In the FBI's Uniform Crime Reports, violent crimes are murder, forcible rape, robbery, and aggravated assault. (4, 22, 43, 48, 59, 66, 152–153, 173, 180, 182, 286, 294)

vision   The planned future direction of an organization. (255)

W

work detail supervisors   Those who oversee the work of individual residents and work crews. (246)

writ of *habeas corpus*   An order that directs the detaining authority to bring the person who is being detained before a judge, who will determine the lawfulness of the imprisonment. (306)

Y

yard officers   Those who supervise incarcerated persons in the prison yard. (246)

CASE INDEX

SUBJECT INDEX

A

Abdel-Rahman, Sheikh Omar, 39, 259
absconding, 88
accreditation
  definition, 151
  jail, 150–151
Acquired immunodeficiency syndrome (AIDS), 341
addiction theory, for women offenders, 136
adjudication, 12
Administrative Maximum (ADX) facility, 189
administrative officers, 246
adults, on parole, 208
Affordable Care Act, 352
age of prison population, 167–168. *See also* older prisoners
aggravating circumstances, 52
agitator inmate role, 275
Alabama
  age of inmates in prison, 168
  age range of inmates, 168
  appeals of death penalty, 54
  caseload size in, 84
  criminal appeals review process, 54
  incarceration cost, 180
  parole boards, 216
  prison conditions, 162
  serious error, 54
  wrongful convictions, 55
Alameda, community service program, 105
Alaska
  adults on probation, 73
  age of inmates in prison, 168
  collateral consequences, 211
  combined jail/prison systems, 44
  conditions of parole in, 219
  incarceration cost, 180
  incarceration cost per person, 180
  legalization of marijuana use, 60
  parole abolished, 227
  standard conditions of parole, 218, 219
Alcatraz, 189
alcohol intoxication in prisons, 281
al-Qaeda, 259
American Academy of Child and Adolescent
  Psychiatry, 58
American Association for Community
  Psychiatrists, 347
American Bar Association
  jail standards, 150

American Correctional Association (ACA)
  code of ethics, 25
  Commission on Accreditation, 26
  demographic characteristics of staff members, 242–243
  on intermediate sanctions, 96
  jail accreditation, 151
  jail standards, 150
  policy statement on discretionary parole, 203
  public correctional policy on community corrections,
    117–118
  public correctional policy on employment of women, 247
  public correctional policy on higher education, 29
  public correctional policy on offenders with special
    needs, 338
  public correctional policy on role of corrections, 16
  public correctional policy on sentencing, 59
American Jail Association (AJA), 27, 131
  on intermediate sanctions, 95
American Medical Association, 58
American Probation and Parole Association (APPA), 27
  caseload standards, 83–84
  on intermediate sanctions, 96
  position statement on parole, 206
  on probation, 71
  recidivism rates, 78
American Psychological Association (APA), 58
Americans with Disabilities Act (ADA), 349
Andrus, Tracy, 248
anesthetics, 50
Angola
  hospice care at prison, 351
Antiterrorsm and Effective Death Penalty Act (AEDPA),
  54
Arizona
  banning execution of juveniles/persons with mental
    impairment, 57
  commercial driver's license (CDL), 178
  correctional program officers (CPOs), 254
  correctional service officers (CSOs), 254
  day fines, 104
  job satisfaction of correctional staff, 254
  licensing barriers reduction, 215
  parole abolished, 227
  private prison population, 186
  women in prison, 165
  wrongful convictions, 55
Arkansas
  banning of execution of juveniles/ persons with mental
    retardation, 57